The SAGE Handbook of

Graduate Employability

SAGE was founded in 1965 by Sara Miller McCune to support the dissemination of usable knowledge by publishing innovative and high-quality research and teaching content. Today, we publish over 900 journals, including those of more than 400 learned societies, more than 800 new books per year, and a growing range of library products including archives, data, case studies, reports, and video. SAGE remains majority-owned by our founder, and after Sara's lifetime will become owned by a charitable trust that secures our continued independence.

Los Angeles | London | New Delhi | Singapore | Washington DC | Melbourne

The SAGE Handbook of

Graduate Employability

Edited by

Tania Broadley

Yuzhuo Cai

Miriam Firth

Emma Hunt and

John Neugebauer

SAGE reference

Los Angeles | London | New Delhi | Singapore | Washington DC | Melbourne

SAGE

Los Angeles | London | New Delhi
Singapore | Washington DC | Melbourne

SAGE Publications Ltd
1 Oliver's Yard
55 City Road
London EC1Y 1SP

SAGE Publications Inc.
2455 Teller Road
Thousand Oaks, California 91320

SAGE Publications India Pvt Ltd
B 1/I 1 Mohan Cooperative Industrial Area
Mathura Road
New Delhi 110 044

SAGE Publications Asia-Pacific Pte Ltd
3 Church Street
#10-04 Samsung Hub
Singapore 049483

Editor: Matthew Waters
Assistant Editor: Colette Wilson
Production Editor: Zoheb Khan
Copyeditor: Sunrise Setting
Proofreader: Genevieve Friar
Indexer: KnowledgeWorks Global Ltd.
Cover Design: Ginkhan Siam
Typeset by KnowledgeWorks Global Ltd.
Printed in the UK

At SAGE we take sustainability seriously. Most of our products are printed in the UK using responsibly sourced papers and boards. When we print overseas we ensure sustainable papers are used as measured by the PREPS grading system. We undertake an annual audit to monitor our sustainability.

Library of Congress Control Number: 2022945692

British Library Cataloguing in Publication data

A catalogue record for this book is available from the British Library

978-1-5297-7184-8

"Few would argue against the notion of higher education being committed to developing students' employability – a notion that implies the capability to function productively in a complex, interconnected and continually evolving world. Some graduates will choose to work locally and perhaps individually, whereas others will collaborate in teams that are national or international in character. The subject(s) chosen for study necessarily influence the emphases given to aspects of employability – consider the different expectations of graduates from programmes in fine art, social science and medicine, for example. This book, importantly, invites readers to consider employability from the perspectives of students, teachers and the world beyond the academy, and to work with an approach appropriate to their particular circumstances."

Mantz Yorke, Formerly Director of Quality Enhancement at the Higher Education Quality Council and Professor of Higher Education at Liverpool John Moores University

This Handbook brings together the latest research on graduate employability into one authoritative volume. Dedicated parts guide readers through topics, key issues and debates relating to delivering, facilitating, achieving and evaluating graduate employability. Chapters offer critical and reflective positions, providing examples of a range of student and graduate destinations, and cover a wide range of topics from employability development, to discipline differences, gender, race and inclusion issues, entrepreneurialism, and beyond. Showcasing positions and voices from diverse communities, industries, political spheres and cultural landscape, this book will support the research of students, researchers and practitioners across a broad range of social science areas.

Part I Facilitating and Achieving Graduate Employability
Part II Segmenting Graduate Employability: Subject by Subject Considerations
Part III Graduate Employability and Inclusion
Part IV Country and Regional Differences
Part V Policy Makers' and Employers' Perceptions on Graduate Employability

This handbook is dedicated to all university graduates. As you navigate the opportunities and challenges of your post–university journey, may you find growth and fulfilment and share the benefits of your university education.

Contents

PART II SEGMENTING GRADUATE EMPLOYABILITY: SUBJECT BY SUBJECT

PART III GRADUATE EMPLOYABILITY AND INCLUSION

List of Figures

List of Tables

Notes on the Editors and Contributors

THE EDITORS

Tania Broadley is Pro Vice-Chancellor Education at the University of Canberra, where she provides leadership and strategic direction for the advancement, development, and improvement of the student learning experience and outcomes. Tania is a teacher educator first and foremost, with experience in academic leadership, university governance, and curriculum development, with research concentrated in the field of educational technologies, teacher education, and academic professional development. Tania was a member of the AITSL National Expert Advisory Group and a foundational member of the QTPA development team at the Queensland University of Technology (QUT).

Yuzhuo Cai is a Senior Lecturer and Adjunct Professor at the Higher Education Group (HEG), Faculty of Management and Business, Tampere University. He has been with the HEG for 20 years and was the Acting Professor of the unit from August 2013 to July 2014. He is the Director of Sino-Finnish Education Research Centre and Deputy Director of Research Centre on Transnationalism and Transformation at Tampere University. He is also Editor-in-Chief of *Triple Helix and Co-Editor of the Journal of Studies in International Education.* His main interests are in higher education research and innovation studies, focusing on interactions between higher education and society. He has published over 100 peer-reviewed publications in these fields, including in top/leading journals, such as *Higher Education, Studies in Higher Education, International Journal of Management Reviews, Technovation, Minerva, Science and Public Policy*, and *European Planning Studies.*

Miriam Firth is a Senior Lecturer in Education Management and Leadership, in the Institute of Education, within the University of Manchester, UK. Her research focuses on Vocational Education, particularly Leisure, Hospitality, Events and Tourism Education. She chairs the AGCAS Creative Industries task group, and leads in Assessment for the Flexible Learning Project across the University of Manchester. With 15 years UK Higher Education lecturing experience Miriam has taught and supervised students on all programme levels. She has worked with the Higher Education Statistics Agency to support development of new national Employability metrics and published textbooks on Employability to support vocational students.

Emma Hunt is the Vice Chancellor of Falmouth University, which specialises in creative and cultural subjects. Professor Hunt has long-standing experience in regional skills policy and has been chair of the Dorset Skills and Advisory Board, which oversaw the implementation of the Dorset Skills Plan and reported annually on implementing national government policy at regional level in England. She is also a member of the Skills Steering Group for the British Academy and a Steering Group member of the Knowledge Exchange Concordat. She has held posts at Derby, Huddersfield and University of Arts London, as well as being a Visiting Professor at Kunming University.

John Neugebauer is a Visiting Fellow at Bristol Business School, University of the West of England. He has held managerial appointments in the UK National Health Service, and senior HR management roles with Lloyds Bank International and Lloyds Bank. He has lectured at undergraduate and postgraduate levels with the University of Bath, University of Bristol, Open University (in the UK and Europe), and the University of the West of England. He has been an external examiner for Bristol Dental School and the University of Plymouth. John has worked as a consultant to small and large organisations, both in his own capacity and as part of Knowledge Exchange activities with higher education institutions. His first degree was from the University of Lancaster, and his postgraduate education degree and PhD from the University of Bristol. He is a qualified coach and Fellow of the Chartered Institute of Personnel and Development.

THE CONTRIBUTORS

Pauline Anderson is Senior Lecturer in the Department of Work, Employment and Organisation, University of Strathclyde Business School. Pauline's research focuses on skills, jobs, and working life, particularly labour market and 'just' transitions, the future of work, skill ecosystems, and healthy workplaces and workers. Her research has a strong public policy/practice focus. She currently serves on the Climate Emergency Skills Action Plan (CESAP) Implementation Strategy Group (Scotland).

Filiz Keser Aschenberger is an Assistant Professor at the University for Continuing Education Krems in the Continuing Education and Educational Technologies Department. After completing her MA degree in Adult Education from Bogazici University, Istanbul, she received her PhD in Educational Administration and Planning from the Middle East Technical University. She is a former Fulbright Scholar who studied and conducted research at University of Wisconsin-Madison. She has taken part in several national/international research projects, and she has been teaching at the University of Vienna in the Educational Sciences Institute for the last nine years. Her research interests include continuing education, lifelong learning, professional development, educational policy, and policy analysis.

Judith Baines is a Principal Fellow of the Higher Education Academy and in 2020 received a Collaborative Award for Teaching Excellence from Advance HE. She has over 20 years' experience in careers and student development services across a range of higher education institutions. Judith is currently Head of Careers and Enterprise at Queen Mary University of London, with responsibility for implementing key strategies to improve employment rates in a contemporary careers service committed to excellent student experience. She is a Trustee for Greenwich Student Union and is active in supporting the Association of Graduate Careers Advisory Services in a range of voluntary roles, including as a professionally accredited trainer, delivering nationally and internationally.

Dawn Bennett is Assistant Provost and Director of the Transformation CoLab with Bond University. She is an experienced senior leader, an educational reformist, and a passionate educator. Dawn's expertise is the enhancement of student success and graduate employability. Dawn is a staunch advocate for student equity and addressing the impacts of disadvantage. She is an internationally known researcher with over 300 academic articles and major reports and AUD$6m in completed research funding. Her EmployABILITY Thinking initiative engages 60 institutions globally and holds the largest dataset of student-derived confidence data in the world.

John Buchanan is an Honorary Industry Fellow at the University of Technology Sydney, where he has worked for 20 years, most recently as an Associate Professor. He has also taught at primary and secondary levels. His research interests focus on teacher quality, recruitment, retention, and working conditions. He has published more than 100 refereed chapters and journal articles in these areas, as well as in his teaching fields of history and geography. He is a past president of the New South Wales Institute for Educational Research. He has been involved in researching Teaching Professional Assessments since their Australian inception.

David F. J. Campbell is a Researcher and Lecturer (Faculty Member) at the Department for Higher Education Research at Danube University Krems (www.donau-uni.ac.at/en/university/organization/employees/person/4295299466) and an Associate Professor (Privat-Dozent) in Political Science at the University of Vienna (https://politikwissenschaft.univie.ac.at/en/about-us/staff/associate-professors/campbell/). David studied political science at the University of Vienna, completing his studies with a doctoral degree in 1996. In 2014, he received his Habilitation (Doctor Habilitatus) from the University of Vienna with a Venia Docendi (entitlement for teaching) for Comparative Political Science. His articles on knowledge, innovation, the knowledge economy, and democracy (knowledge democracy and quality of democracy) have been published in several international journals (citations of his academic work can be followed at http://scholar.google.at/citations?user=GSNvicMAAAAJ&hl=en&oi=ao). His h-index is documented on Scopus (www.scopus.com/authid/detail.uri?authorId=8403349000#top). He has taught at the University of Vienna, Alpen-Adria University of Klagenfurt,

University of Applied Arts Vienna, Danube University Krems, George Washington University (Elliott School of International Affairs), and at THAPAR University (Punjab).

Kate Campbell-Pilling qualified as a solicitor in 1999 and in 2004 moved from practice to teach law at the University of Sheffield. Kate is currently working on student wellbeing, widening participation, and civic engagement projects and leads the school's provision of professional legal skills.

Maria João Carneiro is Assistant Professor of Tourism at the University of Aveiro (UA) and a researcher at its Governance, Competitiveness and Public Policies (GOVCOPP) research unit. She holds a degree in Tourism Management and Planning from UA, an MBA from New University of Lisbon, and a PhD in Tourism from UA. She is the co-author of various papers published in several journals and conference proceedings, as well as of various book chapters. She has also presented several works at conferences and seminars and participated in research projects in the area of tourism. Her research interests are the competitiveness of tourism destinations, consumer behaviour in tourism, and the marketing of tourism destinations.

Jenny Chen is a Senior Lecturer in Human Resource Management at the University of the West of England, where she teaches modules such as critical people analytics and quantitative research methods. She is also an active member of the Human Resources, Work and Employment (HRWE) research group based at the Bristol Business School. She obtained her PhD in Policy Development and Management from the University of Manchester. Her research interests include role theory, identity construction, graduate employability, organisational socialisation, social network and career transition, along with a general research interest in cross-cultural management.

Robert Coelen is Professor of Internationalisation of Higher Education at NHL Stenden University of Applied Sciences. He is also Director of the Centre for Internationalisation of Education, a collaboration between his university and the University of Groningen, Campus Fryslân. Before these roles he was a university executive at four different universities, concerned with the management of internationalisation in Europe and Australia. He is Associate Editor of the *Journal of International Students* and reviews papers for other journals in the field. His research interests relate to internationalisation activities and the impact they have on individuals, institutions, and society in general. He started his academic life as a molecular virologist.

Keren Coney is a Careers and Employability Consultant at Liverpool John Moores University and former Co-Chair of the UK's AGCAS (Association of Graduate Careers Advisory Services) Disability Task Group. With a particular concern for disabled students and graduates and the challenges that exist when many of these individuals seek to enter and succeed in the workplace, Keren regularly speaks on this topic at conferences, events, and training sessions. In addition, Keren is currently studying for a PhD that seeks to explore what is required for autistic students to successfully progress to employment when they graduate, based at the Autism Centre for Education and Research at the University of Birmingham, UK.

Fiona Cosson is Head of School of Humanities and Social Sciences at Anglia Ruskin University, Cambridge. She was previously Deputy Head of the Department of Humanities and Law at Bournemouth University. Fiona is a historian of Modern Britain, with interests in oral history and memory, and public and community history and heritage. She has a professional background in community and cultural engagement and participation with archives, charities, and museums.

Carlos Costa is Full Professor (Professor Catedrático) at the Department (School) of Economics, Management, Industrial Engineering and Tourism (DEGEIT) of the University of Aveiro, and Tourism Expert at the European Commission. He is Editor-in-Chief of the *Journal of Tourism and Development*, and Associate Editor of the *Tourism Review*, *Journal of Destination Marketing Management*, and the *Journal of Hospitality and Tourism Management*. He holds a PhD and MSc in Tourism Management (University of Surrey) and a BSc in Urban and Regional Planning (University of Aveiro). Carlos is the leader of the PhD Tourism Programme of the University of Aveiro and is also the head of the Tourism Research Centre of the University of Aveiro (included in Governance, Competitiveness and Public Policies (GOVCOPP) and evaluated by the Portuguese government as 'Very Good'). He is also Scientific Coordinator of IDTOUR – Unique Solutions, a tourism start-up company (private sector) based at the university.

Victoria Crowe is Senior Careers and Employability Analyst at the Open University. As a psychology graduate, Victoria has worked as a researcher for the police and a national education programme, and as a Senior Lecturer in Psychology, leading on research methods and statistics. Victoria is also a chartered psychologist.

Gemma Dale is a Lecturer in the Business School at Liverpool John Moores University (LJMU), where she teaches programmes on employability and personal and professional development. Prior to joining LJMU, Gemma worked in human resources for 20 years, holding a variety of senior positions. She is the author of *Flexible Working*, and *How to work remotely*, published by Kogan Page, and regularly writes about flexible and remote work. Gemma is a Chartered Fellow of the CIPD, Fellow of the HEA, Certified Management and Business Educator and a qualified mediator and coach. Gemma is a prolific user of social media in a professional and personal context, and writes an award-winning blog about work and human resources.

Stéphanie Devèze is the Deputy Head of the Unit of Education and Employment Relationships within the French Ministry of Higher Education, Research and Innovation. She is responsible for the creation and implementation of mechanisms to best support students' transition throughout their studies and their integration within the workplace. She is the Programme Manager of the EU-funded project SPRINT, which aims to standardise best practices regarding internships. The founder of JURISUP, a network of HE and research lawyers with over 150 institutions, she now serves as its Honorary President. She has presented at numerous conferences throughout Europe regarding internships and work experience, including the 2021 International HRK Modus Conference, sponsored by the German Ministry of Education. She is an active member of the International Association of Student Affairs and Services (IASAS), the Association of Women Leaders in Higher Education, Research and Innovation (AFDESRI), and the Association EVALUE – European Evaluators of the ERASMUS + agency.

Marîlia Durão is Assistant Professor and Head of the Hospitality Management Degree at Universidade Portucalense Infante D. Henrique (UPT). She holds a PhD in Tourism and a MSc in Tourism Planning and Management from the University of Aveiro (UA), and a BSc in Tourism from the Higher Institute of Administration and Management (ISAG). In 2015, she was granted a doctoral scholarship by the Portuguese Foundation for Science and Technology (FCT), and her PhD thesis was devoted to career management, employee retention, and quality of work life in the tourism and hospitality industry. She is also an integrated member of Research on Economics, Management, and Information Technologies (REMIT) (UPT) and a member of Governance, Competitiveness and Public Policies (GOVCOPP) (UA).

Sarah Flynn is an Associate Professor, Principal Fellow of the Higher Education Academy and a National Teaching Fellow. She is Associate Director of Learning and Teaching at the University of Hertfordshire, with responsibility for the development of work-based and flexible learning opportunities. Sarah has many years' experience in academic development and supporting curriculum design processes, specialising in vocationally current curricula and assessment. Her expertise in employability and student placements has been fostered by long-standing work with ASET, the Work-Based and Placement Learning Association, and collaboration with the UK Quality Assurance Agency. Her scholarly activity centres on authentic pedagogy, employability, and equitable experiences and outcomes for all students.

Ken Fox teaches in the School of Creative Arts and Industries, Canterbury Christ Church University. He is School Director of Learning and Teaching, a University Teaching Fellow and a Senior Fellow of the Higher Education Academy. Ken teaches and researches about the representation of landscape and cityscape in cinema and television. He is module leader for the employability strand in the Film Production and Film, Radio and Television degrees. His most recent publications include 'The Authenticity Paradox and the Western', in Lovell and Hitchmough's *Authenticity in North America: Place, Tourism, Heritage, Culture and the Popular Imagination* (2020) and 'Reclaiming the Irish Border in Contemporary Cinema', *Australasian Journal of Irish Studies* (2020).

Leanne Freeman works at Cardiff Metropolitan University, where she currently holds two positions: half of her time is spent within Cardiff School of Sport and

Health Sciences and the other half within the Quality Enhancement Directorate. Her main research interest is gender, within both HE and the family.

Hugo Gaggiotti is Professor in the Bristol Business School at the University of the West of England, Bristol. The focus of his writing is the intersections between professional mindsets and how organisations could contribute to the construction of vulnerability in particular contexts of repetitive change, displacement, transfiguration, and liminality, like international borderlands, multinational assembly plants, and ephemeral project-based work. His work has appeared in a range of interdisciplinary journals, and his books include *Organizational Ethnography: An Experiential and Practical Guide* (2021) and *Origins of Organising* (2019).

Ricky Gee Ricky Gee is a senior lecturer based in the Department of Social and Political Sciences at Nottingham Trent University. Ricky's research focuses on philosophical, sociological and political dimensions of career, influenced via Derridean and decolonial thought. Ricky's research takes a transdisciplinary approach to studying career within contemporary society to explore how social forces influence career trajectory, anticipation, and the seeking of solidarity to challenge modalities of oppression. Ricky is an active member of the NTU Work Futures Research Group and has teaching experience on a range of social science programmes at under- and postgraduate levels, as well as with PhD supervision.

Louise Glover is Director of Employability and Enrichment for University of Sheffield School of Law. She directs the Commercial Law student pro bono clinic at the university, and she has recently co-authored an article on clinical legal education published in the *European Journal of Legal Education*. Louise's interests in employability and professional skills development stem from her background as a solicitor in professional practice prior to joining the Law School.

Vicki Harvey is a Lecturer in People Management at the University of Salford Business School. Prior to a move to academia, she worked as a training and development consultant with the public sector for over 10 years. At present, her research interests are the employability discourse and curricula with higher education and the impact on development for undergraduate students. Vicki is currently working to publish and develop the work from her PhD (completed in 2019) on the student voice in employability within business and management education. This endeavour supports other interests, including the role of capitals, HE policy and ideology, and pedagogy that contributes to our understanding of and practices for employability development.

Scott Hurrell is Senior Lecturer in Human Resource Management and Organisational Behaviour at the Adam Smith Business School, University of Glasgow. His research interests include: transitions from education to work; skills and work organisation; the effect of digital technologies on work and workers; and fighting workplace inequalities. Scott also has an interest in critical realist approaches to studying work, employment, and organisations. He has provided research and consultancy for various organisations and is currently an Associate Editor of *Employee Relations*.

Bob Gilworth, School of Education and Professional Development, University of Huddersfield. Bob has been in leadership roles in higher education careers and employability for around 25 years. Most recently, he was the Director of the Careers Group, University of London. Prior to that, he was Director of the Careers Centre at the University of Leeds for around 13 years and, before that, Head of the Careers Service at the University of Huddersfield. He is now back at Huddersfield in an academic role, teaching on the MA in Careers Guidance and Development and engaging in research and consultancy in the field. Bob is a past president of AGCAS (the Association of Graduate Careers Advisory services), a Fellow of NICEC (National Institute for Career Education and Counselling), and a Principal Fellow of the Higher Education Academy.

Carol Jarvis is Professor in Knowledge Exchange and Innovation in the Bristol Business School at the University of the West of England (UWE). Her research focuses on the application of complexity approaches to leadership, coaching, innovation and entrepreneurship, and the everyday experience of change and innovation. She has an active interest in experiential and team-based approaches to learning, from undergraduate students to participants on executive education programmes, and she played a leading role in designing UWE's suite of team entrepreneurship programmes. Her research is published in *Management Learning*, *Advances in Developing Human Resources*, and *Entrepreneurship Education and Pedagogy*.

Kathy Jordan has been a teacher and teacher educator for over 30 years, most recently as an Associate Professor, and she is currently an Honorary University Fellow with the School of Education, RMIT University. Kathy has a range of research interests, including teacher use of ICT, teacher education policy and practice, and professional experience. She has published widely in these fields and presented at numerous national and international conferences. Kathy has led funded research projects around supporting beginning teachers when new to the profession, encouraging teacher systemic change in using ICT, and innovative models of professional experience.

Selen Kars-Unluoglu is Associate Professor in Organisation Studies in the Bristol Business School at the University of the West England. She researches the ways organisations and entrepreneurs develop and deploy their intangible resources, such as knowledge, capabilities, and networks, to generate growth and achieve learning. Her work is informed by interpretative phenomenology and practice-based approaches with a focus on the micro-level and on lived experience. She has published widely and undertook applied research projects on these topics. Her research has appeared in *Innovation: Management, Theory and Practice*, the *International Small Business Journal*, the *Journal of Management and Organization*, *Leadership* and *Management Learning*.

Siyang Kong currently works as a Survey Data Officer at Netherlands Interdisciplinary Demographic Institute (NIDI) for the Generations and Gender Programme (GGP). She obtained her doctoral degree in sociology in July 2021 at Interuniversity Center for Social Science Theory and Methodology (ICS) at Utrecht University. Her research involves broad research themes in sociology and labour economics. Her research interests concern social inequality and stratification, gender, labour markets, and quantitative methods. Her work appears in reputable international journals, such as *Research in Social Stratification and Mobility*.

Paul Koshy is a Research Fellow at the National Centre for Student Equity in Higher Education (NCSEHE), based at Curtin University in Perth, Western Australia. His research focuses on the influence of disadvantage (equity status) on participation and outcomes in higher education, and the development of policy measures to address it.

Lydia Lauder is a Quality Manager at the Careers and Employability Services at the Open University. Her professional and research interests include quality assurance, professional development and identity, and evidence-based practice. She combines her background in pure and applied science with over 20 years' experience in the field of careers guidance working across adult and community, further and higher education, and public sector careers provision. She represents the Training, Research and Sector Development constituency on the Career Development Institute's Professional Standards Committee.

Anna Levett is a Senior Fellow of the Higher Education Academy and in 2020 received a Collaborative Award for Teaching Excellence from Advance HE. She has over 17 years' experience working in further and higher education, specialising in employability, careers, and enterprise education. Anna is currently Head of Careers and Employment at the University of Hertfordshire. She leads on equality, diversity, and inclusion for the service and works across the institution to ensure all students and recent graduates have access to the careers and enterprise support they need to progress.

Ian Li is Senior Lecturer in Health and Labour Economics, based at the School of Population and Global Health in the University of Western Australia. Ian's research interests include higher education policy and equity, graduate outcomes, and determinants of well-being, and he has a track record of competitive grants and publications in those areas. His teaching has been recognised by several teaching awards, including a national award for Excellence and Innovation in Teaching awarded by the Council of Academic Public Health Institutions Australasia. Ian is an editorial board member of the *Journal of Higher Education Policy and Management*, and he co-edits the *Australian Journal of Labour Economics*. He is a Research Fellow of the IZA Institute of Labor, University of Bonn, and is Senior Fellow of the Higher Education Academy.

Dian Liu is currently Associate Professor at Faculty of Social Sciences, University of Stavanger. Her research combines collaboration between different social science disciplines in the fields of sociology, educational science, and psychology, using analytical lenses including social class, gender, identity, and ethnicity. Her current work comprises four major branches: mobility of university graduates; graduate entrepreneurship across cultures; anti-bullying from the sociocultural perspective; and internationalisation of higher education, underpinned by a strong agenda in achieving social justice through research and public engagement.

Daria Luchinskaya is a Lecturer in the Department of Work, Employment and Organisation, University of Strathclyde Business School. Her research interests are in graduate transitions to employment, skill development and skill utilisation, and in using mixed-methods research approaches. Previously, Daria was a Research Fellow at the Institute for Employment Research, University of Warwick, and a Research Associate at Wales Public Services 2025, hosted by Cardiff Business School.

Katie McAllister is the HE Manager for Business and Education at University Centre Peterborough, part of the Inspire Education Group. She is also the director of a small construction business and manages a portfolio of rental properties. She is currently an education doctorate student, conducting case study research on how higher education providers (HEIs) create alliances with small and medium sized enterprises (SMEs) with the intention of creating a practical guide for HEIs wishing to make incremental or discrete changes to their SME alliance creation practices.

Richard Mendez is the Director of Access, Skills and Apprenticeships at the University of Chester. His work spans the graduate labour market, widening participation, curriculum development, and employer engagement. His work has appeared in a number of publications including research journals, *Times Higher Education*, *Professional Manager* and a book on the topic of supporting dyslexic adults in higher education. He has presented keynote talks and conference papers on the topic of employability and the embedding of employability skills in the curriculum in Spain, Canada, Japan, Hong Kong, Ireland, and the UK. He has held appointments at the University of Leicester, Keele University, and the University of Greenwich. As documented in his chapter, it is in his work at the University of Greenwich that he has led on the progression aspect of the Access and Participation Plan.

Jenny Mercer is a Principal Lecturer and Reader at Cardiff Metropolitan University. Her research in applied psychology spans a number of the cognate disciplines, including education. She has a keen interest in the experiences of students and staff in higher education, illustrated in publications about non-traditional students (e.g. mature age students; those on Erasmus placements), students with mood disorders, and research about collaborative working.

Seamus Needham is a Senior Lecturer and Project Manager: Grants at the Institute for Post-School Studies (IPSS) in the Faculty of Education at the University of the Western Cape (UWC), Cape Town. Seamus has been active in vocational education, policy, and development for about 25 years. His current research interests include technical and vocational education and training (TVET) policy and development, articulation, and dual education. He served on the Ministerial committee of Articulation Policy in 2013, and he has served on the Human Resource Development Council of South Africa (HRDCSA) Further Education and Training (now TVET) Technical Task Team. He is currently the project manager for a five-year TVET Research Programme in collaboration with the Department of Higher Education and Training and the National Skills Fund. Seamus is also the Chairperson of the Council for Higher Education Policy Reference Group, overseeing the development of an articulation policy into and within the Higher Education Qualifications Sub-Framework.

Catherine O'Connor is Pro Vice-Chancellor for Education and Experience at Leeds Trinity University. She has led work to engage with employers around labour market issues in Leeds and developed a number of projects designed to look at how skills gaps can be addressed. Her research interests focus on how universities work with both students and employers to address labour market issues and how students can be given a voice as key stakeholders in this agenda.

Belgin Okay-Somerville is Senior Lecturer of Human Resource Management at the Adam Smith Business School, University of Glasgow. Her research interests include employability, skills utilisation and job quality, career transitions, chance events, and employee wellbeing, especially among younger workers. Belgin is the Youth Employment Lead of the European Association of Work and Organizational Psychology Impact Incubator (EAWOPii) and an Associate Editor of *EAWOP in Practice*.

Attila Pausits is a Full Professor for Higher Education Research and Development and Head of the Department for Higher Education Research at the University of Continuing Education Krems. He is the Academic Director of the Erasmus Mundus Joint Master's Programme Research and Innovation in Higher Education, MSc, spokesman of the Austrian Higher Education Researchers Network, and a member of the newly established European Commission expert group for Quality Investment in Education and Training. Attila has led a number of European and national projects in the field of higher education research and development and authored and co-authored a large number of academic publications, national and international studies, and reports related to policy and institutional development issues in higher education. His research interests include higher education governance, organisational development, the third mission of higher education institutions, and academic continuing education with reference to lifelong learning.

Holly Prescott is currently the Careers Adviser for Postgraduate Researchers at the University of Birmingham. She holds a PhD in Literature and Cultural Geography from the University of Birmingham (2011) and a PGDip (QCG) in Career Guidance from Coventry University (2016). Holly is particularly passionate about developing postgraduate researchers' awareness of career routes beyond and adjacent to academic research, helping them to make transitions into meaningful postdoctoral careers. In February 2021, she founded PostGradual – the PhD Careers Blog: www.phd-careers.co.uk. Her recent publications include 'Beyond the Doctorate: Getting Your First Job' in Townsend et al.'s *How to Keep Your Doctorate on Track* (2020). Holly is also a content writer for the Royal National Institute for Blind People (RNIB).

Josephine Pryce is the Academic Head of MBA Academic Director at James Cook University in Cairns. She is a scholar of organisational behaviour with a keen interest in 'the nature of work'. Josephine came to academia with a strong industry background, having worked for the hotel industry for many years. During that time, she developed a strong appreciation of the challenges faced by workers, employers, and organisations in service industries. Her PhD extended understanding of service predispositions and organisational culture through 'An Examination of the Influence of Organisational Culture in the Hospitality Industry'. Josephine seeks to enrich her research, which leads to better understanding of the working lives of people.

Vianna Renaud is a Placement Development Advisor at Bournemouth University. Supporting students during their sandwich placement in industry, she serves as an independent coach for students and employers to ensure a quality placement experience. She has presented at numerous conferences relating to employability and has published articles in 'What Do Graduates Do?', an annual report by the Association of Graduate and Careers Advisory Services (AGCAS) and Prospects, and the *Journal for Comparative and International Education*, as well as for Diversity Abroad. She is a Trustee of ASET, the UK Work based and Placement Learning Association, and involved with the International Association for Student Affairs and Services. She has co-authored chapters in *Enhancing Employability in Higher Education through Work Based Learning* (2018) and *Global Lean for Higher Education* (2019). She was awarded the 2021 National Undergraduate Employability Award on Outstanding Contribution to Work Experience.

Janice Scarinci is the Coordinator of the Master of International Tourism and Hospitality Management (MITHM) and the Bachelor of Tourism, Hospitality and Events (BTHE) at James Cook University (JCU) in Queensland. Janice earned her PhD in Tourism at JCU whilst on a Rotary Ambassadorial Scholarship from the USA. Janice has taught hospitality and tourism in five countries on three continents and has over 20 years of academic experience as a department chair, director of a hospitality and tourism institute, and a director of teaching and learning. Her research interests include guest satisfaction, motivation, and marketing; sustainable tourism and lodging; and employability skills and experiential learning. Janice is passionate about providing graduates with employability skills to succeed in the tourism, hospitality, and events industry internationally.

Dora Scholarios is Professor of Work Psychology at University of Strathclyde Business School. Her research interests include the relationship between human resource management (HRM) practice and employee health and wellbeing, recruitment and selection, and youth transitions into employment. She was one of the editors-in-chief of the *Human Resource Management* journal from 2016 to 2020, and she is currently a member of several journal editorial boards and professional associations in the fields of psychology, and business and management. She is also a chartered psychologist.

Jessica Schueller is a PhD Student at Miami University (Ohio) in Educational Leadership and Applied Statistics, with a concentration in international higher education research. She holds an Erasmus Mundus Joint Master's degree in Research and Innovation in Higher Education from Tampere University and Danube University Krems. She is also a Research Associate with the Cross-Border Education Research Team (C-BERT). Her work focuses on transnational higher education, international student employability, and the internationalisation of career services.

Mónica Segovia-Pérez has a PhD in Sociology from Universidad Complutense de Madrid and is Associate Professor at Rey Juan Carlos University in Madrid and Head of Sociology. Her main research fields are gender and tourism (working conditions, leadership, glass ceiling, entrepreneurship), gender and technology, and sociology. Over the years, Mónica has taken part in 25 research projects (national and international) and has led nine of them. She is the author of 54 journal articles, some in Q1 (JCR–SJR), books, chapters, and technical reports, and she has participated in 50 congresses, 32 of them international. Mónica is a member of the Board of Directors of Mainstreaming Gender Studies Network in Human, Social and Legal Sciences (GENET, CSIC, Spain), and she is member of the Spanish Association of Scientific Experts in Tourism (AECIT).

Yulia Shumilova is a PhD researcher at the Higher Education Group (HEG), Faculty of Management and Business, Tampere University, focusing on higher education research and international graduate employability in Finland. An Erasmus Mundus Master alumnus, Ms Shumilova has 20 years of experience in international education coordinating academic mobility, joint master's programmes, EU-funded projects and international conferences.

Rebecca Spooner-Lane is Associate Professor at the Queensland University of Technology. Rebecca is the Director of the Quality Teaching Performance Assessment (QTPA) for pre-service teacher education and three partner universities in Australia. In 2020, she was awarded the QUT Vice Chancellor's Excellence Award for her leadership of the QTPA. She has a keen interest in the professional development and career progression of teachers from graduate to lead teacher. She has worked on a number of projects investigating mentoring, school leadership and school improvement, highly accomplished and lead teacher certification, and classroom readiness of graduating teachers.

Kate Terkanian is a Senior Lecturer in Modern History at Bournemouth University. After careers in television production and in the museum sector, she received her PhD in 2018. Kate is the unit leader for Bournemouth University's public history units, including the Graduate Project. Her research focuses on gender and the media. She is particularly interested in public perception of the past.

K. Thirumaran is an academic at the JCU Singapore Business School. He received his PhD from the National University of Singapore. With over 10 years of working experience, both in Singapore and the USA, he continues to combine practice and theory in his teaching pedagogy. Thiru coined the term 'affinity tourism' and has published on a variety of topics focusing on service excellence, luxury, and cultural tourism. He is a keen collaborative researcher with scholars and postgraduates across the world.

Michael Tomlinson is an Associate Professor at the Southampton Education School, University of Southampton, where he has been based since 2011. His interests are in higher education policy and the interplay between higher education and the labour market, focusing on both the perspectives of graduates and employers. He has published extensively in these areas and is the author of three key books in this area, including *Graduate Employability in Context: Theory, Research and Debate* (2017).

Iwi Ugiagbe-Green has worked in higher education for over 20 years in a wide range of professional services and academic roles. She worked as both a management and financial accountant for nearly a decade and wanted to be a finance director, before her heart took her into the brilliant world of accounting education. She is currently a Reader (Accounting, Finance & Banking) & Head of Degree award and progression gaps (Business & Law) at Manchester Metropolitan University. She is the department lead on postgraduate employability and the faculty lead on developing education excellence (DEE). Her current research focuses on intersectionality issues impacting on the racialised experiences of students and degree-awarding gaps in the academy, with particular focus on student transition from higher education to the graduate labour market and postgraduate research. She is the principal investigator of the 2021–25 UKRI/Research Funded project Accomplished Study Programme in Research Excellence (ASPIRE), which seeks to address access, continuation and progression issues for Black scholars into doctoral level study and graduate employment.

Joan Upson has been a Senior University Teacher of Law at Sheffield University for a number of years and is the Director of the LLB Law Programme. She has a particular interest in widening participation and in non-standard entrants, their recruitment, transition, and continued development.

Alison Walker is a Senior Lecturer in Adult Continuing Education at Swansea University. Based in the School of Social Sciences, she runs the part-time degree programme aimed at non-traditional adult learners. Her main research areas are focused on student experience, particularly adult learners, experiential learning, and volunteering.

Acknowledgements

The editorial team wish to express their thanks to Sage Publishing for their support for the project of developing and publishing this book. In particular, we wish to thank Matthew Waters, Publisher, for his initiative in first suggesting the book, and Colette Wilson, for her professional and prompt support throughout the writing process. We also wish to thank, Zoheb Khan and all those who supported the book through its final copy editing, design, publication, and marketing stages.

We thank Professor Paul Gough, Vice Chancellor at the Arts University Bournemouth, for his suggestion on editorial team contributors; Tracey Spiller, RMIT, Australia, for her patient assistance and support as the *Handbook* was developed: and Natasha Coldwell, Arts University Bournemouth, and Natasha Michell, Falmouth University, for their assistance with administration arrangements as the book was developed.

Finally, our thanks to all those who enthusiastically submitted chapter suggestions. Not all these proposals could be included within the space limitations of the book, but they were a reminder of the scale and diversity of interest in graduate employability. Whether or not we have been able to include proposed chapters, we hope that there will be future opportunities to share perspectives of employability knowledge, policy, and practice.

Foreword

Lord Willets

The wide range of chapters in this *Handbook* shows the extraordinary diversity of ways in which universities can contribute to graduate employability. It would be hard for any one higher education institution to cover all these roles and tackle the different challenges that come with them. That is why we should celebrate the diverse missions of different universities. The chapters show that somewhere some institution is seeking to improve the delivery of graduate employability.

It is particularly important for today's debate on higher education that these chapters show that universities can deliver technical training and education. The English debate in particular suffers from the belief that universities that provide a useful education must somehow be betraying their liberal purpose – a belief perpetrated by John Henry Neman's influential writing in the nineteenth century. But more courses than ever provide a licence to practise a particular vocation. As jobs become more complex and demanding so we may expect to see more of them requiring higher education – as had already happened for teaching and now then nursing. That link to employment takes universities back to their medieval origins as training for service in church or state.

Fair access to good employment opportunities is important. We have tended to focus in England on fairness of access to higher education. A lot of progress has been made here though there is still more to do. And it is encouraging that higher education is the one stage of education where students from disadvantaged areas outperform the average. But we are increasingly aware of depressing evidence that for a given level of higher education achievement, graduates from less advantaged backgrounds do less well in the job market than their more advantaged peers. This has led to a new focus for universities on boosting the employability prospects of their more disadvantaged students after graduation. It is a legitimate use of access funding. This *Handbook* includes useful examples of what can be done here.

The focus of attention has tended to be on the employability of graduates who have honours degrees. That is only part of the story, however. Increasing numbers of graduates are staying on for master's degrees and for doctorates. The coverage of such graduates in the *Handbook* is welcome evidence of the breadth and diversity of the collection. Part of the problem is the assumption that for doctoral students the ultimate objective is an academic career. This is a dangerously misleading picture and the chapters on employability outcomes for doctoral students correct the picture by showing the wide range of alternative outcomes that are open to them.

The *Handbook* also covers the key, sensitive issue of skills and subject knowledge as the best means of promoting employability. This debate between knowing stuff and knowing how runs on, with employability as a key focus. The difference between them is, however, increasingly hard to define. It is clear that mathematical and digital are increasingly important for employability but are they subject knowledge of maths or more practical numeracy and digital skills? And many young people develop their skills not in the abstract but through a subject which is of particular interest to them. It is hard to develop skills in the abstract. Even if the skills are the end learning, study can be the means. Even if the skills contribute most to employability in many areas, it is hard to think of many professions and activities without a body of knowledge as their foundation.

This debate on employability is not just British. It is global, reflecting the global growth in participation in higher education. And this is shown in the range of perspectives in these chapters, from over 20 different countries. We can learn from the expertise and historic roles of higher education in many countries. Overseas students bring with them attitudes and assumptions about employability which are a continuous stimulus and challenge. And the divergence is not just national – there are important local and regional studies, too. Sometimes it is one entrepreneurial figure in one place who has tried something new and different from which we can all learn.

There is, of course, more to higher education than employability. And employability itself is a much richer concept than simply earnings. Students themselves recognise this. The chapters in this important collection do not make the mistake of taking employability as the be all and end all of higher education. But it does matter for many students – and funders. This *Handbook* shows the many ways in which universities can contribute to that important but not sole or exclusive ambition.

Looking ahead, key trends are emerging. One is the dramatic opening up of new data that makes it possible to track graduates out into the labour market far better than before. In the medium term, we should be able to see the employment outcomes for different graduates from different universities and with different backgrounds and prior attainments. This will enable us to observe not just absolute attainment but also distance travelled. We may also be able to get valuable micro evidence about particular approaches at particular institutions that are most effective in boosting employability. We will also be able to see performance on metrics other than employability – such as health and mental well-being – and whether success in delivering employability is associated with success on these metrics. We think that we will find evidence that employability complements other benefits from higher education rather than offsetting them. And the evidence we get will create positive feedback loops influencing the behaviour and choices both of students and the educational institutions serving them.

This valuable *Handbook* reviews a wide range of current practice and thinking but it is not the last word in a rapidly evolving and advancing understanding of employability.

David Willetts served as UK Minister for Universities and Science from 2010 to 2014. He is a Visiting Professor at King's College, London. His book *A University Education* is published by Oxford University Press.

Editors' Introduction

Tania Broadley, Yuzhuo Cai, Miriam Firth, Emma Hunt and John Neugebauer

This *Handbook* has been written at the invitation of Sage to provide a scholarly perspective of universities' and higher education's role in the employability of graduates. The aim of the book is to share a diverse range of issues of employability. It is curated as an intentionally eclectic collection, with contributions from academics, careers advisers, and practitioners.

Across the cultural, societal, and political imperatives of their histories and geographies, universities have, and have had, many differently perceived roles. Those roles may be measured by purposes, aims, and – increasingly – metrics, league tables, and word-of-mouth reputations. Whilst the respective weightings of each role may be contentious, few would argue against the importance of the current focus on 'employability', whether from the perspective of the individual graduate or of wider society and the economic benefits.

The intention of the *Handbook* is to provide a wide and informed perspective. Chapters have been written to provide a breadth of academic, best practice, and practical insight. Chapter authors have been selected to include national as well as multinational and international perspectives. We believe that the *Handbook* provides a 'state of the art' insight into employability, though we recognise that not every issue of graduate employability can be covered in a single volume. Therefore, we also hope that it will also stimulate further enquiry and research, not only of the roles of universities, but also within other key employability stakeholders, including graduate destinations and employers.

BACKGROUND

Set against the two millennia of university history, the role of universities and higher education institutes (HEIs) as a place for promotion of graduate employability is relatively recent (Yorke and Knight, 2006) – and that role has been to varying extents accepted and contested.

John Henry Newman (1852) regarded intellectual study at university as a goal in itself – with the 'soul' of a university leaving its mark on the student. In contrast, in *The Wealth of Nations*, Adam Smith (1819: 361) challenged whether the value of content of teaching in schools and universities was 'proper preparation for business'. More recently, this was echoed by Reg Revans (1978), a professor at the University of Manchester, who was critical of the role of university professors, highlighting the important interaction between learning *and* action.

Business in this reference is taken to relate to wider contexts than organisational, profitable, businesses. Students are not simply prepared for paid employment but with the skills and knowledge to tackle any role in graduate life. Those horizons of graduate life appear further off, as retirement ages increase, and less predictable, as employment roles change.

HEIs can therefore prepare students for societal support and engagement, but also enable action via completion of their higher education programmes. Graduate employability is not only an essential component of university curricula, but an imperative series of actions for our graduates to develop for working life.

METHODOLOGY AND SCOPE OF THE BOOK

The chapters of this book have been selected following an open call for contributions, as well as from chapters proposed following invitations from conferences.

The *Handbook* represents knowledge sharing through scholarly and some practical and best-practice contributions. Research methods are both qualitative and quantitative, and include case studies. In this way, the book is intended to inform, and to stimulate further discussion, research, new learning, and practical application across the higher education sector and into working lives.

The focus of the *Handbook* is on employability, but not about which universities lead to the highest salaries or wealth after graduation. This area, and the extent to which so-called elite universities produce the highest returns, is already widely analysed at academic level (for example, see Rivera, 2015; Sullivan, et. al., 2018; Berghaus, 2020), by government organisations and think tanks, and in the more popular media.

No chapters were submitted to analyse professional bodies' and uniformed organisations' perspectives of graduate employability. Yet we are aware of demand and supply mismatches in these areas (for example, UK medical, paramedical, and nurse training). It is not possible to address all areas of the field in one publication. Some disciplines and geographical and occupational sectors have not been included, but it is hoped there will be sufficient stimulation within these chapters to consider applications and approaches that translate into these disciplines and sectors.

CONTEXT AND FUTURE DIRECTIONS

Context

Universities have adapted their focus in response to political, social, and economic challenges over the years. Barnett (2000: 13) noted how universities sought to find a new position and value recognised by an enlarged audience of interested parties.

Political steering by governments in Western nations has been instrumental in how universities have been managed and organised in recent years, with a sustained focus on the vocational outputs of universities, to supply qualified students to the workplace, which has, in turn, seemingly replaced or reduced the emphasis on other attributes of university study, such as the development of an individual's mind and the enhancement of knowledge for its own sake (Becher, 2001).

The stance made here is well known across higher education: either learn for a specific employment role/industry, or develop as a student of a particular subject. However, we contend that universities do not need to be either/or institutions, to prepare for work or develop critical knowledge. Universities can provide an appropriate mixture of learning and application of knowledge to enable skilled workers for the twenty-first century (Trilling and Fadel, 2009). Yorke and Knight (2006) asserted the importance of 'embedding employability': employability does not need to be separate from the core studies in higher education, nor does it need to be an addition to existing curricula; and the 'embedding' of employability is not a hindrance, but a lens through which to identify how and where employability skills and knowledge can be developed within the programme, unit, or class.

The employability of higher education students is now a key area of attention for society, governments, and in graduate life. This attention paid to employability is supported by a focus on research, policy development, metrics, university ranking criteria, and student choice.

FUTURE DIRECTIONS

Extension of Global University Education

There is extensive evidence both globally and within individual states of the growth of university education and the perceived value of the higher education experience.

Between 2010 and 2020, the Organisation for Economic Co-Operation and Development (OECD, 2021: 42) identified a 9% increase in those aged 25-34 with tertiary education. Data from the OECD show that 39% of adults have tertiary education. Even so, participation varies from 20% in some countries to over 50% in countries such as Canada, Ireland, Israel, Luxembourg, the Republic of Korea, the Russian Federation, and the USA (OECD, 2021: 43).

In terms of the value of higher/tertiary education, the OECD (2021) have also shown wider economic, social, and health benefits. For example:

> 58% of 25–34-year-old adults who have not completed upper secondary education are employed compared with 78% among those with upper secondary or post-secondary non-tertiary attainment and 85% among those with tertiary attainment. (OECD, 2021)

Graduate status is also linked with the positive development of employment, per capita income, and health and social outcomes (OECD, 2021). As a further example, the African Union Agenda 2063 states the following as a goal:

> Revitalize and expand tertiary education, research and innovation to address continental challenges and promote global competitiveness as well as harmonising tertiary education qualification across its member states. (African Unity, 2013).

Whilst the debate in some individual communities may be whether a degree is worthwhile, there is an unmistakable global intention and trajectory for future higher education. At a global level, the number of university and HEI graduates has grown, and is expected to grow further.

Co-ordination Between Higher Education and Graduate Destinations

The emphasis of the *Handbook* is on contributions from writers representing employers and graduate-destination organisations, rather than on the destination organisations themselves. Whilst the research reports the voices of these organisations, this is not necessarily the same as destination organisations writing in their own voice of the challenges and benefits of graduate employability. We encourage more research from, and into, destination organisations' perspectives on graduate employability.

Research in progress (but not yet published) by Emma Hunt, a co-editor to this volume highlights some of the benefits, but also the challenges, for higher education, employers and destination organisations, of co-ordinating graduate employability with graduate life opportunities. Hunt's work is based on her reflections and experience as chair of the UK Dorset Skills Board, part of the Dorset Local Enterprise Partnership (LEP).

The UK Dorset Skills Board is made up of private business members, university vice chancellors and college principals, and the local authority. The key aims are to keep the intelligence gathering live and relevant to the strategic economic direction of the Dorset LEP area and to ensure a diversity of voices were sought and acted upon. This work is reported to the main LEP Board and linked firmly to the national policy agenda and access to investment funding.

Hunt observes strong private sector support for the Skills Board as well as funding from national government, which enabled the local labour market to be a strong evidence base. In turn, this enabled the Skills Board members to develop a local skills strategy for the future. Even so, Hunt also observes some of the practical challenges that LEPs (of which there are 37 in the UK) encounter with their work. These challenges include:

> Keeping alive the dialogue, opportunity, and energy in maintaining and responding to changing market opportunities and challenges.
>
> Bringing together a comprehensive and cohesive strategy in a fragmented employment market. As an example, large organisations represent less than 1% of employing organisations in the Dorset LEP region, where Hunt's research is based, but employ approximately 20% of the workforce. Across the region as a whole, employing organisations have an average of 7.3 employees, in contrast with the average in England of 9.5 (Dorset County Council, 2022).
>
> Responding to the dramatic changes faced by both education and destination organisations, arising from the COVID-19 pandemic.
>
> Prioritising investment decisions.

Similar planning challenges are reflected at national and supranational level.

Despite these challenges, it is preferable for HEIs and destination organisations to work together, rather than leaving employability to chance or market forces. Hunt concludes that it is clear that when national governments present the challenge of skills development as a national problem linked to ongoing productivity challenges, the response is most likely to be effective when interpreted by local interests working in partnership, as in the case of the Skills Board. Local know-how supported by local and national data sets has been instrumental in deciding on regional focus and ambition, which might not have been possible through centralised initiatives.

INCLUSION

Measures of the success of higher education and employability are not only about the raw numbers passing through university, but also the balance of opportunity available to all.

In their global study of workplace equality and diversity, the International Labour Office found that progress in many states was slow and patchy, and that issues of discrimination in the workplace were ever-changing – and that 'new challenges arise where old ones remain at best only partially answered' (ILO, 2011: ix). There is evidence from more recent analysis that the progress continues to be progress, but also continues to be patchy and slow.

To illustrate the point with relevance to graduate employability, the OECD (2021) noted that on average across OECD countries, 52% of younger women have a tertiary degree. However, the data also show that women are over-represented in health and welfare, but are under-represented in the broad field of science, technology, engineering, and mathematics (OECD 2021: 42).

Of course, the agenda for equality, diversity, and inclusion is broad and complex, which impacts on all those in working life, including graduates and their employability. Inclusion challenges not only derive from single types of 'difference', but also intersectionality, or combination of disadvantage, such as ethnicity, disability, sexuality, belief, HIV and AIDS, and migration or refugee status.

Within this *Handbook*, we offer chapters on ethnicity, neurodiversity, socio-economic background, and equity status. We do not suggest that these chapters will resolve issues of exclusion in the graduate employability, but they do illustrate the range of challenges we still face.

Employment Requirements

Whether education prepares an individual for 'jobs now' or towards lifetime employment and employability, there have rarely been times in history when the competences, knowledge, and skills required for success have been more challenging to identify.

Organisations such as the World Economic Forum (2020) see opportunity in the future but also rapid change and so a lack of clarity about the types of role that will be available across the paid employment sector. Graduates will have their share of an uncertain and changing wider employment market, where it is forecast that:

> There will be 97 million new job roles, globally. But 85 million jobs displaced;
>
> 50% of all employees will need reskilling by 2025, as adoption of technology increases;
>
> Key skills such as critical thinking and problem-solving, will become even more important in the next five years;
>
> New skills will be required in self-management, active learning, resilience, stress tolerance and flexibility;
>
> 50% of all workers will need to reskill in the next five years, reflecting 'double-disruption' of the economic impacts of the pandemic and increasing automation. (World Economic Forum Jobs Reset Summit, 2020)

Even if these forecasts transpire to be only partly correct, the impacts on employability will be highly significant. Higher education establishments that don't pay attention to employability, or which focus only on contemporary employability criteria, may find they have produced ill-equipped graduates for longer-term working lives. Embedding skills and knowledge on employability is therefore vital for contemporary college and university education providers.

As well as the probable change in roles, rapid growth in the deployment of new technology and the combination of post-COVID-19 pandemic fissures in society and working norms have created a sharp acceleration in how graduates are selected, trained, and inducted for roles, and how they experience the world of work.

Increasingly, graduates may be initially screened through artificial intelligence (AI); be inducted into new organisations through virtual reality (VR) and games technology; need to work with a discerning and critical understanding of the role of AI; and navigate the benefits and disadvantages of work in hybrid office–home settings (for example, see CIPD, 2020). As new technology is adopted, graduates will need to confront new opportunities but also new forms of bias, such as the use of AI in selection (for example, see Moss, 2020; Booth et al., 2021) and video games (Gkorezis et al., 2021). They will need to adapt to where these new techniques are used on a wide scale, and retain the ability to work where more conventional processes of selection and induction are used.

STRUCTURE OF THE BOOK

The *Handbook* is divided into five parts, as follows:

Part I Facilitating and Achieving Graduate Employability

Learning through Uncertainty: Team Learning and the Development of an Entrepreneurial Mindset, Hugo Gaggiotti, Selen Kars-Unluoglu and Carol Jarvis

Key words: entrepreneurial mindset, team learning, social learning, heutagogy, community of practice, friendship, friend leadership

Employability Entrepreneurship for Leveraging Employability capitals, Yulia Shumilova and Yuzhuo Cai

Key words: graduate employability, capital conversion, agency, Bourdieu, conceptual paper

Beyond the Data: Navigating the Struggles of Post-PhD Employability, Holly Prescott

Key words: PhD careers, PhD graduates, PhD employability, employment of PhD graduates, PhD jobs

Quality Assurance in University Careers Guidance – a Student Voice Case Study from the Open University, Lydia Lauder and Victoria Crowe

Key words: student/alumni voice, employability, higher education, careers information, advice and guidance, evidence-based practice, integrative model(s)

The Student Voice in Employability within Tertiary Business and Management Education, Vicki Harvey

Key words: student voice, psychological capital, confidence, continuous development, skills, employability definition

LinkedIn and beyond – Social Media and Employability, Gemma Dale

Key words: social media, LinkedIn, social media recruitment, personal brand

Transitions from Education to Work: Impacts on Perceived Employability in Tourism and Hospitality, Marília Durão, Carlos Costa, Maria João Carneiro and Mónica Segovia-Pérez

Key words: tourism and hospitality industry, careers, skills development, employability, graduates, Portugal

Ready to Get on Board? Facilitating Role Transition of New Graduates, Jenny Chen

Key words: role transition, organisational socialisation, workplace entry, graduate, adaptation

Part II Segmenting Graduate Employability: Subject by Subject

Part III Graduate Employability and Inclusion

Centring Racialised Experiences of Black Students to Mitigate Bias within Graduate Labour Recruitment and Selection Processes, Iwi Ugiagbe-Green

Key words: race, Black students, work-readiness, capitals

Mind the Gap: Efforts to Narrow the Graduate Employment Gap for London Students from Low-participation Neighbourhoods, Richard Mendez

Key words: graduate labour market, low-participation neighbourhood, disadvantaged students, graduate-level employment

Are Higher Education Students from Disadvantaged Backgrounds More or Less Confident than Their Peers? A Study of Perceived Employability with First-year Students at an Australian University, Dawn Bennett, Paul Koshy and Ian Li

Key words: careers, employability, equity, outcomes, race, assessment centres

Critical 'Employability' within the Realms of Sociology – a Movement towards 'Social Justice', Ricky Gee

Key words: career studies, critical pedagogy, critical employability, social justice

Part IV Country and Regional Differences

The Impact of International Student Mobility on Employability, Robert Coelen

Key words: internationalisation, study abroad, employment skills, employer understanding, diversity sources, intercultural competence

Transnational, Multinational, Binational? The Role of International Education in Human Capital Development for Graduate Employability, Jessica Schueller and Filiz Keser Aschenberger

Key words: transnational human capital, international higher education, transnational education, graduate employability, binational human capital, international student mobility, international student employability, graduate employment outcomes, Germany, Turkey

Graduate Employability during the COVID-19 pandemic, Belgin Okay-Somerville, Daria Luchinskaya, Pauline Anderson, Scott Hurrell and Dora Scholarios

Key words: graduates, employability, COVID-19 pandemic, social disadvantage, social background, educational background, career competencies

Graduate Employability and the Labour-market Relevance of Norwegian Higher Education: Perspectives from Students, Dian Liu and Siyang Kong

Key words: graduates, employability, COVID-19 pandemic, social disadvantage, social background, educational background, career competencies

Starting Points and Journeys: Employability Strategy in a Data-rich Environment, R. B. Gilworth

Key words: employability, data, graduate employment, careers registration, career readiness, higher education, UK, international, careers

Part V Policymakers' and Employers' Perspectives on the Practice of Graduate Employability

A renewed Analytical Framework for Understanding Employers' Perceptions of Graduate Employability: Integration of Capital and Institutionalist Perspectives, Yuzhuo Cai and Michael Tomlinson

Key words: employability capital, employers' beliefs, capital theory, institutional theory, conceptual model

Higher Education Institution (HEI) Considerations to Support the Creation of Alliances with Small and Medium-sized Enterprises (SMEs), Katie McAllister

Key words: higher education, universities, small and medium enterprises, SMEs, small and medium businesses, alliance, collaboration

A Living Agenda: The Role of Local Policy In Employability, Catherine O'Connor

Key words: graduate labour market, graduate employability, graduate attributes, skills gap, digital skills

The Role of Dual Education in Graduate Employability: The Comparison between Europe and South Africa, David F. J. Campbell, Attila Pausits and Seamus Needham

Key words: dual education, employability, higher education, higher education institutions (HEIs), innovation, learning, LaTFURE, Mozambique, South Africa

All on the Same Page: The Impact and Importance of Professional Associations Stephanie for Graduate Employability, Vianna Renaud and Stéphanie Devèze

Key words: work based learning, good practice standardisation, professional associations, internship/placement support, student employability, graduate careers, frameworks within HE, ERASMUS

CONCLUSION

In his chapter in this book, Ricky Gee comments that employability approaches need not be confined to single disciplines. Contributors to this *Handbook* come from over 50 different HEI organisations and cover a wide range of disciplines, perspectives, and national and international experience.

From the opportunity and expected benefits of university level education, graduates face existing and new opportunities and challenges in how best to use their learning in their lives.

We invite readers to draw on that background to extend their own understanding of graduate employability and, we hope, to add to the knowledge and practice of how university education can continue to enhance the future of graduates.

REFERENCES

African Unity (2013) Agenda 2063, available at https://au.int/en/agenda2063/overview (accessed 17 March 2022)

Barnett, R. (2000) Realizing the University in an Age of Supercomplexity. Buckingham. Open University Press

Becher, T. and Trowler, P. R. (2001) Academic Tribes and Territories: Intellectual Enquiry and the Culture of Disciplines. Buckingham. The Society for Research into Higher Education and Open University Press

Berghaus, B. (2020) Theory, Measurement, and Consequences of Prestigious Employer Preference. Cham. Springer Nature Switzerland AG

Booth, B. M., Hickman, L., Subburaj, S. K., Tay, L., Woo, S. E. and D'Mello, S. K. (2021) Integrating Psychometrics and Computing Perspectives on Bias and Fairness in Affective Computing: A Case Study of Automated Video Interviews. *IEEE Signal Processing Magazine*, 38(6), 84–95

CIPD (2020) Working from Home: Assessing the Research Evidence, available at www.cipd.co.uk/Images/8051-working-from-home-report_tcm18-84208.pdf accessed 2 July 2022

Dorset Council (2022) www.dorsetcouncil.gov.uk/w/economic-growth?p_l_back_url=%2Fsearch%3Fq%3D7.3%2525, accessed 2 July 2022

Dorset Skills Report (2021), available at www.dorsetlep.co.uk/userfiles/files/Strategy%20and%20plans/Skills%20strategy/Dorset%20Local%20Skills%20Report%202021.pdf accessed 2 July 2022

Gkorezis, P., Georgiou, K., Nikolaou, I. and Kyriazati, A. (2021) Gamified or Traditional Situational Judgement Test? A Moderated Mediation Model of Recommendation Intentions via Organizational Attractiveness. *European Journal of Work and Organizational Psychology*, 30(2), 240–50

International Labour Office (ILO) (2011) Equality at Work: The Continuing Challenge. International Labour Conference, 100th Session 2012. Geneva. ILO, available at www.ilo.org/wcmsp5/groups/public/@ed_norm/@relconf/documents/meetingdocument/wcms_154779.pdf (accessed 4 September 2013)

Moss, H. (2020) Screened out Onscreen: Disability Discrimination, Hiring Bias, and Artificial Intelligence. *Denver Law Review*, 98(4), available at http://dx.doi.org/10.2139/ssrn.3906300 accessed 2 July 2022

Newman, J. H. (1852) The Idea of a University. London and New York. Longman, Green and Co

OECD (2021) Education at a Glance 2021: OECD Indicators. Paris. OECD Publishing, available at www.oecd-ilibrary.org/education/education-at-a-glance-2021_b35a14e5-en accessed 2 July 2022

Revans, R. W. (1978) The ABC of Action Learning: A Review of 25 Years of Experience. Manchester. R.W. Revans

Rivera, L. A. (2015) Pedigree: How Elite Students Get Elite Jobs. Princeton, NJ. Princeton University Press

Smith, A. (1819) An Inquiry into the Nature and Causes of the Wealth of Nations. William Allison and J. Maynard, Edinburgh W. Blair, London

Sullivan, A., Parsons, S., Green, F., Wiggins, R. D. and Ploubidis, G. (2018) Elite Universities, Fields of Study and Top Salaries: Which Degree Will Make You Rich? *British Educational Research Journal*, 44 (4), 663–80

Trilling, B. and Fadel, C. (2009) 21st Century Skills: Learning for Life in Our Times. San Francisco, CA. John Wiley and Sons

World Economic Forum Jobs Reset Summit (2020), available at www.weforum.org/events/the-jobs-reset-summit-2020 (accessed 22 November 2021)

Yorke, M. and Knight, P.T. (2006) Embedding Employability into the Curriculum: Learning & Employability Series 1. The Higher Education Academy, York. www.heacademy.ac.uk/resource/embedding-employability-curriculum, accessed 2 July 2022

PART I

Facilitating and Achieving Graduate Employability

BACKGROUND AND CONTEXT

This Handbook represents a wide range of research into graduate employability, from higher education institutions, employer destination organisations, policy makers, and, of course, the students and graduates themselves.

The first obvious starting point is the graduates themselves, and the education, organisation, and society contexts which may facilitate or obstruct their journeys to employability. A second starting point is the historical (such as already seen from Adam Smith (1819 ed.)) and contemporary criticisms of graduate work readiness. These are the underlying themes of Part I of the Handbook.

In a comprehensive review of graduate readiness for employment in Australia, Pennington and Stanford (2019) set out the opportunities, but considerable challenges, facing Australian graduates (even before Covid 19 global disruption). They comment on the demands for universities to produce candidates who are ready for roles, but challenge the 'distortions' caused by employers' expectations of graduates to be 'fully formed' from the day they start work (p. 99).

This observation appears to be replicated elsewhere. For example, in the UK, the Institute of Student Employers (2021) observed a perceived lack of graduate employability skills. Even so, human resource managers might observe that some of those perceived deficient skills, such as lack of self career management, poor team skills, and poor upward management of the manager, were not confined to graduates, recent or otherwise. Of concern, the same report noted that 78% of employers regarded post placement and internship graduates as better prepared, but that such opportunities had reduced by 25% and 29% respectively. Whilst this illustrates the position in only two countries, the research for the Handbook and many of the chapters suggests that the continued mismatch of expectations are replicated in many other graduate labour markets.

Therefore, this Part I of the Handbook will consider a range of work undertaken to facilitate, achieve, and sustain graduate employability.

The first two chapters (Gaggiotti et al. and Shumilova and Cai) look at work undertaken to develop entrepreneurial skills (and related competences) in future graduates, how this is integrated into the university curriculum, and how research on capital-based employability frameworks may be used and reinterpreted.

For those who might aspire to postgraduate roles, Prescott's chapter examines the employment challenges which still exist for PhD graduates.

Two chapters consider the student voice in employability. The first of these chapters comes from research on the quality of careers services at the UK Open University, whose students study mainly through distance learning. In the second chapter, Harvey looks at employment capital, including the psychology of graduate employability for business and management graduates.

A Handbook of employability cannot ignore the impact of social media on employment. Dale's chapter provides a practical review of how graduates should prepare themselves, and in some cases reposition their social media profiles, for post-university recruitment.

The final two chapters are about transition for university to the workplace. Durão et al. research benefits – and identify gaps – in student work experience in the Portuguese hospitality sector. In the final chapter in this part, Chen looks at a more generalisable model of student transition from university to the workplace.

Each chapter is summarised in more detail below.

Learning through Uncertainty: Team Learning and the Development of an Entrepreneurial Mindset, **Hugo Gaggiotti, Selen Kars-Unluoglu and Carol Jarvis**

This chapter opens with the recognition of the increasingly complex dimensions of work, including attributes such as resilience, adaptability, and proactivity, which the authors see as facets of an entrepreneurial mindset. The attributes also closely relate to the future of work as envisaged by the World Economic Forum (2020).

They follow Lundqvist et al. (2015) to contend that developing these in the context of a higher education programme requires process work that aims to develop these qualities, alongside content work associated with the subject matter of the programme. The chapter explores the influence of team learning on the process of development of entrepreneurial qualities, arising from the learning needs of the students.

Gaggiotti, Kars-Unluoglu and Jarvis identify three key benefits arising from this approach. First, critical independence, and the development of the qualities of an entrepreneurial mindset. Second, learning allows students to operate at the intersection of intellectual and social capital. Third, the contribution of the community of practice to heutagogic learning is underpinned by friendship as an organising principle, encouraging students to prioritise working effectively with others on the (learning) task at hand.

Employability Entrepreneurship for Leveraging Employability Capital, **Yulia Shumilova and Yuzhuo Cai**

Shumilova and Cai observe that the literature seeking to help graduate employability can seem overwhelming. To address this, they suggest moving from the research focus on the skills agenda to capital-based employability frameworks, and the role of agency in graduate transitions.

The chapter recognises conceptual gaps in capital-based frameworks. To mitigate these gaps, the chapter synthesises research literature in order to reinterpret the emerging capital-based employability frameworks in the light of Bourdieu's capital theory, and offers an operational tool for understanding graduate transitions through the concept of employability entrepreneurship.

Beyond the Data: Navigating the Struggles of Post-PhD Employability, **Holly Prescott**

Holly Prescott looks at UK, EU, and North American experiences of employability for holders of PhDs, and the emerging PhD-specific career guidance literature on barriers that PhD graduates encounter with their first post-doctoral jobs.

Prescott finds a clash between PhD career expectations and reality; a need to revise professional identity post-PhD; a danger of being 'over-qualified' *and* 'under-experienced'; and challenges in articulating doctoral skills to employers.

Using research evidence and her own experience as a careers adviser and mentor, Prescott suggests how practitioners, institutions, and PhD graduates can address these employability issues.

Quality Assurance in University Careers Guidance – a Student Voice Case Study from the Open University, **Lydia Lauder and Victoria Crowe**

Alongside the integration of employability with university curricula, universities have had long experience of working with dedicated and integrated careers adviser services.

The chapter recognises that higher education careers providers face unprecedented demands to demonstrate value for public investment, with pressures heightened by the covid pandemic. Lauder and Crowe argue that narrow interpretations of 'employability' inadequately determine the full impact of careers guidance. Their study looks at the Open University's Careers and Employability Service (CES), which has adopted holistic evaluation models to determine the effects of its provision upon students and alumni.

They suggest that evaluative practice at CES against Robertson's (2020) integrative model provides scope for generating multilevel evidence, which is more reflective of the nuanced and complex realities of students' employability. The collateral benefits of advancing an evidence-based organisational culture and thus building the professional and scholastic reputation of careers services across academia and the careers sector are noted. This is achieved through an iterative approach to evaluation, underpinned by a continuous improvement strategy in the evidencing of employability.

The Student Voice in Employability within Tertiary Business and Management Education, **Vicki Harvey**

Developing the theme of the student voice in employability, Harvey's chapter analysis seeks to close the research gap at micro-level concerning the opinions of undergraduates on the topic of employability. The chapter discusses the meaning of employability for business and management undergraduate students from the University of Salford. The focus is to understand the impact of employability skills and the role and influences of various forms of capital, in particular psychological impacts.

LinkedIn and beyond – Social Media and Employability, **Gemma Dale**

Recognising the importance of social media in securing employment, this section includes a practical chapter which is a timely reminder of the practicalities of having the right social media presence as a cornerstone to attract potential recruiters.

Dale's chapter explores the benefits of using social media in a professional context as well as possible pitfalls and challenges. It provides practical information and guidance for those who wish to use social media either personally or to support the use of social media in enabling graduate employability. Beyond LinkedIn, the chapter also discusses the various social media platforms through which professional social networking can take place.

Transitions from Education to Work: Impacts on Perceived Employability in Tourism and Hospitality, **Marília Durão, Carlos Costa, Maria João Carneiro and Mónica Segovia-Pérez**

This study explores internships and graduate employment in the hotel and tourism sector from a perspective of higher education in Portugal. With first-hand accounts from 56 hotel and tourism undergraduates' academic paths and practical learning experiences, and with understanding of the factors influencing career construction and employability, the authors aim to smooth the transition to the labour market and to make full use of their potential upon graduation.

Ready to Get on Board? Facilitating Role Transition of New Graduates, **Jenny Chen**

The final chapter in this section recognises the abundant evidence that student–professional role transition can be problematic and stressful for graduates. Chen analyses how graduates go from the role of a student to that of a professional. The chapter starts by clarifying the key concept of role transition, followed by discussions on the distinguishing characteristics between students and professionals. Drawing on the literature from pedagogical learning, organisational socialisation and role identity, the author proposes a process model for preparing, entering, transforming, and identifying (PETI) to extend our understanding of the student–professional role transition.

CONCLUSION

This section has introduced readers to some of the complexities addressed in the supply side of employability of university graduates, and longer term needs for adaptability to changes in the workplace.

These chapters illustrate the design of university/academic-led activities which contribute towards graduate employability. In some cases, they show that a proportion of undergraduates require greater commitment and engagement with life after university than is evident in the early years at university. The research demonstrates how that engagement can be realised in time for life after university.

Universities will continue to need an agile, robust, and continuously evolving approach to employability. They need to balance some very specific requirements from employer requirements of today, and the more nebulous, but equally demanding world of work, and new competences and skills required for economies, societies, and the world of work as envisaged by organisations such as the World Economic Forum.

Dialogue, knowledge sharing, and partnerships between universities and employers will be key to informing the required preparation. The evidence that this is being undertaken on a consistent basis across all potential graduate destinations is uneven. For some employers and sectors, there is undoubtedly co-operation with the efforts of universities and higher education institutions to balance future needs and preparation. Where other employers and graduate destinations rely on access to a more general graduate market without previous needs analysis and engagement, the results are, predictably, more mixed.

REFERENCES

Smith, A. (1819) *An Inquiry into the Nature and Causes of the Wealth of Nations*. William Allison and J. Maynard, Edinburgh W. Blair, London

Institute of Student Employers (2021) *Graduates lack work-ready skills that businesses need during Covid era, reports ISE Student Development Survey*, available at https://ise.org.uk/page/graduates-lack-work-ready-skills-that-businesses-need-during-covid-era?msclkid=6649341abb6811ec93011f03070489b1

Pennington, A. and Stanford, J. (2019) *The future of work for Australian graduates: the changing landscape of university employment transitions in Australia*, The Australia Institute, Centre for Future Work, Canberra

1

Learning through Uncertainty: Team Learning and the Development of an Entrepreneurial Mindset

Hugo Gaggiotti, Selen Kars-Unluoglu and Carol Jarvis

INTRODUCTION

Relations between humans and work have always been complex. However, the speed, volatility and unpredictability of these relations have been increasing (Stacey, 2010). Consequently, attributes such as resilience, adaptability and pro-activity, facets of a growth or entrepreneurial mindset, are highly prized (Dweck, 2012; Sidhu et al., 2016). The accelerating pace of change places increasing demands on workers to adapt quickly and effectively to project-based work. It requires reaching repetitive milestones and deadlines and working in teams with relatively short lifespans, a practice that has been defined as 'necromanagement' (Gaggiotti and Cicmil, 2019).

This environment calls for *competency* as well as *capability* ('the capacity to use one's competence in novel as well as familiar circumstances') to thrive (Blaschke and Hase, 2015: 26). Developing these in a degree programme requires *process work* to develop personal qualities, alongside *content work* associated with the subject matter of the programme (Lundqvist et al., 2015). The process work involves students in future-oriented thinking, to develop narratives that build from the present to their desired future (Lindberg and Schwartz, 2018). This stands in contrast with traditional approaches that build from the past, applying knowledge from extant theory to experience.

Requiring students to dwell in complexity, future-oriented thinking involves ways of learning that are collaborative, critically reflective and that emerge from informal learning from real-world experience (Blaschke and Hase, 2015). In formal, accredited learning environments, this learning approach can provoke and amplify levels of anxiety that, if not contained, discourage learning (Vince, 1998). Gaggiotti et al. (2020) note the importance of the texture of the learning space in offering a ‘safety net’, ‘that protects against the damage of a hard fall, without limiting movement’ (p. 256). In this chapter, we explore how a programme based on team learning seeks to weave this texture whilst preparing graduates for employment, by contributing to the development of an entrepreneurial mindset and the practice of collaboration.

Our research site is a UK-based undergraduate degree programme with a practice-led, project-based, emancipatory pedagogy (Freire, 1972). Based on team learning through doing and team coaching, it evolved from the Tiimiakatemia (Team Academy) model pioneered in Finland (Partanen, 2012). Students (known as teampreneurs or TEs) are active participants responsible for shaping their own learning and project opportunities. The chapter draws on qualitative research conducted amongst students and staff of the programme, as well as with staff on similar programmes.

THE ORIGINS AND PHILOSOPHY OF TEAM ENTREPRENEURSHIP

In 1993 Johannes Partanen, at Jyväskylä University of Applied Sciences, developed the Tiimiakatemia (henceforth TA) approach to learning by doing in teams. His aim was to develop an undergraduate programme that would provide students with the skills and attributes to create their own jobs. As more institutions have worked with the TA approach, the programme has been adapted to the nuances of local context, however the underpinning philosophy and processes have remained in place.

Forming team companies soon after they start, teampreneurs (henceforth TEs) remain in them throughout their degree. They are set ‘company key performance indicators (KPIs)’ alongside their academic assignments. Each TE has their own learning contract, and these contribute to a team learning contract. Roles in the team company rotate through the course of the programme. A commitment to the development and well-being of the individual, team, community and ecosystem is a cornerstone of the philosophy.

In contributing to KPIs and learning contracts, TEs seek out and negotiate live projects from external organisations in smaller, often cross-team company, teams. Prospective projects are agreed with the team, reviewed and critically reflected on. Whilst there are assessment points to evidence TEs have met learning outcomes, the programme does not follow a predetermined, classroom-based curriculum, centring instead on twice-weekly coached training sessions in team companies. Training sessions provide a space for what Canning and Callan (2010: 74) describe as ‘collaborative reflection’. They are held in a circle and follow the principles of dialogue (Isaacs, 1999). TEs lead the sessions, reflecting on their current learning needs and projects, and engaging with relevant literature to support their learning. The role of the team coach is to facilitate dialogue that will foster a learning culture amongst peers.

ENTREPRENEURIAL LEARNING AND A SHIFT IN MINDSET

Graduates are emerging into a 'learning economy' (Lundvall and Rasmussen, 2016), rather than a 'knowledge economy', that to thrive and enhance employability, requires *capability* – 'the capacity to use one's competence in novel as well as familiar circumstances' (Blaschke and Hase, 2015: 26). Capability development involves *process work* aimed at developing personal qualities, alongside *content work* associated with the subject matter (Lundqvist et al., 2015). Process work requires critical engagement with practice that is both risky and offers the potential for deep learning (Barnett, 2007) when approached with an 'open minded, reflective appraisal that takes account of different perspectives, experiences and assumptions' (Brechin et al., 2000: 26).

The presence of a growth or entrepreneurial mindset (Dweck, 2012; Sidhu et al., 2016) facilitates critical engagement with practice. Mindset is not something that is innate and stable, rather it is influenced by experiences and interactions with others. Dweck (2012: 6) argues a growth mindset 'is based on the belief that your basic qualities are things you can cultivate through your efforts'; valuing challenge and effort are characterised by a desire to improve. Naumann (2017) notes, in the literature, an entrepreneurial mindset is commonly interpreted 'as a way of adaptable thinking and decision-making in complex, uncertain and dynamic environments' (p. 159) yet 'currently no commonly shared concept exists' (p. 169), with authors focussing instead on individual attributes. Like Dweck (2012), Naumann (2017) highlights the importance of awareness, feedback, learning and adaptation in developing two attributes: meta-cognition and cognitive adaptability, noting their importance for inexperienced entrepreneurs in counter-balancing a lack of experience in the field.

Lackéus and Williams Middleton (2015) note the growing interest in experiential learning that emphasises doing entrepreneurship reflexively, aiming to foster the development of meta-cognitive attributes. This approach may be experienced as risky and ambiguous by learners, with heightened anxiety and stress levels by an assumed laissez-faire approach to teaching (Tomkins and Ulus, 2016). However, it is precisely the process of dealing with ambiguity and making meaning out of it that fosters an entrepreneurial mindset and develops meta-cognitive attributes.

Gherardi (2006) argues it is the connectivity produced by the organisational texture that opens up the space to learn. The texture becomes a 'field of practices', capable of producing its own organisational devices to favour, protect, encourage and promote other practices and learning. Practices are connected and interwoven and 'this texture is held together by a certain number of practices which provide anchorage for others' (Gherardi, 2006: 47). An example is the 'safety net' described by Gaggiotti et al. (2020) a device created in the texture of a team-based venture creation programme to 'protect against the damage of a hard fall, without limiting movement' (p. 256).

The 'field of practices' is at the heart of heutagogy to offer a texture for student development as autonomous and self-directed, perceived to be core competencies integral to increasing employability and transition from education to work (Botha, 2012). Hase and Kenyon (2007: 12) describe heutagogy as 'learner-centred learning that sees the learner as the major agent in their own learning, which occurs as a result of personal experiences'. Introducing heutagogy in pedagogical environments involves fundamentally rethinking how students learn, and educators 'teach' in the classroom. It requires students and educators to cross epistemic boundaries as they engage in the challenge of developing autonomy, capability and competency whilst inhabiting an environment structured, to some extent, with a programme curriculum, module lists and specifications. For the student, having full responsibility for their learning is often unfamiliar and experienced as intimidating and uncomfortable; working through this discomfort in a safe environment is, though, important preparation for the world of work. For the instructor, the need to relinquish the desire for control and to flex the learning process and resources to the changing needs of students calls for a change in how they take up their role (Blaschke and Hase, 2015), from an 'expert' with absolute knowledge to a 'coach' and 'co-learner' collaborating with students.

Team Learning and Communities of Practice

In professional contexts people think about real-life problems in highly social situations, as part of communities of practice (Pyrko et al., 2019). Their learning in this social context drives learning in practice, and contributes to becoming a competent professional. Similarly, when a student joins a new educational context, they join a micro-cosmos of knowledge, a 'community of practice' (CoP) who share a common stock of knowledge, a sense of identity and values.

Wenger (1998), who formulated the CoP concept, places emphasis on learning interactions in local situated practices, cohering through mutual engagement to create a common repertoire. Engaging with other members, individuals gradually enact their membership of the community. Lave and Wenger (1991) use the term 'legitimate peripheral participation' to characterise the process during which people move from peripheral members to become more central and legitimate members by gradually increasing the degree of meaningful interaction with other members. As they move from the periphery to the core, members also increase their engagement with the 'situated curriculum' (Gherardi et al., 1998) constituted by a defined, yet not rigid, trajectory of activities to increase capability and competency in practices. CoP membership is multi-layered, with differences in people's 'tenure' in the CoP, time investment in engaging with the curriculum and competence built through engagement. CoPs typically constitute old-timers, who engage regularly with the curriculum and people at the periphery who either aspire to full membership, or for whom less involved participation is sufficient.

CoP members evaluate the practices and conditions of other members, as well as their own, learning through dialoguing in a process of cyclical inquiry (Gajda and Koliba, 2007). Cyclical inquiry implies reflexivity through which members collectively reflect on individual and collective objectives, processes and practices, and their wider environment, adapting their activities accordingly. CoPs, then, exist at the intersection of intellectual and social capital (Snyder et al., 2003). Mastery is a collectively achieved property of the CoP, that is deepened by ongoing interactions, not merely an individual achievement (Lave and Wenger, 1991). With these characteristics, the concept of CoP can allow students to engage with heutagogy as self-directed learners through a situated, relational, communicative and reflexive approach to learning, and can increase the success of transition from education to work through interacting with CoPs in their future workplaces more effectively.

Friendship as an Organising Principle

When we conceptualise enterprise education as situated practices, the student transforms from a passive recipient of knowledge into a committed thinker and actor who develops, tests and evaluates ideas and action in relationship with others (Ramsey, 2014). This has implications for how power and expertise is shared in the classroom and where the leadership and accountability for learning and development resides.

However, as French and Thomas (1999: 5) argue 'instead of the promotion of critical independence, education for tutelage still rules the world'. The student permits others 'to think for [them], direct [them], take responsibility for [them] because, so often, it is simply easier'. The implications of this for learning has been explored, in detail, by Adorno and Becker (1999). Adorno (1969, cited in French and Thomas, 1999) suggests an alternative would be to imagine other relations, such as camaraderie or friendship.

Friendship has always been elusive to study and theorise. Anthropologists Desai and Killick (2010) have suggested that the multiple ways of referring to friendship constitute its major benefit. The possibility of not having to encapsulate friendship into one definition and appreciating its organisational dimension, makes it valuable in explaining heutagogic learning experiences. Experiencing friendship in a learning environment could help to reimagine alternatives usually undermined by old conventions. One example is *friend leadership* (Toivanen, 2014), a term associated with coaching and shared leadership.

Discussing friendship as an organising principle of relations in the classroom, we can unravel different dynamics beyond the traditional understanding of what happens in the classroom amongst students. Friend leadership signals the existence of a community with a sense of us, a close tribe with accompanying norms and rituals (Turner, 1977), a form of 'friendship-in-role' (French and Moore, 2004) that prioritises working together effectively, irrespective of our personal relationship and whether we *like* each other or not. It gives primacy to the relational, bringing to light both the interests of self and other (French and Moore, 2004), highlighting learning as a mutual achievement in the CoP.

As students try to think for themselves, they take faltering steps and fall, like a child learning to walk unaided (French and Thomas, 1999). But with friendship as an organising principle, they have others to help along the way. On their learning journey, friendship enables holding self and others to account – not for the sake of exerting control and surveillance but in line with friends' commitment to each other's development and well-being. This emanates from friendship's capacity to contain conflict and disagreement. The 'readiness to air in public a private argument – the juxtaposition of disagreement and animosity with playful competitiveness and mutual exploration' (French and Thomas, 1999: 10) creates an openness to new insights, ideas, possibilities and to mutual challenges which may facilitate the development of high-performing teams (Katzenbach and Smith, 2015).

METHODOLOGY

Our research took place with students (TEs) and educators (team coaches and external entrepreneurship educators) in an undergraduate entrepreneurship programme developed in partnership between the University of the West of England (UWE) and the Bristol City Robins Foundation, a community-based educational trust established by Bristol City Football Club. The first cohort of TEs joined the programme in September 2017. Our research was conducted from October 2019–November 2020 during the first year that the programme had all three year groups. There were 34 TEs and five team coaches on the programme; all coaches and 25 TEs participated in the research.

In this paper we draw data from three sources. First, we organised two co-creation workshops with TEs (November 2019 and January 2020; named as TE DG1 and 2). They were collaborative and offered space for TEs to reflect on their learning and entrepreneurial development. We utilised creative methods, specifically story-writing and asset-mapping. Second, we conducted three focussed discussion groups with the team coaches (November 2019, January 2020 and May 2020; named as SDG 1, 2 and 3) to seek insight into the role of learning and teaching in the development of an entrepreneurial mindset and its implications for employability. Third, we conducted interviews with five team coaches who were not members of the programme team but were familiar with the programme and the TA approach. These interviews were conducted between September and

October 2020 (named as Ext1–5), after we had completed preliminary analysis of our findings from the other two elements. They provided us with an external view of how the programme was both similar to, and different from, other TA programmes, and explored challenges and enablers for educators working with these methods that enhance employability-relevant student skills and attributes.

FINDINGS AND DISCUSSION

Heutagogic Learning: from Tutelage to Critical Independence

Whilst TEs chose to enrol on the programme, excited by the prospect of this different way of learning, many were taken aback when faced with the reality of independent learning:

> it's a completely different style of learning, even though that's probably the appeal of choosing the course, it's quite difficult and it's a challenge for some of them sometimes to realise that nobody is going to stand in front of them and lecture them for an hour. (SDG1)

Coaches too needed to cross epistemic boundaries and 'to completely un-learn the last 15 years of work experience' (SDG1), to move from expert to co-learner (Blaschke and Hase, 2015). To support this, team coaches work as a 'team company', role modelling the process to TEs, and experiencing similar struggles. Team coaches emphasised the importance of earning 'reciprocal respect', of contracting with the team company about their role, having the courage to stay in role and not rush to 'rescue' when faced with TEs anxiety that they are not learning anything:

> because their development is day to day, continually small amounts, they don't see that they are learning stuff every day, they don't see their personal development. (SDG2)

This was recognised as a slow process, requiring the team coach to judge and work at a pace appropriate to the needs of TEs:

> Nothing's quick, and you almost think sort of nothing's happening, and then you realise so much has happened. And if you try and make stuff happen too quickly you miss the point of the methodology. (Ext5)

Holding training sessions in a circle helped reinforce that staff were co-learners:

> You're in education but you're not sitting at a desk and you're not in a lecture and you're not doing the traditional stuff, you know? You're sat in a circle and your coach is on the same level as you, and they're not an expert. You're empowered by that setting and by that relationship. (Ext5)

This dialogic approach (Isaacs, 1999) provided space for critical reflection that team coaches described as 'the penny drop moment' when TEs realise 'we're responsible for creating our own course of action'. (SDG3). As one TE described it:

> That was almost a confusion for some people, we were like 'why aren't we learning any business at all?' And then it was the case of, actually, we ran all of our own sessions, so we're in charge of what we want to learn. So, if you want to learn marketing, then someone's got to research, plan this session, and come in the next day and teach everyone. And then you teaching everyone makes you know it better as well, and that's the idea (TE, DG1)

Having a number and variety of projects to learn from was important. By 'failing at different things' TEs learned to respond proactively when things didn't go as planned. They began to think differently about failure, to be able 'to be honest about why you've failed and how' (TE DG1):

> I think failing and learning are two different things. You can fail where you don't learn anything and you lose money and vision, that is failing. And then there's learning above that, as long as you learn something from not that ideal [situation] which you had in mind, it's not failing. (TE DG1)

This was viewed as an important attribute of an entrepreneurial mindset, promoting 'positivity, confidence, drive, creativity' (SDG2), requiring TEs to move

> from traditional education to, actually, 'what have I got to lose here? What's the risk involved in this?' 'Potentially just my time. And a dent to my ego if I'm going to take it the wrong way, if I do fail'. (SDG1)

The emphasis placed on acknowledging and reflecting on failure to inform progress is instrumental in future-proofing students for the world of work (QAA, 2018). The assessment placed equal value on learning, whether it emerged from perceived failure or success, providing additional encouragement to take risks. As one TE put it:

> The assignments are targeted for giving us that knowledge, to actually understand it. So, they're not just pointless assignments, these assignments teach you mindset and teach you entrepreneurial activities. Without the assignments, I don't think I'd have the knowledge I do today. (TE, DG1)

It is this ability to transfer learning from one situation to another that defines capability (Blaschke and Hase, 2015) and fosters the ability to thrive in complex working environments. Combining 'the academics' through critical reflection on real-life projects, they felt, meant 'you then learn it forever, rather than just reading it off a board in a lesson' (TE DG1). The formal qualification itself contributes to the 'safety net' (Gaggiotti et al., 2020) as 'at least I have a degree to fall back on'. (TE DG1).

TEs may transform from passive recipients of knowledge into committed thinkers and actors. However, what we observed in this first phase of development is that TEs remain focussed on their own individual learning and have not yet fully connected with the learning and performance of others.

Team Learning and a Community of Practice

If heutagogy 'almost accelerates them into adult life whilst they're still in education', (SDG1), transitioning to understanding the team company as a CoP (Wenger, 1998) was an equally big step.

The team company may start its life as a 'functionalist' entity – stable, run by a range of set mechanisms (training sessions, learning contracts, assignments and externally imposed projects and milestones) instrumental in gaining the degree. As TEs start engaging with heutagogic learning they start building a learning community, recognising the need to identify with each other and recognising that they are similar in things they value. This mutual recognition is crucial in transitioning into a CoP member.

> Colleagues, comrades, people to do the doing with ...The team gives you that. It gives you a wider network of skills, knowledge, abilities, manpower ... The team learning really kind of comes into its own, where it means that the learning's not just about that doing ... We have to engage with other people. (Ext5)

In training sessions TEs were discussing their live projects, considering difficulties, sharing potential solutions from theory and practice in a friendly environment. As Gherardi (2006) observed, connection is fundamental at this stage. Connection is enhanced through dialoguing, allowing TEs to develop confidence and trust in their peers and co-learners, their knowledge and capabilities.

> They're not competitors. There's something about collaboration which I think is particularly unique, whether it's how the TEs work together, whether it's how institutions work together who use the methodology, or anybody who's involved in the methodology, there's something about ... collaboration and co-creation with others that is at the heart of it. (Ext5)

TEs became aware of one another's knowledge and capabilities and turned to the CoP when faced with difficulties: 'We just bounce knowledge and we help each other learn' (TE, DG1) as 'they can pass that down. And maybe we know something that they haven't done yet'. (TE, DG1)

Jack and Anderson (2002: 203) contend that this stage involves more than 'becoming informed' and 'becoming known' issues. It allows TEs to do more than tap into external resources or knowledge held by others, to create a learning community that enables co-creation of new resources and knowledge. As their engagement with the 'situated curriculum' deepened, both they and their entrepreneurial ventures developed:

> I didn't know how to start a project, I wouldn't even think about where to start or what to do it about. But, over the years, I've learnt how to think about projects, do ideation sessions and create ideas and how to use ideas and what to do if I had an idea. My thinking has

> completely changed, if I see something, I'll almost analyse it now, instead of just going straight past it, I'll look at it and process it more. So, my creativity and thinking has improved massively ... I'm looking at everything with an open mindset, thinking how I can turn it into an opportunity? (TE, DG1)

In using the CoP to discuss issues specific to their entrepreneurial and 'student' experience, to share learning resources, knowledge and advice, to give one another help or to jointly initiate projects, TEs started to engage with it as a process of reflexive inquiry, translating dialogues into individual and team actions. In this dialogic relationship, affective learning requirements – seeking encouragement, support and feedback – are as important as cognitive learning expectations, seeking to understand subject knowledge:

> You can get clarification, you can get feedback, validation from teammates, do things together (TE, DG1)

The key learning processes occurring were role modelling and working together with other CoP members that extended beyond the team company. Newcomers learnt from 'old hands' (older year groups) and from the broader TA community through international learning journeys, as well as externals in their ecosystem.

> When you talk about the TE community, their peers are also their role models. The Year 2s and 3s who have gone on and done some amazing projects and stuff. You can see the Year 1s aspire to be some of those, and then you've also got some of the module leaders and team coaches who run their own businesses successfully, are again role models. Whether it's the links with the TEs at UWE or whether it's the ones when they go out to Bilbao or on the learning journeys, there's so much role modelling ... They're all role-modelling for each other, which is really special. (SDG1)

Of course, members made extensive use of other more canonical learning processes, such as academic reading and writing:

> You learn a lot from the books, which you genuinely do apply as well. It's the doing. It's the people. It goes hand in hand. (TE, DG1)

However, the non-canonical learning through shared practice became a source of coherence for the community through a process of mutual engagement, the emergence of a sense of joint interest, goal and values, and the generation of a shared repertoire of resources:

> We struggled ... We genuinely didn't do any projects for like a year ... We had so many good ideas, but we just didn't have the minerals to actually go do it ... As soon as everyone's on board and everyone is trying things continuously, I was not scared of saying 'ooh, no, I couldn't do this'. (TE, DG1)

TEs didn't spend time in classrooms. The dedicated co-working space was significant, reinforcing the CoP's community 'intimacy' which allowed members to work at the intersection of intellectual and social capital:

> We work with each other. There's always conversations. You're not sat in an office on your own. We're all in here. The discussions are always about what's going on in the team, not necessarily just what individual people are doing. (SDG1)

These conversations and discussions had a latent, arguably more important, function, contributing to a sense of belonging, and allowing participants to interact and learn together. TEs built a common vocabulary, creating roles and norms, sharing them with newcomers, thus generating a shared history. This is the moment when TEs start to think about what it means to be a 'teampreneur', a member of the wider TA community.

During this process, accommodating the different layers of CoP membership is perhaps one of the greatest struggles for TEs. Some preferred to stay on the periphery, engaging with the learning experiences in the situated curriculum in a limited way:

> I think, certainly me, I'm holding back this year, which is a really bad move. But hopefully I'm going to make that breakthrough soon and just say 'what have I got to lose'. And just go through everything. (TE, DG1)

A threshold came when they moved from worrying about those who were not there and how they can be forced to engage, to focussing on how best those who are present can work together to meet their goals. Focussing 'on the projects and the things that I can influence, whether that be individual, whether that be team or academic' (SDG3), helps them to build self-confidence and resilience, key enterprising competencies that improve employability:

> [Resilience] is not just the bounce back from failure … Resilience is keep getting projects further, or keep developing that relationship with that individual who either annoys the hell out of them, or is just really quiet and won't contribute … Resilience can look like a lot of different things on this programme. (SDG2)

The shift in attention from a deficit mindset (whose contribution I'm missing) to an appreciative, or growth, mindset (how can I best capitalise on the contributions I've got) allowed the CoP to evolve both in terms of relational dynamics amongst members and of the learning expectations explicitly articulated by its members, formally in learning contracts and informally in daily interactions. It evolved according to the TEs' affective, cognitive and learning needs, enabling holding self and others to account.

> In our teams, we talk about accountability a lot. You can say someone else had let you down or hadn't, but at the end of the day you can only help yourself most of the time. It's too easy to rely on your team and your network, and then blame them for the things that happen. But what role did you play in that? … You've got to be honest about why you've failed and how. (TE, DG1)

We perceived this as a strong indicator of the emergence of a shared in-group identity, supporting a key assumption of the concept of CoP, that learning is not only an individual cognitive process but also the result of a social trajectory within a group. In preparing graduates for work in the 'learning economy' (Lundvall and Rasmussen, 2016), this understanding may foster a commitment to collaboration and shared learning.

Towards Friendship as an Organising Principle

Desai and Killick (2010) refer to the multiple ways of using friendship owing to its elusiveness as a concept that defies a single definition. When our TEs embarked on the programme, they typically had a more partial view of friendship, confined by how much they liked the other person. They aimed to first build bonds through social activities outside the programme:

> The more you socialise with your teammates, the more you get to know them, the stronger bond you'll have, so the more … you'll want to work together. (TE DG1)

Escaping from confining friendship to those we like is central to the CoP. If enterprise education means providing tools to students for lifetime employability (instead of lifetime employment), to cultivate motivation and readiness to engage in relationship-building and skills to use relationships in a productive way is integral to the employability agenda (Parker, 2008). As one team coach put it:

> What I feel is important within the team and with the team coach is to push, push relationships within the team, within the peers. The more they, not like each other, but the more they have those relationships, the more accountable they'll be, the better they'll work together, the more they'll care about other people coming in. (SDG3)

The concept of 'friend leadership' (Toivanen, 2014) is shared across the TA community, suggesting the 'members of the organisation are friends with each other, more than acquaintances, but less than a close friend in the traditional sense'. (p. 7).

'Friendship as an organising principle' (French and Moore, 2004) encouraged TEs to hold themselves and others to account as 'if you've got a good friendship with them, you're not going to want to let them down'. (TE DG1). It fostered a commitment to each other's continuous development and well-being:

> I have seen the shift this year … their mindset has developed from first year, from, 'I am an individual on this course', to actually, 'I have got ten people around me that I can help and I can use for my benefit'. Their mindset develops in terms of the ethos of the 'team-ness'. (SDG2)

In this way TEs became 'partners in the building of their own society' (Ext1), learning to embrace differences and prioritise working effectively with others (French and Thomas, 1999), to 'collaborate well with people' (TE DG1). There was a recognition of 'collectiveness' that held out the possibility of achieving more collectively than alone (Cope et al., 2007); they began to think beyond 'what is best for me', to reflect on 'how can I make my best contribution to this community?'.

As an organising principle, friendship offered a safe space to practise and to learn. In containing disagreement, conflict and contradiction, friendship contributed to the 'good enough' holding of anxiety (Stacey, 2010), so that 'putting themselves in a vulnerable position' (SDG2) felt less risky. Its appreciative mindset encouraged the embracing of difference, to remain open to learning wherever it may come from:

> It's not only the learning of skills but the actual dialogue we have. If I have a project idea and I can put it out there, people will criticise it. Different points of view that I probably didn't see myself. I can look at things different then, in terms of if it was just me by myself, I wouldn't see the strengths and weaknesses from different points of view. (TE, DG1)

As one team coach summed it up:

> They've worked in a team for three years, they might like the people in their team, they may not like the people in their team, they've managed conflict, they've developed relationships, they've led sessions, they're ready to go into a business with practical employability skills. (SDG3)

CONCLUSION

In exploring the development of personal qualities associated with an entrepreneurial mindset through the lens of team learning, we paid particular attention to three elements that we believe contribute to personal and professional development and employability.

First, a *heutagogic approach* encouraging students to develop critical independence can accelerate learning and the confidence to hold oneself and others to account. The texture of the learning environment is woven from a field of *connected* practices (Gherardi, 2006) that support students' personal, as well as academic, development. For example, the lecturer standing at the front of the class is replaced by the team coach as co-learner; the classroom is replaced by a co-working space; and peers can be role models just as well as experienced professionals and team coaches. The learning experiences on the programme demand reframing of how we view failure, which encourages experimentation, critical reflection and reflexivity. This texture has parallels with the world of work and enhances employability. However, as TEs adapt to this way of learning, their learning remains largely centred on and vested in the individual.

Second, this approach to team learning may encourage realising the potential of a community of practice (CoP) (Wenger, 1998) to co-create new resources and knowledge (Jack and Anderson, 2002). Through dialogue in training sessions, TEs become more aware of and confident in one another's knowledge and capabilities; the cliché that we 'learn more and faster together' becomes imbued with meaning, with the team company, wider cohort and TA community perceived as a vehicle for learning. Just as important in this dialogic relationship is the social capital they build, the encouragement, support and feedback they receive.

Operating at the intersection of intellectual and social capital, the CoP and its members develop mastery. And whilst peripheral CoP membership is not without cost (the team will deduct marks from team assignments for individuals who make a lesser contribution), it is accommodated. Thus, as the CoP develops, TEs develop an appreciative mindset that emphasises what can be achieved by the members who are there and with the available resources. They engage with broad and deep internal networks in formal and informal activities to enhance employability by providing support, transmitting reputation or affording access to knowledge and resources. Learning and professional development then is not only an individual cognitive process but also the result of a social trajectory within a group.

Third, this approach to learning is underpinned by *friendship as an organising principle*, fostering a commitment to the well-being and development of others. It encourages TEs to think beyond their personal needs to prioritise working effectively with others on the (learning) task at hand (French and Moore, 2004). When undertaken in the spirit of friendship, giving and receiving feedback and holding self and others to account, it encourages the development of cognitive adaptability and the ability to develop mutually enhancing relationships with unlike others. Taking friendship as an organising principle offers a safe space to practise and learn, to transition from tutelage to autonomy that underpins a growth mindset (Dweck, 2012) and self-directedness in employability competencies.

Our study has limitations. We presented here the potential of the TA approach and its underpinning principles and processes. However, we do not wish to suggest this approach suits all learners or all learning environments. TEs embark on the programme at different points, travel at different speeds and leave at the end of three years in different places, not all having achieved their aspirations; their voyage is far from linear. It is a distinctive and holistic approach, and it would be unwise to assume that different aspects would be effective in isolation from each other. Nonetheless, we would encourage educators to explore how heutagogic learning, team learning as a community of practice and friendship as an organising principle, might be explored in their own learning environments.

Whilst we made a small contribution, the concept of friendship as an organising principle remains under-researched and offers scope for further development in different educational and organisational contexts. What we hope we have highlighted is how it can support learners to develop competency and capability to enhance their employability and to thrive in the complex world of work. After all,

> We have to work with others to make things happen. If we don't learn about how we meet the world and how others meet us and how we can do that better, or maybe we can't do it better, but we can at least understand how it then affects others. (Ext5)

ACKNOWLEDGEMENTS

Research reported in this chapter was supported by British Academy of Management Knowledge and Education (MKE) Award: 2019-116.

REFERENCES

Adorno, T. W. and Becker, H. (1999) Education for maturity and responsibility. *History of the Human Sciences* 12(3): 21–34.

Barnett, R. (2007) *A will to learn: being a student in an age of uncertainty*. Maidenhead: Open University Press.

Blaschke, L. M. and Hase, S. (2015) Heutagogy: a holistic framework for creating twenty-first-century self-determined learners. In: Gros, B., Kinshuk and Maina, M. (eds) *The future of ubiquitous learning: learning designs for emerging pedagogies*. Berlin: Springer, pp. 25–40.

Botha, J. (2012) Graduateness, self-directedness and employability. In: Coetzee, M., Botha, A., Eccles N., Holtzhausen, N. and Nienaber, H. (eds) *Developing student graduateness and employability: issues, provocations, theory and practical guidelines*. Randburg: Knowres Publishing, pp. 385–402.

Brechin, A., Brown, H. and Eby, M. A. (eds) (2000) *Critical practice in health and social care*. Milton Keynes: Sage.

Canning, N. and Callan, S. (2010) Heutagogy: spirals of reflection to empower learners in higher education. *Reflective Practice* 11(1): 71–82.

Cope, J., Jack, S. and Rose, M. B. (2007) Social capital and entrepreneurship: an introduction. *International Small Business Journal* 25(3): 213–219.

Desai, A. and Killick, E. (eds) (2010) *The ways of friendship: anthropological perspectives*. London: Berghahn Books.

Dweck, C. S. (2012) *Mindset: changing the way you think to fulfil your potential*. London: Robinson.

French, R. and Moore, P. (2004) Divided neither in life, nor in death. In: Gabriel, Y. (ed.) *Myths, stories and organizations: premodern narratives for our times*. Oxford: Oxford University Press, pp. 101–115.

French, R. and Thomas, J. (1999) Maturity and education, citizenship and enlightenment: an introduction to Theodor Adorno and Hellmut Becker, 'Education for maturity and responsibility'. *History of the Human Sciences* 12(3): 1–19.

Freire, P. (1972) *Pedagogy of the oppressed*. New York: Penguin.

Gaggiotti, H. and Cicmil, S. (2019) *Necromanagement: dying and resurrecting when labelling work as a project*. In: 37th Standing Conference of Organisational Symbolism (SCOS), York, UK, 8–11 July 2019.

Gaggiotti, H., Jarvis, C. and Richards, J. (2020) The texture of entrepreneurship programs: revisiting experiential entrepreneurship education through the lens of the liminal–liminoid continuum. *Entrepreneurship Education and Pedagogy* 3(3): 236–264.

Gajda, R. and Koliba, C. (2007) Evaluating the imperative of intra-organizational collaboration: a school improvement perspective. *American Journal of Evaluation* 28(1): 26–44.

Gherardi, S. (2006) *Organizational knowledge: the texture of organizing.* London: Blackwell.

Gherardi, S., Nicolini, D. and Odella, F. (1998) Toward a social understanding of how people learn in organizations: the notion of situated curriculum. *Management Learning* 29(3): 273–297.

Hase, S. and Kenyon, C. (2007) Heutagogy: a child of complexity theory. *Complicity: An International Journal of Complexity and Education* 4(1): 111–118.

Isaacs, W. (1999) Dialogic leadership. *The Systems Thinker* 10(1): 1–5.

Jack, S. L. and Anderson, A. R. (2002) The effects of embeddedness on the entrepreneurial process. *Journal of Business Venturing* 17(5): 467–487.

Katzenbach, J. R. and Smith, D. K. (2015) *The wisdom of teams: creating the high-performance organization.* Boston, MA: Harvard Business Review Press.

Lackéus, M. and William Middleton, K. (2015) Venture creation programs: bridging entrepreneurship education and technology transfer. *Education and Training* 57(1): 48–73.

Lave, J. and Wenger, E. (1991) *Situated learning: legitimate peripheral participation.* Cambridge: Cambridge University Press.

Lindberg, J. and Schwartz, B. (2018) Entrepreneurship in societal change: students as reflecting entrepreneurs? In: Berglund, K. and Berduyin, K. (eds) *Revitalizing entrepreneurship education.* London: Routledge, pp. 43–61.

Lundqvist, M., Middleton Williams, K. and Nowell, P. (2015) Entrepreneurial identity and role expectations in nascent entrepreneurship. *Industry and Higher Education* 29(5): 327–344.

Lundvall, B. and Rasmussen, P. (2016) Challenges for adult skill formation in the globalising learning economy: a European perspective. *International Journal of Lifelong Education* 35(4): 448–464.

Naumann, C. (2017) Entrepreneurial mindset: a synthetic literature review. *Entrepreneurial Business and Economics Review* 5(3): 149–172.

Parker, P. (2008) Promoting employability in a 'flat' world. *Journal of Employment Counseling* 45(1): 2–13.

Partanen, J. (2012) *The team coach's best tools.* Jyväskylä: Partus.

Pyrko, I., Dörfler, V. and Eden, C. (2019) Communities of practice in landscapes of practice. *Management Learning* 50(4): 482–499.

QAA (2018) *Enterprise and entrepreneurship education: guidance for UK higher education providers.* [online]. Available at: www.qaa.ac.uk/docs/qaa/about-us/enterprise-and-entrpreneurship-education-2018.pdf?sfvrsn=20e2f581_14. Accessed: 21/6/2022.

Ramsey, C. (2014) Management learning: a scholarship of practice centred on attention? *Management Learning* 45(1): 6–20.

Sidhu, I., Goubet, J. and Xia, Y. (2016) *Measurement of innovation mindset: a method and tool within the Berkeley Innovation Index Framework.* In: International Conference on Engineering, Technology and Innovation/IEEE International Technology Management Conference (ICE/ITMC), Trondheim, Norway, 13–15 June 2016, pp. 1–10.

Snyder, W. M., Wenger, E. and de Sousa Briggs, X. (2003) Communities of practice in government: leveraging knowledge for performance. *The Public Manager* 32(4): 17–22.

Stacey, R. D. (2010) *Complexity and organizational reality.* London: Routledge.

Toivanen, H. (2014) *Friend leadership: a visual inspiration book.* Available at: https://tiimiakatemia.com/wp-content/uploads/2019/03/Toivanen-Friend-leadership-a-visual-inspiration-book.pdf. Accessed: 21/6/200.

Tomkins, L. and Ulus, E. (2016) Oh, was that 'experiential learning'?! Spaces, synergies and surprises with Kolb's learning cycle. *Management Learning* 47(2): 158–178.

Turner, V. (1977) Variations of the theme of liminality. In: Moore, S. and Myerhoff, B. G. (eds) *Secular ritual*. Assen: Van Gorcu, pp. 36–51.

Vince, R. (1998) Behind and beyond Kolb's learning cycle. *Journal of Management Education* 22(3): 304–319.

Wenger, E. (1998) Communities of practice: learning as a social system. *Systems Thinker* 9(5): 2–13.

2

Employability Entrepreneurship for Leveraging Employability Capitals

Yulia Shumilova and Yuzhuo Cai

INTRODUCTION

A number of employability frameworks have been developed lately reflecting the shifts in viewing employability from possessional (as the match between skills possessed and required) and positional (competition) perspectives – towards more relational or processual ones (seeing employability as a negotiation process) (Fugate et al., 2004; Pool & Sewell, 2007; Yorke & Knight, 2007; Bridgstock, 2009; Holmes, 2013; Clarke, 2018). Accordingly, the research perspective has been changing from associating employability with lists of skills to approaching it with the lens of developing employability capitals (Tomlinson, 2017; Pham et al., 2019; Nghia et al., 2020). The employability capital approach emphasises that 'employment outcomes are not simply determined by generic skills, but also by factors such as social class, gender, ethnicity, social networks and university status' (Pham et al., 2019: 395). In such a context, capitals understood as (interdependent) key resources (assets, currencies), accumulated through graduates' educational, social and work experiences, which give them certain advantages when transitioning to the labour market (Tomlinson, 2017a: 17). Specifically, the following forms of capital have been identified: human capital, social capital, identity capital, psychological capital and agentic capital (Korotov et al., 2011; Holmes, 2013; Tomlinson, 2017; Clinkard, 2018; Pham et al., 2019; Nghia et al., 2020).

Thinking about employability in terms of capitals rather than long lists of hard and soft skills may decrease the complexity of graduates' decision making and help researchers understand the differences in the labour market outcomes of graduates with similar backgrounds. However, we have identified several issues with the emerging capital-based approach. First, there is still a lack of consistency in defining and using graduate capitals, which is inevitable in research dealing with such multifaceted phenomena as employability. Second, there is scarce research on how students can develop efficient strategies to better leverage capitals along with understanding employability as a process (Ariss & Syed, 2011; Pham et al., 2019; Nghia et al., 2020). Although the concept of agentic capital has been applied in an attempt to understand international graduate strategies (Pham & Jackson, 2020; Nghia et al., 2020; Pham, 2021), the definition of this capital differs from other capitals according to Tomlinson (2017) and Bourdieu (1986). The latter define capitals as key resources and assets, while agentic capital is defined as a capacity to analyse one's strengths and weaknesses and interlink various capitals and resources (Pham & Jackson, 2020).

These discrepancies may hamper theoretical developments concerning how students/graduates optimise their employability strategies from the perspective of graduate capitals. To bridge the gaps in conceptualising both employability capitals and students' utilisation of capitals, we address two research questions: 1) How can graduate employability capitals identified and applied in extant literature be interpreted from the perspective of Bourdieu's conceptualisation of capital (Bourdieu, 1984, 1986, 1990) and 2) How can students' engagement with capitals to gain a competitive advantage in potential labour markets be conceptualised?

The rest of the chapter is structured as follows. First, the research design is described, focusing on theory synthesis and adaptation used in our conceptual paper. Second, we offer a critical review of modern employability capital through the lens of classical Bourdieu's understanding of capital. Third, we synthesise three streams of literature – on capital conversions, career agency/proactivity and entrepreneurship concepts to develop the employability entrepreneurship process. Finally, the contributions of the study are summarised in the conclusion.

RESEARCH DESIGN

Our study is a conceptual paper based on literature analysis. Our research design follows Jaakkola's (2020) suggestions on methodological approaches to writing conceptual papers. Jaakkola (2020) distinguishes four types of research design in respect of conceptual papers, namely theory synthesis, theory adaptation, typology, and model. The choice of the approach depends on the goals of conceptual papers. Our paper applies both theory adaptation and theory synthesis.

Theory adaptation papers 'seek to amend an existing theory by using other theories' and 'the point of departure for such papers, then, is the problematisation of a particular theory or concept' (Jaakkola, 2020: 23). This reflects the nature of our first research question, which is aimed to improve the shortcomings in the concept of employability capitals by applying the capital theory developed by Bourdieu (1986). Our arguments for answering the research question are not derived from empirical data but through 'the assimilation and combination of evidence in the form of previously developed concepts and theories' (Jaakkola, 2020: 19). Specifically, we will analyse the literature on various employability capitals (Tomlinson, 2017; Nghia et al., 2020) through the lens of Bourdieu's (1986) capital concept.

According to Jaakkola (2020), 'a theory synthesis paper seeks to achieve conceptual integration across multiple theories or literature streams' for offering 'a new or enhanced view of a concept or phenomenon by linking previously unconnected or incompatible pieces in a novel way' (p.2). This is largely in line with the aim of our second research question, in which we try to develop a new concept – employability entrepreneurship to understand students' strategies and actions in enhancing their positional advantage in potential labour markets through synthesising several kinds of literature: 1) studies dealing with relations between entrepreneurship and employability (Moreland, 2006; Moberg et al., 2014; Kucel et al., 2016; Terzaroli, 2019), 2) studies about agentic/proactive behaviour of graduates (Parker & Liao, 2016; Pham et al., 2019; Nghia et al., 2020; Chen & Hong, 2020), and 3) Bourdieu's (1986) elaboration on capital conversions that together help provide understanding for the mechanisms underlying employability entrepreneurship.

FROM FACTORS AFFECTING GRADUATE EMPLOYABILITY TO EMPLOYABILITY CAPITALS

Prior studies have identified a myriad of factors affecting graduate employability that can be grouped into micro-, meso- and macro levels. The micro/individual-level is represented by graduates' skills, competencies, attitudes and socio-economic background; the meso level, by the provision of higher education (such as reputation and type of HEI, study major, availability of career services), parents' influence and employers' beliefs; and the macro level, by labour market policies and employability enhancement programmes (Leuze, 2010; Shumilova & Cai, 2015; Tomlinson & Holmes, 2017). However, the existing research still focuses primarily on what is done by HEIs to improve employment outcomes and on the attributes the employable graduates should possess. In fact, the transition from higher education to the world of work requires the engagement of universities, employers and students (Cai, 2014). Especially, it should emphasise what students could do and are doing for themselves (Hernandez-Lopez et al., 2016).

In recent years, researchers (Fugate et al., 2004; Clark & Zukas, 2013; Tomlinson, 2017; Pham et al., 2019, Nghia et al., 2020) have tried to address this gap by analysing the factors affecting graduate employability from the perspective of graduate capitals. Such a perspective criticises the widely adopted skills agenda for not being able to explain the differences in labour market outcomes among graduates with similar educational backgrounds – differences especially prominent in the international education context (Bridgstock, 2009; Holmes, 2013; Tomlinson, 2017; Clarke, 2018; Clinkard, 2018). The developed framework of employability capitals (Tomlinson, 2017) helps link a variety of factors and resources, going beyond human capital and acknowledging the interconnectedness among capitals. Yet this lens does not sufficiently explain how graduates can utilise their capitals efficiently. Pham et al. (2019) and Nghia et al. (2020) highlight the role of agency in linking the graduate capitals as the first step towards understanding the core of the capital-based framework. In this paper, we would like to re-conceptualise this core by adding an entrepreneurial and capital conversion dimension to it, strengthening the understanding of emerging graduate capitals by comparing them to the classic ones.

A CRITICAL REFLECTION: EMPLOYABILITY CAPITALS MEETING BOURDIEU'S CAPITAL CONCEPT

While the employability capitals approach is useful for students or graduates to better perceive the skills, resources and conditions that affect their employability development, there seems to be a trend of using the term capital freely. For instance, when labelling certain factors or resources as a kind of employability capital, researchers do not always base their definitions on classic sociology understandings of capital, such as Bourdieu's. Here, we discuss the employability capitals mentioned in graduate employability literature in the framework of Bourdieu's conceptualisation of capital (Bourdieu, 1984, 1986, 1990).

According to Bourdieu (1984, 1986), capital can be understood as a currency that affects the position of an individual in the social world; it can be divided into distinct yet interconnected forms, namely economic, social, cultural and symbolic. Economic capital refers to money and ownership of financial means, means of production, material goods and other assets such as property. Social capital can be understood as a network of contacts and the real or virtual sum of resources that could be mobilised through such networks. Cultural capital can be divided into three subtypes: embodied, institutionalised and objectified. The embodied aspect of cultural capital is linked to the dispositions of body and mind shaped by the upbringing and socio-economic background; the institutionalised, in the form of educational qualifications as a 'certificate of cultural competence'; and the objectified – material artefacts with a cultural meaning (Bourdieu, 1986: 246). Symbolic capital is related to the prestige or status attached to certain competencies and values (Bourdieu, 1984). Next, we will compare the modern employability capitals dividing them into two categories: those that are similar to capitals identified by Bourdieu and the ones that fall outside.

GRADUATE CAPITALS THAT FIT BOURDIEU'S CLASSIFICATION OF CAPITAL

Human capital is defined as subject-specific knowledge and soft skills obtained during higher education/work experience (Clarke, 2018). In Bourdieu's theorising, human capital makes up an integral part of cultural capital (Tight, 2018), while in modern employability studies it is kept separately, reflected in the 'skills agenda'. We believe that human capital is rather an extension to institutionalised cultural capital in the Bourdieusian sense. Indeed, in the context of massified higher education and increasingly globalised labour markets, human capital alone is not sufficient for successful labour market integration (Ariss & Syed, 2011; Tomlinson & Holmes, 2017). Researchers of international graduate employability also note that human capital is context-specific or culturally embedded and cannot be easily transferred to a new cultural context without the help of other capitals (Savage et al., 2005; Clark & Zukas, 2013; Nghia et al., 2020). Furthermore, Bourdieu (1986) is critical of human capital theory as failing to account for mechanisms of social reproduction (capital invested by/inherited from family is not taken into account) (Tatli et al., 2014). Finally, human and cultural capitals jointly form the graduates' professional know-how (Korotov et al., 2011), hence can be kept inseparable.

Bourdieu (1986) uses cultural capital to highlight how class differences and upbringing may shape one's access to (prestigious) schools, tutors, higher education and consequently top work positions. This theorising is in line with a positional view on employability (Brown & Hesketh, 2004; Holmes, 2013), according to which, one's socio-economic background shapes the perceptions, level of confidence and actions of graduates, the decisions on which vacancies to apply for (Tomlinson, 2017a). However, such a 'social reproduction' approach appears to be too deterministic in the modern context, where the links between one's family background and career success are not as straightforward (Holmes, 2013). Hence, the later understanding of cultural capital included a set of attributes that can be acquired by students/graduates via internships and coaching such as knowing about the peculiarities of recruitment practices, norms of self-presentation, and interactional styles that are specific to different work environments (Smith, 2010; Tomlinson & Holmes, 2017; Pham et al., 2019). In this sense, cultural capital may serve as the employability enhancer, as it helps graduates develop the 'feel for the game' (Watson, 2013) in the labour market.

Social capital is formed by formal and informal relational ties via networking and implies wider access to resources (Bourdieu, 1986). Bourdieu claims that the volume of the social capital depends not only on the size of the network of connections that one can mobilise, but also on the volume of other capitals (economic, cultural or symbolic) possessed by the network (Bourdieu, 1986; Watson, 2013). Social capital is consistently used by both Bourdieu and modern employability researchers. The key social networks believed to facilitate graduate employability are connections with employers, alumni, supervisors and academics (Nghia et al., 2020). Access to such networks contributes to one's level of insider information on the labour market and affects one's self-efficacy (confidence in one's employability) (Tranquille, 2020). It is argued that graduates' social capital is shaped by social class, type of university attended and type of degree pursued (Holmes, 2013). As is the case with cultural capital, reproduction of social capital requires continuous investments of time and effort, yet it has a multiplier effect – increasing the profitability of the efforts proportionally to the size and quality of accessed social capital (Mayrhofer et al., 2000).

Bourdieu's symbolic capital refers to reflected power (in the form of reputation or prestige) that gives individuals the ability to deploy other types of capital and define the rules of the game (Ariss & Syed, 2011; Tatli et al., 2014). It is accumulated through the mobilisation of any form of capital recognised and valued by society (Ariss & Syed, 2011). In relation to job seeking, and in a more modern sense, symbolic capital may reflect graduates' efforts to strategically manage their careers by building a personal brand or specific graduate identity. Examples of symbolic capital can be letters of reference for one's job application or certificates of achievement that will help a graduate stand out in the pool of other applicants. In this way, symbolic capital is closely related to the concept of identity capital (Cote, 2005; Tomlinson, 2017), which involves aligning one's educational, work and extra-curricular experience to the profiles of targeted employers via tailored cover letters, crafting unique value propositions for employers and storytelling during job interviews (Tomlinson, 2017; Tomlinson & Holmes, 2017).

Finally, economic capital is the most straightforward, liquid and efficient type of capital that is easily convertible to other types (Bourdieu, 1986; Power, 1999; Mayrhofer et al., 2000; Medvetz & Sallaz, 2018). In terms of graduate employability, it can be viewed as both the means and the end. For instance, economic capital can be used as a means to invest in further learning or get access to certain networks via membership fees (Pret et al., 2016) and, as a result, graduates become more employable/get a higher salary. That means the ultimate goal of a graduate is to leverage different forms of employability capitals (including the economic one) and convert them to economic capital in their potential employment. However, in recent capital-based employability frameworks, the economic capital is missing.

GRADUATE CAPITALS OUTSIDE BOURDIEU'S FRAMEWORK

Currently, researchers of graduate employability single out more types of capital that do not strictly fit into Bourdieu's initially identified capitals – for instance, agentic and psychological capitals. The introduction of the agentic capital – as a capacity to analyse one's strengths and weaknesses and interlink various capitals and resources (Pham & Jackson, 2020) was an important attempt to bind the capital-based framework together. Although such understanding is different to other types of capitals that are defined as resources, this was an important step towards highlighting the agentic nature of the graduate capital model.

Psychological capital is a psycho-social resource reflected in ambition, job search self-efficacy, resilience and adaptability that are crucial in the modern context of unstable, unpredictable and highly competitive labour markets (Tomlinson & Holmes, 2017; Tomlinson, 2017). Caballero et al. (2020) reveal that psychological capital is the most relevant of employability capitals followed by social, cultural and human capital. Psychological capital is important as it helps graduates exercise their agency (Tomlinson, 2017). Hence, without diminishing the roles of these capitals, we, however, believe they rather belong to the 'social and psychic energies' that help mobilise the four core capitals (Neveu, 2018).

RE-INTERPRETATION OF MODERN EMPLOYABILITY CAPITALS THROUGH THE LENS OF BOURDIEU'S CAPITAL

To further understand modern employability capitals through the lens of Bourdieu's capital concepts, we adopted Clinkard's (2018) capital-related questions, as they help graduates to reflect on their employability. While theoretical discussions of capitals are useful for researchers, the graduates might be lost in these concepts. Hence, the suggested practically oriented questions can be used for recent graduates to understand the notion of capital and to develop their employability narrative, which is often a weak spot among those without prior work experience. In Table 2.1, we put modern employability-related types of capital in the framework of Bourdieu's capital theory along with three ways of knowing – know-how, know-who and know-why (Korotov et al., 2011).

While interpreting modern employability capitals through the lens of Bourdieu's capital concept, we draw two important implications. First, with the number of capitals proliferating, there is a risk of facing graduate capital inflation and the potential loss of conceptual coherence (DiMaggio, 1979; Neveu, 2018). To mitigate the risk, it is important to give the graduate capitals a clear definition and keep their number limited. We propose to re-define graduate capitals as tangible and intangible resources that students and graduates accumulate, leverage and convert in order to negotiate their employability and get a competitive advantage in the labour market. Table 2.1 also highlights what capital may mean to students/graduates (see Clinkard's self-reflection questions). Second, by further examining the agentic and psychological capitals that are not included in the forms of capital described by Bourdieu, we find that they have a special stance in the graduate capital framework. The elaborations of the two capitals shed light on

Table 2.1 Employability capitals in comparison with Bourdieu's conceptualisation of capital

Bourdieu's capitals	**Modern employability capitals** (Holmes, 2013; Tomlinson, 2017, Pham & Jackson, 2020)	**'ways of knowing'** (adapted from Korotov et al., 2011)	**Questions for graduates' self-reflection** (adapted from Clinkard, 2018, agile reflective tool)
cultural (embodied)	cultural	professional know-how	Do you understand the modern labour market needs, the work culture and peculiarities of recruitment practices in your professional area?
cultural (institutionalised)	human		Have you been proactively seeking learning in all situations (not only at the university but after graduation)?
social	social	know-who (network)	To what extent have you shown the development of 'networking' competencies? (Think of situations in which you have proactively sought out advice, information and support, or have done something to help others)
symbolic	identity	know-why (career motivation and identity)	Who are you? What do you want to become? What impact do you want to have in your professional life? Think about how your identity/professional values have changed over time (being a fresher, an intern, a graduate), and what has belonging to each community enabled you to achieve?
economic	N/A	N/A	Think of your salary expectations and where you can invest the available economic resources to become more employable? What economic value can you bring to the company you apply for?
N/A	agentic	career management know-how	How can you highlight your strengths and hide the weaknesses by combining the available resources to achieve a career goal? (Pham & Jackson, 2020)
	psychological		To what extent have you shown resilience and flexibility (especially when learning from failure through reflection)?

Source: Authors' synthesis of relevant literature.

how graduates can leverage other types of capital for better employability. This leads to our proposed concept of employability entrepreneurship, to be discussed in the next section.

EMPLOYABILITY ENTREPRENEURSHIP TO MAXIMISE THE VALUE OF EMPLOYABILITY CAPITALS

Until recently, employability research streams have mainly focused either on the role of individual attributes or on the hindering–enabling role of contextual factors for graduates' employment outcomes and, as such, the dimension of how graduates can approach the labour market transition efficiently was downplayed. In this part, we synthesise three kinds of studies that help address this gap and tackle the second research goal – to conceptualise students' engagement with the capitals to gain competitive advantage in the labour market. We have identified that the studies on agentic/proactive behaviour of graduates; links between entrepreneurship and graduate employability, and Bourdieu's capital conversion insights will be useful in this respect. Synthesising these studies led us to the development of the employability entrepreneurship concept.

CAPITAL CONVERSIONS

Over one's lifespan, capital can be inherited or otherwise acquired, accumulated and converted from one to another in order to compete and obtain positional advantages in certain fields, such as labour markets (Savage et al., 2005; Pret et al., 2016; Rossier, 2020). To better understand capital conversions, one needs to consider their possible directions, contextuality (feel for the game) and pertinent transaction costs. We discuss these aspects below vis-à-vis graduate employability.

First, Bourdieu (1986) introduced the notion of capital conversions, implying mutual interchangeability of all capitals (in line with his relational approach to sociology), rather than any linear convertibility cycle (Robson & Sanders, 2009). Provided that economic capital is the most convertible one and can be both the means and the end, Bourdieu's conversion model can be presented as a triangular pyramid with economic capital on top (Figure 2.1).

In later studies, there are some alterations to this vision, depicting the conversion cycle as a circular loop of linear transmissions from cultural capital to social, from social to symbolic and from symbolic to economic (Maclean et al., 2005; Pret et al., 2016). Such a vector of conversions can be justified in the case of graduate employability as a recommended path for maximising one's value in the labour market, yet the original idea of capital interchangeability should also be preserved. A practical example of such capital conversion cycle is given in Table 2.3, in the subchapter preceeding the Conclusion.

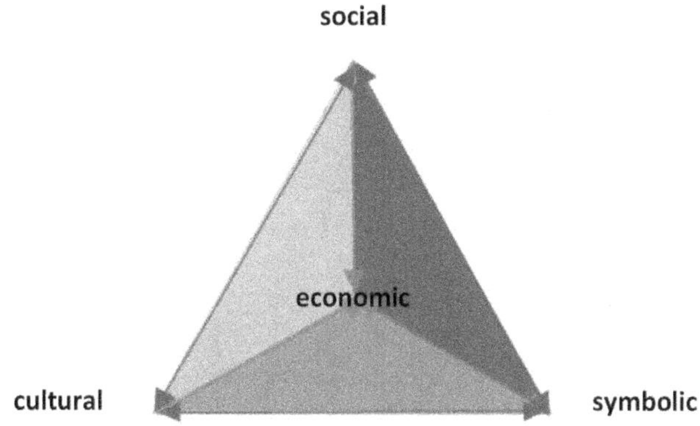

Figure 2.1 Bourdieu's capital conversions

Source: Authors' representation of capital convertibility (Bourdieu, 1986).

Second, when considering a certain capital conversion, graduates should consider the interrelation between a person's socio-economic, educational and cultural background (habitus in Bourdieu's terms) and their specific labour market context (field in Bourdieu's terms) (Medvetz & Sallaz, 2018). As such, one's habitus can act as a filter in the job search. Through this filter, graduates perceive the rules of the game and their position in a specific labour market and match their identity to the employers' demands. However, when moving to a new environment (or a new field), the rules of the game might not be perceived at once. For instance, international graduates in the host country labour market might not know about the implicit recruitment practices, such as hidden jobs that can only be heard of via social networks (Alho, 2020; Joy et al., 2020). Bourdieu (1990) claims that making the rules completely transparent is not feasible, but it is possible to get a better feel for the game via active reflection (Pool & Sewell, 2007), agile learning and asking for feedback (Watson, 2013; Anseel, 2017; Clinkard, 2018).

Third, capitals may have different degrees of convertibility or accompanying transaction costs. Economic capital takes the central role in Bourdieu's conversions as the most liquid asset, yet, even this capital may require the support of other capitals and time for some conversions (Pret et al., 2016; Yüksek, 2018). For instance, money alone cannot immediately be translated to social and cultural capital (networks and qualifications require time commitments) (Firkin, 2001). On the other hand, social, cultural and symbolic capitals can be easily converted to economic capital in terms of obtaining a work position or freelance contract. The principle of conservation of energy is important here, reminding us that 'profits in one area are necessarily paid for by costs in another' (Bourdieu, 1986). Indeed, after capital conversion one usually has more capital, but it is paid for with labour time or money. Therefore, graduates would need to first identify the available capitals and think strategically about which resources can be used to 'pay' to acquire the lacking ones.

To sum up, the capital conversions with their accompanying attributes of transaction costs, economy of time, and reflection needed to get the feel for the game can be useful to further understand graduate transitions. However, as the mechanisms of steering the conversions have not been sufficiently theorised, it is important to continue the discussion on what may structure particular capital conversions in the case of developing graduate employability. Some steps in this direction have been taken with the studies on the role of agency for interlinking the capitals. We want to extend this further in the next section.

AGENCY AND ENTREPRENEURIAL MINDSET AS THE MISSING LINK?

Below we elaborate on how the concepts of agency/proactivity and entrepreneurial mindset can conceptually guide the graduate transition steps. The idea to combine these was inspired by Lackéus et al.'s report (2020) where agency is featured as part of the entrepreneurial employee model. Besides, the concepts proved to converge on a number of aspects and complement each other.

We recognise that while graduates may have limited control over the labour market demand or employers' recruitment practices, they can still exercise some agency in how they approach the higher education-to-work transition (Fugate et al., 2004; Tomlinson, 2017a). Indeed, there have been emerging studies calling for attention to graduate's agency, coupled with relational perspective to graduate employability. Such an approach looks promising, especially in the context where more people acquire similar credentials, requiring extra work to demonstrate one's unique employment value (Beck & Beck-Gernsheim, 2002). The links between agency and employability are reflected in concepts such as proactive career behaviour (Fugate et al., 2004; Uy et al., 2015; Parker & Liao, 2016; Chen & Hong, 2020), career management (Bridgstock, 2009) and agentic capital (Pham & Jackson, 2020).

The concepts of agency and proactivity provide necessary insights that can further strengthen the capital-based employability framework. Generally, a person with strong agency is someone who decides to act in order to reshape their environment and make things happen, rather than letting things happen to them (Lackéus et al., 2020). The process of action-taking is based on one's values and motivations and is supported by reflexivity: analysing past practices and imagining a desirable future (Archer, 2003; Lackéus et al., 2020). Similarly, Parker and Liao (2016) explain that being proactive in one's career: 1) is future-focused (anticipating the needed change); 2) involves change; and 3) is self-initiated (comes from within). They further posit that to make sure one's proactivity leads to successful outcomes, it is important to consider the context, others, and one's own strengths, limitations, values and priorities (ibid.). This binds well with Pham et al.'s (2019) discussion of the role of agency in the capital-based framework, claiming that agency enables graduates to interlink various capitals so that they can make use of their strengths and hide weaknesses. Finally, an important characteristic of the career agency is that it is constructed, exercised and reformed in an iterative way, by requesting feedback on one's actions (Chen & Hong, 2019).

Although the agency and proactivity constructs help to accommodate the complexity of the HE-to-work transition process to some extent, we argue that the entrepreneurial dimension combined with the capital conversion lens should complement them to get a full picture of an efficient graduate transition. The studies linking entrepreneurship and employability mainly focus on the benefits of introducing entrepreneurship courses to the curriculum and the skills developed in such training (Pereira et al., 2019). As such, an entrepreneurial mindset has been argued to aid job searching and articulating one's abilities (Smith et al., 2006) as it involves being alert to opportunities (unseen by others) and proactively making things happen (Bell, 2016); being able to deal with uncertainty (Minniti & Bygrave, 2001); possessing innovativeness, critical thinking and the value creation attitude (Moberg et al., 2014; Kucel et al., 2016; Bacigalupo et al., 2016).

Entrepreneurship, defined as an ability to act on opportunities and transform them into financial, cultural or social value for others (Moberg et al., 2014; Bacigalupo et al., 2016), has a lot in common with the concept of career agency/proactivity (Uy et al., 2015). Moreover, these concepts complement each other in a way that can provide guidance to recent graduates. Besides the ability to make things happen and deal with uncertainty, for example, entrepreneurship, like human agency, is a process of learning (from successes as well as from failures) that involves repetition and experimentation (ibid.). However, the entrepreneurship concept goes a step further than proactivity in its focus on opportunity alertness, risk-taking and creating value for others. In Table 2.2, we summarise the similarities in agency/proactivity and entrepreneurship attributes in relation to employability. These attributes will be further integrated into the employability entrepreneurship process when conceptualising graduates' engagement with capitals in HE-to-work transition.

BINDING ALL TOGETHER: TOWARDS THE CONCEPT OF EMPLOYABILITY ENTREPRENEURSHIP

Building on the importance of both agency/proactivity and an entrepreneurial mindset for graduate labour market integration and the elaborated notion of convertibility of graduate capital, we define the employability entrepreneurship concept as an iterative process of approaching one's higher education-to-work transition in a proactive and entrepreneurial way. It involves leveraging and

Table 2.2 Conceptual comparison of career agency and entrepreneurship attributes

career agency/proactivity	entrepreneurship
(Parker & Liao, 2016; Cheng & Hong, 2020)	(Minniti & Bygrave, 2001; Moberg et al., 2014; Kucel et al., 2016; Bell, 2016; Bacigalupo et al., 2016)
reflexivity, career forethought	critical thinking, opportunity alertness
can do attitude	confidence, risk taking
change making	acting on opportunities; innovativeness
consider the context, others and own strengths	creating value for others
iterative process, getting feedback	repetition and experimentation (testing ideas)
ability to deal with uncertainty	

Source: Authors' summary of the relevant literature.

converting one's graduate capital to create value for oneself, the employers and society in accordance with personal values, goals and strengths.

In Table 2.3, we present the process of employability entrepreneurship in more detail by synthesising the agency and entrepreneurship attributes that help shape the employability steps and integrate the possible capital conversions to these steps. In particular, the employability steps reflect the major attributes of the discussed concepts such as reflexivity, iteration, identifying and acting on opportunities, feedback-seeking, considering the external context and creating value for others, while keeping one's own values in mind and learning from mistakes. As to the graduate capital conversions (inspired by Bourdieu 1986, Maclean et al., 2005; Pret et al., 2016), Table 2.3 reflects some examples of both the cultural-social-symbolic-economic linear conversion cycle (Steps 3–4), the auxiliary conversions (Step 2) and the capital that can be applied at some steps without conversions (Steps 1, 5–7).

By the time of graduation, all students possess cultural capital shaped by their upbringing, education and initial beliefs about the way specific labour markets function. Yet other capital may be lacking and need to be strategically acquired by capital conversion, along with the identified employability entrepreneurship steps. Hence, after reflecting on their available resources and employer needs, the students/ graduates start converting their cultural capital to the social one, by networking with the immediate circle formed during studies, internships and volunteering. The social capital is further converted to the symbolic one by asking for references and developing one's employability narrative (or 'personal brand'). That is, the employers may better recognise the graduates' social and cultural capital when these are converted to the symbolic one, as symbolic capital helps generate trust (Pret et al., 2016). Next, when it is time to pitch one's professional

Table 2.3 The process of employability entrepreneurship

employability steps	**use of graduate capital and possible conversions**			
(Cai, 2012; Korotov et al., 2011)	cultural	social	symbolic	economic
1. Reflect on the available resources, your identity, strong and weak points, values, career goals and labour market context	x	x	x	x
2. Identify employment opportunities/ potential employers relevant for your career goals and analyse their needs (why should they hire you?)		social to cultural: ask your network for advice to identify and better understand potential employers		
3. Gain the lacking resources by converting available capital to the needed ones.	cultural to social: share your expertise via volunteering/ internship to expand your network	social to symbolic: ask your network for references, recommendation letters; build your personal brand in LinkedIn		economic to cultural/ social: invest in continuing education; pay membership fees to a professional association
4. Develop your employability narrative and a unique value proposition for potential employers (pitch, cover letter)			symbolic to economic: in your cover letter/ job interview highlight how your identity can help the company create value	

employability steps	**use of graduate capital and possible conversions**			
(Cai, 2012; Korotov et al., 2011)	cultural	social	symbolic	economic
5. Think of an innovative and proactive way to approach the potential employer/HR to sell your ideas		x		
6. Seek feedback on your job search strategies (CV, cover letter, interview, value proposition)		x		
7. Reflect on the job application process to learn from success/mistakes and adjust your strategy/repertoire of capitals (repeat the cycle)	x	x	x	x

Source: Authors' summary based on the reviewed literature.

identity to the employer via a cover letter or job interview, we assume the graduates will have a higher chance of employment if they think in an entrepreneurial way of what kind of value they can create for the employer (Cai, 2012). Finally, if one application round fails, graduates can use their economic capital to obtain the missing cultural or social capital or reconsider their career path altogether, choosing to become a freelancer or an entrepreneur. Therefore, the employability entrepreneurship process represents an iterative cycle that continues until the satisfying workplace or self-employment is found or created.

The presented employability entrepreneurship process can be used as a self-reflection tool by graduates to shape their employability strategies and better leverage the available capital. The process, based on proactive and entrepreneurial thinking and Bourdieu's capital conversion mechanism, prompts two major questions to keep in mind during one's graduate transition: how can I distinguish myself from the pool of applicants with similar backgrounds? and what added value can I bring? To be able to stand out from the crowd, it is important to start one's employability reflections early. For instance, Steps 1–3 can be made before graduation and preferably with career counsellors, as self-reflection is more efficient when done in a facilitated dialogue (Chen & Hong, 2020). Indeed, capital accumulation takes time (Bourdieu, 1986), yet by investing time in capital conversion, the monetary transaction costs can be brought to a minimum. To be able to bring added value to the target employment, graduates need to develop their reflexivity, opportunity alertness and test their ideas in an agile way – the way entrepreneurs do – by asking for feedback. One way of developing such entrepreneurial thinking can be by joining the student start-up programmes, accelerators or facilitated innovation challenges. We assume that when the three employability capitals are present and the graduate has a unique value proposition for the employer/potential customers or can demonstrate their proactive/entrepreneurial thinking, the chance of obtaining the economic capital in terms of employment or self-employment is higher.

CONCLUSION

In line with the emerging research directions, this conceptual paper treats employability as a graduate transition process in which graduates strategically use various capitals to negotiate their labour market value with employers. This study contributes to the existing literature in both theoretical and practical ways. First, while the recently developed capital-based employability frameworks help graduates better understand their skills, resources and status to gain advantage in the labour market, the employability capitals tend to be used rather freely and their numbers keep proliferating. This challenges the theoretical validity of the concept. Hence, the first research question aims to re-define modern employability capital through the lens of Bourdieu's understanding of capitals. As a result, we have identified that psychological and agentic capitals, for instance, could be categorised as attributes helping the graduate transition process rather than capitals in Bourdieu's sense. Furthermore, we restore the economic capital to the employability framework as an important element, that can be both the means and the end in the graduate transition process.

Second, while the current graduate employability literature has reported a variety of factors affecting employability, there have been fewer discussions on what students/graduates can learn from this knowledge for optimising their strategies of employability development. Accordingly, the second research question aims to conceptualise graduates' engagement with capital to gain competitive advantage in the labour market. When answering this question, it was observed that prior research has overemphasised the importance of individual capital, overlooking the mechanisms of capital convertibility (Pret et al., 2016). Hence, we adapted the capital-based employability framework (Tomlinson, 2017) mainly by introducing Bourdieu's capital conversion cycle and suggesting the mechanisms for optimal progression of conversion. In addition, based on insights from agentic and psychological capitals, we further explored the concepts of career agency and proactivity noting their convergence with the concept of entrepreneurship. By synthesising these relevant studies, we proposed an operational approach of employability entrepreneurship – as a matrix of employability steps and Bourdieu's four convertible capitals to guide students/graduates to maximise their value to employers. It should be noted that we have intentionally avoided developing the concept of entrepreneurial capital to avoid contributing to the inflation of graduate capitals. At the same time, by offering a matrix approach we remain loyal to understanding employability as a process.

Third, this paper offers practical implications for graduates in the form of 1) self-reflection questions about capital (Table 2.1) that will help develop their employability narrative and 2) the employability entrepreneurship process (Table 2.3) that will help structure their thinking about the available resources and how they can be strategically accumulated, used or converted. Nevertheless, as this is a preliminary effort to re-interpret employability capitals from the perspective of Bourdieu's capital theory (including both forms of capital and capital conversion), the conceptual frameworks developed in the chapter need to be further tested in empirical studies. In particular, future research could investigate further the interconnections among graduate capitals; the role of the entrepreneurial mindset in developing capital as well as the role of other enabling and hindering contexts for capital conversion as a way to exercise graduate agency.

While reinterpreting graduate employability through the lens of Bourdieu's capital theory and proposing the concept of employability entrepreneurship, the chapter's conceptualisation is primarily focused on how graduates can better leverage their resources to gain competitive advantage in the labour market. Meanwhile, we understand that it is equally important to understand how employers perceive graduate employability capital and how their perceptions are institutionalised. Such an aspect has been addressed in a chapter of another book (Cai & Tomlinson, forthcoming).

REFERENCES

Al Ariss, A. & Syed, J. (2011). Capital mobilisation of skilled migrants: a relational perspective. *British Journal of Management*, 22(2), 286–304. doi:10.1111/j.1467-8551.2010.00734.x

Alho, R. (2020). 'You need to know someone who knows someone': international students' job search experiences. *Nordic Journal of Working Life Studies*, 10(2). doi:10.18291/njwls.v10i2.120817

Anseel, F. (2017). Agile learning strategies for sustainable careers: a review and integrated model of feedback-seeking behavior and reflection. *Current Opinion in Environmental Sustainability*, 28, 51–57.

Archer, M. S. (2003). *Structure, agency and the internal conversation*. Cambridge: Cambridge University Press.

Bacigalupo, M., Kampylis, P., Punie, Y. & Van den Brande, G. (2016). *EntreComp: the entrepreneurship competence framework*. Luxembourg: Publication Office of the European Union.

Beck, U. & Beck-Gernsheim, E. (2002). *Individualisation. Institutionalised individualism and its social and political consequences*. London: Sage.

Bell, R., (2016). Unpacking the link between entrepreneurialism and employability. An assessment of the relationship between entrepreneurial attitudes and likelihood of graduate employment in a professional field. *Education and Training*, 58(1), 2–17.

Bourdieu, P. (1984). *Distinction: a social critique of the judgement of taste*. Cambridge, Massachusetts: Harvard University Press.

Bourdieu, P. (1986). The forms of capital. In Richardson, J. (ed.), *Handbook of theory and research for the sociology of education* (pp. 241–258). New York: Greenwood.

Bourdieu, P. (1990). *Homo Academicus*. Palo Alto, CA: Stanford University Press.

Bridgstock, R. (2009). The graduate attributes we've overlooked: enhancing graduate employability through career management skills. *Higher Education Research & Development*, 28(1), 31–44, doi:10.1080/07294360802444347

Brown, P. & Hesketh, A. (2004). *The mismanagement of talent: employability and jobs in the knowledge economy*. Oxford: Oxford University Press.

Caballero, G., Álvarez-González, P. & López-Miguens, M. J. (2020). How to promote the employability capital of university students? Developing and validating scales, *Studies in Higher Education*, *45*:12, 2634-2652, DOI: 10.1080/03075079.2020.1807494

Cai, Y. (2012). *Understanding employers' perceptions of international graduates: an investigation of the employment prospects of Finnish-educated Chinese graduates in Finnish companies operating in China*. Tampere, Finland: Tampere University Press.

Cai, Y. (2014). Enhancing overseas Chinese graduate employability: the case of Chinese graduates with Finnish academic qualifications. *Frontiers of Education in China*, 9(3), 377–402. doi:10.3868/s110-003-014-0031-x

Cai, Y. & Tomlinson, M. (Forthcoming). A renewed analytical framework for understanding employers' perceptions of graduate employability: Integration of capital and institutionalist perspectives. In T. Broadley, Y. Cai, M. Firth, E. Hunt & J. Neugebauer (eds), *Sage handbook of graduate employability*. London: Sage.

Chen, C. P. & Hong, J. W. L. (2020). The career human agency theory. *Journal of Counseling & Development*, 98, 193–199.

Clark, M. & Zukas, M. (2013). A Bourdieusian approach to understanding employability: becoming a 'fish in water'. *Journal of Vocational Education & Training*, 65(2), 208–219, doi:10.1080/13636820.2013.782887

Clarke, M. (2018). Rethinking graduate employability: the role of capital, individual attributes and context. *Studies in Higher Education*, 43(11), 1923–1937, doi:10.1080/03075079.2017.1294152

Clinkard, K. (2018). Are employability and entrepreneurial measures for higher education relevant? Introducing AGILE reflection. *Industry and Higher Education*, 32(6), 375–390. doi:10.1177/0950422218808625

Cote, J. (2005). Identity capital, social capital and the wider benefits of learning generating resources facilitative of social cohesion. *London Review of Education*, 3(3), 221–237.

DiMaggio, P. (1979). On Pierre Bourdieu. *American Journal of Sociology*, 84(6), 1460–1474.

Firkin, P. (2001) *Entrepreneurial capital: a resource-based conceptualisation of the entrepreneurial process In: Vol. Labour Market Dynamics Research Programme Working Paper No. 7*. Auckland: Massey University.

Fugate, M., Kinicki, A. J. & Ashforth, B. E. (2004). Employability: a psycho-social construct, its dimensions, and applications. *Journal of Vocational Behavior*, 65, 14–38.

Hernandez-Lopez, L., Garcia-Almeida, D. J. & Ballesteros-Rodriguez, J. L. (2016). Students' perceptions of the lecturer's role in management education: knowledge acquisition and competence development. *International Journal of Management Education*, 14(3), 411–421.

Holmes, L. (2013). Competing perspectives on graduate employability: possession, position or process?, *Studies in Higher Education*, 38(4), 538–554.

Jaakkola, E. (2020). Designing conceptual articles: four approaches. *AMS Review*, 10(1), 18–26. doi:10.1007/s13162-020-00161-0

Joy, S., Game, A. M. & Toshniwal, I. G. (2020). Applying Bourdieu's capital-field-habitus framework to migrant careers: taking stock and adding a transnational perspective, *The International Journal of Human Resource Management*, 31(20), 2541–2564, doi:10.1080/09585192.2018.1454490

Korotov, K., Khapova, S. & Arthur, M. (2011). Career entrepreneurship. *Organizational Dynamics*, 40(2), 127–135.

Kucel, A., Róbert, P., Buil, M. & Masferrer, N. (2016). Entrepreneurial skills and education-job matching of higher education graduates. *European Journal of Education*, 51(1), 73–89. doi:10.1111/ejed.12161

Lackéus, M., Lundqvist, M., Williams Middleton, K. & Inden, J. (2020). In Bacigalupo, M. (ed.) *The entrepreneurial employee in public and private sector – what, why, how* EUR 30108 EN, Publications Office of the European Union, Luxembourg, doi:10.2760/460123, JRC117661.

Leuze, K. (2010). *Smooth path or long and winding road? How institutions shape the transition from higher education to work*. Opladen & Farmington Hills: Budrich UniPress Ltd.

Maclean, M., Harvey, C. & Press, J. (2005). *Business elites and corporate governance in France and the UK*. Basingstoke, UK: Palgrave Macmillan.

Mayrhofer, W., Steyrer, J., Meyer, M., Erten, C., Hermann, A., Iellatchitch, A., Mattl, C. & Strunk, G. (2000). *Towards a habitus based concept of managerial careers*. Paper presented at the Annual Meeting of the Academy of Management, Toronto, Canada.

Medvetz, T. & Sallaz, J. J. (2018). *The Oxford handbook of Pierre Bourdieu*. New York, NY: Oxford University Press.

Minniti, M., & Bygrave, W. (2001). A dynamic model of entrepreneurial learning. *Entrepreneurship Theory and Practice, 25*(3), 5–16. https://doi.org/10.1177/104225870102500301

Moberg, K., Fosse, H. B., Hoffman, A. & Junge, M. (2014). *Impact of entrepreneurship education in Denmark 2014*. Odense, Denmark: Fonden for Entreprenørskab.

Moreland, N. (2006). *Entrepreneurship and higher education: an employability perspective*. York, England: The Higher Education Academy.

Neveu, E. (2018). Bourdieu's capital(s): sociologizing an economic concept. In Medvetz, T. & Sallaz, J. J. (eds) *The Oxford handbook of Pierre Bourdieu*. New York, NY: Oxford University Press.

Nghia, T. L. H., Tomlinson, M., Medica, K., Thompson, C., Pham, T. & Thompson, C. (eds) (2020). *Developing and utilising employability capitals: graduates' strategies across labour markets*. Abingdon, Oxon; New York, NY: Routledge. doi:10.4324/9781003004660

Parker, S. K. & Liao, J. (2016). Wise proactivity: how to be proactive and wise in building your career. *Organizational Dynamics* 45, 217–227. doi:10.1016/j.orgdyn.2016.07.007

Pereira, E. T., Vilas-Boas, M. & Rebelo, C. (2019). Does entrepreneurship and innovative education matter to increase employability skills? In Carvalho, L. C. and Daniel, A. D. (eds) *Global considerations in entrepreneurship education and training*. Hershey, PA: IGI Global. doi:10.4018/978-1-5225-7675-4.ch013

Pham, T., Tomlinson, M. & Thompson, C. (2019). Forms of capital and agency as mediations in negotiating employability of international graduate migrants. *Globalisation, Societies and Education*, 17(3), 394–405, doi:10.1080/14767724.2019.1583091

Pham, T. and Jackson, D. (2020). Employability and determinants of employment outcomes. In Nghia, T. L. H., Tomlinson, M., Medica, K., Thompson, C., Pham, T. & Thompson, C. (eds) (2020). *Developing and utilising employability capitals: graduates' strategies across labour markets*. Abingdon, Oxon; New York, NY: Routledge. doi:10.4324/9781003004660

Pham, T. (2021). *Navigating the host labour market: international graduates need more than credentials*. (Centre for Global Higher Education working paper series; No. 64). University of Oxford.

Pool, L. D. & Sewell, P. (2007). The key to employability: developing a practical model of graduate employability. *Education & Training*, 49(4), 277–289.

Power, E.M. (1999). An introduction to Pierre Bourdieu's key theoretical concepts. *Journal for the Study of Food and Society*, 3(1), 48–52, doi:10.2752/152897999786690753

Pret, T., Shaw, E. & Drakopoulou Dodd, S. (2016). Painting the full picture: the conversion of economic, cultural, social and symbolic capital. *International Small Business Journal: Researching Entrepreneurship*, 34(8), 1004–1027. doi:10.1177/0266242615595450

Robson, K. & Sanders, C. (eds) (2009). *Quantifying theory: Pierre Bourdieu*. Toronto, CA: Springer.

Rossier, T. (2020). Accumulation and conversion of capitals in professorial careers. The importance of scientific reputation, network relations, and internationality in economics and business studies. *Higher Education*, 80(6), 1061–1080. doi:10.1007/s10734-020-00508-3

Savage, M., Warde, A. & Devine, F. (2005). Capitals, assets, and resources: some critical issues. *British Journal of Sociology*, 56(1), 31–47. doi:10.1111/j.1468-4446.2005.00045.x

Shumilova, Y. & Cai, Y. (2015). Factors affecting the employability of international graduates. *Universities and Leadership*. 1(1), 24–30.

Smith, A. J., Collins, L. A. and Hannon, P. D. (2006). Embedding new entrepreneurship programmes in UK higher education institutions: challenges and considerations, *Education and Training*, 48 (8/9), 555–567.

Smith, V. (2010). Review article. Enhancing employability: human, cultural, and social capital in an era of turbulent unpredictability. *Human Relations*, 63(2), 279–303, doi:10.1177/0018726709353639

Tatli, A., Vassilopoulou, J., Özbilgin, M., Forson, C. & Slutskaya, N. (2014). A Bourdieuan relational perspective for entrepreneurship research. *Journal of Small Business Management*, 52(4), 615–632. doi:10.1111/jsbm.12122

Terzaroli, C. (2019). Entrepreneurship as a special pathway for employability. *Fostering Employability in Adult and Higher Education: An International Perspective*. 2019,(163), 121–131, doi:10.1002/ace.20346

Tight, M. (2018). Human and social capital and their application in higher education research, *Theory and Method in Higher Education Research* (4), 209–223. https://doi.org/10.1108/S2056-375220180000004013

Tomlinson, M. (2017). Forms of graduate capital and their relationship to graduate employability. *Education and Training*, 59(4), 338–352. doi:10.1108/ET-05-2016-0090.

Tomlinson, M. (2017a). Introduction: graduate employability in context: charting a complex, contested and multi-faceted policy and research field. In Tomlinson, M. & Holmes, L. (eds) (2017). *Graduate employability in context. Theory, research and debate*. London: Palgrave Macmillan, UK. doi:10.1057/978-1-137-57168-7

Tomlinson, M. & Holmes, L. (eds) (2017). *Graduate employability in context. Theory, research and debate*. London: Palgrave Macmillan, UK. doi:10.1057/978-1-137-57168-7

Tranquille, M. D. (2020). Circumnavigation: supporting employability by developing capitals. In Nghia, T. L. H., Tomlinson, M., Medica, K., Thompson, C., Pham, T., & Thompson, C. (eds) (2020). *Developing and utilising employability capitals: graduates' strategies across labour markets*. Abingdon, Oxon; New York, NY: Routledge. doi:10.4324/9781003004660

Uy, M. A., Chan, K.-Y., Sam, Y. L., Ho, M. H. R. & Chernyshenko, O. S. (2015). Proactivity, adaptability and boundaryless career attitudes: the mediating role of entrepreneurial alertness. *Journal of Vocational Behavior*, 86, 115–123. doi:10.1016/j.jvb.2014.11.005

Watson, J. (2013). Profitable portfolios: capital that counts in higher education. *British Journal of Sociology of Education*, 34(3), 412–430. doi:10.1080/01425692.2012.710005

Yorke, M. & Knight, P. (2007). Embedding employability into the curriculum. Evidence-informed pedagogy and the enhancement of student employability. *Teaching in Higher Education*, 12(2), 157–170.

Yüksek, A. D. (2018). Evaluating the importance of social capital for the conversion of the forms of capital: a critical approach to the Bourdieusian model, *Gaziantep University Journal of Social Sciences*, 17(3), 1090–1106.

3

Beyond the Data: Navigating the Struggles of Post-PhD Employability

Holly Prescott

INTRODUCTION

The employability and career destinations of PhD graduates have attracted increasing attention in the early twenty-first century. One factor driving such attention has been the implication of postgraduate research in national agendas for economic growth, in which doctoral graduates and their skills are portrayed as strategically vital to the productivity of a country's or region's knowledge economy and capacity for innovation (Department for Business, Energy and Industrial Strategy, 2020; Leitch, 2006; LERU, 2007). Positioning PhD graduates as a highly skilled potential workforce central to national productivity therefore suggests that such graduates can look forward to healthy employability prospects. The full picture is, however, rather more complex, as policy narratives encouraging increases in doctoral student numbers are often contested by concerns that the supply of PhD graduates already exceeds labour market demand for such candidates, as well as arguments that the current structure and content of PhD programmes require an overhaul if graduates' employability prospects are to be preserved (Hancock et al., 2019: 5).

Indeed, evidence from a range of countries suggests that these concerns are supported by the lived experiences of PhD graduates. Boulos (2016) questions incentives to increase PhD student numbers based on her own difficulties finding work to match her qualifications and skills in Europe. Whilst using data from

1,002 PhD graduates in Catalonia, Di Paolo and Mañé found that 26% appeared to be in jobs requiring neither a PhD nor the skills developed during postgraduate research (2016: 438). The prospects of such underemployment not only impact the mental health of individuals involved (Guthrie et al., 2017); they also represent a potential 'underutilization of publicly-funded human capital therefore limiting knowledge-based economic growth' (Hayter and Parker, 2019: 557). Meanwhile in Canada, the Council of Canadian Academies (CCA) report a national situation in which the creation of new 'tenure-track' academic jobs has not kept pace with the increase in PhD graduate numbers, whilst sectors beyond academia do not, in turn, appear to have significantly enhanced their recruitment of PhD graduates (2021: xviii).

Internationally therefore, PhD graduates' employability prospects appear more complex than the policy narratives outlined above may suggest. In this chapter, I attempt to unpick some of this complexity by focusing on some of the key challenges that PhD graduates face when entering the job market, taken both from relevant literature and from my own career guidance work with postgraduate researchers. I begin by outlining top-level employment data that appears to give PhD graduates in the UK, USA and Canada cause to be optimistic about their employability prospects. I then outline some key limitations of this data, reviewing studies which highlight specific employability challenges faced by PhD graduates. Specifically, I assess how the lived experiences of PhD researchers and graduates are impacted by: the clash of their career expectations with reality; the need to revise professional identity post-PhD; the phenomenon of feeling simultaneously over-qualified and under-experienced; and difficulties in articulating doctoral skills to employers. This analysis will also offer suggestions of how practitioners, institutions, and PhD researchers alike can address these struggles and prepare PhD graduates to enter the labour market. Whilst particular attention will be paid to evidence from the UK as this is the context of my own practice, accounts from other European nations and from North America will also be used to demonstrate the international prevalence of the featured challenges in post-PhD employability.

EMPLOYMENT DATA ON PHD EMPLOYABILITY

At first glance, employment data from the UK, USA and Canada suggests that PhD graduates can look forward to lower unemployment rates than their bachelor-level counterparts. At the time of writing, the most recent data from the UK's Graduate Outcomes survey as reported by the UK Council for Graduate Education (UKCGE) shows that 15 months after graduation, 8% of doctoral graduates were unemployed compared with 11% of those graduating with an undergraduate degree (UKCGE, 2020: 2). In the USA, data from 2020 shows the unemployment rate for all doctoral graduates over the age of 25 (2.5%) to be below that of masters (4.1%) and bachelor graduates (5.5%) (US Bureau of Labor Statistics, 2020). Meanwhile in Canada, the most recent census at the time of writing shows the unemployment rate of all PhD graduates at 5.1%, compared to 5.6% for all masters and 5.5% for all bachelor graduates (CCA, 2021: 95).

This doctoral premium appears to persist in other measures of job market performance, including salary and feelings of being valued by one's employer. Of those graduating in 2017–18, 87% of doctoral graduates in the UK were earning more than £30,000 per year 15 months after graduation, compared with 43% of taught masters graduates and 23% of those with an undergraduate degree (UKCGE, 2020: 2). Meanwhile, data from all doctoral graduates shows higher median salaries than for those with bachelor's and master's degrees in both the USA (US Bureau of Labor Statistics, 2020) and Canada (CCA, 2021: 104). More qualitatively, studies have shown that doctoral graduates feel valued by their employers for their specialist knowledge, research abilities, and transferable skills (Bryan and Guccione, 2018; Diamond et al., 2014), and are considered vital to the success and productivity of many of their employers (Diamond et al., 2014). They are also more likely than those with taught masters or undergraduate degrees to report that they are applying their learning to their current work (UKCGE, 2020: 4).

Nevertheless, this top-level employment data conceals significant variations regarding characteristics such as subject area, work experience, and age. For instance, evidence from several countries suggests higher unemployment rates amongst PhD graduates from humanities disciplines than other subject areas (Auriol, 2010; European Science Foundation, 2017; Mellors-Bourne et al., 2013). In the UK, humanities PhD graduates also report higher incidences of part-time employment and employment on fixed-term contracts shorter than 12 months (Mellors-Bourne et al., 2013). Discrepancies also exist between gender and age groups. For example, the CCA report that female PhD graduates in Canada are more likely to experience unemployment than their male colleagues, with the economic return-on-investment of a PhD in Canada appearing lower for graduates under the age of 40 compared with the general PhD-qualified population (2021: 94).

As well as these variations, studies also reveal growing concerns around the suitability of PhD programmes to adequately prepare graduates for professional life beyond the PhD. For example, despite the common portrayal of the PhD as an 'apprenticeship' for academia (Hancock et al., 2019: 4), PhD graduates still report a lack of understanding of how academia operates, including how academic careers are structured and what is expected of candidates (Radden and Sung, 2009). PhD programmes across Europe and North America have also been criticised for failing to adequately prepare graduates for academic teaching-focused careers (Kyvik and Olsen, 2012; Rogers, 2020). Simultaneously, commentators have questioned the extent to which PhD study prepares candidates for careers beyond academia, with both employers and PhD graduates citing factors including lack of commercial awareness, overspecialisation and adaptation to non-academic work environments as stumbling blocks for PhDs in non-academic recruitment processes (Boyd and McAlinden, 2016; Council for Industry and Higher Education, 2010; Rubio and Hooley, 2010).

As awareness has spread of the proportions of PhD graduates leaving academia, the employability of PhD graduates in sectors beyond academia has attracted particular attention. In the UK, for example, longitudinal data found that three-and-a-half years after graduation, 70% of PhD graduates had left academia (Hancock, 2020). Nevertheless, the extent to which their decisions to leave are undertaken out of necessity or agency appears unclear. Disparities between growing numbers of PhDs being awarded and relatively stagnant numbers of academic job postings have been cited as one key reason why so many PhD graduates must now look beyond the academy for longer-term employment (Parada and Peacock, 2015: 593). Moreover, whilst evidence from the UK shows that recent doctoral graduates are significantly more likely than master's and bachelor's graduates to be on fixed-term contracts 15 months after graduation (UKCGE, 2020: 3), OECD data suggests significant variation between countries, with nations including Belgium, the Czech Republic, Germany and Spain showing especially high proportions of PhD graduates on temporary contracts even five years post-graduation (Auriol, 2010: 13). Indeed, according to an international survey of PhD graduates undertaken by Wellcome, 45% of those who left academia cited job insecurities and difficulties in finding a job amongst their reasons for leaving (2020; 16). Despite evidence that some postgraduate researchers undertake a PhD without any desire to pursue an academic career (Hancock, 2019; Mangematin, 2000), such data suggests that uncertainties around establishing a secure academic career play a significant part in some PhD graduates' departures from academia.

As Hancock therefore contends, when it comes to exploring issues of post-PhD employability, an over-dependence upon employability statistics and survey data means that 'the lived experiences associated with particular employment outcomes are seldom addressed' (2021: 5). It is therefore to the lived experiences of PhD graduates themselves to which we now turn, to highlight some of the key challenges that this cohort face when entering the job market, and to envision how careers practitioners, institutions, and PhD graduates alike might address these challenges.

CAREER EXPECTATIONS VS REALITY

Despite the data shown above indicating that most PhD graduates eventually leave academia, studies also show that high proportions of doctoral and postdoctoral researchers nonetheless expect a career in academia to be their most likely destination (Cornell, 2020; Parada and Peacock, 2015). When placed next to data on the likelihood of securing a permanent academic position, these expectations appear unfounded. In the UK for example, the Royal Society reported that only 3.5% of scientific PhD graduates secure permanent jobs in academic research, with 0.45% becoming professors (2010: 14). In the United States, Caterine concludes from a range of sources that fewer than one in ten PhD graduates secure a 'tenure-track' (secure) academic position, with only 1.2% of arts and humanities PhDs appointed to such positions at leading universities (2020: 7).

This disparity suggests that PhD and postdoctoral researchers hold unrealistic expectations of the likelihood of securing a long-term academic position (Parada and Peacock, 2015). PhD researchers in the early and mid-stages of their doctorates may also be susceptible to a lack of awareness of academic workloads and career paths, envisioning academic jobs in an 'abstract' fashion (McAlpine and Turner, 2012: 544). In my own career guidance practice, I frequently hear doctoral researchers who favour an academic career state the 'freedom to research what I want' as a principal motivation towards academic work. This further suggests unrealistic expectations of the academic workload, and limited knowledge of the ways in which factors such as metrics and increasing expectations on research staff profoundly impact the time they have to undertake such research (Wellcome, 2020: 12).

This therefore suggests that significant numbers of PhD candidates find themselves working towards ill-defined academic career goals, unsure of both the steps to take towards these goals and what these goals look like once they are achieved. It is therefore unsurprising that 'disillusionment with academia' has been cited as another key driver in encouraging PhD graduates to leave academia for other sectors (Diamond et al., 2014: 49). As my own career guidance practice with postgraduate researchers has emphasised, however, the centrality of postgraduate researchers' relationships with their supervisors to their academic experience can also play a part in career expectations. Attitudes amongst some academic supervisors which prioritise the placement of PhD graduates into academic positions may lead them to evade engagement with alternative career options (CCA, 2021; Sauermann and Roach, 2012), resulting in PhD researchers feeling vilified if they express wishes to pursue a career in a different industry (Hayter and Parker, 2019; Jackson, 2007). Furthermore, PhD researchers' engagement with career guidance can also be impacted by the extent to which PhD supervisors support and enable participation in such activity (The British Academy, 2020: 19).

However, my own practice emphasises another important aspect of postgraduate researchers' career expectations that the literature reviewed so far neglects. This is linked to the ways in which limited (or even discouraged) exposure to wider career options can impact PhD candidates' abilities to envision themselves in future destinations other than academia. According to Hodkinson's influential theory of careership, someone's career choices are circumscribed by their 'horizons for action', that is, by the possibilities that are visible to them from their current position (2008: 6). The more their horizons for action are thus restricted to academic work activities, environments and role models, the less able doctoral researchers are to imagine what professional futures may be open to them beyond these horizons. Consequently, data demonstrating that high proportions of PhD candidates expect to pursue an academic career post-PhD may not simply demonstrate PhDs' unrealistic expectations of their employability prospects within academia; it may also belie their lack of knowledge of potential prospects in other sectors.

LEAVING ACADEMIA AND 'IDENTITY CRISES'

With so many PhD candidates apparently expecting to pursue longer-term academic careers, yet with so few ultimately securing such positions, another challenge faced by many PhD graduates comes in revisioning their professional identity post-PhD. The mid-2010s onwards have seen a surge in publications addressing the struggles faced by PhD graduates entering the labour market; often referred to as 'Quit Lit' and written by PhD graduates and former faculty members who have left academia, many of these texts describe a loss of identity when transitioning out of academia. For example, Melissa Dalgleish (2018) explains how academic culture can lead researchers to conflate their identities with the research that they undertake, leading to fears that 'if you don't continue to work as an academic, you'll be nothing', and risking a 'painful identity crisis when the professoriate becomes an unachievable dream' (p.21). This identity crisis is exacerbated, Lisa Munro suggests, for PhD candidates who move straight through from school to university to PhD, for whom 'school may feel like not just what you do in life, but who you are' (2018: 37). I have often seen these identity struggles at play in my own career guidance practice with PhD candidates. With limited exposure to careers beyond academia, and subsequent difficulties in envisioning themselves as anything other than academics, PhD graduates may struggle to reconfigure their professional identity post-PhD, especially if they went through that PhD expecting an academic job to come next.

Introducing PhD researchers to real-life role models and stories of PhD alumni living fulfilling professional lives in sectors beyond the academy would therefore appear a priority (British Academy, 2020; Council for Canadian Academies, 2021). What is equally crucial, I would argue, is raising PhD researchers' awareness that 'leaving academia' does *not* necessitate the complete abandonment of one's academic identity. In so many of the PhD graduates I have worked with over the years, I see bright and motivated people bringing elements of their 'academic' approach to a range of jobs beyond academia. The ancient history PhD graduate who now holds a lecturer-graded position in academic practice and skills. The former literature PhD who applies her knowledge of narrative theory to working with clients' career stories. As Katina Rogers describes, many doctoral graduates doing work beyond academic research and teaching 'tend to [...] incorporate scholarly methods into the way that work is done. They engage in work with the same intellectual curiosity that fuelled the desire to go to graduate school in the first place' (Rogers, 2020: 13). In other words, many PhD holders approach their apparently 'non-academic' jobs with an 'academic' mindset, thus problematising the boundaries often drawn between 'academic' and 'non-academic' work. Career guidance therefore has an important part to play in helping PhD researchers to navigate the struggles of post-PhD identity crisis. This comes, however, not just in increasing exposure to role models beyond academia; it also comes in helping doctoral researchers to identify what being 'academic' means to them, and in supporting them to explore roles in which they can continue to actualise these aspects of their identities beyond 'traditional' academia.

'OVERQUALIFIED' YET 'UNDEREXPERIENCED'

This state of feeling 'in-between' identities is not the only liminality experienced by PhD graduates seeking employment beyond academia. In my own guidance practice, I often hear postgraduate researchers worry that they occupy a strange hinterland between fresh graduate and experienced professional. As Chris Caterine warns in his semi-autobiographical companion guide *Leaving Academia*, one of the greatest challenges that PhD graduates face in non-academic job markets 'is the perception that you're overqualified for entry-level positions, but underqualified for more senior listings' (2020: 88). Indeed, many postgraduate researchers I work with in the UK struggle to determine what 'level' of role to apply for beyond academia, fearing that employers may discount them as overqualified in terms of theoretical knowledge, but lacking practical skills and experience applicable to the workplace (Boulos, 2016).

There is indeed evidence to suggest that these worries are widespread. Studying over 1,800 doctoral graduates in the UK, Diamond et al. (2014) found that some respondents experienced their PhD as a stumbling block in non-academic recruitment processes. This appeared especially pertinent for those applying for lower, entry-level roles, be this to switch sectors, to return to work after taking time out, or to find work in a particular location. Afraid that their PhDs would brandish them as overqualified, some of these graduates disclosed that they had removed their PhD from their CV (Diamond et al., 2014: 54). Furthermore, many postgraduate researchers do not consider themselves 'graduates' in the same way as their bachelor-qualified counterparts, yet are simultaneously unsure where they stand in applying for positions above graduate level. It is therefore no surprise that many PhD graduates looking to leave academia experience great uncertainty about their next moves.

My own practice suggests that this simultaneously over- and under-qualified *Catch 22* presents for several reasons, each of which hints at what can be done to remedy this challenge for PhD graduates job hunting beyond academia. First is the need to consider what 'overqualification' means in this context, especially from employers' points-of-view. My own conversations with recruiters suggest that many such reservations are around PhD graduates' motivations and commitment. As Bielczyk describes, employers may assume that when someone has achieved the highest degree possible, they are more likely to have other options on the table (2020: 95). Personally, I have also heard some employers voice fears that their vacancies would not hold the attention of someone with a doctoral qualification. Overall however, employers' hesitancy around 'overqualification' often comes down to what Bielczyk describes as a question of loyalty: that if a PhD graduate accepts a job with them, employers may fear that they will leave as soon as a 'better offer' comes along (ibid.). To avoid being viewed as a potential flight risk therefore, it is paramount that PhD graduates clearly articulate within applications and interviews that the opportunity in question is a conscious career choice for them, and formulate a convincing narrative as to why they want to make this move. Demonstrating their commitment to the new sector or career area, be that through relevant commercial awareness, research into the hiring organisation, relevant experience, or anything else that shows an investment into the intended new field, is also imperative.

A further reason why PhD candidates and graduates often experience confusion over how and where they fit into non-academic labour markets comes in the fact that many potentially relevant employers do not specify a PhD as a necessary criterion when hiring. In Australia, a machine learning analysis of over 29,000 job postings by Mewburn et al. concluded that 80% of job postings seeking candidates with high-level research skills did not specify a PhD degree as a requirement to apply (2018: 807). Research from the UK further demonstrates that only a small minority of employers actively target doctoral graduates and have recruitment strategies to do so (Rubio and Hooley, 2010). Even when employers tend to recruit candidates with PhDs, and see demonstrable benefits in doing so, they may not specify a PhD in their hiring criteria to prevent restricting their hiring pool (Diamond et al., 2014: 75). In such situations, PhD graduates are simply picked up by organisations in their general recruitment processes, with many employers hiring people with PhDs without the specific intention to do so (Council for Industry and Higher Education, 2010; Diamond et al., 2014; Elias et al., 2005).

Beyond industries such as pharmaceuticals, life sciences and other R&D functions which hire for specific technical skills and subject knowledge, employers are therefore more likely to recruit based on candidates' broader skills rather than on specific levels of academic qualification. This means that many jobs for which PhD graduates may be suited, and which might value their skills, remain somewhat 'hidden' from potential candidates who are unable to use search terms based on their qualification level to identify them. For example, in my own career guidance practice, I see many postgraduate researchers use search terms such as 'PhD [history/psychology/ X subject] jobs' to guide their initial job hunt beyond academia. These searches result in frustration and an apparent lack of options, due to the mismatch between the search terms being used by candidates to identify jobs (academic credentials and subject area), and the terms being used by employers to identify suitable candidates (broader skills and abilities). The result is often further confusion as to what type of job PhD graduates are 'qualified for'. If a job does not explicitly ask for a PhD, many worry that they will be perceived as overqualified.

Effective career guidance for PhD candidates and graduates, therefore, should support them to devise more productive search terms to uncover relevant and appropriate options. This might, for example, involve supporting PhDs to identify which of their skills they most want to use on a regular basis in their work, and focusing on options that involve the day-to-day application of these skills. It might also involve helping them to tap into their values and the kind of difference they want their work to make, thus focusing the search on companies and organisations whose mission aligns with these priorities. This allows them to move away from the restrictive search terms based on credentials ('what jobs can I do with a psychology PhD?') and towards terms that are based on employers' hiring needs ('what types of jobs will use my quantitative and data analysis skills on a regular basis?'). Using current contacts or networking platforms such as LinkedIn to identify the types of roles and organisations that PhD graduates from similar backgrounds have moved into can also be reassuring. This creates 'real-life' examples of roles that might use one's doctoral-level skills, or organisations who value what someone with a PhD can bring to their workplace. Even for STEM PhD graduates who are able to use their training to move into relevant technical positions in industry, Lee et al. found that 7–10 years after graduation, 60% had moved into non-technical positions such as management, business services or consultancy (2010: 875). This therefore suggests that careers support can help such PhD graduates to leverage their existing technical skills to transition into an industry role for which they are deemed 'qualified', but can also empower them with strategies to use this first role to explore wider options, and to assess where they want to position themselves longer-term.

ARTICULATING DOCTORAL-LEVEL SKILLS BEYOND ACADEMIA

With considerable proportions of PhD graduates now leaving academia, another key aspect in tackling their dismissal as being theoretically 'overqualified' but practically 'underqualified' is the effective articulation of their skills. Indeed, evidence shows that 'translating' academic experience into terms that resonate with employers beyond academia is a widespread employability struggle for PhD graduates, with employers specifying the articulation or marketing of skills as a particular weakness amongst candidates with research degrees (Council for Industry and Higher Education, 2010; Souter, 2005). PhD graduates may also struggle to even recognise their transferable skills (Jackson, 2007) and to quantify these skills in a way that is of interest to employers (Boyd and McAlinden, 2016: 18). It is therefore no surprise that these challenges have become a common focus of the proliferation of PhD career guidance literature that has emerged over the past five years. Drawing on his own experiences of transitioning into work beyond academia, Caterine encourages PhD graduates to move away from presenting themselves as subject matter experts by focusing on *how* they carry out their research, rather than on the esoteric details of *what* they research (2020: 126). Meanwhile, Berdahl and Malloy encourage doctoral graduates to approach the job hunt from the employer's perspective, communicating themselves as the 'solution' to an employer's problems or hiring needs (2018: 157).

This advice suggests that PhD graduates' difficulties in communicating their skills effectively come down to the fact that academia operates according to a different value system than many other industries. Where academia prioritises research 'quality' as assessed through publications, for example, these criteria are far less definitive in private sector recruitment processes (Mangematin, 2000: 749). Supporting PhD researchers to recognise the differences between these value systems, and creating opportunities for them to hear from a range of employers on what they value most when recruiting, are therefore important to factor into employability support for PhD researchers and graduates. Once they understand the skills and abilities that are of greatest value to employers in their sector(s) of interest, PhD graduates often still need support in recognising their own skills and putting these skills into words. I speak to many postgraduate researchers who find it difficult to think of themselves as 'having skills', and who struggle to tease out transferable skills from the minutiae of their academic work. Consequently, exercises which 'zoom out' from the PhD and allow candidates to view it from others' perspectives can help researchers to identify, quantify and articulate the skills they have demonstrated during their PhD work. Linder et al. suggest a particularly useful activity in which doctoral researchers are encouraged to turn their PhD into a job description, as if it were to be advertised as a vacancy (2020: 58). In my own work with PhD candidates, asking them to draw up sets of instructions as if they were handing over their PhD duties to someone else has similarly helped some to understand *how* they do what they do, and the abilities they demonstrate in the process.

On the other side of this challenge is the lack of understanding displayed by many potential employers regarding what a PhD entails, and the subsequent skills and value that PhD graduates can bring to their organisations (Kyvik and Olsen, 2012: 214). Evidence shows that employers without direct experience of hiring candidates with doctoral degrees are more likely to hold negative stereotypes towards PhD graduates' potential overspecialisation, narrow skillset, and lack of interpersonal skills (Morgavi et al., 2007; Rubio and Hooley, 2010). On the other hand, companies who have previously hired PhD graduates appear more likely to view such candidates positively, producing a 'cumulative effect' in which firms with a track record of employing candidates with PhDs are more likely to hire further PhD-qualified employees (Garcia-Quevedo et al., 2012: 618). This evidence suggests a self-perpetuating two-tier job market, in which the recruitment of PhD graduates remains restricted to pockets of employers with existing experience of hiring such candidates. Outside of these pockets meanwhile, a lack of awareness of doctoral programmes and skills maintains the scepticism and reservations that some employers hold towards PhD graduates.

Consequently, increased contact and mobility between researchers and industries beyond academia have been highlighted as vital in challenging such reservations, and in introducing a wider range of potential employers to the benefits that doctoral graduates can bring to their businesses (CCA, 2021; Garcia-Quevedo et al., 2012). This is especially crucial in the arts, humanities and social sciences where 'industrial' applications of PhD research and skills may appear less obvious than in STEM disciplines. Initiatives set up to tackle this include 'co-op' programmes, such as the Arts Co-op Program at the University of British Columbia, in which PhD researchers from English and History undertake paid work placements in a variety of settings beyond academia (CCA, 2021: 162). In the United States, Fellows Programs support knowledge exchange between PhD researchers and a variety of sectors, such as the Mellon/ACLS Public Fellows Program which promotes the value of a humanities PhD through creating placements for doctoral researchers within the public and non-profit sectors (ibid.: 170). Other initiatives have a more direct remit to increase national economic growth and innovation by connecting researchers (including doctoral students) to research partners in industry, such as Mitacs in Canada.

CONCLUSION

The initiatives highlighted above awaken long-standing debates as to whether PhD programmes should focus on academic training, or whether they should also equip candidates with employability skills needed to succeed beyond academia. I want to conclude this chapter, however, by challenging this dichotomous portrayal of the PhD as *either* training for academia *or* training for industry. As Kyvik and Olsen (2012) deduce from their study of the relevance of doctoral training to labour markets in Norway, it is perhaps not so much that PhD programmes need to respond to the diverse needs of potential PhD employers; rather, it is that PhD training must reflect the fact that academic practice itself is changing, placing increasing emphasis on work practices including collaboration, project management, and impact (p. 222). Increasingly therefore, the skills required to succeed within academic research environments develop significant crossover with those coveted by non-academic employers.

Throughout this chapter, we have seen how PhD graduates' lived experiences of job-hunting are impacted by their limited understanding of contemporary academic working practices, and their reservations around whether they have the skills needed for jobs beyond academia. On top of these issues, we have also seen how some employers' perceptions of PhD graduates can exacerbate these frustrations. We must recognise, therefore, that some employers' reservations about PhD graduates, including their difficulty fitting into a team environment (Souter, 2005: 14) and their inability to look beyond their own research towards the bigger picture of wider business needs (Council for Industry and Higher Education, 2010: 13), are based around concerns that PhD graduates lack some of the very skills highlighted by Kyvik and Olsen as becoming increasingly vital to academic practice itself. This recognition that developing PhD researchers for modern academic environments has much in common with training them to succeed beyond academia is therefore vital for PhD employability. Training PhD researchers to confidently discuss concepts such as their main stakeholders, how they spot gaps and opportunities, and how their work can be applied and communicated in non-academic contexts prepares them to compete in modern academia. Simultaneously, it helps to address the employer perceptions noted above, whilst also alleviating the difficulties in articulating academic experience in ways that resonate in other sectors.

It goes without saying, however, that some of the policies that have heralded these changes to academic work practices are viewed by many as controversial. For example, in their international study of over 4,000 academic researchers, Wellcome found significant proportions of researchers reporting that increased metrics and administrative demands stifle their creativity and prioritise metrics over research quality (2020: 8, 12). On the other hand, the same study revealed that whilst a significant majority of researchers in managerial roles said that they enjoy managing people (79%), only 48% reported receiving training in doing so (ibid.: 22). This suggests that whilst researchers view some aspects of the 'business-ification' of academia as detrimental to their work, some enjoyable aspects of their roles could be enhanced were academic culture to embrace more explicit professional development in traditionally 'non-academic' professional skills such as people management. This example therefore suggests that activities which support postgraduate researchers to succeed beyond academia can also equip them with skills essential to academic career progression (Rogers, 2020: 15). Furthermore, the development of academic hiring practices that prioritise such transferable and interpersonal skills could also help to address the toxicity reported by many employed within academic research, where workplace bullying is reported to be common and most often perpetrated by supervisors or managers (Wellcome, 2020: 27).

To suggest that a widespread academic culture change is required to address the PhD employability challenges discussed throughout this chapter is indeed aspirational. Nevertheless, for as long as employability and skills training remain largely extra-curricular exercises for PhD researchers in countries such as the UK, USA and Canada, so will they continue to exclude those whose professional, familial or other commitments mean they are unable to invest in such training (Rogers, 2020: 74). In the UK specifically, PhD programmes often do not have a 'curriculum' as such. Subsequently, embedding career guidance and employability skills within such programmes proves more elusive than for taught degrees. This poses further questions over equity and accessibility: for example, with 45% of black doctoral researchers in the UK being enrolled part-time, this makes black PhD researchers more likely to be self-funded (The British Academy, 2020: 22), and thus less able to prioritise extra-curricular training over paid work and other responsibilities. Subsequently, institutions, funders, governments, and individuals alike must work together to cultivate academic cultures in which investment in continued professional development is prioritised (Hodge, 2010: 37). Building such professional development into the structure of the PhD itself addresses the aforementioned equity issues, and offers spaces within the PhD to formally acknowledge the intersections between academic and other professional practices.

REFERENCES

Auriol, L. (2010). Careers of Doctorate Holders: Employment and Mobility Patterns [online]. *OECD Science, Technology and Industry Working Papers* 2010/04. Paris: OECD Publishing. [Viewed 19 May 2021]. Available from: DOI: 10.1787/5kmh8phxvvf5-en.

Berdahl, L. and Malloy, J. (2018). *Work your career: get what you want from your social sciences or humanities PhD.* North York: University of Toronto Press.

Bielczyk, N. (2020). *What is out there for me? The landscape of post-PhD career tracks.* 2nd edn. Nijmegen, Netherlands: Welcome Solutions.

Boulos, A. (2016). The labour market relevance of PhDs: an issue for academic research and policymakers. *Studies in Higher Education* [online]. 41(5), pp. 901–913. [Viewed 24 May 2021]. Available from: DOI: 10.1080/03075079.2016.1147719

Boyd, R. and McAlinden, S. (2016). *PhD study to employment: experiences of transition* [online]. [Viewed 5 May 2021]. Available from: https://luminate.prospects.ac.uk/phd-study-to-employment-experiences-of-transition

The British Academy (2020). *Good practice in providing careers guidance for postgraduate research students* [online]. London: The British Academy. [Viewed 12 May 2021]. Available from: www.thebritishacademy.ac.uk/publications/career-pathways-postgraduate-research-students-good-practice/

Bryan, B. and Guccione, K. (2018). Was it worth it? A qualitative exploration into graduate perceptions of doctoral value. *Higher Education Research & Development* [online]. 37(6), pp. 1124–1140. [Viewed 26 May 2021]. Available from: DOI: 10.1080/07294360.2018.1479378

Caterine, C. (2020). *Leaving academia: a practical guide.* Princeton: Princeton University Press.

Cornell, B. (2020). *PhD students and their careers* [online]. HEPI Policy Note 25. London: Higher Education Policy Institute. [Viewed 28 April 2021]. Available from: www.hepi.ac.uk/wp-content/uploads/2020/07/HEPI-Policy-Note-25_PhD-students-careers_FINAL.pdf

Council of Canadian Academies (2021). *Degrees of success* [online]. Ottawa (ON): The Expert Panel on the Labour Market Transition of PhD Graduates, CCA. [Viewed 3 May 2021]. Available from: https://cca-reports.ca/reports/the-labour-market-transition-of-phd-graduates/

Council for Industry and Higher Education (2010). *Talent fishing: what businesses want from postgraduates* [online]. London: CIHE. [Viewed 28 April 2021]. Available from: www.ncub.co.uk/reports/talent-fishing-what-businesses-want-from-postgraduates.html

Dalgleish, M. (2018). The things I wish I'd known during my PhD. In J. Fruscione and K. J. Baker (eds) *Succeeding outside the academy: career paths beyond the humanities, social sciences and STEM,* 1st edn. Lawrence: Kansas University Press, pp. 11–22

Department for Business, Energy and Industrial Strategy (2020). *UK research and development roadmap.* [online]. [Viewed 28 April 2021]. Available from: www.gov.uk/government/publications/uk-research-and-development-roadmap

Di Paolo, A. and Mañé, F. (2016). Misusing our talent? Overeducation, overskilling and skill underutilisation among Spanish PhD graduates. *The Economic and Labour Relations Review* [online]. 27(4), pp. 432–452. [Viewed 18 May 2021]. Available from: DOI: 10.1177/1035304616657479

Diamond, A., Ball, C., Vorley, T., Hughes, T., Moreton, R., Howe, P. and Nathwani, T. (2014). *The impact of doctoral careers* [online]. Leicester: CFE Research. [Viewed 12 May 2021]. Available from: www.ncub.co.uk/wp-content/uploads/2015/01/Impact-1.pdf

Elias, P., Purcell, K., Durbin, S., Davies, R. and Warren, S. (2005). *The employment of social science PhDs in academic and non-academic jobs: research skills and postgraduate training* [online]. Swindon: Economic and Social Research Council. [Viewed 14 May 2021]. Available from: https://warwick.ac.uk/fac/soc/ier/publications/2005/final_draft_socsci_phds _06_june_2005.pdf

European Science Foundation (2017). *2017 Career tracking survey of doctorate holders* [online]. Strasbourg: European Science Foundation. [Viewed 14 May 2021]. Available from: www.esf.org/fileadmin/user_upload/esf/F-FINAL-Career_Tracking_Survey_2017_Project_ Report.pdf

Garcia-Quevedo, J., Mas-Verdú, F. and Polo-Otero, J. (2012). Which firms want PhDs? An analysis of the determinants of the demand. *Higher Education* [online]. 63(5), pp. 607–620. [Viewed 26 May 2021]. Available from: DOI: 10.1007/s10734-011-9461-8

Guthrie, S., Lichten, C. A., van Belle, J., Ball, S., Knack, A. and Hofman, J. (2017). *Understanding mental health in the research environment: a rapid evidence assessment* [online]. Santa Monica, CA: RAND Corporation. [Viewed 18 May 2021]. Available from DOI: 10.7249/RR2022

Hancock, S. (2019). A future in the knowledge economy? Analysing the career strategies of doctoral scientists through the principles of game theory. *Higher Education* [online]. 78(1), pp. 33–49. [Viewed 26 May 2021]. Available from: DOI: 10.1007/s10734-018-0329-z

Hancock, S. (2020). The employment of PhD graduates in the UK: what do we know? 17 February. *Higher Education Policy Institute blog* [online]. [Viewed 18 April 2021]. Available from: www.hepi.ac.uk/2020/02/17/the-employment-of-phd-graduates-in-the-uk-what-do-we-know/

Hancock, S. (2021). What is known about doctoral employment? Reflections from a UK study and directions for future research. *Journal of Higher Education Policy and Management* [online]. 43(5), pp. 520–536. [Viewed 28 May 2021]. Available from: DOI: 10.1080/1360080X.2020.1870027

Hancock, S., Wakeling, P. and Chubb, J. (2019). *21st century PhDs: why we need better methods of tracking doctoral access, experiences and outcomes* [online]. RoRI Working Paper No.2. London: Research on Research Institute. [Viewed 8 May 2021]. Available from: DOI: 10.6084/m9.figshare.9917813

Hayter, C. and Parker, M. (2019). Factors that influence the transition of university post-docs to non-academic scientific careers: an exploratory study. *Research Policy* [online]. 48(3), pp. 556–570. [Viewed 24 May 2021]. Available from: DOI: 10.1016/j.respol.2018.09.009

Hodge, A. (2010). *Review of progress in implementing the recommendations of Sir Gareth Roberts regarding employability and career development of PhD students and research staff: a report for Research Councils UK by an independent review panel October 2010.* [online]. Research Councils UK. [Viewed 28 May 2021]. Available from: https://research.aston.ac.uk/en/publications/review-of-progress-in-implementing-the-recommendations-of-sir-gar

Hodkinson, P. (2008). Understanding career decision making and progression: careership revisited. *The Journal of the National Institute for Career Education and Counselling* [online]. 21, pp. 4–17. [Viewed 18 May 2021]. Available from: https://secure.toolkit-files. co.uk/ clients/29820/sitedata/Journal_Archive_Secure/nicec-journal-issue-21-winter-2009.pdf

Jackson, C. (2007). *Recruiting PhDs: what works?* [online]. Cambridge: The Careers Research and Advisory Centre and UK GRAD Programme. [Viewed 3 June 2021]. Available from: https://sociologie.cuso.ch/fileadmin/sociologie/Jackson-2007-.pdf

Kyvik, S. and Olsen, T. B. (2012). The relevance of doctoral training in different labour markets. *Journal of Education and Work* [online]. 25(2), pp. 205–224. [Viewed 24 May 2021]. Available from: DOI: 10.1080/13639080.2010.538376

League of European Research Universities (2007). *LERU statement on doctoral training and The Bologna Process* [online]. Leuven: LERU Office. [Viewed 14 May 2021]. Available from: http://ehea.info/media.ehea.info/file/20070305-06_Berlin/54/3/LERU_Statement _doctoral_training_February2007_585543.pdf

Lee, H. F., Miozzo, M. and Laredo, P. (2010). Career patterns and competences of PhDs in science and engineering in the knowledge economy: the case of graduates from a UK research-based university. *Research Policy* [online]. 39(7), pp. 869–881. [Viewed 21 May 2021]. Available from: DOI: 10.1016/j.respol.2010.05.001

Leitch, S. (2006). *Leitch review of skills: prosperity for all in the global economy – world-class skills* [online]. London: HM Treasury. [Viewed 28 May 2021]. Available from: www.gov.uk/government/publications/prosperity-for-all-in-the-global-economy-world-class-skills-final-report

Linder, K. E., Kelly, K. and Tobin, J. (2020). *Going Alt-Ac: a guide to alternative academic careers.* Sterling, Virginia: Stylus.

Mangematin, V. (2000). PhD job market: professional trajectories and incentives during the PhD. *Research Policy* [online]. 29, pp. 741–756. [Viewed 18 May 2021]. Available from: DOI: 10.1016/S0048-7333(99)00047-5

McAlpine, L. and Turner, G. (2012). Imagined and emerging career patterns: perceptions of doctoral students and research staff. *Journal of Further and Higher Education* [online]. 36(4), pp. 535–548. [Viewed 25 May 2021]. Available from: DOI: 10.1080/0309877X.2011.643777

Mellors-Bourne, R., Metcalfe, J. and Pollard, P. (2013). *What do researchers do? Early career progression of doctoral graduates.* Cambridge: Vitae.

Mewburn, I., Grant, W. J., Suominen, H. and Kizimchuk, S. (2018). A machine learning analysis of the non-academic employment opportunities for Ph.D. graduates in

Australia. *Higher Education Policy* [online]. 33, pp. 799–813. [Viewed 1 June 2021] Available from: DOI: 10.1057/s41307-018-0098-4

Morgavi, A. C., McCarthy, M. and Metcalfe, J. (2007). *Employers' views of researchers' skills* [online]. London: The Rugby Team and UK GRAD Programme. [Viewed 4 June 2021]. Available from: www.dur.ac.uk/resources/cel/views-of-researchers-skills-Sept2007.pdf

Munro, L. (2018). Finding footholds, finding your way. In J. Fruscione and K. J. Baker (eds), *Succeeding outside the academy: career paths beyond the humanities, social sciences and STEM,* 1st edn. Lawrence: Kansas University Press, pp. 34–43

Parada, F. and Peacock, J. (2015). The quality of doctoral training and employability of doctorate holders: the views of doctoral candidates and junior researchers. In A. Curaj, L. Matei, R. Pricopie, J. Salmi and P. Scott eds, *The European higher education area: between critical reflections and future policies*. Berlin: Springer, pp. 593–612

Radden, A. and Sung, J. (2009). *The career choices and impact of PhD graduates in the UK: a synthesis review* [online]. University of Leicester, Economic and Social Research Council and Research Councils UK. [Viewed 18 May 2021]. Available from: https://esrc.ukri.org/files/public-engagement/public-dialogues/full-report-phd-graduates-career-choices/

Rogers, K. (2020). *Putting the humanities PhD to work: thriving in and beyond the classroom*. Durham (NC) and London: Duke University Press.

The Royal Society (2010). *The scientific century: securing our future prosperity* [online]. RS Policy document 02/10. London: The Royal Society. [Viewed 15 June 2021]. Available from: https://royalsociety.org/topics-policy/publications/2010/scientific-century/

Rubio, M. and Hooley, T. (2010). *Recruiting researchers: survey of employer practice 2009* [online]. Cambridge: The Careers Research and Advisory Centre. [Viewed 28 April 2021]. Available from: http://hdl.handle.net/10545/583862

Sauermann, H. and Roach, M. (2012). Science PhD career preferences: levels, changes, and advisor encouragement. *PLoS One* [online]. 7(5):e36307. [Viewed 15 May 2021]. Available from: DOI: 10.1371/journal.pone.0036307

Souter, C. (2005). *EMPRESS: Employers' perceptions of recruiting research staff and students* [online]. Leeds: University of Leeds Careers Centre. [Viewed 28 May 2021]. Available from: http://careerweb.leeds.ac.uk/download/downloads/id/268/researchers_guide_to_employability_skills

UK Council for Graduate Education (2020). *Graduate outcomes for postgraduates 2017/18 – policy briefing* [online]. Lichfield: UK Council for Graduate Education. [Viewed 28 April 2021]. Available from: www.ukcge.ac.uk/article/graduate-outcomes-17_18-policy-briefing-464.aspx

US Bureau of Labor Statistics (2020). *Employment projections* [online]. [Viewed 2 May 2021]. Available from: www.bls.gov/emp/tables/unemployment-earnings-education.htm

Wellcome (2020). *What researchers think of the culture they work in* [online]. London: Wellcome. [Viewed 28 April 2021]. Available from: https://wellcome.org/sites/default/files/what-researchers-think-about-the-culture-they-work-in.pdf

4

Quality Assurance in University Careers Guidance – a Student Voice Case Study from The Open University

Lydia Lauder and Victoria Crowe

INTRODUCTION

The Cogency of Student Voice and Comprehensive Approaches in Evaluating Employability

There is no greater agency than the student and alumni voice when measuring employability. Under the cataclysmic change inflicted by the Covid-19 pandemic, the resourcing of higher education faces distinctive challenges. In the transition to a new world, service provision will mean a heightened focus on activities that improve student outcomes and thus a return for investment (AGCAS, 2020). Equally, students are making more discerning choices and seeking to ensure the best returns on their investment. National data collections and external regulators have increasingly sought to use students' experiences and assurance judgements as lead indicators of excellence in service provision. Student and alumni voices are thus a critical layer within the new regulatory ecosystem.

Evidencing the impact of employability service provision holds significant benefits for the careers professional and indeed the ongoing professionalisation of the careers sector itself. Determining and calibrating the impact of careers provision on student employability also poses obdurate challenges.

The definition of what careers information, advice and guidance is, and the varying perceptions or indeterminateness adopted by various stakeholders (policy-makers, regulators, institutional governance structures, students, careers professionals) constitutes a fundamental difficulty. Indeed, given that guidance is often more an art than a science, this raises questions about the extent to which it is possible to illustrate success. Many models of impact assessment are implicitly medical and are thus problematic for the social nature of careers work. Thus, the challenges of defining career outcomes, methodological considerations, cause and effect linkages and other complexities are constrictions to evaluation.

More recent work however sheds new light on developing evidence-based practice within careers. Hughes and Percy (2020) outline a blended approach between qualitative, quantitative and theory-led techniques for evaluation. Robertson's quadruple model (2020) calls for: practitioner expertise and judgement, evidence from the local context, a critical evaluation of research and the perspectives of the user.

For 30 years The Open University's Careers and Employability Services has allowed the unique exploration and exegesis of various impact assessment models within a remote learning context. Building on this expertise we have developed an impact assessment framework incorporating the newer models mentioned above. Our approach places the student and alumni voice at its centre, within timely, robust, and low burden evaluation methodologies. This chapter therefore aims to:

- Demonstrate the principles and application of holistic models to evidence-based practice.
- Provide vignettes of these evaluation approaches from our extensive online service provision.
- Illustrate the efficacies of the digital infrastructure via the range of tools developed to support evaluation.

We therefore seek to deepen the understanding on ways that the student and alumni voice can be effectively heard despite the challenges of careers work and with greater cogency as higher education service provision transits to a post Covid-19, more digitised world.

INTRODUCING THE OPEN UNIVERSITY AND ITS CAREERS SERVICE

The Open University (OU) is the largest university in Europe, with 175,178 students (October 2021). Since launching in 1969, more than 2.2 million people worldwide have studied at a distance through Supported Open Learning. It has no academic prerequisites for admission to its undergraduate provision (with the exception of a small number of modules), and students enrol with a wide range of study goals and previous educational experience. There are entry requirements for taught postgraduate level and research degrees. The OU comprises students of all ages, normally 16 years or over with no upper age boundaries, who study by remote learning. OU students account for 41% of the part-time, undergraduate UK higher education population. Student numbers are currently expanding, and most modules and qualifications are available throughout Europe and some worldwide, with over 7,700 international students directly studying with the OU (October 2021).

The OU mission is 'to be open to people, places, methods and ideas'. This is reflected in the institutional definition of employability, which is deliberately broad in its scope, recognising personal development goals alongside those that are more career focused: 'A set of capabilities and achievements that support students in developing their careers, raising their aspirations and enhancing their contribution to society'. As part of this, the University integrates the requirements from all UK nation governments linked to funding agreements into its strategic approach to student employability.

Careers and Employability Services (CES) is part of Academic Services and is organised under Student Support, working to deliver the pan-University Student Employability Strategy. Its staff deliver services across two teams: first, qualification teams in faculties, responsible for the development of the curriculum, supported by careers and employability consultants for Learning and Teaching. Second, Student Support Teams, responsible for supporting students to successfully navigate their studies, supported by student-facing careers and employability consultants. In addition, the CES Employer Engagement Team prospects relationships with employers across the UK to provide a variety of opportunities for students to access during and after study.

Given the university's sizeable and diverse student population, CES provides support to a variety of cohorts many of whom fall within the characteristic of widening participation. These include students in secure environments, those with disabilities (including a specific team to support disabled veterans), mature students, students based internationally, students with low prior educational qualifications. Services are offered to all registered students as well as alumni, for up to three years after they stop studying with the university. A blend of individual guidance by phone, email and video is complimented by a programme of 'one to many' events and resources. These are designed to support students and alumni at scale given the vast size of the potential CES population (317,540 at July 2021). These include a comprehensive website, webinars, forums, podcasts, employer events, plus tools to write and review CVs, develop interview skills and consider career options. Provision is particularly tailored to support the needs of part-time OU students (75% approximately) who are balancing work and study and are looking for information, advice and guidance on career development and / or change rather than help with starting their careers.

The scale and breadth of CES activities within an institution of such magnitude demands service-level and individual levels of accountability, implemented through effective performance and quality management systems. The CES quality infrastructure offers a case study for the integrative evaluation of practice in evidencing employability as the ultimate arbiter of student success and the raison d'etre for the service.

THE CHALLENGES OF EVALUATING CAREERS WORK

Evaluation of career guidance work requires expansion beyond narrow economic considerations through breadth and depth of focus and outcome evidence. The case for evaluation (that is, the process by which we form judgements about the value of guidance, Killeen, 1996b) in careers work has been well made over 50 years of related research. McMahon (2019) traces the long history of career assessment from over a century ago and the work of Frank Parsons in 1909 (who is widely regarded as the founder of vocational career guidance and counselling) to the present day.

The wealth of studies that have attempted to penetrate the domain of career guidance evaluation has exposed a number of challenges. Some of these relate to the tangling up of evaluation with the macro-politics and resource allocation infrastructures that govern the sector. There are issues of definitional clarity in terms of what guidance is, its intended outcomes and the methods used for measuring these. Simon (2014) for example notes that there is no universal understanding of what quality assurance in guidance involves and McMahon (2019) outlines difficulties in conceptualising qualitative career assessment. Killeen (1996b) explains how evaluation is 'extraordinarily diverse' with respect to the various stakeholders and distinctions between the seven types of process evaluation and six forms of outcome-based evaluation activity in career guidance.

Of the more irrefragable issues are those associated with methodological techniques. Research evaluation is most commonly centred on short-term studies often due to budgetary constraints and thus fails to determine the true and longitudinal impacts of career guidance for individuals, organisations and society. This in turn procures difficulties of incorporating control groups or counterfactuals and placebos. The evidence is often thus biased towards the 'hard' outcomes from immediate individual learning at the cost of ascertaining the longer-term 'softer measures' of attitudinal shifts and behavioural changes and wider social and economic impacts from career guidance. Where evidence for the positive outcomes of career guidance interventions does exist, definitive conclusions regarding casual mechanisms are difficult to draw due to the 'very nature of the guidance process and its inter-relatedness with a multiplicity of factors' (Maguire, 2004).

The philosophical paradigms of evaluative studies present additional dilemmas. Robertson (2020) requisitions that the ontological and epistemological assumptions within studies are made explicit whilst recognising that much of career development research so far has adopted traditional, positivist perspectives mechanised through quantitative methodologies. For example, there are meta-analytical studies which apply a statistical procedure to combine results from multiple studies into an average effect size so that the effect of an intervention can be detected more confidently (Robertson, 2020). Meta-analyses have proved useful in growing the evidence for the effectiveness of career interventions internationally (Whiston et al., 2019) but cultural and contextual transferability is constrained. Qualitative research has much to offer in demonstrating linkages between the guidance process and its outcomes; it is however undervalued, under-researched and underrepresented in published literature (McMahon, 2019; Robertson, 2020). McMahon (2019) elucidates the merits of qualitative careers assessments as strongly aligned to social and constructivist theory, emphasising individual agency, meaning making and context. To answer its critics on the grounds of inadequate scientific rigour, McMahon (2019) appeals to the adoption of idiographic and interpretative, phenomenological criteria for its interpretation. A higher profile of qualitative assessments is called for in the current zeitgeist with the rapidly changing world of work and complex needs of diverse client groups. This does not mean, however, that one paradigmatic position should be espoused to the exclusion of the other. In recognising the complementarity of quantitative and qualitative methodologies, the needs of the client should be the primary driving force in the selection of assessment techniques (McMahon, 2019) and 'the approach to data analysis should correspond to the philosophical foundation of the guidance interventions' (Whiston et al., 2019). It is to such comprehensive assessment models that we will now turn our attention for career guidance evaluation.

ADVANCING EVALUATION PRACTICE: HOLISTIC MODELS FOR CAREER GUIDANCE EVALUATION

Theory of Change Principles

A recent framework offered by Hughes and Percy (2020) recognises the individual, economic (primary, secondary and macro-economic benefits) and non-economic impacts from career guidance. In the assessment of these impacts a blended model combining qualitative, quantitative and theory-led approaches is suggested. Techniques include a comprehensive approach of process evaluation, ascertaining direct beneficiary and stakeholder benefits as well as wider community building influences. Rudimentary principles governing impact assessment are outlined which originate from 'theory of change' enquiries. As Hooley (2018) notes, 'the theory of change describes the steps that need to take place between what you do and the impact that you hope to achieve. It helps you to think about what you are doing and why. It also helps you to establish a framework for evaluation and quality assurance'. The construction of a theory of change process is propounded in designing outcomes and assessing levels of impact within a robust evaluation cycle. For career guidance a theory of change approach goes a good way towards determining cause and effect linkages and hence distinguishing what a 'good' career outcome is. As Roberston (2020) elucidates, 'a career intervention is an attempt to bring about change (for the better) and requires a theory of change or a change of actions through which an intervention leads to impact'.

The Pivotal Role of Practitioners

In the formidable challenge of determining efficacious outcome measures there is strong evidence from the literature to suggest that the role of the practitioner is pivotal. For the purposes of our examination, we will adapt the definition offered by the Career Development Institute (2021) Blueprint of Learning Outcomes for professional roles in the Career Development Sector. That is, a career development practitioner is a qualified individual engaged in the provision of career development services, who regards careers education, information, advice and guidance as their main professional activity, underpinned by the tenets of professionalism. Different terms or titles may be used to describe the same functions by various employers or institutions (for example, 'careers adviser', 'careers consultant' and 'careers counsellor'). Evangelista (2003) proposes a tri-variable model of the quality assurance of guidance services where 'the production of quality products requires the availability of optimum productive factors which are then utilised by qualified human resources (guidance counsellors) with optimum processes'. In his view, counsellors play a central role in establishing and regulating quality standards in career guidance services. Given 'their experience, they are able to easily define the objectives and identify the optimum combination of factors. In this way, they can be directly involved (and therefore motivated) in the improvement of the service'. This involves a 'bottom-up' ethos to service evaluation within a multi-factorial approach pillared by practitioners' professionalism, training and expertise.

In reality however, the interplay of drivers determining what is meant by successful guidance outcomes often produces conflict. As contributors to NGRF (2020) describe when conflict occurs, it may be that the dominant driver becomes the economic imperative, irrespective of the front-line experiences of guidance practitioners. This creates a dilemma. In relation to impact analysis there is a need for joined-up thinking as some studies are too narrow in focus to take into account the broader context of the work they attempt to evaluate. Impact analysis therefore needs to address these conflicting drivers and evolve a mechanism for a wider range of possible outcomes that is sufficiently robust to be meaningful.

Designs limited to the confines of economistic and positivist paradigms such as Randomised Controlled Trials (RCT) may have strong internal validity but weak ecological validity (Robertson, 2020). The wealth of contextual knowledge owned by practitioners and necessary for holistic evaluation is therefore excluded.

Thus, efforts to converge the two opposing vantage points (Maguire, 2004) of policymakers (concerned with macroeconomic issues and quantitative outcomes) and practitioners (focusing on micro-level and qualitative quality outcomes) must be made through integrative evaluation approaches. Killeen (1996b) asserts that 'guidance practitioners cannot routinely assess economic effects. So, should they abandon all hope of outcome evaluation?' Instead he notes practitioners' involvement in the assessment of learning outcomes through their mundane (and reflective) practice as 'legitimate because they correspond to things guidance practitioners say they are trying to achieve'. Through 'a division of labour and an interchange between summative economic evaluators and formative practitioner-evaluators' Killeen (1996a) envisages learning outcomes fulfilling education and practice-related outcomes whilst simultaneously serving as 'proxies' for economic ones. In this way, notions of irrelevance, dismissal or threatening responses by practitioners (NGRF, 2020) towards impact assessment can be avoided. Rather, the value of sound evaluation practice and the indubitable benefits it holds for their professional development, performance and satisfaction can be embraced.

The Client Prerogative in Evaluation

Of equal parity to the other components within holistic impact assessment models is the client's own evaluation of the service. This accords with the principal ideology of careers guidance: that of respecting the client's judgement and promoting client autonomy (Evangelista, 2003). The voice of the service user also bears pragmatic value in evaluation, in determining the effectiveness and potential democratisation of services (Robertson, 2020). With policy now observing a keen interest in social equity and social justice issues, including mental health and racial equity, evaluation methodologies must become more user-centred and designed around client experiences. The WikiJob Team (2021) herald the need for the recognition of the rights of the marginalised, international students, part-time students and the 'transformative value' of services to students from less affluent backgrounds in methods assessing graduate employment. Moreover, prospective students themselves 'want to know more about the longer-term return on investment for their career prospects and many are aware that there are numerous ways to measure their own "career success" beyond job title and salary' (WikiJob Team, 2021). This demands broader research tools than destination and satisfaction surveys with their limited concepts of employability (Kellett and Clifton, 2017). The socio-economic cultural forces and complex labour market infrastructures in which clients function must be accommodated for within agile evaluative systems capable of reflecting these phenomena. For UK university careers services in a post-Covid-19 world, the primary challenge is 'to understand their student cohort: to gather data on the students they have and deeply understand them' (WikiJob Team, 2021). Thus, client-centric holistic evaluation models are those where the 'recipients of guidance are crucial to an understanding of the impact of the guidance process' (Maguire, 2004) as well as its 'harder' outcomes.

Quality Assurance Infrastructure

Evidence generated from an evaluation of policy or provision secures assumptions upon which quality assurance can be based (Killeen, 1996a). The author suggests that quality assurance should be developed in tandem with 'all kinds of outcome research'. Killeen (1996a) outlines a five-fold body of evaluation evidence that quality assurance can use for process monitoring and optimisation and performance management purposes. Hooley (2018) considers the interconnectedness between turning the cycle of continuous improvement into an evaluation cycle with career guidance systems ultimately focusing on the individual, supporting learning and progression and ensuring quality through assuring and evaluating provision. Evangelista (2003) considers six industrial methods to quality and applies these within his tri-variable model to the ongoing evaluation of career guidance services. Distinctions between continuous improvement practices and the impact evaluation of services are therefore often blurred in practice.

Simon's (2014) examination of university career guidance services in England, France and Spain demonstrated independent developments of quality models across the institutions to suit their own requirements. Her investigation determined that there was no common quality assurance framework for the delivery of guidance in higher education in Europe. Some services followed generic industrial standards (such as ISO 9001) based on models of procedural rather than performance assessment whilst others assumed performance indicators and principles for quality assurance. Standards more specifically measuring the quality of career guidance were identified in the UK and, since the timing of that research, they have been further revised and honed. These include the Quality Assurance Agency's Quality Code (2018) with accompanying principles for career information, advice and guidance, the matrix standard (2020) and the AGCAS Membership Quality Standard (2020). These can provide a synergistic vehicle for quality assurance for organisations propelled by internal and external motivators (Simon, 2014). With the dramatic changes to labour markets and student engagement precipitated further by the Covid-19 pandemic, university career services have needed to broaden their focus to a wider range of stakeholders and adapt and innovate provision accordingly. A strategic focus on quality is therefore needed covering all aspects of guidance service delivery: input, process and outcomes. A strong quality management system therefore supports both the ends and means of comprehensive impact evaluation.

An Integrative Model for Evidence-Based Practice

The four tenets of career guidance evaluation outlined above converge within an integrative conception of evidence-based practice. This is defined as 'making decisions through the conscientious, explicit and judicious use of four sources of information: practitioner expertise and judgement, evidence from the local context, a critical evaluation of the best available research evidence and the perspectives of the people who might be affected by the decision' (Robertson, 2020). These concepts have been extended into a pragmatic model for evaluation and improvement of practice (Figure 4.1). It combines a wide range of pragmatic knowledge with reflective practice and is to be used iteratively within a continuous improvement cycle.

We suggest that this model offers a nexus of opportunity for evidencing employability in careers provision where the axioms of career guidance and the values and mission of The Open University's Careers and Employability Services (CES) align. We will seek to demonstrate the efficacies of this model to evaluative practice at CES in the remainder of this chapter.

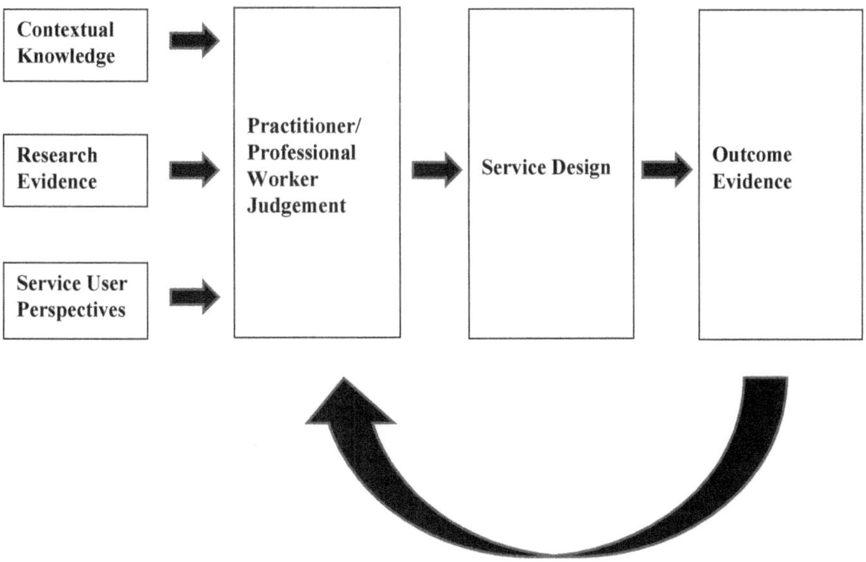

Figure 4.1 An integrated model for evidence-based practice (Robertson, 2020)

CONTEXTUAL KNOWLEDGE: CULTIVATING A CONTINUOUS IMPROVEMENT CULTURE

The OECD's definition of career guidance refers to 'services and activities intended to assist individuals, of any age, and at any point of their lives, to make educational, training and occupational choices and to manage their careers' (OECD, 2004). At CES we have adopted this broad perspective to support the needs of our extensive student population as career starters, changers or developers. The governing principle for delivery is stipulated as 'student focused, enabling career management and planning, confidence building and supporting employability and career progression'. Policy-driven distinctions (albeit semantic in nature) between information and advice also require consideration. Information refers to the provision of facts and figures relating to learning and careers, but without discussion about the relative merits of different options. Employability advice, however, provides 'an immediate response to the needs of clients who present an enquiry or reveal a need that requires more than a straightforward information response. Advice is usually limited to helping with the interpretation of information and with meeting needs already clearly understood by the client' (Corney and Watts, 1998). The CES infrastructure thus comprises information and advice provision supported by employability advisers, and careers guidance is offered by a team of careers consultants. Interventions involve initial triaging, directing the student to the most suitable offer of personalised support, inclusive of information/advice and guidance interventions. The operational model is responsive and provides a flexible approach to meeting student needs, allowing intra-referrals between information/advice and guidance support (Figure 4.2). The service offer provides one or multiple careers interventions at the right time via mediated and self-help activities and resources, so career planning, management, employability and progression can be successfully achieved.

CES quality standards and skills frameworks for one-to-one delivery, one-to-many and faculty-facing work are informed by the theoretical and political definitions of CEIAG as well as wider quality and institutional desiderata. The service operates to the Association of Graduate Careers Advisory Services (AGCAS) and Quality Assurance Agency Codes of Practice, the national matrix standard and The Open University's Equality Scheme. CES is also part of the OU's Quality Assurance Agency's Quality Enhancement Review and is accreditation via the Middle States Commission on Higher Education. These regulatory frameworks and quality schemes provide holistic determinants of the effectiveness and continuous improvement of the service.

Careful consideration was given to the establishment of the continuous improvement and quality strategy at CES. Hooley and Rice (2018) propose a series of domains and a typology of quality assurance approaches: regulatory, advisory, competitive and organic. Organic approaches view quality as being co-defined by the provider and the professional. So, although the CES Quality Development and

Information (Discover)/Advice (Understand and Decide – offer / options) (Delivered by Employability Advisers or Careers Consultants):	**Careers Guidance (Understand and Decide – offer/options and self)** (Delivered by Careers Consultants):
1. Delivered by phone, email, Skype and in person at events.	1. Delivered by phone, email and Skype.
2. If telephone interventions are conducted, calls are managed in a structured, friendly and professional manner and effective communication skills deployed to ensure meeting of student need.	2. If telephone interventions are conducted, calls are managed in a structured, friendly and professional manner and effective communication skills deployed to ensure meeting of student need.
3. Staff use appropriate questioning to gain an understanding of circumstances that will enable clarification and identification of need.	3. Guidance is the process of providing in-depth advice and support to meet students' needs. It involves deeper applications of career theories than information and advice and is a complex interaction between practitioner and student that depends on the skill of the practitioner to elicit, interpret and feedback from both verbal and written communication.
4. Information and advice supports students' informed decision making and planning through: supporting students' understanding of information available; how to research information themselves; providing suggestions on available options and agreeing on what action to take to progress.	4. Guidance involves identifying and clarifying needs and exploring ideas and values in relation to study opportunities, supporting life ambitions and identifying career goals.
5. Staff may need to interpret, clarify or contextualise information and assess when signposting to more specialist support or guidance is needed.	5. In the process, guidance should involve motivating, encouraging and challenging unrealistic expectations as well as referral to more specialist guidance and support.

Figure 4.2 Open University CES operational model – efficiencies in CEIAG delivery

Data Teams ensure that we continually improve, develop analytics and evaluate our performance, the strategisation and operationalisation of continuous improvement involves the full professional community of managers and practitioners.

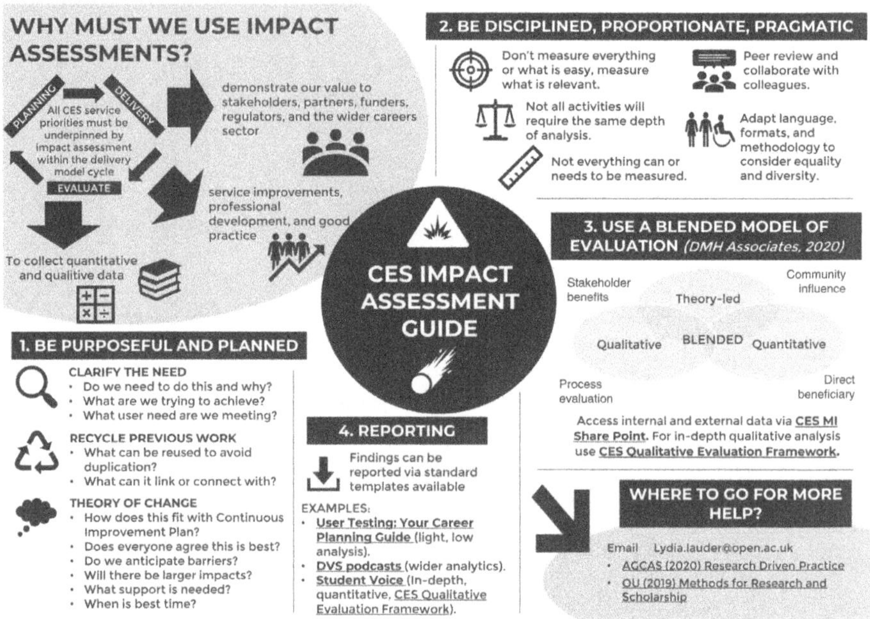

Figure 4.3 Open University CES Impact Assessment Guide.

Author: Lydia Lauder

Systems which privilege professional autonomy such as community of practice fora, peer observation, staff consultations and self-evaluation underpin continuous improvement. Our strategies are often presented as guidelines which serve as voluntaristic frameworks for the improvement of quality. Evaluation models focus on internal self-review against these guidelines and improvements driven by intrinsic professional values and the desire to do a good job rather than external drivers of compliance or regulatory and competitive mandates. For example, an impact assessment guide (Figure 4.3) encourages staff to plan, deliver and evaluate service delivery considering the impact on students and alumni. Within this approach a theory of change rubric and levels of analysis are required rudiments towards conceptualising the best outcomes for service evaluation and improvement. The normalisation of a data-informed and evidence culture within the service, however, carries its own challenges which will now be considered.

SERVICE DESIGN AND OUTCOME EVIDENCE: DATA DRIVEN APPROACHES – CONSTRICTORS OR EMANCIPATORS TO EVALUATING EMPLOYABILITY?

As Cobb (2019) notes, 'the volume, variety and velocity of data in higher education is increasing'. Data analysis has been key to designing the service and evidencing outcomes at CES. A data-driven approach underpins our service business plan and facilitates strategic and operational decision-making. Our operational measures and key performance indicators (KPIs) are one example. These measures inform management team meetings and our progress is monitored monthly by assigning RAG (red-amber-green) statuses against expected progress to the targets we set. We collect measures across five different aspects of the service:

- CES reputation and recognition (e.g., proportion of students who would recommend the service)
- OU partnerships (e.g., number of student-facing collaborative activities)
- Services to students and alumni (e.g., proportion of appointments conducted by video)
- Employer engagement (e.g., number of employer relationships)
- Quality enhancement (e.g., number of students responding to feedback surveys)

Measures such as these may be ascribed to the configuration of public management systems. However, we have sought to adopt a more tangential approach considering both static data at specific points in the student journey and fluid data (through their regular digital careers interactions at CES). This allows for a richer insight into student needs through an examination of the narrative substrata around KPIs and measures. The definitions of outcome measures and distance travelled indicators as well as the design of data collection instruments (large-scale surveys such as our Employability of Qualifiers Survey) consider the embedded social and life contexts and psychological and behavioural concepts affecting career progression. The impact of our employability-enhancing activities is thus gauged over the course of the student and alumnus lifecycle.

Demonstrating returns on investment solicits a focus on the transformative value of our provision to all students particularly those who may be more disadvantaged. Our approach to service design has been informed by the analysis of student engagement data and the development of an engagement data dashboard. This work collates data on the students who engage with our service, often across a number of different platforms. This includes our one-to-one provision, users of guidance consultations and email advice, and our one-to-many offering, such as visitors to webinars, forums, podcasts, online careers fairs, employer insight days and those who access our vacancy platform and interactive online resources. These data have not only enabled us to know how many students we are reaching, but also to examine the proportions of engaged students from APS (access, participation and success) cohorts. We are keen to see if such students are representative in our engaged population, enabling us to know if we are reaching the more vulnerable students via our services.

This work has also provided us with an insight into student behaviour, for example in examining the proportion of students who access only one aspect of the service. Our aim is to encourage students to access the full range of resources that we have available, to sample from the 'CES buffet' instead of just sticking to the one dish. The data also enable us to ask those difficult questions about resource versus return. When our ambition is to reach as many students as possible, we can now make decisions about whether we 'spend' resource on a product that we can see from visitor numbers is not popular with students.

The interactive data dashboard has enabled staff to self-serve, to filter and drill down to data that are relevant to their role and their curriculum area. This has further fostered the culture shift in data usage within the service, encouraging staff to question assumptions and base their work in evidence.

Considering value-added dimensions within our data strategy to capture the broader complexities of students' employability has involved the creation of the Employability of Qualifiers Survey (EQS). This survey gathers data on both careers and personal goals, employability skills, reflections on studying at the OU, as well as feedback on careers service provision. The survey runs annually and collects insights from alumni approximately three years after qualifying. It was felt that a three-year period post qualification allowed time for those OU students who were already working to reflect and act on the impact from their studies, as well as recognise the added value towards broader goals relating to personal and social development.

Certain features of the EQS have provided additional contextual insight into our understanding of student outcomes. The use of the benchmark comparison group has been a particular strength. The benchmark data, comparing responses from OU alumni to responses from alumni from other higher education institutions, has enabled us to contextualise OU performance. For example, the EQS surveys found that career motivation was reported by more benchmark alumni (79%[1]) than OU alumni (58%). Earning potential was more important for the benchmark alumni (50%) than for the OU alumni (36%), and that personal development was the converse – more important for OU respondents (77%) when compared with the benchmark respondents (71%). These data provide a deeper perspective and context when considering longitudinal education outcomes (LEO) salary data and the Teaching Excellence Framework (TEF) metrics, illustrating that perceived benefit for students is not solely based on salary.

In considering these examples of the operational measures, student engagement data and EQS, data driven approaches pose both an opportunity and challenge. Access to the data is sometimes problematic – our IT infrastructure is configured for operational purposes and not for management information and analytical requirements. Staff competency in using data is nascent but confidence is being fostered by better access to more intuitive data through the platforms such as data dashboards. The benefits of implementing a data culture for the service are beginning to be reaped through increased reputability across the institution. Our approach has become a 'critical value layer' (Cobb, 2019) for strategic decision-making at service and institutional levels. We have demonstrated the value of multifarious data including career surveys (Cobb, 2019; Jackson, 2018) which allow a focus on the whole delivery system, shape service policy and strategy, providing persuasive quantitative evidence for decision-making and understanding employability outcomes over time for varying student cohorts. In these ways the constrictions of data-driven approaches can be surmounted. Above all, our experience has shown that for a data-driven strategy to be more emancipatory in evaluating careers practice, then a holistic scope for evidencing employability must be adopted.

SERVICE USER PERSPECTIVES: STUDENT AND ALUMNI VOICES – HARBINGERS OF IMPACT

The CES philosophy offers the fulcrum upon which the service is delivered and evaluated. That is 'to empower OU students to realise their career and life ambitions by building their confidence to articulate their capabilities and skills helping them carve out their career journey and navigate the job market and connecting them to new opportunities'. Service users are recognised as recipients, evaluators and co-creators of provision. Our student voice strategy enables the proactive gathering of the student voice through a variety of consultation methodologies (such as a bespoke student panel of 900 students and alumni; large-scale surveys and focus groups) to achieve the CES mission and vision. Students and alumni are offered a ladder of engagement opportunities from informants, to consultants to collaborators and ultimately up to partners of service design and decision-making. Partnership, for example, is expressed through student representation at our strategic CES Student Voice Steering Group. At the information end of this spectrum, all service users can participate in feedback surveys issued to recipients at each service touch point. Students and alumni are invited to complete initial and secondary deeper-dive insight questionnaires. The results are collated within an interactive dashboard supported by full qualitative content analyses to enable comprehensive impact evaluation.

National instruments of measuring employability are inadequate to capture the complex realties of employability for part-time and distance learners such as those at the OU (Kellett and Clifton, 2017). A more nuanced three gains model is offered of learning, working and personal gains. Killeen's (1996a) model of guidance determinants also provides a useful corollary with immediate, intermediate and ultimate outcomes at individual and systemic levels. Immediate and intermediate outcomes capture changes in knowledge and skills, attitudes, decision-making, search-ability and motivational commitment. Career management indicators are also set out in the Blueprint for Careers UK (LSIS, 2013). Our feedback surveys draw upon all these paradigms to capture the holistic scope of guidance impact upon the service user.

These approaches allow for a deep opportunity for the student and alumni voice to be heard as well as heuristic comparisons to be made with other voices in service arbitration – such as the practitioner's judgements.

PRACTITIONER / PROFESSIONAL WORKER JUDGEMENTS AND RESEARCH EVIDENCE: EFFECTIVE PROFESSIONALS, REFLECTIVE PRACTITIONERS AND EMERGENT EVALUATORS

The ambition to increase evaluative practices at CES via a strategic approach has signalled the need for creating staff awareness, upskilling and improving their confidence as evaluators. Our experience so far, affirms Whiston et al.'s (2019) findings that impact evaluation is not an easy task such that practitioners 'may avoid evaluating a career programme because they are unfamiliar with appropriate instruments or measures'. The CES Impact Assessment Guide (Figure 4.3) propels all levels of staff to consider the fundamentals of evaluation and whether this needs to be formative or summative. The principles also encourage a holistic evaluation approach including relevant perspectives and interests from a full range of stakeholders. This is particularly relevant as the OU's target market is not focused upon the narrow confines of graduating students but is inclusive of the wide range of students at all levels, alumni, employers, faculty and wider external stakeholders and accountability bodies. Feedback and insights from our Employer Engagement Team's activities, for example, are therefore critical in contributing to the impact evaluation of the service.

Practitioners' tacit knowledge also provides an indispensable measure for determining impact. Opportunities for self-reflective and objective critiques of practice are afforded through online communities of practice forums and quality monitoring mechanisms (such as observation frameworks for email, telephone and skype CEIAG delivery). These focus on examination of the socio-cultural, ethical and professional body principles influencing practice and are more to do with improving value for students and enhancing staff skills than measures for gathering statistics. This model combining reflective practice and pragmatic knowledge within a service improvement cycle is consistent with an action research approach (Robertson, 2020). Scholarship and research projects relating to student insight as well as careers activity supporting learning and teaching are encouraged at CES. A practitioner-led, dedicated CES Scholarship Team accesses funding opportunities internal and external to the OU to carry out action research activities. Strategic themes for scholarship include the OU's Open Degree Programme, diversity (diversity strategy) and nations, digital experience and online innovation and student voice. Research outputs and publications ensure that CES grows and maintains its visibility, reputability and competitive value inter alia across the university and CEIAG sector. Promulgating an evidence-based approach within the service also supports its cultural progressivity as its staff not only carry out their functions as effective professionals but are coetaneous in their advancement as reflective practitioners and emergent evaluators.

INTEGRATIVE EVALUATION AND INTERNATIONAL PERSPECTIVES

This chapter cannot be closed without reference being made to the extensive reach of The Open University to international contexts. Watts (1996) provides formidable, illustrative evidence into the complexity of factors impacting careers guidance across different countries. These include a country's stage of economic development, socio-political and cultural factors, educational and training systems to professional and organisational structures. Contextualising career guidance within these divergent variants for international students is challenging. Discrepancies in the recognition of distance learning qualifications across countries, further constricted by the complications of post-Brexit labour markets are demanding for both the OU student and careers practitioner to navigate. Integrative evaluation provides opportunities for nuanced practice and seeking out professional convergencies or example, empowering students to explore solutions within respective ministerial, industrial, and professional body organisations; development of clear online resources for students and staff, capitalising upon relevant, external organisational expertise on qualification recognition and immigration requirements.

Beyond such techniques, however, lies the more fundamental notion that careers guidance transcends time and culture as it is based on the ultimate, universal human value of self-actualisation (Watts, 1996). Therefore, the practice and evaluation of career guidance at CES is universal and egalitarian as we seek to uphold these values, irrespective of whether it is a UK or international student that is being supported. For ultimately, the impact of a careers guidance service is judged by the extent of its 'contribution to the self-actualization of the individual' (Watts, 1996). In our experience, successful integrative evaluation means observing contextual sensitivities but remaining resolutely dedicated to the central dogma of the career guidance philosophy, that of individual respect, growth and development.

CONCLUSION

In this chapter we have outlined the increasing pressures of the current zeitgeist upon higher education careers services to demonstrate returns on investment in a post-pandemic world. We have argued from literature evidence, that under these socio-political forces and labour market singularities, more holistic models of evaluation are needed in order for careers providers to show their true value for money in evidencing 'employability'. Using The Open University's Careers and Employability Services as an example, we have depicted how the tenets of integrative evaluation, notably Robertson's (2020) model, can be applied in practice. Impact assessment principles of this kind offer a counterbalance to the methodological challenges associated with evaluating careers guidance and provide a means for evidencing the multi-level impacts of guidance beyond the preoccupation with economistic measures. Comprehensive evaluation frameworks, such as these, allow for an 'interchange between summative economic evaluators and practitioner-evaluators' (Killeen, 1996b). Evidence generated in this way at an organisational level can offer proxies for longer-term economic assessments (Maguire, 2004) for policy-makers and funders to consider. Our experience at the OU's CES suggests that careers services can be 'data-rich but insights-poor' with an abundance of evidence at our fingertips but we need to learn how to better use it to evaluate and improve our provision. This demands an integrated evaluation approach allowing for an array of voices to be clearly heard, not least those of the students and alumnus. We propose that both the outcomes and the process of evaluation itself must be used iteratively within a continuous improvement cycle if employability is to be meaningfully evidenced.

Note

1 Data taken from the 2020 EQS

REFERENCES

AGCAS (2020) *AGCAS HE Careers Service Resourcing Survey 2020* www.agcas.org.uk/Latest/agcas-he-careers-service-survey-2020

Career Development Institute (2021) *Blueprint of learning outcomes for professional roles in the career development sector*. CDI [On line]. Available at: www.thecdi.net/CDI-Blueprint-for-Professional-Roles (Accessed: 23 October, 2021).

Cobb, F. (2019) 'There's no going back': the transformation of HE careers services using big data, *Journal of the National Institute for Career Education and Counselling*, 42:1, 18–25.

Corney, M. and Watts, A. G. (1998) *Individual learning accounts: the role of information, advice and guidance*. CRAC/NICEC Conference Briefing. Cambridge: Careers Research and Advisory Centre.

Hughes, D. & Percy, C. (2020) *The career development landscape: evidence and impact assessment*. Webinar presentation, Exeter: DMH Associates [On line]. Available at: https://dmhassociates.org/wp-content/uploads/2020/09/080920-The-career-development-landscape-webinar-FINAL-VERSION.pdf (Accessed: 16 November, 2020).

Evangelista, L. (2003). *Quality assurance in guidance services – a tri-variable model*. ACADEMIA [On line]. Available at: www.academia.edu/10016383/Quality_assurance_in_career_guidance_services_a_tri-variable_model (Accessed: 3 July, 2021).

Hooley, T. (2018) *Evidence based practice and evaluation in career guidance. Adventures in career development [Online].* Available at: https://adventuresincareerdevelopment.wordpress.com/2018/11/24/7023/ (Accessed: 2 July, 2021).

Hooley, T. and Rice, S. (2018) Ensuring quality in career guidance: a critical review, *British Journal of Guidance & Counselling,* 47:6, 1–15.

Jackson, C. (2018) The role of career surveys: identifying issues and evaluating practice, *Journal of the National Institute for Career Education and Counselling*, 41:1, 18–25.

Kellett, M. and Clifton, G. (2017) *Measuring gains and employability for part-time students*. WONKHE [On line]. Available at: https://wonkhe.com/blogs/analysis-measuring-gains-and-employability-for-part-time-students/ (Accessed: 23 June, 2021).

Killeen, J. (1996a) The learning and economic outcomes of guidance. In: Watts, A. G., Law, B., Killeen, J., Kidd, J. M. and Hawthorn, R. (1996) *Rethinking careers education and guidance*, London: Routledge, pp. 72–91.

Killeen, J. (1996b) Evaluation. In: Watts, A. G., Law, B., Killeen, J., Kidd, J. M. and Hawthorn, R. (1996) *Rethinking careers education and guidance*, London: Routledge, pp. 331–348.

Learning and Skills Improvement Service (LSIS) (2013) *The blueprint for careers: a guide for users. Excellence Gateway [Online].* Available at: https://repository.excellencegateway.org.uk/LSIS2013-04a-BlueprintForCareersUserGuide.pdf (Accessed: 23 June, 2021).

Maguire, M. (2004) Measuring the outcomes of career guidance, *International Journal Educational and Vocational Guidance,* 4: 179–192.

McMahon, M. (2019) Qualitative career assessment: a higher profile in the twenty-first century? In: Athanasou, J. A. and Perera, H. N. (eds) *International handbook of career guidance*, Springer Nature Switzerland AG, pp. 735–754. Available at: https://link.springer.com/ book/10.1007/978-3-030-25153-6?page=2#toc

NGRF (2020) *Discussions on what matters and what counts in guidance*. Extracted from https://warwick.ac.uk/fac/soc/ier/ngrf/effectiveguidance/impact/assessing/outcomes on 7 October, 2020.

Simon, A. (2014) Quality assurance in university guidance services, *British Journal of Guidance & Counselling,* 42:2, 181–198.

Watts, A. G. (1996) International perspectives. In: Watts, A. G., Law, B., Killeen, J., Kidd, J. M. and Hawthorn, R. (1996) *Rethinking careers education and guidance*, London: Routledge, pp. 366–379.

Whiston, S. C., Mitts, G. N. and Li, Y. (2019) Evaluation of career guidance programs. In: Athanasou, J. A. and Perera, H. N. (eds) *International handbook of career guidance*, Springer Nature Switzerland AG, pp. 815–834. Available at: https://link.springer.com/book/10.1007/978-3-030-25153-6?page=3#toc

WikiJob Team (2021) *What are the main challenges facing university careers services?* WikiJob [On line]. Available at: www.wikijob.co.uk/content/features/ universities/what-are-main-challenges-facing-university-careers-services (Accessed: 27 July, 2021).

5

The Student Voice in Employability within Tertiary Business and Management Education

Vicki Harvey

INTRODUCTION

One of the challenges for the education sector, in preparing people to develop employability skills, is to exploit the advances of rapid technology which has changed the nature of work and demand for skills. A problem therefore lies in how the education sector understands employability requirements so it can respond and implement actions that prepare people not only for the labour market, but also for a life beyond work.

This chapter concerns employability in higher education (HE) for business and management degree programmes placing the focus on the undergraduate student voice. Much of the empirical research to date has focused upon employability of graduates, employability definitions and models. There is a gap at a micro-level concerning the opinions of undergraduates. This chapter draws upon a study that addresses this gap. By accepting the premise of Bridgstock (2017: 352) in relation to employability, HE can be more effective in preparing students for the future of work and society, then the student voice should be heard.

In terms of work, it is estimated that 65% of children entering primary schools today are likely to work in new jobs and functions that do not currently exist (Universities UK, 2018). A future aspect of employability will require changes in the type of work we do, how we go about that work and through developing flexibility in skills.

To tackle the future challenges, organisations such as the Chartered Institute for Personnel and Development (CIPD) argue that a range of qualifications will be needed (Brinkley and Crowley, 2017). Alongside qualifications, there is increasing demand for employability skills. These are required in subject-specific topics, professional and technical areas, supported by core transferable skills. Employability has therefore become a significant focus for the tertiary education sector (Artess et al., 2017).

This chapter discusses the meaning of employability for business and management (B&M) undergraduate students from the University of Salford. The focus is to understand the impact of employability skills and the role and influences of various forms of capital, in particular psychological. This chapter discusses findings of an empirical study that applied the concepts of capital resources and the socio-analytical tools of Bourdieu as a lens to understand the student voice in relation to employability. From data collected, the definition of skills within employability to understand the relative emphasis in an HE context is interrogated.

THE SIGNIFICANCE OF EMPLOYABILITY

As this book demonstrates, employability remains a major topic for research, upon which a single agreed position has not been attained and it covers many areas from policies in HE through to ideologies, practices, and models to embed employability within the curriculum (Tymon, 2013; Tomlinson and Holmes, 2017). However, employability remains a critical part of the public policy rationale of higher education today (Artess et al., 2017).

As a result, higher education institutions (HEIs) have made significant efforts to embed employability into the undergraduate curriculum and provide support (Cole and Tibby, 2013). Yet there remains a lack of consensus as to how HE should implement employability initiatives.

Furthermore, there is a lack of student voice in relation to employability. A major literature review conducted by the Higher Education Academy (HEA) from Artess et al. (2017) suggests much of the research explored focuses upon graduate outcomes rather than undergraduate input or undergraduate views (Bryson, 2015).

Following from themes of the literature, it can be said the very expression, 'the degree is not enough', captures a range of challenges at the heart of the current student and graduate experience (Tomlinson, 2017a:16). There is widespread agreement and evidence in terms of policy, practice, and research that employability skills are an essential outcome of participation in HE (Tomlinson, 2012). Consequently, Wilson et al. (2013) and Bryson (2015) suggest there is a narrowing of focus towards outcomes, or a mechanistic tick-box approach to 'skills acquisition', rather than consideration of inputs aimed at developing employability capability to expand opportunities for achievement upon graduation. It is also suggested students themselves cannot see the value of undertaking employability skills development (Tymon, 2013; Wilson et al., 2013; Bryson, 2015).

There are concerns and counterarguments that the purpose of education is not just to produce graduates that serve the needs of a shifting economy and prepare people for the world of work. Wheelahan (2015: 751) suggests the reduction of education in several cases is towards the skills needed to get a job, resulting in the subordination of knowledge. If we accept employability should be an integral part of HE, then we should consider the impact that this perspective has upon the value of knowledge versus skills.

Such comments follow from the argument of Maton (2005) suggesting HE should work to enable students to access several forms of capital to support the development of both skills and knowledge. Furthermore, HE should integrate opportunities to develop capital into teaching and learning for students to convert such capital and the resources conferred by them, in a more explicit manner (Maton, 2005).

CONTEXT

Data was collected using volunteer student focus groups (labelled FG) and individual interviews (labelled STU), from which data was analysed to generate a set of questions posed to represent the student voice, to employers and members of staff from the University of Salford Business School (located within the north-west of England). Employers and staff were then asked to respond to the student views to establish a further understanding of the student voice. The study is an examination of the meaning of employability for students within HE, who studied a range of bachelor's degree business and management (B&M) programmes.

Across twelve B&M degree programmes, all students undertake a professional development module as part of their studies. The compulsory level 5 module aims to develop competencies, attributes, knowledge, and attitudes in students so they develop confidence and competence in identifying and addressing their own employability needs and goals. Each student completed an employability self-assessment and followed a typical labour market recruitment process via a constructively aligned learning, teaching, and assessment experience.

INFLUENCES UPON EMPLOYABILITY

With the increasing emphasis within HEIs upon employability, tension is created due to competing agendas. There is a significant body of literature relating to employability and, in this chapter, it is not possible to summarise all of the work. However, three key areas of influence will be examined, embedding of employability in HE curricula, definitions of employability and psychological capital.

It can be useful to consider employability (both from academic literature and policy) as broadly divided into 'supply-side' and 'demand-side' perspectives and factors. This distinction is drawn from the work of Hillage and Pollard (1998) and McQuaid and Lindsay (2005). Supply-side refers to the responsibilities of the individual-centred components of employability, whereby the emphasis is placed upon the individual to develop and demonstrate employability to gain employment. For this chapter, HE is also considered as the supply-side, given the responsibility now placed upon it for developing employability with students.

Demand-side considers employability outcomes in the labour market and therefore the skills requirement or demands of employers. Traditionally speaking, demand-side factors were those of labour market conditions, such as availability of jobs and macroeconomic conditions. However, the shift in focus towards employability factors from those of labour market conditions, has placed more importance on the skills required by employers (McQuaid and Lindsay, 2005).

The emphasis upon employability within HEI creates tension due to competing agendas. This is exemplified by a meta study from the Higher Education Academy (HEA) which undertook a review of 187 pieces of research from the period of 2012 to 2016 (Artess et al., 2017). The review of the literature for the study draws significantly from this period whilst paying attention to some older research for valuable context.

The following points highlight the significant issues raised from the review of Artess et al. (2017) that informs this research:

1. There has been a significant amount of change within the landscape of HE. Such change is continuous and there are multiple policy reviews.
2. There is a wide range of terminology or definitions surrounding employability.
3. There is pressure placed upon HEIs to provide adequate support for student employability, but a lack of consensus as to how this should be done.
4. There is a lack of a clear student voice, the review revealed only limited evidence of student views of employability provision.
5. There is a consensus that there is value in engaging with employability.
6. There are several frameworks and models that attempt to measure the outcomes of graduate attributes and employability but these often focus upon graduate employment.

EMPLOYABILITY DEFINITIONS

As stated, the approach in the literature is broadly along the lines of supply-side and demand-side of high-level skills for the labour market. The definition of employability has shifted throughout history but appears to be based upon the premise of these two key perspectives. The position developed by researchers and policy makers, suggests a demand-side, i.e. an employer concern, which is focused upon individuals to develop the skills and capability to do a job. Skills to *do a job* are defined from the differing needs of the employer and may be developed through or by them. Whereas a focus upon the supply-side concept concerns skills and attributes to get a job, skills to *get a job* concern individual 'capability to gain initial employment, maintain employment and obtain new employment if required' through possessed assets of knowledge, skills, and attitudes (Hillage and Pollard, 1998:1).

SUPPLY-SIDE EMPLOYABILITY

There is a sense of challenge within the field in defining employability. McQuaid and Lindsay (2005: 205) assert that employability 'should be understood as being derived from, and affected by, individual characteristics and circumstances and broader, external (social, institutional and economic) factors influence a person's ability to get a job'. In attempts to consider definitions therefore, Barrie (2006: 217) contends that there is a bewildering array of terms that have emerged in describing student skills. Within the literature the description of skills may include 'transferable skills', 'generic skills', 'attributes', 'qualities', 'professional skills' and so on (Yorke, 2006; Biggs and Tang, 2007). Some or all categories of 'skills' listed may be attributed to employability, but this assumes an agreed definition, upon which some caution is urged by both Harvey (2005) and Yorke (2006). The reasoning of Harvey (2005: 13) lies within a plethora of micro-interpretations and a probabilistic focus upon gaining employment rather than a process of enhancing abilities.

The academics Harvey and Yorke have both studied aspects of employability extensively and remain widely cited. It is from such work and the external increasing political pressure upon HEIs to concentrate resources on employability, that pedagogical approaches were developed. The influential definition here is:

> A set of achievements – skills, understandings and personal attributes – that make individuals more likely to gain employment and be successful in their chosen occupations, which benefits themselves, the workforce, the community and the economy. (Yorke, 2006: 8)

In the UK, embedding employability within the curriculum has become a major activity for universities. A significant document resulting from this work is 'Pedagogy for employability', from Cole and Tibby (2013) which clearly places employability as of the utmost importance, as follows:

> Embedding employability into the core of higher education will continue to be a key priority of Government, universities and colleges, and employers. This will bring significant private and public benefit, demonstrating higher education's broader role in contributing to economic growth as well as its vital role in social and cultural development. (HEFCE, 2011:5 cited in Cole and Tibby, 2013:5)

DEMAND-SIDE EMPLOYABILITY

Definitions have also emerged from the demand-side. Besides coexisting definitions, another key point is between employability as both continuous and distinct from employment. The point being employability, regardless of your employment status is a continuous development process, contextualised by factors of the external environment (Harvey, 2001 cited in Williams et al., 2016: 878).

As a key stakeholder, employers are the functional drivers from which a practical shift from the theoretical to the strategic and practical application of employment and employability occurs. It is perhaps obvious that employers tend to view employability as primarily a characteristic of the individual. Leaving aside the arguments for graduate 'work-readiness', the Confederation of British Industry (CBI) subsequently collaborated with the National Union of Students (NUS) to produce a document 'working towards your future'. This work produced a new definition to focus upon generic attributes required by employers:

> A set of attributes, skills and knowledge that all labour market participants should possess to ensure they have the capability of being effective in the workplace – to the benefit of themselves, their employer and the wider economy. (CBI/NUS, 2011:14, cited in Cole and Tibby, 2013: 8)

The compatibility between these two approaches is clear in terms of the individualised nature of graduate attributes and the need for personal qualities. However, both have a reliance on the supply-side, developing as an individual who has the required set of skills and attributes (Morrison, 2019). There is no suggestion of a developmental contribution from the demand-side within the definitions.

Drawing upon the supply and demand elements, Tomlinson (2017a:23) asks the question: 'what are the views employers have about graduates and universities'. Tomlinson also poses other questions, for example, 'for employability; to what extent do graduates meet the organisational demands and how can the relationship between HE and employer organisations be better understood and coordinated?' (Tomlinson, 2017a:14).

EMBEDDING EMPLOYABILITY IN THE HE CURRICULA

An expectation of responsiveness is required from HEIs to consider their primary role to 'develop graduates as lifelong learners, transform students by *enhancing* their knowledge, skills, attitudes, and abilities while simultaneously *empowering* them as lifelong critical, reflective learners' (Harvey, 2000: 3, emphasis in the original).

Strathdee (2009) uses the concepts of cultural and social capital to theorise the links between HE and the labour market, raising an interesting question about how universities are understood and judged by employers when recruiting. Brown and Hesketh (2004, cited in Strathdee, 2009: 86) argue that meeting the competitive pressures of advanced capitalist economies has led employers to demand graduates immediately add value to their enterprises. This may be attributable to the move to a market-driven HE, with an agenda for the provision for employability support.

There are several academic arguments from HE in response to employers' views on employability, summarised as follows:

Skills development: how can such skills be effectively developed within HE? Whilst there is no overall current consensus, it is important to consider B&M studies as semi-vocational with careers more variable in both job content and context (Wilton, 2008). If the primary focus is upon the marketability of cumulative personal skills, there is a need to consider the balance between academic skills and skills for business environments, or rather being equipped to do a job (Harvey, 2001).

Transferability: can skills be readily transferred into employment without either work experience or suitable work-based training and development? Wilton (2008:156) suggests the employer perspective is an 'unrealistic wish-list of skills and an attempt to pass the cost of pre-employment training on to HE'. However, embedded employability has become a focal point for HE (Artess et al., 2017).

Demand: there are questions over the potential for an imbalance between supply and demand (Brown et al., 2003; Ball, 2019).

Recruitment practices: another contrasting factor is noted by Wilton (2014) surrounding complex recruitment and selection processes. Wilton (2014) takes the perspective that the processes lack coherence and clarity in recruitment criteria.

Research from Cai (2013:458) suggests that employers have changing perceptions of workers with similar qualifications. These dynamic attitudes vary according to their different traditions, political biases, and other factors (Teichler, 2009 cited in Cai, 2013). The conclusion, in line with the consensus presented here, is that universities should provide support for students to enter the labour market. Following from Cai (2013) the responsibility falls to HE to engage and inform employers, through relationships and networks, to influence their beliefs.

THE ROLE OF CAPITALS

Capitals are defined as key resources that confer power or status and, in a graduate context, give benefits and advantages (Maton, 2005; Tomlinson, 2017b). Capitals comprise multiple forms, such as human, social, cultural, identity, and psychological. The role of capital is also expressed in the work of Bourdieu (2004), in his research-based tools for socio-analysis. A capitals-based concept developed by Bourdieu (1984) considers HE as a field forming a setting in which agents and their social positions are located. The focus upon employability has resulted in an increasing consideration upon forms of capital as resources that confer employability.

From contemporary research, expanding upon Bourdieusian research, Tomlinson (2017b) has developed a conceptualisation of graduate employability based on graduate capitals. The combination of capital-based concepts of Bourdieu and Tomlinson is a valuable approach to understanding graduate employability and the challenges faced in the transition to the labour market, having implications for developing employability strategies for HE.

Capitals can be understood as key resources accumulated through graduates' education, social and initial employment experiences, and which equip them favourably when transitioning to the job market. Some sources of capital are rooted in graduates' formal education and socio-cultural milieu, and are converted into subsequent economic value (Bourdieu, 1986).

Maton (2005) suggests that HE should enable students to access forms of capital (both skills and knowledge). Therefore, the HE field could allow for the opportunity for students to convert capital and the resources conferred by them in a more explicit manner if they are integrated into teaching and learning (Maton, 2005). In other words, capital developed within or gained from HE (the field) will determine the chances of success for practices, in this case, employability (Bourdieu, 1986).

A focus for this chapter is psychological capital. Psychological capital is described as 'positively oriented human resource strengths and psychological capacities that can be measured, developed, and effectively managed for performance improvement in today's workplace' (Luthans, 2002: 59). The principle is to build upon strengths to flourish in organisational settings and develop a locus of self-control (Çavuş and Gökçen, 2014). Psychological capital includes states such as confidence, hope, resilience, positive self-evaluation, and personality traits such as conscientiousness. The essence of psychological capital lies in resilience, adaptability and even emotional security, and is an affective relation of social capital (Rattray, 2016).

The successful development of psychological capital is dependent on the ability of an individual to cope within challenging environments (or negative experiences) and find alternate pathways. Applied to employability this involves developing strategies to expand the scope of employment opportunity and respond to a changing job context (Savickas and Porfeli, 2012). It also entails being proactive and even re-orientating goals based on labour market change. Self-efficacy is associated with the concept of psychological capital, where Bandura (1995:2) determines 'efficacy beliefs influence how people think, feel, motivate themselves and act'. Crucially, according to Dacre-Pool and Sewell (2007:285) in their early employability model work, self-efficacy and self-confidence provide a link between knowledge, understanding, skills, experience and personal attributes and employability'.

The work of Luthans et al. (2007:245) focuses on the idea of 'who you are becoming rather than who you are' and is an important aspect as this study is examining undergraduate students who are working towards becoming graduates. The development of psychological capital is said by Luthans et al. (2007: 245) to contribute to a better understanding of thoughts and emotions that shape personal behaviours.

Furthermore, it is argued that forms of capital can play a considerable role in shaping graduates' transitional experience and early employment outcomes (Tomlinson et al., 2017: 29). Therefore capital (psychological capital) can be conceptualised for employability and 'conceived as key resources that confer benefits and advantages onto individuals' (Tomlinson, 2017a).

WHAT DOES EMPLOYABILITY MEAN TO STUDENTS?

The purposefully selected data presented in this chapter is drawn from an extensive analysis of a larger PhD study conducted by the author (Harvey, 2019). All data is presented anonymously with participants' permission.

SKILLS TO *DO* AND SKILLS TO *GET* A JOB

The picture for students for employability overall is complex, and meaning is constructed from many influences. Initially during focus groups, when asked about employability, discussions quickly began by simply listing skills, but then moved towards the challenges of getting to grips with the many aspects of employability. Analysis of the discussions show the students understood the complexity and attempted to communicate the 'interwoven' (FG4-4) or 'overlapping' (FG5-2) nature of what employability meant to them.

Drawing from the literature, Williams et al. (2016) conclude that the debate continues in attempting to define employability and the associated skills. It is therefore important to recognise that skills have a broader relevance beyond an employability context and have a bearing in HE and in everyday life.

Within the literature, employability as a concept has moved from a person being employable, to include a whole range of stakeholder perspectives. This includes terms which have subsequently been used interchangeably and relate to differences in outcomes of 'skills' and outcomes described as 'attitudes' (Barrie, 2006). The driver behind the questioning of employability meaning therefore reinforces the point made by Williams et al. (2016: 878) 'in reality, one must first identify the perspective from which the term is being applied'. The findings show it is now possible to add the undergraduate perspective.

The analysis of participant data showed that students could clearly identify a variety of skills for employability. The evaluation determines those factors the

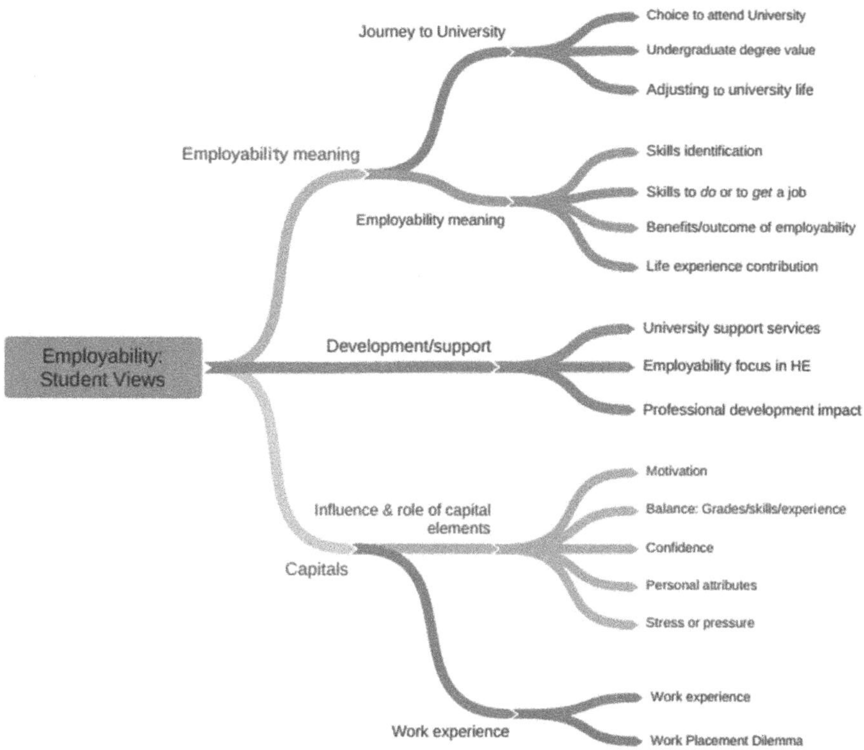

Figure 5.1 Mind Map analysis of student view of employability (Harvey, 2019)

students considered to have an impact upon the meaning of employability. The most listed skills included communication, teamwork, IT, and organisational skills. The analysis generated a list of skills nodes from the data, subsequently interpreted as skills to do a job in Figure 5.1.

It is not surprising the students began by identifying specific skills before going into more depth of meaning, as this is quite often what students are presented with in HE. A review by Tymon (2013:844) summarises skills and attributes from several employability frameworks, highlighting that communication and teamwork are the most cited. Other writers with a critical stance of employability where the concept is frequently presented simply as skills identification, results in a 'tick-box approach to the acquisition of skills' or that employability becomes a buzzword (Wilson et al., 2013: 1223).

Therefore, by asking students 'what does employability mean to them' rather than what it is, allowed the participants to reflect further upon their experiences and learning, whereupon students made the distinction between skills for getting and doing a job. For example, STU-3 described the different paths of getting and doing a job in relation to employability skills as 'talking the talk and walking the walk'.

The results reflect the distinction as a common element, where students understand employability as two processes rather than the identification of specific skills.

The student views reflect the literature in terms of the connection between employability skills for doing and those for getting a job. This invokes the views of Gazier (1998) that the concept of employability (in this setting), has a dynamic adaptive and multidimensional nature. The students understand employability as being complex with interwoven aspects, from which they need to adapt their approach if they are to demonstrate their own capability to employers.

The findings show employability skills to get a job include the need for competence in elements of the job selection process, for example producing CVs, and performing well in assessments and interviews. For participant FG3-1, the idea of 'getting a foot in the door' and 'grabbing the attention' was an important aspect of employability for getting a job. Based on the agreement of several participants, the theme developed as one of being able to 'sell yourself' and your skills as an employable person to employers.

The analysis shows it is a case of using skills *to get* a job and to be able to provide evidence of your ability in terms of skills *to do* a job. This dual purpose for employability means 'a lot of getting a job is selling yourself' (FG5-2) to employers. The students were clear they understood the skills to do a job could be developed later whilst in the workplace. As participant FG3-1 pointed out 'once you are in a job you can develop yourself and learn skills that are required'.

As the agenda has developed in HE systems globally, the articulation of employability has shifted according to the needs of a wider stakeholder base (Kalfa and Taksa, 2015). This relates to labour market factors of 'supply' and 'demand' discussed by Hillage and Pollard (1998), moving to a singular focus upon the individual and their skills as stated by McQuaid and Lindsay (2005). Placing a focus upon the 'supply' side means consequently concern lies with the individual to develop employability through possessed assets of knowledge, skills, and attitudes (Hillage and Pollard, 1998:1).

The findings which explained the meaning of employability for doing a job relate to the application of skills in various situational workplace contexts. The students linked this combination or 'overlap'. Students explained how they should articulate proof of their individual skills, as it is difficult to convey employability without application or realisation of contexts of skills to do a job. This is where the shift from 'selling yourself' to demonstrating your ability to perform occurs, thereby adding to the complexity and challenge of what employability is and what it means.

As FG5-5 commented, you may have skills on paper (a CV) but felt they were meaningless without back-up from some work experience. STU-11 felt it was important to draw upon experience to show that he was employable. Students provided examples of their range of work experiences, where skills such as teamwork and customer service, in companies such as McDonalds (STU-4) or in the retail industry (FG4-4) can be 'transferred' and therefore applied to a graduate role context.

However, it is important to note that students are aware employability not only comes from work experience. The students also discussed life experiences and education that could contribute to their employability. As argued by McQuaid and Lindsay (2005), employability is a framework built upon 'individual factors, personal circumstances and external factors, which acknowledges the importance of both supply-side and demand-side factors'.

The original analysis shows that capitals are a feature of many aspects of employability (Table 5.1, Figure 5.1). The findings are broadly in line with the literature, in the interpretation that various capitals accumulate from developing employability (Figure 5.2). As stated, the purpose here is to focus upon psychological capital.

Table 5.1 Results summary (Harvey, 2019)

Question	Results
What does employability mean?	• Employability involves a number of factors and is interwoven in nature • Distinction between skills to *do* a job and *get* a job • Skills developed from work and life experiences, and becoming independent by attending university all contribute to developing employability • Self-assessment that evaluates both personality and emotional traits are important for understanding one's own employability • Achieving a balance between academic and employability development is challenging • The purpose of HE and obtaining a degree is to get a job. University is a natural progression from secondary education
What is the student opinion regarding employability development?	• Employability should be included in HE curricula • Employability development is a cause of stress or pressure • Developing employability has benefits beyond working life
What is the role and influence of capitals?	• Employability teaching experiences have are important for building confidence and motivation • A situation where a work placement dilemma occurs, influenced by factors of human and psychological capitals • A lack of maturity can be a barrier to employability
Is there variation in opinion with stakeholders?	• Employability should be described as a continuous development process • Appropriate work experience is important to develop employability • Achieving a balance between academic and employability development should be challenging • Barriers to employability include demonstrating organisational fit, describing skills, and understanding recruitment processes

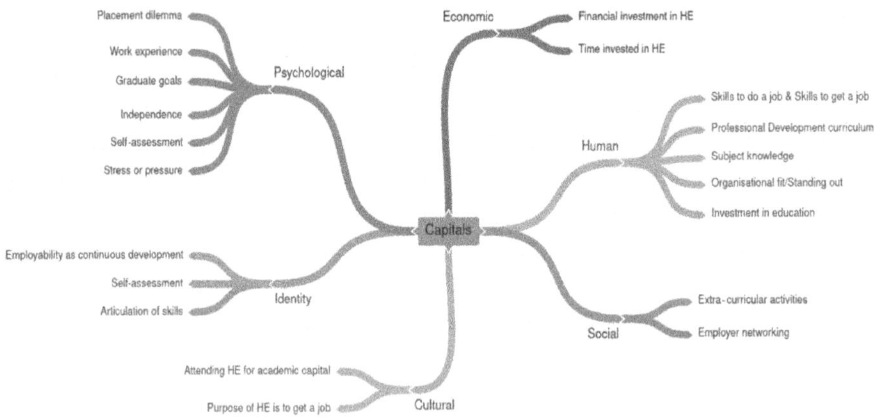

Figure 5.2 Mind Map analysis role and impact of capitals (Harvey, 2019)

The theoretical understanding of capitals feature in many studies that conceptualise employability, with psychological capital cited as 'capacity offering strengths within the job market' (Williams et al., 2016: 890) or to 'adapt and respond proactively to inevitable career challenges' (Tomlinson, 2017b: 347). More fundamentally, psychological capital has features that impact upon a positive situation for personal development (Çavuş and Gökçen, 2014). Confidence or self-efficacy is a basic component of psychological capital that an internal locus of self-control can exert, resulting in motivation and positive behaviours (Luthans et al., 2007).

It was found that confidence is a significant theme. The building of confidence and motivation in the field of HE was found to emanate from several situations identified by the students. One aspect is the knowledge and understanding of employability as processes (skills *to do* and *to get* a job) and their current abilities. For example, FG8-5 stated, 'you need to have a certain level of confidence to get a job', and the learning from the professional development module gave a sense of confidence and preparedness for tackling the job market.

From an employability standpoint, psychological capital is closely associated with human and social capital affecting the individual ability to perform well within a given role, and adapt to change, alongside drawing upon relationships in the workplace (Luthans, 2002; Luthans et al., 2007; Williams et al., 2016). Psychological capital is also said to be a form of psycho-social resource allowing career adaptability and resilience when faced with career challenges (Tomlinson, 2017b). What is most applicable in this research is the differentiation made by Luthans et al. (2007) that psychological capital focuses on 'who you are becoming' rather than 'who you are'. This point is important in terms of the focus upon undergraduate development as applied to employability and the future graduate self.

Confidence and motivation were linked by the students to several different aspects of employability and were said to impact upon the ability to get and to do a job. According to the students, confidence builds from several sources and, for many, confidence was boosted by participating in the professional development module. From the comments, two activities gave the students confidence. First, in undertaking a self-assessment and second, via gaining understanding of the overall awareness of the selection process. The successful completion of these activities built confidence as students became clear in knowing what is required from employers and themselves. The results show through the students learning experiences that they understand the strategies for future job seeking and coping with the challenges of the job market. For some students, it could be said that the psychological capital gained from starting to develop employability skills has allowed them to establish a high locus of self-control (Seligman and Csikszentmihalyi, 2000; Tomlinson, 2017b: 347).

Discussing confidence, motivation was an associated factor resulting from developing confidence. FG11-7 stated he has built confidence from his development at university that he felt brought him closer to his goal. This point was reiterated by FG4-2; by improving his employability he could meet his goals of a 'better job, better pay and a better life', but he also said you needed to be motivated to achieve these goals. The literature demonstrates that the combination of motivation and confidence-building are forms of psychological capital that are linked to self-efficacy (Bandura, 1995). Self-efficacy can therefore be an important factor in how these students perceive themselves and use the employability skills to achieve their goals, whilst they are developing within HE (Tomlinson, 2017b: 347).

The results show that success for many students, beyond obtaining a degree, is dependent upon motivation and building confidence through work experience. Several participants also raised part-time working, undertaken whilst at university, as a source of confidence. STU-12 for example, said her part-time job built confidence in communication skills, dealing with problems and managing people. As a result, she felt employability skills were transferable into her chosen field of human resources. However, some students were concerned and felt less confident by not having any work experience. FG7-4 for example, worried about her 'lack of experience'.

Comments from STU-3 illustrate the point; the gains from his work placement in terms of skills had given him confidence and 'new little building blocks that I want to build on'. The confidence of having developed skills and the motivation that drives future career plans, and becoming a graduate, form the key elements of psychological capital seen from the interpretation of the data. This also ties in with the literature in terms of self-efficacy from Bandura (1995). Dacre-Pool and Sewell (2007) have applied the concept concluding that 'mastery experiences' such as work placements are a key source of generating self-confidence and motivation. However, the employability model of Dacre-Pool and Sewell (2007) and the research cited above, does not consider confidence as a form of capital, only a factor of employability.

Other facets of developing confidence and generating motivation are identified in the data as originating from: life experiences (STU-4), becoming independent by attending university (STU-5 and STU-10) and students having realised employability skills can be developed from extracurricular activities such as sport (STU-7 and STU-13). As has been discussed across this chapter, other forms of capital interact, such as social and cultural capital, but the results show that confidence is also generated from the type of experiences which occur beyond direct learning in HE.

Psychological capital, applied to the context of employability, is significant, based on the emotional demands extending from the job-seeking process (Tomlinson, 2017b). Emotional demands form part of the undergraduate landscape; as FG10-5 states, 'we live in such a competitive world and the university environment is so competitive', for this student and several others this can be 'overwhelming' and 'stresses them out' (FG5-5). The need to develop employability for many students can cause stress and pressure, which will test the level of psychological capital that is developed.

Following Holmes (2015: 219), this study aimed to look at the capitals that are recognised as important at undergraduate level, with a view to gaining a better understanding of employability. The understanding should not be encumbered by what he describes as the 'flawed notion' of a complex network of 'skills' and 'attribute' definitions. From this study, confidence was seen to be by far the most valuable form of psychological capital that can support employability and therefore employment.

INTERROGATION OF THE DEFINITION OF EMPLOYABILITY

The discussion culminates in the interrogation of the definition of employability based on new insight brought together from the findings and the literature. The works of Bourdieu and Tomlinson, particularly in relation to capital, have provided a robust framework to examine employability.

The definition of employability that provides the reference point for this chapter is in the section on supply-side employability.

Based on the interpretation of the data, the definition of employability should include a long-term outlook and take account of the role of confidence in developing employability that is of any consequence to the individual. Therefore, a definition could be described as:

> Employability is a set of skills, understandings, and personal attributes, achieved through continuous lifelong development. Success requires support for positive psychological capital to build strengths that are used to one's advantage. The results make individuals more likely to gain employment and be successful in their chosen occupations, which benefits themselves, the workforce, the community, and the economy.

It can be said therefore, within HE, it is possible to provide curricula support for developing skills *to get* a job and the development of psychological capital. This leads to improved employability and possible labour market outcomes. In terms of employability practice, it is continuous in development when entering the workplace using skills *to do* a job and skills that contribute for a life beyond work.

The revised definition takes account of the student voice and incorporates the stakeholder response. The revision presents an opportunity for a common easily understandable language, that is, instilling the idea of continuous development. Employability does not end with the degree award or the first graduate job. To improve support for undergraduate students, HE must emphasise the continuous development aspect of employability; getting a degree is not the end but rather one of the steps of developing the practice of employability. HEIs should work with employers to support the principle of lifelong learning. Moreover, this point supports both philosophical and practical perspectives for the sustainability of skills and knowledge for a life beyond work.

FUTURE DIRECTIONS

The study design could be replicated as it would be valuable to explore and compare the views of students from different student cohorts, different faculties from across the University of Salford, and even different institutions (particularly 'elite' institutions). Though this study focuses upon B&M students, the same analysis and lessons could be developed across a range of different HR disciplines. This type of study would add further empirical research for the student voice, following the conclusion of Artess et al. (2017) and provide further data on what shapes employers' attitudes to employability (following from Cai, 2013). A longitudinal study should be considered.

This research could be followed up with some action research applied to the employability curricula within Salford Business School. It may be possible to collaborate with programme leaders to examine the lifelong learning emphasis of the teaching to embed the proposed revised definition of employability into the curriculum. At the same time, research could be conducted to develop methods to enable a focus upon building confidence and psychological capital for students across employability and other curricular aspects.

Research that focuses upon psychological capital in relation to employability is currently limited. This could be an area to build upon with both theoretical and practical implications for this concept and its relevance in employability development.

The concept of continuous development is not new, however employability as continuous development or as lifelong learning lacks emphasis in the literature. The examination of this concept and the role of stakeholders in this process, with the aim of improving shared understanding and collaborative processes, would be an interesting extension of this project.

CONCLUSION

With respect to the meaning of employability for the students, two important aspects of the findings determined the concept as principally skills to *do* and *get* a job. The employability inputs received (in the form of a professional development module), were shown to be important to students in understanding their own skills and how they might transfer into the workplace. The empirical findings also support the view that employability includes the development of skills as well as dispositions for conduct in workplace contexts.

Psychological capital is often associated in the literature as capacity for workplace and organisational performance, and indeed the students recognised this function. In other literature, the aspects of resilience and adaptability of psychological capital is highlighted as important for graduate employability (Tomlinson, 2017b). The theme of psychological capital in the form of confidence developed in the study is a much more fundamental resource, reflecting the position of the undergraduate student. It is therefore concluded that psychological capital for building confidence is important as it focuses on 'who you are becoming' rather than 'who you are' (Luthans et al., 2007). This outcome draws together the threads of employability as a longer-term development process, which by focusing on developing confidence rather than just a wish list of skills can better meet the needs of students. The inclusion of psychological capital in the employability discourse has the potential to reduce pressure on students and their perception to be an 'oven-ready' graduate.

The experience of the students saw them reflecting upon the meaning of employability and development needs, through the challenges of self-assessment and understanding of selection processes. Students claimed that much of the confidence they gained was supported by the curricula inputs in the form of a professional development module.

REFERENCES

Artess, J., Mellors-Bourne, R. and Hooley, T. (2017) *Employability: a review of the literature 2012-2016*. York, UK: Higher Education Academy.

Ball, C. (2019) Graduate labour market myths. In C. Burke and F. Christie (eds) *Graduate careers in context: research, policy and practice*. Oxon: UK: Routledge, pp. 57–70.

Bandura, A. (1995) *Self-efficacy in changing societies*. Cambridge: Cambridge University Press.

Barrie, S. C. (2006) Understanding what we mean by the generic attributes of graduates. *Higher Education*, 51(2) pp. 215–241.

Biggs, J. and Tang, C. (2007) *Teaching for quality learning at university*. 3rd edn. Berkshire, England: Open University Press.

Bridgstock, R. (2017) The university and the knowledge network: a new educational model for twenty-first century learning and employability. In M. Tomlinson and L. Holmes (eds) *Graduate employability in context: theory, research and debate*. London: Palgrave Macmillan, pp. 339–358.

Brinkley, I. and Crowley, E. (2017) *From 'inadequate' to making the UK's skills system world class*. CIPD: London.

Brown, P., Hesketh, A. and Williams, S. (2003) Employability in a knowledge-driven economy. *Journal of Education and Work*, 16(2) pp. 107–126.

Bourdieu, P. (1984) *Distinction: a social critique of the judgement of taste*. London, UK: Routledge.

Bourdieu, P. (1986) The forms of capital. In Richardson, J. G. (ed.) *Handbook of theory and research of the sociology of education*. Westport, CT: Greenwood Press Inc., pp. 241–258.

Bourdieu, P. (2004) *Science of science and reflexivity*. Polity Press & The University of Chicago Press.

Bryson, J. (2015) Putting skill in its place. *Journal of Education and Work*, 28(5) pp. 551–570.

Cai, Y. (2013) Graduate employability: a conceptual framework for understanding employers' perceptions. *Higher Education*, 65(4) pp. 457–469.

Çavuş, M. and Gökçen, A. (2014) Psychological capital: definition, components and effects. *British Journal of Education, Society & Behavioural Science*, 5(3) pp. 244–255.

CBI/NUS (2011) *Working towards your future: making the most of your time in higher education*. CBI: London.

Cole, D. and Tibby, M. (2013) *HEA employability framework – defining and developing your approach to employability*. HEA: York.

Dacre-Pool, L. and Sewell, P. (2007) The key to employability: developing a practical model of graduate employability. *Education and Training*, 49(4) pp. 277–289.

Gazier, B. (1998) *Employability: concepts and policies – report*. Berlin: Institute for Applied Socio-Economics: European Employment Observatory: European Commission.

Harvey, L. (2000) New realities: the relationship between higher education and employment. *Tertiary Education and Management*, 6(1) pp. 3–17.

Harvey, L. (2001) Quality in higher education: defining and measuring employability. *Quality in Higher Education*, 7(2) pp. 96–109.

Harvey, L. (2005) Embedding and integrating employability. *New Directions for Institutional Research*, 2005(128) pp. 13–28.

Harvey, V. M. (2019) *The student voice in employability within tertiary business and management education*, PhD thesis, University of Salford.

HEFCE (2011) *Opportunity, choice and excellence in higher education*. Bristol: HEFCE.

Hillage, J. and Pollard, E. (1998) No 85 employability: developing a framework for policy analysis: Institute for Employment Studies. *Labour Market Trends*, 107(85).

Holmes, L. M. (2015) Becoming a graduate: the warranting of an emergent identity. *Education and Training*, 57(2) pp. 219–238.

Kalfa, S. and Taksa, L. (2015) Cultural capital in business higher education: reconsidering the graduate attributes movement and the focus on employability. *Studies in Higher Education*, 40(4) pp. 580–595.

Luthans, F. (2002) Positive organizational behavior: developing and managing psychological strengths. *Academy of Management Executive*, 16(1) pp. 57–72.

Luthans, F., Youssef, C. and Avolio, B. (2007) *Psychological capital: developing the human competitive edge*. Oxford: Oxford University Press.

Maton, K. (2005) A question of autonomy: Bourdieu's field approach and higher education policy. *Journal of Education Policy*, 20(6) pp. 687–704.

McQuaid, R. W. and Lindsay, C. (2005) The concept of employability. *Urban Studies*, 42(2) pp. 197–219.

Morrison, A. (2019) Whose employability? In C. Burke and F. Christie (eds) *Graduate careers in context: research, policy and practice*. Oxon, UK: Routledge, pp. 29–40.

Rattray, J. (2016) Affective dimensions of liminality. In R. Land, J. H. F. Meyer and M. T. Flanagan (eds) *Threshold concepts in practice*. Rotterdam: Sense Publishers, pp. 67–76.

Savickas, M. L. and Porfeli, E. J. (2012) Career adapt-abilities scale: construction, reliability, and measurement equivalence across 13 countries. *Journal of Vocational Behavior*, 80(3) pp. 661–673.

Seligman, M. E. P. and Csikszentmihalyi, M. (2000) Positive psychology: an introduction. *American Psychologist*, 55(1) pp. 5–14.

Strathdee, R. (2009) Reputation in the sociology of education. *British Journal of Sociology of Education*, 30(1) pp. 83–96.

Tomlinson, M. and Holmes, L. (2017) *Graduate employability in context*. In M. Tomlinson and L. Holmes (eds) *Graduate employability in context: theory, research and debate*. London: Palgrave Macmillan.

Tomlinson, M. (2012) Graduate employability: a review of conceptual and empirical themes. *Higher Education Policy*, 25(4) pp. 407–431.

Tomlinson, M. (2017a) Introduction: graduate employability in context: charting a complex, contested and multi-faceted policy and research field. In *Graduate employability in context: theory, research and debate*. London: Palgrave Macmillan, pp. 1–40.

Tomlinson, M. (2017b) Forms of graduate capital and their relationship to graduate employability. *Education and Training*, 59(4) pp. 338–352.

Tomlinson, M., Mccafferty, H., Fuge, H. and Wood, K. (2017) Resources and readiness: the graduate capital perspective as a new approach to graduate employability. *Journal of the National Institute for Career Education and Counselling*, 38 pp. 28–35.

Tymon, A. (2013) The student perspective on employability. *Studies in Higher Education*, 38(6) pp. 841–856.

Universities UK (2018) *Solving Future Skills Challenges*. London.

Wheelahan, L. (2015) Not just skills: what a focus on knowledge means for vocational education. *Journal of Curriculum Studies*, 47(6) pp. 750–762.

Williams, S., Dodd, L. J., Steele, C. and Randall, R. (2016) A systematic review of current understandings of employability. *Journal of Education and Work*, 29(8) pp. 877–901.

Wilson, A., Åkerlind, G., Walsh, B., Stevens, B., Turner, B. and Shield, A. (2013) Making 'professionalism' meaningful to students in higher education. *Studies in Higher Education*, 38(8) pp. 1222–1238.

Wilton, N. (2008) Business graduates and management jobs: an employability match made in heaven? *Journal of Education and Work*, 21(2) pp. 143–158.

Wilton, N. (2014) Employability is in the eye of the beholder: employer decision-making in the recruitment of work placement students. *Higher Education, Skills and Work-based Learning*, 4(3) pp. 242–255.

Yorke, M. (2006) Employability in higher education: what it is – what it is not. *Learning & Employability: Series One*. York, UK: Higher Education Academy. www.advance-he.ac.uk/knowledge-hub/employability-higher-education-what-it-what-it-not [Accessed 16/10/21].

6

LinkedIn and Beyond – Social Media and Employability

Gemma Dale

INTRODUCTION

Social media is a broad collective term used to describe a range of online platforms that allow individuals to connect with each other and easily share information such as photographs, links to online content or personal updates. Social media sites vary significantly and include platforms focused primarily on photo or video sharing, some that are community or network based, and others that are created for longer form written posts like blogs. Social media platforms can also be differentiated by whether they are intended for predominantly professional or personal use.

Social media began to emerge from the mid-2000s and whilst particular platforms have risen and fallen in popularity and usage over that time, both the overall number of users and total number of sites have increased continuously. New platforms emerge frequently and some quickly gain new users and momentum. For example TikTok, a short-form video-sharing platform, launched in September 2016. By mid-2018 it had reached half a billion users worldwide, gaining on average 20 million new users each month (Our World in Data, 2019). Social media usage data clearly illustrates that the use of online social networks is now firmly embedded into everyday life for many people.

By April 2021 there were over 4.33 billion social media users globally; a year on year increase of 13.7%, or 521 million users. Users aged 16–25 spend on average each day two hours and 22 minutes on social media (not including accessing other digital services such as music streaming, listening to podcasts, playing games or streaming films or television). The world's top ten visited websites include four social media sites: YouTube, Facebook, Instagram and Twitter. People use social media for a range of reasons; according to users the most popular of which is keeping in touch with friends and family; 22.6% of users also say that they use social networking sites to undertake work-related networking and research. Globally, the most used social media platforms are Facebook, YouTube and WhatsApp (Digital 2021, 2021). Although LinkedIn is not in this list of most used platforms overall, it is perhaps one of the best known and most popular sites for online professional networking, making it important for graduate employability purposes.

Like most organisations today, higher education institutions are regular users of social media, utilising it in student recruitment, communication and engagement activities as well as in teaching and learning. Social media touches every part of the student experience lifecycle (Benson and Morgan, 2014). Universities also use social media to engage with staff and wider communities. For some time now universities have been well aware of the importance of social media for graduate employability, and provide learning and training accordingly (Swan, 2012). It would be rare today to find a university careers or employability service that is not offering at least some basic training on professional platforms such as LinkedIn. In this fast-moving field, however, this alone may not be sufficient to fully prepare and equip students for a graduate hiring market that is increasingly digital. Today's students, graduates and early career professionals need to be aware, accomplished and active with social media if they are to maximise its potential benefits for job seeking and longer-term careers.

SOCIAL MEDIA AND EMPLOYABILITY

The use of social media to enhance employability is an established norm (Meacham and Ross, 2018) and having a LinkedIn profile is now considered to be a social–professional norm (Nikitkov and Sainty, 2014). The use of social media can benefit employability in a number of ways. First, it can connect individuals to existing job opportunities. Graduate recruiters are regular users of social media platforms, advertising specific jobs as well as proactively identifying potentially suitable candidates. It is not unusual for today's undergraduate students to be contacted directly by recruiters making use of LinkedIn's specialist recruitment features. Social media can be a valuable source of information when researching employers in advance of recruitment and selection procedures, and employer review sites such as Glassdoor can provide useful insight into an organisation's culture and working practices.

More broadly, social media can support both job-seeking and career development activities by helping individuals to create an effective online presence and personal brand (a subject that will be discussed later in this chapter), as well as build a professional virtual network that can benefit an entire career. Finally, social media can support continuing professional development through providing access to a wide range of learning content and new perspectives.

Despite its name, social media is far from a merely social activity; it is a key business communication tool and a widely used technology. In a fast-moving digital age, demonstrating competence with current technologies is a necessity rather than an advantage (Meacham and Ross, 2018) or an optional 'nice to have'. Competence with social media has been described as a 'non-negotiable 21st century skill' (Kleppinger and Cain, 2015). English et al. (2021) also highlight the particular relevance of social media for those wishing to pursue a portfolio career and self-employment – both of which have continued to rise in recent years.

Today's students are often described as digital natives (Hewitt, 2019). They have grown up with technology as part of their everyday lives as well as their schooling. However, whilst young people are often proficient in the use of technology in general (and social media specifically) in their personal lives, it does not necessarily follow that they will be able to use these skills effectively in a professional context. Nor will students necessarily fully appreciate the employability benefits of social media (English et al., 2021) or indeed the potential problems or pitfalls. In fact, research suggests that students may underestimate the skills required to be effective professional social media users and be overconfident about their overall online capabilities (Benson and Morgan, 2016). Social media skills should therefore be included in higher education in order to equip students with these important competencies whilst also enhancing their employability. The need for these skills crosses academic disciplines; they are required for every student and not just those wishing to enter specific careers.

Students will benefit from education on social media platforms throughout their education. Training can help students to bridge the gap between personal and informal use of social media and learn how to use it effectively. In particular it can also help them to address issues that research suggests are common, specifically lack of confidence in using social media professionally and a lack of awareness of its application in a workplace context (Sutherland and Ho, 2017). Students can thus be supported to build 'connected capabilities' (English et al., 2021).

Benson et al. (2014) recommend a tiered approach to social media training, with learning taking place across multiple years of study, starting with supporting undergraduates initially to develop basic skills such as setting up a LinkedIn profile. This would progress to much deeper levels of understanding and competence by the final year of study, including the ability of students to use social media to research potential employers and develop awareness of theories on social capital.

Students may believe themselves to already have a good understanding of social media through their personal and informal use of networks; the teaching and learning approach therefore needs to overcome these perceptions and illustrate the important differences between personal and professional use.

Requirements for this type of learning and support requires higher education institutions to have staff who possess the skills themselves to support such learning. Educators require practical and technical skills; they need to be able to competently use those social media platforms that students need to navigate, to provide specific advice on platform suitability and to act as effective social media role models and advocates.

Not only will HE educators need to be sufficiently knowledgeable about social media to deliver the requisite learning, they will also need to keep up to date to ensure they can provide the most relevant advice (Benson and Morgan, 2016), particularly given its fast evolving context. Here too, understanding LinkedIn is not enough; learning and support needs to include a range of social media platforms – those that are popular today and those that are yet to launch. Not all institutions will have this core competency amongst existing faculty and therefore may need to support staff in developing these skills for themselves, or bring in external experts.

PROFESSIONAL NETWORKING

A professional network can be described as a series of relationships or ties linking people together, and which enables them to exchange information, provide practical help and build relationships (Nikitkov and Sainty, 2014). The process of professional networking specifically includes building and maintaining relationships and using them to enhance career success (Wolff and Moser, 2009). Social capital theories have established the many benefits of being well connected and having a wide professional network. From obtaining that first graduate role to a positive correlation between networking and salary growth (Wolff and Moser, 2009) the importance of networking perhaps cannot be overstated. As the cliché tells us 'it isn't what you know, it is who you know'.

From an employability perspective, networking is a behaviour that can be taught (Batistic and Tymon, 2017) and, taking into account its importance for employability, should form part of higher education teaching and learning activities. As well as providing students with important skills, having a well-developed professional network can help graduates to make a smooth transition into employment (English et al., 2021).

Professional networking is of course nothing new; social media simply provides a new and virtual approach to building a network of contacts and relationships. It has been described as a 'networking enabler' (Benson and Morgan, 2014). Personal networks are typically made of both strong ties (those with whom we are generally closest) and weak ties – those with whom we have limited involvement or infrequent contact (Granovetter, 1973). In a social media context we can consider those weaker ties as being people with whom we are connected (on a site such as LinkedIn) or follow or follow us (such as Twitter) but with whom there is little or irregular personal interaction or engagement. Even without active engagement, the very nature of social media means that weak ties will still be able to view and interact with each other's content. Granovetter (1973) considers these weak ties to be important, serving as bridges to other people – or job and career opportunities. A key characteristic of LinkedIn is that both companies and individuals use it to share job opportunities. A larger number of connections therefore, even if they are predominantly weak ties, may well increase the likelihood of a user identifying a new career opportunity. Professional networking has always been a valuable tool for finding jobs; it is well known that not all job opportunities are advertised through traditional channels and are instead fulfilled through personal connections, recommendations or word of mouth. Social media itself is often described casually as 'word of mouth on steroids'.

Social media networking provides one additional and important benefit over more traditional forms of networking: its potential to support geographically broad networks. It is relatively simple when using social media to build connections in any location – very different from the face-to-face networking events of the pre-social media age.

PERSONAL BRAND

Social media provides an opportunity to develop an online personal brand. Leading business and management writer Tom Peters first introduced the idea of personal branding in the late 1990s; he argued that individuals should take lessons from corporate marketing, defining their own unique qualities and characteristics and then promoting these accordingly, focusing on building personal visibility. He describes this process as deciding 'what I want to be famous for' (Peters, 1997). Although developed well before the rise of social media, his ideas are now arguably easier to implement in a digital age. Personal branding has also been defined as the process through which individuals stand out from the crowd by developing their unique value proposition (another familiar marketing term) which is then shared to build credibility and reputation (Schawbel, 2009). Helping students and graduates to craft their own online personal brand, introducing them first to the concept but then also the practical actions that will shape it, can form part of the overall approach to developing social media skills in higher education. It can, however, take time for students to determine and then adopt their professional identity (English et al., 2021).

Social media platforms allow professionals to proactively craft and shape their public image for the purposes of benefiting their careers. Indeed failing to have a digital identity may be problematic in itself, potentially signalling a lack of competence with digital communication (Kleppinger and Cain, 2015). Personal branding activity through social media can be a long-term game; building and maintaining an online profile will take ongoing time and effort, as will learning new tools and technologies (Harris and Rae, 2011). It can however be a worthwhile investment; effective personal branding can be a key differentiator in terms of career progression (Harris and Rae, 2011). Part of personal branding will inevitably involve sharing one's achievements and successes. Doing so in an appropriate way is also a learned skill.

Peters (1997) also popularised the idea of the personal 'pitch', another term borrowed from corporate marketing. The term elevator pitch is now in common use to describe a short personal introduction to an individual, one that could be delivered in the time it takes to travel from one floor to another in an elevator. Elevator pitches can be used in any networking situation (or indeed in a job interview process); in a face-to-face environment they are delivered verbally and in person whereas on social media platforms they are typically replicated digitally through a profile or 'about' section. Whether physical or digital, this brief form of introduction is likely to be the first piece of information shared about the individual in question.

Many social media platforms limit the length of biography or 'about' sections. Typical advice for a verbal elevator pitch is to keep it to less than two minutes or 100 words; in the digital sphere it may need to be fewer than 160 characters. Brevity, clarity and creativity are all important when crafting the social media elevator pitch, as social media and marketing specialists Hootsuite (2019) say in their guidance: 'bios matter'. They also recommend including an element of personality and humble self-promotion. A well-written social media elevator pitch will support personal brand, provide useful information about the individual and help to create that crucial first impression. As a well-crafted and in-person elevator pitch will encourage further conversation, its digital comparator will encourage further interaction with the social media profile.

LinkedIn

LinkedIn is a professional social media platform that first launched in 2003. It describes itself as the world's largest professional network with 756 million members in more than 200 countries. LinkedIn state that their mission is to connect the world's professionals to make them more productive and successful (LinkedIn, 2021). Like many platforms it offers a free basic model with additional, optional paid-for services for both businesses and individuals. LinkedIn is now the standard way to build personal networks (Peterson and Dover, 2014). The site allows individuals to create a personal profile page, detailing their career, education and accomplishments. Users can post short updates and links or write and publish long-form posts akin to blogs. Individuals have choice over how much information they share in their personal profile, and with whom they share it, although LinkedIn's algorithms favour the most complete profiles. LinkedIn is essentially an online CV or resume, detailing education, employment history, skills and accomplishments.

As well as a professional networking site, LinkedIn operates as a recruitment platform. Organisations can pay to post job opportunities on the site, or even create whole career sites within LinkedIn, providing company and vacancy information. Additional functionality can also be purchased that allows recruiters to have greater access to profiles, supporting headhunting and direct approaches. As well as formal recruitment advertising, members often organically share job vacancies they are personally aware of, and users can opt to include an 'open to work' badge on their profile to highlight that they welcome information about new opportunities. LinkedIn state that three people are hired every minute on the site with 40 million people using it each week to search for work (LinkedIn, 2021). It is therefore a critical space for most professionals, and students and graduates in particular, providing not only opportunities to take part in professional networking but also vital links to recruiters and jobs.

The importance of having a LinkedIn profile is recognised by students, graduates and career services departments. Many universities will include training or resources on developing an effective professional LinkedIn profile. However, it is far from the only platform that will support graduate employability and where individuals can showcase their talent and personal brand to maximum employment opportunities and career development.

Beyond LinkedIn

As discussed, having a complete and active LinkedIn profile is arguably a minimum criterion for today's students and early career professionals. Individuals can, however, go further in their social media use, becoming original content creators on relevant platforms (Hewitt, 2019). There is no one other social media platform that a student or graduate should adopt; different platforms have different audiences and demographics, and lend themselves to creating and sharing different types of content. What is the 'best' platform for a student or graduate to use will therefore depend on the industry and desired career path, as well as aims and objectives for use. For example, a student undertaking a creative degree seeking a career in design may wish to focus efforts on platforms that can visually showcase their work such as (currently) Instagram or Pinterest. A law student or graduate may find that joining the active legal community on Twitter where they can follow and even engage directly with other lawyers an effective use of their time. However, what might be determined as the most appropriate platform currently may change over time, and the speed of social media evolution is such that decisions should be regularly reviewed. Any advice provided to students or graduates will be time-bound and possibly quickly out of date. Whatever the platform choice, using one or two forms of social media efficiently and actively will generally be more effective than using multiple platforms intermittently or poorly. Those wishing to use social media professionally and strategically are therefore advised to focus on which platform will deliver the most value for their specific goals and to review current usage and demographic data prior to decision making.

Blogging

Unlike websites, blogs are interactive, allowing readers to like and comment on content. Informal in tone, posts are usually short, focusing on one key message or theme. Blogs are relatively simple and free to set up (some sites have additional, paid for services that can enhance the appearance and experience of the site), and content can be easily shared across other social media platforms such as Twitter or LinkedIn. Popular blogging platforms include WordPress, Tumbler and Medium.

There are numerous potential career benefits that can be gained from blogging. Setting up a blog and writing regularly can help to build digital skills, desirable for many organisations. Blog writing can also improve written communication and creativity. For relevant roles, a well-written blog can act as a showcase for skills and talent as well as highlight enthusiasm for a subject or profession. Blog posts also provide content to share on other sites such as LinkedIn, enhancing the blogger's profile there too.

Blogs can support the enhancement of personal brand, as well as contribute to the building of professional networks. They can position bloggers as knowledgeable in their specialist areas (Harris and Rae, 2011), or even as thought leaders.

Writing blog posts demands a time investment; good blogs are updated regularly with fresh and interesting content. There are millions of blogs, and standing out can be difficult. However, well-written blogs can both attract an audience, thereby building more personal connections and expanding further a professional network, as well as being a valuable addition to a CV or resume (Schwabel, 2009). A blog can help to differentiate a job applicant from other candidates, helping an application to stand out from others – a useful attribute in a crowded graduate candidate market.

Twitter

Twitter is a platform based on short form posts, where users can share (or tweet) short messages (of no more than 280 characters). Users can include a photograph and short 'bio' that also allows for links to other sites such as a blog or LinkedIn profile. The platform is based on people following each other where they can then view and share each other's content. Posts (or tweets) can include text, images and video as well as links to other online content.

From a professional point of view Twitter can perhaps best be thought of as a cross-over platform; it can be and is used both professionally and personally, and unlike LinkedIn which is predominantly used by professionals sharing business-related content, many users share content from both spheres of their life. Content is often curated via the use of hashtags. It is perhaps a more social form of social network than those purely professional sites, based on ease of interaction and supporting 'real time' conversation.

Twitter is used by organisations to share job opportunities and for marketing purposes, but is also used for professional networking, sharing output from conferences and events and 'Twitter Chats' where professionals join together online at specified times to discuss professional issues and questions. It is relatively simple to search for and follow relevant professions and hashtags and also make professional content easy to find. Twitter allows users to access a broad range of content in one feed from a job vacancy to breaking news. This can help users keep up to date with relevant information and current trends quickly and easily. Very few businesses today do not have a Twitter feed, so for the job seeker it can present a rich stream of information about a particular organisation and the people that work for it.

As with other social media platforms, Twitter can provide a place where professionals can build their network through connecting with others, showcase their skills and abilities and position personal brand.

Instagram

Instagram is a popular image-sharing site that supports photographs and video content. It also provides for the sharing of 'stories', short videos of up to 15 seconds that last on a user's site for just 24 hours.

Like many other social media platforms it is based on individuals following each other in order to view their content. Accounts can be private (restricted to viewers approved by the user) or public and as such visible to anyone. The site is popular with celebrities and influencers, and has over 1 billion users globally. It therefore has the potential to support personal branding and employability. Many organisations and brands have Instagram accounts, making it another useful source of information when researching potential employers.

Although there are fewer opportunities to build connections and have real-time dialogue on Instagram when compared with sites such as LinkedIn and Twitter it can be a useful place to showcase relevant talents. Any creative career, especially those with a visual output or end product such as photography, art or design can benefit from an Instagram account. The overall account can act as a visual CV or resume. A well curated Instagram account can provide content to share across other social media platforms, as well as enhance a traditional CV or resume.

Enterprise Social Networks

Social media platforms internal to organisations (with access restricted to its own employees) are also common in many businesses today. These platforms are referred to as Enterprise Social Networks and are usually dedicated to connecting colleagues and sharing internal communications. Yammer and Workplace are two examples of these platforms. Functionality and terminology is generally similar to more familiar social media sites (Workplace is owned by Facebook). Joining and actively participating in these platforms can help employees, especially new entrants, build internal relationships and contribute to personal branding efforts.

Employee participation in enterprise social networks can increase the visibility of individuals, their communications and outputs of their work. The benefits of this visibility extend beyond the individual; others can view these communications, in real-time or later, providing the opportunity to learn from them (Leonardi et al., 2013). Enterprise social networks can also act as what Leonardi et al. describe as a 'social lubricant', providing insights into what other people are doing, making it easy to initiate new connections and maintain established ones. Such networks are ultimately new ways to connect people within organisations, making them essential tools for early career professionals and a key part of any personal social media strategy.

SOCIAL MEDIA PROBLEMS AND PITFALLS

Stories of social media misuse resulting in negative career implications are not unusual. Neither too are tales of disciplinary action or even dismissal. Job applicants can be similarly impacted; a survey by website CareerBuilder found that 70% of employers use social networking sites to research candidates during the recruitment process and more than half of respondents had found content that resulted in them not making an offer of employment. Such content included sharing inappropriate information or photographs, evidence of them drinking or using drugs or making discriminatory posts (CareerBuilder, 2018).

Successful management of personal brand or digital footprint (the collective available information held about an individual online) must include minimising the impact of negative material that might be online or available via social media platforms (Harris and Rae, 2011). Active management of privacy settings, removal of content that may conflict with desired personal brand, and regular checks via search engines are simple steps that any individual can take to manage their online identity. Careers services or employability tutors should consider educating students on these issues; effective social media use cannot end with setting up LinkedIn profiles but must also include avoiding some of the potential problems that can arise from ill-considered use.

Some professional associations issue their own guidance on using social media. Members (or potential future members) of these organisations or associations should familiarise themselves with any such requirements to ensure that there is no inadvertent breach of rules.

SUCCESSFUL PROFESSIONAL SOCIAL MEDIA USE

As well as avoiding problems and pitfalls on social media, there are a number of steps that users can take to ensure that use of chosen platforms is successful, both in terms of personal branding, building a professional network and connecting with job opportunities. Advice on effective use is plentiful, including through the platforms themselves.

In terms of employability, the specific social media platform itself does matter; perhaps unsurprisingly research suggests that being present and undertaking regular activity on LinkedIn has strong and consistent associations with professional success. Sites such as Twitter and Facebook, however, have been found to have little impact on career prospects, and in the case of poor or inappropriate use may even adversely affect success (Nikitkov and Sainty, 2014). This research, however, in social media terms at least, is potentially now dated and more research into professional use of different platforms is now overdue.

Merely signing up to a social media site and establishing a profile is unlikely to lead to success. Regular activity on the chosen platform is essential. Unfortunately research suggests that after joining professional social networks and initial activity there is often a decline in platform use by undergraduates, potentially because of unrealistic expectations or lack of ability to use professional sites to best effect (Benson et al., 2014).

Authenticity in social media activity is seen as critical; it helps to build trust and reputation (Harris and Rae, 2011). So too is consistency, aiming for a coherent presentation across all professionally used social media platforms. This has been described as 'brand fluidity' which can help create a strong personal impression (Kelly, 2016).

Consideration should be given to the specific development needs of undergraduate students to ensure that they can attain success. Sutherland and Ho (2017) asked students to consider the topics that they wanted to see included in social media pedagogy. Respondents identified learning needs in respect of developing personal brand, technical skills, professional networking and online safety. Benson and Morgan (2016) propose a number of competencies that graduates need in order to use social media networks to maximise their social capital. These include general communication skills, technical efficacy, ethics of social media use (including responsible content posting) and reputation management. It is the job of employability educators and higher education institutions to provide these critical skills for current and future students. In this ever changing field however, we should be mindful that needs will change too, and as such we may need to undertake regular dialogue with students to determine their most up to date learning needs.

Taking into account these factors for success, how best can these ideas be translated into practical, everyday actions for individuals?

PRACTICAL ACTIONS

Undergraduates and early career professionals can take a number of actions to enhance their use of professional social media, on LinkedIn and beyond. The guidance presented here is generic rather than platform specific, and these proposed 'rules' can apply to all forms of social media for professional use. These actions are categorised under three headings; aware, accomplished and active.

Aware

Awareness of social media refers firstly to its importance professionally, but also awareness of specific platforms and which are the most appropriate for the individual's aims and goals. Actions on social media need to be conscious and deliberate and sometimes even strategic. In this context, therefore, awareness also refers to being aware of one's own professional image and personal brand, and how any given post, update or action on social media can enhance or detract from it. Posting on social media should have purpose. Finally, users should be aware of their audience and give consideration to both building that audience (and network) and tailoring messages accordingly.

Accomplished

To be an accomplished user of social media, professionals need to be able to effectively use their chosen social media platforms. This includes understanding the functionality of the platform, its terminology and use etiquette which can vary from site to site. On LinkedIn for example, it is considered polite to send a brief note with a connection request introducing oneself or explaining the purpose of the request. Different platforms also have varying levels of informality; these can be learned either through formal training or simply by what is sometimes known as 'lurking' (watching and consuming content rather than actively posting or commenting) to learn from the activities of others.

Active

As already discussed, merely having a presence on a social media site or sites is not enough on its own to generate any real professional or career benefits.

Professional networks need to be actively developed and cultivated (English et al., 2021). Social media profiles and platforms also need to be in regular use. Those who wish to demonstrate their competence and build valuable connections need to post regularly, engage in discussions, chats or groups, share their accomplishments and make proactive connection requests or follow others depending on the particular platform. Until social media use becomes an established habit or users reach a level of competence, this may require deliberate time set aside on a weekly or even daily basis. Curating a strong personal brand will require investment and regular engagement with the platform itself and other users within it. What is considered active is relative to the platform. On a blog, weekly or bi-weekly may be sufficient. On Twitter, daily activity is more typical as the site is faster and content shorter to consume.

In addition to these rules, users of social media for professional purposes may also wish to consider some or all of the following:

- Determining the most appropriate platforms for their specific career aims and goals.
- Reviewing privacy settings and making informed decisions about access to content.
- Clearly differentiating between personal and private social media, and enabling privacy settings accordingly.
- Presenting a consistent brand image (including photograph and biography) across all platforms used for professional purposes.

CONCLUSION

Effective use of social media is a key skill for business and professional success at all stages of a career. Higher education institutions therefore need to include social media skills in employability programmes in order to ensure students and graduates build these critical skills, both to meet the immediate challenge of securing a first postgraduate role or internship, but also for longer term career success and development. Successful networking behaviour can be taught through a range of approaches from standalone, extracurricular activities through to embedding the development of these skills into the curriculum (Batistic and Tymon, 2017).

Such skills need to go beyond merely practical sessions to help students in establishing a LinkedIn profile, but must also build awareness and appreciation of the importance of professional networks. Students must also gain a broader understanding of social media as a tool for communication and career success and personal development, as well as how to avoid any negative career implications of social media use. To enable the provision of this development, higher education institutions will also need to ensure that they have the internal skills to support delivery. Social media training should not be an add-on to careers education, a 'nice to have', or delivered just to relevant degree programmes such as marketing or communication, but a central element within employability training and development for all students and courses, in order to equip them for the future of work. The very nature of social media means that it will be a continually evolving communication medium. New platforms will emerge and others will fade away. Established sites will also continue to evolve their features and how they are used. The demographics of platform users will also shift over time. Those who therefore wish to use professional networking sites to support professional success and career development will need to keep skills current and potentially consider using a range of social media sites over the course of their careers. Social media use is a lifelong learning requirement.

More research is required into the outcomes of different forms of social media to establish their impact upon career success. In particular, research is needed into the use of a variety of different platforms including those that have emerged in recent years, including those that might not be typically seen as 'professional' social media sites. In this fast moving and ever evolving field, it is to be expected that the research may always be somewhat behind the practice. Further research into specific learning activities and their outcomes would also benefit our understanding of how students and graduates can be supported in developing knowledge and skills.

REFERENCES

Batistic, S. and Tymon, A. (2017) 'Networking behaviour, graduate employability: a social capital perspective', *Education and Training*, 59(4), 374–288.

Benson, V. and Morgan, S. (2014) *Cutting edge technologies and social media in higher education*. Hershey, US: IGI Global.

Benson, V. and Morgan, S. (2016) 'Social university challenge: constructing pragmatic competencies for social networking', *British Journal of Educational Technology*, 47(3), 465–473.

Benson, V., Morgan, S. and Filippaios, F. (2014) 'Social media management: social media and employability skills gap', *Computers in Human Behaviour*, 30, 519–525.

CareerBuilder (2018) *'More than half of employers have found content on social media that caused them NOT to hire a candidate'*, [Accessed 17 June 2021] http://press.careerbuilder.com/2018-08-09-More-Than-Half-of-Employers-Have-Found-Content-on-Social-Media-That-Caused-Them-NOT-to-Hire-a-Candidate-According-to-Recent-CareerBuilder-Survey

Digital 2021 April Global Statshot Report (2021) [Accessed 30 May 2021] https://hootsuite.widen.net/s/xlbzrttkxl/digital2021_aprilstatshot_report_en

English, P., de Villiers Scheepers, M. J., Fleischman, D., Burgess, J. and Crimmins, G. (2021) 'Developing professional networks: the missing link to graduate employability', *Education and Training*, 63(4), 647–661.

Granovetter, M. (1973) 'The strength of weak ties', *American Journal of Sociology*, 78, 1360–1380.

Harris, L. and Rae, A. (2011) 'Building a personal brand through social networking', *Journal of Business Strategy*, 32(5), 14–21.

Hewitt, M. (2019) 'Social media: employability skills for the 21st century', *Techniques Magazine* [Accessed 17 June 2021] http://digital.graphcompubs.com/ publication/?i=607763&p=8&pp=1&view=issueViewer

Hootsuite (2019) *'How to write a good Twitter bio: tips, ideas, and examples'* [Accessed 19 July 2021] https://blog.hootsuite.com/twitter-bio-ideas/

Kelly, M. (2016) *Social media for your student and graduate job search.* London: Palgrave.

Kleppinger, C. and Cain, J. (2015) 'Personal digital branding as a professional asset in the digital age', *American Journal of Pharmaceutical Education*, 79(6) Article 79.

Leonardi, P., Huysman, M. and Steinfeld, C. (2013) 'Enterprise social media: definition, history, and prospects for the study of social technologies in organizations', *Journal of Computer-Mediated Communication*, 19, 1–19.

LinkedIn (2021) *'About LinkedIn'* [Accessed 30 May 2021] https://about.linkedin.com/#:~:text=About%20LinkedIn&text=Welcome%20to%20LinkedIn%2C%20the%20world's,200%20countries%20and%20territories%20worldwide.

Meacham, S. and Ross, M. (2018) *'Development of social media skills to enhance employability'* [Accessed 17 June 2021] www.researchgate.net/publication/275769489_Development_of_Social_Media_Skills_to_Enhance_Employability

Nikitkov, A. and Sainty, B. (2014) 'The role of social media in influencing career success' *International Journal of Accounting and Information Management*, 22(4), 273–294.

Our World in Data (2019) *'The rise of social media* [Accessed 30 May 2021] https://ourworldindata.org/rise-of-social-media

Peters, T. (1997) 'The brand called you', *Fast Company* [Accessed 17 June 2021] www.fastcompany.com/28905/brand-called-you

Peterson, R. and Dover, H. (2014) 'Building student networks with LinkedIn: the potential for connections, internships and jobs', *Marketing Education Review*, 24(1),15–40.

Swan, G. (2012) 'Using social media to boost student employability', *The Guardian* [Accessed 17 June 2021] www.theguardian.com/higher-education-network/blog/2012/ jun/18/social-media-to-boost-student-employability]

Schawbel, D. (2009) *'Me 2.0, build a powerful brand to achieve career success'*, Kaplan Publishing, New York.

Sutherland, K. and Ho, S. (2017) 'Undergraduate perceptions of social media proficiency and graduate employability', *Higher Education Skills and Work-Based Learning*, 7(3), 261–274.

Wolff, H., and Moser, K. (2009) 'Effects of networking on career success: a longitudinal study', *Applied Psychology*, 94, 196–206.

7

Transitions from Education to Work: Impacts on Perceived Employability in Tourism and Hospitality

Marília Durão, Carlos Costa, Maria João Carneiro and Mónica Segovia-Pérez

INTRODUCTION

The tourism and hospitality (T&H) industry has a significant and widely known multiplier effect on employment. But as it is difficult to find structured careers opportunities in which individuals are given genuine prospects of career development and growth, one of the major challenges for the industry is to retain highly educated and skilled employees (Kusluvan, 2003; Ladkin and Kichuk, 2017). Despite its reputation of precarious working conditions and high turnover rates, the T&H industry has become a growing career choice. The role of higher education in meeting the needs of both the industry and the graduates has been receiving growing attention and it is not an exclusive concern of this occupational field (Tomlinson, 2012). The provision of T&H-dedicated higher education has grown significantly in recent years in Portugal, both fuelling and being fuelled by a growing interest of young students in this professional area. Yet little is known of the circumstances of the graduates from these programmes.

Higher education institutions (HEI) play a pivotal role in the training and skills development of future T&H managers, being expected to endow students with fundamental skills and prepare them for a successful career in various segments of the T&H industry. Hence, HEIs have been increasingly pressured to produce both marketable and market-ready graduates (Ruhanen, 2005; Barron and Ali-Knight, 2017). Marketability, in the sense that individuals' job security is anchored to their skill portfolio and employability, rather than to an organisation, is precisely at the core of 'new' career models such as boundary-less careers (McGuire, 2014). Internships, in particular, have the general goal of providing a positive learning experience that supplements classroom learning, hence helping students in their transition to the labour market (Calvo, 2011).

This study sets out to explore and gain a better understanding of the education-to-work transition process in the T&H field, focusing on the academic paths and practical learning experiences of highly qualified individuals. To this end, perceptions on the extent to which these individuals feel prepared for a working life in the T&H industry, the importance of on-the-job experience as an essential part of their curricula, and the fundamental skill set for graduates' employability and successful career in the industry, are explored. In the face of globally significant changes in labour markets and in mainstream employment relations, an improved understanding of the factors underpinning and influencing the T&H industry's potential for attracting and retaining highly qualified individuals is critical to these same graduates, to HEI offering T&H programmes, and to the T&H industry alike. The findings should assist both educators and employers in understanding how to better prepare graduates for a smooth transition into the labour market and to make full use of their potential upon graduation.

LITERATURE REVIEW

Higher Level Qualifications in T&H

The growing provision of T&H degree courses have been a route for qualification and professionalisation (King et al., 2003), and there is evidence to suggest that many people working in the industry are now highly educated (Szivas et al., 2003; González et al., 2016). However, there is still a significant predominance of T&H workers with low academic qualifications, which is related to the high availability of low-skilled jobs that require little or no formal training and few conceptual or knowledge-driven attributes, although many tourism jobs require a combination of soft and technical skills, as well as higher level skills. Due to the perception of hospitality work as unskilled, the industry poses low entry barriers, despite a quarter of service positions being estimated to be supervisory or skilled occupations at managerial, professional or technical level (ILO, 2010; Stacey, 2015). However, Brien et al. (2017) interestingly note that defining hotel jobs as low-skilled may be beneficial for hotels to justify the low levels of pay, when in reality low skills are not what hotels are looking for in prospective employees.

Furthermore, some employers are sceptical about formal qualifications, as they do not perceive them as a guarantee of good performance or fit to the job from the new employee, and consider vocation, flexibility, mobility, work experience and operational competencies more relevant than academic achievements (Kusluvan, 2003; Ayres, 2006; Nachmias et al., 2017). It is frequently assumed that the knowledge and skills required to work in T&H can be easily learned by on-the-job training (Kusluvan, 2003; ILO, 2010; Stacey, 2015). This view is enhanced by the fact that many hospitality managers do not have appropriate qualifications themselves and fail to meet the demands of managerial work, perpetuating an 'amateur' management style (Guerrier and Deery, 1998).

Qualification is pivotal to keep employees competitive in a continuously changing economic environment and to ensure the standard of service quality that is delivered to customers. Skills development aims to prepare graduates for future job responsibilities through the acquisition of new competencies, knowledge, experiences and attitudes. The role of higher education in meeting the needs of both the industry and the graduates has been receiving growing attention (Correia et al., 2017; Swarbrooke and Gibson, 2017; Thompson et al., 2017). Curriculum design is often the outcome of a 'triangular relationship between students, industry and the academy, which results in a strong vocational (and therefore practical) focus in hospitality programmes' (Thompson et al., 2017: 19). Curricula must reflect students' expectations and the industry needs, providing the skills and knowledge that is needed to 'fit' hospitality organisations, and preparing both operationally skilled and business-oriented graduates. Hospitality programmes are also expected to transmit fundamental cultural traits of the industry, so students can be more closely aligned with work in firms that comply with these characteristics (Dawson, 2014).

Expectations in Education-to-Work Transition

T&H is an educational popular choice, with students exhibiting high enthusiastic and high expectations about their future work opportunities. However, many graduates seem to become quickly disillusioned with this field of employment, therefore contributing to the high turnover rates in the industry (Iverson and Deery, 1997). Several researchers suggested the discrepancy between what students and newcomers expect and what they experience once in the job, is one of the main reasons why people leave the T&H industry; sometimes employees leave if they don't experience at a high enough level factors which they consider important (Kusluvan and Kusluvan, 2000; Dewar et al., 2002; Blomme et al., 2009).

Previous research has examined attitudes towards careers in the hospitality industry and found that students' perceptions and expectations of careers and working conditions in the hospitality industry might not be very clear, therefore reporting not being willing to remain in the industry. Expectations were, therefore, considered significantly relevant for career choice (Richardson, 2009). But while some authors (Kusluvan and Kusluvan, 2000) suggest that realistic expectations may influence hospitality graduates to remain in the T&H industry, others (Dickerson, 2009; Lu and Adler, 2009) found that even when students are provided with more realistic expectations and have some work experience, they might also form negative perceptions of the industry.

Real experiences of what a certain job is like, such as work simulations, work tours or internships, can help individuals in forming more realistic pre-employment expectations about what type of job environment they may be entering. Prior and accurate information on the nature of the job, expected roles, type of rewards that one can possibly receive in exchange of his/her participation, the likelihood of achieving success and the personality profile required thereof, and on the positive and negative aspects of the job, is one of the ways of creating realistic job previews (Wanous et al., 1992; Dickerson, 2009). Internships are perceived as critical experiences in influencing students' decisions to join the T&H workforce (Robinson et al., 2016; Correia et al., 2017).

PRACTICAL LEARNING EXPERIENCES

Learning experiences influence people's career exploration and career development process (Lent et al., 2006). Taking on-the-job training, working face-to-face with customers, and taking on a variety of tasks a valuable way to complement classroom learning. Higher education internships represent an active learning experience which is seen as a valuable route to enter the labour market. Through internships, students can develop and apply the skills, theories and concepts learned in their study programmes, as well as gaining industry-specific knowledge and competencies, hence enhancing their employability.

The value of internships is particularly relevant in a dynamic and multidisciplinary industry such as T&H, which requires a workforce with a wide variety of skills. Within-degree internships are, precisely, one strategy for embedding active, on-the-job learning experience into the curriculum, and this is an important feature of most T&H degrees (Correia et al., 2017; Farmaki, 2018).

Prior knowledge of the hospitality industry via on-the-job experience is interpreted as a warranty of the training, skills and abilities of new entrants, and as an indication of work readiness, especially considering that although dependent on organisational size and structure, the hospitality industry is often fast paced and there may not be a lot of time devoted to training of new entrants. As interviews do not allow for candidates to demonstrate their abilities, nor allow employers to gather enough information regarding an applicant's potential performance, past work experience becomes the requisite (Walsh et al., 2011). Although an entry-level job equates to a job that requires basic skills and little job experience (such as that obtained during an internship), hence being suited for recent graduates who are initiating their careers in the industry, T&H companies typically seek work readiness among graduates in entry-level positions (Jiang and Alexakis, 2017).

RESEARCH METHODOLOGY

This study draws upon qualitative research carried out in the scope of a doctoral thesis. A constructivist–interpretivist stance with a critical orientation was adopted and, following the researcher's reflexivity, data collection was based on an interactive and co-operative researcher–participant relationship. In-depth semi-structured interviews were carried out with a total of 56 informants (52% female and 48% male; mean age 32), with different job positions in the Portuguese hotel sector, at different career stages:

- 30 employees, T&H graduates currently employed in the industry,
- 14 leavers, T&H graduates formerly employed in the industry, who voluntarily left their job, with the deliberate intention of getting a job in a different occupational field, and
- 12 newcomers, students majoring in T&H-related degrees having first contact with hospitality work (internship) with potential to become future workers in the industry.

Data collection took place between November 2018 and June 2019. Interviews, conducted either in person or by web conferencing, provided an opportunity to explore participants' views on their career initiation, as informed by their personal expectations, experiences and conceptions. Data analysis was carried out alongside data collection and an interim analysis informed adaptation of the topic guide and ongoing participant selection. When no new insights emerged from the analysis of an additional case, data saturation/informational redundancy was deemed achieved (Sandelowski, 1995; Given, 2008). An adapted thematic analysis, combined with narrative elements (Braun and Clarke, 2006; Ayres, 2008; Carvalho, 2017), was used to offer new or deeper explanations about the phenomenon being studied. Data was analysed with the assistance of the qualitative data analysis software NVivo 12.

SELECTION AND PROFILE OF RESEARCH PARTICIPANTS

Research participants were selected purposively. As for the main criterion for choosing the participants, all interviewees held a higher education degree in the T&H field or, in the case of newcomers, were close to graduation and completion of their degrees.

Within the hospitality industry, participants were chosen from the same occupational field: the hotel sector. Hotels were chosen as the research setting due to the pivotal role that accommodation plays within the T&H industry in terms of job creation. Because the hotel sector presents one of the most structured employment sectors in terms of a hierarchy, it made it easier to trace career patterns (Ladkin and Kichuk, 2017).

Table 7.1 Main characteristics of the study's informants

Employees	Leavers	Newcomers
43% female and 47% male Mean age: 33 80% Millennials Mean years in the industry: 10 53% in operational positions 30% in top management	79% female and 21% male Mean age: 38 57% Gen Xers Mean years in the industry: 7 Mean years out of the industry: 7 14% in operational positions 50% in top management	42% female and 58% male Mean age: 22 100% Millennials Mean number of internship experiences: 2 Mean duration of internships: 6 months

Source: The authors.

The heterogeneity of the employees and leavers groups was also enhanced by the inclusion of both back and front-of-house staff in the sample, as well as a variety of functional levels (staff/operational, supervisory and managerial) and job positions (up to 15 different positions). Newcomers completed from one to four different internships over their higher education programme, which were hosted by up to six different departments and ranged from 2 to 15 months in length. A short profile of each group of respondents is outlined in Table 7.1.

FINDINGS

Preparedness for the Labour Market

For half of the research participants, the choice of T&H as a study programme and anticipated long-term career in the industry was highly motivated by the promising employability prospects that the industry offers. As employability and marketability constitute important attributes of 'new' career models such as boundary-less careers (McGuire, 2014), research participants were asked to comment on the level of educational preparation that they expected and received for their future careers in T&H.

A significant number of interviewees (n=12) believed they had received adequate preparation for their working lives in the industry, emphasising several positive aspects of their academic programmes. Their degrees were described as interesting and well-structured (despite some topics being approached quite superficially), comprising demanding assignments (including field work, industry-applied assignments) and contact with industry players (fostering networking), providing the necessary theoretical fundamentals, and contributing to their personal growth and development. Some interviewees also mentioned that nowadays students are given many opportunities to improve their resumes, for example, by attending lectures with invited speakers, attending events and trade fairs, doing extracurricular internships, visiting local T&H companies, or by doing a study or a placement period in another country with Erasmus programmes. References were also made to the important role educators play in shaping students' expectations and competencies for the sector, as many research participants considered that being made aware of the specificities of the industry was an important requirement in higher education.

From a less positive perspective, a second set of research participants (n=16) considered their study programmes to have inadequately or insufficiently prepared them for the labour market, lacking sufficient practical knowledge and experiential learning. Several interviewees mentioned that although the theoretical component was valuable, the practical component was clearly insufficient. This divide between academic knowledge and practical skills is a persistent condition and challenge in T&H management education (Ruhanen, 2005; Thompson et al., 2017). For this reason, when starting their internships, many of them felt lost and unprepared. Coinciding with findings from previous research, some interviewees questioned the validity of some subjects/courses which they did not perceive as relevant for their future jobs in the industry (Mooney and Jameson, 2018). It should be noted that most of the participants in this study opted for a generalist degree, which is aimed at widening students' understanding of the various facets of the tourism sector, thus offering them a more comprehensive picture and a wider range of employment prospects (not limited to the hotel industry). A higher proportion of research participants had also graduated in polytechnic institutions (rather than universities).

Another interesting topic that stood out from participants' interviews was that most T&H degrees, and very likely most of the higher education degrees, do not foresee any course content directed to prepare future graduates for their roles as workers. Graduates are, therefore, left to deal with issues such as work contracts, employment legislation, collective bargaining, employment categories, wage policy or tax-related issues, solely when first engaging with the labour market, with little advice and guidance. Most T&H degrees include some type of legislation-related courses, which focus exclusively on implementation and classification of hotels. One of the leavers exemplified such limitations when explaining that it was only in her first job that she first saw a work contract or payslip. This issue, which is also related to broader themes such as the lack of transparency in exchange relationships or job security, is indicative that many graduates are not fully conscious and well-informed of their legal duties and rights as future workers, which puts them in a vulnerable position, especially in their first employment relations.

Internships and Learning Experiences

Participants' references to on-the-job training are also closely related to the role, form and content of curricular internships which is, for most undergraduates, a first contact with the labour market. Most of the study programmes in HEI include at least one mandatory internship experience, while some even have a one-per-year ratio. Ten of the 12 newcomers enrolled in curricular internships and five opted for extracurricular programmes to broaden their experience and build a stronger resume.

Perceptions and attitudes built on direct, first-hand experiences can give students a stronger and more realistic view of the industry, playing a decisive role in shaping their future behaviour. For five research participants who were undecided about their career choice, the internship was critical in confirming their orientation towards hospitality, hence improving their perceptions of occupational fit. This may positively contribute to more realistic expectations, more informed career choices, and more effective job search behaviours. Previous research has found that students who have some type of work experience in the industry before graduating hold more realistic expectations. These are also more likely to lead to negative perceptions of the industry (Kusluvan and Kusluvan, 2000; Richardson, 2009). Most of the research participants who actively embraced these experimental learning opportunities, even by voluntarily enrolling in extracurricular internships, considered that they had been given a clearer view of the different job positions and functional departments they would like to (or not) work in, in the future. For one of the newcomers, her internship had contributed to a redefinition of career goals; her initial aspirations of becoming a food and beverage manager were replaced by a resolute decision not to look for a job in this functional area.

Overall average duration of newcomers' internships was six months. Some newcomers did more than one internship during their degree, but with an average duration of only three months. Some organisations do not consider this time frame for a more complete and efficient cross-training programme, which may explain why so few newcomers enrolled in this type of internship. The duration of the internships is deemed a determinant issue in employers' perceptions of undergraduates' worth as future professionals. Considering that all internships have (or should have) an integration phase, if the internship is too short, when the trainee is ready to independently perform tasks, the training period is over. Short internships do not allow organisations to get a return on the investment in training and staff time, neither do they provide trainees with a meaningful experience (Calvo, 2011). The longer the internship, the higher the adaptability to a new job will be, which may positively impact the recognition of the trainees' competencies. Short-term, it may also convey to companies the idea that the trainee does not have enough mastery of the role, and as such, will be solely assigned to operational roles.

Based on participants' reports, the food and beverage (F&B) department hosted most of the trainees. Both in F&B and in the front-of-house departments, all the trainees were assigned specific tasks, but none were offered the possibility of accompanying the respective manager/supervisor in his/her daily routine. For almost all the newcomers in this study, internship plans were designed solely to include operational functional levels. As previous research also suggests, 'the work experience components that are common to many hospitality degrees are primarily, or even exclusively, comprised of operational experiences and rarely do students get any exposure to management activities' (Raybould and Wilkins, 2005: 212). Disappointment with the lack of opportunities for internships in which trainees could become more familiar with management-related positions, for example by observing/accompanying an assistant manager, was also reported. Only three newcomers were given this opportunity. This raises some doubts as to whether most internships actually suit T&H management trainees, as would be expected for future T&H management graduates.

Although many hotel companies offer rotational internship programmes, only two interviewees among the newcomers were offered such opportunity, which is also largely contingent on the internship duration. These two newcomers, who aspire to management positions, described this internship plan as the most appropriate for any future manager. Some interviewees engaged with different roles but only within a single department, which could also configure a type of rotational internship (Calvo, 2011). This type of experience is particularly interesting; if the students have the opportunity to enrol in several single-department rotational internships across their academic preparation, when graduating they will benefit from a global, in-depth view of hotel management. Rotational internships allow new entrants to experience a diverse range of roles and responsibilities, which can help them 'assess their skills and interest in a number of positions' (while employers can also evaluate their potential future employees while performing various roles) and improve their adaptability when joining the labour market (although the transferability of skills from one context to another should not be taken for granted) (Calvo, 2011: 8).

Only one newcomer was offered a paid internship. This was an in-service training experience with a three-month duration in peak season, clearly interpreted as an exception. Although the issue of payment is quite controversial, several key players of the industry are found to be in favour either of full or partial payment of trainee's work, which could only improve the image of T&H jobs, as it could contribute to an employer's mindset change (Durão, 2021). For organisations, internships can be akin to an extended interview, which allow a more accurate identification of young talent. Internships make it possible to determine whether a candidate will be the best fit prior to formal hiring. Unfortunately, as reported by several research participants, internships in T&H are usually seen as free labour.

As T&H is facing severe labour shortages, coupled with other HR management issues, organisations frequently use trainees (not only from HEI but also from vocational schools) to leverage the gap in some critical functional areas where manpower is lacking. This may partially explain the reasons why most trainees are assigned to operational-oriented (only) internships. F&B operations are largely mentioned as one of, or even the most critical department with regard to employee turnover. Therefore, it is not surprising that this is the department hosting a more significant number of trainees. Participants holding supervisory duties acknowledged this common practice by referring to the many new entrants being invited to work with full responsibilities as regular workers after the end of their internships, for a second experimental period at zero cost. This is partially justified with the greater capacity – in terms of dimension, structure and scope of duties – of operational areas, such as F&B or front-office, to accommodate trainees. On the other hand, if a hotel only has one assistant manager, he/she will be able to mentor and supervise only one trainee.

When recalling their experiences as trainees, many newcomers, as well as some employees and leavers, complained about not having received appropriate training and on-the-job guidance, being left to themselves, or relying on fellow employees' generosity. Newcomers also reported that internship agreements are not always implemented, often resulting in the need to work additional hours without any compensation, lack of feedback, lack of appreciation for their efforts, or the complete absence of follow-up meetings with the on-site supervisor assigned by the organisation. Previous studies, such as that of Dagsland et al. (2015), have also found that unacceptable treatment, lack of interaction with supervisors and lack of follow-up, were reported as having negatively impacted the learning process. It is important that trainees, identified as such, are given responsibilities and allowed to independently perform the agreed roles and corresponding tasks, beyond simple observation. Most of the internship experiences take place solely 'in-service' as hardly any interviewees mentioned having gone through a duly structured or especially designed integration process. Trainees are often left to be hands-on, active on the job, as if they were already familiar with the work procedures. This raises some concerns regarding the extent internships are effective learning experiences for most T&H new entrants. Many operational jobs (such as waitering) are associated with 'easily' performed jobs, which anyone – qualified or not – can do, when in fact these jobs highly impact service quality, much more significantly than other back-office jobs.

This type of practice fails to promote students' professional growth – failing to meet the inner objectives of any internship – but can also irreversibly undermine undergraduates' career intentions (Durão, 2021). Although some organisations are perceived as having good practices, these are the exception, not the rule, as the number of trainees who are given an authentic learning opportunity, highly increasing their chances of occupying an entry-level management position, is very small.

The insufficient training and support that several newcomers experienced is perceived as symptomatic of the extent to which organisations resort to internships as an alternative to formally hiring employees. If organisations rely on a reduced core pool of employees (considering that under-staffing is a well-documented practice of the industry (Baum, 2002)), this may constitute a disadvantage not only for trainees, who receive limited coaching and guidance (considering the low availability of mentoring staff), but also for the core employees, who are given the additional burden of supervising trainees while performing their usual tasks. This is a frequent situation, particularly in peak season and in highly visited tourist destinations, often reported to supervisory authorities, yet largely overlooked.

Valuable Employability Skills

Employability skills are expected to ensure that graduates are able to effectively and innovatively apply their expertise in the workplace (Jackson, 2014). However, research participants were asked to identify, based on personal work experiences and knowledge of the sector, which skills they perceived to be valued by employers when selecting and recruiting potential employees.

Communication skills (mentioned by 10 participants) were described as highly important in a people-industry as in the case of T&H. Such a skill set encompasses the ability to communicate with all type of customers (politeness, oral expression, negotiation), to generate empathy (by listening and relating to others), and easily connecting with other people. This has been mentioned in previous research as one of the most desired graduate employability skills, although graduate oral communication skills are frequently reported (by employers) to inadequately meet the industry expectations (Jackson, 2014). Having good communication skills is an important relational tool at the workplace, not only with customers but also, and more significantly, with managers, peers, subordinates and other external stakeholders. Hence, all relevant managerial activity requires good communication skills. This is particularly relevant when operating in different cultural contexts and with a diverse workforce (Kirton and Greene, 2015).

Emotional intelligence, which can be defined as the ability to understand one's own emotions and the emotions of others, was perceived by eight interviewees as involving self-control, behavioural flexibility and discipline, and the ability to deal with pressure/stress tolerance. Some interviewees referred to this characteristic as one's ability not to 'lose their head' regardless of the nature of customer demands. One participant specifically mentioned one's ability to perform genuine and authentic interactions. This reinforces the notion that the T&H industry is highly prone to emotional labour.

Other skills and competencies were also mentioned, such as: adaptability (to understand and accept change and to positively adapt to new scenarios and constantly changing workplaces), willingness/ability to learn, professional attitude (referring to a skill set consisting of body language, etiquette and good manners, hospitable personality, and presentation), problem-solving/resourcefulness, flexibility, open-mindedness, responsibility and collaboration/team orientation. It should be noted that, mostly due to the nature of the question (which focused on skills new entrants thought employers most valued), flexibility should be interpreted as 'employer-friendly flexibility', which is meant to benefit the employer following an increased competitiveness and profitability rationale (Costa et al., 2017). The modest references (only two) to team orientation were quite surprising, considering both the relevance this characteristic has been given in previous studies and the general literature (Jiang and Alexakis, 2017), and the high importance research participants place on interpersonal and supportive relations at work.

As far as hard skills are concerned, there is strong consensus that foreign language proficiency is a key, highly valuable skill (mentioned by 19 participants). In most participants' opinion, very few employees are fluent in more than one language. English is not only regarded as the most relevant, but also as a minimum requirement. Other languages (especially other than Spanish or French) are highly valued, especially because these are considered resources that organisations lack.

Occupational and job-specific technical skills were mentioned only by three interviewees. Technical knowledge and skills are associated with the specific work that a given organisation does and its different functional levels. Digital competencies are also highlighted, with regard both to hotel-specific software (training which some study programmes provide), and to channel management, social media management or other digital tools proficiency. Some interviewees (in supervisory/managerial positions) suggested that having such technical skills when joining the organisation are not that relevant in comparison to other types of skills, as many companies are now willing to provide specific training to fulfil this limitation, as long as the prospective employee positively matches other relevant recruitment criteria (the right attitude and motivation).

CONCLUSION

A variety of views regarding higher education learning outcomes and improvement needs were found in this study, based on the participants' reflections on the educational preparation they received for their future careers in T&H and its impact on their future employability.

T&H study programmes are generally perceived as offering challenging and exciting career opportunities, as most participants give a very positive evaluation of the curriculum which they consider to have prepared them well for their working lives in the industry, as far as possible. HEI are perceived, by most participants, as gradually making efforts to adjust their delivery models. With regard to their condition as workers (labour law, terms of employment, workers' rights) there seems to be a generalised lack of preparation for future new entrants. Those holding a more negative perspective tended to focus on the lack of practical knowledge and experiential learning, although none of the interviewees started their careers in the hotel industry without having been, at least, enrolled in a curricular internship.

In view of such a diverse labour market, the role and responsibility of employing companies in preparing new entrants to the labour market is also discussed, as a 3/4-year degree is unlikely to prepare graduates to fit into any organisation. If the companies' role is assessed based on the participants' active learning experiences in their internships, the overall view is not very flattering. A more profound analysis of the design and implementation of curricular internships is deemed necessary, as many organisations are considered to be failing, to some extent, in meeting internships' goals. Training and on-the-job guidance, which are the core of any internship programme, are often deemed to be missing. In addition, most trainees are assigned to solely operational-oriented internships, which raises some doubts as to whether most internships actually suit T&H management trainees, as would be expected for future T&H management graduates.

The recurrent issue of internships as free labour was also addressed by the interviewees, to which companies resort to address labour shortages. Trainees are expected to be productive workers, more than to be thought how to 'labour'. Although this may not necessarily hamper their employability or stop them from accessing more permanent jobs, it fails to promote students' professional growth, as it can irreversibly undermine their career intentions. This study did not target individuals who had left hospitality careers after internships failed to meet their expectations. However, it can be perceived from participants' accounts of their internships that negative experiences gave them a greater distrust of their employers' ability to reciprocate in the future, as the norms of reciprocity that form the basis of psychological contracts presuppose (Siegrist, 2017).

As previous research also emphasises, the skills portfolio for the T&H draws on a bundle of hard and soft skills, which are associated with general human capital, hence transversal to other professional areas. A review of previous research shows that soft competencies are considered the most important for success in hospitality management (Sisson and Adams, 2013); similarly, in this study, higher importance is placed on soft skills, particularly at entry-level. This highly transferable skill set allows individuals to move across the labour market more easily, by enhancing their employability potential. This is perceived to constitute both an advantage and a disadvantage for individuals with dedicated T&H higher education qualifications, as well as for the industry itself. This transferable skill set allows these individuals to move across the labour market more easily, by enhancing their employability potential (Baruch, 2009). This can be perceived as an opportunity to get a higher quality job elsewhere, particularly in the services sector, if the T&H industry fails to meet their needs and expectations. Many participants believe that other sectors highly value the type of skills and competencies that T&H employees typically possess, making it easier to enrol in a new, different occupation. This may result in the irreversible loss of valuable and talented employees. However, the chances are that workers from other sectors can also easily migrate into the T&H industry, hence increasing competition for the same job positions. Many employers in the industry are redirecting their recruitment efforts towards graduates from other fields rather than T&H, many of them with more focused, specific qualifications for the hiring departments (social media management, finance, economics), which naturally poses more challenges for candidates with T&H dedicated qualifications (Durão, 2021).

Some caution is necessary with this employability rhetoric that connects skills acquisition to certain employment outcomes, as many of these skills typically develop over time, with work experience. Practical training in a work environment, such as that provided by internships, contributes to the development of such skills, but recent graduates tend to face resistance in seeing their skills recognised as sufficient to meet the requirements of certain job positions due to employers' perceived lack of experience (Raybould and Wilkins, 2005).

The research presented here is part of a broader study (Durão, 2021), thus is not able to reflect all the complex ramifications of these themes. The major limitation of the research is one of scale, as generalisation is not possible. Findings have drawn on the most prominent facts emerging from the data; arguably not limited to these presented.

ACKNOWLEDGEMENTS

Marília Durão would like to thank the support of the Portuguese Foundation for Science and Technology (Fundação para a Ciência e a Tecnologia), for the PhD Grant SFRH/BD/101236/2014.

REFERENCES

Ayres, H. (2006) 'Education and opportunity as influences on career development: findings from a preliminary study in Eastern Australian tourism', *Journal of Hospitality Leisure Sport and Tourism*, 5(1), pp. 16–27. doi: 10.3794/johlste.51.101.

Ayres, L. (2008) 'Narrative interview', in Given, L. (ed.) *The Sage encyclopedia of qualitative research methods*. Thousand Oaks, CA/London, UK: Sage, p. 545.

Barron, P. and Ali-Knight, J. (2017) 'Aspirations and progression of event management graduates: a study of career development', *Journal of Hospitality and Tourism Management*, 30, pp. 29–38. doi: https://doi.org/10.1016/j.jhtm.2017.01.005.

Baruch, Y. (2009) 'Fostering career development in organizations', in R. J. Burke & C. L. Cooper (eds.) *The peak performing organization*, Routledge, pp. 92–107.

Baum, T. (2002) 'Skills and training for the hospitality sector: a review of issues', *Journal of Vocational Education and Training*, 54(3), pp. 343–364. doi: 10.1080/13636820200200204.

Blomme, R. J., Van Rheede, A. and Tromp, D. (2009) 'The hospitality industry: an attractive employer? An exploration of students' and industry workers' perceptions of hospitality as a career field', *Journal of Hospitality and Tourism Education*, 21(2), pp. 6–14. doi: 10.1080/10963758.2009.10696939.

Braun, V. and Clarke, V. (2006) 'Using thematic analysis in psychology', *Qualitative Research in Psychology*, 3(2), pp. 77–101. doi: 10.1191/1478088706qp063oa.

Brien, A., Thomas, N. J. and Brown, E. A. (2017) 'How hotel employee job-identity impacts the hotel industry: the uncomfortable truth', *Journal of Hospitality and Tourism Management*, 31, pp. 235–243. doi: https://doi.org/10.1016/j.jhtm.2017.03.005.

Calvo, J. (2011) *Internships between higher education and work: theoretical considerations and analysis for reflection*. OCIDES: Kassel, Germany.

Carvalho, I. (2017) *Gendering the tourism sector: women managers' experiences in hotel and travel businesses in Portugal*. Universidade de Aveiro: Portugal.

Correia, L. M. M., Salgado, M. A. B. and Costa, C. (2017) 'Higher education in BF hospitality: curricular internship in degree', *Revista Turismo and Desenvolvimento/Journal of Tourism and Development*, 27/28(1), pp. 1785–1795.

Costa, C., Bakas, F. E., Breda, Z., Durão, M., Carvalho, I. and Caçador, S. (2017) 'Gender, flexibility and the "ideal tourism worker"', *Annals of Tourism Research*, 64, pp. 64–75. doi: https://doi.org/10.1016/j.annals.2017.03.002.

Dagsland, Å. H. B., Mykletun, R. J. and Einarsen, S. (2015) '"We're not slaves – we are actually the future!" A follow-up study of apprentices' experiences in the Norwegian hospitality industry', *Journal of Vocational Education and Training*, 67(4), pp. 460–481.

Dawson, M. E. (2014) 'Preparing students to fit within the hospitality industry culture: does the educational background make a difference?', *Journal of Teaching in Travel and Tourism*, 14(1), pp. 53–68. doi: 10.1080/15313220.2014.872900.

Dewar, K., Sayers, J. and Meyer, D. (2002) 'Hopes, dreams and reality: an investigation into the expectations and experiences of tourism graduates', *Journal of Teaching in Travel and Tourism*, 2(1), pp. 1–18. doi: 10.1300/J172v02n01_01.

Dickerson, J. P. (2009) 'The realistic preview may not yield career satisfaction', *International Journal of Hospitality Management*, 28(2), pp. 297–299. doi: 10.1016/j.ijhm.2008.06.015.

Durão, M. (2021) *Managing retention, careers and quality of working life of qualified human resources in tourism and hospitality: the case of Portugal*. University of Aveiro, Portugal.

Farmaki, A. (2018) 'Tourism and hospitality internships: a prologue to career intentions?', *Journal of Hospitality, Leisure, Sport and Tourism Education*, 23, pp. 50–58. doi: https://doi.org/10.1016/j.jhlste.2018.06.002.

Given, L. M. (ed.) (2008) *The Sage encyclopedia of qualitative research methods*. Thousand Oaks, CA/London, UK: Sage.

González, F., Sánchez, S. M. and López-Guzmán, T. (2016) 'The effect of educational level on job satisfaction and organizational commitment: a case study in hospitality', *International Journal of Hospitality and Tourism Administration*, 17(3), pp. 243–259. doi: 10.1080/15256480.2016.1183547.

Guerrier, Y. and Deery, M. (1998) 'Research in hospitality human resource management and organizational behaviour', *International Journal of Hospitality Management*, 17(2), pp. 145–160. doi: 10.1016/S0278-4319(98)00017-6.

ILO (2010) *Developments and challenges in the hospitality and tourism sector: issues paper for discussion at the Global Dialogue Forum for the Hotels, Catering, Tourism Sector*. Geneva, CH.

Iverson, R. D. and Deery, M. (1997) 'Turnover culture in the hospitality industry', *Human Resource Management Journal*, 7(4), pp. 71–82.

Jackson, D. (2014) 'Business graduate performance in oral communication skills and strategies for improvement', *The International Journal of Management Education*, 12(1), pp. 22–34. doi: https://doi.org/10.1016/j.ijme.2013.08.001.

Jiang, L. and Alexakis, G. (2017) 'Comparing students' and managers' perceptions of essential entry-level management competencies in the hospitality industry: an empirical study', *Journal of Hospitality, Leisure, Sport and Tourism Education*, 20, pp. 32–46. doi: https://doi.org/10.1016/j.jhlste.2017.01.001.

King, B., McKercher, B. and Waryszak, R. (2003) 'A comparative study of hospitality and tourism graduates in Australia and Hong Kong', *International Journal of Tourism Research*, 5(6), pp. 409–420. doi: 10.1002/jtr.447.

Kirton, G. and Greene, A. (2015) *The dynamics of managing diversity: a critical approach*. Oxon/New York: Routledge.

Kusluvan, S. (2003) 'Characteristics of employment and human resources management in the tourism and hospitality industry', in Kusluvan, S. (ed.) *Managing Employee Attitudes and Behaviors in the Tourism and Hospitality Industry*. New York, NY: Nova Science Publishers, pp. 3–24.

Kusluvan, S. and Kusluvan, Z. (2000) 'Perceptions and attitudes of undergraduate tourism students towards working in the tourism industry in Turkey', *Tourism Management*, 21(3), pp. 251–269. doi: 10.1016/S0261-5177(99)00057-6.

Ladkin, A. and Kichuk, A. (2017) 'Career progression in hospitality and tourism settings', in Horner, S. (ed.) *Talent management in hospitality and tourism*. Oxford, UK: Goodfellow Publishers, pp. 69–83.

Lent, R. W., Brown, S. D. and Hackett, G. (2006) 'Social cognitive career theory', in Greenhaus, J. H. and Callanan, G. A. (eds) *Encyclopedia of career development*. Thousand Oaks, CA/ London, UK: Sage, pp. 750–754.

Lu, T. (Ying) and Adler, H. (2009) 'Career goals and expectations of hospitality and tourism students in China', *Journal of Teaching in Travel and Tourism*, 9(1–2), pp. 63–80. doi: 10.1080/15313220903041972.

McGuire, D. (2014) 'Career development', in McGuire, D. (ed.) *Human resource development*. 2nd edn. Thousand Oaks, CA: Sage, pp. 53–68.

Mooney, S. and Jameson, S. (2018) 'The career constructions of hospitality students: a rocky road', *Hospitality and Society*, 8(1), pp. 45–67. doi: 10.1386/hosp.8.1.45_1.

Nachmias, S., Walmsley, A. and Orphanidou, Y. (2017) 'Students' perception towards hospitality education: an Anglo-Cypriot critical study', *Journal of Hospitality, Leisure, Sport and Tourism Education*, 20, pp. 134–145. doi: https://doi.org/10.1016/j.jhlste.2017.04.007.

Raybould, M. and Wilkins, H. (2005) 'Over qualified and under experienced', *International Journal of Contemporary Hospitality Management*, 17(3), pp. 203–216. doi: 10.1108/09596110510591891.

Richardson, S. (2009) 'Undergraduates' perceptions of tourism and hospitality as a career choice', *International Journal of Hospitality Management*, 28(3), pp. 382–388. doi: 10.1016/j.ijhm.2008.10.006.

Robinson, R. N. S., Ruhanen, L. and Breakey, N. M. (2016) 'Tourism and hospitality internships: influences on student career aspirations', *Current Issues in Tourism*, 19(6), pp. 513–527. doi: 10.1080/13683500.2015.1020772.

Ruhanen, L. (2005) 'Bridging the divide between theory and practice', *Journal of Teaching in Travel and Tourism*, 5(4), pp. 33–51. doi: 10.1300/J172v05n04_03.

Sandelowski, M. (1995) 'Sample size in qualitative research', *Research in Nursing and Health*, 18(2), pp. 179–183. doi: 10.1002/nur.4770180211.

Siegrist, J. (2017) 'The effort–reward imbalance model', *The handbook of stress and health*. (Wiley Online Books), pp. 24–35. doi:10.1002/9781118993811.ch2.

Sisson, L. G. and Adams, A. R. (2013) 'Essential hospitality management competencies: the importance of soft skills', *Journal of Hospitality and Tourism Education*, 25(3), pp. 131–145. doi: 10.1080/10963758.2013.826975.

Stacey, J. (2015) *Supporting quality jobs in tourism, OECD Tourism Papers*. 2015/02. Paris, FR. doi: https://doi.org/10.1787/5js4rv0g7szr-en.

Swarbrooke, J. and Gibson, P. (2017) 'Talent management in the hospitality and tourism context', in Horner, S. (ed.) *Talent management in hospitality and tourism*. Oxford, UK: Goodfellow Publishers. doi: 10.23912/978-1-910158-66-1-3327.

Szivas, E., Riley, M. and Airey, D. (2003) 'Labor mobility into tourism: attraction and satisfaction', *Annals of Tourism Research*, 30(1), pp. 64–76. doi: https://doi.org/10.1016/S0160-7383(02)00036-1.

Thompson, D., Poulston, J. and Neill, L. (2017) 'How satisfying is real work? An analysis of student feedback on applied learning in a hospitality degree', *Journal of Hospitality, Leisure, Sport and Tourism Education*, 20, pp. 110–121. doi: https://doi.org/10.1016/j.jhlste.2017.04.006.

Tomlinson, M. (2012) 'Graduate employability: a review of conceptual and empirical themes', *Higher Education Policy*, 25(4), pp. 407–431. doi: 10.1057/hep.2011.26.

Walsh, K., Sturman, M. C. and Carroll, B. (2011) *'Preparing for a successful career in the hospitality industry'*, Cornell University, School of Hospitality Administration.

Wanous, J. P., Poland, D. T., Premack, S. L. and Davis, K. S. (1992) 'The effects of met expectations on newcomer attitudes and behaviors: a review and meta-analysis', *Journal of Applied Psychology*, 77(3), pp. 288–297. doi: 10.1037/0021-9010.77.3.288.

8

Ready to Get on Board? Facilitating Role Transition of New Graduates

Jenny Chen

INTRODUCTION

Role transition is often a normative yet challenging process in graduates' careers. If graduates manage their transition from college to the professional world well, it boosts their confidence and enables them to construct professional identities faster; if not, it can decrease their functioning and induce anxiety (Molinsky and Pisman, 2019). To facilitate student–professional role transition in the work environment, many universities provide work-integrated learning opportunities such as fieldwork and internship (Nadelson et al., 2017) and career-related interventions such as career counselling and self-assessment service (Langher et al., 2018). However, previous empirical evidence shows that young graduates often fail to cope with upcoming challenges or meet work expectations after entering organisations (Trede et al., 2012). In fact, many graduates leave their first post-graduate jobs after less than one year (Sturges and Guest, 2001; Marshall and Butler, 2015).

In response, to improve our understanding on new graduates' role transition, this chapter covers questions such as: What are the key differences between being students and being professionals? How do graduates adapt successfully after entering the workplace? How do graduates make use of personal and contextual resources to facilitate their professional role learning? By integrating the broader research lines of pedagogical learning, organisational socialisation and role identity, I have developed a four-stage *PETI* (*P* = Preparing; *E* = Entering, *T* = Transforming, and *I* = Identifying) model to illustrate key processes involved in the role transition from student to professional. This model can be used by educators, career consultants, graduates and practitioners when considering the psychological and behavioural aspects to facilitate student–professional role transition. This chapter first clarifies the fundamental concepts of role transition, followed by discussions on key differences between being students and professionals. After this, a *PETI* model is introduced and discussed, including a series of stages and influential factors. The chapter closes by discussing future research directions.

ROLE TRANSITION

Broadly speaking, role transition refers to 'the process through which individuals psychologically (and if relevant, physically) exit one role and enter another' (Ashforth, 2001: 167). This role transition process does not happen within one day but is a continuous change process. Individuals' prior learning and experiences influence subsequent transition and outcomes. This chapter focuses on how graduates navigate their role transition to construct their professional identities in their initial employment. A professional role here reflects specialised knowledge, certain tasks and associated accountabilities embedded in the social system, and a professional identity occurs when an individual occupies a role and then identifies the self by the role (Ashforth, 2001; Pratt et al., 2006).

From the literature on higher education, the key perspectives exploring the student–professional role transition lie in the contextual predictors of professional identities, such as practice-based pedagogical learning (Clouder, 2005), and the dynamic processes of the development and construction of professional identities in the academic learning environment (Reid et al., 2008). Clearly, college learning promotes students' professional identity development, but as Trede et al. (2012) noticed, researchers have also shown an abundant interest in exploring how individuals form their professional identities at work (Ibarra, 1999; Pratt et al., 2006). That being said, although previous management studies also emphasise the pre-socialisation stage (Wendlandt and Rochlenz, 2008, Tharenou and Kulik, 2020), these studies usually adopt a limited time frame, focusing primarily on the prior-entry workplace experiences such as recruitment and selection or newcomers' existing institutional assumptions, without really linking to graduates' learning experience at college. The knowledge on graduates' transition experience from education to the workplace is indeed limited (Grosemans and De Cuyper, 2021). Without a more complete understanding of graduates' experiences before and after graduation, it is not possible to combine both educators and management when discussing how to help graduates develop professional identities at work.

ROLE REQUIREMENTS: STUDENTS VS PROFESSIONALS

As a means of facilitating discussions on role transition from students to professionals, a summary of distinguishing characteristics of role requirements is developed (see Table 8.1).

Task Features

When individuals view themselves as 'students', they are supposed to be engaged in academic activities such as attending lectures and seminars, preparing and doing assignments and examinations given by tutors and professors. Learning arrangements in the college are often structured and formalised, and they are incorporated into the curriculum to help students progress gradually. Long holiday periods and reading weeks (non-teaching weeks) also provide students with much autonomous time to explore and engage in extracurricular and student-led learning activities (Macaskill and Taylor, 2010). Experience shows that effective time management is a skill that undergraduate and postgraduate students often take time to master (Fazey and Fazey, 2001).

On the other hand, being a professional implies that an individual is not only supposed to complete the allocated tasks by management, take new challenges and make decisions when necessary, but may also have to manage upwards and inform their own views (Pfeffer, 2010), for example, by suggesting solutions to problems and letting managers know their preferences. It must be noted, however, that daily routine tasks (meetings, checking invoices) are also an essential part of professionals' work role, which may be repetitive and learning may not always occur, although self-directed learning is often encouraged and promoted at the workplace (Noe et al., 2014). Moreover, unlike students, professionals may be less likely to have frequent breaks and holidays, and, perhaps due to task interdependence, they may have less control over time-management.

Social Interactions

At college, the role of the student is complementary to the counter-role of tutors and professors. When a student acts like a student by attending lectures and doing assignments, this in turn allows tutors and professors to carry out their obligations and verify their role identities. Indeed, the pedagogical literature has indicated that student identity is shaped through social contacts with tutors, professors and classmates. Interactions with tutors and professors facilitate students' academic achievements, while informal contacts with classmates can help to develop voluntary friendships and improve the enjoyment of college life (Anderson and Fowers, 2020).

Table 8.1 Summary of different key aspects of role requirements of students and professionals

	Students		Professionals
Task features	*Generic learning-oriented activities*	→	*Value-based impacts at work*
	– structured and organised learning activities – tasks assigned by tutors – relatively more autonomous time		– new challenges and decision-making, but often routine tasks – manage upwards if necessary – less control over irregular events
Social interactions	*Homogeneous and affect-based*	→	*Diverse and collaborative*
	– tutor/professor-student – classmates of relatively similar backgrounds – voluntary friendships		– manager-subordinate – colleagues and/or clients with more diverse backgrounds – work-based relationships
Thinking patterns	*Process-oriented with short-term focus*	→	*Result-driven with long-term focus*
	– process-oriented, focusing on learning – relatively short and event-focused – perhaps with a customer mindset		– result-driven, focusing on delivery and outcomes – continuously improving – team- and/or client-focused
Levels of responsibility	*Self-focused and relatively simplistic*	→	*Profession-defined and more complex*
	– following academic and research ethical standards – being responsible for one's own learning outcomes – holding responsibility if deviations occur		– accepting and internalising professional ethical standards – being responsible for the quality of one's own work – taking responsibility if deviations occur

In contrast, professionals are normally embedded within manager–subordinate relationships at work, which are often based on the power structure in the organisation. They may need to develop connections with a more diverse group of colleagues (age, ethnicity, work experience and interests) and/or clients (expectations, requirements, personality traits). Professionals also form and develop workplace friendships, but studies show some potential risks associated with workplace friendships, such as conflict of interest situations (Berman et al., 2002). Also, unlike students at college, professionals sometimes have to manage difficult relationships in the professional world even though they may not like that manager or clients (Molinsky and Pisman, 2019).

Thinking Patterns

Thinking patterns, also understood as mental models or mindsets, concern how people think (Senge, 1990). Students may be inclined to cultivate a process-oriented mindset; it is the process of learning that matters. In a related vein, as college learning often consists of different assignments and activities, this can also result in a short and event-focused mindset. In addition, although the relationship between students and the college is not a superficial consumer transaction purely based on economic value, there is a growing tendency towards being more market-driven (Brown and Carasso, 2013). Such changes that have taken place in higher education may further influence students' wider sense of the self as service-users associated with rights as fee-payers (Tomlinson, 2017).

At the workplace, managers are different from tutors and professors. They are responsible for the whole team's performance, not just for one person's learning, and need to report satisfactory progress to their own managers. They may be less likely to tolerate errors and delay as the quality of an individual's performance can influence team performance and effectiveness (Mathieu et al., 2008). Serious mistakes at work can even harm the company's reputation (Molinsky and Pisman, 2019). Therefore, professionals are more likely to develop result-oriented mindsets, with the emphasis on delivery and outcomes. Related to this, some workplace projects may last a few years, and a continuous learning mindset may be encouraged after entering the workplace. In fact, to provide good service to the clients, professionals often see themselves as continuous learners to improve the procedures and products. Managers can provide inputs and/or resources, but it is the professional's own responsibility to acquire the relevant knowledge and skills to be a professional.

Levels of Responsibility

University students are experiencing a life developmental phase called 'emerging adulthood', which offers more freedom compared with adolescence, but less responsibility compared with adulthood (Arnett, 2000). No matter whether individuals like it or not, responsibility directs how individuals react to rules and situations (Frink and Klimoski, 1998). As students, they are agents of their own learning and academic achievement. If they are internally obligated to take the ownership of learning, they are more likely to build up knowledge and achieve academic success. However, given that students have not practised as full professional members, they would not have experienced the responsibilities and hold more formal obligations (accountability) associated with professional roles.

Compared with students, professionals are not just being responsible for the quality of their own work but are also accountable to the team, to the department, and to the company (Molinsky and Pisman, 2019). Professionals are also answerable for any deviations from professional conduct and ethical standards (Vriens et al., 2018). For example, when facing an ethical dilemma, solicitors must follow a code of conduct and make ethical judgments when providing services. In this way, it allows the occupants of counter-roles (e.g., a judge in this case) to carry out their duties. Similarly, other professionals such as nurses are also required to be accountable for their ethical behaviours and conduct (NMC, 2008).

AN INTEGRATIVE MODEL: FROM STUDENTS TO PROFESSIONALS

Drawing on studies on pedagogical learning, organisational socialisation and role identity, an integrative *PETI* model is developed by focusing graduates' experiences of student–professional role transition. As illustrated in Figure 8.1,

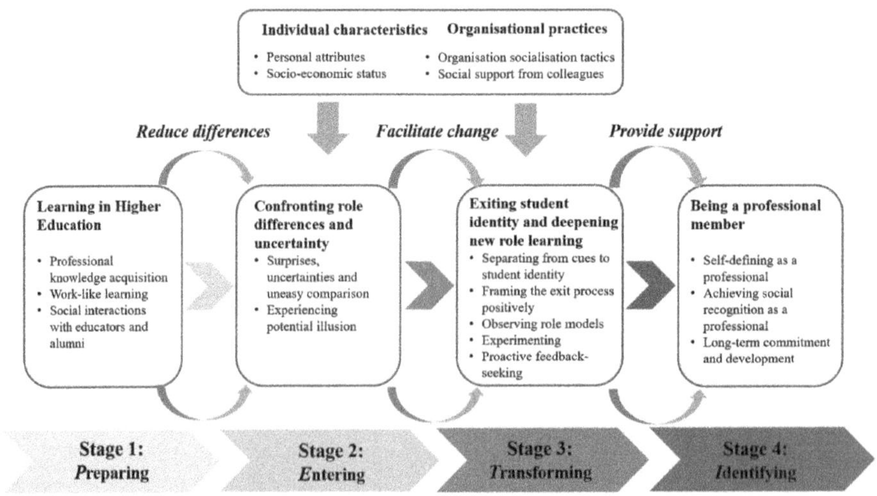

Figure 8.1 The *PETI* model of role transition from student to professional

college learning and social interactions with educators and alumni serve as critical resources to help graduates reduce surprises and uncertainties after organisational entry. This in turn further facilitates student role exit and professional role learning, and, accordingly, professional identification. The *PETI* model also acknowledges individual and situational factors in this role transition process. Details are illustrated and discussed below.

Stage 1: Preparing – learning at college

A critical issue across professions is that the expectations, standards and rules have been established in the social systems before individuals enter (Ibarra, 1999). Once graduates join the organisation, they would be expected to act professionally even if they may have not fully understood or internalised professional standards and role requirements. To make this possible, learning at college plays a key role in preparing graduates to get ready for the role transition at work (Reid et al., 2008). For example, learning technical terms and specialised knowledge of the discipline provide a starting point with which college students can identify. Trede and colleagues (2012) further suggest that the college provides a rich setting for students to acquire pre-professional identities through learning specialised knowledge. Jackson (2016) also emphasises the essence of 'embracing pre-professional identity' into college learning.

Moreover, to facilitate graduates' adaptation into work environments, considerable efforts have been expended on designing work-related pedagogical curricula and providing a work-like learning environment. For example, Ronfeldt and Grossman (2008) found that fieldwork may have the most influence on professional identity development due to the extensive opportunities to experiment with the professional role. Nadelson and colleagues (2017) further found that science, technology, engineering and mathematics (STEM) students were more likely to develop professional identities if they engaged in learning activities that were similar to the working activities of STEM professionals. In this sense, work-like learning helps graduates understand professional roles and prepare for the anticipatory student–professional role transition at work.

Moreover, Ronfeldt and Grossman (2008) found that students' prior teachers can be an inspiring drive for those students to enter the profession in the first place. Jensen and Jetten (2016) also suggest that social interactions between students and faculty members are essential for students to develop some awareness of a professional identity. That being said, it is worth noting that they did not find any evidence to show that social interactions with peers can also support the development of professional identity. However, social interaction with alumni may help students keep up to date on professional development, and this may be useful in preparing graduates for the upcoming role transition at the workplace.

Stage 2: Entering – confronting role differences and uncertainty

After entering the organisation, Louis (1980) points out that individuals were inclined to appraise their environment by interrelating new settings with their previous experiences. As discussed in Table 8.1, students and professionals may experience different role requirements and expectations. These distinguishing characteristics can bring surprises and a 'transition shock' after graduates enter the workplace (Duchscher, 2009), especially for those who have no experience of work-like learning (internship and fieldwork). These negative entry experiences may be related to a lack of understanding of the profession (Olson and Bialocerkowski, 2014).

Moreover, the student–professional role transition is associated with potential threats of identity change as graduates will have to, sooner or later, accommodate themselves to different professional role expectations and requirements, and let go of their student identity which had formed a part of the self. This thus opens the possibility of experiencing identity lingering (Wittman, 2019). When graduates face challenges and difficult situations at work, they may continuously be posturing themselves as students who are learning at the workplace instead of professional workers delivering values and impacts at work. Such sustained illusion allows graduates to stay in their comfort zone and protect their self-views and psychological well-being (Folkman and Lazarus, 1984), but enduring lingering identities can result in ongoing struggles to meet external work requirements and being internally 'stuck in the past' (Wittman, 2019).

Stage 3: Transforming – exiting student identity and deepening new role learning

The role transition involves a process of leaving a former role or losing some familiarity while moving into a new role (Marshall and Butler, 2015). The former role here refers to the certain tasks and behaviours associated with the student identity whereas the new role means the professional worker is associated with relevant expectations, standards and rules at work. To strip away values and beliefs associated with the student identity, leaving room for new professional roles, individuals need to distance themselves from familiar cues that may activate their established self-views (Wrzesniewski et al., 2003). For example, graduates can tailor their social interactions by creating more opportunities to communicate with colleagues and other professionals in after-work social events, rather than just staying within the existing social networking with prior friends and classmates. Through more contacts with professionals, graduates can acquire a way of thinking and acting like professionals by imitation, and leave their student role behind. Further, to avoid the continuity of student identity at work, graduates could start with relatively small changes such as dressing, body and written language and then move towards more complex changes such as values, beliefs and working styles. All of these changes are necessary to reflect a professional identity at the individual level.

Further, to satisfy the needs of reducing discrepancies between student and professional role expectations, graduates can employ psychological tools to maintain the sense of self-control and reduce potential stresses during role transition. Here, one of these tools is positive framing. This is a cognitive self-management mechanism enabling new members 'to alter their understanding of a situation by explicitly controlling the cognitive frame they place on the situation' (Ashford and Black, 1996: 202). In the organisational socialisation literature, positive framing is found to be a useful coping mechanism to facilitate the process of fitting in (Kim et al., 2005) and to increase job satisfaction in the early tenure (Wanberg and Kammeyer-Mueller, 2000). Positively framing the process of exiting the student identity may help graduates foster the personal resource of positive affect to counteract potential negative emotions and stress (Tice et al., 2007).

Having discussed the potential challenges associated with the entry stage, we will now discuss three proactive behaviours that can facilitate professional role learning. First, grounded in social learning theory (Bandura, 1977), professional role learning involves observing the context, including people and situational cues, to learn the role and standardised ways of doing things (Ostroff and Kozlowski, 1992; Ashford and Black, 1996). Observation is useful to understand the discrepancies between standards and actual responses, which can motivate the change of behaviour to measure up to these role standards (Bandura, 1977). Miller and Jablin (1991) suggest that new members are able to learn about role requirements by observing their colleagues' behaviours that result in rewards or punishments. Takeuchi and Takeuchi (2009) also emphasise observation of role models by new members comparing themselves with more experienced co-workers.

Second, when young professionals observe others, they generate a repertoire of potential identities that serve as the basis for 'experimenting their provisional selves' by testing themselves in the practices (Ibarra, 1999). While individuals may develop a different repertoire of selves due to different prior experiences and social influences (Slay and Smith, 2011), research has confirmed the use of experimenting as a strategy for role learning. Ibarra (1999) suggests that experimenting can help to 'bridge the gap between their current capacities and self-conceptions and the representations they hold about what attitudes and behaviours are expected in the new role' (p. 765). In the organisational socialisation literature, experimenting, as a proactive behaviour, also facilitates role learning and facilitates newcomer adaptation (Ostroff and Kozlowski, 1992; Cooper-Thomas and Burke, 2012).

Further, it is known that contextual uncertainty will stimulate transforming self-conception and assimilating all aspects of one's attitudes, feelings and behaviours to the in-group prototype (Hogg, 2000). This is unlike the learning experience at college, where tutors and professors help students confront misconceptions, and the minds of the students are usually in good care. Personalised advice and feedback are often provided through assignments and personal meetings at college (Molinsky and Pisman, 2019). At the workplace, new members are expected to seek feedback proactively from insiders and acquire the necessary information to perform the tasks (Allen et al., 2017). Those who make the effort of seeking feedback from role models have more opportunities to efficiently interpret professional behavioural standards and role requirements. Prior socialisation literature has indeed suggested that feedback-seeking is associated with better role learning, task mastery and lower intention to leave (Vandenberghe et al., 2021).

Individual Characteristics and Organisational Practices of Role Transition

Research on role transition and organisational socialisation also emphasises the importance of individual characteristics and organisational practices (Allen et al., 2017; Tharenou and Kulik, 2020). Understanding individual characteristics helps to improve our insights on what types of individuals are more likely to engage in role learning and developing professional identities. Identification of organisational practices can also help to design effective interventions to facilitate student–professional role transition. In the following, the impacts of individual characteristics (personal traits and social-economic status) on role transition are discussed first, followed by organisational practices (organisational socialisation tactics and social support).

Previous empirical studies have identified various individual differences that may influence new members' behaviours and performance after organisational entry. For example, research has shown that new members' desire and ability to learn can influence their adjustment (Ashforth et al., 2007); and new members' curiosity serves as an antecedent to taking charge and job performance (Harrison et al., 2011). Moreover, it is widely acknowledged that those from a higher socio-economic status have more social capital than those with lower socio-economic status (Tierney and Jun, 2001). Research has shown that social capital has a significant impact on the growth and identity development of college students (Tierney, 2000). Those graduates with more social capital and networks may have more chances to meet and interact with people holding similar professional roles (parents and other family members). This experience can also benefit professional role identification at work.

Further, formalised and structured organisational socialisation tactics are found to facilitate new member adaptation and role learning (Jones, 1986). In particular, Pratt (2000) treated divestiture tactics as a 'sense breaking' practice to influence members' self-evaluation. Contrary to investiture tactics, divestiture tactics invalidate the self by disconfirming the 'incoming identity' of a new member (Van Maanen and Schein, 1979). Hence, under divestiture tactics, new members are more likely to alter the self, increasing professional role learning. In addition, social support also appears to be essential to speed up role learning and adaptation (Korte and Lin, 2013). Supervisors and line managers are commonly considered as essential agents in supporting employees to realise their obligations to the organisation. With social support, new graduates are likely to assume that the environment in the new workplace is friendly and supportive, which may contribute to their information acquisition. It seems logical to expect graduates with such social support to learn new role behaviours and standards more readily.

Stage 4: Identifying – being a professional member

Given the distinguishing characteristics of being students and professionals, as illustrated in Table 8.1, the role transition process does not always occur successfully, and some graduates may fail to develop professional identities at work. Individuals are expected to resolve the challenges associated with a previous stage before transitioning to the next stage (Ashforth et al., 2007). New graduates who have successfully gone through the professional role learning should ultimately come to this stage of identifying with the profession. When conceptualising the self as 'professional', one's professional identity serves as an organising framework for an individual's self-concept (Stryker, 2007). The construction of a professional identity offers meaning and purpose for individuals (Caza and Creary, 2016). Individuals who behave and act as members of the profession are highly identified with their professions and see their own beliefs about the profession as self-defining (Pratt, 2000).

Further, one's professional identity provides behavioural guidance (Ibarra, 1999). When graduates fulfil professional role requirements and provide profession-defined quality and service to the clients, they are more likely to achieve social recognition and gain credibility. Yet one can imagine a new graduate being rejected by the other group members due to a misalignment with professional standards and work styles. Such deviations seem to easily evoke more disliking and stress in the workplace (Janssen, 2003). This is not hard to understand from the similarity-attraction paradigm (Byrne, 1971), which suggests that people sharing similar characteristics are attracted to each other and generally have better affective consequences than people who are different. According to this principle of functional antagonism, existing members display interpersonal attraction toward those new members who share similar attitudes and perspectives. When new graduates align with professional role standards, they are thus more welcomed and accepted. Otherwise, they may face negative consequences including exclusion from formal and informal interactions.

Identifying with the profession also indicates long-term commitment (Bucher and Stelling, 1977). New professionals continue to accumulate relevant knowledge and skills and to provide profession-defined quality (Freidson, 2001). In this way, the professional role identity is internalised as a cognitive framework influencing how individuals think, behave and feel. In Tan et al.'s (2017) study, they also state that 'professional identity is the self that has been developed with the commitment to perform competently and legitimately in the context of the profession' (p. 1505).

PRACTICAL IMPLICATIONS

To facilitate seamless student–professional role transition, it becomes important for college students to not only acquire specialised knowledge and techniques but also to improve their awareness of profession-defined behaviours and standards to reduce potential surprises after entering the organisation. In addition, given that traditional academic training may not address the practical work-related problems directly, instructors are expected to include more work-related information in the delivery and cultivate a work-like learning environment whenever possible. In doing so, students have more chances to apply what they have learnt in the work settings and therefore reduce unrealistic expectations which may in turn facilitate transition after graduation.

Moreover, the differences between students and professionals go further than knowledge and skill sets, as shown in Table 8.1, but also include levels of responsibility and thinking patterns. Thus, the student–professional role differences and their associated implications for role transition after organisational entry should become a part of employability programmes, along with other training such as how to develop a CV and advice on job hunting. These structured programmes can help to improve the awareness of differences and future challenges, help graduates prepare for the potential surprises and get ready for anticipatory changes after organisational entry.

Further, as graduates progress from stages of entering to transforming, their professional role learning becomes increasingly reliant on organisational and social support (Boulamatsi et al., 2020). The *PETI* model indicates that organisational socialisation tactics and social support are essential to facilitate role change and reduce anxiety during the transforming stage. Managers are thus encouraged to motivate more tenured employees to support new graduates' adjustment and develop professional identities. Perhaps a well-designed mentoring programme or buddy system can be used to provide graduates with an opportunity to deepen their learning about the profession, to help them internalise the professional rules and values, and to facilitate their role transition.

FUTURE RESEARCH DIRECTIONS

To take a step further, researchers can find ways to study the entire spectrum of professional identity construction by connecting the developmental roots of professional choices. As we know, the formulation and development of professional preferences is a lifelong journey. The *PETI* model discussed in this chapter attempts to bridge the episodes before and after college graduation, but the importance of childhood and adolescence cannot be ignored. It would be interesting to explore if there are any psychological differences in role transition at different stages of life. It is likely that the exploration of how individuals gradually develop their occupational preferences and construct their professional identities may not only help to refine the theory surrounding the role transition literature but may also provide practical insights for educators and recent graduates on how to adapt to the workplace and build up professional identity smoothly.

Moreover, it has been noted that graduates do not always follow the anticipated professions after graduation. For example, a law school student may choose to become an HRM officer instead of pursuing a career as a solicitor. Research can strive to investigate whether internal personal characteristics or critical events in their college learning may have influenced their professional choices to ones not directly relevant to their subjects/disciplines after graduation. It may be useful to determine whether there are any differences in terms of professional identity construction for those graduates who change professions. Also, given the time and resources needed to learn the specialised knowledge at college, it may be useful for researchers to find out how students perceive their fit towards their profession while still at college, and whether their perceived fit affects their role transition after graduation.

Additionally, it is worth noting that most empirical studies investigating role transition experiences are based on western contexts such as the United States. Although it is likely that some of the findings may be true for a non-western context, the student–professional transition process may have new characteristics in other cultures. In fact, research has shown that in Asian cultures such as that in China, employees' behaviours and attitudes are deeply influenced by the Confucianism that emphasises collectivism and interpersonal harmony (Hwang, 1987). Therefore, it may be interesting to explore whether there are key features observed in western graduates during role transition similar to those of graduates from eastern cultures, or whether eastern graduates report different challenges during role transition after graduation. Although the available population necessarily becomes more limited, it would be interesting to explore the role transition of students from one culture moving to another culture. It is believed that examining this issue in a non-western context may expand our view and understanding about how professional identity construction works across cultural boundaries.

Finally, this chapter mainly focuses on one side of the coin – recent graduates' behaviour during the student–professional role transition. It is reasonable to expect they may also experience cognitive (linear –> non-linear reasoning) and emotional (moody –> stable) changes during role transition. If so, then to what extent do cognitive changes interact with contextual factors to influence new graduates' construction of professional identities at work? Are there distinct patterns of relationships between cognitive, emotional and behavioural changes? How do new graduates manage their emotions when faced with surprises and uncertainties during organisational entry? What other contextual factors, beyond organisational socialisation tactics and social support, influence cognitive and emotional changes? Such analysis certainly invites further research to advance insights for improving the learning and working experience to achieve the desired professional identity effectively.

CONCLUSION

With an increasingly agile workforce, it becomes more essential for new graduates to understand how to be able to transition into professional roles more effectively and function as professional employees more quickly. To maximise the benefit from their recruitment process, it is equally essential for organisations to determine how to facilitate the transition of new graduates into their workplaces. In this chapter, drawing on the literature from pedagogical learning, organisational socialisation and role identity, the *PETI* model is developed focusing on how new graduates form and develop their professional identities. By discussing such a process model, this chapter helps to advance our understanding of the student–professional role transition and should stimulate further thinking and research on role transition into postgraduation employment.

REFERENCES

Allen, T. D., Eby, L. T., Chao, G. T. and Bauer, T. N. (2017). Taking stock of two relational aspects of organizational life: tracing the history and shaping the future of socialization and mentoring research. *Journal of Applied Psychology*, *102*, 324–337.

Anderson, R. A. and Fowers, B. J. (2020). An exploratory study of friendship characteristics and their relations with hedonic and eudaimonic well-being. *Journal of Social and Personal Relationships*, *37*, 260–280.

Ashford, S. J. and Black, J. S. (1996). Proactivity during organizational entry: the role of desire for control. *Journal of Applied Psychology, 81*, 199–214.

Ashforth, B. E. (2001). *Role transitions in organizational life: an identity-based perspective*. Mahwah, NJ: Erlbaum.

Ashforth, B. E., Sluss, D. M. and Harrison, S. H. (2007). Socialization in organizational contexts. In G. P. Hodgkinson and J. K. Ford (eds), *International review of industrial and organizational psychology* (pp. 1–70), Wiley: Chichester.

Arnett, J. J. (2000). Emerging adulthood: a theory of development from the late teens through the twenties. *American Psychologist, 55*, 469–480.

Bandura, A. (1977). Self-efficacy: toward a unifying theory of behavioral change. *Psychological Review, 84*, 191–215.

Berman, E. M., West, J. P. and Richter, Jr. M. N. (2002). Workplace relations: friendship patterns and consequences (according to managers), *Public Administration Review, 62*, 217–230.

Boulamatsi, A., Liu, S. Q., Lambert, L. S., Yao, X., Guo, R. and Yin, J. F. (2020). How and when are learning-adaptable newcomers innovative? Examining mechanisms and constraints, *Personal Psychology, 74*, 751–772.

Brown, R. and Carasso, H. (2013). *Everything for sale: the marketization of UK higher education*. London: Routledge.

Byrne, D. (1971). *The attraction paradigm*. New York: Academic Press.

Bucher, R. and Stelling, J. G. (1977). *Becoming professional*. Beverly Hills, CA: Sage.

Caza, B. B. and Creary, S. (2016). The construction of professional identity. In A. Wilkinson, D. Hislop and C. Coupland (eds), *Perspectives on contemporary professional work: challenges and experiences* (pp. 259–285). Cheltenham, UK: Elgar.

Clouder, L. (2005). Caring as a 'threshold concept': transforming students in higher education into health(care) professionals. *Teaching in Higher Education, 10*, 505–517.

Cooper-Thomas, H. D. and Burke, S. E. (2012). Newcomer proactive behavior: can there be too much of a good thing (pp. 56–77). In C. Wanberg (ed.), *The Oxford handbook of organizational socialization*. Oxford: University Press.

Duchscher, J. B. (2009). Transition shock: the initial stage of role adaptation for newly graduated registered nurses. *Journal of Advanced Nursing, 65*, 1103–1113.

Fazey, D. M. A. and Fazey, J. A. (2001). The potential for autonomy in learning: perceptions of competence, motivation and locus of control in first-year undergraduate students. *Studies in Higher Education, 26*, 345–361.

Folkman, S. and Lazarus, R. S. (1984). *Stress, appraisal and coping*. New York: Springer Co.

Friedson, E. (2001). *Professionalism: the third logic*. Chicago: University of Chicago Press.

Frink, D. D. and Klimoski, R. J. (1998). Toward a theory of accountability in organizations and human resource management. *Research in Personnel and Human Resources Management, 17*, 1–51.

Grosemans, I. and De Cuyper, N. (2021). Career competencies in the transition from higher education to the labor market: examining developmental trajectories. *Journal of Vocational Behavior, 128*, 103602.

Harrison, S. H., Sluss, D. M. and Ashforth, B. E. (2011). Curiosity adapted the cat: the role of trait curiosity in newcomer adaption. *Journal of Applied Psychology, 96*, 211–220.

Hogg, M. A. (2000). Subjective uncertainty reduction through self-categorization: a motivational theory of social identity processes. *European Review of Social Psychology, 11*, 223–255.

Hwang, K. K. (1987). Face and favor: the Chinese power game. *American Journal of Sociology, 92*, 944–974.

Jackson, D. (2016). Conceptualising graduate employability: the construction of pre-professional identity in the higher education landscape of practice. *Higher Education Research and Development*, *35*, 925–939.

Janssen, O. (2003). Innovative behavior and job involvement at the price of conflict and less satisfactory relations with co-workers. *Journal of Occupational and Organizational Psychology*, *76*, 347–364.

Jensen, D. H. and Jetten, J. (2016). The importance of developing students' academic and professional identities in higher education. *Journal of College Student Development*, *57*, 1027–1042.

Jones, G. R. (1986). Socialization tactics, self-efficacy, and newcomers' adjustments to organizations. *Academy of Management Journal*, *29*, 262–279.

Kim, T., Cable, D. M. and Kim, S. (2005). Socialization tactics, employee proactivity, and person–organization fit. *Journal of Applied Psychology*, *90*, 232–241.

Korte, R. and Lin, S. (2013). Getting on board: organizational socialization and the contribution of social capital. *Human Relations*, *66*, 407–428.

Ibarra, H. (1999). Provisional selves: experimenting with image and identity in professional adaptation. *Administrative Science Quarterly*, *44*, 764–791.

Langher, V., Nannini, V. and Caputo, A. (2018). What do university or graduate students need to make the cut? A meta-analysis on career intervention effectiveness. *Journal of Educational, Cultural and Psychological Studies*, *17*, 21–43.

Louis, M. R. (1980). Surprise and sensemaking: what newcomers experience in entering unfamiliar organizational settings. *Administrative Science Quarterly*, *25*, 226–251.

Macaskill, A. and Taylor, E. (2010). The development of a brief measure of learner autonomy in college students. *Studies in Higher Education*, *35*, 351–359.

Marshall, A. E. and Butler, K. (2015). School-to-work transitions in emerging adulthood. In J. J. Arnett (ed.), *The Oxford handbook of emerging adulthood* (pp. 316–333). Oxford, UK: Oxford University Press.

Mathieu, J., Maynard, M. T., Rapp, T. and Gilson, L. (2008). Team effectiveness 1997–2007: a review of recent advancements and a glimpse into the future. *Journal of Management*, *34*, 410–476.

Miller, V. D. and Jablin, F. C. (1991). Information seeking during organizational entry: influences, tactics, and a model of the process. *Academy of Management Review*, *16*, 92–120.

Molinsky, A. and Pisman, S. (2019). The biggest hurdles recent graduates face entering the workforce. *Harvard Business Review Digital Articles*, 2–6.

Nadelson, L., McGuire, S., Davis, K., Farid, A. K., Hardy, K. K., Hsu, Y-C., Kaiser, U., Nagarajan, R. and Wang, S. (2017). Am I a STEM professional? Documenting STEM student professional identity development. *Studies in Higher Education*, *42*, 701–720.

Noe, R. A., Clarke, A. D. M. and Klein, H. J. (2014). Learning in the twenty-first-century workplace. *Annual Review of Organizational Psychology and Organizational Behavior*, *1*, 245–275.

Nursing and Midwifery Council (2008). *The code: standards of conduct, performance and ethics for nurses and midwives*. London.

Olson, R. and Bialocerkowski, A. (2014). Interprofessional education in allied health: a systematic review. *Medical Education*, *48*, 236–246.

Ostroff, C. and Kozlowski, S. W. J. (1992). Organizational socialization as a learning process: the role of information acquisition. *Personnel Psychology*, *45*, 849–874.

Pfeffer, J. (2010). *Power: why some people have it and others don't*. New York: Harper Business.

Pratt, M. G. (2000). The good, the bad, and the ambivalent: managing identification among Amway distributors. *Administrative Science Quarterly*, *45*, 456–493.

Pratt, M. G., Rockmann, K. W. and Kaufman, J. B. (2006). Constructing professional identity: the role of work and identity learning cycles in the customization of identity among medical residents. *Academy of Management Journal*, *49*, 235–262.

Reid, A., Dahlgren, L. O., Petocz, P. and Dahlgren, M. A. (2008). Identity and engagement for professional formation. *Studies in Higher Education*, *33*, 729–742.

Ronfeldt, M. and Grossman, P. (2008). Becoming a professional: experimenting with possible selves in professional preparation. *Teacher Education Quarterly*, *35*, 41–60.

Senge, P. (1990), *The art and practice of the learning organization*, New York: Doubleday /Currency.

Slay, H. S. and Smith, D. A. (2011). Professional identity construction: using narrative to understand the negotiation of professional and stigmatized cultural identities. *Human Relation*, *64*, 85–107.

Stryker, S. (2007). Identity theory and personality theory: mutual relevance. *Journal of Personality*, *75*, 1083–1102.

Sturges, J. and Guest, D. (2001). Don't leave me this way! A qualitative study of influences on the organisational commitment and turnover intentions of graduates early in their career. *British Journal of Guidance and Counselling*, *29*, 447–462.

Takeuchi, N. and Takeuchi, T. (2009). A longitudinal investigation on the factors affecting newcomers' adjustment: evidence from Japanese organizations. *International Journal of Human Resource Management*, *20*, 928–952.

Tan, J., Choo, S., Kang, T. and Liem, G. (2017). Educating for twenty-first-century competencies and future-ready learners: research perspectives from Singapore. *Asia Pacific Journal of Education*, *37*, 425–436.

Tharenou, P. and Kulik, C. T. (2020). Skilled migrants employed in developed, mature economies: from newcomers to organizational insiders. *Journal of Management*, *46*, 1156–1181.

Tice, D. M., Baumeister, R. F., Shmueli, D. and Muraven, M. (2007). Restoring the self: positive affect helps improve self-regulation following ego depletion. *Journal of Experimental Social Psychology*, *43*, 379–384.

Tierney, W. G. (2000). Power, identity, and the dilemma of college student departure. In J. M. Braxton (ed.), *Reworking the departure puzzle* (pp. 213–234). Nashville, TN: Vanderbilt University Press.

Tierney, W. G. and Jun, A. (2001). A college helps prepare low income youths for college: tracking school success. *Journal of Higher Education*, *72*, 205–225.

Tomlinson, M. (2017). Student perceptions of themselves as 'consumers' of higher education. *British Journal of Sociology of Education*, *38*, 450–467.

Trede, F., Macklin, R. and Bridges, D. (2012). Professional identity development: a review of the Higher Education literature. *Studies in Higher Education*, *37*, 365–384.

Vandenberghe, C., Landry, G., Bentein, K., Anseel, F., Mignonac, K. and Roussel, P. (2021). A dynamic model of the effects of feedback-seeking behavior and organizational commitment on newcomer turnover. *Journal of Management*, *47*, 519–544.

Van Maanen, J. and Schein, E. H. (1979). Toward a theory of organizational socialization. In B. M. Staw (ed.) *Research in organizational behavior* (pp. 209–264). Greenwich, CT: JAI Press.

Vriens, D., Vosselman, E. and GroB, C. (2018). Public professional accountability: a conditional approach. *Journal of Business Ethics*, *153*, 1179–1196.

Wanberg, C. R. and Kammeyer-Mueller, J. D. (2000). Predictors and outcomes of proactivity in the socialization process. *Journal of Applied Psychology*, *85*, 373–385.

Wendlandt, N. M. and Rochlenz, A. B. (2008). Addressing the college-to-work transition: implications for university career counselors. *Journal of Career Development*, *35*, 151–165.

Wittman, S. (2019). Lingering identities. *Academy of Management Review*, *44*, 724–745.

Wrzesniewski, A., Dutton, J. E. and Debebe, G. (2003). Interpersonal sensemaking and the meaning of work. In R. M. Kramer and B. M. Staw (eds), *Research in organizational behavior*, (Vol. 25, pp. 93–135) Amsterdam: Elsevier.

PART II

Segmenting Graduate Employability: Subject by Subject

BACKGROUND AND CONTEXT

To situate this part, and the chapters therein, graduate employability is aligned to industry, society, and academic contexts for students studying higher education. This background context offers the lens from which the chapters can be aligned in policy development and education practice to enhance student employability.

Society and industry have often been linked with the research and programmes of study within higher education institutions (HEIs). Universities and colleges[1] are founded upon inquiry of society, and supported to meet the research needs of expanding industry. HEIs not only mirror the needs of these external contexts, but seek to develop methods, processes, products, and knowledge to engage in development to support social and industrial development. As such, graduate employability should naturally be entrenched within the curriculum as it enables students to apply their knowledge in work and societal-based contexts. However, embedding employability (Yorke and Knight, 2006) is a relatively recent development in the history of HEIs.

The later part of the twentieth century saw the start of mass marketization of HEIs and the sector began growth to attract and include a wider range of students. No longer were HEI programmes accessible to the elite minority (Kelly et al., 2017), but were open to students from all backgrounds and life experiences (Hinton-Smith, 2012). This shift created new types of programmes, but also new ways of studying and funding in higher education (Gornitzka et al., 2005). A resulting consequence of the mass marketization of HEIs was the development of metrics to assess the quality and standards of the education provided (Gunn, 2018; Yorke, 2009). Included in this began the analysis of graduate transitions into successful graduate employment (Madsen, 2021). During the 2010s this increased in pace, and employability is now core in most curriculum review and development exercises completed in HEIs (for examples, see McCowan et al., 2018; Heydenrych and Case, 2018; Kuráth and Sipos, 2020). Therefore, academics are not only required to analyse data on graduate employability, but also seek to develop curricula and pedagogy to design and embed employability for successful employment.

Assessing how employability is designed and embedded within programmes enables policy makers and education practitioners' case study insights into how employability can be effective for HEI students. However, academic disciplines[2] research, write, and value employability in vastly different ways (O'Leary, 2017). It could also be argued that employability is a model which could be applied universally by simply adding graduate perspectives to the curriculum (Firth, 2022). As such, it is important to consider the different knowledge and values of employability provided for these discipline-based students. These chapters offer a lens on graduate employability in providing case examples of enhancing employability in different programmes of study. These exemplify 'on the ground' curriculum review and development exercises completed in support of graduate employability.

SUBJECT CONSIDERATIONS OF EMPLOYABILITY

Whilst there is no body of research focussing on 'disciplines of study and employability', there are bodies of knowledge within specific disciplines, and also in interdisciplinary employability development through competency, skill and knowledge progress. As such, the literature themes addressed briefly here are employability competencies, and discipline/interdisciplinary employability development.

Employability competencies are a useful, and yet contested, framework from which to consider effective and successful embedding of employability within HEI discipline curricula. A competency is often required by employers and noted within job adverts or role description criteria. As these are assessed and necessary for initial recruitment they are naturally considered for developing graduate employability. However, looking to develop competencies for a specific role, in a singular organisation, limits the range and application of the competency. Bridges (1993) argues this point in noting that competency development is not as sophisticated as the development of professional behaviour which is based upon intellectual and personal reflections from experiences. In this way, a competency can be included within discipline employability development, but has to be transversal (Leoni, 2014) in order to support lifelong employment in a range of organisations and roles.

The debate between discipline-specific employability and interdisciplinary employability can be noted due to the scholarship nature of the inquiry. A researcher asking 'How do I embed employability?' will naturally seek to research this within their own field of knowledge and teaching practice. When considering discipline-based employability, O'Leary (2017) found that even though students select a discipline-focussed programme within a HEI, students want varied employability skills and knowledge developed from their course and module directors. This is the motivating precursor to the development of HEI careers departments, and university-wide employability awards. However, these still do not universally support all students for the range of employment opportunities presented in their working life. Another way to weave interdisciplinary knowledge and embed employability is via industry and academic input. Römgens et al. (2020) argue this case in noting that work and study based employability development can reinforce each other in an interdisciplinary and integrated way. Embedding industry stakeholder positions with academic topics can enable students to critically appraise employability development in a range of contexts. This case study approach can be limiting if the same industry context is applied to the same topic area though. Further, Boahin and Hofman (2013) found that students wanted vocationally based employability developed from their programmes of study. This would follow in the same concept of competency developments and could lead to narrow skill and knowledge development.

The themes of competency and disciplinary/interdisciplinary employability for students are common perspectives to consider when looking within programme curricula development. They enable discussion of learning outcomes, assessment and critical analysis for employability to successfully embed and develop graduate employability.

OVERVIEW OF THE CHAPTERS IN THIS PART: ISSUES, THEMES AND RESEARCH

The chapters presented in this part offer a range of research outcomes, themes and issues emerging in support of graduate employability. The chapters cover case study research of graduate employability for arts industry students (Fox), law programmes (Glover et al.), psychology programmes (Walker et al.), history (Terkanian and Cosson), initial teacher education (Spooner-Lane et al.) and tourism and hospitality (Scarincini et al.). Although the chapters present different discipline-based analysis, they can all be utilized in developing policy and curricula for graduate employability.

***Integrated, Holistic and Inclusive*, Louise Glover, Joan Upson and Kate Campbell-Pilling**

Glover et al. have an interest in the emotional aspects of progression, and student wellbeing and resilience. Their chapter considers embedding employability across a cohort of students studying law. Although law is a traditionally vocational discipline, the authors are interested in how holistic employability curricula can support widening participation students, diverse cohorts, and inclusive education for employability. They focus on integrated employability, self-managed professional development, and learner wellbeing. The conclusions identify that law students require support for wider skillsets in order to fully support student employability for successful transitions into legal, and non-legal careers.

***We Need to Talk about Albert*, Ken Fox**

Fox's article offers exploration of a sustainability certificate for arts and creative industry university students. In this chapter Fox reflects on the benefits of an extra-curricular certificate for sustainability and aligns the student outcomes with their employability development. Fox notes that there needs to be a faster pedagogical response to support climate change issues as this is not online important for sustainability of the planet, but employability development for successful graduate transitions into arts and creative industry roles.

Through Others We Become Ourselves: How Service-learning Develops Graduate Identity, **Alison Walker, Jenny Mercer and Leanne Freeman**

From psychology, Walker et al. offer a new model, the 'Quadruple Helix', to demonstrate how graduate identity is developed through service-learning. The Helix model presented in this chapter includes management of emotions, developing purpose, establishing identity and moving towards independence. These are noted as important areas for graduate identity and the authors conclude that their model facets are required to develop the skills and attributes necessary for effective graduate employability and graduate identity.

The Graduate Project: A Model for Embedded Employability in Arts and Humanities Undergraduate Education, **Fiona Cosson and Kate Terkanian**

Terkanian and Cosson's chapter discusses a graduate project in history, a humanities subject, for undergraduate students. Through small workgroups students project-manage a new resource for society on behalf of an external 'client.' Not only does this project embed employability into history curricula, it also engages wider communities with the university and students and allows for analysis of research in new local communities.

Informing the Curriculum: Graduate Employability Skills for the Tourism and Hospitality Industry in Australia during a Pandemic, **Janice Scarinci, Josephine Pryce and K. Thirumaran**

Scarinci et al. outline the importance of graduate employability for tourism and hospitality graduates set against the backdrop of the COVID 19 pandemic. Thematic analysis of job advertisements in Australia offers an industry perspective of the changing skill and knowledge requirements employers have for new graduates from these fields of study. Transferable and industry-relevant skills, a curriculum which embeds external employers, and consistent curriculum review and development are noted as key to ensuring students can transition successfully into graduate employment.

The Teaching Performing Assessment (TPA) and Its Impact on Graduates' Preparedness for Employment, Rebecca Spooner-Lane, Kathy Jordan, John Buchanan and Tania Broadley

The Teaching Performance Assessment for Initial Teacher Education is analysed in three Australian Universities for Spooner-Lane et al.'s chapter. Through analysis of teacher perspectives this chapter critically explores the use of an additional capstone assessment to further develop school teacher employability. Conclusions note how school teacher employability is not fixed, nor finite, but developed over many years in practice and employment.

These chapters provide unique insights into case studies on embedding employability within disciplines of study in higher education. Authors are not only investigating improvements in curriculum design, but seeking to understand how best to embed and assess employability for students. A limitation of this part is that the chapters do not consider postgraduate, apprenticeship nor research based programmes of study, but these are reflected upon in other chapters within the book.

AREAS OF FURTHER RESEARCH RECOMMENDED:

- International comparisons of employability for specific disciplines is needed. Existing research in disciplines tends to focus within national borders or across similar types of HEIs. International comparisons would enable a more sophisticated understanding of graduate employability for transnational flows of graduates;
- Discipline research for employability tends to focus upon undergraduate studies and there is a gap in knowledge for postgraduate students. Research is needed to understand the employability needs of postgraduate taught and postgraduate research students;
- Programmes of study that are not explicitly linked with a vocation, or employment routes, should ensure transferable skills are developed effectively. Analysis of effective, transferable and life-long employability skills and knowledge is needed for an effective model to implement in HEIs;
- The balance between quality higher education, and higher education that effectively prepares students for graduate life does not need to be in opposition. Research is needed to test this position to further enable HEIs to effectively embed employability across all programmes of study;
- Researching an interdisciplinary approach to the inclusion of industry professionals and thought leaders within the curriculum;
- Analysis of portfolio careers and the skills and knowledge graduates need to complete these.

NOTES

1 Higher Education establishments in North America, not secondary education providers in the UK
2 Topics of study, or faculties of study

REFERENCES

Boahin, P. and Hofman, A. (2013). A disciplinary perspective of competency-based training on the acquisition of employability skills. *Journal of Vocational Education & Training*, 65(3), 385–401.

Bridges, D. (1993). Transferable skills: a philosophical perspective. *Studies in Higher Education*, 18(1), 43–51.

Firth, M. (2022). Why higher education needs graduate workers' perspectives, *WONKHE Blog post*, accessed at https://wonkhe.com/blogs/why-higher-education-needs-graduate-workers-perspectives/ (Accessed: May 30 2022).

Gornitzka, A., Kogan, M. and Amaral, A. (2005). *Reform and change in higher education: analysing policy implementation*. A. Gornitzka, M. Kogan & A. Amaral (eds) Dordrecht: Springer Netherlands.

Gunn, A. (2018). Metrics and methodologies for measuring teaching quality in higher education: developing the Teaching Excellence Framework (TEF). *Educational Review* (Birmingham), 70(2), 129–148.

Heydenrych, H. and Case, J. M. (2018). Researching graduate destinations using LinkedIn: an exploratory analysis of South African chemical engineering graduates. *European Journal of Engineering Education*, 43(5), 693–705.

Hinton-Smith, T. (2012). *Widening participation in higher education: casting the net wide?* Houndmills, Basingstoke, Hampshire; Palgrave Macmillan.

Kelly, P., Fair, N. and Evans, C. (2017). The engaged student ideal in UK higher education policy. *Higher Education Policy*, 30(1), 105–122.

Kuráth, G. and Sipos, N. (2020). Competencies and success measured by net income among Hungarian HE graduates. *Education & Training* (London), 63(3), 417–439.

Leoni, R. (2014). Graduate employability and the development of competencies. The incomplete reform of the 'Bologna Process'. *International Journal of Manpower*, 35(4), 448–469.

Madsen, M. (2021). The configurative agency of metrics in education: a research agenda involving a different engagement with data. *Journal of Education Policy*, 36(1), 64–83.

McCowan, T., Oanda, I. and Oketch, M. O. (2018). Towards a national graduate destinations survey in Kenya: an exploratory study of three universities. *Higher Education Policy*, 31(1), 97–119.

O'Leary, S. (2017). Graduates' experiences of, and attitudes towards, the inclusion of employability-related support in undergraduate degree programmes: trends and variations by subject discipline and gender. *Journal of Education and Work*, 30(1), 84–105.

Römgens, I., Scoupe, R. and Beausaert, S. (2020). Unraveling the concept of employability, bringing together research on employability in higher education and the workplace. *Studies in Higher Education*, 45(12), 2588–2603.

Yorke, M. (2009). 'Student experience' surveys: some methodological considerations and an empirical investigation. *Assessment and Evaluation in Higher Education*, 34(6), 721–739.

Yorke, M. and Knight, P. (2006). *Embedding employability into the curriculum*. York: Higher Education Academy.

9

Integrated, Holistic and Inclusive: A Law School Employability and Skills Model Working to Maximise Opportunity and Support for All

Louise Glover, Joan Upson and Kate Campbell-Pilling

In this chapter we examine the importance of employability provision that is integrated, holistic and inclusive across a full cohort of students and appropriate to all levels of the degree programme.

DEFINING AND LEARNING FOR EMPLOYABILITY THROUGH AN ACADEMIC DISCIPLINE

The earliest universities in Europe were founded to teach law; Irnerius, commonly considered the founder of the University of Bologna was a judge and professor of Roman law during the late eleventh century and early twelfth century (University of Bologna, 2022). Today many law schools including our own play a civic role within their community by the provision of free legal advice (University of Sheffield, 2022). Within a law school where students focus upon law and/or criminology, obvious career pathways may continue to suggest a narrow, practice-focused approach to employability. However, as with all disciplines, many of our students have wider perspectives from the outset, or change their aims as they recognise the breadth of opportunities available to them due to their legal studies, or more broadly as a graduate. This reflects the norm in the

UK that a law degree is an undergraduate rather than postgraduate degree and therefore students' career ambitions may evolve or change dramatically during the course of their studies.

In our chapter, we endorse a definition of employability that is broader than merely *recruitability* into employment but looks forward to the individual's future success within it. As Yorke (2006, p. 8) explains, employability is: 'a set of achievements – skills, understandings and personal attributes – that makes graduates more likely to gain employment and be successful in their chosen occupations, which benefits themselves, the workforce, the community and the economy'.

This reflects an approach to higher education as giving life long skills or graduate attributes. These broader approaches accord with an increasing focus within institutions on employability in a wide sense and recognition that employability is not a discrete task that is done outside and in addition to students' degrees, but developed through their degree as well as other aspects of their life before and at university. As Speight et al. (2013: 115) explain '[t]he model is not academic learning and learning for employability, but learning for employability through the academic discipline'.

Within our own institution, this principle is encapsulated in the Sheffield Graduate Attributes (2021), which include attributes linked to learning as well as personal impact and self-management. The graduate attributes are dynamic, transitional and transferable tools; they are the 'attributes which the university community and external partners have agreed are likely to be particularly beneficial to academic success, personal development and employability' and they will be 'developed and enriched through academic programmes and all extra-curricular activities, learning and work experiences' (University of Sheffield, 2021).

This formulation recognises the holistic impact on student development of a range of activities within and out with a students' degree programme. Defining a wider range of experiences as contributing to graduate attributes suggests that the experiences are linked in some way to the degree programme, even if their provision is not integral to it. For example, the inclusion of work experience may refer to a placement undertaken as part of a degree programme but would also include experience on employer vacation placements secured independently of the university but to which students gain access due to their educational status.

By implication, this wider definition also recognises the limitations of academic study alone to extend or assess an individual's capabilities, a trend that is reflected both in employer expectations and academic literature on employability. Eraut (2011) explains the importance and complexity of informal learning in the workplace, which he defines to include student participation in higher education itself as well as the more obvious places where paid work is carried out. Gbadamosi et al. (2019) highlight the important role that both placements and part-time work play in developing students' soft skills and confidence, and in creating a pathway to further opportunities.

IMPLICATIONS OF WIDER CHANGES IN THE SECTORAL LANDSCAPE

Taking a step back, as we are aware, the global transition from elite to mass higher education as observed by Trow (1974) and Tight (2017) amongst many others, impacted upon the growth of both university and student numbers across OECD nations during the latter part of the twentieth century and into the twenty-first century. This was further emphasised in the domestic context by the UK Labour Government policy of the late 1990s to increase the number of students attending university domestically to 50% of all 18-year-olds, although Augar (2019) would suggest that we cannot presume that that direction of travel will be maintained going forward. This increase brought with it the need to expand both university provision and the pool of potential students to sustain growth, thus increasing the opportunities of access to university education and encouraging social inclusion in terms of recruitment.

In the UK this growth has generally focused upon a push for social inclusion through widening participation; the push for widening participation allowing new social groups to gain the economic and other benefits of higher education, in addition to the more general benefits to the wider economy. Beyond the perspective of social justice, extending the opportunities of higher education may, as suggested by Warrington (2008), of course also be viewed as ensuring a continued supply of appropriate skills and expertise to support the emergent knowledge economy. However, the needs of the economy may sometimes be erratic, challenging those embarking upon their career pathway to do the best that they can individually, calling upon formal and informal skills, learning and employability experience. From the perspective of those engaged in learning and teaching in higher education a key focus should be knowing and understanding who our students are currently, rather than assuming that they are representative of the same schools, the same qualifications, the same social background that they may theoretically have been in the past. The character of our students and their pre and post university experience should influence how we choose to enable transition, learning and best facilitate them to succeed in their chosen career route through our employability strategies. Our strategies should, therefore, seek to maximise the benefit of the student experience whatever the economic backdrop of the individual may be.

The growth in higher education provision has provided not only an opportunity for universities, but also an obligation to commit to the support of students across all social backgrounds to maintain their progress at each stage of their undergraduate experience, through selection, recruitment, transition and final attainment. This expectation is not just to allow universities free rein to service their own interest in maintaining and/or expanding recruitment numbers, but in the interests of widening participation (WP), as a condition of licensed HEI status eligibility for those recruited to gain the support of the Student Loan Company at the current fee rate. To maintain their position, universities must commit their support to WP students not least through the Access Agreement, with the Office for Students as regulator focusing their interest on outputs rather than inputs.

Access and recruitment on the basis of widening participation and social inclusivity has been an important trend, but opportunity alone does not create an equal experience, as the periodic reports of the Social Mobility Commission evidence (2019, 2020).

A further feature of the sectoral landscape which 'sets the scene' for the growing focus on employability within institutions and the students whom they serve is the consumerisation of higher education (see for example guidance on consumer law by the UK's Competition and Markets Authority (CMA, 2015)) as part of a wider process of marketisation (Tomlinson, 2018). Employability statistics such as the UK's Graduate Outcomes metrics lend themselves readily to this approach as a measurable comparator of value in an increasingly commoditised higher education sector in which added value or quality may be hard to assess by other means.

DEFINING WIDENING PARTICIPATION AND RECOGNISING POSSIBLE IMPLICATIONS FOR EMPLOYABILITY PROVISION

'Widening participation' as a category and widening participation students cannot be represented by a single definition, although thematically some strands may have much in common. Moore et al. (2013) reporting to HEFCE and OFFA included:

- Lower socio-economic groups
- Mature students
- Part-time learners
- Learners from ethnic minority groups
- Vocational and work-based learners
- Disabled learners
- Care leavers

Although for some purposes, and some higher education institutions, the definition adopted may be broad enough to identify attendance at a state school as sufficient to fall within the widest spectrum. What is clear from our perspective is that although students from this grouping *may* have family and/or friends within the legal profession or allied legal or criminological careers, they are likely to be in the minority, with the remainder having no access to the intrinsic knowledge of those professionals that may be passed on painlessly to some other students. This may be viewed as an aspect of 'social and cultural capital' as highlighted by Bourdieu (1986). Reflecting upon this Francis (2015: 179) observed 'those without the appropriate habitus have their possibilities for action severely constrained'.

Reference to this concept is particularly significant in relation to students who are seeking a legal career. For law students, an early insight into the professions and recruitment processes may mean that a student is already ahead of the game. An important feature of the employability agenda in a *law school* therefore, is that it must engage students early in their first year and ensure that they buy into the cadence of events, rather than considering employability and career aspirations to be something for the future.

Whilst the focus of attention in relation to students who might be viewed as being representative of widening participation remains largely upon recruitment, transition and attainment, it may be argued that for some this might miss the point. The legal profession has made movements towards increasing diversity during the twenty-first century, as Sommerlad et al. (2010) observe, but further support and guidance within their substantive, employability and extra-curricular studies may better support overall learning and help all students to launch their individual careers. The point was well made by Bamber and Tett (2000) that 'for its part the university must accept that the implications of offering access to non-traditional students does not end, but rather begins at the point of entry'.

For all students, transitioning to university may bring with it a certain anxiety as they seek to reach the position of, in the words of Meehan and Howells (2019), 'being, belonging and becoming'. For students from a widening participation background this may however, in some instances, be more difficult as they may be more prone to feeling 'othered', assuming that everyone else knows what they are doing both in the immediate and longer term. The impact may range from a defensive preference not to fully take part in group discussions or learning activities to perhaps a greater incidence of consequent mental health issues as observed by Olaniyan (2021). What this does prompt is careful consideration of those employability events and skills sessions that are of clear importance to all, suggesting that at least a minimal employability provision ought to have *required* attendance.

Our own model of holistic integration was developed with this in mind, but also acknowledged the practical difficulties that may be faced by some in attending non-timetabled and extra-curricular events. This is in line with the observations of Tinto (2008), but is something that we had observed ourselves anecdotally, prompting us to reconfigure and reschedule some of our employability provision. Prior to our current employability template we had a number of compulsory first year events which were then followed by non-compulsory provision in the second and final years. A brief reflection upon student attendance of these events over just a few years suggested that whilst the first-year sessions attracted equal numbers of students from widening participation and non-widening participation backgrounds, in the second and final years there were twice as many non-widening participation students in attendance. Whilst this was little more than an observation, it did support a concern that we already had and informed us as we looked to develop the current model.

A more unfortunate aspect of differential attendance of extra-curricular activities as between widening participation students and their counterparts, however, is that widening participation students may be less involved in such activities than other student groups (Moore et al., 2013).

This remains a distinguishing feature of many widening participation students and may be for a whole range of reasons. Not all have children or are carers, part/full-time workers, commuters, remaining living at home with their existing infrastructure around them and some may not be aware of the significance of becoming an engaged citizen of their university. Many, however, will have their own stories to tell that will inform potential employers of their efforts inside and beyond the classroom, and employability provision should seek to help individuals to validate these activities as well as any formal extra-curricular opportunities.

WEAKNESSES OF THE TRADITIONAL EMPLOYABILITY MODEL

Whilst as a Law School we have always presented a strong employability provision it was traditionally based upon optionality and student proactivity with events and opportunities being extra-curricular. However, our reflections on this model identified a number of weaknesses.

The timetable for showing interest in legally focused careers starts from the first year of the degree programme, with increasing numbers of employers, predominantly large international commercial law firms offering short structured internships even at this early stage. Strong performance on a first year scheme may secure the candidate a place on the law firm's penultimate year schemes that can lead to the offer of a graduate job or, more unusually, may even allow the student to secure a graduate job at the end of their first year (see international law firm Clifford Chance's 2021 SPARK scheme). Students therefore need an awareness of deadlines for those opportunities and the expectations of them as candidates at a very early stage in the degree.

These early opportunities are highly competitive and should be seen in the context that in 2018–19 there were 6,344 trainee solicitor placements in England and Wales (the largest branch of the legal profession), compared to 16,499 students graduating from law degrees. The number of law graduates represents a 22.8% increase from 2009. The average age of qualification as a solicitor was 29.6 years in 2018–19 (The Law Society, 2020) who report that more up-to-date data has been delayed by technical issues. Not only is qualification as a solicitor a long process, it is inevitable that many graduating students will go on to careers outside the traditional legal professions and these factors must be reflected in an effective employability model.

The optional model therefore principally favours those who were already in a position to 'know'. Without this knowledge, the natural instinct to focus on their studies and deal with careers at a later date also worked against groups of students who did not have the background knowledge to embrace employability provision from the outset, perhaps being particularly detrimental to those who may be categorised as widening participation students.

This early timetable for career focus within prestigious parts of the legal profession may lead to an instrumental approach to employability to facilitate students securing work experience or a graduate role. In our Law School we run employability events at least once a week and often more frequently during term time. Common events include alumni explaining their own career journey and employers providing students with information or mentoring, often using well-known employers to encourage students to sign up voluntarily as well as skills sessions such as networking, mooting training, legal tech and commercial awareness sessions.

While there are clear knowledge-sharing benefits to such events, the importance of reflective practice to development is now well established by Kolb (1984) and others, including an assessment of the benefits of reflective practice within our own School of Law (Blandy, 2019). Without such a process, there may be substantial variance in students' ability to recognise the employability skills that they have acquired (Burke et al., 2005). Nicholson (2020) argues that a 'product' (such as a law degree) may have a true value that is not fully appreciated by its 'consumer' (or student), and this argument also holds for broader aspects of that student's experience. The discipline required for effective reflective practice may be more difficult in an extra-curricular setting than within a curriculum in which students anticipate, and may be compelled to participate in, study commitments. We encourage this by packaging some of our extra-curricular events into certificates that can be added to student CVs and require students to engage with a programme of events and undertake a reflective exercise rather than simply attending on an ad hoc basis. In our curricular module we are able to go further by requiring students to complete a compulsory e-portfolio; a method with recognised positive effects (Belcher et al., 2014) but also some barriers to use such as privacy concerns.

MOVE TO AN INTEGRATED, HOLISTIC APPROACH

For employability to be truly integral to the degree it needs to contain elements that are embedded within the degree to be experienced by all members of a cohort rather than to take place in extra-curricular spaces accessed in practice by only some of its members. It needs to be visible so that students can reflect upon, 'name and claim' their expertise for '[e]mployability as "hidden" within the curriculum serves no one as it cannot be articulated' (Speight et al., 2013: 124).

Students increasingly acquire transferable skills not merely through experiences provided in or through their institution but also independently of it, such as part-time work. A diverse student body means that other students will arrive at university with a diverse range of transferable skills (for example a mature student who has enjoyed a prior career). Students may struggle to recognise the benefits of unnamed skills gained by non-traditional means to graduate employment though they may readily recognise benefits from a 'university sponsored' experience such as an integrated placement, as Gbadamosi et al. (2019: 210) noted in relation to part-time work. One aim of a holistic, embedded and reflective approach to employability should be to facilitate all students within its body who may have diverse backgrounds, routes to university and lifestyles to perceive the contribution of their individual journey to their unique mix of capabilities, character and values. We argue that a holistic model of learning for employability through the academic discipline may encourage the same academic and employability benefits to attach to students' diverse non-university experience that are seen in relation to initiatives that are more obviously integral to the university experience or 'university sponsored'. This model may also foster inclusion and avoid the perception of 'othering'.

A further argument for embedding employability-related skills is that such transferable skills are also necessary *during* university, to enable students to transition effectively from their 'before' life (whether that is secondary education or otherwise) *through* university (enabling adjustment to the increasing requirements of their degree) and beyond to create a valuable life after university. On this view, employability is best seen as 'preparation for life rather than a specific job, it is about capabilities rather than specific skills, and about being rather than having' (Bamber and Tett, 2000: 123).

Focusing on capabilities removes one of the weaknesses of the narrow, profession-based approach. We recognise that we cannot cater for all potential career routes within the School, though we can signpost to support elsewhere. More fundamentally, we can encourage all students to be curious and confident in exploring the range of options open to them. The curricular model can give all members of the cohort the inspiration and, we hope, the freedom to do so.

EMBEDDING EMPLOYABILITY IN A SCHOOL OF LAW

We present here our case study of measures that we have taken in our Law School to respond to the issues discussed above. An assessment of their impact, opportunities for future growth and how best to address these will be the subject of future work.

In our compulsory skills module, employability activities sit alongside academic skills development through legal, professional and academic skills toolkits and activities. This starts early in each new intake's journey when they work in teams to take part in a moot (a mock judicial proceeding set up to examine a hypothetical case as an academic exercise) during the first few weeks of their degree. Participation in the moot is compulsory for all students, who may take a team role as an advocate or judge, as well as researching the relevant law and preparing the team's skeleton or outline argument. During the pandemic, the moot has reflected the adjustments that have taken place in real-life courtrooms as reported upon by the House of Lords' Select Committee on the Constitution (House of Lords, 2021) by taking place with students working not merely remotely from the staff judges but from the other members of their own team. As part of their e-portfolio, students must reflect upon the moot and the skills they have employed or developed in taking part.

Students take part in a peer-to-peer CV review exercise intended to encourage them to reflect further on their own skills and, as we discuss below, to normalise conversations around skills and employability and to build support and resilience within their personal tutor groups.

Continuing our focus on 'capabilities', students take part in a workshop on teamwork to give structure to their own group work for academic credit during core law modules. They meet a panel of alumni and employers from a range of occupations which include, but are broader than, the legal professions who explain the relevance of teamwork to their working lives.

Graduate employers explain how teamwork is one of the core competencies that they seek from candidates and how and why they use assessment centres to map candidates' capabilities. Students take part in a group work exercise with more senior students acting as facilitators and assessors, similar to the type of exercise that might be used in an employer assessment centre. Once more, students reflect upon these experiences in their e-portfolios.

ACADEMIC PERFORMANCE

Our primary reason for developing the module was to give students the skills they require in order to succeed on the degree. Such skills are transferable to employability but are also transferable from employability activities to academic pursuits. Binder et al. (2015) explain that employability activities such as work placements and involvement in student societies do not merely develop soft skills but also improve academic performance. This benefit also extends to first year students (Harris-Reeves and Mahoney, 2017). In a pilot 'convenience' study, students involved in pro bono volunteering in our own School of Law perceived the positive effect on their curricular learning, including on their ability to apply law to facts, to carry out accurate and well-organised research and in the development of their understanding of complex issues (Barrow et al., 2020). We suggest that universities and those who work in them should clearly articulate the benefit of participation in skills-based activities *for students' current studies* as well as future employability ambitions. One further benefit of embedding such activities may be to regulate the time that students allocate to them, as studies suggest that the benefit to academic work of extra-curricular activities is strongest at low to moderate levels of activity but levels off and declines if excessive levels prevent students dedicating the necessary time to their academic studies (Seow and Pan, 2014).

WELLBEING

We have become increasingly interested in the emotional aspects of progression, student wellbeing and resilience in relation to postgraduation career plans. This chapter relates to a module delivered within a law school where there can be a perception of a particular career path. Some students may be comfortable not yet planning for the future or not knowing what they might want that future to hold. However, in light of this perception, others may judge themselves against peers who appear to have a firm idea of their future and seem well advanced on that path. Those students may then be detrimentally impacted by what they see as their own failing, in comparison, which may exacerbate their own perceived or potentially real reduced employability opportunities. As Francis (2015) notes, drawing on Markus and Nurius (1986), 'possible selves can only include those selves that it is possible for that individual to perceive'. There is a real need for this to be addressed.

The association between ongoing unemployment and reduced subjective wellbeing is now well established and much information is readily available on this topic. However, before reaching such a point it is necessary to consider young people just leaving full-time education and moving into employment. As the What Works Centre for Wellbeing (2018) states:

> The transition from full-time education into employment can be a testing time for many young people. Helping young people find employment has been a key policy objective for many years, and indeed the percentage of young people not in education, employment or training (NEETs) is now part of the United Nations SDG framework. Using five years of longitudinal data from the UK Understanding Society Survey, this study finds that young people with lower levels of life satisfaction are less likely to go on to find a job.

This study then continues to note that 'while most demographic factors are fixed, life satisfaction is something that can be improved within the education system … As such, actors looking to improve the employability of young people – particularly introverts, should consider interventions that improve their life satisfaction'.

In accepting this statement, wellbeing must be viewed as integral to the student journey. There has been a pivot in our approach to student support and in particular wellbeing support. This used to be seen as the exclusive domain of the personal tutor. Now it is the remit of both a newly created and dedicated Wellbeing Team and the skills module designers. This facilitates wellbeing to be embedded from the ground level upwards enabling it to be fully integrated into the student experience. It fuses wellbeing with the development of legal academic and employability skills. The wellbeing support, particularly in relation to employability, aims to negate the effect any barriers students may face or indeed themselves create in relation to the development of such skills where they do not yet have a definite career plan mapped out.

Wellbeing is at the core of the personal tutor system but it can often feel forced and difficult for a student who has had little contact with their allocated member of staff. This is well recognised but, to remedy this and with straightforward action, we revised the compulsory skills module. Small group face-to-face sessions are delivered, in the case of the Level 1 entrants, intensively in the early weeks of the first semester. These are now led exclusively by the students' personal tutor. This has a raft of benefits, the first being that the relationship between student and personal tutor is established at the start of the student journey. This relationship is likely to last for the duration of their studies and a solid foundation to build from is essential. Second, it brings together small groups of students, new to higher education who can share their experiences, hopes and fears. In particular the frequent contact can help the quieter, less outgoing students to find their place within the group. Such groups can become high functioning, passing through the stages of Tuckman's model (1965) so providing a solid peer support network for each other throughout their time at university. Third, as the same tutor delivers the sessions it provides a consistent point of contact. By drawing these benefits together we aim to reduce some of the well-known anxieties of starting university (such as, not being as able as other students on that course, not having a postgraduation plan, not having enough experience of the expected career path the course leads to) through the two-level wellbeing support system wrapping around them. Such a support system should also naturally foster the space for the students to develop resilience with the comforting knowledge that both peer and tutor support underpins them.

Turner et al. (2016) in their first finding noted that amongst the benefits of engaging in skills-based activities within a degree programme was the student perception of their enhanced employability. By drawing on this conclusion, such enhancement can be argued to have a direct positive impact on the wellbeing of the participants, thus reinforcing the importance of the fusion of the two pillars of employability and wellbeing.

To complement this provision at modular level the School has a dedicated wellbeing team comprising staff with significant experience of pastoral care and specially trained wellbeing advisors to support holistic wellbeing. The team has developed and implemented a strategy to work proactively to enhance the wellbeing of all students guided by the overarching university student mental health strategies. Following these priorities the team has created and delivered interactive sessions to help raise awareness and understanding of the importance of wellbeing and to foster a culture where wellbeing is openly acknowledged and discussed. Regular drop-in sessions and tailored support during the summer vacation period are also offered to ensure that the support is ongoing and accessible for continuing student needs.

The wellbeing provision goes beyond the examples drawn above but one further particular example is worthy of discussion in this chapter with its focus on employability skills. Within the compulsory skills module, students in those same small groups are required to perform tasks in relation to CVs, both of their peers and their own. Carefully structured to engender engagement through a range of activities, the students gradually critique their own skill set and identify and develop how to demonstrate such skills. The premise is twofold: improvement of their own CV leading to enhanced awareness of their employability skills but also crucially the awareness that skills gained beyond the vocational field can be wide ranging and varied. By having to discuss skills and analyse them, the students gain insight into their own abilities. They also have direct sight of the skills of their peers and their career aspirations. This can nurture resilience. A clear example of this is their discussion of employment setbacks they have experienced. Those discussions bring such disappointments into the light. They can be seen as learning points and part of developing employability skills rather than failures. We believe that this feeds directly into wellbeing by students becoming aware that whilst some of their peers, even at this early stage, have chosen career paths, many of their peers are not in that position and that this is normal and usual. They understand that not having a career mapped out ahead of them at any stage is not failing. Talking about your own feelings is a well-accepted mental health strategy and its benefit is widely promoted. By giving time and space in the curriculum to do this, the module reinforces the importance of this within an employability context.

Whilst this section has primarily focused on the Level 1 provision, the compulsory skills module is delivered across all levels and continues to work in tandem with the wellbeing provision within the School. This perhaps sits with the theory argued by Jackson (2016) that whilst students are responsible for the control of their own identities some responsibility also lies with others who seek to strengthen their employability.

Despite the compulsory skills module being centred around legal academic and employability skills this model of integrated wellbeing is transferable to other disciplines and arguably more so to less clearly vocational programmes, and to both national and international degree programmes. The overriding aim at all levels of normalising an absence of a planned career path and indeed resilience within such an area is something to be developed, honed, worked on and talked about. That is the key message here.

CONCLUSION

The development of our integrated, holistic and inclusive approach linking employability with legal and wider academic skills therefore works to favour and support *all* students throughout their studies and beyond, and represents a model of wider interest. Having worked through our initial development and reappraisal of this model we now find ourselves, as everyone else, facing the strains of employability at a time of the Covid-19 pandemic. Our embedded curriculum has proved surprisingly adaptable to moving online. Some aspects have been more successful than others: for example, peer CV review has faced similar challenges for student engagement with online group work to that which we have experienced in mainstream academic learning. Again, like others, we find ourselves reviewing what has worked well online and what works best in a face-to-face setting.

In these current circumstances our model extends support not only to the positive route to future careers, but works to enhance wellbeing by enabling students to give themselves 'permission' not to follow established pathways, or schedules. Such self-management is particularly important in a vocational degree programme but we feel that it may feature to one extent or another across academic programmes at all levels.

REFERENCES

Augar, P. (2019) Review of post-18 education and funding, Department for Education, London.

Bamber, J. and Tett, L. (2000) Transforming the learning experience of non-traditional students: a perspective from higher education *Studies in Continuing Education*, 22(1), pp. 57–75.

Barrow, D., Glover, L. and Hervey, T. (2020) Pro bono develops Pericles and plumbers: the roles of clinical legal education in contemporary European law schools *European Journal of Legal Education*, 1(1), pp. 117–154.

Belcher R., Jones, A., Smith, L., Vincent, T., Bhaarrati Naidu, S., Montgomery, J., Haq, I., and Gill, D. (2014) Qualitative study of the impact of an authentic electronic portfolio in undergraduate medical education *BMC Medical Education* 14(265).

Binder, J., Baguley, T., Crook, C. and Miller, F. (2015) The academic value of internships: benefits across disciplines and student backgrounds *Contemporary Educational Psychology* 41, pp. 73–82.

Blandy, S. (2019) Enhancing employability through student engagement in pro bono projects *International Journal of Clinical Legal Education*, 26(1), pp. 7–45.

Bourdieu, P. (1986) The form of capital. *Handbook of theory and research and the sociology of education*, New York: Greenwood, pp. 241–258.

Buckley, P. and Lee, P. (2021) The impact of extra-curricular activity on the student experience *Active Learning in Higher Education*, 22(1), pp. 37–48.

Burke, V., Jones, I. and Doherty, M. (2005) Analysing student perceptions of transferable skills via undergraduate degree programmes *Active Learning in Higher Education*, 6(2), pp. 132–144.

Chance, C. (2021) *What we offer.* Available at: https://careers.cliffordchance.com/london/what-we-offer/spark.html. (Accessed 7 July 2021).

Competition and Markets Authority (2015) *Higher education: consumer law advice for providers.* Available at: www.gov.uk/government/publications/higher-education-consumer-law-advice-for-providers (Accessed 24 October 2021).

Eraut, M. (2011) Informal learning in the workplace: evidence on the real value of work-based learning *Development and Learning in Organizations*, 25(5): pp. 8–12.

Francis, A. (2015) Legal education, social mobility, and employability: possible selves, curriculum intervention, and the role of legal work experience *Journal of Law and Society*, 42(2), pp. 173–201.

Harris-Reeves, B. and Mahoney, J. (2017) Brief work-integrated learning opportunities and first year university students' perceptions of employability and academic performance *Australian Journal of Career Development*, 26(1), pp. 32–37.

Jackson, D. (2016) Re-conceptualising graduate employability: the importance of pre-professional identity *Higher Education Research & Development*, 35(5), pp. 925–939.

Gbadamosi, G., Evans, C., Jones, K., Hickman, M. and Rudley, H. (2019) The perceived value of work placements and part-time work and its diminution with time *Journal of Education and Work*, 32(2), pp. 196–214.

House of Lords (2021) Select Committee on the Constitution 22nd Report of Session 2019–21 *Covid-19 and the Courts.* Available at https://publications.parliament.uk/pa/ld5801/ldselect/ldconst/257/257.pdf (Accessed 12 July 2021).

Interim Conclusion of the Review of Post-18 Education and Funding (2021), Department for Education, GOV.UK

Kolb, D. A. (1984) Experiential learning: experience as the source of learning and development. Englewood Cliffs, New Jersey: Prentice-Hall.

Markus, H. and Nurius, P. (1986) Possible selves *American Psychologist*, 41(9), pp. 954–969.

Meehan, C. and Howells, K. (2019) In search of the feeling of 'belonging' in higher education: undergraduate student transitions into higher education *Journal of Further and Higher Education*, 43(10), pp. 1376–1390.

Moore, J., Sanders, J. and Higham, L. (2013) *Literature review of research into widening participation to higher education*, Report to HEFCE and OFFA by ARC Network.

Nicholson, A. (2020) The value of a law degree, *The Law Teacher*, 54(2), pp. 194–208.

Olaniyan, F. (2021) Paying the widening participation penalty: racial and ethnic minority students and mental health in British Universities *Analyses of Social Issues and Public Policy*, 21(1), pp. 761–783.

Seow, P. and Pan, G. (2014) A literature review of the impact of extracurricular activities participation on students' academic performance *Journal of Education for Business*, 89(7): pp. 361–366.

Social Mobility Commission, *State of the Nation 2018–19: Social Mobility in Great Britain*, Social Mobility Commission, GOV.UK.

Speight, S., Lackovic, N. and Cooker, L. (2013) The contested curriculum: academic learning and employability in higher education *Tertiary Education and Management*, 19(2), pp. 112–116.

Sommerlad, H., Webley, L., Duff, L., Muzia, D., Tomlinson, J. and Parnham, R. (2010) *Diversity in the legal profession in England and Wales: a qualitative study of barriers and individual choices,* University of Westminster Law Press.

The Law Society (2020).

Tight, M. (2017) Mass higher education and massification *Higher Education Policy*, 32, pp. 93–108.

Tinto, V. (2008) *Access without support is not opportunity: keynote address at the 36th Annual Institute for Chief Academic Officers*, The Council of Independent Colleges, Seattle, Washington.

Tomlinson, M. (2018) Conceptions of the value of higher education in a measured market *Higher Education*, 75, pp. 711–727.

Trow, M. (1974) Problems in the transition from elite to mass higher education, Carnegie Commission on Higher Education.

Turner, J., Bone, A. and Ashton, J. (2016) Reasons why law students should have access to learning law through a skills-based approach *The Law Teacher*, 52(1), pp. 1–16.

Tuckman, B. W. (1965) Developmental sequence in small groups *Psychological Bulletin*, 63(6), pp. 384–399.

University of Bologna (2022) Irnerius [Viewed 16 March 2022]. Available at: www.unibo.it/en/university/who-we-are/our-history/famous-people-and-students/Irnerius.

University of Sheffield (2022) *School of Law*, Pro Bono [Viewed 16 March 2022]. Available at: www.sheffield.ac.uk/law/undergraduate/probono.

University of Sheffield (2021) The Sheffield Graduate Attributes [Viewed 7 July 2021]. Available at: www.sheffield.ac.uk/skills/sga.

Warrington, M. (2008) Decisions and transitions: meeting the needs of the knowledge economy *Environmental and Planning Government and Policy*, 26, pp. 924–937.

What Works Centre for Wellbeing (2018) Education to employment: the role of wellbeing. Available at: https://whatworkswellbeing.org/resources/education-to-employment-the-role-of-wellbeing/ (Accessed 11 July 2021).

Yorke, M. (2006) *Employability in higher education: what it is, what it is not*, Higher Education Academy. Available at www.voced.edu.au/content/ngv%3A16446 (Accessed 24 October 2021).

10

We Need to Talk about Albert: Sustainability is Employability

Ken Fox

INTRODUCTION

The title of Lionel Shriver's novel (2003), *We Need to Talk about Kevin*, and the film of the same name released in 2013 is a catchy hook on which to hang the title of this chapter but the inspiration drawn from the book in particular is the need to confront the reality of our situation.

Lionel Shriver's central female character does not wish to have children but when she does, in the shape of Kevin, who goes on to take part in a Columbine-like school massacre, every facet of motherhood is questioned. In talking about Kevin, she and her husband, through the epistolatory style of the novel try to confront their own culpability but also make sense of how they raised a sociopathic son. The central theme of the book may seem a long way from a discussion of education for sustainable development and employability. However, the impetus of the novel to question the very nature of the maternal instinct leaves no doubt that talking about what is feared, what is repressed, and sometimes what is denied is the only way forward.

As George Marshall's book (2014) *Don't Even Think About It: Why Our Brains Are Wired To Ignore Climate Change* notes, talking or thinking about climate change does not arrive without direction, encouragement and the empowerment of individuals. Kingsnorth's review of Marshall's book in the *London Review of Books* (2014) captures the author's message:

> Marshall suggests we change the narrative: instead of seeing climate change as a war, we could see it as a quest, which would give people of all persuasions a chance to take part in solving the problem. Doing anything useful about climate change requires everyone to lever themselves out of their comfort zones.

Without education for sustainable development and the incentive of employability this leverage out of our comfort zones might still prove difficult despite repeated evidence that we are in a climate emergency. We also need to be mindful, as Kahneman (2011: 4) observes in his experiment on people's perception known as the 'gorilla study', where participants were asked to watch very closely one task taking place, as someone in a gorilla suit passed through the observed scene: 'The gorilla study illustrates two important facts about our minds: we can be blind to the obvious and we can be blind to our blindness'. Education for sustainable development coupled with the focus on employability through the Albert certification provides a dual purpose, self-interest in terms of employability prospects in the creative industries and survival of the planet to ensure the future for us all: two very good incentives to recognise one's blindness and do something about it.

It might be argued that employability and sustainability within the context of higher education provides two opposing mind-sets that represent what many universities have become, under the influence of neo-liberal ideology, where value for money and graduate outcomes outweigh pedagogical and research purposes (Collini, 2012; Rustin, 2016). On the other hand, the drive to be more sustainable, to use Barnett's (2018) title, to become 'the ecological university' puts the emphasis on how central to the university's mission should be the public good. Are these positions incompatible? On the surface it would seem so, but under the surface both the higher education sector, educators of future graduates for the screen industries, and the screen industries themselves must recognise the intersections of sustainability and employability as a necessary working paradox. What both mind-sets need to accept is that unsustainability is not an option. This case study on the Albert certificate delivered through the Pebblepad e-portfolio focuses on the intersectionality of employability and sustainability. The positive way in which the students engaged with the work, and the 100% success of the cohort in achieving Albert certification, is a measure of their commitment to sustainable media production practices as well as a recognition that securing employment in the creative industries and working sustainably are imbricated. The overlapping nature of employability and sustainability has been explored in other higher education subject areas such as science and engineering (Pritchard & Atlay, 2015) and business (Winfield & Ndvolu, 2019) but the Albert certificate and the educational partnership has facilitated an engagement with this intersectionality among screen studies courses. This case study will be the first of many to emerge, as the Albert educational partnership expands and becomes more global.

WHAT IS ALBERT?

The screen industries make a significant contribution to carbon emissions due to their production practices. With this in mind, the Albert sustainability consortium was set up in 2011 by the British Association of Film and Television Arts (BAFTA) in the UK to encourage broadcasters, streaming services and film productions companies to adopt the Albert sustainability initiative which would be applied as an industry kitemark. Since 2015, the Albert educational partnership has grown out of this industry initiative to include over 20 higher education institutions in the UK where screen studies courses are taught. The number of higher education partners grows each year as do the numbers of industry partners. The Albert logo is now a familiar sight at the end credits of all BBC, ITV, Channel 4 and Sky programmes in the UK.

Evidence that the screen industries are taking the Albert kitemark seriously can be seen in the Screen Skills Assessment report (Bratzanti et al., 2021) which provides a summary of skills issues affecting the UK screen industries in the period from January 2020 to January 2021. The report reflects on the emergence of sustainability as a key driver in future production processes, suggesting a skills gap will need to be filled. 'Supporting the ethos of the Albert, BFI, and Arup report (2020) on sustainability in film production, nearly half of employers and just over half of the workforce surveyed thought that by 2026 the sector will be deploying more environmentally sustainable practices' (2021: 6).

Against this backdrop of recognition by screen industry employers and employees that more environmentally sustainable practices will be essential moving forward, and also the growing awareness of a skills gap, makes the introduction of Albert certification timely.

The Albert consortium now includes, among others, BBC, ITV, SKY, Channel 4, Channel 5, NBC Universal and Warner Bros. International and Netflix and a whole range of smaller production companies who have signed up to train their production staff in the implementation of the carbon calculator tool to calculate carbon emissions arising from their productions and reduce them. Most major film and TV production companies in the United Kingdom need to have an Albert certified production plan to gain green light status for their production. Albert's industry-based initiative now has a range of international partners and when UK-based productions take place in other countries the Albert initiative is used to ensure equity, fairness in hiring and resource usage in line with the host country's production practices.

Albert engages with a range of global organisations to bring about changes to their screen industries. These include:

- Reel Green (http://mppia.com/links/reelgreen),
- Screen Greening (http://www.screengreening.com/),

- NTR (www.ntrplc.com/about-us/sustainable-investing), Green Screen (www.interregeurope.eu/greenscreen/), and
- NRK (www.nordiskfilmogtvfond.com/news/stories/finland-shows-the-way-in-green-production-and-practices).

The move to expand Albert as an industry-based resource and an educational partnership is being explored by BAFTA as demand from across the world for greener media production processes and graduate engagement increases.

Key objectives of Albert include:

1. Inspire: empowering the industry to create content that supports a vision for a sustainable future
2. Restore: enabling the industry to make positive contributions to the environment while actively eliminating waste and carbon emissions from production (https://weareAlbert.org)

ALBERT AS AN INDUSTRY-BASED DEVELOPMENT AND THE GROWTH OF THE ALBERT EDUCATIONAL PARTNERSHIP

Having focused on the film and television production industries since its inception in 2011, the development of an educational partnership in 2015 with those higher education providers in the UK who offer screen studies degree courses provides an organic link to the creative industries workforce of the future.

Adapting industry training for higher education purposes posed a significant challenge but also provided an opportunity for synergies between what is offered to current creative industry professionals and those graduates who seek to gain employment in the creative industries.

A key aspect of embedding Albert certification at Canterbury Christ Church University is its inclusion in the taught and assessed curriculum as part of an existing employability module. The location of the Albert certification within this module enabled the intersections between sustainability and employability to be made visible to the students. Signing up to the educational partnership involves an annual fee but the cost/benefit analysis for the students in gaining Albert certification indicates a strong case for investment. When planning to introduce Albert certification as part of an employability module for final year undergraduate students it was necessary for the tutor to undertake training in how to use the carbon calculator as well as study the material presented to complete the four assessments and ensure the assessment could be incorporated in the learning outcomes for the module and the overall course. Employability and learning was twofold, working for both the students and the tutor. To embed the Albert certificate into an existing module involved a university quality and standards assurance process. While this was necessary in terms of the Albert certificate meeting the standards for university assessment, the slowness of the process is an example of what Kemp and Scoffham (2020) describe as the fast/slow paradox in higher education. We are all keen to teach and talk about sustainability but sometimes the machinery of higher education slows this down. The arrival of the pandemic and subsequent lockdown and the social distancing and blended learning options meant that the materials for the certificate needed to be transferred to an online format. As the students had already used the e-portfolio tool Pebblepad (2004) as part of Professional Perspectives in Year 1 and Year 2 it made sense to adapt the work for Pebblepad use. Pebblepad is one of many possible e-portfolio tools that could be used but as the University has an institutional account it seemed sensible to utilise this online system to deliver the Albert certificate work.

Having used Pebblepad in the first two years of their degree, tutors and students find it valuable as an e-portfolio to build on it each year and take with them after university as evidence of continuing professional development. In their systematic scoping of a range of e-portfolio systems used in education Mitchell et al. (2021) identified some of the benefits for employability of using e-portfolios such as Pebblepad to gather student resources as examples of ongoing learner development: professional work, curriculum vitae, work experience, skills audits, videos and photos. The addition of the Albert certificate within their e-portfolio, focusing as it does on employability and sustainability skills, aims to frame our students as future-ready graduates. As Kaminski (2020) notes in the study of the use of Pebblepad with nursing students, the professional practice element is well served by the meaningful and well organised way that Pebblepad operates. This also applies to the integration of the Albert certificate as an industry-facing sustainability skills production workbook with the potential for positive graduate employability outcomes.

Paul Wallis (2017) at Confetti Institute of Creative Technologies, part of Nottingham Trent University, adapted the work as an online portfolio suitable for blended learning. Canterbury Christ Church University uses Pebblepad to deliver online portfolio work. With a number of training sessions and lots of helpful input from Paul and our faculty's digital academic developer, Simon Starr, the Pebblepad version of Albert was made ready for student use. The students' previous experience of using Pebblepad for assessment enabled them to complete the certificate work successfully and all 57 in the cohort achieved certification. The student feedback on the use of Pebblepad to deliver the Albert certification was very positive with many students commenting on the well-structured nature of the information and the clear lay out of assessment tasks.

The Albert workbook on Pebblepad includes four sections. Each section contains a number of sub-sections that relate to individual assessments or activities built around the information on the science of climate change. Section 1 focuses on the science of climate change and this is reinforced with a multiple choice quiz assessment. Section 2 focuses on how individual and groups working in the media industries can make a difference and impact on environmental sustainability by making a commitment to be involved in sustainable productions. Section 3 introduces case studies of sustainable productions from film and television and provides detailed information on how the carbon calculator works for media productions. Students learn to use the carbon calculator as part of the assessment for this section as well as drawing up an action plan for how changes can be made to ensure media productions meet the criteria to gain the Albert industry kitemark. Section 4 offers examples of how the message of sustainability can be included in media productions by providing activities and examples from film and television output and an assessment which encourages the students to provide their own editorial content with a sustainability message.

The Albert certificate was first used as a training tool for creative industry professionals, and the adaptation of the work for academic purposes raises many questions about pedagogical approaches in terms of presentation and engagement. The tendency in the industry approach was to focus on powerpoint slide presentations with less opportunity for participant interaction. This more didactic model has been adapted for the demands of higher education where student engagement puts the emphasis on student interaction, learner initiative and student-led inquiry. A positive aspect of the move online for the Albert workbook material, or teaching deck, is the insertion of a range of learner activities that emerge from each section. These learner activities involve group discussion, further enquiry, and role-playing exercises. These enhance the experience of learning about climate change while also enabling students to participate in skills-based training that is industry certified.

EMPLOYABILITY AND SUSTAINABILITY: FUTURE 360

Placing employability as a key component in all three years of our Film Production and Film, Radio and Television degrees is underpinned by a vision of employability that owes much to Harvey's (2003) definition. Harvey's outline avoids the reductionist principles of many other similar summaries and considers the necessary mix of intellectual development and skills training that marries, still rather uncomfortably, utility and intellect.

> Employability is not just about getting a job. Conversely, just because a student is on a vocational course does not mean that somehow employability is automatic. Employability is more than about developing attributes, techniques, or experience just to enable a student to get a job, or to progress within a current career. It is about learning, and the emphasis is less on 'employ' and more on 'ability'. In essence, the emphasis is on developing critical, reflective abilities, with a view to empowering and enhancing the learner (Harvey, 2003:2).

Since the emergence of employability as a key priority in higher education in the UK in the past two decades, greater pressure is now placed on institutions to record graduate outcomes, provide value for money and wrestle with the tension that exists between a narrowly focused vision of employability and one that offers a more holistic approach. As Stoten (2018: 9) suggests:

> Whereas the traditional priority of attending university was to obtain a degree, nowadays a university education is much more concerned with a 'package deal' that prepares graduates to confront the multifarious challenges of the twenty-first century. Employability is one component within the 'package deal' but is likely to become even more important as students become ever-more conversant with the HE market that has developed in recent years and will continue to evolve with differential fees structures.

The Covid pandemic has brought this 'package deal' into greater focus with the curtailing of work experience, shadowing and industry placements as well as more limited face-to-face teaching. In the UK higher education sector where funding for universities comes through a fees system paid by students, it is unsurprising that students are calling for refunds for a package deal where some of the components were absent or below expected thresholds.

The introduction of a media industry sustainability skills-based (Albert) certificate within an existing employability module follows the suggestion by Marshall (2014) to see our collective response to climate change as a quest rather than a war. This skills-based certificate created by Albert.org empowers students, in the case of this module, Year 3 students who are in their final year of a Film Production or Film, Radio and Television degree to ask questions about the creative industries in terms of how they impact on climate change. The learning materials in the certificate provide the students with ways to develop their own response to sustainability issues and the skills to calculate the carbon footprint of their own or other creative productions with a view to moving from a development stage to a final carbon footprint to show the changes they would make to ensure film and television productions are more sustainable.

As Ehiyazaryan and Barraclough (2009) point out, the integration of real world experiences in the curriculum enhances the student's readiness for engagement with the world of work. A key component of the Albert certificate work is that it is already grounded in industry training, so it involves a combination of real world (climate change) problems and industry-led experience.

Embedding the Albert certificate in an existing employability module was framed and encouraged by two key factors within my own institution. The first is the overall strength of the employability and enterprise framework rolled out by colleagues in the careers and enterprise service which helps underpin our employability modules. The second is the forward thinking nature of the university's sustainability team, the Student Green Office and the commitment of the university at an institutional level to encourage students and staff to adopt a climate change focus in curricula, assessment and use of resources.

The Future 360 Framework (2019) for developing enterprising, professional graduates was put in place as the first year cohort of Film Production and Film, Radio and Television students started their courses. The Professional Perspectives in the Creative Industries module is taught in all three years of these courses and is a core module. The central themes of the Framework are used in these modules to offer a sense of progression and differentiation between each year's curriculum content and assessment practices. Year 1 focuses on Thinking about Self, Year 2, Thinking about your Potential, and Year 3 Thinking about your Future. Clearly, there is some overlap in how these themes are integrated through curriculum content and assessment practices but, on the whole, the nature of the students' work in these modules leads them to focus on their future by the time they reach Year 3. One might consider that this would occur naturally, but many students in their final year put off thinking about their transition from university as it becomes their own 'elephant in the room'. This temporary blindness has become more acute during the uncertainties in the jobs market caused by the pandemic.

Drawing upon Tomlinson's (2017) Graduate Capital model, the Future 360 Framework provides a scaffolding for the curriculum activities in the modules but also encourages extra-curricular activity to enhance the student's employability options. Graduate Capital is defined as 'key resources that confer benefits and advantages in the labour market' (Tomlinson, 2017: 1), and the addition of the Albert certificate fits very effectively into the elements of the framework.

The introduction of the Albert certificate occurred in the middle of a pandemic through which we are all still living, a pandemic that consumed every waking minute of our lives and obliterated a range of other societal concerns from the agendas of governments, people and the media. To avert the looming climate catastrophe, we need a similar global response as we have had to the pandemic to empower people to take responsibility through their own actions to achieve sustainability. The imminence of the danger to humanity from climate change is evident but it still appears not to have reached high priority status in most people's minds. In a phrase that is attributed to Ernest Hemingway in *The Sun Also Rises* (1926) when describing how people go broke, he notes this happens, gradually, then suddenly. Novelist and essayist John Lanchester (Allardice, 2019) in an interview about his eco-novel *The Wall* borrows this phrase to reflect upon the climate crisis as a way of explaining humanity's response to climate change. The gradual nature of the changes in our climate will at some point soon give way to sudden catastrophe. It is very difficult to avoid being the harbinger of doom when teaching about climate change but as Susannah Rustin (2021) notes in her *Guardian* article: 'how we talk about climate crisis is increasingly crucial to tackling it'.

From my perspective as an educator/lecturer, one of the positive features about the work contained in the Albert certificate is its focus on education about climate change, but it also nudges participants towards individual responsibility and a skills-based approach to effect change in their own production practices and a commitment to working more sustainably once they enter the creative industries.

THE STRUCTURE OF THE WORK

Drawing from the work of Bearman et al. (2014), *Guide to the assessment design decisions framework*, a key aspect of the assessment for gaining Albert certification is around learner development. Through a minor modification process colleagues who teach this strand through the three years of the degree were able to shift some of the work of Year 3 to Year 2 and so leave space for Albert. The certification work is worth 40% of the overall module marks. Beyond the achievement of marks, which students, on the whole, are most concerned with, it was important to the nature of the subject matter that the assessment tasks focused on initial skills development but more importantly ongoing learner development about sustainability.

The four assessment tasks target learning on the science of climate change, the global impact of a changing climate, solutions for a sustainable society, an overview on international, national industry action, how the industry measures its carbon impact, sustainable production solutions and creating content with a strategic environmental purpose.

Assessment 1, a multiple-choice quiz, provides evidence of a general understanding of the science of climate change and its impacts drawn from the material presented in the workbook. This was an iterative process where the students needed to achieve a pass mark of 70%. Even when they reached the pass threshold many students returned to the questionnaire to gain 100% which indicated their interest in understanding more about the science of climate change.

Ongoing learner development was promoted through assessment 2 as students are required to write or record a personal commitment to sustainability which will evidence their commitment to creating a greener industry in a future role they would like to hold.

The students came to the commitment statement having calculated their own personal carbon footprint from a questionnaire embedded in the online course material. Asked about their diet, how they travel, their home and things they buy for leisure, personal use, or their studies, the personal carbon calculator fed directly into the commitment statement. While the course leader was wary that the students would not take this sustainability commitment as seriously as other elements of the assessment, that fear was unfounded. Some of the most effective reflective writing arose from this assessment based on the evidence of their own personal carbon footprint score. After completing their carbon footprint, the students also discussed and took part in a 'play your carbon right' online exercise that helped them consider positive environmental actions they can make as an individual. The students found this activity and personal footprint calculation empowering as it focused on changing the discourse around how the narrative of sustainability can be represented as a personal as well as a global response. It also fed into their employability skills as it highlighted the need for self-reflection in terms of how their future career in the creative industries could focus on sustainable options for media productions, another alignment between sustainability and employability.

Evidence that the students are willing to take personal responsibility can be seen in their commitment to sustainability statements and the focus of the questions offers them the opportunity to be more hopeful in terms of what they contribute in their own lives and in their prospective careers in the creative industries – a quest rather than a war.

STUDENT A

January 1st, 2020, I decided to become a vegetarian. I think, so far, this is the most significant step I have taken towards making a difference to climate change. Leaning into a plant-based diet has had wonderful personal effects on my health and wellbeing, as well as my attitude towards the meat industry and its impact on the environment. I am not looking back on this and intend to remain a vegetarian. I've recently discovered various dairy-free products and foods that are entirely vegan which can further the positive impact I make personally.

ALBERT is a wonderful resource of information and knowledge. Third year seems a bit late in my university life to learn about it. I think the university could introduce this immediately on their media courses. Promoting ethical, professional work cannot be understated.

STUDENT B

Climate change is a large problem that affects everyone and will have an increasing effect on our future. As a student and as a worker in an arts industry, it is important to aim towards sustainability.

The largest impact my life has on climate change is through technology and home appliances, which I upgrade more often than ideal. This leads to a lot of waste, as these items take a lot of energy to make and are often hard to recycle.

To reduce my impact, I won't upgrade technology unless necessary, and will buy second-hand technology when suitable.

Overall, I feel this commitment to long lasting change will be an important factor of any production moving forward, and I hope to continue my learning journey.

STUDENT C

Despite the actions in the past, I am becoming more educated on the problems in the world and the issues which contribute to climate change, therefore I am going to work towards changing aspects of my personal daily life and future professional life in order to do my part to reduce global warming.

The emphasis in the comments above on students taking responsibility for their own climate change quest and the promise to take this commitment into their working lives in the creative industries is very positive. This is evident in the professional work attitudes taken up by the students in relation to their Albert certification and their recognition that they can play a part in making sustainable productions in the future. This alignment between employability and sustainability is noted by the students themselves; a self-realisation encouraged by their Albert certification work. This group of students who underwent Albert certification are not the exception, they are becoming the norm. The positive responses of the students to the importance of teaching about sustainable development is given wider resonance in the evidence of the 2020 National Union of Students (NUS) Skills Survey '91% of respondents agreed their place of study should actively incorporate SD – up from 88% in 2014; while 83% would like to see SD actively incorporated and promoted across all courses – up from 71% in 2014' (Education for Sustainable Education, Advance HE and QAA Guidance, 2021:5).

Taking up personal responsibility in terms of a commitment to sustainability could be seen as overpromising in order to gain marks but the depth of feeling in most of the commitment statements suggests a real sense of purpose. However, I am mindful of Biesta's (2020:103) injunction in relation to how their commitments to sustainability can 'meet the world'.

> Education as subjectification is therefore not about asking students for their opinions or providing them with opportunities to express themselves 'without limits'. This doesn't mean that subjectification is about forbidding students to express themselves. It is rather about making sure that what students express can 'meet' the world so that a reality check, as I have put it, becomes possible.

The reality check for these commitment statements comes in the shape of formative feedback and discussion of the work but also how their commitment statement is underpinned by the completion of their own carbon footprint through the Albert workbook.

The considerations given to Assessments 3 and 4 focus on equipping the students with the skills necessary to measure the carbon impact of productions but also how to create content with a strategic environmental purpose. Assessment 3, the completion of a carbon calculation for a case study production, supplied in the workbook, or a template for calculating the carbon emissions of their own productions, is drawn directly from the industry training. This proved to be the most difficult task for many students as it involved the completion of an online form with statistical information supplied in the case study. Students with learning differences found transferring the information from one spreadsheet to another quite a challenge and much tutorial time was spent on overcoming these difficulties. As well as the e-portfolio version, the workbook was also available as a static powerpoint which was more appropriate for some students in terms of accessibility.

Greater consideration needs to be given to ensuring accessibility is central to how the workbook is constructed, and this has been fed into the latest iteration of the workbook being prepared for use in September 2021. Additional work on signposting of assessments had to be done and regular online tutorials with these students were established to help them maintain workflow. As this was the first time Albert was delivered via an e-portfolio, glitches arose in student log-on and completion of the production carbon calculator. These problems were solved through contact with BAFTA Albert enquiries, but it did create a considerable amount of extra work for the tutor. The streamlining of the log-on process and the updating of the carbon calculator tool for the 2021 iteration of Albert should help address these problems. It was exciting to see approximately 30% of the students opt to create a carbon footprint for their own productions as opposed to using the case studies within the workbook.

Assessment 4 required the students to present editorial ideas /a story board/ an elevator pitch as evidence they can present editorial ideas for a production that could engage audiences with positive solutions to climate change. The submission could be written or recorded but the focus is on identifying strategies that would engage audiences with environmental sustainability. The students were also required to reflect on whether their ideas passed the Planet Test. Using Alison Bechdel's Test as a model, the Planet Test asks users to reflect on three questions. Does your editorial idea acknowledge that the natural world exists? Are negative environmental behaviours shown as negative character traits? Does one person in your idea do something to make the world a better place?

Matched against UNESCO's (2017: 16) key competencies for sustainability the Albert certificate works well as ways of thinking and practising and ways of being. The table below illustrates how the Albert assessment aligns with employability and sustainability skills and competencies.

Embedded within the Albert Certificate workbook on Pebblepad or using it as a free-standing educational resource outside the e-portfolio system, the links with education for sustainable development are evident in the close attention given to understanding climate science, and how to use this knowledge to inform sustainable media productions.

FUTURE CONSIDERATIONS

The presence of Albert as part of the assessment process encouraged all students to take it seriously. What Kemp and Scoffham (2020) identify as the fast/slow paradox in our response to the climate emergency in higher education is evident here. We need a fast response in our curriculum development, but the institutional architecture of universities moves very slowly. However, signs of hope exist as Kemp and Scoffham (2020: 13) also note 'The way that the covid-19 pandemic has revealed a surprising flexibility and adaptability within the HE sector opens up new possibilities for educational responses to the environmental crisis'.

Although other institutions may deliver Albert certification as an extra-curricular or non-assessed activity, having it embedded in the curriculum provides a stamp of legitimacy in the students' eyes. Ideally, the Albert certificate involves

Table 10.1 Aligning Albert assessments with Employability and ESD competencies

Albert assessments	UNESCO's Key competencies for Sustainability (Reickman)	Employability Skills (adapted from Confederation of British Industries list)
Assessment 1 The Science of Climate Change	Systems competency, showing awareness of how systems are embedded within different domains and scales	Self-management International & Cultural Awareness
Assessment 2 Commitment to Sustainability	Self-awareness and critical thinking competencies	Self-management Problem solving
Assessment 3 Carbon Calculator and Action Plan for productions	Anticipatory (future thinking competency) Integrated problem solving competency	Numeracy, application of information technology Problem solving
Assessment 4 Editorial Content and passing the Planet Test	Strategic and collaboration competencies	Audience awareness Communication and Literacy

work all students should be motivated to do, but given the way in which assessment activities have become the driving force in education policy and practice, rightly or wrongly, assessment confers legitimacy. What emerges from this case study is that embedding as part of assessment Albert or other forms of sustainability/employability work leads to higher student engagement. Students responded positively to the intersectionality of sustainability and employability as they went through the Albert workbook which included many examples of creative industry figures emphasising the importance of sustainable production practices. The fact that it is now mandatory for most broadcasting services in the United Kingdom to have a carbon calculation for their productions in order to go into production also focused the students' attention on their future employment in the creative industries.

The apparent success of the Albert certification work in terms of student responses in tying sustainability and employability together moves away from the notion that 'sustainability education is a linear process involving the transmission of knowledge about sustainability issues' (Kemp & Scoffham, 2020: 8). The commitment to sustainability in Assessment 1 leans towards lifelong learning and the industry-centred carbon calculation in Assessment 3 moves beyond this linear process and engages students with real world problems and some of the tools to mitigate these problems. Biesta's (2020) three domains of education are helpful here to identify how the Albert assessment and student engagement encompass qualification, the promotion of socialisation and subjectification, opportunities for students to engage with the world and their place in it. The assessments highlight the ongoing education about sustainability and the clear links with the screen industry's workplace environment. Gaining the Albert qualification is only the starting point and the impetus provided by the assessments focus on the next steps in a screen industry getting ready to embrace sustainable production practices through action-oriented and transformative education.

The publication of Education for Sustainable Development guidance by Advance Higher Academy (HE), which provides continuing professional development for tutors, and the Quality Assurance Agency (QAA), which oversees benchmark statements in all areas of curricula in the UK higher education sector in 2021 offers a clear recognition that education for sustainable development needs to be at the heart of curriculum change. Although framed as guidance, the material backed by QAA is likely to have a very positive impact on the embedding of education for sustainable development within the UK higher education sector.

> ESD is best achieved when:
>
> 1. ESD objectives, targets and KPIs are part of the institution's strategic priorities and subsequent strategies and policies.
> 2. The framing of ESD within the curriculum is included in the validation of new courses and ongoing review of existing courses.
>
> (*Education for Sustainable Development Guidance – Executive Summary*. March 2021: 3)

The Albert certificate work outlined in this case study, although it took over a year to set up as part of the Film Production and Film, Radio and Television course, frames ESD within the curriculum and provides a model for how other employability-based modules in the creative industry subjects can link sustainability with employability. BAFTA is working with Albert to set up international partnerships that will not only embrace the industry-led carbon calculation initiative but also form educational partnerships. As a model for employability/sustainability work the Albert certificate has much to recommend it. To ensure the climate-based information is kept up to date a new iteration of the Albert workbook is produced annually.

Employability and sustainability can be seen as contested terms but what is difficult to contest is the notion of unsustainability. The screen industries in the United Kingdom have come together to develop an industry kitemark around carbon emissions and the reduction of carbon footprint. The adoption of the Albert sustainability protocols is driven by industry with the considerable help of BAFTA, and the offshoot educational partnership that has grown out of this industry initiative is an effective and growing model of industry/education synergies.

Stoten (2018: 10) identifies employability as a contested concept and elaborates how some of the assumptions and discourse around employability can be questioned. 'Whereas the post-war social democratic model of the State was based on rigid structures and rules, the neo-liberal State operates on the premise that responsible citizens can manage their own lives without significant intervention from Government. It is within this political context that employability has evolved'.

The Covid pandemic appears to have upended the neo-liberal model with large-scale government interventions in all aspects of our daily lives so it will be interesting to see, post-pandemic, if there is a rebalancing of the role of government but also if a broader notion of employability might emerge where, for example, home working becomes much more integrated into our work schemas. The Aviva Business Report, *Thriving in the Age of Ambiguity*, (2021:19) identifies how 'the journey towards the workplace of the future has been accelerated by the pandemic, from decreasing office space and increased homeworking to widespread digitalisation and non-linear careers'.

Covid has been the great disruptor and it may be that out of this shock to societal systems, including education, more effective forms of pedagogy might emerge that move forward, rather than look back, with a renewed sense of purpose about how gaining employment and saving the planet are inextricably linked.

One of the priority actions for the Screen Skills Assessment Report (Bratzanti et al. 2021:11) is to 'support the efforts to mobilise environmentally sustainable practice'. This gives a strong indication that employability opportunities for those students with Albert certification will increase as they will be well placed to fill the skills gap around environmentally sustainable practice identified in the report. Moving forward, sustainability and employability are likely to emerge as twin drivers of industry and education policies as we attempt to come to terms with our imminent planet test and this will need a global and local response.

REFERENCES

Allardice, L. (2019) '"The Wall", interview with John Lanchester'. *The Guardian*, January 11, 2019

Aviva Business Report (2021) *Thriving in an age of ambiguity: building resilience for the new realities of work.* Available at https://www.aviva.co.uk/business/business-perspectives/featured-articles-hub/how-employers-can-thrive/ (Accessed on 25/6/21).

Advance HE, QAA (2021) *Education for sustainable development guidance.* https://www.advance-he.ac.uk/teaching-and-learning/education-sustainable-development-higher-education#guidance (Accessed on 28/3/21).

Barnett, R. (2018) *The ecological university*, London: Routledge.

Bearman, M., Dawson, P., Boud, D., Hall, M., Bennett, S., Molloy, E. & Joughin, G. (2014) *Guide to the assessment design decisions framework.* Available at http://www.assessmentdecisions.org/wp-content/uploads/2014/09/Guide-to-the-Assessment-Design-Decisions-Framework.pdf

Biesta, G. (2020) Risking ourselves in education: qualification, socialization, and subjectification revisited, *Educational Theory*, Volume 70, No.1, pp. 89–104.

Branzanti, C., Howe, L. & Cortvriend, J. (2021) *ScreenSkills Assessment Report (2021)* https://www.screenskills.com/media/4587/2021-06-08-screenskills-assessment-2021.pdf (Accessed on 25/6/21)

Collini, S. (2012) *What are universities for?* London: Penguin.

Confederation of British Industries Skills Framework. Available at https://www.cbi.org.uk/media/1914/cbi-skills-framework.pdf

Ehiyazaryan, E. and Barraclough, N. (2009) Enhancing employability: integrating real world experiences in the curriculum, *Education and Training*, Volume 51, No. 4, pp. 292–308.

Future 360 Framework, (2019) *Canterbury Christ Church University Careers and Enterprise*. Available at https://www.canterbury.ac.uk/career-development/docs/112-CH-19-CE-framework.pdf

Harvey, L. (2003) *Transitions from higher education to work: a briefing paper prepared by Lee Harvey (Centre for Research and Evaluation, Sheffield Hallam University), with advice from ESECT and LTSN Generic Centre colleagues.* Available from: http://bit.ly/oeCgqW [Accessed on 13 February 2012].

Kahneman, D. (2011) *Thinking, fast and slow*. London: Penguin.

Kaminski, J. (2020) The promise of PebblePad for dynamic learning. *Canadian Journal of Nursing Informatics*, Volume 15, No. 3. Available at https://tinyurl.com/yy9vctqs

Kemp, N. and Scoffham, S. (2020) The paradox model: towards a conceptual framework for engaging with sustainability in higher education. *International Journal of Sustainability in Higher Education*. https://doi.org/10.1108/IJSHE-08-2020-0311

Kingsnorth, P. (2014) The four degrees. *London Review of Books*, Volume 26, No. 20, 23 October.

Marshall, G. (2014) *Don't Even Think About It: How our brains are wired to ignore climate change*. USA: Bloomsbury.

Mitchell, L., Campbell, C., Somerville, M., Cardell, E. & Williams, L. T. (2021) Enhancing graduate employability through targeting ePortfolios to employer expectations: a systematic scoping review. *Journal of Teaching and Learning for Graduate Employability*, Volume 12, No. 2, pp. 82–98. Available at: https://ojs.deakin.edu.au/index.php/jtlge/article/view /1003/1060

Pebblepad (2006) https://www.pebblepad.co.uk/

Pritchard, D. & Atlay, M. (2015) Sustainability and employability: alliances at the University of Bedfordshire. In: Leal Filho, W., Azeiteiro, U., Caeiro, S. & Alves, F. (eds) *Integrating sustainability thinking in science and engineering curricula*. World Sustainability Series. Springer, Cham. https://doi.org/10.1007/978-3-319-09474-8_4

Rieckman, M. (2019) "Learning to transform the world: key competencies in ESD" in Leicht, A., Heiss, J. & Byun, Won Jung. (eds) *Issues and trends in education for sustainable development*. Available at https://unesdoc.unesco.org/ark:/48223/pf0000261445

Rustin, M. (2016) The neoliberal university and its alternatives, *Soundings*, No. 63, July, pp. 147–176.

Rustin, S. (2021) 'How we talk about the climate crisis', *The Guardian,* 17 May.

Shriver, L. (2003) *We need to talk about Kevin*. Berkeley, CA.: Counterpoint Press.

Stoten, D. (2018) Employability: a contested concept in higher education, *Journal of Pedagogic Development,* Volume 7, No. 1, pp. 9–17.

Tomlinson, M. (2017) Forms of graduate capital and their relationship to graduate employability, *Education and Training*, Volume 59, No. 4, pp. 338–352.

UNESCO Education for Sustainable Development Goals: Learning Objectives. 2017. https://unesdoc.unesco.org/ark:/48223/pf0000247444 (Accessed on 20/5/21)

Wallis, P. (2017) *Closing the gap between higher education and the UK screen art industries: collaborating with BAFTA Albert to create and embed the 'Applied Skills for a Sustainable Media Industry' training module into existing UK higher education film and TV programmes of learning*. https://globalgreenmediaproduction.wordpress.com/ (Accessed on 28/6/21)

Winfield, F. & Ndlovu, T. (2019) 'Future proof your degree': embedding sustainability and employability in Nottingham Business School. *International Journal of Sustainability in Higher Education*, Volume 20, No. 8, pp. 29–42.

11

Through Others We Become Ourselves: How Service-learning Develops Graduate Identity

Alison Walker, Jenny Mercer and Leanne Freeman

INTRODUCTION

In this chapter we introduce a 'Quadruple Helix' to illustrate the development of graduate identity through service-learning (SL). This approach is an adaptation of Chickering and Braskamp's (2009) four vectors of psychosocial development, onto which we have mapped findings from our research with psychology undergraduates who completed an SL module. It offers a framework to understand the processes through which SL can facilitate identity development and provides a model for creating a more holistic approach to embedding employability and graduate attributes in HE.

BACKGROUND CONTEXT

UK universities have traditionally broadened students' employability skills through industrial work experience, corporate placements and internships. Here, business is used as the foundation for experiential learning. In contrast, SL offers a flexible community-based learning experience which can help to develop social agency in addition to developing graduate identity.

SL is an experiential pedagogy, a structured learning experience that combines community service with explicit learning objectives, preparation and reflection.

Students undertaking an SL placement are expected to provide community service, but also to learn from the community partner with which they are placed, about their roles as citizens, community issues and the symbiotic relationship between their experience and their academic coursework (Seifer, 1998).

SL has much in common with other types of voluntary and community service programmes, yet it differs from others in that its aim is to equally benefit both the students and the recipients of their service in the community (Sigmon, 1979). It is, therefore, unlike other forms of experiential learning that focus on student learning, such as internships, work placements or vocational training, and it differs from volunteering which is primarily focused on the beneficiaries and does not include structured learning (Deeley, 2010; Furco, 1996). SL stresses the importance of reciprocity between the server and the served. This avoids the paternalistic one-way model where an individual or group share their resources 'charitably' with those who lack resources (Deeley, 2015). In SL the needs of the community should determine the focus of the service provided and support the students to ensure their work is of use (Stanton et al., 1999).

SL is originally a US pedagogy, but one which has spread across the globe. SL is not a culture-neutral pedagogy but draws on national and local histories and socio-economic needs pertinent to each education system around the world, with countries adapting the idea to suit their own needs. Despite using the US term, service-learning, its meaning, understanding and practice vary from country to country (Bheekie & van Huyssteen, 2015).

In Europe, different countries are using SL to meet their socio-economic needs to different degrees but helping to meet the economic and community needs of the country are common purposes. Traditionally, European universities have had two main missions: teaching and research. Yet, universities' engagement with society is another aim increasingly upheld as a third mission. Despite reforms carried out in recent years within the European higher education area, there is still a greater need for the development of community engagement (Gerholz & Losch, 2015; Heras-Colàs et al., 2017). In Asia, SL is often used to promote the concept of indigenous or local and culturally specific knowledge or systems of knowledge (Xing & Ma, 2010), which differ across different regions. In Latin America, SL has developed from varied cultural contexts of the component countries. Often referred to as *aprendizaje-servicio solidario*, the idea of *solidaridad* is a key concept in Latin American SL. It means helping others in an organised and effective way, working together for the common cause, standing as a group or as a nation to defend rights and face natural disasters or economic crises (Liou, 2018).

Despite cultural and socio-economic differences, Mueller and Lee (2010), in a review of SL courses in Asia, Europe and the USA, found that there were no significant differences in the students' learning outcomes. Despite the focus and sophistication of the SL projects varying greatly amongst countries, the personal and social learning outcomes were found to be similar for all the students involved. Nearly all students expressed feeling emotions such as fear, guilt and admiration, having developed a better understanding of the contexts of people's lives and of wanting to make a difference in their own lives.

In the UK, SL has also been recognised as a transformative pedagogy which often creates learning from discomfort (Asghar & Rowe, 2018; Carnicelli & Boluk, 2017). Students' concerns before starting SL centre around anxiety related to not being accepted, or saying or doing the wrong thing, and a lack of confidence going into a new environment (Asghar & Rowe, 2018). Students' fears and discomfort are the catalyst for change; they overcome their fears as they develop their confidence. Students learn more from difficult situations, or when plans go awry, as it enables them to develop a more flexible approach and the ability to think on their feet. As they become more accomplished, they revise their sense of purpose and their view of the roles they undertake, and change their understanding of the work, the people they work with, increasing their sense of agency. Reflection is an integral part of the learning process as it is a crucial factor in working alongside people from marginalised groups without reinforcing oppressive and stigmatising beliefs and practices (Asghar & Rowe, 2017, 2018; Deeley, 2010).

Commonly reported outcomes of SL are increased confidence, self-efficacy and self-esteem (Saylor et al., 2018; Whitley et al., 2017). It can also impact on individuals' sense of social agency through working with disadvantaged groups (Bailey, 2017; Coffey et al., 2017). However, less attention has been paid to *the process* through which this potentially transformative pedagogy impacts students, in turn facilitating identity development. This chapter offers a lens through which this can be done by mapping findings of our study with students on a university SL module onto a quadruple helix of identity development.

DEVELOPING THE QUADRUPLE HELIX TO ILLUSTRATE HOW SL HELPS TO DEVELOP GRADUATE IDENTITY

Our study explored, within the context of an HEI in Wales, the practice of SL as a tool for developing graduate identity. The experiences of students who completed an SL module as part of a psychology degree were gathered via semi-structured interviews. These took place pre and post the module. Nineteen students took part, who had undertaken a range of different community-based roles (see Table 11.1).

Table 11.1 Participant profiles

Pseudonym	Age	Placement	Role
Aasef	21	Secondary School	Mentor
Abby	23	Hospital Ward	Befriender
Alice	20	Cycling Charity	Bike Assistant
Brian	23	Hospital Ward	Befriender
Chelsea	20	Secondary School	Mentor
Daisy	26	Secondary School	Mentor
Gemma	23	Recovery Centre	Support Assistant
Grace	22	Homeless Day Centre	Activities Assistant
James	21	Sports Psychology Department	Research Assistant
Jane	20	Offending Triage Project	Triage Assistant
Joe	21	Mental Health Crisis Centre	Support Assistant
Kelly	32	Hospital Ward	Befriender
Lauren	26	Secondary School	Mentor
Lolly	21	Supported Living Project	Befriender
Luke	24	Community Gardens Project	Research Assistant
Nelly	22	Community Farm	Befriender
Rosie	21	Primary School	Teaching Assistant
Ruby	21	After School Club	Club Leader
Theo	22	Primary School	Teaching Assistant

Perceptions of the opportunities and challenges that the placements offered were analysed using a reflexive thematic analysis (Braun & Clark, 2006).

Themes identified were:

1. *'through a different lens'* which encapsulated the shifting views and perspectives that participants encountered in relation to SL, developing a better understanding of social justice and increased plurality in their thinking;
2. *'learned nothing; learned a lot', in which participants discussed the opportunities that the SL experience offered. They demonstrated the power of experiential learning to make the abstract real, to develop skills, aptitudes and passions and to raise awareness of social issues.*
3. *'outside the comfort zone' focused on the challenges that the participants faced: practical, emotional and educational. Most participants lacked confidence and needed to overcome their fear of the unknown, and all grappled with maintaining motivation.*

The themes presented a picture of a challenging and sometimes uncomfortable mode of learning that in its juxtaposition with new life experiences provided opportunities for students to question their beliefs and attitudes and reassess their worldview. We were interested also in what their narratives revealed about the ways in which SL impacted their identity development. Chickering and Braskamp's (2009) four vectors of psychosocial development were used as a framework to understand how this development takes place. In recognition of the interconnectedness of the vectors, the process is represented as a quadruple helix, a spiralling chain of events and experiences, linking and overlapping to create the learning process. Each student will find their own journey, making better progress in some helixes than others. It can also be an iterative process, as reflection may initiate a pause or retreat to increase understanding, and then builds again to enable further development. What follows is an account of this, using quotations from our study to illustrate the process.

Figure 11.1 Quadruple helix to illustrate the development of graduate identity through service-learning

HELIX ONE: MOVING THROUGH AUTONOMY TOWARD INTERDEPENDENCE

The first helix represents the process of emotional and instrumental independence that students undergo when encountering new contexts and experiences. Chickering and Reisser (1993) identify three components: *emotional independence*, freedom from the need for reassurance and approval; *instrumental independence*, the ability to carry out activities and problem-solving in a self-reliant manner; *interdependence*, a developing awareness of one's role in society and its relationship with the welfare of the greater community. SL supports the development of these components.

EMOTIONAL INDEPENDENCE

When young adults move to university, they need to adjust to their new environment. SL offers opportunities to develop emotional independence by providing new environments and expectations for developing new skills, confidence and self-efficacy.

> I was quite, I felt quite daunted by the whole experience (Brian, theme 3).

The participants in our study were at different stages of the emotional independence continuum. Many had left home, whilst others were living with parents. A few had already worked full time and developed an independent lifestyle before entering HE. Selecting the module was itself a step closer to emotional independence. Students had to make decisions about what level of commitment they could offer the community partner, managing their time and work schedule, whilst juggling academic work with the demands of the placement and other responsibilities. SL facilitates emotional independence by providing the opportunity to make independent decisions.

> I feel if I was doing a similar role, or something like this in the future, I'd know where my errors are (Luke, Theme 2).

Initiative was a common attribute that community partners looked for in an SL student. Some developed their initiative and faced the challenge, whilst others were less able to assert themselves and accepted a more passive attitude to the placement. Some had to accept quite a high level of responsibility, including for the safety of others and themselves. Being in a position of responsibility was a new experience for many. They were not used to having to take the 'adult' role in a relationship and this could be challenging.

> It's a lot of pressure when if you miss something, or you don't record that they've taken the meds key out, or something (Joe, theme 3).

> I'm very patient with kids, but I just didn't expect you'd need as much, but they are a very challenging class. [...] I think that's another good thing about the experience, because I've, I feel like I've been dropped in the deep end, kind of thing, so, it can only go up, really (Rosie, theme 3).

INSTRUMENTAL INDEPENDENCE

Chickering and Reisser (1993) identify two major components to instrumental independence: the ability to carry out activities on one's own and to be self-sufficient, and the ability to leave one place and function well in another (p. 132). Both of these attributes have the potential to be developed by the SL process.

Because SL requires students to work in a community setting, it helps to develop their instrumental independence by taking them away from the security of the university campus, to areas that are unfamiliar. They work with people who may have very different life experiences from their own and are of varied ages and capabilities.

> working alongside other people who might interact differently and use different kind of methods of you know, like tone of voice and body language and things like that. Um, sometimes I felt, this is kind of a bigger challenge for me (Nelly, Theme 3).

Brundage and MacKeracher (1980) applied processes in response to social change and trauma to the process of entering a new learning situation. Their four-stage approach is a synthesis of various models of student autonomy:

ENTRY

Entry begins when students enter an unfamiliar situation. They may experience stress and feel disoriented or inhibited, typically retreating from active participation to being an observer until they feel comfortable. Everyone described feeling like this at the start of their placement, but the challenge of discomfort is an important aspect of developing independence, to increase self-efficacy and develop new skills and attributes.

> I didn't know what to expect really. I had this idea of what it could be, which it was, but there was nothing kind of concrete as it was a new environment for me (Aasef, theme 3).

REACTIVE

Learners move into the reactive stage when either they start to settle in and feel more independent, or if they view the environment as unreliable or unsupportive. A few participants who felt their placement was unsupportive seemed unable to get beyond this stage.

> I thought I'd have a bit more support and there'd be weekly meetings and I'd be emailed helpful information and things like that (Luke, theme 3).

PROACTIVE

When learners begin to feel more comfortable in the community setting, they enter the proactive stage, beginning to gain a better understanding of those that they interact with, viewing others' experiences in relation to their own and looking to develop shared norms. Most participants reached and remained at this stage.

> I've definitely learned that it's um, not easy and that it's going to be difficult to- and challenging is, I guess, a better word, it's not so negative, because it's good to be challenged (Lauren, theme 3).

INTEGRATIVE

The integrative stage is reached when students integrate others' perspectives with their own, developing a balance between their own views and others, and developing relationships, accepting multiple behaviours, different interpretations of experience and valuing the experience. Four participants reached this stage, recognising others' worldviews, limitations and abilities, accepting others' differences, sharing their own experiences and learning to value individuals and groups. By the end of their SL experience, their views and attitudes had changed, and their self-awareness was increased.

> It's helped me realise how much I have changed [...] I think I'm a lot more sympathetic, empathetic [...] I thought that I'd make a really big change to her, but she's actually made a hell of a lot of change to me, without even realising it, she is just living her life exactly the way she would even if I wasn't there, and just her doing that has completely changed my whole perspective on a lot of things (Lolly, theme 2).

INTERDEPENDENCE

Once students develop a sense of autonomy, it is important for them to understand that although they can be independent in their thinking and choices, their actions impact on others and vice versa. SL is a good opportunity for developing a sense of one's place in society and the impact that different life events can have on people's lives. With greater understanding of the impact each individual can have on another, and that freedom must be bound by responsibilities, students can learn about reciprocity, compromise, sacrifice and a commitment to the wider community (Chickering & Reisser, 1993).

> I think the reflective process is quite important in the sort of experience of work experience, because it can help you see how much you've changed, and how much you've made a difference and how much the difference has been made to you as well (Lolly, theme 1).

Participants felt that they had learned about the social problems faced by disadvantaged and marginalised people.

> You always just hear about the victims and how it affected them and how it's ruined their lives, you never hear about, maybe all the traumatic stuff that the offenders had, whether they've had domestic violence at home or something, (Jane, theme 1).

They learned about responsibility and commitment and about the importance of having somewhere to go for help and support.

> Some people have phoned in ill with minor things on the project [...] but kind of knowing that people are depending on you, you think, oh, you can't let these people down, you know, (Kelly, theme 3).
>
> and they were saying that um, like how being at [name] has sort of helped them see that they're not alone and it's a really isolating thing, but it's not now that they're at [name] (Gemma, theme 1).

In reflecting on their experience, they felt that they had learned even more about themselves than about other people or social issues, and it was this increased self-awareness that helped them to put their experience into a context where they could develop their understanding of their own needs and plan for their future.

> I still needed to know that I didn't enjoy the experience, because otherwise I would have just had this image in my head of how I would have loved it, or whatever, and gone on the wrong career path and wasted a lot of money and time (Abby, theme 2).

HELIX TWO: ESTABLISHING IDENTITY

There are several theories of identity development which relate to students and young adults and the fundamental theme is the gradual emergence of an internal voice to evaluate external influences and manage one's life. Before the cultivation of this internal voice, one's identity is an echo of the voice of external authority (Baxter Magolda, 2009).

SL is a good way of developing personal and social skills and increased cultural competency (Leonard et al., 2022). These developments are born from changes in students' thinking and attitude which comes from spending time with people from diverse backgrounds that are different from their own and reflecting on that experience. In this way, the learning is affective, as well as cognitive in nature, and helps the students to develop and frame their own sense of personal and graduate identity. Some participants were more successful than others in being able to frame their different identities and switch between them and those that could easily switch experienced a greater impact as this is an integral part of the learning process.

IDENTITY DEVELOPMENT

Participants associated their usual identity as a 'student identity'. Some, however, related to professional identities also. The developing professional identities were noted as emerging from participants who completed paid or voluntary work. Participants who did not work did not appear to have professional identities. The emergence of a professional identity was seen to be key to their performance on placement. Those who worked in jobs with a level of responsibility were able to draw on that professional identity to use their skills in a new context.

> I can work with patients who are suffering from mental illness and organic illness as well, um, that I have the skills, [...] some of the skills that I need, to be able to work in that environment and that was something that I wanted to do, so it's kind of confirmed that yes, you know, that is probably a good option for you (Kelly, theme 3).

Those who did not have that experience found it harder to develop initiative, to step out of a passive role and into a role with emerging responsibility. Whilst some were able to switch between student and graduate identities, others were less able to do so.

> Yeah, I think that was like, poor communication for me, so I thought I had, I, I had good communication skills, but obviously you have to apply it differently to different people, you can't be the same for everyone (Alice, theme 2).

In order to understand how this process may work, we need to draw on two key ideas from other contexts: identity framing and frame switching.

IDENTITY FRAMING

Identity framing illustrates the various ways in which people view themselves in specific contexts, but it also allows us to explore how individuals who are part of a larger group are influenced by their affiliation with, and participation in, that group (Gardner, 2016).

Frames are cognitive shortcuts that people use to understand complex information; they help individuals to interpret the world. When a person frames a phenomenon, they give meaning to some aspects of what is observed or experienced, while discounting other aspects that may appear irrelevant at that time (Kaufman et al., 2016).

Identity frames are born of an individual's self-conception and group affiliations. One might frame oneself as a particular gender, nationality or social group.

> It's important to help others, I've always been brought up that that is what you do. If you can help someone, you just do it (Joe, theme 1).

Everyone reported feeling varying levels of discomfort at the start of their placement and this was due to the change of context. A significant aspect of identity framing is the attachment to context. The context within which an individual develops their identity can provide stability and continuity. A change in context can result in feelings of displacement (Scanlon et al., 2007). The change from the frame of a student identity to a new framing which may be unclear at the start of the placement was responsible for much of the unease the participants felt.

> I am capable and perhaps in the beginning I was quite nervous, it was a new experience, but I feel that I've learned that I would be able to do something like this (Lauren, theme 2).
>
> I think I'm more aware of things now, [...] like what I would say. I would have to choose what I would say, um, being aware of others really, just knowing what they're going through and how like I choose to um, communicate with them (Ruby, theme 2).

FRAME-SWITCHING

Frame-switching is the process of changing from one cultural stream to another, when entering a situation that calls for a specific type of response (Schwartz et al., 2017).

The part-time nature of SL placements, unlike full-time placement years, requires students to assume different identities (student/developing graduate) depending on the day, and the task in hand. Participants were required to develop a new identity, consistent with the new context, before they could start the process of frame-switching.

> I thought I'd be better at it I guess, and thought I'd be a little bit more resilient to everything, but I wasn't and it was like, quite intimidating and when there is an incident like, you're a bit clueless on what to do (Abby theme 3).

Children learn from a young age to frame-switch between identities. Many parents will identify with teachers describing their child quite differently from their own experience and this is an example of just how well young children learn to adapt their identities to the context. If young adults are already proficient in frame-switching, why do some struggle to move from a student to a graduate identity? The answer lies in the notion of saliency. Student identity is salient, is hierarchically superior, to any developing graduate identity, and for those who have yet to develop a graduate identity, they do not have an appropriate frame to switch to.

The development of 'soft' skills and attributes is increasingly seen as important in higher education. The soft skills and attributes that participants developed, the increased confidence and self-efficacy, the recognition that it is not selfish to want to feel good in your daily work, has provided them with a conviction that they are capable and they can make a difference.

HELIX THREE: DEVELOPING PURPOSE

A sense of purpose has been described as a critical developmental asset for young adults. Developing purpose entails an increasing ability to be intentional, to assess interests and options, to clarify goals, to make plans and to persist despite obstacles. Damon (2009) suggests that Generation Z lacks purpose as the world is so fast-paced and change is so common that they are unable to map their futures as previous generations have done. He claims that education enriches the intellectual and personal lives of students but fails in guiding them towards future paths that they will find rewarding and meaningful. With a societal focus on monetary success, students can find that they are aiming for a future which focuses on earnings rather than fulfilment.

As a motivator, purpose helps to clarify life goals and daily decisions by directing the use of personal resources, such as time, energy and effort, towards prosocial aims. When a young person identifies a purpose in life and connects that purpose to their academic experience, learning can take on a relevance and personal meaning that it might otherwise lack. In this way, purpose can serve as an important source of motivation (Cotton Bronk et al., 2009; Damon,

2009). This prosocial dimension in SL is important for understanding where the sense of purpose ultimately leads. A sense of purpose is scaffolded by various factors, including family activity and social role fulfilment, personal reflection on past events and formal educational experiences. These experiences increase students' awareness and their openness to new experiences and alternative ways to examine themselves and the outside world (Cotton Bronk et al., 2009).

> You WILL come out with that idea of 'Man, I feel better about myself', because I've done something for people or community, or society (Brian, theme 1).

SL enables students to participate in meaningful community activities and reflect on the experience. SL is the most likely educational experience to match all four dimensions of purpose: personal meaningfulness, future intention, active engagement and beyond-the-self impact (Damon, 2009). This is because, by definition, it engages in actions expected to positively impact others and the common good. Students can reflect on the personal meaning of the SL experience that can give rise to intentions for prosocial contributions later in life.

> To help people, kind of, you're helping the future, I guess. Um, but also, it's kind of a personal thing, where um, in school, my teachers used to really help me and stuff, and it's sort of, help others (Aasef, theme 1).

The participants' purpose in doing the module ranged from gaining experience related to career goals, learning about specific groups or issues and helping others.

> It's more about me, kind of, consolidating my education now, so I can help others in the future. [...] personal about myself, CV, like learn more about myself and things... (Brian, theme 1).

> I feel like I'm not doing this to feel better about myself, I'm doing it to help others feel better about themselves, which in turn will make me feel better, but that's like a knock-on effect rather than a reason I'm doing it (Gemma, theme 1).

Some did not get the experience they anticipated; some were dreamers who had aspirations which were not realistic, a couple were dabblers engaging in what seemed to be purposeful activities but showing little awareness beyond the present or any real sense of what they wanted to do with their lives.

> I went into the placement thinking it was going to be maybe more, it was more of one that was sort of towards counselling, thinking it was like helping people. But when I've actually seen the criminal side of it, I think that's far more interesting (Jane, theme 1).

Most were purposeful, finding something meaningful to give their time and attention, or clarified what they did was meaningful and realised they needed to explore new areas of interest (Damon, 2009).

> It helps you to decide if that's the career for you or not, because there's obviously different aspects of it, but then it also helps you grow as a person, I think personally, well it has for me, anyway (Lolly, theme 1).

HELIX FOUR: MANAGING EMOTIONS

The final helix focuses on how the participants dealt with difficulties and challenges, building resilience and flexibility. Helix one discussed discomfort and fear at entering a new environment. Everyone overcame these fears to complete the placement, and managing emotions is essential for wellbeing, good communication and dealing with diverse situations and people. It demands realistic and productive responses and being able to control feelings of anger, depression, guilt and fear. The ability to manage emotions becomes critical if we wish to effectively tackle social problems, bringing together diverse communities and perspectives (Chickering & Braskamp, 2009).

SL exposes students to people, ideas and situations and this can disrupt accepted ways of thinking. It is this disruption that allows for new understandings, but it can also be overwhelming and emotionally intense. Noyes et al. (2015) categorised the emotions encountered in SL into four categories: excitement/joy, anger/frustration, sad/upset and rewarded/inspired.

Participants reported feeling excitement and joy during their placement. Usually this was a response to the individuals they were working with. Sometimes the joy came from just spending time with them, but often it came from watching them develop in small but meaningful ways. Finding joy in SL comes from suppressing previous assumptions and accepting individual circumstances and limitations. Once done, it is easier to take pleasure from the small details: a smile, a laugh, a welcome back.

> Oh yeah, it's amazing, [...] they give you that sense that you were needed [...] it was great, it made me sort of, it does like, sort of, encourage you to want to go back, you want to keep feeling that feeling more often, don't you, a bit like an addictive feeling, like of helping them (Theo, theme 3).

Many felt anger and frustration during SL, caused by different issues and aimed at different people and situations. Some felt angry or frustrated with workers or volunteers if they felt that their behaviour was inappropriate. Sometimes they felt angry with themselves when they felt their own responses had not been appropriate and sometimes they were angry with the situations that others found themselves in and a society that allowed people to be marginalised.

The only people they did not report getting angry or frustrated with were the service-users, though those who worked in secondary schools found themselves very challenged by the behaviours they encountered.

> I've been surprised at sort of how out of control some of the pupils have been (Lauren, theme 2).

Overall, participants discussed very positive experiences, but they were often saddened by the situations that the service-users found themselves in. Some were upset by the effects of illness, addiction and disability, others by the social stigma that service-users faced. Again, the root cause of this sadness was social injustice or the restricting nature of illness.

> you learn how difficult it can be for them to sort of live just the daily life, and you know, they go to a coffee shop, or whatever, there's a little kid there, [...] will just say something like, 'oh, look at that person, what's wrong with them' (Lolly, theme 2).

Finally, participants spoke at length about their reward and inspiration, for despite the frustration and sadness with an imperfect world, the service-users and staff and sometimes the organisations that they worked with were inspirational. They were rewarded for their time and commitment with friendship, warmth and gratitude. They felt both wanted and needed and were inspired by the stories of the people they met.

> As it went on, it was really good. Um, each session got better. It got a lot easier just to talk to them. I felt more and more comfortable. By the end of it I could just sit there [...]. I really enjoyed that. He was there laughing next to me (Brian, theme 2).

SL settings have more power to produce emotional experiences than traditional classroom settings.

> People aren't textbooks and people aren't lectures and notes, they're real people, doing real things and you can write down the basis of things, but to actually fully experience it, that is a lot more important (Lolly, theme 2).

Noyes et al. (2015) believe it allows for a better understanding of subjective experience and its relationship with academic outcomes. It illustrates how thoughts and feelings are interlinked with cognition and emotion co-creating to achieve a greater degree of critical thinking and reflection, informed action and a greater sense of wellbeing for both individuals and their communities.

CONTRIBUTIONS TO KNOWLEDGE

The purpose of this study was to evaluate the effectiveness of the SL model for learning and understand the opportunities and challenges faced by the students. It set out to fill a gap in the UK literature on SL as the first study to evaluate SL in Wales. It finds that SL is an effective pedagogy as it provides students with opportunities to meet new people with diverse backgrounds, to learn about marginalisation, deprivation and social justice issues, to develop skills and understandings and to develop greater self-awareness and their graduate identity.

The study also contributes to the SL literature by developing the quadruple helix to illustrate the development of graduate identity through service-learning. It provides a new insight into how SL supports developing graduate identity and how this could be used to develop a more holistic approach to employability and graduate attributes.

LIMITATIONS

As a qualitative study, it did not set out to generalise results, but there are limitations to the study. First, this study ends with the completion of the placement. As such, there is no investigation of the long-term impact of SL on the students' future volunteering intentions or work focus.

Second, the study focuses on those who chose to participate and so it provides no explanation of the motivations for those who chose not to participate in an SL module. The paradox of self-efficacy is that students with low self-efficacy regulate their behaviour to avoid failure. In doing so, they reduce their opportunity for participating in opportunities that may help to increase their self-efficacy.

Third, it maps the quadruple helix only to the SL model, with further research it could be evaluated for its relevance to other forms of placement or experiential learning.

CONCLUSION

The quadruple helix maps the ways in which students learn from experience and the ways in which they develop skills and attributes that relate to both graduate identity and employability. SL provides opportunities to meet new people from diverse backgrounds, to learn about marginalisation, deprivation and social justice issues, to develop skills and understandings and to develop greater self-awareness and graduate identity. The challenges lie in dealing with new places and people, overcoming discomfort, dealing with different attitudes and recognising their own limitations. Opportunities can be challenges and challenges can be opportunities, depending on the situation and the individual.

Our study revealed SL to be an individual process, different for every student. As such we should be careful about trying to generalise the benefits, and should not claim that it *is* transformative, but that it *can be* transformative. Students benefit in many ways and to differing degrees.

There is one aspect of SL which we expected to rank highly in the ways in which students learn through SL, but was not recognised as a major factor by the participants. Reflection is an integral part of the experiential learning process and yet few participants noted its importance in their learning. Its power for learning was not appreciated by students. Future research could explore students' attitudes to learning through reflection. How do they understand the reflective learning process and why is there sometimes a negative response to the use of reflection in academic learning?

SL has an important role to play in students developing a graduate identity and recognising their career goals and values. This is an aspect of student development which has not been previously discussed in the SL literature. Developing a graduate identity and the ability to switch between different identities in different situations has an impact on the success of a placement as it differentiates those who sit passively from those who actively involve themselves in the work. From the data, we can see that most participants learned a lot from the SL experience, but a minority learned less. In trying to discover the difference between those who had a meaningful experience and those who did not, there seems to be a link between the ability to frame-switch and a positive SL experience. The student identity is often a passive one; a work environment demands a more proactive identity. This is an important outcome if SL is to be seen as a pedagogy that meets the needs of both civic mission and the employability agenda. The quadruple helix would make a flexible and holistic framework for developing graduate attributes, as, in the UK, we still see graduate attributes largely in terms of skills rather than individualised personal and professional development. In other countries, research into student development is much more advanced than in the UK and we could learn a lot about developing employable graduates by focusing on the affective learning process, developing independent and socially aware graduates, rather than trying to force everyone into a specified skillset which inevitably will not be relevant to all students' future careers.

REFERENCES

Asghar, M. & Rowe, N. (2017). Reciprocity and critical reflection as the key to social justice in service learning: a case study. *Innovations in Education and Teaching International*, *54*(2), 117–125. https://doi.org/10.1080/14703297.2016.1273788

Asghar, M. & Rowe, N. (2018). Learning from the unfamiliar: how does working with people who use mental health services impact on students' learning and development? *Journal of Further and Higher Education*, *42*(3), 339–351. https://doi.org/10.1080/0309877X.2016.1261095

Bailey, M. S. (2017). Why 'where' matters: exploring the role of space in service-learning. *Michigan Journal of Community Service Learning*, *24*(1), 38–48. http://dx.doi.org/10.3998/mjcsloa.3239521.0024.104

Baxter Magolda, M. B. (2009). The activity of meaning making: a holistic perspective on college student development. *Journal of College Student Development*, *50*(6), 621–639. https://doi.org/10.1353/csd.0.0106

Bheekie, A. & van Huyssteen, M. (2015). Be mindful of your discomfort: an approach to contextualized learning. *International Journal for Research on Service-Learning and Community Engagement, 3*(1). https://doi.org/10.37333/001c.21560

Braun, V., & Clarke, V. (2006). Using thematic analysis in psychology. *Qualitative research in psychology, 3*(2), 77-101.

Brundage, D. H. & MacKeracher, D. (1980). *Adult learning principles and their application to program planning.* Ontario Ministry of Education, Toronto, Canada.

Carnicelli, S. & Boluk, K. (2017). The promotion of social justice: service learning for transformative education. *Journal of Hospitality, Leisure, Sport & Tourism Education,* 21, 126–134. https://doi.org/10.1016/j.jhlste.2017.01.003

Chickering, A. W. & Braskamp, L. A. (2009). Developing a global perspective for personal and social responsibility. *Peer Review*, 11(4), 27–30. www.aacu.org/peerreview/2009/fall/chickering-braskamp

Chickering, A. W. & Reisser, L. (1993). *Education and identity*. Jossey-Bass Publishers, San Francisco, CA.

Coffey, H., Harden, S. B., Brown, K. E. & Williams, M. (2017). Civic minor in urban youth and communities: a new service-learning curriculum disrupts traditional teacher education. In B. H. Hall & H. Ashley (eds) *Community engagement program implementation and teacher preparation for 21st century education* (pp. 48–65). Hershey PA: IGI Global.

Cotton Bronk, K., Hill, P. L., Lapsley, D. K., Talib, T. L. & Finch, H. (2009). Purpose, hope, and life satisfaction in three age groups. *The Journal of Positive Psychology,* 4(6), 500–510. https://doi.org/10.1080/17439760903271439

Damon, W. (2009). *The path to purpose: how young people find their calling in life*. New York: Simon and Schuster.

Deeley, S. J. (2010). Service-learning: thinking outside the box. *Active Learning in Higher Education*, 11(1), 43–53. https://doi.org/10.1177/1469787409355870

Deeley, S. J. (2015). *Critical perspectives on service-learning in higher education.* Basingstoke, UK: Palgrave Macmillan.

Furco, A. (1996). Service-learning: a balanced approach to experiential education. In B. Taylor (ed.) *Expanding boundaries: serving and learning.* Corporation for National Service. https://digitalcommons.unomaha.edu/slceslgen/128/ [Accessed 30 May 2017].

Gardner, R. (2016, July 6). *Identity frames* [Text]. Beyond intractability. www.beyondintractability.org/essay/identity-frames [accessed: 16 February 2018].

Gerholz, K.-H. & Losch, S. (2015). Can service learning foster a social responsibility among students? A didactical analysis and empirical case-study in business education at a German university. In L. O'Riordan, P. Zmuda & S. Heinemann (eds) *New perspectives on corporate social responsibility: locating the missing link* (pp. 603–626). Wiesbaden: Springer Fachmedien. https://doi.org/10.1007/978-3-658-06794-6_30

Heras-Colàs, R., Masgrau-Juanola, M. & Soler-Masó, P. (2017). The institutionalization of service-learning at Spanish universities. *The International Journal of Research on Service-Learning and Community Engagement*, 5(1). https://journals.sfu.ca/iarslce/index.php/journal/article/view/268

Kaufman, S., Elliott, M. & Schmueli, D. (2016, July 6). *Frames, framing and reframing* [Text]. Beyond intractability [24 March 2018].

Leonard, G., Lassiter, J. W., Hammill, R. & LeCrom, C. W. (2022). Service-learning and the development of interpersonal skills in pre-professional undergraduate students. *Pedagogy in Health Promotion*, 23733799221074624. https://doi.org/10.1177/23733799221074626

Liou, C. P. (2018). Learning from experience: from psychotherapy to service-learning. *Asia Pacific Journal of Counselling and Psychotherapy*, *9*(1), 77-85.

Mueller, J. & Lee, D. (2010). How actions can become learning: the cross-cultural effectiveness of service-learning in Asia. In J. Xing & C. H. K. Ma (eds) *Service-learning in Asia: curricular models and practices* (Vol. 1). Hong Kong University Press.

Noyes, E., Darby, A. & Leupold, C. (2015). Students' emotions in academic service-learning. *Journal of Higher Education Outreach and Engagement*, 19(4), 63–84. https://eric.ed.gov/?id=EJ1086106

Saylor, J., Hertsenberg, L., McQuillan, M., O'Connell, A., Shoe, K. & Calamaro, C. J. (2018). Effects of a service learning experience on confidence and clinical skills in baccalaureate nursing students. *Nurse Education Today*, 61, 43–48. https://doi.org/10.1016/j.nedt.2017.11.009

Scanlon, D. L., Rowling, L. & Weber, Z. (2007). 'You don't have like an identity … you are just lost in a crowd': forming a student identity in the first-year transition to university. *Journal of Youth Studies,* 10(2), 223–241. https://doi.org/10.1080/13676260600983684

Schwartz, S. J., Birman, D., Benet-Martinez, V. & Unger, J. (2017). Biculturalism: negotiating multiple cultural streams. In S. J. Schwartz & J. Unger (eds) *The Oxford handbook of acculturation and health*. New York: Oxford University Press.

Seifer, S. D. (1998). Service-learning: community-campus partnerships for health professions education. *Academic Medicine*, 73(3), 273–277. www.ncbi.nlm.nih.gov/pubmed/9526454

Sigmon, R. (1979). Service-learning: three principles. *Synergist,* 8(1), 9–11. https://nsee.memberclicks.net/assets/docs/KnowledgeCenter/IntegratingExpEduc/BooksReports/55.%20service%20learning%20three%20principles.pdf

Stanton, T. K., Giles Jr, D. E. & Cruz, N. I. (1999). *Service-learning: a movement's pioneers reflect on its origins, practice, and future.* Jossey-Bass Higher and Adult Education Series. San Francisco, CA: Jossey-Bass Publishers.

Whitley, M. A., Walsh, D., Hayden, L. & Gould, D. (2017). Narratives of experiential learning: students' engagement in a physical activity-based service-learning course. *Journal of Teaching in Physical Education*, 36(4), 419–429. https://doi.org/10.1123/jtpe.2016-0141

Xing, J. & Ma, C. H. K. (2010). *Service-learning in Asia: curricular models and practices.* Hong Kong University Press.

12

The Graduate Project: A Model for Embedded Employability in Arts and Humanities Undergraduate Education

Fiona Cosson and Kate Terkanian

INTRODUCTION: UNIVERSITIES AND THE EMPLOYABILITY AGENDA

Ensuring that graduates are highly employable after their university studies has become increasingly important to governments, universities, employers, and the public. Whilst it is widely acknowledged a university education should not only be about job prospects, and there have been many criticisms of the ‘employability agenda’, it also remains the case that for students, job prospects after their degree are an important motivator for pursuing university education. In turn, higher education providers have a role to play in ensuring their graduates are equipped with the experiences, skills, and attributes to allow them to obtain employment in their chosen fields, and to adapt and change with the labour market in the future.

The higher education sector in England has undergone rapid and radical changes in the last 20 years (Wales and Scotland operate on different funding and tuition fee systems). Since Blair’s New Labour government introduced £1,000 tuition fees for students in England in 1998, there have been multiple increases in tuition fees for universities in England – to £3,000 in 2006, and £9,000 in 2012, and £9,250 per year in 2021–22 (Willetts, 2010).[1] The result of tuition fees and the marketisation of English higher education has been a shift in the discourse and understanding of higher education, from an investment in human and intellectual capital for the benefit of society, to instead a personal investment in one's future job prospects and earning potential – a 'significant private benefit' afforded by substantial personal debt to be repaid over a graduate's lifetime (Johnson, 2017; Bolton, 2021).

These shifts in how and why higher education is pursued and valued, funded and delivered has had profound consequences across all aspects of higher education provision. One key consequence has been the changing relationship between universities, students, and the labour market. With claims such as graduates earn £500,000 more than non-graduates over their lifetimes, the link between university education, 'value', and financial success has been progressively cemented in public discourse (Institute for Fiscal Studies, 2016).[2] With students required to financially invest in their education, with the promise of better jobs and higher wages than their non-university educated peers, the result is that students increasingly perceive their learning as an investment in their employability 'that will give them direct benefits in the labour market' (Tomlinson, 2008: 49).

Like many terms in the higher education sector ('widening participation', 'student experience') the term 'employability' is widely used but lacks clear definition, and might be seen by some as yet another 'buzzword' (Philpott, 1999; Baker, 2011). Early scholarship on employability (Hillage and Pollard, 1998) understood it as simply gaining and retaining work after graduation, and thus little different from 'employment'. Since then, some definitions (Walker and Zhu, 2013) have sought to emphasise individual endeavour and ability, such as 'the propensity of the individual student to get employment'. Elsewhere (Cole and Tibby, 2013), there is an emphasis that employability is not only about securing employment but also about 'adaptability', 'life-long learning' and 'success'.

Whatever its definition, universities are more concerned than ever about their graduates' potential to obtain work after they leave university. Indeed, a key indicator, used in most UK university league tables is graduate destination after leaving university (Higher Education Statistics Agency, c. 2021). At the same time, there has been attention to the alleged deficiencies in the skills and experiences of newly graduated students, and universities are accused of not doing enough to equip their students with the skills needed in graduate employment or by graduate recruiters (Saunders and Zuzel, 2010: 1–15; Mason and Rincon-Aznar, 2015; Steed, 2018). According to a Universities UK report (2015), employers say that university and college leavers lack a mix of job-specific and general employability-related skills, as well as a lack of work experience.

One of the poorest relations in this debate are perhaps the students and graduates of programmes in the arts, humanities, and social sciences whose courses are regularly lampooned by government (Williamson, 2021) and the press as 'dead-end' and low value.[3] Correspondingly, Donald et al.'s research (2019: 610) noted a tendency for humanities students to view themselves less employable than graduates with clearer career paths, and that these distinctions had a gendered dimension as female students viewed themselves as less employable than male ones (609–12). Those who teach undergraduates in arts, humanities, and social sciences know the abundance of transferable knowledge and skills that are acquired by the study of these disciplines – critical thinking; research, selection, and interpretation; argument, persuasion, and communication. But these are not always apparent to students and employers alike. Furthermore, students in these fields do not always have the opportunity to *apply* their subject knowledge, get *experience* of professional work settings, or transferable skills in ways that they are later able to *articulate* and *evidence* to employers.

Pressure on universities to prepare their students for the labour market has resulted in a number of approaches and initiatives to boost graduate employability. In the UK, this has seen employability become central to some university degree programmes themselves evident, for example, in the rise of vocation-orientated degree programmes such as journalism, marketing, and hospitality. Here the curricula itself supports students in pursuing clear paths of employment and career development. Universities also increasingly engage with the professional, statutory, and regulatory bodies (Higher Education Better Regulation Group, 2011) for programme accreditation, which can help students access or fast-track into a route to qualified, chartered, or professional status.

Elsewhere, employability activity has expanded from the peripheries of university education services, such as careers services and job fairs, to include increasingly sophisticated personal and career development programmes, events, and activities. Many UK universities now offer opportunities to their students including work placements, either as summer activities, embedded in their modules, or as a 'sandwich' placement year, extending their undergraduate course by a year. Elsewhere, employability development has been offered to students through 'Careers with' modules, which focus on the discipline-specific career options (Scott et al., 2019). Additionally, there has been an increase in universities working with regional and national organisations to engage students on research and project briefs. Employability passports are also widely used in UK, North American and Australian universities as a means of recording and evidencing students' work-related skills and experiences. Finally, students are also further encouraged to consider how the experience and skills they may gain from volunteering, involvement with student clubs and societies, and paid employment also contribute to their employability.

One of these methods of developing employability is project-based learning (PBL) which teaches skills through group projects executed within modules. PBL can provide more intensive experiences for students than extra-curricular or short-duration activities (Thune and Storen, 2015). By pairing student groups with community organisations or industrial partners to teach specific skills or provide industry experience, different disciplines across the globe have embraced PBL to enhance understanding and ultimately employability. In Brazil (Arentes do Amarala and Motohashi Matsusaki, 2017), MBA students learn project management by working directly with community organisations. In South

Africa (Davidson, 2020), employability for engineering postgraduate students is bolstered through research collaboration with industry partners. In Botswana (Moalosi et al., 2012), students work with local companies on packaging design projects. In the US (Hall, 2018), humanities students explore communication, investigation, and disability studies through 3D printing technologies. These initiatives highlight the benefits of working on live, in-depth projects, but this type of learning is offered more often to postgraduate students or in disciplines where practice periods and projects are the norm – engineering, social sciences, medical degrees, business and education.

Thune and Storen (2015) note that humanities degrees are much less likely to integrate practical elements into their curriculum, but that these same students dramatically increase their employability when participating in project-based learning. Their 2015 Norway-based study indicated that post-study employment difficulties for humanities masters' students was cut in half when they had participated in project work or practice periods (712–16). Thune and Storen further suggest (2015: 718) that short-term interactions such as site visits and extra-curricular activities are less effective than these longer-term interactions.

Integrating employability into the curriculum gives students space to reflect on their learning and see the value of their education beyond the classroom. Barrie (2006: 224–30) proposes that enabling students to understand and express core graduate attributes are essential elements in developing employability in higher education, and that there are four ways of conceptualising how employability can be incorporated into a university curriculum. Precursor skills assume students arrive with abilities that they can apply on their own. Complement skills are bolted on top of subject-based curricula; these are the types of attributes that are developed through career services, workshops, and employability passport schemes. Transform and enable models marry discipline-specific skills with desired graduate attributes. For humanities students, this would be understanding that the analytical and writing skills learned through subject study are valuable tools (transform), as well as comprehending how these skills can be applied in other disciplines or workplaces (enable). Hall's 3D printing project (2018) is an excellent example of enabling, as humanities students used their communicative and investigative abilities to design a prosthetic limb for an outside client.

It is against this backdrop that the Bournemouth University's BA History programme developed the Graduate Project. Students *transform* the skills they have developed over the course of their degree by applying them in a live project. As a result, their ability to see the myriad of applications of history-specific skills beyond both the discipline and academia is *enabled.* They are then able to experience, articulate, and evidence their transferable and employability skills. The chapter now discusses the Graduate Project at Bournemouth University as an example of embedded employability undergraduate education, and then suggests how the Graduate Project model has potential wider application in employability education for arts, humanities and social science programmes.

THE GRADUATE PROJECT AT BOURNEMOUTH UNIVERSITY

The Graduate Project is a final-year core module on the BA (Hons) history programme at Bournemouth University (UK). The module can stretch across the whole academic year or be confined to a single semester. Working in small teams of three to four, students design, develop and deliver a project, event, or resource for an outside organisation, 'the client'. Clients provide a project brief which the students use as a base to interpret and develop an achievable output. The students then manage their project, their competing workload, and their team, with support and supervision from their lecturers and their client, before presenting and transferring the final project output over to the client at the end of the module.

From its inception in 2015, the BA (Hons) history programme at Bournemouth University has incorporated practical elements into its curriculum. Mandatory summer placements and group work at all year levels are typical. Students are also encouraged to take part in an optional 'sandwich' placement, a year-long, career-orientated stint with a degree-related employer. Students learn how history is practised both inside and outside of academia and are encouraged from their first year to envision how they can put a history degree to work once they have finished their studies.

The first time the Graduate Project module ran was in the 2017–2018 academic year, in the third year of the degree programme. The initial clients were local to Dorset and included the regional archive, a county museum, a heritage site, a literary festival and a primary school. In advance of the module launch, lecturers started to build up relations with arts, cultural, community, and heritage organisations in the Bournemouth region as there were no pre-existing relationships. Subsequent recruitment has been aided by referral from previous clients, repeat clients, and Bournemouth University Community Liaison Officers. Local institutions and organisations have been eager to establish relationships with the university, and increasingly organisations such as heritage organisations and the local council has asked for assistance in carrying out funded projects. The Graduate Project is an excellent tool to boost community engagement, and repeat clients indicate that the projects are beneficial to the community groups as well as the students.

Certain aspects of the Graduate Project, such as the module goals, expected outcomes and academic weight, were predetermined, but specifics of the module were intentionally brief, a 'shell' to be filled and developed. The flexibility of the module design has allowed the lecturers to adapt and shape the module year-to-year depending on the needs of the projects. In addition to fulfilling the requirement of the UK Quality Assurance Agency for Higher Education (2014b) to train history students to communicate history to the public, the Graduate Project also explicitly focusses on developing employability-related skills and experiences with final-year students by helping students to:

- identify their strengths, interests and skills and put them to use
- further develop skills and attributes about which they may be less confident or experienced
- showcase their skills and experience to future places of work or study
- stand out from the crowd in having not only gained knowledge and skills during their degree, but also to have applied them to real-world clients and projects

Students are encouraged and supported to develop a range of professional skills and experiences including project management, presentations and pitches, curation and exhibition, educational resources, events-programming, archival research, writing and publishing – valuable transferable skills for future aspirations and careers. Other aspects enable and support the development of skills and attributes commonly required in graduate-level employment, including performing effectively both independently and in group work; confidence in communicating and networking; allocating and evaluating time, tasks, and resources, and planning. The end goal is to provide history students with a greater understanding of the ways historical skills can be utilised in the workplace, thus avoiding leaving students to discover these possible paths on their own after graduation.

The module represents a progression of the history degree learning goals and enables students to apply the historical skills and knowledge that they have gained over their years as history undergraduates. In order to scaffold both the confidence and the skills needed to work with outside organisations, students learn historical skills and are introduced to public history concepts and small-group projects in the first year of study. In the second year, the students conduct oral history interviews and then develop an outward-facing group project built on the interviews. By the time students reach their third and final year, they are equipped to undertake original historical research with the aim of communicating this research and information to public audiences, with an awareness of the many ways in which history can be interpreted and communicated to the public. This aligns with the UK Quality Assurance Agency for Higher Education's (2014a) descriptions and history degree benchmarks regarding communicating information, ideas, problems, and solutions to specialist and public audiences.

Whilst the delivery and assessment have been tweaked over the years, the essential elements – groups of three to four students working with an outside client to produce a history-related output – have remained the same. What has been most striking about the module is the students' creativity and adaptability in the face of daunting topics and circumstances. From the first cohort, the lecturers have seen both high-performing students excel, and under-performing students blossom, and witnessed the production of excellent pieces of public history.

MODULE DELIVERY AND STRUCTURE

Three elements are central to the student experience and the development of skills. The first is the provision of masterclass workshops tailored to fit the range of projects on any given year. Second, project supervision to offer guidance and intercede with client issues is also essential. The third aspect is the module assessments which are geared towards tracking group progress, instilling time-management and project-management skills, and the production of tangible material and skills that assist in postgraduation job searches. These summative elements are also supplemented by formative engagement activities. Students and clients participate in an initial meet-the-client session at the start of the module, arrange site visits with the clients where appropriate, and participate in an end-of-module project showcase.

MASTERCLASS WORKSHOPS

In the main, student progress on their projects is self-directed, supported by supervision with lecturers and by masterclasses. Masterclasses are workshops that assist students with the execution of the projects and development of employability skills. These sessions vary from year-to-year, but typically include sessions on project and time management, pitching a project, exhibition design, networking, CVs, cover letters and interview preparation, and audio/visual production techniques.

Whilst the module lecturers conduct some of these sessions, the workshop format enables other Bournemouth University staff, outside professionals, including clients, and former students to share their expertise and knowledge. For example, in the masterclass on networking, Bournemouth University's Community Engagement Officer provides links with other individuals and community groups and offers concrete ways in which the students can promote their projects to the wider community. Elsewhere, Bournemouth University experts in audio and video production get the students to think creatively about their outputs and connect them with media production students who provide technical assistance to the groups. Repeat client, the Museum of East Dorset, conducts a hands-on workshop in display design and label composition (Figure 12.1). A former student who is now a small business owner offers his expertise in running social media campaigns.

Figure 12.1 Exhibition design masterclass

As the masterclass format is flexible, specialist guest lecturers can be incorporated as needed. One year, an expert on crowd-sourcing and online archive platforms was brought in when clients wanted to develop electronic archives. The masterclass format provides maximum flexibility for designing the course and ensuring the students receive appropriate skills, broadening their knowledge base. The inclusion of people active in the sector also widens the students' professional network and increases their confidence. Students are empowered by directly exploring their employability through the inclusion of job-seeking sessions and contact with outside professionals.

SUPERVISION

The module aims to instil strong group-work relationships and to bolster individual confidence, and the students are consequently given charge of client relationships. However, each project team is also assigned a supervisor. Supervision is not intended to actively mediate the relationship between the student groups and the clients, but to act as a monitor should relationships or communication break down. The second function of supervision is to track progress and inspire the students. Supervisors suggest ways in which the teams can improve or expand on their intended outcomes. Supervision is a vital part of the Graduate Project and is conducted at regular intervals. Whilst there are no assessment points tied to this aspect of the module, some of the assignments detailed below feed into the supervision process.

ASSESSMENT

Whilst research (Gammie and Matson, 2007: 186–99) has shown that group work is a way to prepare students for working environments, many students fear group work, and anxieties around group work are linked to inequities in performance. In order to mitigate this perception, the module is assessed on an individual level and a group level (Table 12.1). A peer assessment element also allows the students to evaluate group members to offset worries about unequal effort. The clients have no direct role in assessment, but students often seek feedback from their client. The successful completion of the project is the end goal, but the milestones along the way are equally important. Setbacks and changes in direction are all part of the process and students are counselled on these inevitabilities. The stress is placed on the learning aspects of group work and how this mirrors experiences that they will encounter in the workplace. Former students have reported (Anonymous respondents, 2021, personal communication) that they have been able to use their successes and challenges in the Graduate Project to obtain employment and in day-to-day practice.

Table 12.1 Assessments and weightings for the Graduate Project module

Assessment		Weight	Group / Individual
Client Project Pitch		10%	Group
Project Progress Log		10%	Individual
Project Portfolio made up of:	(a) Project Output	40%	Group
	(b) Project Report	25%	Individual
	(c) Cover Letter & CV	10%	Individual
	(d) Peer Assessment	5%	Individual

There are four sub-elements for the individual assessment – project progress reports, a CV and cover letter, a project report and a peer evaluation. Together they comprise 50% of the module mark. The project progress reports (10% of the module mark) take the form of a survey/questionnaire and there are four submission points during the semester. These are used during supervision to monitor progress and to allow the students the space to discreetly disclose conflicts or concerns. It also serves as a diary and can help with the completion of the final project report. The CV and cover letter (10% of the module mark) are directly linked with employability. Students are expected to highlight skills gained from both the module and their degree in their CVs and cover letters, encouraging them to directly consider what they have learned at university and how their experiences relate to future employment. Some students have used live job advertisements to complete this element and subsequently secured employment, taking the first steps on their intended career path.

The final two individual elements are the project report and the peer evaluation. The project report (25% of the module mark) encourages the students to both evaluate the project and reflect on the learning process. Bournemouth University history students are exposed to report writing in both their first and second years of study. Therefore, the format of a report is familiar. They are encouraged to use reflective cycles and evaluation techniques typical for project reporting. The format also allows them to consider the learning process and, like the CV and cover letter, think about how the degree has improved their employability. The peer evaluation (5% of the module mark) allows the team members to rate the performance of the other members and offer constructive feedback. This information is collected through an online survey, and lecturers reserve the right to exclude unnecessarily punitive reviews. Research indicates (Lejk and Wyvill, 2001a: 61–70, 2001b: 552–9; Gammie and Matson, 2007: 189, 196; Onyia and Allen, 2012: 1–20) that a barrier to successful peer evaluation can be low response rates, but when handled properly peer evaluation can be an effective tool. Bournemouth University history students face no penalty for non-participation in the peer evaluation process, and yet nearly all students have taken part in this aspect of the assessment.

There are two group assessments for the module – a project pitch and the final project output, which constitute 50% of the module mark. The project pitch (10% of the module mark) is weighted significantly lower than the final project output and is the first opportunity for students to demonstrate their understanding of their client needs. Students create an oral presentation and pitch the project to the lecturers. The pitch relays the students' comprehension of the brief, their determination of what is achievable in the time frame, and indicates that wider sector research has been conducted. After presenting to the lecturers, the students then pitch the project to the clients in a separate session.

The **project output** is the major piece of work for the project, constituting 40% of the module mark. Each project has its own parameters and as such is judged on its merits. The emphasis is on determining whether the groups have achieved the objectives set by the client, if they have created a successful piece of public history, and if they have used their research and writing skills to achieve these objectives. BA (Hons) history students have created websites, e-books, pamphlets, walking tours and exhibitions, and have also held community events, conducted oral history interviews, and hosted public forums. Please see the 'Additional Resources' at the end of this chapter for publicly available examples.

STUDENT EXPERIENCE AND GRADUATE OUTCOMES

Given the flexibility of a history degree, the graduate destinations for Bournemouth University's history students are varied. Some have pursued higher education, become teachers, account executives, trainee accountants, recruitment consultants, and started their own businesses. What many of the graduates have in common is their assessment of the benefits of the Graduate Project in their professional lives. In a survey, graduates were asked how they have used the skills learned both in applying for positions and on-the-job. Many of the responses indicated that their CVs feature their client relationships and project development, and that the module served as a useful example during interviews. One former student who is now a secondary school teacher stated (Anonymous respondent, 2021, personal communication) that 'the graduate project was a centre of conversation in all my job interviews that I attended. All employers were really impressed at the experience it had given me and it allowed me to stand out from other applicants'.

These student expressions echo what Barton et al. (2019: 453–63) term 'that extra sparkle' – soft skills that make graduates more attractive candidates. There are some differences between the Graduate Project as a core module and the volunteering activities described by Barton et al. (2019: 455–62), but the added benefit to student employability of experience with outside organisations is strikingly similar. The link between successful job searches and experiential learning, or soft skills, acquired through voluntary work experience resonates with the Graduate Project outcomes. The Graduate Project has the added benefit of embedding the development of soft skills within the degree. Developmental activities such as voluntary work and involvement in extra-curricular organisations can be exclusionary. Non-traditional students whose community, family and work commitments make voluntary work and involvement in student clubs difficult or unattractive are subsequently disadvantaged in acquiring skills that help attain post-university employment (Hordósy and Clark, 2018: 414–35). By allowing all students to work with outside clients, mimicking voluntary work and civic involvement, the Graduate Project creates a more inclusive paradigm. As a former student relates (Anonymous respondent, 2021, personal communication), the module is '[s]omething that is completely opposite ... to the normal essay writing and exam sitting, I think it is key to helping students get jobs post-graduation'.

As a former polytechnical institution, Bournemouth University has retained a strong emphasis on practical skills, and the practical aspects of the module are what students have indicated have best served them on the job. Teamwork and time management were noted as the top skills that former students use day-to-day on their jobs. The survey responses also indicated that these aspects were ones the students found to be the most challenging. Two graduates who are now teachers indicated that the Graduate Project inspired them to model local history modules for their own students (Anonymous respondents, 2021, personal communication), and in one school, the whole department had adopted the graduate's work scheme and lessons. Whilst the feedback from this survey is qualitative, the responses indicate that the goals of the module have been comprehended by the students. They have been able to utilise skills learned in both applying for work, during the interview process, and on the job.

As a final testament to the efficacy of the Graduate Project in emphasising both traditional humanities skills and their practical application, this unsolicited response from a recent graduate is indicative:

> the graduate project was absolutely incredible and I was blessed to be surrounded by amazing people ... I'm still in a state of shock at how well we've done! I put that down to [the lecturers] and the brilliant masterclasses that helped inspire us along the way! We honestly felt like detectives as we sieved through information and used all tools at our disposal to understand these people, their lives, and their struggles (Anonymous, 2021, personal communication).

MAKING AN IMPACT

Beyond the employability skills and experiences that the Graduate Project provides for students that have been discussed so far, the Graduate Project model has, further, added social value for universities and their communities. By facilitating the creation and development of positive relationships and partnership-working between staff, students, and the community-based external clients, the Graduate Project model can act as a driver to start, expand, or deepen a university's engagement with its communities, whilst also fulfilling sector and institutional drivers and metrics relating to public engagement, co-production, and research impact agendas (University Partnership Programme Foundation Civic University Commission, 2019).

As the UK higher education sector increasingly assumes more corporate, market-like behaviour, universities simultaneously seek to demonstrate their social value to 'engage' and 'impact' their communities and the public. Initiatives such as the UK National Co-ordinating Centre for Public Engagement, which was founded in 2008, and the UK Civic University Network, launched in 2020 and backed by the University Partnership Programme Foundation has more than 50 UK university members, indicating a growing appetite within the higher education sector for public and community engagement. These engagements and relationships are also increasingly being measured by the sector assessments and metrics; since 2014, the UK Research Excellence Framework has sought to assess the benefits of research outside of academia through its Impact agenda, and 2021 saw the first iteration of the UK Knowledge Exchange Framework, set up to measure knowledge exchange activities between universities and external partners for the benefit of the economy and society. As such, both institutional targets and a genuine desire to connect and include their communities and the public with their work means that universities are keener than ever on outreach and partnership work. The Graduate Project enables universities to connect with organisations in their region and beyond, allowing the development of relationships, projects, and ways of working, with the potential to progress to more formal partnerships and collaborations, through memorandums of understanding, funding bids, and contract research.

There are benefits to the clients in participating in the Graduate Project. Of course, there is input needed from the project clients into the Graduate Project; principally, this is time rather than money. As above, clients are asked to complete a project brief, attend meetings with students to help steer the project through feedback and planning, and attend a showcase of the students' work at the end of the module. In return, there can be significant payback for the clients. Enlisting students on a project can bring practical benefits in terms of extra support, activity or resources on an existing client project, helping to plug the volunteer gap, and boost projects that have lost momentum. For clients, working with a student team can also bring new insights, approaches, and ideas, such as ways to engage younger audiences, or ways to expand the use of digital technologies. Elsewhere, student input to client projects sees students use their disciplinary skills, knowledge, and passion. Additionally, the structure of the Graduate Project model encourages the development of projects and relationships with and between university staff, students and client organisations; projects can be built on year after year by subsequent cohorts. Finally, and more broadly, there can also be kudos for organisations to work with universities, to illustrate their reach or relevance, and to demonstrate partnership-working to funders, governors, or regulatory bodies.

CONCLUSION

Degrees in the arts, humanities, and social sciences allow their students to gain a wide range of skills and attributes, including research, interpretation, communication, flexibility, and adaptability, but this broad skillset is also one of the reasons students can struggle with the direction of their job search post-university. Emphases on employability and graduate outcomes concentrate on high-paying technology-related degrees. However, Adam J. Smith (2018, 1037–44) posits that humanities graduates, whose education is rooted in resilience and humanity, are more prepared for a future environment that is adaptable to the economic precarity that new graduates will meet in the modern workplace. Yet, graduates from these programmes are not always able to recognise or articulate the skills they have as a result of their studies. The Graduate Project overcomes this by giving students the opportunity to apply, experience, articulate, and evidence their employability skills and experiences. The Graduate Project has potential wider application, and presents a model for employability education in arts, humanities, and social science programme undergraduate curricula, to embed, expand, and enrich undergraduate employability opportunities and experiences to support students' future careers.

The Graduate Project model could be applied to politics undergraduates, with client projects with local government and councillors, activism and campaigning, and political media organisations. Students studying English or linguistics might work with literacy and reading charities, book and poetry festivals, and publishers. Sociology undergraduates could work with equality, policy, and youth organisations. Further, the Graduate Project model could also function at postgraduate level, allowing specialised projects, individual or group, with discipline or industry-relevant projects embedded into a taught MA programme. In terms of location, the Graduate Project detailed here has principally worked with organisations local to the region but, given the experience of universities and organisations in remote working as a result of COVID-19, there are also possibilities for working with national and international organisations and companies as project clients. Finally, if the Graduate Project model was employed by universities at an institutional level, an administrative channel would enable companies and organisations to approach the university. A wider range of clients and projects might be recruited and supported to take part in the Graduate Project, delivering projects for organisations and industries, and furnishing students with career capital to take forward into their graduate futures.

The skills, confidence, and sense of achievement gained from completing a high-quality Graduate Project is invaluable to students who will soon be leaving university to pursue employment or further study. Working with clients gives students a taste of real-world, professional working environments, projects, and communications in a way traditional university-based learning cannot, giving them a better idea of what they are capable of and the myriad of opportunities they can follow.

ADDITIONAL RESOURCES

Bournemouth Blind Society – eBook, audio book and interactive map www.bournemouthblindsociety.uk/home-2/student-history-project/

Dorchester Town Council Heritage Tourism – Dorchester Hidden Histories walking trail https://geotourist.com/tours/4406

Dorset History Centre – The Treves Trail walking trail, Dorchester. https://geotourist.com/tours/1908

Golden Arrow: The Roads Less Travelled online exhibition https://nationalmotormuseum.org.uk/online-exhibitions/golden-arrow-the-roads-less-travelled/

Queen's Park Forum – Memories of Charminster walking trail https://pocketsights.com/tours/tour/405-B3063-Bournemouth-BH8-9QT-UK-Memories-of-Charminster-2983

St Barbe Museum & Art Gallery Timeline www.stbarbe-museum.org.uk/our-collections/collections-timeline/

Notes

1 When introduced in 2012, the figure of £9,000 was supposed to be an 'absolute limit' charged only in 'exceptional circumstances' but, in fact, almost all universities chose immediately to charge the maximum tuition fees and continue to do so, with tuition fees in 2021–22 in England at £9,250 per year.

2 Johnson's figures were later challenged, and, amongst other errors, these figures did not include the cost of student loan repayments or tax, nor take into account other aspects that shape graduate outcomes, including family background and education.

3 It might be noted that Gavin Williamson studied Social Sciences at the University of Bradford from 1994 to 1997.

REFERENCES

Arantes do Amarala, J. A. and Motohashi Matsusaki, C. T. (2017) 'The dynamics of connecting universities, non-governmental organizations and community members by means of academic projects directed at people in need'. *Educational Action Research* 25(2): 280–99.

Baker, M. (2011) 'Employability: the new student buzzword at universities'. *BBC News* 9 April. Available at: www.bbc.co.uk/news/education-13013994 (accessed 6 August 2021).

Barrie, S. (2006) 'Understanding what we mean by generic attributes of graduates'. *Higher Education* 51: 215–41.

Barton, E., Bates, E. A. and O'Donovan, R. (2019) '"That extra sparkle": students' experiences of volunteering and the impact on satisfaction and employability in higher education'. *Journal of Further and Higher Education* 43(4): 453–66.

Bolton, P. (2021) *Student loan statistics*. House of Commons Library Briefing Paper 01079. London: House of Commons. Available at: https://commonslibrary.parliament.uk/research-briefings/sn01079 (accessed 6 August 2021).

Cole, D. and Tibby, M. (2013) *Defining and developing your approach to employability: a framework for higher education institutions*. Heslington: The Higher Education Academy. Available at: www.heacademy.ac.uk/system/files/resources/employability_framework.pdf (accessed 6 August 2021).

Davidson, I. E. (2020) 'Successes in university – industry partnerships – perspectives from Durban University of Technology'. *2020 International SAUPEC/RobMech/PRASA Conference*, doi: 10.1109/SAUPEC/RobMech/PRASA48453.2020.9041128.

Donald, W. E., Baruch, Y. and Ashleigh, M. (2019) 'The undergraduate self-perception of employability: human capital, careers advice, and career ownership'. *Studies in Higher Education* 44(4): 599–614.

Gammie, E. and Matson, M. (2007) 'Group assessment at final degree level: an evaluation'. *Accounting Education: an International Journal* 16(2): 185–206.

Hall, A. (2018) 'From tchotchke to techne: project-based learning in the arts and humanities'. *Currents in Teaching and Learning* 10(2): 36–50.

Higher Education Better Regulation Group (2011) *Professional, statutory and regulatory bodies: an exploration of their engagement with higher education*. London. Available at: www.universitiesuk.ac.uk/policy-and-analysis/reports/Documents/2011/hebrg-professional-bodies.pdf (accessed 6 August 2021).

Higher Education Statistics Agency (c. 2021) *'HE graduate outcomes data'*. Available at: www.hesa.ac.uk/data-and-analysis/graduates. (accessed 6 August 2021).

Hillage, J. and Pollard, E. (1998) *Employability: developing a framework for policy analysis*. Suffolk: Department for Education and Employment.

Hordósy, R. and Clark, T. (2018) 'Beyond the compulsory: a critical exploration of the experiences of extracurricular activity and employability in a northern red brick university'. *Research in Post-Compulsory Education* 23(3): 414–35.

Institute for Fiscal Studies (2016) *'What and where you study matter for graduate earnings – but so does parents' income'*. Press release, 13 April. Available at: www.ifs.org.uk/uploads/publications/pr/graduate_earnings_130416.pdf (accessed 6 August 2021).

Johnson, J. (2017) 'Delivering value for money for students and taxpayers'. *Speaking to the Higher Education sector at Reform*, London, 20 July. Available at: www.gov.uk/government/speeches/jo-johnson-delivering-value-for-money-for-students-and-taxpayers (accessed 6 August 2021).

Lejk, M. and Wyvill, M. (2001a) 'Peer assessment of contributions to a group project: a comparison of holistic and category-based approaches'. *Assessment & Evaluation in Higher Education* 26(1): 61–72.

Lejk, M. and Wyvill, M. (2001b) 'The effect of the inclusion of self-assessment with peer assessment of contributions to a group project: a quantitative study of secret and agreed assessments'. *Assessment & Evaluation in Higher Education* 26(6): 551–61.

Mason, G. and Rincon-Aznar, A. (2015) 'Appendix – skills and productivity in the UK, US, France and Germany: a literature review' *House of Commons Business, Innovation and Skills and Education Committees Education, Skills and Productivity: Commissioned*

Research. First Special Joint Report HC 565. London: The Stationery Office. Available at: https://publications.parliament.uk/pa/cm201516/cmselect/cmbis/565/565.pdf (accessed 6 August 2021).

Moalosi, R., Molokwane, S. and Mothibedi, G. (2012) 'Using a design-orientated project to attain graduate attributes'. *Design and Technology Education* 17(1): 30–43.

Onyia, P. and Allen, S. (2012) 'Peer assessments of GPW: infusing fairness into students' assessments of peer contributions'. *Research in Higher Education Journal* 17:1–20.

Philpott, J. (1999) *Behind the buzzword: employability*. London: Employment Policy Institute.

Quality Assurance Agency for Higher Education (2014a) *Subject benchmark statement: history*. Gloucester.

Quality Assurance Agency for Higher Education (2014b) *UK Quality Code for Higher Education: part a: setting and maintaining academic standards*. Gloucester.

Saunders, V. and Zuzel, K. (2010) 'Evaluating employability skills: employer and student perceptions' *Bioscience Education* 15(1): 1–15.

Scott, F. J., Connell, P., Thomson, L. A. and Willison, D. (2019) 'Empowering students by enhancing their employability skills'. *Journal of Further and Higher Education* 43(5): 692–702.

Smith, A. J. (2018) 'Economic precarity, modern liberal arts and creating a resilient graduate'. *Educational Philosophy and Theory* 50(11): 1037–44.

Steed, S. (2018) 'Too many graduates are mismatched to their jobs. What's going wrong?' *The Guardian*, 25 January.

Thune, T. and Storen, L. A. (2015) 'Study and labour market effects of graduate students' interaction with work organisations during education – a cohort study'. *Education and Training* 57(7): 702–22.

Tomlinson, M. (2008) '"The degree is not enough": students' perceptions of the role of higher education credentials for graduate work and employability'. *British Journal of Sociology of Education* 29(1): 49–61.

University Partnership Programme Foundation Civic University Commission (2019) *Truly civic: strengthening the connection between universities and their places*. Available at: www.upp-foundation.org (accessed 6 August 2021).

Universities UK (2015) *Supply and demand for higher-level skills*. London.

Walker, I. and Zhu, Y. (2013) *The impact of university degrees on the lifecycle of earnings: some further analysis*. Department for Business, Innovation and Skills Research Paper 112. London: Department for Business, Innovation and Skills. Available at: https://assets.publishing.service.gov.uk/government/uploads/system/uploads/attachment_data/file/229498/bis-13-899-the-impact-of-university-degrees-on-the-lifecycle-of-earnings-further-analysis.pdf (accessed 6 August 2021).

Willetts, D. (2010) *Oral statement to parliament: statement on higher education funding and student finance*. Department for Business, Innovation & Skills, 3 November. Available at: www.gov.uk/government/speeches/statement-on-higher-education-funding-and-student-finance–2 (accessed 6 August 2021).

Williamson, G. (2021) 'Education Secretary speaks at launch of Digital Learning Review'. *Department for Education, Office for Students*, 25 February. Available at: www.gov.uk/government/speeches/education-secretary-speaks-at-launch-of-digital-learning-review (accessed 6 August 2021).

13

Informing the Curriculum: Graduate Employability Skills for the Tourism and Hospitality Industry in Australia during a Pandemic

Janice Scarinci, Josephine Pryce and K. Thirumaran

INTRODUCTION

Our study addresses the importance of tourism and hospitality (T&H) for the Australian economy in the provision of tertiary education and training. A review of the Australian T&H landscape and tertiary education offers interesting education histories and trajectories parallel to economic growth patterns. Our study seeks to build capability within the T&H industry and showcase the relevance of T&H tertiary education in responding to the impact of global health issues, such as COVID-19. The findings contribute not only to the T&H industry, but also have parity with retail, service, and leisure industries globally.

According to the Australian Tourism Labour Force Report, 69% of T&H businesses identified skills deficiencies in their staff. This deficit represented a 50% increase in lack of skills since 2011, potentially affecting productivity and competitiveness, and creating problems for effective business operations (Deloitte Access Economics, 2015).

According to the Australian Trade Commission's Australian Tourism Labour Force Report: 2015–2020, severe labour shortages in the T&H industry in Australia persist. The report identified a shortage of over 38,000 positions in the

T&H industry and a projected growth of over 123,000 jobs by 2020. Businesses reported that, 'an additional 150,000 workers will be needed to close this gap' (Deloitte Access Economics, 2015: i).

COVID 19 and the associated disruptions in the service industries internationally have amplified the need for qualified employees. According to the Australian Trade and Investment Commission (2020) (Austrade, 2020), COVID-19 has resulted in a drop in employment figures by 18%, from 748,200 in 2019 to 611,700 by June 2020. This decline has resulted in shortages of qualified and long-term employees as parts of the economy rebounded in 2021. Austrade together with Tourism Australia conducted a series of workshops, industry consultations and studies which culminated in the Beyond Tourism 2020 Industry Workshop Report (Austrade, 2020). This report outlines the opportunities, challenges, and recommendations that will reimagine and set forth a development path that will drive the Australian tourism industry to 2030. One of the highlights recommended in the document was the emphasis on training and learning that will lead to qualified and rewarding career pathways for graduates in the hospitality and tourism industry.

Since the pandemic, COVID-19 interruption means further reviews of graduate attributes and relevant skill sets, and the importance of educating future leaders for the T&H Industry is paramount. Furthermore, when the economy has recovered, data from the Australian Industry and Skills Committee (2020) forecasts that by 2024 in the post-COVID-19 era, there will be 1.94 million people needed in the T&H sector or, more specifically, the accommodation and food service sector.

The National Careers Institute (2021) identified the hospitality sector as a growth area focusing on restaurants, pubs, and taverns. Another area of growth is the sporting events and festivals as domestic visitation continues to play a significant role in the 50 billion dollar annual Australian tourism receipts (Tourism Research Australia, 2021). The demand in the industry, especially in regional areas, highlights that the T&H industry is facing a serious shortage of skilled applicants. To mitigate this shortage, the Queensland government has allocated AUD$7.5 million dollars, part of which contains benefits and incentives to encourage young people to join the T&H industry (Queensland Government, 2021). Also known as the 'Work in Paradise' scheme, this stimulus package which started on July 1, 2021, provides $1500 for relocation expenses and another $250 for travel purposes. In addition, there is an impetus on tertiary educational providers to ensure that specialisations in T&H are options for students in order to meet the educational needs of the T&H industry workforce. Universities need to act fast to fill this gap and to ensure a successful future for graduates and for the T&H industry.

Australia has several public universities offering a distinctive range of T&H degrees and as such, it has a longer tradition of training generations of students in readiness for the workforce, from junior to middle management. As of April 2021, data from SEEK (a job recruitment portal) reported a drastic 20% deficit in qualified people to resource the T&H industry (Cluff, 2021). More than 46,000 people were needed to urgently fill various positions with 8,060 vacancies for chefs and another 140,261 people reportedly needed to fill positions such as restaurant and café managers (Harris, 2021). These shortfalls in the industry are sounding urgent calls for young people to consider careers in T&H.

Therefore, it is imperative to study the effectiveness of the role of tertiary institutions in resourcing the industry. In response to this need, the research reported here involves an inductive thematic text analysis of job advertisements across a range of positions in the T&H industry. We expect that by studying the employability skills that employers are advertising, we will be able to contribute valuable direction to tertiary institutions for enhancement of their programmes, leading to more job-ready graduates. Hence, our research has the potential to fill the skills gap in the T&H industry in Australia, as the economy rebounds following the COVID-19 pandemic.

AUSTRALIAN HISTORY OF TOURISM AND HOSPITALITY EDUCATION

Dredge et al. (2013) identified four phases of the evolution and development of higher education in Australia. The first phase began in the 1800s before Australia was a nation and was based on traditional disciplines. The second phase began after the war and served to accommodate the growing interest in higher education; new disciplines were developed to reflect the contemporary emphasis of an inter-disciplinary approach to research and education. The third phase paralleled the late 1980s Government's Dawkins Reforms which witnessed the shift from government-funded education to student contribution of tuition through taxation after graduation. This change created competition amongst universities and has led to a reliance on student-paid tuition to fund universities. The focus of education changed to reflect emerging technologies, skills and trades that were promoting economic development. The fourth phase in the higher education landscape expanded in the 2000s to include private universities, degree-granting vocational colleges, and campuses of international universities.

In the late 1990s, immigration policies changed to facilitate new pathways to citizenship in Australia through education. In 2012 the National Tertiary Education Quality Standards Agency (TEQSA), was established to enforce quality assurance and compliance. The trifecta of government influences such as the decrease in government funding, university enrolment quotas being lifted, and continued competition amongst universities to attract more students has created a challenging environment for universities in Australia. The current phase of higher education requires universities to establish innovative curriculum design and strategic development to meet the demands from the T&H industry to provide jobs, careers, and future-ready graduates.

This research is timely, relevant, and necessary due to demands from industry, government, and universities for job-ready graduates. Nearly every industry in Australia is experiencing labour and skills shortages due to COVID-19. The Australia Parliament has created a Higher Education Support Amendment Bill 2020, known as the Job-ready Graduates Package; it was passed in parliament on October 19, 2020. This Bill links the Commonwealth funding to courses that produce 'job-ready' graduates. The purpose of the package was designed to deliver job-ready graduates in the regional areas of Australia and in disciplines that are needed the most to drive the nation's economic recovery from COVID-19 (Australia Government, 2021; Parliament of Australia, 2020).

The fifth phase of the evolution of education in Australia is preparing 'job-ready graduates'. The 'job-ready graduates' programmes may include work experience in industry (WEI) or work integrated learning (WIL), engaging with industry partners to co-create subject material, and job placements. WIL can be considered as any application or approach within a course which integrates theory with the practices necessary within the workforce (Patrick et al., 2008). The following section will elaborate on the importance of WIL in higher education and highlight the urgency and relevance of our research.

IMPORTANCE OF WORK INTEGRATED LEARNING (WIL) IN HIGHER EDUCATION

According to Australia's Higher Education Standards Framework, created by TEQSA, higher education learning outcomes must include employability skills for all degree courses (TEQSA 2021). TEQSA (2021) notes that 'all providers of higher education must meet the requirements of Part A and satisfy the requirements set out under the "Institute of Higher Education" category in order to gain registration by TEQSA' (p. 17). Jackson (2015) highlights that WIL is widely accepted to provide graduates with employability skills to function well in the workplace. Jackson (2015) defines WIL as 'the practice of combining traditional academic study, or formal learning, with student exposure to the world-of-work in their chosen profession, has a core aim of better preparing undergraduates for entry into the workforce' (p. 350). The value of WIL programmes is emphasised in a study conducted by Lillis and Bravenboer (2020) where they evaluated best practices in WIL programmes at four public degree apprenticeships in London, UK. They found that signature pedagogy best practices were transferable from professions and sectors of the industry.

According to Jackson (2015) there are numerous forms of WIL opportunities. If the practice involves authentic work practices and application of skills and knowledge in the 'real-world' context it can be included as WIL. Some of these opportunities include internships, work placement, field work, sandwich year degrees, cooperative education, and job shadowing. Clinton and Thomas

(2011) expanded on this definition of WIL and included volunteering and service-learning opportunities if they involve development of professional skills that will provide service and benefit the community.

Precision Consultancy (2007) note that WIL is a general term used to describe a combination of experiences at the workplace which is integrated as part of the course of study. The Business, Industry, and Higher Education Collaboration Council (BIECC) was developed in 2004 with the sole purpose of advising the Australian Government of ways to develop collaboration between businesses, higher education, and the community. One of the main priorities is ‘engaging the higher education and business sectors in the development of a best practice framework for the development, teaching, assessment and reporting of generic and employability skill of graduates’ (Precision Consultancy, 2007: 14).

There has been a focus on employability skills in Australia since 2001 when the Australian Chamber of Commerce and Industry (ACCI) and the Business Council of Australia (BCA) conducted research on the generic and employability skills needed by industry. The outcome was a document entitled ‘Employability Skills for the Future’ which was provided by the Department of Education, Science and Training (DEST) with industry views on key skills that were needed in business (DEST, 2002). Precision Consultancy (2007) acknowledged that ‘since that time, all Australian universities have been required to develop policy statements which specify their generic graduate attributes as part of funding and reporting arrangements with the Department of Education, Science and Training’ (p. 19). This shows the importance and urgency of our research and how the results can be applied to university curricula to increase the employability skills in our graduates.

IDENTIFYING KEY ATTRIBUTES AND SKILLS NEEDED IN THE WORKPLACE

It is increasingly recognised that there is a shortfall in the employability skills necessary for university graduates to work in the T&H industry (Wardle & Ashwell, 2018). The T&H industry, the government and the universities have the same goals to create work-ready graduates. Employers are demanding a capable workforce, but the research indicates that the set goals are not being met (Jackson et al., 2016; Li et al., 2015; Suarta et al., 2018).

The employability skills that are important to employers in the T&H industry have been identified in numerous studies. According to Scarinci et al. (2021, in press) communication, teamwork and problem-solving skills were the most desired skills identified by employers in the T&H industry in Australia and Singapore. The DEST (2002) Employability Framework was used to identify the employability skills in the job descriptions to determine if the skills had changed in the past 10 years, including during the emergence of COVID-19. Through a deductive analysis that utilised the Employability Skills Framework, the results indicated that the same employability skills were still needed in 2020 that were deemed necessary from industry in 2002 by DEST and included:

1 communication skills that contribute to productive and harmonious relations between employees and customers
2 teamwork skills that contribute to productive working relationships and outcomes
3 problem-solving skills that contribute to productive outcomes
4 initiative and enterprise skills that contribute to innovative outcomes
5 planning and organising skills that contribute to long-term and short-term strategic planning
6 self-management skills that contribute to employee satisfaction and growth
7 learning skills that contribute to ongoing improvement and expansion in employee and company operations and outcome
8 technology skills that contribute to effective execution of tasks (DEST, 2002: 7).

Messum et al. (2016) also utilised a content analysis of job advertisements and identified communication and teamwork as the top two skills. Olawale (2015) conducted a similar study using content analysis of job advertisements in the construction industry and identified similar results, with teamwork, communication, and problem-solving skills being the most frequently recognised skills needed. Suarta et al. (2018) analysed 57 job advertisements and identified 272 employability skills for entry level workers. The top four skills were communication skills, self-management, teamwork, and problem solving. In a study conducted by Warwick and Howard (2015), similar findings were identified for accounting graduates, with communication skills, analytical, problem solving, interpersonal and teamwork being the most important skills noted. Finally, McMurray et al. (2016) conducted a similar study on the preferred employability skills in Scotland and found communication and teamwork skills to be amongst the top skills identified by employers. The findings from these studies are similar across countries and industries with the most frequently identified skills in each of the studies being communication skills, teamwork, and problem solving. These studies highlight the international and universal nature of the employability skills being sought by the T&H industry.

Oliver (2011) conducted a study to determine the attributes that Australian universities identified as their most important attributes or skills based on the universities' learning outcomes. The most common skills across multiple disciplines were nearly identical, with written and oral communication, critical and analytical thinking and problem solving as the top three skills identified across 40 out of the 42 universities in Australia. Based on the results of the 2011 and 2015 studies, Oliver and Jorre de St Jorre (2018) recommend that all educational providers need to make graduate attributes and employability skills more visible to the public. Universities need to be sure that the students are aware of the graduate attributes that are deemed most important to employers and embed them in the curriculum, especially assessment materials. Also, universities need to communicate and explain the graduate attributes frequently throughout the course. Additionally, they recommended using stakeholder perceptions to measure the outcomes and continue to emphasise attributes associated with global citizenship, teamwork, and communication. They recommended more emphasis on independence, critical thinking and problem-solving, and the fundamental skills of written and spoken communication. Finally, they recommended reviewing and revising the attributes regularly to ensure currency in the rapidly changing global environment. This point emphasises the timeliness and relevance of our study as a review of employability skills, as the T&H industry emerges from the tumultuous upheaval realised during COVID-19.

There is a plethora of literature identifying the generic skills, attributes and foundation skills (such as communication) that are needed in our graduates (DEST, 2002; Jackson et al., 2016; Li et al., 2015; McMurray et al., 2016; Messum et al., 2016; Olawale, 2015; Oliver et al., 2018; Oliver, 2011; Scarinci et al., 2021; Suarta et al., 2017, 2018; Wardle & Ashwell, 2018; Warwick & Howard, 2015). Yet, there are few studies that explore the higher-level employability skills necessary for job-ready graduates who aspire to be managers in the T&H industry. In addition, there have been no other studies that have adopted an inductive thematic approach to identify the common employability skills that were deemed important by employers as a pandemic emerged into the economic landscape. Our study will make a substantial contribution to the body of knowledge and provide a practical application for educators to design and develop high-level employability skills to provide 'job-ready graduates'. Our study goes above and beyond the traditional generic skills, attributes, and foundation skills that previous studies have reported. It highlights the calibre of graduates required for the T&H industry and the veracity and value of having a career in the T&H industry.

MEASURING EMPLOYABILITY SKILLS OUTCOMES

National studies such as the Quality Indicators for Learning and Teaching (QILT, 2020) were funded by the Australian Government Department of Education, Skills and Employment. They have developed several national higher education surveys that are designed to report on the attributes and skills students need to acquire and develop throughout their degree, and the skills needed to prepare them for employment. The four national surveys that were developed include the Student Experience Survey (SES), the Graduate Employment Survey, the Graduate Satisfaction Survey, and the Employer Satisfaction Survey. For our study, we reported the findings that relate specifically to employability skills that are necessary for future employment (QILT, 2021).

The Student Experience Survey (SES) is designed to assist institutions to provide continuous improvement and offer information for potential students to make a more informed decision about their education. There are five distinct areas of the students' experience measured by the SES. The first is skill development, second is learner engagement, third is teaching quality, fourth is student support and fifth is learning resources. For our study the skill development results were reported. The overall skills development score has declined from 81% in 2019 to only 78% in 2020. This represents a decrease of three percentage points during COVID 19. This is understandable since universities had to quickly pivot and begin teaching remotely. Prior to 2020 the skills development scores remained consistent at 81% from 2014–2019. It was noted in the report that the scores from 2013 are not comparable to the 2014–2020 data, for they were reported as a percentage of positive scores rather than an average scale score (QILT, 2021).

The Graduate Outcomes Survey (GOS) has been administered since 2016 and replaced the Australian Graduate Survey (AGS). The 2020 GOS was primarily conducted online due to COVID 19 to 112 higher institutions and 71 Non-University Higher Education Institutions (NUHEIs). There was a total response rate of 131,780 which represents a response rate of 42.3%. This response rate is only slightly lower than 2019 which reached a 44.2% response rate. The GOS includes a section on satisfaction which asks coursework graduates, four months after they have graduated, to rate on a five-point scale their satisfaction with the generic skills. The undergraduate satisfaction with the generic skills learned at university increased from 82.4% in 2019 to 82.9% in 2020. The postgraduate coursework graduates were also asked to rate their generic skills on a scale from 1 to 5 and, in 2019, 79.5% reported satisfaction with their generic skills and this increased to 80.7% in 2020 (QILT, 2020).

Another study that QILT has administered annually since 2016 is The Employer Satisfaction Survey. This survey sought to determine the employers' view of recent graduates' attributes. In 2020 the study had 3,430 employers respond. This survey seeks to determine the readiness of graduates to enter the workforce. This is evaluated by the employers' views of technical skills, generic skills, and work readiness. Direct supervisors of our graduates were presented with a survey that contained the 'Graduate Attributes Scale' and supervisors were asked to rate each skill or attribute and evaluate whether they agreed (or disagreed) that graduates' degrees prepared them for their job. If the skill was not required for the job the employer was asked to answer 'not applicable'. The graduate attributes included foundation skills, adaptive skills, collaborative skills, technical skills, and employability skills (QILT, 2021a).

The results indicate that higher education is doing an outstanding job with 93.7% satisfaction rating in 2020 at preparing our graduates with the foundation skills. Notably, foundation skills included communication skills, numeracy and general literacy and the ability to integrate knowledge. This is consistent with previous research on the foundation and generic skills (DEST, 2002; Jackson et al., 2016; Li et al., 2015; McMurray et al., 2016; Messum et al., 2016; Olawale,

2015; Oliver et al., 2018; Oliver, 2011; Scarinci et al., in press; Suarta et al., 2017, 2018; Wardle & Ashwell, 2018; Warwick & Howard, 2015).

Employability skills received the lowest satisfaction score, with 86.8% satisfaction by employers. The variables used in this section of the survey included (QILT, 2021a; 23):

- Ability to work under pressure
- Capacity to be flexible in the workplace
- Ability to meet deadlines
- Understanding the nature of your business or organisation
- Demonstrating leadership skills
- Demonstrating management skills
- Taking responsibility for personal professional development
- Demonstrating initiative in the workplace

As the previous literature indicated, employability skills are best learned on the job during some form of 'work integrated learning' and 'learning integrated work' experiences (Clinton & Thomas, 2011; DEST, 2002; Jackson, 2015; Lillis & Bravenboer, 2002; Precision Consultancy, 2007; TEQSA, 2021; Von Treuer et al., 2010). The T&H service industry is a hands-on industry that requires graduates to have hands-on experience to attain the employability skills to prepare them for their career in T&H. Our study aims to advance previous work by conducting a thematic content analysis of 300 job descriptions in the T&H industry to determine the higher-level employability skills needed for our graduates to be successful in a COVID-19 environment. The results will be compared with the literature, and recommendations will be made based on these findings to inform the curriculum to ensure our graduates are job-ready.

RESEARCH DESIGN

Our study employed a thematic content analysis of the employability skills deemed important to the T&H industry in Australia, as extracted from job advertisements. Three hundred job advertisements were gathered from two prominent websites promoting hospitality jobs in Australia. The websites were: www.seek.com.au/ and au.jora.com

The data collection of the job descriptions was from March 2020 to the end of November 2020. The search for job advertisements were from a range of positions from frontline to back-of-house and from supervisory to executive level positions. Fifteen positions were chosen using a process that considered positions in the industry and positions advertised. For each of the positions, 20 job descriptions were selected, resulting in a total of 300 job descriptions for analysis. Please refer to Table 13.1 for a list of the positions that were used in our study.

Table 13.1 Position titles searched

General Manager	Sales & Marketing Manager	Public Relations
Assistant General Manager	Front Office Manager	Customer Service Manager
Duty Manager	Food & Beverage Manager	Chefs
Recruitment Consultant/ HR Manager	Housekeeping Manager	Concierge
Revenue/Financial Manager	Events Coordinator	Hotel Manager

The data were collated for each job position and entered into NVivo 12.0 for analysis. Employability skills were determined for all the positions collectively and then, for a comparative examination of each position individually, and for each of the top skills separately.

FINDINGS AND DISCUSSION

In the first instance, the data were auto coded in NVivo. The resultant codes were examined for commonalities, resulting in 32 employability-related skills. Please refer to Figure 13.1 for the nodes (themes) from NVivo auto-coding.

Figure 13.1 shows that the number 1 node was 'being a manager' which was repeated over 500 times in the 300 job advertisements. The second ranked node was 'experience' with just under 500 references. The third node was 'skills' with just over 400 references.

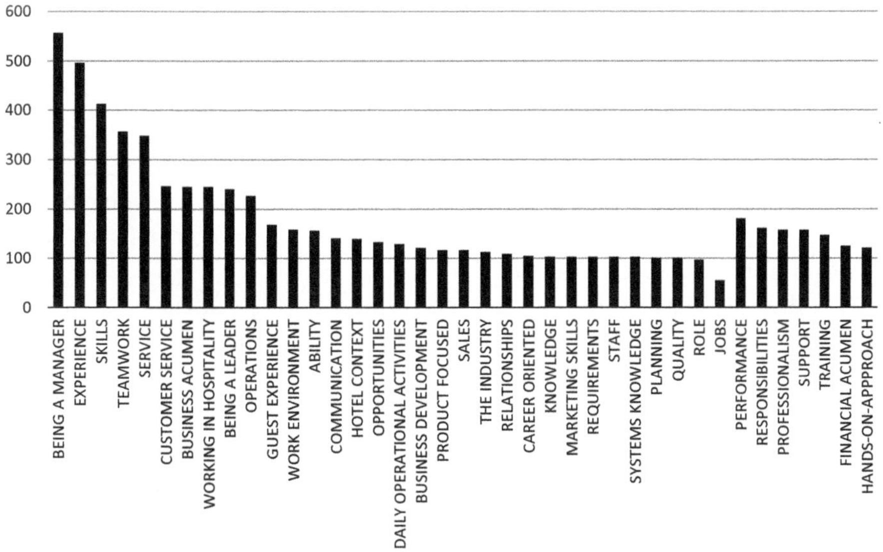

Figure 13.1 Nodes from NVivo auto-coding

These results are consistent with the QILT 2021 results on employability skills. The following employability skills received the lowest satisfaction scores by employers in the QILT 2021 survey.

- Ability to work under pressure
- Capacity to be flexible in the workplace
- Ability to meet deadlines
- Understanding the nature of your business or organisation
- Demonstrating leadership skills
- Demonstrating management skills
- Taking responsibility for personal professional development
- Demonstrating initiative in the workplace

The areas of management, leadership, and experience need to be integrated into the curriculum by tertiary institutions in order to fill this employability gap and provide 'job-ready graduates'.

To further assess the validity of the nodes, a frequency search was conducted, and seven other employability skills were identified: performance, responsibilities, professionalism, support, training, financial acumen, and a hands-on approach. The collective top employability skills from the auto-coding and frequency analysis are captured in the word cloud below (Figure 13.2). Of these skills, the paper focuses on the top five employability skills areas (themes) identified from the Australian job advertisements: being a manager, having experience, customer service and the guest experience, teamwork and being a leader, and business acumen.

BEING A MANAGER

According to QILT (2021) management, leadership skills, and having experience are also identified by industry as being areas that need improvement. These higher-level skills need to be applied in the classroom. Being an outstanding leader and manager needs to be integrated into the curriculum. Providing opportunities for practice, application, and evaluation need to be implemented in the classroom and in WIL experiences.

The data showed that 'being a manager' required skills that related to managing including budgets, business development projects, customer service delivery, departments, projects, quality service standards, revenue goals, risk, and site operations. The skills that were highlighted included effective skills in: people management, time management, relationship management, financial management (including yield and revenue management, and risk management). Repeatedly, the level of skills required in relationship to 'being a manager' were referred to as having to be 'excellent', 'exceptional', 'exemplary', 'great', or 'strong'. The skills are captured in the cluster analysis below (Figure 13.3).

Figure 13.2 Word cloud depicting the top employability skills areas from Australian job advertisements

The main five clusters in Figure 13.3 show the most common skills necessary under the 'being a manager' category which included: communication, negotiation, interpersonal, problem-solving, leadership, time management, planning, and financial acumen. These results are consistent with the previous literature with communication skills, problem solving, and teamwork being the most important foundation skills to employers (DEST, 2002; Messum et al., 2016; McMurray et al., 2016; Olawale, 2015; Oliver, 2011; QILT, 2021a; Scarinci et al., 2021, Suarta et al., 2017, 2018; Warwick & Howard, 2015).

Cotronei-Baird (2020), in a study based on action theory, also found that communication, problem solving, critical thinking and teamwork skills continue to be what academics perceive as essential for work readiness, informed by academic interviews, curriculum and subject data mined. This resonates with our findings where the data were derived directly from employers, extracted through job advertisements. Contronei-Baird (2020) study continued to find gaps in fully integrating employability skills into the curriculum approach. Our findings support Valeria's conclusions and show that there is an employability gap in the essential employability skills being integrated in the curriculum (Contronei-Baird, 2020).

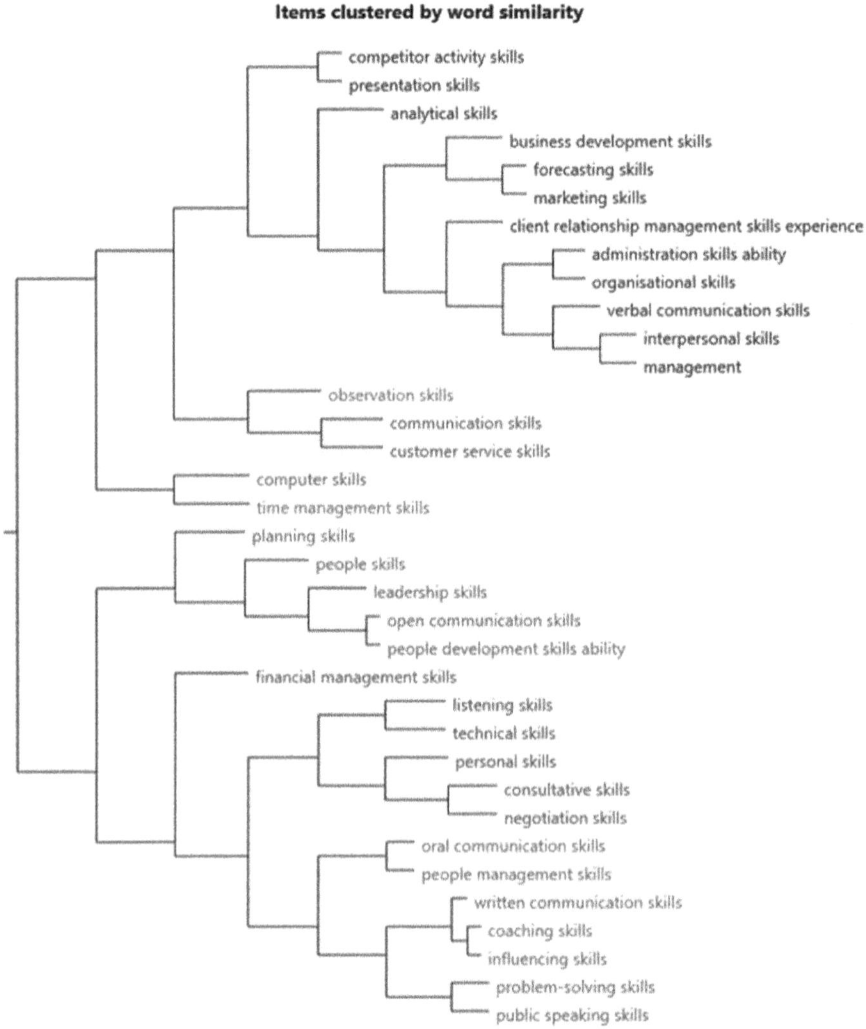

Figure 13.3 Employability skills for 'being a manager'

The findings suggest that the best way graduates acquire these skills is while they are on the job. Therefore, 'work integrated learning' and 'learning integrated work' experiences can provide students with vital and valuable opportunities to learn how to work under pressure and what it is like to be in the workplace. In addition, many universities are forming partnerships with Technical and Further Education NSW (TAFE) and other Registered Training Organisations (RTOs) in order to provide meaningful skills and work placement in the T&H industry. T&H and service industries are hands-on industries that require graduates to have employability skills for them to be 'job-ready graduates'.

HAVING EXPERIENCE

In evaluating 'experience' for the various positions examined, the key aspects that were considered important included: years of experience and type of experience (administration, people, or operations). More specifically, the data highlighted that the experience required was in a range of management areas, such as management of conflict, projects, people, business development, technology, and customer service (see Figure 13.4).

The five general clusters from Figure 13.4 include:

1 Guest or industry experience
2 Management experience
3 People management
4 Operational experience
5 Technology experience

Figure 13.4 Experience required for employability in the tourism and hospitality industry

Most of the universities in Australia only require 100 hours of work experience as part of their WIL programme. This is not enough to meet the industry standard of years of experience in administration, people, and operations. The Australian WIL programme needs to be integrated over the three years of an undergraduate degree to ensure that the students are gaining at least three years of experience to be 'job-ready graduates'. The WIL work requirements need to be reviewed and revised to meet the needs of the T&H and service industries. Many universities in the United States and Europe offer semester-long internships of up to 1200 hours of work experience. Additionally, they require their students to complete hundreds of hours of volunteer work throughout their university education, and they provide practical work experience opportunities in the classes as part of their assessments. It is recommended that a national and international assessment of the WIL work requirements are identified to ensure that the Australian minimum WIL requirements are up to the international standards worldwide and are fully integrated into the curriculum over three years.

The data relating to experience also presented qualifying terms for the experience required, 'essential', 'exemplary', 'relevant' and 'solid' (see Figure 13.5). These suggest the importance of experience to employability. Figure 13.5 shows that 'previous' and 'proven' experience is important for management positions in the tourism and hospitality industry.

Figures 13.4 and 13.5 highlight that 'having experience' is an important aspect of employability in the tourism and hospitality industry. These findings are consistent with the literature, and while we have had WIL programmes implemented in higher education for many years, perhaps the quality and quantity of these work experiences can be reviewed for effectiveness and efficiency. Some of the areas identified in the job descriptions such as management areas, management of conflict, projects, people, business development, technology, and customer

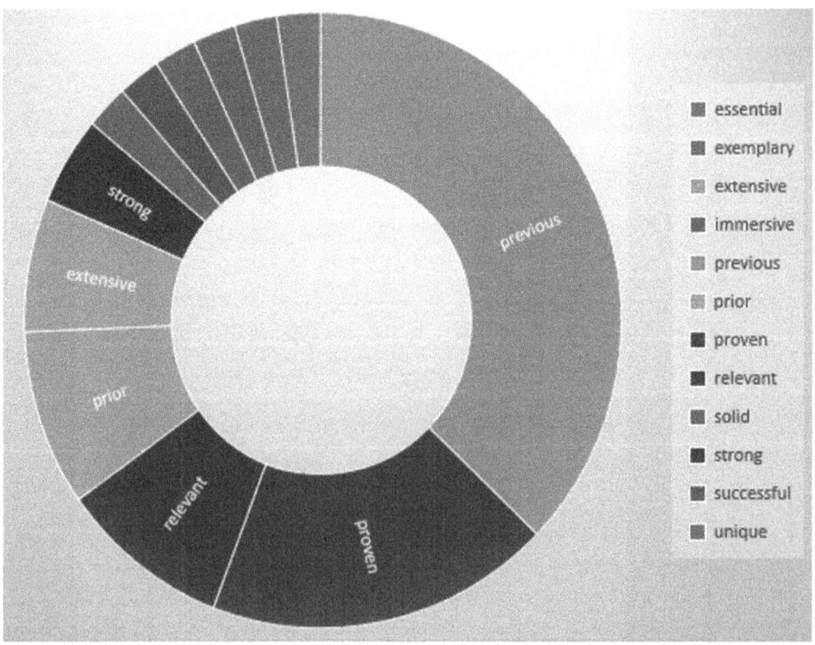

Figure 13.5 Experience descriptors

service need to be integrated into the curriculum and the WIL programmes throughout Australia. Based on the findings, it is recommended that the curriculum be reviewed to ensure that the subjects/topics are included in the tourism and hospitality curriculum (Firth, 2020; Kift, 2019).

CUSTOMER SERVICE AND THE GUEST EXPERIENCE

The customer service data highlights in detail the employability skills required to address this area. Some of the skills in the customer service and guest experience include resolving customer issues, maintaining customer satisfaction, and developing high-touch customer relationships. Please refer to Figure 13.6 for clusters of similar words/phrases.

The five general clusters in Figure 13.6 that relate to customer service and guest experience include:

1 Customer service
2 Customer business strategies
3 Customer relations

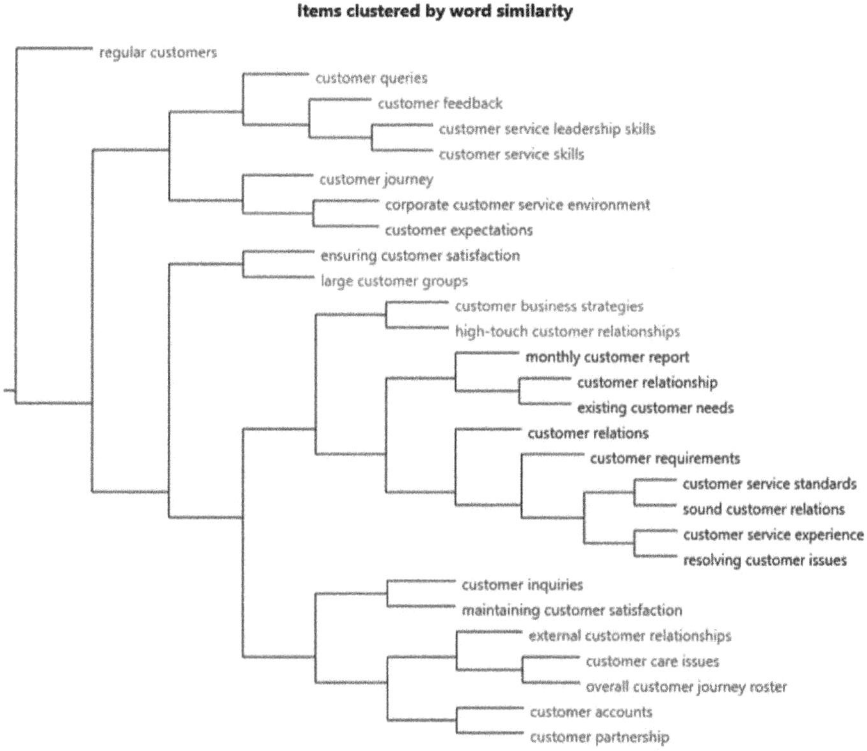

Figure 13.6 Items clustered by word similarity

4 Maintaining customer satisfaction
5 Customer relationships

A study by Adeyinka-Ojo et al. (2020), despite the pandemic situation pushing students to learn online, provided opportunities for students to develop their digital customer service skills, as many of the service sector industries, be it retail, healthcare or hospitality, are increasingly using digital technology to communicate with customers. This suggests that the skills required in the T&H industry are increasingly universal and transferrable to the broader service sector such as retail, leisure, and healthcare globally.

Despite the value of technologies, it remains that the best way to gain customer service experience is with hands-on experience opportunities in the workplace such as WIL placements and volunteering. Yiu and Law (2012) found, through a survey of key stakeholders, that graduates developed customer service skills through internships and that employers were keen on including this key element in their structured training programme. It is recommended that each service degree includes at least one customer service subject and that there is an opportunity to volunteer or conduct research with the industry partners in customer satisfaction. This will provide opportunities for students to gain valuable experience in customer service, relationships, satisfaction, and business strategies to achieve increased customer satisfaction.

TEAMWORK AND BEING A LEADER

The themes of 'teamwork' and 'leadership' appeared as prominent aspects of employability in the job advertisements. Within these themes, evidence of the skills required included ability, understanding one's role, knowledge of operations, communication, and ability to lead (see Figure 13.7). Other skills included support, planning, managing, and setting of goals and objectives.

Teamwork was one of the top three employability skills identified in the Scarinci et al. (2021, in press) study along with problem solving and communication. Planning and organising and self-management were fifth and sixth respectively. Messum et al. (2016), Olawale (2015), Suarta et al. (2017, 2018), Warwick and Howard (2015) and McMurray et al. (2016) identified communication and teamwork as the top skills deemed by employers. These foundation skills need to be integrated into the curriculum and used as assessments throughout a university degree. It is becoming recognised that when students are assigned a group project, there is a need to provide students with instructions and activities on how to work in a team and how to be an effective team leader (Poort et al., 2020). Teamwork exercises can be implemented in-class and opportunities to practise their leadership and planning skills in class provide the students with confidence and continuous learning opportunities. It is not enough to have a group project,

Figure 13.7 Themes of teamwork and leadership

but we must teach students how to perform as a cohesive team, how to set goals, plan and implement a plan, for this is what employers need.

BUSINESS ACUMEN

The theme of business acumen encompassed a range of aspects of running a business that constitute employability skills for the tourism and hospitality industry. These include: setting business goals; building business partnerships; ensuring business performance; having a business mindset; being strategic; and setting innovative business strategies (see Figure 13.8).

The post Covid-19 recovery stage may provide opportunities for graduates to mint their own start-up businesses. This affords opportunities for courses within and relevant to the T&H industry to enable and empower students with the relevant knowledge and skills. This will provide graduates with experience during their studies that assist in building the technical skills and expertise in order to operate their own businesses (Edet, 2020). On the other hand, the pandemic has also led to the demise of many T&H businesses and managers who

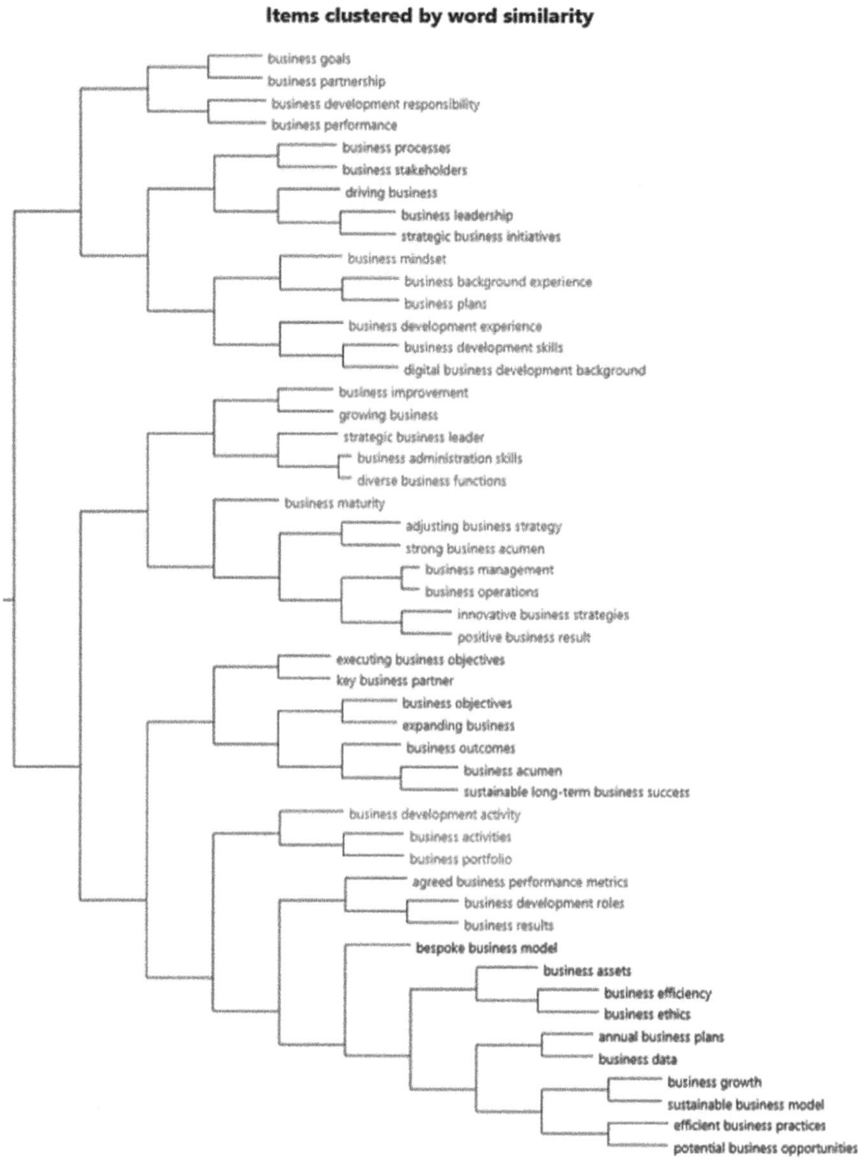

Figure 13.8 Themes of business acumen

were previously employed in the industry to settle into alternative industries. Therefore, it is timely for emerging graduates to seek work in the T&H industry that is meaningful and utilises what they have learnt in their degree. Equally, the values of work experience provide the cutting edge for such graduates because it is recognised that graduates with considerable professional internships of 3–6 months stand a strong chance of progressing up the professional ladder quickly

(Edet, 2020). Research shows that work experience builds technical and managerial skills and influences the attitudes of students working in the T&H industry upon graduation (Chan, 2017). That is, work experience allows students to exhibit qualities of agility, being fast learners, an ability to show that they can work both as a team player and lead a team as well as being able to articulate their broader planning and critical thinking skills translated into good big picture visionaries. Affording opportunities to allow students to build and enhance these skills, enables graduates to attain managerial and equally high-level positions in the T&H industry.

CONCLUSION

Table 13.2 presents a summary of some of the research examining employability skills to highlight parallels with our study.

Table 13.2 shows that there is consistency across the literature in identifying the most important employability skills. In particular, the top recurring skills are communication, teamwork, people skills, leadership, and problem-solving. Our study has added to the literature by not only supporting these main skills, but also highlighting how these skills are clustered to accommodate 'higher order' employability skills that are required of graduates seeking to work toward managerial jobs in the T&H industry. Table 13.3 presents a collective overview of the five themes above and the associated employability skills in our study, for comparison to previous studies.

Table 13.3 shows that 'being a manager' includes the top employability skills from the literature including communication, problem-solving, and teamwork. Most of these skills are learned on the job and therefore it is recommended that the WIL programmes begin in the first year of study and continue throughout the three-year degree. As maintained throughout this chapter, it is recommended that the curriculum includes work experience; equally, emphasis can be given to projects with industry, guest speakers, field trips and mentorship programmes to give the students an opportunity to network with industry professionals and learn about the T&H industry. As Bilsland et al. (2020) point out, internships play a very important role in educating the next generation of tourism skilled workforce.

A further recommendation is that 'quality customer service' be included in the T&H curriculum and 'teamwork and leadership' be taught and embedded in assessments. Finally, it is recommended that the T&H degrees are exposed to the business discipline, so students are acquiring 'business acumen' including setting business goals, building business partnerships, ensuring business performance, having a business mindset, setting innovative business strategies, and understanding sustainable and ethical business practices. Most importantly, the findings show that a holistic approach needs to be taken such that the complexities of managerial roles in T&H are captured. By understanding that various aspects

Table 13.2 Most important employability skills by author and year of publication

Author and year	Most Important Employability Skills
DEST (2002) Employability Framework	Communication Teamwork Problem-solving Initiative and enterprise Planning and organising Self-management Learning Technology
Scarinci, Pryce and Thirumaran (2021)	Communication Teamwork Problem-solving
Mussum, et al. (2016)	Communication Teamwork
Olawale (2015)	Communication Problem-solving Teamwork
Suarta, Suwintana, Fajar & Hariyanti (2017 & 2018)	Communication Self-management Teamwork Problem solving
Warwick and Howard (2015)	Communication Analytical Problem solving Interpersonal and teamwork
McMurray et al. (2016)	Communication Teamwork
Oliver (2011)	Written and oral communication Critical and analytical thinking Problem solving
QILT 2020	Ability to work under pressure Capacity to be flexible in the workplace Ability to meet deadlines Understanding the nature of your business or organisation Demonstrating leadership skills Demonstrating management skills Taking responsibility for personal professional development Demonstrating initiative in the workplace

Table 13.3 General themes from the current study highlighting employability skills from this study and from previous research noted in Table 13.2

Main Themes from this study	Employability Skills from this study and from Table 13.2
Being a manager	Communication People Skills/Leadership Listening and personal skills Oral and Written Communication Problem Solving Analytical Forecasting Marketing Interpersonal skills
Experience	Guest or industry experience Management experience People management Operational experience
Customer service & guest experience	Customer service Customer business strategies Customer relations Maintaining customer satisfaction Customer relationships
Teamwork and being a leader	Ability Understanding one's role Knowledge of operations Communication Ability to lead
Business acumen	Setting of business goals Building of business partnerships Ensuring business performance Having a business mindset Being strategic Setting innovative business strategies

of managerial roles, the main themes from our study (being a manager, having experience, and business acumen), can contribute to building a curriculum that has the appropriate employability skills embedded within it can make graduates ready for employment in the T&H industry, ensuring that universities are producing 'job-ready graduates'.

Previous literature highlights foundation skills such as communication, problem-solving and teamwork. Our study dives deeper into the 'higher order skills' that are demanded of future managers of the T&H industry, such as being a manager, having experience, and business acumen. These skills highlight that employability in the T&H industry is described by a clustering of skills that define the roles that will be assumed by graduates who aspire to be managers in the T&H industry. For example, business acumen captures the need for prospective managers to know about business development and have experience in planning and strategy while adopting a hands-on approach. Equally, the manager working in the T&H industry will be a master of customer service and guest experience with knowledge of products and product development and understand quality while ensuring training meets the operational needs of the T&H industry. When viewed in this holistic way and as a cluster of roles, it is incumbent upon education providers to ensure that the curriculum has the richness, depth and breadth to ensure graduates have the employability skills that the T&H industry expects of its managers and future leaders.

Though our data did not emphasise digital technology use in the space of tourism and hospitality, the nature of the Australian T&H sector calls for a focus on a more personable touch given the key variables such as communication skills and the creation of guests' experiences. This is in sync with the demands as mentioned in the introduction where accommodation, taverns and pubs continue to drive tourism as the four largest contributors to the Australian economy (Tourism Australia, 2020). Therefore, as the economy rebounds from COVID-19, the practices of tertiary T&H education in blended learning through web 2.0 and virtual internships that have continued to act as a medium of nurturing the primary skills relevant to resourcing the industry, can be supplemented by internships in workplaces. In doing so, it is recommended that the current Australian WIL and internship requirements, number of hours and assessments be reviewed and compared to the international standards in order for Australian graduates to be 'job-ready graduates' and be able to 'fit' into the T&H industry or other service-related positions in Australia or internationally.

Our study set out to extend current thought on the employability skills for graduates in the T&H industry during COVID-19. The findings contribute to current literature that emphasises the relevant fundamental skills during a pandemic environment. The findings also suggest a reason for a strong curriculum that embeds skills transferability while graduates are journeying through tertiary education. A curriculum that emphasises the integration of industry-driven learned skills is also emphasised in Firth's (2020) comprehensive book that studied the tourism, hospitality and events sector and how students and educators can learn to gain future anchors in industry through tertiary education experience, one that is employability skills focused. This means that more resources should be placed on such activities that include industry professionals who are engaged as thought leaders, sharing their insights and as guest speakers enlivening the learning experiences of students on specific industry topics and specialisations. It means that emerging skills, such as digital literacy, are integrated into the curriculum and that known factors, such as the importance of WIL, are given increased attention and importance. Such shifts in curriculum will mean that graduates will be equipped with employability skills that serve a range of complementary service industries. It is on the horizon that graduates of the future will demand employability skills that empower them to apply for and fit in a range of employment options. In a salute to Handy (2011), the age of the portfolio career is well and truly here. As a response, it is incumbent upon educators to ensure graduates have the diversity of employability skills required for their inclusion into the workforce of the future.

REFERENCES

Adeyinka-Ojo, S., Lee, S., Abdullah, S. K. and Teo, J. (2020). 'Hospitality and tourism education in an emerging digital economy', *Worldwide Hospitality and Tourism Themes*, 12(2),113–125. https://doi.org/10.1108/WHATT-12-2019-0075

Austrade (2020). *'Beyond Tourism 2020 Industry Workshop Report. Australian Government'*. Retrieved from www.austrade.gov.au/australian/tourism/policy-and-strategy/tourism-2030

Australia Government (2021, February 15). *'Department of Education, Skills and Employment'*. Retrieved from Job-ready Graduates Package: www.dese.gov.au/job-ready

Australian Industry and Skills Committee (2020). *'Tourism, Travel and Hospitality. National Centre for Vocational Education Research'*. Retrieved from https://nationalindustryinsights.aisc.net.au/industries/tourism-travel-and-hospitality.

Australian Trade and Investment Commission (2020). *'Labour and Skills. Australian Government'*. Retrieved from www.austrade.gov.au/australian/tourism/policy-and-strategy/labour-and-skills.

Bilsland, C., Nagy, H. and Smith, P. (2020). 'Virtual internships and work-integrated learning in hospitality and tourism in a post-COVID-19 world'. *International Journal of Work – Integrated Learning*, 21(4), 425–437.

Chan, M. C. (2017). *'Exploring how hospitality undergraduate students' perceptions and attitudes towards a career in the hospitality industry are affected by their work experience: a New Zealand quantitative study'* (Doctoral dissertation, Auckland University of Technology).

Clinton, I. and Thomas, T. (2011). 'Business students' experience of community service learning'. *Asia-Pacific Journal of Cooperative Education*, 12(1), 51–66.

Cluff, R. (2021, May 20). '$1500 incentive to lure hospitality workers to North Qld'. *Topic Now*. Retrieved on June 18, 2021 from www.tropicnow.com.au/2021/may/20/1500-incentive-to-lure-hospitality-workers-to-northqld#:~:text=%241500%20incentive%20to%20lure%20 hospitality%20workers%20to%20North%20Queensland,for%20up%20to%20six%20months.

Cotronei-Baird, V.S. (2020). Academic hindrances in the integration of employability skills development in teaching and assessment practice. *Higher Education* 79, 203–223.

Deloitte Access Economics (2015). *'Australian Tourism Labour Force Report: 2015–2020'*. Retrieved on June 18, 2021 from www.tra.gov.au/Archive-TRA-Old-site/Research/

View-all-publications/All-Publications/australian-tourism-labour-force-report-2015-2020

DEST (2002). *'Employability skills for the future, a report by the Australian Chamber of Commerce and Industry and the Business Council of Australia for the Department of Education, Science and Training, Canberra'.*

Dredge, D., Benckendorff, P., Day, M., Gross, M., Walo, M., Weeks, P. and Whitelaw, P. (2013). 'Drivers of change in tourism, hospitality, and event management education: an Australian perspective'. *Journal of Hospitality & Tourism Education*, 25(2), 89–102, DOI: 10.1080/10963758.2013.805091

Edet, D. A. (2020). 'Curriculum content, ownership of universities, work experience and acquisition of employability skills among business education graduates of universities in Cross River state, Nigeria'. *American Journal of Educational Research and Reviews*, 5(73).

Firth, M. (2020). *Employability and skills handbook for tourism, hospitality and events students*. London: Routledge.

Handy, C. (2011). *Beyond certainty: the changing worlds of organisations*. London: Arrow Books.

Harris, R. (2021, May 15). *'Restaurant industry facing critical shortage of chefs, managers, and sommeliers'*. Retrieved on June 18, 2021 from www.smh.com.au/politics/federal/restaurant-industry-facing-critical-shortage-of-chefs-managers-and-sommeliers-20210513-p57rn1.html

Jackson, D., Rowbottom, D., Ferns, S. and McLaren, D. (2016). 'Employer understanding of work integrated learning and the challenges of engaging in work placement opportunities'. *Studies in Continuing Education*, DOI: 10.1080/0158037X.2016.1228624

Jackson, D. (2015). 'Employability skill development in work-integrated learning: barriers and best practice'. *Studies in Higher Education*, 40(2), 350–367. https://doi.org/10.1080/03075079.2013.842221

Kift, S. (2019). 'Holistic curriculum design for employability'. In Higgs, J., Crisp, G. and Letts, W. J. (eds) *Education for Employability*, pp. 155–164. Leiden: Brill Sense.

Li, I., Malvin, M. and Simonson, R. D. (2015). 'Over-education and employment mismatch: wage penalties for college degrees in business'. *Journal of Education for Business*, 90(3), 119–125.

Lillis, F. and Bravenboer, D. (2020). 'The best practice in work-integrated pedagogy for degree apprenticeships in a post-viral future'. *Higher Education, Skills and Work-Based Learning*, 10(5), 727–739. https://doi.org/10.1108/HESWBL-04-2020-0071

McMurray, S., Dutton, M., McQuaid, R. and Richard, A. (2016). 'Employer demands from business graduates'. *Education and Training*, 58(1), 112–132. https://doi.org/10.1108/ET-02-2014-0017

Messum, D., Wilkes, L., Peters, K. and Jackson, D. (2016). 'Content analysis of vacancy advertisements for employability skills: challenges and opportunities for informing curriculum development'. *Journal of Teaching and Learning for Graduate Employability*, 6(1), 72–86. https://doi.org/10.21153/jtlge2016vol7no1art582

National Careers Institute (2021). *'Tourism and Hospitality. Australian Government'*. Retrieved on June 18, 2021 from www.myskills.gov.au/industries/tourism-hospitality

Olawale, Y. (2015). *'The employability skills provision within a construction project management degree programme'*. Raidén, A. B. and Aboagye-Nimo, E. (eds) Procs 31 Annual ARCOM Conference (pp. 959–968). Lincoln, UK: Association of Researchers in Construction Management.

Oliver, B. (2011). *'Assuring graduate outcomes good practice report'*. Sydney: Australian Learning and Teaching Council. Retrieved from www.jcu.edu.au/__data/assets/pdf_file/0019/122842/jcu_086521.pdf

Oliver, B. and Jorre de St Jorre, T. (2018). 'Graduate attributes for 2020 and beyond: recommendations for Australian higher education providers'. *Higher Education Research & Development*, 37(4), 821–836, DOI: 10.1080/07294360.2018.1446415

Parliament of Australia (2020, October 3). *'Higher Education Support Amendment (Job-ready Graduates and Supporting Regional and Remote Students) Bill 2020'*. Retrieved on June 18, 2021 from Parliament of Australia: www.aph.gov.au/Parliamentary_Business/Bills_Legislation/ bd/bd2021a/21bd012

Patrick, C-J., Peach, D., Pocknee, C., Webb, F., Fletcher, M. and Pretto, G. (2008, December). *'The WIL [Work Integrated Learning] report: a national scoping study'* [Australian Learning and Teaching Council (ALTC) Final report]. Brisbane: Queensland University of Technology. Available online at: www.altc.edu.au and www.acen.edu.au

Poort, I., Jansen, E. and Hofman, A. (2020). 'Does the group matter? Effects of trust, cultural diversity, and group formation on engagement in group work in higher education'. *Higher Education Research & Development*, 1–16.

Precision Consultancy (2007). *'Graduate employability skills'*. Business, Industry, and Higher Education Collaboration Council. Retrieved on August 6, 2021 from https://apo.org.au/node/1505

QILT (2020). *'2020 Graduate Outcomes Survey National Report'*. Australian Government Department of Education and Training. Retrieved on August 6, 2021 from www.qilt.edu.au/docs/default-source/gos-reports/2020-gos/2020-gos-national-report.pdf?sfvrsn=be0bec3c_2

QILT (2021). *'2020 Student Experience Survey national report'*. Australian Government
Department of Education and Training. Retrieved on August 6, 2021 from www.qilt.edu.au/docs/default-source/ses/ses-2020/2020-ses-national-report.pdf?sfvrsn=a3ffed3c_2

QILT (2021a). *'Employer Satisfaction Survey National Report'*. Australian Government Department of Education and Training. Retrieved on August 6, 2021 from www.qilt.edu.au/docs/default-source/ess/ess-2020/2020-ess-national-report.pdf?sfvrsn=2f3ed3c_2

Queensland Government (2021, May 20). *'Premier calls on Australians to Work in Paradise with new tourism campaign'*. Department of the Premier and Cabinet. Retrieved on August 6, 2021 from https://statements.qld.gov.au/statements/92144

Scarinci, J., Pryce, J. and Thirumaran, K. (in press). 'A new world during COVID-19: employability skills in tourism, hospitality and events'. In *Domestic tourism and hospitality management: issues, scope, and challenges amid the COVID-19 pandemic*. Burlington, Canada: Apple Academic Press.

Suarta, M. I., Suwintana, K. I., Fajar, P. S. and Hariyanti, D. N. (2017). 'Employability skills required by the 21st-century workplace: a literature review of labour market demand'. *Advances in Social Science, Education and Humanities Research*, 102, 337–342.

Suarta, M. I., Suwintana, K. I., Fajar, P. S. and Hariyanti, D. N. (2018, December). 'Employability skills for entry level workers: a content analysis of job advertisements in Indonesia'. *Journal of Technical Education and Training*, 49–61. doi:10.30880/jtet.2018.10.02.005

Tertiary Education Quality and Standards Agency (TEQSA) (2021). *'Higher Education Standards Framework (Threshold Standards) 2021'*. Retrieved on August 28, 2021 from www.legislation.gov.au/Details/F2021L00488

Tourism Australia (2020). *'The economic importance of tourism'*. Retrieved on August 28, 2021 from www.tourism.australia.com/en/markets-and-stats/tourism-statistics/the-economic-importance-of-tourism.html

Tourism Research Australia (2021). *'Measuring the impact of COVID-19'*. Australian Government. Retrieved August 28, 2021 from www.tra.gov.au/

Von Treuer, K., V. Sturre, S. Keele, and J. McLeod. (2010). *Evaluation methodology for work integrated learning – placements*. Paper presented at 3rd Biannual ACEN National Conference, September 27–October 1, in Perth, Australia.

Wardle, K. M. and Ashwell, J. Closing the capability gap: Enhancing the employability of hospitality graduates [online]. In: Young, T., Stolk, P., and McGinnis, G. (Eds). CAUTHE 2018: Get Smart: Paradoxes and Possibilities in Tourism, Hospitality and Events Education and Research. Newcastle, NSW: Newcastle Business School, The University of Newcastle, 2018: 733-736.

Warwick, J., & Howard, A. (2015). A note on structuring employability skills for accounting students. *International Journal of Academic Research in Business and Social Sciences*, *5*(10), 165-174.

Yiu, M., & Law, R. (2012). A review of hospitality internship: Different perspectives of students, employers, and educators. *Journal of teaching in Travel & Tourism*, *12*(4), 377-402.

14

The Teaching Performing Assessment (TPA) and Its Impact on Graduates' Preparedness for Employment

Rebecca Spooner-Lane, Kathy Jordan, John Buchanan and Tania Broadley

INTRODUCTION

This chapter focuses on education and employability for pre-service teachers transitioning into the school teaching profession. The development and nurturing of a quality teacher workforce, has been a central issue of OECD countries for some time (OECD, 2005; Schwartz et al., 2007). While some countries focus attention on the attraction and recruitment of teachers, others are grappling with increasing quality and preparedness for employment. In Australia, high quality Initial Teacher Education (ITE) is seen as vital to addressing many of these concerns. However, national reports and reviews, such as the Top of the Class report (Standing Committee on Education and Vocational Education, 2007), the Productivity Commission Report on Schools Workforce (2012) and the Teacher Education Ministerial Advisory Group (TEMAG, 2014) continue to argue that programme quality and graduate standards are inconsistent and in need of reform, leading to an increasing regulatory and standards-driven system. With such a focus on the quality of the graduate teacher for employment outcomes, the notion of graduate employability for life in this graduate cohort is also of importance to consider.

EMPLOYMENT AND EMPLOYABILITY

ITE providers have a core role in preparing the next generation of teachers (Walker et al., 2019). On the face of it, Australian providers appear highly successful, with recent data showing high levels of graduate employment (AITSL, 2019). Yet there are problems in retention, with large-scale studies also showing frequent movement between schools, which can be considered both positive and negative in terms of beginning teacher experience (McKenzie et al., 2014). It is these early experiences that will shape subsequent years of teaching (Bartell, 2004) and ultimately might be considered foundational to the employability of these graduates. Beginning teachers require approximately three to five years' teaching experience to become effective teachers and improve student learning outcomes (Rivkin et al., 2005).

For the most part, ITE programmes prepare graduates for employment as teachers. Yet the notion of work readiness is changing because of increasing unemployment or under-employment leading to interest in graduates having a stronger sense of employability and a capacity to work in a range of contexts (Jackson, 2018). Bennett (2018) argues the terms employment and employability are often used interchangeably and posits that the two terms need to be distinguishable. She advocates for the term employment as job-getting, and employability as the ability to create and sustain work over time. Higher education institutions, she argues, need to focus less on employment and more on educating for employability for life. Such an approach, she suggests, encourages students to understand 'why they think the way they think, how to critique and learn the unfamiliar, and how their values, beliefs and assumptions can inform and be informed by their learning, lives and careers' (Bennett, 2018: iv).

This view put forward by Bennett (2018), is seemingly at odds with the teacher education agenda in Australia. This agenda is primarily focused on reforming teacher education programmes so that graduates are classroom-ready and a teaching performance assessment (TPA) has been introduced to measure and provide assurance of this readiness. Thus, the focus is currently on immediate employment as classroom teachers rather than longer term employability.

ACCREDITATION OF ITE IN AUSTRALIA

In Australia, national accreditation of ITE is 'an important part of the agenda for improving teaching quality' (Productivity Commission, 2012: 13). All programmes, for example, need to comply with design, development and delivery standards (AITSL, 2015; AITSL, 2018) as well as a set of Australian Professional Standards for Teachers (AITSL, 2011). Meeting these programme and professional standard requirements is intended to ensure that ITE programmes are preparing high quality graduate teachers with the knowledge and skills to be employed and effective as teachers in Australia's schools. (AITSL, 2015). Yet a year following the introduction of national accreditation, a further review was called.

The TEMAG group (2014) was established 'to provide advice on how initial teacher education programs could be improved to better prepare new teachers with the practical skills needed for the classroom' (TEMAG, 2014: 1). The Advisory Group (TEMAG, 2014) argued that there was too great a variation in the quality of classroom teaching, and there was no guarantee that graduates from teacher education programmes were classroom-ready. Teacher education was then seen as a problem needing to be fixed. The final report, *Action Now: Classroom Ready Teachers*, recommended reform in six key areas including a robust assessment of pre-service teacher classroom readiness, the focus of this chapter.

Thus, in Australia, greater regulation of teacher education has been identified by policymakers as key to producing a quality teacher workforce, one with the skills perceived to prepare graduates for employment. Commonly, a deficit discourse, in which teacher education is perceived as failing to produce classroom-ready graduates is used to justify the need for greater quality assurance and tighter regulation.

EMPLOYERS AND THE TPA

The TPA was introduced as a measure of pre-service teacher achievement of classroom readiness based on the Australian Professional Standards for Teachers. Professional experience, the time when pre-service teachers undertake teaching practice in schools, is integral to the TPA as it is during their final placement that they are required to undertake this assessment.

While the TPA is relatively new in Australia, capstone assessments are common in some international contexts, particularly in the United States (Stacey et al., 2020). Australia's TPA has been included as a requirement for national accreditation for graduation from a teacher education programme. The TPA is positioned as an authentic, rigorous assessment to measure demonstrable graduate classroom readiness. Such an assessment, it is then argued, will lead to 'the right' teachers being employed, those who will improve student performance. Yet little is known about how individual providers approached the development, implementation and evaluation of the TPA, to what extent the TPA prepares graduates for employment as teachers, and how the TPA influences perceptions of classroom readiness.

THE STUDY

In this chapter we examine pre-service teacher perceptions and experiences of the TPA at three different ITE institutions. Each institution developed its own TPA and were at various stages of development when the TPA agenda was in its infancy in this country. The three institutions were the Queensland University of Technology (QUT), the Royal Melbourne Institute of Technology University (RMIT), and the University of Technology Sydney (UTS).

Fifty-five graduating teachers who were completing various ITE programmes (undergraduate and postgraduate, early childhood, primary and secondary) at the three institutions participated in our study. Focus groups and interviews of approximately 30–40 minutes were conducted from July–November 2018. Both data collection methods focused on graduating teacher perceptions and experiences of the TPA including their initial thoughts about the task and their preparation for undertaking it, as well as their views about the impact of the TPA experience on their confidence to teach and classroom readiness.

Focus groups and interviews were led by employed researchers who were not directly involved in the larger study, to remove any potential bias or power relations. Data were transcribed and de-identified where necessary, with participants recoded as a numerical number to protect anonymity. Data were then thematically coded (Braun & Clarke, 2019) for analysis of recurring themes and outlying responses and were then cross-checked to maximise inter-rater reliability. Findings are organised around the key themes: provider preparation for the TPA; impact of the TPA on classroom readiness; and impact of the TPA on student learning. Comments by graduating teachers are recorded by institution, followed by form of data collection (either focus group or interview) and then numerical number of the participant. For example, RMIT, FG2P10 refers to data from RMIT, from the second focus group, and participant number 10.

This chapter draws on data from a larger study funded in 2018 by the Australian Technology Network (ATN) (Broadley et al., 2019). This study produced institutional case studies, using a survey instrument developed by Spooner-Lane et al. (2017), interviews and focus groups. For the purposes of this chapter, which is to examine graduate teacher perceptions of the TPA and its impact on employability, only focus group and interview data with graduating teachers is used.

PREPARING STUDENTS FOR THE TPA

For the most part, graduating teachers from each of the three institutions commented favourably on the learning gained from their provider in preparation for the TPA. Pre-service teachers mostly came to the view that the TPA was straightforward, once they realised it was 'documenting what we do anyway'. (UTS, FG2P6). As one graduating teacher reported:

> I found them [assessment tasks] all to be really valuable in preparing us to go out there, to know the standards, know what we've achieved collecting that evidence and that's all practical-stuff that we're going to need to apply for jobs, which is great. (RMIT, FG1P5).

Another pre-service teacher commented:

> We've learned heaps of different teaching strategies at the university, we've learned how to do lesson planning, learned how to make rubrics, the importance of pre-assessment. The course has been pretty good in informing us of that. (QUT, IP2).

However, some graduating teachers were more critical of the additional assessment hurdle at graduation, expressing concerns about a lack of preparation time and an inability to demonstrate everything they knew. One graduating teacher lamented,

> I could've written a lot more than what I put in there, but we were stuck to a word limit … It was really hard though to limit it to what we felt was most appropriate and most valuable in our teaching practice. (QUT, IP2).

Another graduating teacher explained it this way.

> The in-class time allocated to the content, there was so much content there that we didn't really get a great chance to go back over it and to discuss it and to develop that understanding before the interview, which was a shame. (RMIT, FG1P9).

Some graduating teachers commented that more time would have led to a higher quality TPA. For example, 'The volume of work was so overwhelming that the quality got lost within that and I think that's a shame'. (RMIT, FG1P8).

IMPACT OF SCHOOL PLACEMENT

While the TPA aims to assess authentic tasks associated with teaching, students felt variability in professional experience placements may be a hindering factor in meeting the TPA requirements. One graduate stated:

> The high absenteeism of students, something that unfortunately is out of your control, … ultimately affects how well you can analyse your impact as a teacher. (UTS, FG3P7).

Graduate teachers studying more practical based units such as health and physical education noted that 'it was more challenging to assess impact on student learning'. (QUT, IP3). One graduating teacher summed it up as:

> Depending on schools and where their schools were, and where their classes were at, it could have been a hard time to actually see the overall impact that they had. Yeah, so for me I was lucky because I still had content to do in my classes, so I could see that impact. (QUT, IP2).

For some, fulfilling an additional hurdle of a TPA undermined their focus and sense of engagement during their final placement experience.

> I almost felt like I couldn't enjoy my placement because I just had in the back of my head all this stuff I had to do and I just – I felt like I almost wasn't present. Expecting us to do all that while we're still expected to teach, plan lessons – you're just exhausted as it is and it was just too much. (RMIT, FG2P3).

And similarly,

> After school at night you would be sitting there doing your lesson plans and then doing assignment stuff and then looking at the TPA. It was like hours and hours of work when you might have just had a staff meeting and be back until seven o'clock at night, get up and do it all again. (RMIT, FG2P7).

INFLUENCE OF SUPERVISING TEACHER

Some graduate teachers discussed the influence of the supervising or mentor teacher on their capacity to both implement the TPA and develop classroom readiness. This is typified in the following comments,

Look, I feel like I was really fortunate that the placement set me up really well to complete the TPA, but I've got to say that the big factor in that was the fact I had a great mentor. I feel like if you didn't have a mentor that was really dedicated you're at a severe disadvantage to complete that TPA. (RMIT, FG1P4)

While uni has really broadened my expectations of teaching and of teachers, and certainly helped me develop some ideas, it was really that guidance from my mentor teacher that helped me. (QUT, IP1)

If you're lucky enough to have a good mentor teacher, they will provide opportunities for you to show evidence. But if you don't have a good relationship with your mentor teacher, you'll really struggle with some of those points. (RMIT, FG2P8)

Graduating teachers from one institution also recognised the demands the TPA placed on supervisor teachers, particularly the time commitment. This is shown in the following comments from RMIT graduating students,

> I obviously gave my mentor the TPA (assessment guide) at the beginning, but she was unable to complete it until right at the end. I tried to meet with her throughout and it was just too challenging. So, obviously near the end a lot of things that happened weeks one to three had been forgotten. She just rushed through it, did dot points and I just felt it wasn't an accurate representation of what I'd completed. So, that was a bit frustrating. (RMIT, FG1P3).

> I actually find my mentor was incredibly supportive, but he was overwhelmed with what was going on within the school reporting time. Therefore, he didn't have a lot of spare time to sit with me and go through it and I found that it was really frustrating to sit there and know that I had all this evidence that I needed to collect and knowing that the chances of that happening from, with assistance from him, was going to be negligent, no, negligible sorry, negligible. (RMIT, FG1P8).

Some pre-service teachers discussed the effect that completing this task had on the mentor relationship. For example, 'I had a really great mentor relationship, and then towards the end it became quite strained because I felt like I had to put my foot down and say, we need to do this together'. As she later added, 'it seemed really sad to have this great relationship with your mentor and then be like, well the uni is making me do this and I don't want to fail'. (RMIT, FG1P7).

IMPACT OF TPA ON CLASSROOM READINESS

Graduating teachers from each institution spoke about the TPA helping their classroom readiness, especially their confidence to teach. These comments were always expressed in enthusiastic terms. The three comments below, one from each institution, are typical of comments provided.

This was probably the most beneficial assignment I've done in the last four years. So, it actually made me a lot more confident that I'd practised these things and I could talk about them. (QUT, IP3).

I found it like really boosted my confidence because I became more aware of them and it was in, like throughout my placement. (RMIT, FG1P10).

The TPA gave me a solid direction. Especially given the fact that it was my final practicum. I mean it will never capture the entirety of what teaching actually is, but it was a good leg up into what I kind of expect I'm going to have to do once I get into the actual classroom. (UTS, FG1P3).

Some also identified the TPA as a tool or a prompt for practice or reflection on practice as shown in the following comments:

Using it as a tool to remind me to be collecting the evidence of what I'd done in the classroom to show that I can identify students' needs, plan for those needs and then help them get to an agreed upon goal to show them that they have developed in that way and they have completed the learning. (QUT, IP1.)

The fact that there was a TPA prompted me to be a little bit more formal with my formative assessments … the choice of the three [focus] kids was interesting, too … the choice of those three did influence the way I, what I got out of the prac, actually. Partly it was thinking about which kind of three I'd be interested in thinking most about. You know, that was something I would not otherwise have necessarily done. (UTS, FG1P2).

IMPACT OF TPA ON PROFESSIONAL DEVELOPMENT

Graduating teachers from QUT also explained how enacting the TPA helped to build their sense of identity as a teacher and confidence in being able to contribute positively to student learning and achievement.

> I would say for me I could see that my students learnt something. I could see from the data and from the formative assessment that I had set and received back that I had impacted my students' learning. (QUT, IP2).
>
> I think it really helped us to reflect on who we are as a teacher, how our teaching practice is beneficial for our students and how we need to improve, which I definitely think prepares you for next year coming out as a first year, where you stand, your ability, your knowledge, what you need to work on. (QUT, IP1).

EMPLOYABILITY FOR TEACHER EDUCATORS

There is growing research to suggest that higher education needs to also focus on building the employability of graduates as well as their employment (Rees, 2019). Being a graduate of a higher education programme is now no longer a guarantee of securing employment. Embedding employability into programmes, that enable graduates to develop the knowledge, skills and attributes to be employed across their lifespan is therefore recommended. This is a significant shift in thinking especially for programmes such as teacher education.

Teacher education programmes concern themselves with education and teachers, educating and teaching, and not merely 'training' students to be teachers. While students who undertake a teacher education programme have various motivations, many are motivated to become teachers. Thus, teacher education programmes have had an employment purpose as a raison d'être.

For the most part, graduates of teacher education programmes in Australia gain employment as teachers, if not in the first year, then most likely within three years. Yet there are widely reported issues around teacher retention, with considerable evidence to suggest that a high number of teachers leave the profession within the first five years (Ingersoll, 2001). Little is reported, however, about what they do subsequently. Given Bennett's argument (Bennett, 2018) that we should focus more on supporting the long-term employability of graduates, teacher education providers focusing on their graduates' employment in schools will face challenges. To date, teacher education programmes have not wrestled with this broader notion of employability, and the TPA, because of its focus on being classroom-ready, adds to this quandary.

THE TPA

In the TEMAG review, ITE programmes are depicted as out of touch and being overly preoccupied with theory; rather than being evidence- and research-based (TEMAG, 2014) and supporting the development of classroom-ready graduates. This concern about the quality of ITE programmes and graduates is not new.

According to Mayer (2014), 'Teacher education is, and has been, a highly scrutinised domain in Australia' (p. 462). The TEMAG review, therefore, can be seen as symptomatic of reviews and another effort by government aimed at fixing perceived problems.

The TPA, as conceptualised by TEMAG (2014) and implemented by AITSL, aims to provide greater quality assurance of graduate readiness to teach. The Australian Teacher Professional Standards are used as the basis for such an assessment. While we acknowledge some merits in using these standards, we are concerned that they might 'draw attention to specific kinds of performances, outcomes and dispositions that frame teaching as a technical activity' (Mayer & Mills, 2020: 3). Teaching is a complex activity and such a narrow focus on technical knowledge and skill can operate to the detriment of other valuable learning.

The TPA has been quickly introduced in Australia. While providers have had some experience in designing programmes to ensure that these standards are met, this is not a long period, in the context of other, competing demands, in which to implement such a change. It is important to note that programmes are accredited for a five-year period, yet the TPA, as well as other reforms emerging from TEMAG (2014) were implemented as additional requirements of accreditation. We recognise that designing and implementing a TPA is challenging. AITSL in leading this development has supported these efforts through establishing a national grant process. However, this process took considerable time, as there were resultant issues around copyright. Two consortia, the Learning Sciences Institute of Australia at the Australian Catholic University, and the Melbourne Graduate School of Education at the Melbourne University, were successfully funded to develop two nationally endorsed TPAs. Upon receiving endorsement, both consortia sought interest from ITE providers across Australia to join their efforts and use their TPA for a fee. AITSL also set up an Expert Advisory Group to support providers and ensure compliance with requirements, such as reliability and validity. However, AITSL later announced that providers had to incorporate an EAG-endorsed TPA by 2019. It is likely that some providers may have felt pressure to join one of the consortia rather than develop a TPA independently, and seeking and gaining approved by the EAG. Thus, it seems likely that provider independence in designing a TPA to suit their own needs and context may have been compromised.

PROVIDER PREPARATION FOR TPA

It is to be noted that each of the three providers reported in this chapter were at this initial stage of implementation of the TPA, and all developed and implemented different instruments. For the most part, pre-service teachers felt their providers prepared them for the TPA. We feel that this is a welcome finding, given that our timelines for developing the TPA meant that consortium models had not been developed. We acknowledge that there were concerns, however, especially regarding the workload involved in the TPA.

IMPACT OF TPA ON CLASSROOM READINESS

As indicated by the title of the TEMAG review (2014), *Action Now: Classroom Ready Teachers* (2014), classroom readiness of graduate teachers is at the crux of the review. Yet while achieving classroom readiness is elevated as an imperative by government, it is not well defined. As Mayer and Mills (2020: 6) suggest, the assumption seems to be that meeting the Australian Professional Standards for Teachers equates to classroom readiness and 'that what was needed was a tighter accountability framework around using them'. As the term is not explained, this may infer that it is self-explanatory. Such an assumption leaves readers to make their own meaning, and it is highly likely that this may mean different things to different stakeholders. Moreover, 'classroom readiness' is presented as an absolute; one is either classroom ready or one is not. As such, this does not allow readers to appreciate the various degrees of classroom readiness that one may have at a particular time, as well as ignoring the important notion that teachers grow and develop throughout their professional lives.

We recognise that teacher education providers have a responsibility to help graduates achieve the necessary knowledge and skills to gain employment as teachers. Yet we also think that a focus on 'classroom readiness' may be at the expense of other important teacher attributes that cannot be neatly categorised (such as effective communication skills, rapport with diverse learners in the classroom). Teacher education is not merely about skilling. Classroom readiness can be such an alluring mantra, but it presupposes understanding 'classroom', or, more importantly, what happens in a classroom. It harks back to Lortie's (1975) deprecation of 'apprenticeship of observation'. One might learn many things by imitating one's teacher (how to draw, or to write a haiku), but learning to teach effectively is less easy to mimic, in the absence of an understanding of knowledge and theories that drive the teacher's decisions. This may play into popular notions that teaching comprises 'knowing and telling'. In the long term, such a discourse can be highly problematic for the profession as too much of an emphasis on classroom readiness can reduce the complex toolkit that teachers need, for those skills that can be easily measured. There is risk, then, that an ITE qualification will focus exclusively on teaching rather than educating and thus be reduced to a narrowly defined and assessed set of knowledge and skills.

Despite the TPA's narrow focus on classroom readiness, most pre-service teachers in this study valued the TPA as they appreciated its focus on practice and observed that they would get return for effort; that putting in the effort to complete it would aid them in their careers as teachers. Research has clearly shown that pre-service teachers value practical components of their programmes (Walker et al., 2019). While we agree that programmes should incorporate a practical focus, we also acknowledge that without theoretical frames, graduates are unable to make sense of these practices and their proper application.

Many of the participating pre-service teachers commented that the teacher mentor was highly influential in their capacity to undertake the TPA. Some commented that a supportive mentor made the task more do-able. Teacher mentors could support, for example, collection of data and interpretation of impact on student learning. Several pre-service teachers commented that their teacher mentors were not forthcoming in supporting their efforts, and that many were constrained by their own teaching obligations.

The role of the teacher mentor in supporting pre-service teacher learning, including their knowledge and skills to teach, is well documented in the literature. It is also well documented that schools are under no obligation to host pre-service teachers during professional experience and that finding supervisors is an ongoing problem, with decisions often being made for administrative convenience. Training of teacher mentors, while recommended by AITSL, is optional and no additional funding has been provided to assist with it. There has been considerable research that shows the teacher mentor and pre-service teacher relationship is an important one and that mentoring itself requires knowledge and skills, other than having classroom experience (Adoniou, 2013). Many mentor teachers are motivated to undertake the role from an altruistic desire to contribute to the profession. While being a mentor is now required for career progression, mentoring is largely unrewarded and increases teacher workload. Pre-service teachers in this study felt that the TPA placed additional responsibility on teacher supervisors or mentors.

The dominant discourse permeating recent reviews and reports of ITE in Australia is that graduates lack the teacher knowledge and skills to be classroom-ready. In this discourse, the role of the supervising teacher in supporting graduating teachers' efforts to attain classroom readiness is understated. This is of particular concern given the extensive literature that has highlighted the importance of having quality supervision. As well, this discourse emphasises 'the right people' coming into the profession. As Mayer and Mills argue, 'This focus on the person (i.e., teachers not their teaching) resulted in recommendations about required academic skills and desirable personal attributes and characteristics' (2020, p. 7).

IMPACT OF TPA ON STUDENT LEARNING

The inclusion of the phrase 'impact on student learning' was an addition to the revised national accreditation standards and procedures. Its inclusion appears to have emerged from the TEMAG review, which was concerned that providers were not designing programmes that were evidence- and research-based. While we dispute this view, we agree that teacher practice should positively impact student learning but we have concerns that this has been oversimplified, perhaps presenting a false impression of the profession and its demands. Moreover, it is the 'teacher' who impacts learning; therefore, denying due attention to the importance of context, socio-economic background and school priorities is misdirected.

Defining impact and collecting data as evidence of impact is not simple. Yet the TPA may encourage a narrow, superficial view of impact as data that can be easily used rather than impact taking time, and as involving multiple attempts, fits and starts.

While the TPA provides a limited opportunity for pre-service teachers to engage in the full planning, teaching, assessing and reflecting cycle, enacting the TPA resulted in pre-service teachers engaging in self-reflection and self-realisation about their future potential impact on student learning. Graduate teachers started to develop a sense of teacher identity and confidence in their teaching. It could be argued that fulfilling the TPA requirements may assist pre-service teachers to reflect on the meaningful work of teachers. Bennett (2018: 33) argues that long-term employability is associated with securing employment that brings 'personal meaning and societal worth'. It could therefore be argued that the TPA may play an important first step in prompting pre-service teachers to consider the meaningful impact teachers have on student lives.

CONCLUSION

The quality of education and the teaching workforce in OECD countries remains high on the agenda. This focus assists countries to continue to increase the knowledge and skills of its citizens for better lives and employment, to generate prosperity and promote social inclusion. In Australia, the development of accreditation requirements, including the TPA, have been implemented to raise the quality of beginning teachers and prepare them for employment in classrooms, referred to as 'classroom ready'. We argue that classroom readiness is not an absolute and that teachers grow and develop throughout their professional lives. Our findings highlight the impact of the TPA on employment readiness. In line with the literature on employability, we propose that higher education ITE providers should consider the longer term employability of graduates by recognising the range of interdisciplinary knowledge and skills (skills in written and oral communication, IT and research) acquired by pre-service teachers during their programme, as well as their initial employment. Not all teacher graduates seek to work inside the classroom. Some graduates use their education qualification in other fields.

While the UK and other countries are moving away from preparing teachers in the university system, Australia is committed to strengthening the partnership between schools and universities to further solidify the nexus between practice and theory. The quality of partnerships between the school and the university continues to be critical to the approach and is reflected in the programme standards for providers, alongside the goal to strengthen employability outcomes.

Further research could examine this more closely and investigate the knowledge, skills and attributes that could be embedded into teacher education programmes to support broader graduate employability, within and beyond the classroom.

REFERENCES

Adoniou, M. (2013). Preparing teachers – the importance of connecting contexts in teacher education. *Australian Journal of Teacher Education,* 38(8), 47–60.

Australian Institute for Teaching and School Leadership (AITSL) (2015). *Accreditation of initial teacher education programs in Australia: standards and procedures*. Melbourne: AITSL.

Australian Institute for Teaching and School Leadership (AITSL) (2011). *Australian Professional Standards for Teachers*. Melbourne: AITSL. www.aitsl.edu.au/docs/default-source/national-policy-framework/australian-professional-standards-for-teachers.pdf Retrieved January 20 2022.

Australian Institute for Teaching and School Leadership (AITSL) (2017). *Teaching performance assessments: an overview for schools.* www.aitsl.edu.au/deliver-ite-programs/teaching-performance-assessment/teaching-performance-assessments-an-overview-for-schools. Retrieved January 22 2022.

Australian Institute for Teaching and School Leadership (AITSL) (2018). *Accreditation of initial teacher education programs in Australia: standards and procedures*. Melbourne: AITSL.

Australian Institute for Teaching and School Leadership (2019). *Initial teacher education: data report 2019.* Melbourne: AITSL.

Bartell, C. A. (2004). *Cultivating high-quality teaching through induction and mentoring*. Thousand Oaks, CA: Corwin Press, a SAGE Publications Company.

Bennett, D. (2018). Graduate employability and higher education: past, present and future. *HERDSA Review of Higher Education*, 5, 31–61.

Braun, V. & Clarke, V. (2019). Reflecting on reflexive thematic analysis. *Qualitative Research in Sport, Exercise and Health*, 11(4), 589–597, DOI: 10.1080/2159676X.2019.1628806

Broadley, T., Spooner-Lane, R., Buchanan, J., Hardy, G. & Jordan, K. (2019). *A case study of teacher graduate preparedness: developing a national capstone assessment.* (ATN Final Report). https://eprints.qut.edu.au/201752/ Accessed February 2 2022.

Ingersoll, R. (2001). Teacher turnover and teacher shortages: an organisational analysis. *American Educational Research Journal*, 38(3), 499–534. DOI:10.3102/00028312038003499

Jackson, D. (2018). Developing graduate career readiness in Australia: shifting from extra-curricular internships to work-integrated learning. *International Journal of Work-Integrated Learning*, 19(1), 23–35.

Lortie, D. (1975). *Schoolteacher: a sociological study*. London: University of Chicago Press.

McKenzie, P., Weldon, P., Rowley, G., Murphy, M. & McMillan, J. (2014). *Staff in Australia's Schools 2013: Main Report on the Survey*. Canberra: Department of Education.

Mayer, D. (2014). Forty years of teacher education in Australia: 1974–2014. *Journal of Education for Teaching*, 40(5), 461–473 DOI: 10.1080/02607476.2014.956536.

Mayer, D. & Mills, M. (2020). Professionalism and teacher education in Australia and England. *European Journal of Teacher Education*, 44(1), 45–61. DOI: 10.1080/02619768.2020.1832987

Organisation for Economic Co-operation and Development (OECD) (2005). *Teachers matter: attracting, developing and retaining effective teachers*. DOI: 10.1787/19901496

Rees, S. (2019). Re-imagining employability: an ontology of employability best practice in higher education institutions. *Teaching in Higher Education*, 26(6), 1–16. https://doi.org/10.1080/13562517.2019.1670637

Rivikin, S. G., Hanushek, E., & Kain, J. F. (2005). Teachers, schools and academic achievement. *Econometrica*, 73(2), 417-458.

Schwartz, R. B., Wurtzel, J. & Olson, L. (2007). Attracting and retaining teachers. *OECD Observer*, 261 (May), 27–28.

Spooner-Lane, R., Thompson, G. & Shield, P. (2017). *Graduate Teacher Preparedness Survey*. Unpublished manuscript. Faculty of Education, Queensland University of Technology, Brisbane, Queensland. Australia.

Stacey, M., Talbot, D., Buchanan, J. and Mayer, D. (2020). The development of an Australian teacher performance assessment: lessons from the international literature. *Asia-Pacific Journal of Teacher Education*, 48(5), 508–519. https://doi.org/10.1080/1359866X.2019.1669137

Standing Committee on Education and Vocational Education (2007). *Top of the class: report of the inquiry into teacher education*. Retrieved from www.aph.gov.au/parliamentary_business/committees/house_of_representatives_committees?url=evt/teachereduc/report/fullreport.pdf. Accessed January 05 2022.

Teacher Education Ministerial Advisory Group (TEMAG) (2014). *Action now: classroom ready teachers*. Canberra: Department of Education.

Walker, R., Morrison, C. & Hay, I. (2019). Evaluating quality in professional experience partnerships for graduate teacher employability. *Journal of Teaching and Learning for Graduate Employability*, 10(1), 118–137.

PART III

Graduate Employability and Inclusion

BACKGROUND AND CONTEXT

Despite the extension of higher education opportunities globally, it does not always follow that the employment opportunities for graduates are proportionately or equitably balanced, nor that the individual, organisational, or society potentials are fully achieved. In this part, we consider issues related to improving the inclusivity of all graduates in economic and social activity.

In each case, authors have reviewed relevant literature in addition to the input from their own qualitative and quantitative research, and case studies. In many cases, this helpfully includes student voice and perspectives.

CHAPTERS IN THIS SECTION

***Working towards Equitable Outcomes for All through Embedding Activities in the Curriculum,* Sarah Flynn, Anna Levett and Judith Baines**

The study looks at awarding gaps between different groups of students, in relation to both the classification of degrees awarded and progression into graduate level employment. Their case study (n=3,000) considers a students' outcomes case study from a curriculum-embedded, immersive assessment centre experience. It underlines the importance of institutional commitment to equitable employability outcomes, including those from socially and economically disadvantaged backgrounds.

The chapter explores the previous research backgrounds and approaches, and is helpfully supported by student qualitative research and voice. Resonating from other chapters in this book, the case study reinforces the value of partnerships, in this case between the careers and employment team, Smart Resourcing Solutions (SRS), academics, employers, and students. The outcomes from this work were recognised by Advance HE in 2020 in their Collaborative Awards for Teaching Excellence.

***Supporting the Employability of Neurodivergent Graduates,* Keren Coney**

Coney considers the increased proportions of neurodiverse students now at higher education institutions. Coney notes that the employability outcomes for these graduates are often disappointing when compared with those with no known disability. The chapter considers how neurodiverse graduates may be perceived, and supported, including the development of inclusive working environments. Of concern are Coney's observation that whilst larger (and well-resourced organisations) have been more proactive with policies and support, this is less evident internationally, in small and medium-sized organisations which account for well over half of all graduate employment.

Coney calls for consideration of further research and support for resourcing and work environments for those lesser-resourced smaller companies, and for international perspectives. She also advocates exploring how successful neurodiverse individuals obtained employment and ascertaining what accommodations could be put in place to enable individuals to realise their potential.

Centring Racialised Experiences of Black Students to Mitigate Bias within Graduate Labour Recruitment and Selection Processes, Iwi Ugiagbe-Green

The first of two chapters we include which particularly focus on Black students and mitigation of bias within graduate labour recruitment and selection processes.

Ugiagbe-Green uses a work-readiness framework (Ugiagbe-Green and Southall, 2020) based on research with 28 employers and 17 graduate recruiters. The framework was then used as a tool of empirical analysis to explore the racialised experiences of 10 Black students, seeking student graduate opportunities in the labour market. The analysis highlights the importance of graduate identity and signalling theory (Spence, 2020) to employers, and the associated subjectiveness/bias that is systemically embedded into graduate recruitment and selection practices.

Ugiagbe-Green concludes with a Call to Action to address inequitable outcomes for Black students which lead to unacceptable, and life-diminishing graduate labour pay gaps, higher levels of graduate unemployment, under-representation in senior leadership and executive roles, lower levels of accumulated wealth, home ownership, pensions and other forms of economic and social gaps. In turn, each of these factors reflect back into society and the community, not simply the graduate and the workplace.

Ugiagbe-Green highlights the work of the 100 Black Interns Scheme (www.10000blackinterns.com/100-black-interns-programme), offering positions to Black undergraduates from over 200 finance/investment management organisations.

Ugiagbe-Green concludes with the ongoing need to engage in open, constructive dialogue about recruitment bias, signalling and the role of perception of identity in our conversations with students, careers provisions, and employers.

Mind the Gap: Efforts to Narrow the Graduate Employment Gap for London Students from Low-participation Neighbourhoods, Richard Mendez

We are reminded that The Office for Students (2021) in the United Kingdom asserts that graduates from more deprived backgrounds are less likely to progress into higher skilled employment. Echoing warnings ('Mind the Gap!', the call familiar to passengers on London's rail system), Mendez reminds us that the Covid 19 pandemic has most likely exacerbated these existing socio-economic outcome differences – gaps – with the London region experiencing some of the greatest dips, and so competition for roles, in online advertised job vacancies compared with 2019 averages.

The chapter explores Mendez's university bespoke employability interventions that have been designed or repurposed, to place emphasis on students and graduates from low participation neighbourhoods and those most likely to suffer unemployment or under-employment. This includes technology-blended support for employability for working with local employers on a semi-exclusive basis, and the growth of mentoring schemes.

Mendez calls for future discussions to improve participation and employment success for students from disadvantaged backgrounds to remain as an important objective for the UK's higher education sector.

Are Higher Education Students from Disadvantaged Backgrounds More or Less Confident than Their Peers? Dawn Bennett, Paul Koshy and Ian Li

Based on qualitative and quantitative research in Australia, Bennett, Koshy and Li point out that Australian and international studies have repeatedly demonstrated that socio-economic, geographical, cultural or medical disadvantage (in Australia, referred to as 'equity status') among students extends to the labour market. While this necessitates measures to remove barriers to entry–level positions, more broadly it brings into focus the need for student engagement with intentional employability thinking, preparing students to conceptualise, plan and undertake actions that connect their studies to graduate careers.

They find that narrow psychological, individualistic or discipline–bound conceptions of employability can, however, overlook labour market conditions and disadvantages. Therefore, students need to appraise and develop their employability strengths and learning needs within a metacognitive frame. This frame involves the development of inner–value capitals such as self–awareness, self–esteem, self–efficacy, and confidence within the context of broader industrial, professional, and societal awareness.

Their study considers first-year students at a large, urban university in Australia. The findings extend the analysis of student self–assessment of inner–value capitals with a variety of control variables for family background, academic preparedness, academic achievement, gender, and measures of disadvantage relating to socio–economic, migrant background, regional or remote location, and disability status.

Critical 'Employability' within the Realms of Sociology – a Movement toward 'Social Justice', Ricky Gee

In conclusion to this part of the Handbook, Gee starts with reference to the Browne Report (2010) on higher education and student finance which, in the UK, amplified the issue of employability as a key issue in higher education outcomes. Gee's case studies examine in more detail career education and guidance (CEG) activity aiding transition from education to work, and how students inform their own career development with a combination of career development as well as critical theory, to provide a form of critical career studies. Gee observes that students were able to assess how their own social position influences their career, leading to consideration of how career-enactment could aid movements toward 'social justice' at personal and collective levels.

Gee concludes by observing that although his research and the critical nature of learning was undertaken within a cohort studying sociology, the findings and lessons should be applied across other academic disciplines.

CONCLUSION

Inclusion and failure to make the most use of graduate ability and talent are very broad-based, but penetrating, challenges. Furthermore, we know from wider work on diversity and inclusion that even where the technical analysis has been understood, this does not, in itself, drive engagement for corrective action.

In this Handbook with its breadth of view of employability, it has only been possible to illustrate some of the themes of non-inclusion. Gender, sexuality and identification, ethnicity, physical disability, age, caste, and class are further examples of areas of exclusion. Any of these single elements may be further compounded by 'inter-sectionality', or 'combination', where more than one area of exclusion conflates and provides additional obstruction to the identification, selection, and development of all graduate talents.

These chapters illustrate the significant challenges for inclusion, but show that progress is possible and can be achieved. The major challenge to higher education, policy makers, workplaces, and societies is of a scale and complexity to realise the full potential and talents of all those who have benefitted from higher education.

15

Working towards Equitable Outcomes for All through Embedding Activities in the Curriculum

Sarah Flynn, Anna Levett and Judith Baines

INTRODUCTION

Higher education (HE) providers in the UK operate within a political landscape which places expectations on universities to eliminate performance gaps between different groups of students, in relation to a range of data points from recruitment, retention, progression, classification of degrees awarded and progression to highly skilled employment. The Office for Students (OfS)[1], are responsible for ensuring 'every student, whatever their background, has a fulfilling experience of higher education that enriches their lives and careers' (OfS, 2018a).

These expectations have led to considerable institutional change in terms of structures of universities, mission statements, strategic and operational planning. Fullan (1999) argues that for change to be effective it needs to happen not just at institutional level but also at middle-leadership and grassroots levels.

Eliminating awarding[2] gaps between different groups of students, in relation to both the classification of degrees awarded and progression into graduate level employment is a critical imperative for UK HE. Engagement in optional career development activities is more typical for on-campus students and those who have the social and cultural capital to understand its value in securing graduate employment.

Research by The Bridge Group (2017) found that students from lower socio-economic backgrounds participate less often in activities that have greatest currency amongst employers, particularly where these sit outside the curriculum. To address these challenges there is a need to engage with academics across the disciplines, and with student groups with differential outcomes to build confidence and social capital. This requires a significant institutional commitment to equitable employability outcomes.

THE POLITICAL LANDSCAPE FOR ADDRESSING INEQUITY IN STUDENT OUTCOMES

Employability is defined by Advance HE[3] as 'providing the opportunities to develop knowledge, skills, experiences, behaviours, attributes, achievements and attitudes to enable graduates to make successful transitions and contributions, benefitting them, the economy and their communities' (Advance HE, 2016).

This is amongst a political backdrop of several decades of the expansion of UK HE, the introduction and increase of tuition fees, and the codification of achievements in league tables. In England, the OfS are clear that as a marker of students receiving a value-for-money experience, all students from all backgrounds should be able to progress into employment or further study, often expressed as an employability indicator.

Data have been collected for many years on the post-university destinations of graduates and published by the Higher Education Statistics Agency (HESA), formerly as the Destinations of Leavers from Higher Education (DLHE) and since 2020 as Graduate Outcomes. These data have often featured in league tables, comparing one university to another, making the employability of graduates more transparent to prospective students, their families and advisers, and to the general public. The visibility of such employability data has seen a parallel explosion of declarations in institutional strategic plans and visions to the centrality of employability to the student experience.

Academic discourse now acknowledges the role of capital in the employment prospects of students. Tomlinson (2017: 340) argues that we need to move away from dominant skills approaches to employability and 'conceptualise(s) employability as constituting a range of dynamic, interactive forms of capital which are acquired through graduates' lived experiences'. There can be no doubt that the social and cultural capital of students has an impact on their prior experiences, the opportunities available to them, and their inherent awareness and understanding of the value of employability-building activities.

The monitoring of progress towards eliminating gaps in outcomes is supported by access and participation plans which the Office for Students (OfS) require English universities to publish. These focus on comparable outcomes for all non-traditional students by level of economic disadvantage, ethnicity, disability, age, study mode, and experience of care. Universities are now, more than ever, collecting and analysing their own data but also responding and reacting to more data being in the public domain. There is both the expectation for HE to offer value-for-money for those who pay for it, and to offer an equitable experience for those who participate in it.

OUTCOMES FOR NON-TRADITIONAL STUDENTS AND SECTOR-WIDE CHALLENGES

This chapter is offered from a UK perspective, under English policy oversight as HE is a devolved responsibility. It is important to acknowledge that differences in outcomes for the various demographic groups of students is a global concern, as extensively explored in Mountford-Zimdars et al.'s work (2015). Examining perspectives from the United States, Australia, Denmark and Germany alongside that of the UK showed similarities but also important differences in emphasis of areas for concern. In the USA, retention and completion are of most significant concern as the country has 'one of the lowest HE completion rates of OECD countries with only 65.1% of students completing in 6 years … for community colleges that offer Associate Degrees, the rate is 33%' (2015: 8). This issue is compounded by a distinct divide in typical student populations between four-year colleges and community colleges, the latter of which have a much higher proportion of the least advantaged students. Australian institutions have similar concerns about retention and invest heavily in supporting students to complete their studies, whereas the focus is different in Denmark where retention 'does not vary greatly by social origin. Focus is instead on differentials in attainment. Here, there are differences by social class, gender (boys lacking behind) … and ethnicity, often in combination with gender (ethnic minority girls faring better than ethnic minority boys)' (Mountford-Zimdars et al., 2015: 9).

The international sector challenges may vary in their emphasis, but it is fair to say that HE providers, funding bodies and Governments are under increasing public scrutiny and pressure to address differences in access, retention, progression, achievement and the passage into graduate study and employment.

The UK is getting better at understanding the differential outcomes for students. Inequalities exist in terms of where students study, retention, the proportion awarded a good degree, and their prospects for graduate employment (OfS, 2018b) with the most significant disparities being seen between White and BAME[4] students, and within the BAME student population for Black students. Universities UK are clear in their assessment that 'attainment differentials unfairly disadvantage BAME students, with the potential for long-term effects on students' lives after graduation' (2019: 7). In the same report, Universities UK challenged the sector to look at their curricula and ensure that they were diverse, inclusive, and representative, noting that the design of the curriculum 'can have a significant impact on the way that students from different backgrounds and ethnicities respond' (2019: 17).

There is important and equal distinction given to both what is taught and how it is taught, with a greater awareness across HE providers now on what Benson Snyder first termed the hidden curriculum in 1971 – the influence of not only what is said and taught, but what is unsaid, assumed and culturally implied via the norms and values of teachers and institutions.

There has been extensive work in the UK on inclusive curriculum models (Advance HE, 2011) and the introduction of the Race Equality Charter Mark[5] with the guiding principles of:

- Racial inequalities remain significantly manifested within HE, as in everyday situations.
- UK HE cannot reach its full potential until individuals from all ethnic backgrounds can benefit equally from the opportunities it affords.
- Long-term institutional culture change must be the goal, avoiding a deficit approach.
- The complexities of different experiences within the group of BAME staff and students needs to be considered in analysing data and developing actions.
- The intersection of the multiple identities an individual has should be considered wherever possible.

(Advance HE, 2021)

AWARDING GAPS AND THE IMPACT ON GRADUATE EMPLOYMENT

Students from BAME backgrounds are less likely to be awarded a good degree (first or upper second classification[6]) compared with White students (Bunce et al., 2021; Moores et al., 2017; Richardson, 2015). This still applies even when allowing for prior achievement (Bunce et al., 2021) and is applicable in several countries, including the UK, the Netherlands and the USA (Moores et al., 2017). The degree awarding gap between different groups of students has been highlighted for over 20 years (Richardson, 2015) and yet it persists. The overall numbers of students being awarded a good degree has increased over the last decade but the gap in differential outcomes between students from different ethnicities remains (Moores et al., 2017). Being awarded a lower class of degree can limit the opportunities available to graduates, as many employers require at least an upper second for graduate level roles, and universities may not accept a candidate with a lower second on a higher-level course (Moores et al., 2017).

During the last few decades there has been a significant increase in the number of people from BAME backgrounds attending universities to complete degree level study (Singh, 2009). This could be connected to a perceived need from people from these backgrounds that they must gain a degree in order to evidence their skills so they can progress into higher level employment (Connor et al., 2004). Despite this increase in participation and a more diverse student cohort, there is a growing body of evidence which shows students from BAME backgrounds are discriminated against at all stages of their university experience, from recruitment, retention, student satisfaction and classification of degree awarded (Connor et al., 2003, 2004). BAME graduates in the UK are 5 to 15% more likely to be unemployed than White UK graduates six months after they graduate (Zwysen & Longhi, 2018). The underlying reasons for the difference in results are complex.

The opportunities for and experiences of students from BAME communities can be affected in a variety of ways, both inside of university and beyond (Goldenburg, 2014). Measuring employability outcomes is difficult and can overlook the complexities behind inequalities in the labour market (Cranmer, 2006) and the fact that some graduates will take low-level jobs because of financial burdens, not having the luxury to wait longer for a graduate level role (Dacre Pool & Sewell, 2007). There are other contributing aspects that impact on the employment outcomes of graduates, for example the labour market, the distribution of jobs and discrimination in recruitment practices (McCowan, 2015). There is evidence that social class and the university someone attends has some impact on the employment outcomes of graduates (Clarke, 2018). Connor et al. (2003, 2004) noted evidence that BAME students can be clustered at certain universities, mainly post-1992s[7], with low numbers attending other types of university. This will also impact on employment outcomes for BAME graduates as some employers favour universities perceived to be more prestigious over post-1992 institutions, which in turn will impact the diversity of the graduates they recruit.

ENGAGEMENT CHALLENGES IN OPTIONAL CAREER DEVELOPMENT ACTIVITIES

Unfortunately, social background remains a factor in who gets access to graduate programmes and as more people enter the labour market with degrees, the value of qualifications for screening purposes declines, encouraging an increased focus on personal qualities, which in turn can enhance inequalities in accessing graduate roles, especially for those perceived to have less social capital (Brown et al., 2003; Clarke, 2018). Students often leave university unprepared to enter the labour market and the impact of early career indecisiveness can be a precursor to struggling to find meaningful employment (Clark, 2005; Greenbank, 2011). Having a career plan is an important factor in moving forwards with career decisions, especially if done before the student graduates which will increase the likelihood of finding a graduate level opportunity (Clark, 2005; Shury et al., 2017).

Universities need to ensure their graduates are equipped not just with the skills needed for this global labour market, but also the social capital required to compete with other, more privileged graduates. Careers professionals often struggle to get students to focus on taking steps to plan their careers whilst they are still studying and many students suffer with procrastination and unrealistic career expectations, as well as not fully understanding how their studies and university experiences relate to the future world of work (Clark, 2005). We know from research carried out by The Bridge Group (2017) that students from low socio-economic groups usually have lower participation rates when it comes to the activities that employers see as most valuable. Engagement with opt-in employability activities can be more common with academically high-achieving students, those living in halls of residence or those who have more privileged backgrounds. Students who might benefit most from additional support are not usually the ones who are able or are choosing to engage with extra-curricular programmes (The Bridge Group, 2017). There are differences in engagement from other under-represented groups, such as mature students, who may not engage with extra-curricular activities at all, partly due to caring commitments at home, whereas the opposite is true of more 'traditional' students studying at an elite university (Bathmaker et al., 2013).

Often a key factor in why students do not engage with extra-curricular activities is because they do not see how the activities could be linked to helping them compete in the graduate labour market (Greenbank, 2015). Some students also wait and see if opportunities come their way, leaving things to fate instead of proactively engaging in activities that could be of benefit to them (Greenbank, 2015). This technique is rarely successful, and moving careers education and employability into the curriculum ensures that all students get the benefit in a timely manner. If these activities are only offered as extra-curricular then there will be unequal access to the types of social capital development which are valued by employers, as widening participation[8] students are less likely to engage with extra-curricular activities than students from more 'traditional' backgrounds (Stuart et al., 2011).

VALUE OF CURRICULUM-BASED ACTIVITIES

With the pressure on universities to improve graduate employment outcomes, it is no wonder that there has been increased interest in embedding employability skills development activities in undergraduate modules. Students are encouraged to enhance their employability skills, and therefore social capital, through additional activities within and outside of their studies (Bathmaker et al., 2013). Embedding activities which help to develop social capital or allow students to practice in work-related environments, gives widening participation, often first in family, working-class students an increased chance of succeeding in gaining graduate level roles against their more privileged peers.

For graduates to stand a good chance of finding a graduate level role they are happy in, career learning is essential (Dacre Pool & Sewell, 2007). Generally, in universities in the UK, the approach has been to offer extra-curricular provision for developing employability capital or to embed skills development activities within the curriculum (Cranmer, 2006). Students want employability skills to be embedded within their degrees as standard (Crowne et al., 2020), and it is recommended by the National Association of Colleges and Employers (NACE) that this is done from the first year (Crowne et al., 2020). Embedding activities is more effective than offering optional programmes (Cranmer, 2006) and career readiness activities have been shown in some studies to enhance academic outcomes for students (Crowne et al., 2020). Often, this type of training is offered by careers services as an extra-curricular activity, which can result in a missed opportunity to make links between the world of work and the programme of study (Crowne et al., 2020). The chance to embed this content within modules offers the opportunity to make activities credit-bearing which demonstrates their importance and makes the activities more valuable to students, whilst increasing participation (Crowne et al., 2020). Providing chances for students to practise recruitment activities, followed by self-evaluation and reflection can increase self-efficacy which in turn can increase the chance of a graduate being successful in gaining a role they want (Dacre Pool & Sewell, 2007).

Academics play an important part in the career development of undergraduate students, both formally and informally, as part of the curriculum and beyond (Schlesinger et al., 2021). Students will often approach academics they know to discuss career options and can be more likely to turn to them, and friends or family, than to approach university careers professionals, who they may not know as well. Even where academics are willing to discuss career plans with students, there can be barriers, such as lack of time or confidence in advising on a wide range of career goals, different to their own experiences (Schlesinger et al., 2021).

Bringing careers professionals into the curriculum as part of embedded activities can solve both these problems. Academics are supported by qualified experts who can cover a wide range of job opportunities and sectors, and students get the chance to meet careers professionals as a core part of their studies. This provides equality of access to professional careers support, rather than forcing a decision from a student between taking a shift at their part-time job or having to sort out additional support for caring responsibilities to attend an appointment with a careers professional outside of teaching time. Many students would not be able to prioritise the careers appointment and may therefore miss out altogether. Having careers education content embedded in courses helps to make the careers service a core part of the university experience and not just a standalone office that students are referred to (Dey & Cruzvergara, 2014).

DIVERSITY CHALLENGES FOR EMPLOYERS

It is important to employers to increase the diversity of their graduate intake, especially since the introduction of the Equality Act in 2010 and more recent global campaigns, such as Black Lives Matter. There are sound economic reasons for them doing this:

- If social mobility in the UK increased to the average level in Western Europe, gross domestic product could be roughly 2% higher (Sutton Trust, 2019).
- It benefits a company if the workforce reflects the diversity of its current and potential clients.
- A diverse workforce leads to diversity of thought and creativity, leading to innovation.

- 'Business leaders need to see that by tackling race and adopting an inclusive culture, they can improve almost all parts of their organisation, including wellbeing, engagement, sustainability and innovation – which all then contribute to the bottom line'. (Pasha, 2021: 2).

The dialogue around bias in recruitment practices is long-standing. Rare (2011) found that assessment activities range from the well designed, effectively managed face-to-face assessments which could eliminate bias, to badly designed assessments that lead to blatant bias. The report recommended that all assessors are trained in unconscious bias and cultural differences and examine their recruitment practices. Revisiting recruitment processes for bias was also supported by a recommendation in a UK Government research paper (BIS, 2015) which advised employers to monitor the social mobility of candidates. Manstead (2018) highlighted that if a workplace is prone to middle-class values this could lead students from lower socio-economic backgrounds to feel out of place during the recruitment process. In addition, the UK Government (2015) recommended employers give helpful feedback to rejected candidates to help them improve early in the recruitment process. Careers services are also keen for candidate feedback as they can then help students improve their performance in the future.

The global pandemic of 2020 necessitated a swift move to online recruitment processes for employers. The Institute of Student Employers (ISE) Recruitment Survey 2020 found that 87% of organisations revised processes to improve diversity focussing on removing barriers to recruitment, often based on protected characteristics. However, socio-economic factors such as family background, income and education are not always monitored. The survey showed that 62% of employers had formal diversity targets and 89% were taking a range of actions to increase diversity. At the top of the target list was sex and gender (48%), race (47%) and social mobility (24%). Overall, targeting groups, targeting different universities and tailored marketing materials were popular activities for attracting potential candidates in 2019/20.

However, 46% of employers found psychometric tests the most effective way to narrow down the field which Rare (2011) cited as presenting barriers to students from BAME and lower socio-economic backgrounds. Employers appear to be reluctant to make more radical changes to the recruitment process itself. Therefore, students need support from careers services to navigate the system.

Despite taking actions to increase diversity, the ISE/Debut Survey 2020 shows that there is more that needs to be done as employers still face barriers in their aims to increase diversity:

- Jobseekers are sceptical about the fairness of recruitment processes.
- Candidates want to see that they fit with the organisation and hear about the experiences of diverse employees; this is more important to non-white and female candidates, key target groups for ISE employers.

Visibility, and representation, are important, and recognised by the Institute of Student Employers: 'It is important for students to be able to see people who look like them or somewhat represent them, and for students to be able to say "Hey, they're like me, if they can do it so can I"' (ISE, 2019).

Around 87% of employers engaged in careers fairs in 2019/20; contributing to the curriculum was only used by 15% of those surveyed (ISE, 2020). Yet careers services are increasingly moving to embedding their work within the curriculum to achieve equality of access to opportunities and scalability. Experience tells us that the larger employers who engage within curricula often do so to raise awareness of or change perceptions of their brand. Large employers do not have infinite resources to visit all universities and have tended to engage with a small number that are often the more elite universities with smaller numbers of diverse students. The global pandemic of 2020 has levelled the playing field somewhat as employers have been able to push out their own events via their own digital platforms without number restrictions, enabling students from a wider range of universities to attend, however this is still outside of the curriculum and difficult for time-poor students to attend. Also, it is not yet known whether these activities will continue in the post-pandemic recruitment landscape.

University approaches to teaching and learning are becoming more blended and hybrid in a post-pandemic and more digitally enabled environment, with one potential impact being students less likely to be on campus as often and therefore reducing opportunities to be involved in extra and co-curricular activities. This makes curriculum engagement even more important moving forward, whether it is face-to-face or blended. The ISE/Debut Survey (2020) found that respondents from post-92 universities are more likely to find academics helpful for their careers and all students rated 'how to succeed at assessment centres' as one of their top topics on what they wanted to know from employers.

This makes the Assessment Centre Experience (ACE), the case study within the chapter, the perfect employer vehicle for engaging students.

CASE STUDY OF UNIVERSITY OF HERTFORDSHIRE'S ASSESSMENT CENTRE EXPERIENCE

Context

The Assessment Centre Experience (ACE) is embedded within modules for over 3,000 students per year at the University of Hertfordshire (UH). This provides equal access opportunity for all students. Around 70% of undergraduate UK/EU students at UH come from widening participation backgrounds. These students may be less likely to have strong networks with graduate employers, work experience in relevant organisations or the socio-economic capital that is often required to access the opportunities that support employability skills development or network expansion (Peeters et al., 2019). Working with Smart Resourcing Solutions, an external partner, ACE provides students with a realistic and safe environment to practise recruitment activities and get feedback so they can prepare for recruitment processes.

Aims of the Activity

This case study was based around the following research questions:

- How does having an assessment centre simulation embedded in modules impact undergraduate students?
- Would undergraduate students prefer employability activities to be embedded within their degree, as extra-curricular activity or not at all at university?
- Do undergraduate students think it is the responsibility of universities to offer employability skills development activities?

Description

Eleven students who had been involved in the ACE in 2020 completed a questionnaire. They included representatives from all but one of the academic schools that take part in ACE. Of the participants, 73% self-identified as women and 27% as men, 55% were international students and 45% home/EU students. Around 18% self-identified as White, 73% were Black/Black British or Asian/Asian British and 9% preferred not to state their ethnicity. Of these, 17% were first-generation to attend university from their family, 91% of participants were aged 18–24, with one mature student aged 45–54 taking part. Three students were interviewed. One identified as a woman and two as men. Two were UK/home students and one international. They were all from different academic schools of study, with two aged 18–24 and one mature student. Thematic analysis was used to interpret the data collected.

DISCUSSION

How Does Having an Assessment Centre Simulation Embedded in Modules Impact Undergraduate Students?

Fourteen out of fifteen participants referred to the ACE as a positive, developmental experience. A key topic that emerged was how people related the ACE to their professional development, or to real-life recruitment activities and how they now knew what to expect or how to improve. The chance to practise and get feedback gives people the opportunity to improve and become more at ease with the situation (de Janasz and Forret, 2008).

Participant 1 (questionnaire) stated:

> I'm better prepared and more confident to go through an actual placement or job application. The feedback was extremely valuable and helpful as it highlighted both my strengths and weaknesses.

Do Undergraduate Students Think it is the Responsibility of Universities to Offer Employability Skills Development Activities?

Around 86% of responses showed that the participants felt that the university had a responsibility to offer employability activities as part of their degree. This aligns with the pressure on universities from a variety of stakeholders to ensure students are ready for employment as soon as they graduate (Bridgstock, 2009). Employers regularly feed back to universities that they expect graduates to have had employability skills developed alongside their studies (Clarke, 2018) and this matched the views of most of the participants.

Participant 1 (questionnaire):

> A degree is to prepare a student to, ultimately, get absorbed in the job market. It's important that universities help students to better market themselves.

Participant 11 (questionnaire):

> Getting help in preparing for a career after graduation is very important.

Interviewee C, a mature student, had their own grown-up children of typical university age. They expressed how important employability activities were for all students, not just who they described as 'the youngsters', referring to 18–24-year-olds, but also for mature students, who had never experienced the graduate labour market and recruitment processes for graduate level jobs. They felt these were very different from the more informal interview processes or 'chats' they had taken part in previously for non-graduate roles. Graduate level recruitment can be different to other types, and we know that many recent graduates have been found to be ill-equipped to do well in interviews (Crowne et al., 2020).

Interviewee C:

> I think absolutely they have a responsibility. It's not just taking your money and saying good luck ... ... and they can't guarantee everybody getting a job or anything, absolutely not, but they need to get that foundation in there. And I think ACE is one of the steps of making you ready, ready for, whatever life is going to throw at you when you finish uni.

Would Undergraduate Students Prefer Employability Activities to be Embedded within their Degree, as Extra-curricular Activity or not at all at University?

Around 79% of participants thought that employability or careers-related activities should be embedded within the curriculum. No one thought they should not be offered at all by the university. A key theme that emerged was the importance of having the employability/careers related activities embedded within the curriculum, highlighting the pressure on universities to deliver these skills for students as well as other stakeholders (Bridgstock, 2009; Caballero et al., 2020; Cranmer, 2006; Tomlinson, 2017).

Participant 3 (questionnaire):

> I consider it necessary to have employability/ careers activities in my course.

Interviewee A:

> So, this actually teaches you how to get a real-life job. Like, they give you a list of jobs, you chose the job you interviewed [for]. Group work is the same [as for a real assessment centre], and even the presentation is the same, so I'd 100% say that yes, this should be part of the modules.

Interviewee C:

> [This should be compulsory] because otherwise people like me who actually need this kind of thing wouldn't do it. And I absolutely think it should be compulsory. I think it's essential …

Another key part of this theme was that many of the participants would not have or could not have taken part in the ACE if it had not been part of their module. This aligns with the findings of The Bridge Group (2017) whose research found that those from more disadvantaged backgrounds were unable to or less likely to engage with the extra-curricular activities that employers tend to value.

Participant 3 (questionnaire):

> I might have ignored it as there is already so much pressure this year.

Time, work pressures, lack of confidence and financial pressures were all quoted as possible barriers to taking part if the employability activities were not included in the curriculum. By not being able to take part in extra-curricular activities students could be missing out on valuable social and cultural capital, putting them at a disadvantage when applying for jobs (de Janasz and Forret, 2008).

Interviewee A stated:

> Yeah, I would have done it, but in all honesty, I would have not done it this year because I wouldn't have had the time, 'cause if it wasn't part of my module, then I had other assignments, work, and lectures to attend, so depending on the time that I had I would do it. I would definitely want to do it, but then, maybe time would have not allowed me to do it.

They also referred to the amount of credit the module was worth and how students sometimes made choices on how hard to work on an assignment/topic, based on how much weighting the assignment was given. Making an activity credit-bearing demonstrates its value to students and increases engagement (Crowne et al., 2020).

The interviewees stated it was important to make ACE compulsory, as people needed the practice and the beneficial outcomes of taking part. Many universities offer these sorts of activities as opt-in (Cranmer, 2006), but we can see how the students in this study value these activities being embedded. Students expect these skills to be embedded as standard (Crowne et al., 2020) and having the activities embedded is more impactful than stand-alone programmes (Cranmer, 2006).

Interviewee C:

> I don't think I'm good enough. Therefore, I wouldn't have attended it if it had been voluntary, and I think that's a big shame … it needs to be compulsory, otherwise they'll miss out on it. And, and it's a shame.

Key Learning

Students involved in the research valued the ACE and found it beneficial to their professional development, helping to build their confidence. The students felt that universities had a responsibility to be offering employability activities and that these should be embedded within their degree. The ACE exemplifies this approach as a true partnership between the careers and employment team, Smart Resourcing Solutions (SRS), academics, employers, and students, and it has been recognised by Advance HE in 2020 in their Collaborative Awards for Teaching Excellence.

CONCLUSION

A contemporary careers service acts as a connector of all stakeholders, bringing them together into an employability ecosystem, creating 'connected communities' as described by Cruzvergara and Dey 'forward-thinking career professionals will recognize the opportunity to activate the large and complex network that exists on a college campus in order to connect key stakeholders' (2014: 11).

This is particularly important with regard to social mobility, as students need to be connected to supportive communities, offering a range of experiences and networks helping them to navigate recruitment processes and to learn about the full range of options open to them after graduation. A key aim for a careers service should be to deliver personalised but scalable services underpinned by strong networks. The ACE is an example of this with students given the chance to choose exercises that fit with their potential careers, scaled up via integration into the curriculum supported by flexible online and technological approaches.

Whereas, in the past, careers services used to protect their territory in the employability space, often seeing others offering careers support as diluting their expertise; they had to make the shift to utilise all stakeholders and influencers effectively to build a university-wide community of support for students. Employability and student success are the shared responsibility of the university community, and the careers services can reach out and help to embed that culture change, to be the 'orchestrators of opportunities' (Dhindsa, 2019). This extends beyond the university-wide community and embraces employers, alumni, professional bodies, and third-party providers, plus others.

Until HE has eliminated the awarding gaps between different groups of students, in relation to both the classification of degrees awarded and progression into graduate level employment, work to embed employability development in the curriculum must continue. It is no longer acceptable to rely on student engagement in optional career development activities as the path to developing the necessary social and cultural capital that will assist them in securing graduate employment. We must meet the needs and support the successful outcomes of all our students, and work across our universities and disciplines to achieve this. Endeavours such as those described here require clear, unequivocal institutional commitment to the development of employability outcomes. Employability strategies must focus on those students for whom gaps in progression and graduate employment exist, and must offer a full range of curriculum-based interventions and approaches as a foundation to the student experience.

Notes

1 The independent regulator of higher education in England maintains the register of approved degree-awarding bodies and provides the governance structure for quality and standards.
2 The literature uses attainment/ awarding to refer to the classification of degree given to a student. Our preference is for awarding as this de-centres the student as the source of the gap and centres the actions and inactions of the awarding body.
3 Advance HE is a member-led, sector-owned body with strategic goals to enhance confidence and trust in higher education, address inequalities and advance education to meet the evolving needs of students.
4 BAME, Black, Asian and Minority Ethnic students, who elsewhere might be referred to as students of colour or global majority students. We acknowledge that the use of such a term fails to adequately recognise the individual ethnicities represented within and welcome moves across the sector to move to more precise populations. However, much of the literature on this topic makes a simple delineation

between White and BAME students and therefore is retained here when referring to sources and data where it is used this way.

5 The Race Equality Charter Mark provides a framework through which institutions work to identify and self-reflect on institutional and cultural barriers standing in the way of BAME staff and students.

6 UK degree classification relates to a grade point average as first class 4.0+, upper second 3.25–3.75, lower second as 2.5–3.0 and third as 1.75–2.25.

7 Universities who gained their degree-awarding powers in 1992 following an expansion of higher education in the UK; these universities typically followed vocational and technical curricula although they have since diversified.

8 Widening participation is used to describe students who belong to a demographic population who access university in lower proportions than average. It is typically linked to age, race, socio-economic status, disability, or experience of living in state-supported care.

REFERENCES

Advance HE (2011) *Inclusive curriculum design in HE*, available at www.advance-he.ac.uk/knowledge-hub/inclusive-curriculum-design-higher-education (Accessed: 30 June 2022).

Advance HE (2016) *Embedding employability in higher education*, Advance HE frameWORKS series – Essential frameworks for enhancing student success.

Advance HE (2021) *The Race Equality Charter Mark,* available at www.advance-he.ac.uk/equality-charters/race-equality-charter#overview (Accessed: 30 June 2022).

Bathmaker, A., Ingram, N. & Waller, R. (2013) Higher education, social class and the mobilisation of capitals: recognising and playing the game, *British Journal of Sociology of Education*, 34(5-6), 723–743.

Business, Information and Skills BIS (2015) *Understanding employers' graduate recruitment and selection practices*, Research paper no. 231, BIS, HM Government.

Bridgstock, R. (2009) The graduate attributes we've overlooked: enhancing graduate employability through career management skills, *Higher Education Research and Development*, 28(1), 31–44.

Brown, P., Hesketh, A. & Williams, S. (2003) Employability in a knowledge-driven economy, *Journal of Education and Work*, 16(2), 107–126.

Bunce, L., King, N., Saran, S. & Talib, N. (2021) Experiences of black and minority ethnic (BME) students in higher education: applying self-determination theory to understand the BME attainment gap, *Studies in Higher Education*, 46(3), 534–547.

Caballero, G., Álvarez-González, P. & López-Miguens, M. J. (2020) How to promote the employability capital of university students? Developing and validating scales, *Studies in Higher Education*, 45(12), 1–19.

Clark, T. (2005) The business profession: a mandatory, noncredit, cocurricular career preparation program for undergraduate business majors, *Business Communication Quarterly*, 68(3), 271–289.

Clarke, M. (2018) Rethinking graduate employability: the role of capital, individual attributes and context, *Studies in Higher Education*, 43(11), 1923–1937.

Connor, H., Tyers, C., Davis, S. & Tackey, N. D. (with contributions from Modood, T.) (2003) *Minority ethnic students in higher education: interim report*, Institute for Employment Studies (Research Report No. 448). London: Department for Education and Skills.

Connor, H., Tyers, C., Modood, T. & Hillage, J. (2004) *Why the difference? A closer look at higher education minority ethnic students and graduates* (Research Report No. 552). London: Department for Education and Skills. Report RR448.

Cranmer, S. (2006) Enhancing graduate employability: best intentions and mixed outcomes, *Studies in Higher Education*, 31(2), 169–184.

Crowne, K. A., Brown, M., Durant, D., Baburaj, Y., Hornberger, P., McCloskey, D. & Vike, L. (2020) A program for embedding career activities in multiple core business courses, *The International Journal of Management Education*, 18(3), 100421.

Dacre Pool, L. & Sewell, P. (2007) The key to employability: developing a practical model of graduate employability, *Education & Training*, 49(4), 277–289.

Dey, F. & Cruzvergara, C. Y. (2014) Evolution of career services in higher education, *New Directions for Student Services*, 148, 5–15. Available from: www.nacada.ksu.edu/Portals/0/ Clearinghouse/advisingissues/documents/Dey%20Cruzvergara%202014.pdf

Dhindsa, A. M. (2019) *What's next for career services: increasing well-being and preparing students for the future of work,* Master of Applied Positive Psychology (MAPP) Capstone Projects, 162. https://repository.upenn.edu/mapp_capstone/162

Fullan, M. (1999) *Change forces: the sequel*. London: Falmer.

Goldenberg, B.M. (2014) White Teachers in Urban Classrooms: Embracing Non-White Students' Cultural Capital For Better Teaching and Learning, *Urban Education,*49(1), 111-144.

Greenbank, P. (2011) 'I'd rather talk to someone I know' – the role of network in undergraduate career decision-making, *Research in Post-Compulsory Education,* 16(1), 31–45.

Greenbank, P. (2015) Still focusing on the 'essential 2:1': exploring student attitudes to extra-curricular activities, *Education & Training*, 57(2), 184–203.

Institute of Student Employers (2019) *The student employer: diversity matters but action matters more*, no.8, summer. London: ISE.

Institute of Student Employers (2020) *Student recruitment survey 2020: challenge and resilience in the year of Covid-19*. London: ISE.

Institute of Student Employers & Debut (2020) *What do students want? Listening to the voices of young jobseekers*. London: ISE & Debut.

de Janasz, S. C. & Forret, M. L. (2008) Learning the art of networking: a critical skill for enhancing social capital and career success, *Journal of Management Education*, 32(5), 629–650.

Manstead, A. S. R. (2018) The psychology of social class: how socioeconomic status impacts thought, feelings, and behaviour, *British Journal of Social Psychology*, 57(2), 267–291.

McCowan, T. (2015) Should universities promote employability?, *Theory and Research in Education*, 13(3), 267–285.

Moores, E., Birdi, G. K. & Higson, H. E. (2017) Placement work experience may mitigate lower achievement levels of Black and Asian vs. White students at university, *Frontiers in Psychology*, 8(1518).

Mountford-Zimdars, A., Sabri, D., Moore, J., Sanders, J., Jones, S. & Higham, L. (2015) *Causes of differences in student outcomes*, a report to HEFCE by King's College London, ARC Network and the University of Manchester, available at https://dera.ioe.ac.uk/23653/1/HEFCE2015_diffout.pdf (Accessed: 30 June 2022).

Office for Students (2018a) *Office for Students Strategy 2018–2021, Open Government Licence 3.0*, available from www.nationalarchives.gov.uk/doc/open-government-licence/ version/3/ (Accessed: 30 June 2022).

Office for Students (2018b) *Topic briefing: black and minority ethnic (BAME) students,* available at https://www.officeforstudents.org.uk/publications/office-for-students-strategy-2018-to-2021/ (Accessed: 30 June 2022).

Pasha, N. (2021) *The equity effect*, Henley Business School, University of Reading.

Peeters, E. R. R., Nelissen, J., De Cuyper, N., Forrier, A., Verbruggen, M. & De Witte, H. (2019) Employability capital: a conceptual framework tested through expert analysis, *Journal of Career Development,* 46(2), 79–93.

Rare (2011) *Class, race and graduate recruitment: best practices*, available from www.rarerecruitment.co.uk/static/research/2011_Class_race_and_graduate_recruitment.pdf (Accessed: 30 June 2022).

Richardson, J. T. E. (2015) The under-attainment of ethnic minority students in UK higher education: what we know and what we don't know, *Journal of Further and Higher Education*, 39(2), 278–291.

Schlesinger, J., O'Shea, C. & Blesso, J. (2021) Undergraduate student career development and career center services: faculty perspectives, *The Career Development Quarterly*, 69(2), 145–157.

Shury, J., Vivian, D., Turner, C. & Downing, C. (2017) *Planning for success: graduates' career planning and its effect on graduate outcomes*, DfE research report, no. DFE-RR668, Department for Education, Manchester, available from https://assets.publishing.service.gov.uk/government/uploads/system/uploads/attachment_data/file/604170/Graduates__career_planning_and_its_effect_on_their_outcomes.pdf (Accessed: 30 June 2022).

Singh, G. (2009) *A synthesis of research evidence. Black and minority ethnic (BME) students' participation in higher education: improving retention and success.* London: Higher Education Academy.

Stuart, M., Lido, C., Morgan, J., Solomon, L. & May, S. (2011) The impact of engagement with extracurricular activities on the student experience and graduate outcomes for widening participation populations, *Active Learning in Higher Education*, 12(3), 203–215.

Sutton Trust (2019) *Social mobility in the workplace: an employer's guide.* London: The Sutton Trust.

The Bridge Group (2017) *Social mobility and university careers services*, A report by the Bridge Group, funded by the UPP Foundation. London: The Bridge Group.

Tomlinson, M. (2017) Forms of graduate capital and their relationship to graduate employability, *Education & Training*, 59(4), 338–352.

Universities UK and the National Union of Students (2019) *Black, Asian and minority ethnic student attainment at UK universities: #ClosingTheGap.* London: Universities UK.

Zwysen, W. & Longhi, S. (2018) Employment and earning differences in the early career of ethnic minority British graduates: the importance of university career, parental background and area characteristics, *Journal of Ethnic and Migration Studies,* 44(1), 154–172.

16

Supporting the Employability of Neurodivergent Graduates

Keren Coney

INTRODUCTION

Neurodiversity is a term first defined by sociologist Judy Singer, who argued that the 'neurologically different' should have a political category of their own (to add to the familiar categories of race, gender and class), in order to promote understanding of the social model of disability (Singer, 1999). As noted by Griffin and Pollak (2009), the term provides a less negative and more empowering concept of 'difference' rather than 'deficit'; it also acknowledges the comorbidity and even overlapping of some conditions. Although the term has become popular within the media and in international documentaries, from an academic perspective, neurodiversity suffers from conflicting definitions (Doyle, 2020). For many, neurodiversity is an umbrella term and includes dyspraxia, dyslexia, autism, dyscalculia, attention deficit hyperactivity disorder (ADHD) and Tourette syndrome (Clouder et al., 2020). Others adhere to a broader concept of neurodiversity, which includes conditions such as personality disorders that are responses to early trauma, changes to cognitive ability due to brain injury or mental health conditions. For the purposes of this chapter, this broader definition of neurodiversity will be assumed; the terms 'disability' and 'disabled' are adopted when referring to studies, models or employment-related terminology where these descriptions have been used. It should be noted that one element shared by all neurodivergent individuals is the fact that their conditions are non-visible and therefore not necessarily apparent; this can lead to misunderstanding from others.

The past two decades have seen a steady rise in the numbers of disabled students in higher education institutions in many countries, including Australia (Veitch et al., 2018), Israel (Lipka et al., 2020), the USA (Smith et al., 2019), Norway (Svendby, 2020), Italy (Biggeri et al., 2020) and Spain (Morina & Perera, 2020). This increase is also observed regarding numbers of neurodivergent students (Clouder et al., 2020). Reasons for this increase include the introduction of international disability legislation, such as the United Nations Conventions on Rights of Persons with Disabilities (UN, 2006) and the subsequent reiteration of these rights in the 2030 Agenda for Sustainable Development (UN, 2015), which highlights the importance of ensuring equal access for disabled people to all levels of education by 2030 (Biggeri et al., 2020). Another suggested cause for the larger proportions of disabled students is the greater recognition of disabilities, particularly those which were previously poorly understood, such as some neurodivergent conditions, as well as increased diagnosis (Veitch et al., 2018), in addition to a greater recognition of the capabilities of disabled individuals by society. The incorporation of new technologies to assist with learning in education could also have led to more disabled people viewing higher education as a viable option (Morina & Perera, 2020).

When it comes to employment, some neurodivergent graduates have historically fared less well than neurotypical graduates, both in terms of un- and under-employment (Krzeminska et al., 2019). A recent UK-based study of the destinations of graduates found that of all disabled graduates, those with autism are least likely to be employed, while those autistic individuals who were in employment were least likely to indicate that their qualification level had been required for their job role (Allen & Coney, 2021). Unfortunately, these disappointing outcomes for autistic graduates in particular are widely recognised in the literature (Bublitz et al., 2017; Pesonen et al., 2021). Doyle (2020) notes that there is persistent evidence of greater proportions of neurodivergent individuals within prison populations and long-term unemployment and urges that there are economic, social and moral imperatives for more to be done to support these individuals.

Work is recognised as a way in which people find purpose, status in the community, self-confidence and economic wellbeing (Pratt et al., 2014); being employed is a human right (Nolan & Gleeson, 2017). Unemployment therefore has implications for fulfilment of potential and for independence; there is also greater vulnerability to mental health conditions for individuals who are not in work (WHO, 2011). Conversely, the benefits of employment include opportunities for social interaction, a sense of achievement, an opportunity to contribute to society, better health outcomes and an improved quality of life and wellbeing, in addition to income (Chen et al., 2015; Waddell & Burton, 2006). In recent years, the increased use of 'social value' measures at an organisational level has provided growing evidence of the case for including disabled people in the workplace; these measures indicate that the benefits reach beyond the disabled individuals themselves and instead are of real benefit to organisations and broader society (CSJ, 2021). One US-based study found that companies that had improved their disability inclusion policies and practices were four times more likely to have shareholder returns that outperformed their peers (Accenture, 2018).

MODELS OF DISABILITY

There are a number of models which seek to define disability and provide a basis for creating strategies on how best to meet the needs of individuals. The medical, or biological, model defines individuals as disabled by their impairments and views these differences as the cause of challenges for those individuals. In some countries, however, the social model of disability is proposed as an effective approach to support disabled individuals, highlighting the need for society to take responsibility for the removal of any barriers, rather than the individuals. Sayce (2011) concurs with this view of disability as a social construct, noting that individuals are often 'disabled' by barriers to participation as much as by any physical or cognitive disability. These barriers to participation can include the attitudes and perceptions of those in the workplace (McMullin & Shuey, 2006). Yusof et al. (2020: 1146) note that the social model, while only a limited explanation of the barriers disabled individuals may face and not fully adopted in all countries, 'can be a tool to improve their lives'.

The World Health Organisation International Classification of Functioning Disability and Health (ICF) utilises a biopsychosocial model to describe health-related functioning (World Health Organisation, 2002). This biopsychosocial model captures the biological factors of disability that will in turn have an impact on how an individual processes the world (psychological factors), while their experiences will also be influenced by their environment and context (social factors). Shakespeare and Watson (2001: 24, in Guldberg, 2020) argue that there is a need for consideration of how 'impairments' can have individual and social consequences and state that these factors cannot be easily separated. Svendby (2020) concurs with this, opting for a relational understanding that both acknowledges disability as a biological phenomenon (drawing from the medical model) and as a restriction of involvement that individuals experience due to social oppression and inequality (referring to the social model). Guldberg (2020) goes one step further by endorsing a biopsychosocial-insider model, which considers how the medical, psychological and social factors interrelate and have an impact on the experiences of an individual. Guldberg asserts that the insider perspective – that of the disabled individual – must be at the forefront of considerations relating to them.

What are the practical implications of these varying models of disability? Doyle (2020: 114) notes that using the biopsychosocial model in employment settings leads to an approach which becomes 'more about adjusting the fit between the person and their environment, than about treating a disorder'. There is no legal obligation for the individual to change according to their workplace; the requirement sits with the employing organisation (Doyle, 2020). However, given that the biopsychosocial model also requires an understanding of how the neurodivergent condition affects an individual, it would perhaps be helpful if that person were able to articulate this when seeking to enter employment. Booth (2016: 15), an autistic author and co-chair of the UK's TUC Disabled Workers' Committee, advocates that workplaces should change without waiting for an individual to request this change: 'it would be far better for an autistic individual to arrive at an autism-friendly workplace rather than confronting many distressing factors, identifying each one individually and demanding adjustments'. In light of this, employers could consider ways in which they can provide recruitment processes and workplaces that are accessible to all. Following the biopsychosocial-insider model, employers could gain the 'insider' perspective by consulting with neurodivergent graduates and, in doing so, radically enhance their understanding and increase the accessibility of the workplace for these individuals.

CHALLENGES FOR NEURODIVERGENT GRADUATES SEEKING TO ENTER EMPLOYMENT

Neurodivergent students and graduates may encounter a number of challenges when seeking to enter the labour market, including concerns around sharing information about their disability and uncertainty regarding adjustments. Employers may have a lack of understanding of neurodiversity, or have uncertainty about how to provide effective adjustments. Challenges relating to disclosure, adjustments, the recruitment process and employer neurodiversity awareness are outlined below.

Disclosure and Adjustments

Disclosure is a term frequently used to describe the action of an individual sharing information about their disability or health condition with an employer. In recent times, some in the disability community have voiced a dislike for this term, due to the suggestion that disclosure implies the sharing of information that is in some way embarrassing, causing a number of people in support roles to use terms such as 'sharing' your disability instead. The challenge can be that due to its use for many years, students and graduates tend to be more familiar with utilising the term 'disclosure of disability' and understand the meaning of this.

Madaus (2006) notes that the decision to share information about a disability with an employer adds complexity to the job search and interview process for a graduate. Some studies have found that individuals with invisible disabilities are likely to perceive more barriers to disclosure than those with physical disabilities (Norstedt, 2019); Nolan and Gleeson (2017) reported that graduates with mental health conditions were less likely to disclose, due to fears of stigma and discrimination. These fears can be related to past negative experiences of sharing information about their disability, either with a recruiter, a line manager or even with colleagues. One UK-based study of disabled graduates (Cooke, 2015) found that 76% of disabled graduates were concerned that potential employers would discriminate against them; other specific concerns were that they would be seen as a hassle or nuisance (72%). This can lead to non-disclosure, which Cooke (2015) highlights as an issue of great importance: if an employer is unaware of an applicant or employee's disability, they are unable to make the adjustments required. This issue has implications for the employee's rights, in addition to the employer's legal responsibilities and can result in a disabled person underperforming, or missing out on the opportunity to demonstrate their potential in the recruitment process or workplace. However, some studies have found that sharing information about a disability did not lead to a positive response from employers or to suitable adjustments (Bublitz et al., 2017; von Schrader et al., 2014). In many cases, this may not be due to negative attitudes towards disabled applicants, but rather a lack of understanding or awareness on the part of employers.

The Recruitment Process

One of the key reasons why the proportions of neurodivergent graduates entering employment are lower than non-disabled graduates are the challenges experienced in the recruitment process. These can include issues with timed online psychometric tests for those with processing challenges and misunderstanding of meaning in interview questions for those who may take a literal understanding of vague questions such as 'tell us about yourself'. Even with recent technological developments, which have resulted in areas of the recruitment process being conducted virtually, new barriers have been experienced. One example of this is the lack of opportunity to clarify the meaning of a question during automated online interviews, where there is no interviewer present at the time of the recorded interview. Moss (2021: 805), a neurodivergent author and attorney, argues that technology used by employers to screen video interviews demonstrates bias against disabled candidates: 'while AI promises to streamline and reduce costs associated with recruitment and hiring, it has had a prejudicial effect on job seekers with disabilities who already experience systematic oppression'.

Some neurodivergent graduates may have particular challenges with interviews, due to the complex social interaction involved with these situations. These could include issues with interpreting the body language of the interviewers, making appropriate amounts of eye contact and moderating tone of voice while also seeking to focus on effectively answering the interview questions. Graduates can be supported by careers practitioners in universities to prepare for these situations (Chen et al., 2015), but Sarrett (2018) notes that real benefits for disabled individuals would occur if employers modified social aspects of job interviews to make them more accessible, rather than there being a need for individuals to be trained to navigate the interview process. Perhaps then, in addition to supporting neurodivergent students and graduates to prepare for interviews, employers should consider how they assess the abilities of candidates and explore other ways to do this; some examples of employers who are innovating with different approaches are described later in this chapter.

Employer Perceptions

The perceptions and attitudes of employers towards neurodiversity are significant in determining recruitment practices. Gillies (2012) states that there are persistent systemic barriers for disabled graduates, which prevent them from obtaining meaningful employment. Workplace discrimination can occur where employer attitudes, and particularly those responsible for recruitment, are negative (Brostrand, 2006; von Schrader et al., 2014). Kim and Williams (2012) note that the social stigmas related to disabled people may have been internalised by some non-disabled individuals leading to biased opinions about the ability of a disabled individual in the workplace; Norstedt (2019: 15) states that individuals with hidden disabilities (such as neurodivergent conditions) are 'often met with distrust because they do not look disabled or ill'. Remington and Pellicano (2019) assert that the 'double empathy' issue (Milton, 2012) causes challenges for autistic individuals, where misapprehension and misinterpretation is bi-directional and non-autistic managers and colleagues may lack understanding of the needs of those with autism. Negative attitudes can also be due to misconceptions about the costs of workplace adjustments, the competences of disabled individuals and the fear of disruption in the workplace (Fisher & Purcal, 2017). Another issue is that many employers consider themselves to be positive about employing individuals with disabilities, but consider themselves to lack the required knowledge and capability (Waterhouse et al., 2010).

WHAT WORKS? EXAMPLES OF GOOD PRACTICE

Given the number of challenges facing neurodivergent graduates seeking to enter employment, it is important that the remainder of this chapter focuses on what can be done to alleviate this situation. The UK's Centre for Social Justice (CSJ, 2021) highlights two important elements: the need to enhance the support disabled individuals are offered to prepare for employment and also the need to forge inclusive working environments. If this latter aim is not achieved and employers do not recognise their responsibility to improve accessibility of the workplace, then efforts to support individuals will not be effective. This section contains examples of good practice for both preparing neurodivergent individuals and encouraging employers to create inclusive recruitment processes and work environments.

University-based Employability Support for Neurodivergent Students and Graduates

It is widely held that higher education institutions should integrate the development of employability skills and preparation for future life into the learning experiences of disabled students (Butterwick & Benjamin, 2006). Vickerman and Blundell (2010) assert that in doing so, universities provide disabled individuals with opportunities to explore and address potential challenges associated with the workplace and future employment. A number of ways in which universities may provide these opportunities are outlined below.

Individual Support

In some universities, employability support for neurodivergent students that is tailored and person-centred is available for individuals. Examples of this include one-to-one careers guidance appointments (sometimes called career counselling), where an individual will meet with a practitioner to discuss their career ideas, issues around sharing their disability with employers and navigating the recruitment process. These meetings are focused on a non-directive and non-judgmental approach based on Rogers' foundational premises: first, that people are their own best experts and therefore best placed to make their own decisions, and second, that the natural human tendency is to strive towards self-actualisation (Van Nieuwerburgh, 2017). Chen (2021) notes that one of the central aims of career counselling in higher education is to promote equality, diversity and social justice by increasing the accessibility of careers services; he asserts that effective collaboration between services seeking to support disabled students (the careers service, disability service, mental health and counselling support) is required to ensure that individuals are aware of the support available.

Many neurodivergent students and graduates have not considered how to communicate their condition to an employer and may be uncertain about how to approach this. Careers practitioners in universities can provide key support at this point, in helping the individual to articulate their needs; students may be familiar with study support adjustments they need to help while at university, but be unaware that different accommodations could assist them in the recruitment process and workplace. This is a key life skill for the individual: to be an expert in their own neurodiversity, how to describe this to employers and therefore to successfully navigate the recruitment process – for their first role and for the rest of their working career. It is also of particular importance that individuals are encouraged to consider any strengths they have due to their neurodiversity. Examples of these strengths could include excellent attention to detail due to their autism and an ability to demonstrate empathy due to their experience of a mental health condition. This process of identifying how their condition has actually helped them to develop certain proficiencies can lead to empowerment and increased confidence regarding sharing information and provide evidence to the employer about why the individual is an eligible candidate for the role.

Mentoring Programmes

Another form of tailored support is mentoring programmes, where individual students or graduates are paired with a mentor who can provide advice or support related to employment. These mentors may be university staff, employers or even university peers. As noted by Lucas and James (2018), mentoring can promote the employability and psycho-social wellbeing of mentees. Madaus (2006: 90) recommends using disabled graduates in employment as mentors, to provide advice, insights and to act as a 'sounding board' for students with hidden disabilities preparing to transition into the workplace. Mentoring has been found to increase job-seeking self-efficacy, career adaptability and assertiveness in job hunting (O'Mally & Antonelli, 2016). Research also indicates that acting as a mentor can increase job satisfaction, provide fulfilment and act as a 'morale booster' for mentors (James, 2014).

Work Experience Programmes

Obtaining work experience is recognised as important for many reasons, including informing future career choice and to develop employability skills (Bennett, 2016). Experience of employment supports neurodivergent students in their transition to the workplace as graduates, by providing opportunities to gain confidence and an understanding of work roles (Remington et al., 2021), as well as equipping students with the abilities to cope and succeed in the workplace (Georgiou et al., 2012). It is also well established that employers look for evidence of work experience in candidates' applications (Nolan & Gleeson, 2017). Work placement programmes or internships for neurodivergent students and graduates can enable these individuals to obtain this vital experience in a supported environment. Such experiences can support disabled individuals in gaining an understanding of suitable adjustments required and, simultaneously, perspectives about employing individuals with disabilities can be positively influenced (Briel & Getzel, 2001). In some countries, relevant charities have collaborated with universities to offer work experience opportunities to neurodivergent individuals (the Neurodiversity Hub community of practice in Australia and Ambitious About Autism's 'Employ Autism' project in the UK); these collaborations bring together collective expertise for the benefit of neurodivergent students and graduates.

Entrepreneurial Support

One recent study found that greater proportions of disabled graduates pursued self-employment after leaving university, when compared to graduates who had not disclosed a disability (Allen & Coney, 2019). Self-employment support offered by institutions for disabled students and graduates who are keen to explore setting up their own businesses can be of real benefit; indeed Landstrom (2005) argues that universities have a key role in promoting entrepreneurship aspirations. This support could include entrepreneurship education, the provision of role models or mentors and opportunities to engage with 'action mechanisms' (defined by Dakung et al. (2017: 286) as 'the stepping stones to self-employment initiatives'). Dakung et al. (2017) also assert that when universities offer inclusive entrepreneurship education, disabled students will be aided in the development of their entrepreneurial ideas and knowledge. The case study below illustrates how support while at university assisted one neurodivergent student in developing their own business.

Case Study: the Positive Impact of Entrepreneurial Support at University

Eva, an autistic illustrator, had always known that she was creative and loved art, which led her to choose to study for a degree in illustration at university. Eva had started selling her work at local craft fairs while at school and continued to do this once she started her degree course. During her second year, a member of the university careers service attended one of Eva's classes to talk about entrepreneurship and self-employment and mentioned that grants were available to help with business start-ups for students. Eva spoke to the careers practitioner and was encouraged to apply for a grant, which she was subsequently successful in gaining; she used this to pay to become a seller at a prestigious national fair. Unbeknown to Eva, the owner of a national clothing brand was present at this fair, scouting for new products to sell on his website. This owner spotted Eva's work and later invited her to sell her products on his website; Eva is still successfully doing this several years on and her presence on this website has greatly helped her promote her illustrations.

Embracing the Student/Graduate Voice

Vickerman and Blundell (2010) assert that hearing the voices of disabled students in higher education is important, so that universities can be aware of the challenges faced by them. It is vital that those in institutions seeking to support disabled students and graduates as they prepare for the workplace learn first-hand from the lived experiences and perspectives of these individuals. In their study, Vickerman and Blundell (2010) found that only 50% of disabled students had engaged with their careers service; they suggest that careers practitioners should consult with the disabled students and graduates they are seeking to help. In recognition of this, one university-based careers practitioner sought to involve students in each stage of a careers and employability programme; this is described in the case study below.

Case Study: a Participatory Approach to Planning the Careers Support for Autistic Students

Understanding that graduates with autism have some of the lowest levels of employment, the careers practitioner was keen to provide some targeted provision for this group at the university she worked in. Recognising the importance of consulting those she was seeking to support, the careers practitioner first conducted a survey of all autistic students at the university, asking them what careers provision they would like. Next, she recruited a group of autistic student consultants, to co-analyse the findings of this survey. With the support of these consultants, a series of online workshops was designed, on the topics the autistic students had deemed to be of most importance to them: disclosure of their neurodiversity, reasonable adjustments and hearing about the experiences of autistic graduates. The autistic student consultants identified elements that would help these workshops to be more inclusive. Through collecting data regarding the impact of the online workshops using before and after surveys, a notable positive shift in the self-perceptions of these autistic students was observed, in terms of their knowledge relating to their legal rights and their understanding of disclosure and reasonable adjustments. As a result of their involvement in the co-design and delivery of the programme, several of the autistic consultants stated that they had gained self-awareness and a greater understanding of their capabilities and two described how they felt empowered to pursue work related to promoting diversity and inclusion issues in the workplace. The impact of this project on the careers practitioner included a richer understanding of the needs and concerns of autistic students regarding employment and a conviction that participatory approaches are vital in order to ensure effective provision of careers support.

Developing Inclusive Workplaces

As described in an earlier section of this chapter, it is vital that employers are encouraged to consider ways to improve the accessibility of their recruitment processes and workplaces. Many employers have indicated a desire to increase the diversity of their workforce; in order to achieve this, clearly there must be accessibility in the recruitment process. This would allow neurodivergent graduates the opportunity to compete on more equal terms with other applicants. In addition, employers must seek to adopt attitudes of respect and understanding in the workplace and to reflect on biases or preconceived ideas of disabled graduates that they may have (Gillies, 2012).

Improving Employer Awareness

This chapter has already alluded to the responsibilities of the employer and noted that some of the described issues could perhaps be alleviated if organisations were to be more cognisant of the needs of neurodivergent employees; it is therefore clear that improving employer awareness is key. A greater understanding of the needs and concerns of neurodivergent individuals could lead to more inclusion and less discrimination. Von Schrader et al. (2014) recommend that disability awareness training for all employees could reduce misunderstandings about the competencies of disabled individuals. They also assert that this training could increase supervisors' confidence in discussing adjustments with disabled individuals. Reverse mentoring, described by Chaudhuri and Ghosh (2012) as a social exchange tool which seeks to increase appreciation of different needs and perceptions, could be a useful means to achieving understanding.

Case Study: Reverse Mentoring

Steve, a disabled graduate working for a central government organisation, had observed first-hand the challenges of disabled individuals seeking to navigate the recruitment process. In particular, he felt that people with disabilities were experiencing direct and indirect discrimination due to employers' lack of understanding of what they needed to do to meet their employees' needs. To improve this situation, Steve created a reverse mentoring scheme, which matches business leaders, HR professionals and board members with disabled mentors. These mentors are recognised as having expertise through their lived experiences and are generally recent graduates, or students with experience of the recruitment process. Mentors meet with their mentees every month for six months and share their unique insights and the challenges of obtaining and maintaining employment. Managers and business leaders have used their experiences and learning as mentees to inform their reformation of policies, reasonable adjustment processes and to raise awareness of disability in their workplaces. This reverse mentoring scheme is still in its first year of existence, but there has been such interest that Steve is looking to expand this successful and innovative approach to raising awareness of the needs and strengths of individuals with disabilities.

Once organisations have improved their accessibility in the recruitment process and the workplace, it is advisable that they market themselves effectively as inclusive employers to prospective employees. Cooke (2015) notes that those seeking to attract disabled graduates must outline their commitment to disability and make this readily available on their websites; information included should outline support available for applicants and profiles of current disabled employees.

Removing Attitudinal Barriers

In response to attitudinal barriers in the workplace, Brostrand (2006) describes how the Tilting at Windmills programme was introduced in the USA to use activities and discussions to promote awareness of attitudes. A key determining factor for employers' willingness to hire disabled individuals is previous positive experiences of people with disabilities (Gustafsson et al., 2014). One strategy that can lead to successful employment of individuals with disabilities is seeking to develop an accessible culture through effective leadership, which 'places both ethical and practical value on creating a workforce that is inclusive of employees with disabilities' (Waterhouse et al., 2010: 22). This method of using a positive experience of employing a neurodivergent student to effect change in attitude and practice by liaising with company leaders is illustrated in the case study below.

Case Study: an Employer Consulting with a Neurodivergent Student in order to Develop Inclusivity in the Workplace

Jack is a second year 'Education with Inclusion' student who has been diagnosed with dyspraxia and autism. As an element of his degree programme, he completed a virtual internship with a company that is part of a global corporation. While there, Jack was asked to conduct a research project exploring how the company could develop a policy to support colleagues with unseen disabilities. This was aligned to the company's plans to develop their accessibility and diversify the workforce in the next few years. The recommendations in the report Jack created were found to be so helpful by senior management that he was asked to present these findings to the board. The organisation has now created 'Affinity Groups' and Jack has been invited to be a member of the disability group in order to implement some of the recommendations he made. It is clear to Jack that by sharing his perspectives and by developing recommendations, he has been able to make a real contribution to the organisation's approach to diversity and inclusion.

Positive Employer Responses

It should be noted that some organisations have developed inclusive work programmes to encourage the employment of neurodivergent individuals. This is not just driven by an employer's determination to be seen to be 'doing a good deed', although this can be one motivation (Pisano & Austin, 2016); instead, a number of organisations are recognising the business benefits of hiring neurodivergent employees. GCHQ, the UK's intelligence, security and cyber agency, has collaborated with the charity 'Made by Dyslexia' to promote the recruitment of individuals with dyslexia (McLoughlin, 2020). The international software company SAP, assert that their 'Autism at Work' programme has not only aided their talent shortage issue, but has resulted in higher than anticipated levels of ability in their recruits (Krzeminska et al., 2019). This programme at SAP seeks to provide support for autistic individuals during the recruitment process and once in the workplace, through a buddy, mentor and coach. Similar approaches have been introduced by other organisations, such as EY, who have developed Neurodiverse Centres of Excellence in many countries, including Canada, India, Poland, Spain, the USA and the UK. Interestingly, recruiting neurodivergent employees can be found to have wider positive implications, including increased clarity in communications and the redesigning of processes (Austin, 2018, in Krzeminska et al., 2019).

CONCLUSION

To summarise, there are increasing numbers of neurodivergent graduates internationally; it is essential that these graduates are supported to successfully enter and progress in the workplace. This has been identified to be of great importance not only for the individual, in terms of realising their potential and opportunities to contribute to society and for universities, who are measured on their graduate outcomes, but also for employers, in ensuring a diverse and inclusive workforce and potentially greater profitability. For this to occur, it is important that all relevant parties do what they can to support these students and graduates; there is a need to both enhance the support neurodivergent individuals are offered to prepare for employment and to forge inclusive working environments.

Universities must ensure that adequate funding is allocated so that effective careers and employability support can be provided. Colleagues within universities, including careers staff and disability services staff, should work closely together, to seek the most streamlined support for disabled students and graduates (Coney, 2021; Nolan & Gleeson, 2017). Employers must be encouraged to see the benefits of improving their accessibility and increasing proportions of neurodivergent graduates in the workplace; this could be done by celebrating success stories and doing more to communicate the economic value of having a diverse workforce. So far, it appears to be large, well-resourced organisations who have sought ways to enhance accessibility for neurodivergent graduates; however, it is known that in many countries, small and medium-sized organisations account for well over half of all graduate employment. An important next step is to consider what can be done to support these smaller companies, with fewer resources, to develop inclusive recruitment processes and work environments.

In addition, it is recommended that research is conducted into effective practice, both in universities and also in the workplace. In order to change the current disadvantages experienced by neurodivergent graduates, it is important that understanding is gained into how successful individuals obtained employment and to ascertain what accommodations could be put in place to enable individuals to realise their potential. While much research has been undertaken regarding the transitions of neurodivergent individuals from school to employment, there is a paucity of international research regarding graduate transitions. Evidence gained from such research could be used to promote the need for additional resources to support neurodivergent graduates in the workplace and to bring about changes in policy at institutional, national and international levels. In this way, neurodivergent graduates could look forward to a future without economic and societal disadvantage and instead enjoy accessibility and inclusion in the workplace, to the advantage of all.

REFERENCES

Accenture (2018). *Getting to equal: the disability inclusion advantage.* Available at: www.accenture.com/_acnmedia/PDF-89/Accenture-Disability-Inclusion-Research-Report.pdf (accessed 25.06.21).

Allen, M. & Coney, K. (2019). *AGCAS. What happens next? A report on the outcomes of 2017 disabled graduates.* www.agcas.org.uk/write/MediaUploads/ Resources/ Disability%20TG/ What_Happens_Next_report_2019.pdf (accessed 29.06.21).

Allen, M. & Coney, K. (2021). *AGCAS. What happens next? A report on the outcomes of 2018 disabled graduates.* Available at: www.agcas.org.uk/News/what-happens-next-2021/268397 (accessed 29.06.21).

Bennett, D. (2016). *Enacting strategies for graduate employability: how universities can best support students to develop generic skills.* Available at: https://melbourne-cshe.unimelb.edu.au/__data/assets/pdf_file/0011/1874774/SP13-3258_Curtin_Bennett_Graduate-Employability_Final-Report_Part-A_20163.pdf (accessed 08.05.21).

Biggeri, M., Di Masi, D. & Bellacicco, R. (2020). Disability and higher education: assessing students' capabilities in two Italian universities using structured focus group discussions. *Studies in Higher Education.* 45:4, 909–924.

Booth, J. (2016). *Autism equality in the workplace: removing barriers and challenging discrimination.* London: Jessica Kingsley.

Briel, L. W. & Getzel, E. E. (2001). Internships in higher education: promoting success for students with disabilities. *Disabled Studies Quarterly.* 20:1.

Brostrand, H. L. (2006). Tilting at windmills: changing attitudes toward people with disabilities. *Journal of Rehabilitation.* 72, 4–9.

Bublitz, D. J., Fitzgerald, K., Alarcon, M., D'Onofrio, J. & Gillespie-Lynch, K. (2017). Verbal behaviors during employment interviews of college students with and without ASD. *Journal of Vocational Rehabilitation.* 47:1, 79–92.

Butterwick, S. & Benjamin, A. (2006). The road to employability through personal development: a critical analysis of the silences and ambiguities of the British Columbia (Canada) life skills curriculum. *International Journal of Lifelong Education.* 25:1, 75–86.

Centre for Social Justice (CSJ) (2021). *Now is the time.* Available online: CSJJ8819-Disability-Report-190408.pdf (centreforsocialjustice.org.uk) (accessed 21.06.21).

Chaudhuri, S. & Ghosh, R. (2012). Reverse mentoring: a social exchange tool for keeping the boomers engaged and millennials committed. *Human Resource Development Review.* 11:1, 55–76.

Chen, C. P. (2021) Career counselling university students with learning disabilities. *British Journal of Guidance & Counselling*. 49:1, 44–56.

Chen, J. L., Leader, G., Sung, C. and Leahy, M. (2015). Trends in employment for individuals with autism spectrum disorder: a review of the research literature. *Journal of Autism Developmental Disorders*. 115–127.

Clouder, L., Karakus, M., Cinotti, A., Ferreyra, M. V., Fierros, G. A. & Rojo, P. (2020). Neurodiversity in higher education: a narrative synthesis. *Higher Education*. 80, 757–778.

Coney, K. (2021). What should be done to ensure autistic graduates succeed in the workplace? *Journal of Inclusive Practice in Further and Higher Education*. 13:1, 106–126.

Cooke, H. (2015). *Openness: understanding why students are reluctant to be open with employers about their disability*. Windsor: My Plus Consulting Ltd.

Dakung, R. J., Munene, J. C., Balunywa, W., Orobia, L. & Ngoma, M. (2017). Self-employability initiative: developing a practical model of disabled students' self-employment careers. *Africa Journal of Management*. 3:3–4, 280–309.

Doyle, N. (2020). Neurodiversity at work: a biopsychosocial model and the impact on working adults. *British Medical Bulletin*. 135: 108–125.

Fisher, K. R. and Purcal, C. (2017). Policies to change attitudes to people with disabilities. *Scandinavian Journal of Disability Research*. 19:2, 161–174.

Gillies, J. (2012). University graduates with a disability: the transition to the workforce. *Disability Studies Quarterly*. 32:3. Available at: https://dsq-sds.org/article/view/3281/3115 (accessed 28.06.21).

Georgiou, C. E., Espahbodi, S. & De Souza, L. H. (2012). Preparing for the world of work: an exploratory study of disabled students' experiences of work placement. *Journal of Education and Work*. 25:5, 523–536.

Griffin, E. & Pollak, D. (2009). Student experiences of neurodiversity in higher education: insights from the BRAINHE project. *Dyslexia*. 15, 23–41.

Guldberg, K. (2020). *Developing excellence in autism practice*. Oxon: Routledge.

Gustafsson, J., Peralta, J. P. & Danermark, B. (2014). The employer's perspective: employment of people with disabilities in wage subsidized employments. *Scandinavian Journal of Disability Research*. 16:3, 249–266.

James, A. I. (2014). Cross-age mentoring to support A-level pupils' transition into higher education and undergraduate students' employability. *Psychology Teaching Review: Special Issue: Pedagogical Action Research*. 20:2, 79–94.

Kim, M. M. & Williams, B. C. (2012). Lived employment experiences of college students and graduates with physical disabilities in the United States. *Disability and Society*. 21:6, 837–852.

Krzeminska, A., Austin, R. D., Bruyere, S. M. & Hedley, D. (2019). The advantages and challenges of neurodiversity employment in organisations. *Journal of Management & Organisation*. 25, 453–463.

Landström, H. (2005). *Pioneers in entrepreneurship and small business research*. New York: Springer.

Lipka, O., Sarid, M., Zorach, I. A., Bufman, A., Hagag, A. A. & Peretz, H. (2020). Adjustment to higher education: a comparison of students with and without disabilities. *Frontiers in Psychology*. Available at: www.frontiersin.org/articles/ 10.3389/fpsyg.2020.00923/full (accessed 20.06.21).

Lucas, R. & James, A. I. (2018). An evaluation of specialist mentoring for university students with autism spectrum disorders and mental health conditions. *Journal of Autism Development Disorders*. 48, 694–707.

Madaus, J. W. (2006). Improving the transition to career for college students with learning disabilities: suggestions from graduates. *Journal of Postsecondary Education and Disability*. 19:1, 85–93.

McLoughlin, L. (2020). 'Hello world': GCHQ, Twitter and social media engagement. *Intelligence and National Security*. 35, 233–251.

McMullin, J. A. & Shuey, K. M. (2006). Ageing, disability and workplace accommodations. *Ageing & Society*. 26:6, 831–847.

Milton, D. E. M. (2012). On the ontological status of autism: the 'double empathy problem'. *Disability and Society*. 27:6, 883–887.

Morina, A. & Perera, V. H. (2020). Inclusive higher education in Spain: students with disabilities speak out. *Journal of Hispanic Higher Education*. 19:3, 215–231.

Moss, H. (2021). Screened out onscreen: disability discrimination, hiring bias, and artificial intelligence. *Denver Law Review*. 98:4, 775–805.

Nolan, C. & Gleeson, C. I. (2017). The transition to employment: the perspectives of students and graduates with disabilities. *Scandinavian Journal of Disability Research*. 19:3, 230–244.

Norstedt, M. (2019). Work and invisible disabilities: practices, experiences and understandings of (non)disclosure. *Scandinavian Journal of Disability Research*, 21:1, 14–24.

O'Mally, J. & Antonelli, K. (2016). The effect of career mentoring on employment outcomes for college students who are legally blind. *Journal of Visual Impairment and Blindness*. 295–307.

Pesonen, H., Waltz, M., Fabri, M., Syurina, E., Krückels, S., Algner, M., Monthubert, B. & Lorenz, T. (2021). Stakeholders' views on effective employment support strategies for autistic university students and graduates entering the world of work. *Advances in Autism*. 7:1, 16–27.

Pisano, G. P. & Austin, R. A. (2016). *Hewlett Packard Enterprise: The Dandelion Program*. Boston, MA: Harvard Business School.

Pratt, C. W., Gill, K. J., Barrett, N. M. & Roberts, M. M. (2014). *Employment in psychiatric rehabilitation*. 3rd edn. London: Elsevier.

Remington, A. & Pellicano, E. (2019). Sometimes you just need someone to take a chance on you: an internship programme for autistic graduates at Deutsche Bank, UK. *Journal of Management & Organization*. 25, 516–534.

Remington, A., Heasman, B., Romualdez, A. M. & Pellicano, E. (2021). Experiences of autistic and non-autistic individuals participating in a corporate internship scheme. *Autism*. 1–16.

Sayce, L. (2011). *Getting in, staying in and getting on: disability employment support fit for the future*. Review to Government. Department for Work and Pensions.

Sarrett, J. (2018). Interviews, disclosures, and misperceptions: autistic adults' perspectives on employment related challenges. *Disability Studies Quarterly*. 37:2. Available at: https://dsq-sds.org/article/view/5524/4652 (accessed 08.05.21).

Singer, J. (1999). Why can't you be normal for once in your life? From a problem with no name to a new category of disability. In Corker, M. & French, S. (eds) *Disability Discourse*. Milton Keynes: Open University Press.

Smith, S. A., Woodhead, E. & Chin-Newman, C. (2019). Disclosing accommodation needs: exploring experiences of higher education students with disabilities. *International Journal of Inclusive Education*. Available at: www.tandfonline.com/ doi/abs/10.1080/13603116.2019.1610087 (accessed 29.06.21).

Svendby, R. (2020). Lecturers' teaching experiences with invisibly disabled students in higher education: connecting and aiming at inclusion. *Scandinavian Journal of Disability Research*. 22:1, 275–284.

United Nations (UN) (2006). *Convention of the Rights of Persons with Disabilities.* Available at: www.un.org/development/desa/disabilities/convention-on-the-rights-of-persons-with-disabilities.html (accessed 29.06.21).

United Nations (UN) (2015). *Transforming our world: the 2030 Agenda for Sustainable Development.* Available at: https://sdgs.un.org/2030agenda (accessed 25.06.21).

van Nieuwerburgh, C. (2017) *An introduction to coaching skills: a practical guide*, 2nd edn. London: Sage.

Veitch, S., Strehlow, K. & Boyd, J. (2018). Supporting university students with socially challenging behaviours through professional development for teaching staff. *Journal of Academic Language & Learning*. 12:1, 156–167.

Vickerman, P. & Blundell, M. (2010). Hearing the voices of disabled students in higher education. *Disability & Society*. 25:1, 21–32.

von Schrader, S., Malzer, V. & Bruyere, S. (2014). Perspectives on disability disclosure: the importance of employer practices and workplace climate. *Employee Responsibilities and Rights Journal*. 26, 237–255.

Waddell, G. & Burton, A. K. (2006). *Is work good for your health and well-being?* London: TSO. Available at: https://assets.publishing.service.gov.uk/government/uploads/system/uploads/attachment_data/file/214326/hwwb-is-work-good-for-you.pdf (accessed 25.06.21).

Waterhouse, P. H., Kimberley, H., Jonas, P. & Glover, J. (2010). *What would it take? Employer perspectives on employing people with a disability*. National Centre for Vocational Education Research (NCVER). Available at: www.ncver.edu.au/__data/assets/file/0018/3726/2219.pdf (accessed 14.06.21).

World Health Organisation (WHO) (2002). *Towards a common language for functioning, disability and health: the international classification of functioning, disability and health*. Geneva: World Health Organisation. Available at: www.who.int/classifications/icf/icfbeginnersguide.pdf (accessed 29.06.21).

World Health Organisation (WHO) (2011). *Impact of economic crises on mental health*. Copenhagen: World Health Organisation. Available at: www.euro.who.int/ __data/assets/pdf_file/0008/134999/e94837.pdf (accessed 25.06.21).

Yusof, Y., Chan, C. C., Hillaluddin, A. H., Ramli, F. Z. A. & Saad, Z. M. (2020). Improving inclusion of students with disabilities in Malaysian higher education. *Disability & Society*. 35:7, 1145–1170.

17

Centring Racialised Experiences of Black Students to Mitigate Bias within Graduate Labour Recruitment and Selection Processes

Iwi Ugiagbe-Green

INTRODUCTION

Critical writers of employability suggest that as educators, we need to engage with the graduate employability agenda in higher education and instil more radical and critical content (Hooley, 2015; Jameson et al., 2012; Kalfa and Taksa, 2015; Reid, 2016; Rooney and Rawlinson, 2016).

This chapter provides a radical and critical examination of the valorisation of graduate identity by employers, in forming perceptions of their work readiness. In this examination, particular emphasis is placed on the impact that valorisation of graduate identity by employers has on the racialised experiences of Black students.

The chapter starts with an exploration of the context of graduate employability. The context of employability extends beyond the personal, broadened beyond to what Tholen (2012, 2017) calls 'the arena', and to what Bourdieu (1986) refers to as 'the field'. This distinction is important because of the relational effect of context on graduate identity formation itself.

The author conducted a study in 2020 with 28 UK-based employers (17 of which are graduate recruiters) to explore job market signalling (Spence, 1973) from an employer perspective. From this work, a research-informed work-readiness framework (Ugiagbe-Green and Southall, 2019) was developed. The work-readiness framework uses the concept of capitals (Bourdieu, 1986) as proxies of what students are perceived to need in order to be successful in 'the field'. Although 'capital' can be a problematic term (largely due to its association with capitalism), in this context, capitals is associated with value. The capitals describe, at an individual level, dimensions of graduate identity associated with the perception of being prepared for success in the workforce.

Through questionnaires and focus groups, this study explored the racialised experiences of 10 Black accounting/banking and finance students who attended a Russell Group[1] University in the UK. All students identified as Black with intersecting characteristics (e.g. race, sex and disability). They were actively engaged in a process of developing their graduate identity – for example, seeking industrial placement during their studies (of which none of the Black students on the study were able to get).

The research highlights that some Black students suffered with early career engagement issues. Students expressed a lack of confidence in and with career development opportunities at their university. However, when students did progress to recruitment and selection stages with employers, they faced many issues. Emergent themes from the analysis stage of the study include micro-aggressions and othering due to issues with persistent negative perceptions of their work readiness. Micro-aggression is the communication of hostile, derogatory or negative attitudes toward marginalised groups (Johnson and Joseph-Salisbury, 2018). Othering is a set of dynamics, processes and structures that engender marginality and persistent inequality across any of the full range of human differences based on group identities (Powell and Menendian, 2016).

The author proposes that there is a need to collectively build career provision that firstly recognises and secondly mitigates bias and othering, which are systemic within graduate labour recruitment and selection processes. Career education with students and soon-to-be graduates should not be centred on skills acquisition and articulation. It should be a holistic dialogic experience that centres around the development of their graduate identity and how best to navigate the field in order to develop their work readiness.

EMPLOYABILITY IS DEVELOPED IN THE FIELD, NOT JUST A PERSONALISED CONTEXT

Individuals acquire the beliefs, behaviours and values that predominate or are valued in a culture, thus permitting competent membership in that culture (Mehan, 1979). Jarvis (1983: 88) explains that it is the 'process by which the objective world of reality is internalized and becomes subjectively meaningful'. This process is referred to as 'socialisation': the acquisition of skills, knowledge and dispositions that enable the individual to participate in his or her group or society (Sivan, 1986). Weidman et al. (2001: 4) define socialisation in a broad sense as 'the process by which persons acquire the knowledge, skills and disposition that makes them more or less effective members of society'.

The process of socialisation is relational and contextual. Shulman and Carey (1984) describe this as 'social constructivism'. They explain that it is representative of a paradigmatic shift toward viewing the construction of meaning or psychological events through the reciprocal influence of individual and context. As students become socialised and develop their employability, they develop a better understanding of labour market processes and employers' recruitment practices (Roberts, 2009).

Students' understanding of themselves, the development of their skills, knowledge and attitudes and their transition to the labour market are influenced by their positioning, in what Bourdieu (1986) refers to as 'the field'. Personalised contexts are bound by spatial and time constraints relating to the individual. However, social fields are environments in which competition between individuals and between groups takes place. The difference between a field and personalised context is ultimately hegemonic. Tholen (2012, 2017) acknowledges the influence of hegemony in this context, referring to it as 'the arena': a field is a competitive 'arena' of production, circulation, appropriation, exchange of labour, skills, knowledge and status across multiple stakeholders (other students, graduates, universities, employers), not just that of the individual.

JOB SIGNALLING – PERCEPTIONS OF WORK READINESS BY GRADUATE RECRUITERS

Signalling theory is important to human resource management, where a number of studies have examined signalling that occurs during the recruitment process (Suazo et al., 2009). Recruiters tend to turn to statistical reasoning and to rely on easily observable signals that are expected to provide reliable information, when faced with information asymmetry, on the quality of candidates. Spence (1973) pointed out that the observable features that can have signalling value are of two kinds: those that cannot be changed by the applicant (gender, race, nationality, age), which he calls 'indices', and those that, in contrast, can be modified by a candidate, which he calls 'signals'. Spence (2002) considers that education is a capability signal to employers, separating potentially high- and low-capability workers. Tom Fryer in HEPI (May 2021) suggests that it is possible some aspects of higher education influences employment, but it is also perfectly possible that graduate employment rates are influenced mainly by factors other than higher education.

Concerns that education alone is insufficient to develop the employability of graduates may in part explain the use of placements and internships as a graduate recruitment scheme in its own right, especially in technical or professional fields (UKCES, 2009). The BIS Understanding Employers' Graduate Recruitment and Selection Practices: Main Report (Pollard et al., 2015) explains that most graduates are recruited with the expectation that they would go on to progress to medium-term professional and managerial 'talent pipelines.'

The Wilson (2012) report recommends that universities increase opportunities for students to acquire relevant work experience during their studies by means of 'sandwich' degrees and internships, before taking up graduate opportunities. Internships provide an opportunity for students to 'enhance graduate skills levels to ensure a smooth and effective transition between university and business environments' (Wilson, 2012). They also offer employers and students reduced commitment to permanent employment and thus reduced risk (The Understanding Employers' Graduate Recruitment and Selection Practices: Main report, 2015).

At its core, this 'try before you buy' approach to graduate employment is an organising logic of the capitalist mode of production. Through internships and placements, organisations are able to appropriate value with reduced risk within an asymmetric information context. Internships are treated as proxies for 'appropriate attitudes and dispositions' (Cook et al., 2012: 1758).

IMPORTANCE OF INTERNSHIPS/PLACEMENTS AND LINKS TO GRADUATE EMPLOYABILITY

From employers' perspectives, placements bring new skills into their organisations and provide good-quality and good-value workers, often later recruited to permanent positions (see e.g. Brooks and Youngson, 2016; Maertz et al., 2014). From students' perspectives, placements provide valuable real-life learning experiences, improve their employment prospects and inform their career plans (BIS Research, 2016; Pegg and Caddell, 2016). Indeed, the 'majority of those who had not undertaken any form of work experience later rued this decision' (BIS Research, 2016: 8) indicating, with hindsight, an appreciation of a placement as a lost opportunity to enhance employment prospects, develop industry contacts and enhance study-based skills and knowledge. Similarly, Wilton (2014) found that graduates who had completed placement unanimously felt both the experience and new contacts had provided them with an advantage to access opportunities in the graduate labour market.

Most studies that examine the importance of internships and placements conclude that they improve the academic performances of students. Using student record data on graduates from Aston University (England) and the Ulster University (Northern Ireland), a study conducted by Jones et al. (2017) found that 'the effect of taking an integrated sandwich work placement appears still to have a positive and significant impact on final year academic performance'. The estimated positive impact according to the paper is in the range of 2%–4% across both institutions. These results are somewhat comparable to other estimates reported in the literature. The Gomez et al. (2004: 378) study uses multivariate regression analysis, in which they conclude 'students taking a sandwich placement exhibit improved academic performance in the final year. On average, placement students gain an advantage of 4%'. Equally, in a study carried out by Surridge (2008) – also using regression analysis – found that a cohort of Accounting and Finance students experienced an average improvement of 3.6%. Brooks and Youngson (2016) found evidence of work placements leading to better degree outcomes and contributing to easier routes to graduate jobs. Other, wider benefits reported from studies as a result of work experience include the development of skills and confidence (Linn, 2015; Matsouka and Mihail, 2016).

Some studies, however, maintain that placements do not improve academic performance. Chillas et al. (2015) found that not all placements provided opportunities for learning. A notable study is Duignan (2002: 214), which concludes that '[n]o significant difference (in achievement) was found between those who undertook a placement and those who did not'.

EMPLOYMENT CAPITAL

Anderson-Gough et al. (1998) suggest that credentialism in itself does not have intrinsic value. Their study suggests that conduct is used by employers as a tool to assume control over employees and maintain a uniformity of behaviour and values in work. Organisations control the 'terms, conditions, goals and content' of their work (Freidson, 2001: 60). Interactions during the professional socialisation process happen during professional encounters in the workplace and communities of practice. Cooper and Robson (2006: 415) explain that organisations where these encounters occur are 'sites where professional identities are mediated, formed and transformed, and where important conceptions of personal [and] professional [...] are transmitted'.

Ugiagbe-Green and Southall (2019) explain that employment capital is the differentiated occupational behaviours, judgements and moral orientations valorised by employers. In short, those graduates who have been successfully socialised into their specific organisation's approach to work practices navigate entry into employment in an organisation far more easily than those graduates who have no organisation-specific work experience. It is an altered form of closure 'and one where exclusion is formed within the graduate population' (Chillas, 2010).

GRADUATE IDENTITY

Holmes (2006: 9) explores the concept of graduate identity, in response to a dissatisfaction with the prevailing concept of graduate employability in terms of skills acquisition. He observes that identity is to be taken 'non-essentially, as relational, the emergent outcome of situated social processes [...] identity is thus socially constructed and negotiated, always subject to possible contestation and so fragile'.

Graduate identity is formed and reformed through a wide range of experiences during their studies. The socialisation of students who undertake placements and internships to adopt the accepted norms and behaviours of workers within the organisation is what Mats Alvesson (2001) refers to as 'identity regulation'. Alvesson and Willmott (2002: 622) state that 'through identity regulation, employees incorporate specific managerial instructions into their personal narratives of self-identity.

Chatman (1991) explains that students who possess prior experience of working within the firm they are applying to demonstrate the most potential for a seamless 'fit' in terms of values, norms and practices of the organisation. It is these students who demonstrate the 'graduate identity' sought by the organisation who are most likely to gain employment. Hinchliffe and Jolly (2010) suggest that graduate identity is made up of four strands: values, intellect, performance and engagement. They highlight the importance of the performative element of employability, as an employer's view that a graduate will be successful in the organisation can only be based on perception, not actual performance.

WORK READINESS

A number of factors differentiate graduate recruitment and selection from other contexts, the most important being that graduates generally lack job-related experience (Caballero and Walker, 2010). Work readiness has emerged in the literature as a selection criterion for predicting graduate potential and capability (AC Nielsen Research Services, 2000; Casner-Lotto and Barrington, 2006; Hart, 2008). It is defined as being 'the level to which graduate students are *perceived* as possessing attitudes and attributes that enable them to be prepared for success in the workforce'. Work readiness is of high priority for employers (Keep and Mayhew, 2004) and is thus an influencing factor in selection (Chillas, 2010).

RACIALISED EXPERIENCE – BLACK STUDENTS

The 'Access to What?' project (Blasko et al., 2002) shows that relative chances of selection are not the same for all students with equivalent qualifications – some groups face systematic labour market disadvantage. Research shows how Black, Asian and other racially minoritised students are very often subject to social disadvantage and structural inequality (Arday, 2020) within education. In relation to employability and career development, these disadvantages and inequalities are experienced in areas such as access to industry contacts, understanding how to articulate experience or being in a position to undertake an internship or placement (McGregor-Smith, 2017).

Riach and Rich (2002: 499) provide a systematic analysis of the results of racial discrimination audits conducted in nine countries (including Britain) over a period of 30 years and conclude that (with the exception of the USA) 'the rate of net discrimination recorded against blacks, Asians, and Arabs has never been less than 25% [...] in view of the number of studies involved and their geographical extent this is compelling evidence of enduring and pervasive racial discrimination in employment'.

The Equality Act (UK Government, 2010) states that it is against the law to discriminate against anyone because of protected characteristics including that of 'race including colour, nationality, ethnic or national origin'. Yet, persistent inequitable outcomes across different racialised student and graduate groups exist, right across the student life cycle. During the period 2003/4 to 2019/20, at no stage have Black, Asian and minority ethnic (BAME) undergraduate students outperformed white students in terms of the awarding of 'good degrees' – that is, a 2:1 or 1:1 classification in the UK. If the same trajectory of achievement of good degrees continues into the future, the white–Black awarding gap will close in 2085–6.

These inequitable outcomes are not due to lack of effort on the part of Black students in higher education. Black students report the highest levels of engagement and participation at university (Neves, 2019). Black students are over-represented in higher education in England and Wales. Black students make up 8% of the undergraduate student population, yet only 4% of 18- to 30-year-olds in England and Wales are racialised as Black (HESA, 2020). Despite this, a Black student entering higher education with AAA A-level grades is less likely to be awarded a 'good degree' than a white student with BBB A-level grades (Universities UK and National Union of Students, 2019).

A snapshot of the first graduate-outcomes dataset conducted by the Higher Education Statistics Agency (HESA) – the experts in UK higher education data and the designated data body for England – shows that 61.6% of white graduates from 2017/18 gained full-time employment 15 months after graduation, compared with 53.5% of BAME graduates. 'Other Black students' are the ethnic group with the lowest proportion of graduates in full-time employment (47.4%). More Asian (27.3%) and Black (21.7%) 2017/18 graduates went into further education than any other ethnic groups. However, a white male undergraduate earns more than a Black postgraduate at the same point of their post-graduation lifecycle. Black graduates across all age groups are the lowest paid, with median earnings of £25,500, compared with the median of £35,000 for white graduates (JISC/Prospects, 2020).

IT DOES MATTER IF YOU'RE BLACK OR WHITE (LIVED EXPERIENCES OF BLACK STUDENTS)

Black students are over-represented in the post-1992 institutions (Connor et al., 2004), and as such, a deficit model and stereotype bias is often associated with this racialised group. Morley and Aynsley (2007: 229) concluded that '[T]he hierarchy of opportunity within the labour market often appeared to correspond to a highly stratified higher education sector'.

However, the report 'Causes of differences in student outcomes' (Mountford-Zimdars et al. (2015), commissioned by the Higher Education Funding Council for England (HEFCE), contains a multivariate analysis of the post-graduation outcomes of undergraduates from Russell Group universities over the three academic years (2009/10 to 2011/12) at six months after graduation (controlling for age, degree class, subject, higher education institution and year of graduation), and it shows that the educational characteristics are not sufficient to explain the ethnic-group differences. The higher rates of unemployment among ethnic minority Russell Group graduates are highlighted as a particular cause for concern (Lessard-Phillips et al., 2014).

In 2019, the author of this chapter conducted a mixed-methods research study that sought to explore the experiences of 87 second-year accounting/banking and finance students in seeking internships and placements at a highly ranked Russell Group university in the UK. Analysis of the survey data showed very stark results of the 10 Black student respondents when compared with other racialised groups surveyed. All Black students had achieved the required academic credentials to study one of the most highly ranked accounting/banking and finance courses in England.

As a racialised group, Black students who completed the survey scored the lowest self-reported professional identity scores and skills-awareness scores. Not one (0%) of the Black students on the second-year accounting/banking and finance course had secured a UK internship or placement since the commencement of their university course, with some relying on family and friend contacts in other countries to gain experience.

To explore these racialised experiences further, two focus groups were conducted with eight (two male and six female) of the Black student respondents of the survey. All Black students shared experiences of feeling isolated, experiencing little sense of belonging outside of friendship groups, displacement within academic settings, hypervisibility (singled out when discussing race in learning environments), invisibility (being ignored and experiences being invalidated) and indirect and overt racism during employment selection processes, feeling that they could not be their authentic self and be successful and also shared feelings of lacking confidence. These racialised experiences had undoubtedly negatively impacted on their student experience, motivation and self-efficacy. Students expressed that those feelings of isolation had made their experience so much more difficult and that their struggles in navigating the academy had led to an accumulation of missed opportunities.

Another significant theme of this study is what Yosso (2005) refers to as 'community cultural wealth'. During focus groups, Black students consistently referred to experiences where their cultural knowledge, skills, abilities and contacts were unrecognised and unacknowledged by others during the recruitment and selection process. Examples of this included experience gained in volunteering in faith and cultural communities, treasury management and leadership roles in cultural societies that were not valued by agencies and organisations that were recruiting for student internships and placements. Students shared that they purposefully employed strategies to remove these cultural markers from their graduate identity in the hope that this would enhance the likelihood that they would gain employment and be successful in their chosen occupations.

WORK-READINESS FRAMEWORK

Work readiness is a relatively new concept, and as such, there is very little framing of this concept in the literature. The focus group data collected from our study, as well as literature from philosophy and sociology, were used to develop a framework of work readiness.

The resultant work-readiness framework (Ugiagbe-Green and Southall, 2019) scaffolds dimensions of graduate identity valorised by employers in forming perceptions relating to the level to which graduate students were *perceived* as possessing attitudes and attributes that enable them to be prepared for success in the workforce.

Figure 17.1 Work-readiness capitals (Ugiagbe-Green & Southall, 2019)

CAPITALS EXPLAINED

1 Human capital: The skills and knowledge of the graduate, as evidenced by their qualifications and experience (e.g. degree classification, degree subject, prior work experience).
2 Social capital: The graduate's network of personal and professional relationships, as well as their capability to form professional relationships (e.g. graduate having friends or family in their desired industry/sector).
3 Cultural capital: The graduate's embodiment of organisational professionalism (e.g. the way in which the graduate dresses or the way in which they speak).
4 Identity capital: The ability of the graduate to demonstrate self-reflexive understanding of their positioning in the graduate labour market field (e.g. having set career goals, being able to communicate one's skills and experiences in the language of the employer).
5 Employment capital: The differentiated occupational behaviours, judgements and moral orientations that are valued by employers (e.g. business acumen, situational judgement and ability to manage up).
6 Economic capital: The ability of a graduate to bear financial risks related to employment opportunities (e.g. whether or not there are financial barriers to geographical mobility or taking on unpaid work experience).

Whilst these capitals are conceptualised as being generalisable to all individuals, they do represent a framework that assumes some degree of individual agency of the student/graduate. In reality, institutional systems, structures, policies, practices and students' interactions within wider social systems outside of the field mean that students with different intersectional characteristics will experience access to opportunities in the field differently. Students will have differing levels of ability, opportunity and success in navigating 'the field' and their resultant transition to graduate labour market.

Often, so-called 'marginalised' and 'minoritised' students are positioned as 'disadvantaged'. This framing of students who are not the dominant normative group demonstrates the hegemonic inter-play across and between different student groups. In the context of graduate recruitment, this is important. Signalling theory posits that successful navigation by students of 'the field' is positional and relational. As such, so-called 'disadvantaged' students – that is, minoritised and marginalised students – are competing with 'advantaged' students in both developing and demonstrating their work readiness to others as they transition from higher education to the graduate labour market. The information asymmetry associated with the graduate labour market relies on perception, bias and subjective practices.

OTHERING OF BLACK STUDENTS

Black students who took part in our study shared deeply personal racialised experiences during recruitment and selection process in which they experienced being 'othered'. As individuals, they felt marginalised and experienced being displaced (confirmed through feedback), due to negative perceptions of their graduate identity expressed by employers. These negative perceptions were evidenced by things that were said and by visceral reactions.

None of the Black students interviewed had secured a placement or internship. They highlighted instances when they had to deal with these visceral reactions when already feeling under pressure and nervous. For example, when a Black student with a very English-sounding name turned up for an interview, it was made very clear that they (the student) were not who the employer was expecting.

Examples of verbalised micro-aggressions that have led Black students to conclude that they are othered during recruitment and selection processes include 'oh, you speak really well', or 'so you're active in the Church…mmm', with some of the commentators of these micro-aggressions concluding in the feedback when the student has been told that they are unsuccessful, 'I just don't think you are the right fit for the team'.

IT DOES MATTER IF YOU'RE BLACK OR WHITE – EMPLOYERS' PERSPECTIVE

Following the survey and focus groups, we undertook a follow-up survey with 28 UK-based employers (17 of which are graduate recruiters), in which we sought affirmation of the work-readiness framework and associated insights relating to work readiness from an employers' perspective.

Employment, identity and human capital were identified by the employers surveyed as being most important in informing and shaping their perceptions that students possess the attitudes and attributes that enable them to be prepared for success in the workforce. When employers were asked 'which capitals do you think graduates lack the most?', identity, employment and economic capitals ranked the highest.

These results confirm important themes that were emergent from focus groups with Black students and that surfaced from the literature review. Black students are less likely to have done a placement/internship (sites where employment capital is developed) than other racialised student groups. Black students who participated in our study scored the lowest level of identity capital (using the Professional Identity Five Factor Scale in Tan et al., 2015) of all five racialised groups represented in the survey. Black students are generally less likely to achieve a 'good degree' (a proxy for human capital) than any other racialised group.

The study has revealed that there is some fantastic work being undertaken by employers via, for example, heritage schemes, to attract more Black talent to their organisations. Many of the graduate employers pointed to reviews of recruitment and selection practices that sought to mitigate bias – for example, removing the 'good degree' requirement, blind CV reviews, video interviews that are watched by at least two people, tests that seek to identify potential and gender-diverse interview panels. However, employers also shared that, in truth, there was a preference for specific higher institutions of study (i.e. Russell Group universities) and that algorithms used to write competence tests were based on 'what good looks like' according to the existing performance evaluation practices, modelled on the existing workforce and talent in the organisation. In short, whilst practices have been reviewed to be more 'inclusive', the assumptions regarding 'success' based on easily observable signals have not.

COLLECTIVE RESPONSIBILITY – A CALL TO ACTION

Those of us with an interest in graduate employability must ask ourselves, how is it that a student group who is over-represented in higher education and is reportedly the most engaged student group within higher education goes on year after year after year to be awarded the lowest graduate outcomes (i.e. 'good degrees' and graduate employment rates)? These inequitable outcomes lead to unacceptable and life-diminishing graduate labour pay gaps, higher levels of graduate unemployment, under-representation in senior leadership and executive roles and lower levels of accumulated wealth, home ownership, pensions – the list goes on and on. These persistent inequitable outcomes have a broader societal impact and create exclusionary spaces and structures of opportunity that mean employers are missing out on diverse, distinctive, unique and value-adding talent.

On 20th October 2020, the 100 Black Interns scheme (www.10000blackinterns.com/) was launched and then successfully piloted. It was later scaled up to the current 10,000 Black Interns scheme. The scheme is transforming the prospects and horizons of young Black people in the UK interested in working in the investment management industry. It offers 10,000 internships over five years across 24 sectors and involving more than 700 companies to Black African, Black Caribbean and/or Black British candidates in the UK. Accessible opportunities for training, development and mentorship are made available for Black students. Training and insights into the different sectors of the industry are delivered by industry professionals. Engagement with the scheme means that Black students develop their work-readiness (identity, human, employment, social, cultural and economic) capital through a sustainable cycle of mentorship, sponsorship and development opportunity.

The scheme is proving to be very successful in opening up opportunities for organisations to recruit new Black talent. The UK Health Data Research Alliance (HDR Alliance) is launching an internship programme this summer, as part of its response to the heavy under-representation of Black people in the science, technology, engineering and maths (STEM) community. They report, 'through partnership with the 10,000 Black Interns initiative, HDR UK has recruited 54 interns, including over 30 women (HDR UK, 2021).

We must progress the conversation of graduate recruitment beyond that of skills development, skills articulation and understandings (though, these remain fundamental) to graduate employability. We must engage in open, constructive dialogue about recruitment bias, signalling and the role of perception of identity in our conversations with students. Career provision should encourage students to access opportunities to develop their graduate identity and work-readiness. We must work with stakeholders in 'the field' to lower hegemonic barriers to structures of opportunity for students and with employers to identify, acknowledge and mitigate bias baked into their recruitment and selection processes. This requires sustained, systematic, dialogic work that encourages disruption to the status quo and normative practices, enabling the shifting of 'community cultural wealth' and the framing of 'what good looks like' to really challenge existing mindsets as well as graduate recruitment and selection practices. This work is not benevolence; it is necessary and important in unlocking new talent, adding value to both business and society as a whole.

NOTE

1 'The Russell Group' is a catch-all term for a group of universities with a shared focus on research and a reputation for academic achievement (www.theuniguide.co.uk/advice/choosing-a-course/what-is-the-russell-group)

REFERENCES

100 Black Interns (n.d.) Home page. www.10000blackinterns.com/

AC Nielsen Research Services (2000) *Employer Satisfaction with Graduate Skills: Research Report*. Canberra: Department of Education Training and Youth Affairs.

Alvesson, M. (2001) Knowledge work: Ambiguity, image and identity. *Human Relations*, 54(7): 863–86.

Alvesson, M. and Willmott, H. (2002) Identity regulation as organizational control: Producing the appropriate individual. *Journal of Management Studies*, 39(5): 619–44.

Anderson-Gough, F., Grey, C. and Robson, K. (1998) 'Work Hard, Play Hard': An analysis of organizational cliché in two accountancy practices. *Organization*, 5(4): 565–92.

Arday, J. (2020) Fighting the tide: Understanding the difficulties facing Black, Asian and Minority Ethnic (BAME) Doctoral Students' pursuing a career in Academia. *Educational Philosophy and Theory*, 53: 972–79.

Blasko, Z., Brennan, J., Little, B. and Shah, T. (2002) *Access to What? Analysis of Factors Determining Graduate Employability*. A report to HEFCE. London: Open University, Centre for Higher Education Research and Information.

Bourdieu, P. (1986) The Forms of Capital. In J.G. Richardson (Ed.), *Handbook of Theory and Research for the Sociology of Education* (pp. 241–58). New York: Greenwood Press.

Brooks, R. and Youngson, P.L. (2016) Undergraduate work placements: An analysis of the effects on career progression. *Studies in Higher Education*, 41(9): 1563–78.

Pollard, E., Hirsh, W., Williams, M., Buzzeo, J., Marvell, R., Tassinari, A., Bertram, C. and Fletcher, L., Artess, J., Redman, J. and Ball, C. (2015) *Understanding Employers' Graduate Recruitment and Selection Practices: Main Report.*, Department for Business, Innovation and Skills, BIS Research paper, no. 231. https://core.ac.uk/download/pdf/74379837.pdf

Business, Innovation and Skills (BIS) Research (2016). *Computer Science Graduate Employability: Qualitative Interviews with Graduates*. Department for Business, Innovation and Skills, BIS Research paper, no. 274. www.gov.uk/government/uploads/system/uploads/attachment_data/file/523079/bis-16-114-computer-science-graduate-employability.pdf

Caballero, C. and Walker, A. (2010) Work readiness in graduate recruitment and selection: A review of current assessment methods. *The Journal of Teaching and Learning*, 1(1): 13–25.

Casner-Lotto, J., & Barrington, L. (2006). *Are they really ready to work? Employers' perspectives on the basic knowledge and applied skills of new entrants to the 21st century U.S. workforce*. USA: The Conference Board, Inc., the Partnership for 21st Century Skills, Corporate Voices for Working Families, and the Society for Human Resources Management.

Chatman, J. (1991) Matching people and organizations: Selection and socialization in public accounting firms. *Administrative Science Quarterly*, 36: 459–84.

Chillas, S. A. (2010). *Work-readiness: what employers really want of graduates*. Paper presented at International Labour Process, New Jersey, United States.

Chillas, S., Marks, A. and Galloway, L. (2015) Learning to labour: An evaluation of internships and employability in the ICT sector. *New Technology, Work & Employment*, 30(1): 1–15.

Cooper, D. J. and Robson, K. (2006) Accounting, professions and regulation: Locating the sites of professionalization, *Accounting, Organizations and Society,* Volume 31, Issues 4–5, 2006, Pages 415–444, ISSN 0361-3682.

Connor, H., Tyers, C., Modood, T. and Hillage, J. (2004) *Why the Difference: A Closer Look at Ethnic Minority Students and Graduates*. Research report, no. 552. London: DfES.

Duignan, J. (2002). *'Undergraduate Work Placement and Academic Performance: Failing by Doing.'* Quality Conversations: Proceedings of the 25th HERDSA Annual Conference, Perth, Western Australia, July 7–10, 214–21.

Freidson, E. (2001). *Professionalism: The Third Logic*. Cambridge: Polity Press.

Fryer, T. (2019) *What is a graduate outcome? Higher Education Policy Institute (HEPI)*, May 2019, https://www.hepi.ac.uk/2021/05/28/what-is-a-graduate-outcome/

Gomez, S., Lush, D. and Clements, M. (2004) Work placements enhance the academic performance of bioscience undergraduates. *Journal of Vocational Education & Training*, 56(3): 373–85.

Hart, P. D. (2008). *How should colleges assess and improve student learning? Employers' views on the accountability challenge, A survey of employers conducted on behalf of: The Association of American Colleges and Universities*. Washington, DC: Peter D. Hart Research Associates, Inc.

Health Data Research (HDR) UK (2020) *Health Data Research UK announces Black internship programme starting Summer* 2021. www.hdruk.ac.uk/news/10000-black-interns-programme-launched/

HESA (2020) *Higher Education Graduate Outcomes Statistics UK*, 2017/18. www.hesa.ac.uk/news/18-06-2020/sb257-higher-education-graduate-outcomes-statistics

Hinchliffe, G.W., and Jolly, A. (2010) *'Graduate identity and employability'*, British Educational Research Journal, iFirst Article, 1–22.

Holmes, L. (2006) *Reconsidering graduate employability: beyond possessive-individualism*, paper presented at the Seventh International Conference on HRD Research and Practice across Europe, Tilburg, The Netherlands, 22–24 May.

Hooley, T. (2015) Who wins the rat race? Social justice and the graduate labour market. *Graduate Market Trends*, Autumn: 8–9.

Jameson, J., Strudwick, K., Bond-Taylor, S. and Jones, M. (2012) Academic principles versus employability pressures: a modern power struggle or a creative opportunity? *Teaching in Higher Education*, 17(1): 25–37.

Jarvis, P. (1983) *Professional Education*. Kent: Croom Helm.

JISC/Prospects (2020) *What do Graduates do? (2020/21)*. Annual report. https://graduatemarkettrends.cdn.prismic.io/graduatemarkettrends/a484bd37-501e-4585-8e7d-47ab61ca463f_what-do-graduates-do-2020-21.pdf

Johnson, A. and Joseph-Salisbury, R. (2018) 'Are You Supposed to Be in Here?' Racial Microaggressions and Knowledge Production in Higher Education. In J. Arday and H. Mirza (eds), *Dismantling Race in Higher Education: Racism, Whiteness and Decolonising the Academy* (pp. 143–60). Cham: Palgrave Macmillan.

Jones, C.M., Green, J.P. and Higson, H.E. (2017) Do work placements improve final year academic performance or do high-calibre students choose to do work placements? *Studies in Higher Education*, 42(6): 976–92.

Kalfa, S. and Taksa, L. (2015) Cultural capital in business higher education: Reconsidering the graduate attributes movement and the focus on employability. *Studies in Higher Education*, 40(4): 580–95.

Keep, E. and Mayhew, K. (2004) The economic and distributional implications of current policies on higher education. *Oxford Review of Economic Policy*, 20(2): 298–314.

Linn, P. (2015) A lifespan perspective on cooperative education learning: A grounded theory. *Asia-Pacific Journal of Cooperative Education*, 16(4): 301–26.

Maertz Jr, P., Stoeberl, C.A. and Marks, J. (2014) Building successful internships: lessons from the research for interns, schools, and employers. *Career Development International*, 19(1): 123–42.

Matsouka, K. and Mihail, D.M. (2016) Graduates' employability: What do graduates and employers think? *Industry and Higher Education*, 30(5): 321–26.

McGregor-Smith (2017) *Race in the Workplace: The McGregor-Smith Review*. Independent review by Baroness McGregor-Smith considering the issues affecting black and minority ethnic (BME) groups in the workplace. https://assets.publishing.service.gov.uk/government/uploads/system/uploads/attachment_data/file/594336/race-in-workplace-mcgregor-smith-review.pdf

Mehan, H. (1979) *Learning Lessons*. Cambridge: Harvard University Press.

Morley, L. and Aynsley, S. (2007) Employers, quality and standards in higher education: Shared values and vocabularies or elitism and inequalities? *Higher Education Quarterly*, 61(3): 229–49.

Mountford-Zimdars, A., Sabri, D., Moore, J., Sanders, J., Jones, S. and Higham, L. (2015) *Causes of Differences in Student Outcomes*. London. Report to HEFCE by King's College London, ARC Network and The University of Manchester.

Murray, S. (2018) An internship could be your golden ticket to a graduate job. *The Guardian*, 8th July. www.theguardian.com/education/2018/jul/09/internship-golden-ticket-graduate-job

Neves, J. (2019) UK Engagement Survey 2019 highlights the untapped potential of black students. *Advance HE*, 31st October. www.advance-he.ac.uk/news-and-views/ukes-2019-highlights-untapped-potential-black-students

Pegg, A. and Caddell, M. (2016) Workplaces and policy spaces: insights from third sector internships, Scotland. *Higher Education, Skills and Work-Based Learning*, 6(2): 162–77.

Powell, J., & Menendian, S. (2016). The Problem of Othering: Towards Inclusiveness and Belonging. *Othering and Belonging: Expanding the Circle of Human Concern*, (2): 14–39.

Reid, J. (2016) Redefining 'employability' as something to be achieved. *Higher Education, Skills and Work-Based Learning*, 6(1): 55–68.

Riach, A. and Rich, J. (2002) Field experiments of discrimination in the market place. *The Economic Journal*, 112(483): F480–F518.

Rooney, S. and Rawlinson, M. (2016) Narrowing participation? Contesting the dominant discourse of employability in contemporary higher education. *Journal of the National Institute for Career Education and Counselling*, 36: 20–29.

Lessard-Phillips, L., Swain, D., Pampaka, M. & Nwabuzo, O. (2014). *When education isn't enough Labour market outcomes of ethnic minority graduates at elite universities.* Runnymede Trust.

Lessard-Phillips, L., Swain, D., Pampaka, M. & Nwabuzo, O. (2014), *When education isn't enough Labour market outcomes of ethnic minority graduates at elite universities. Runnymede Trust.*

Schultz, T.W. (1961) Investment in human capital. *The American Economic Review*, 51(1): 1–17.

Shulman, L.S. and Carey, N.B. (1984) Psychology and the limitations of individual rationality: Implications for the study of reasoning and civility. *Review of Education Research*, 54(4): 501–24.

Sivan, E. (1986) Motivation in social constructivist theory. *Educational Psychologist*, 21(3): 209–33.

Spence, M. (1973) *The Quarterly Journal of Economics*, 87(3): 355–74.

Spence, M. (2002) Signaling in retrospect and the informational structure of markets. *American Economic Review*, 92: 434–59.

Surridge, I. (2008) Accounting and Finance Degrees: Is the Academic Performance of Placement Students Better? *Accounting Education*, 18(4/5): 471–85.

Tan, C.P., Van der Molen, H.T. and Schmidt, H.G. (2015) A measure of professional identity development for professional education. *Studies in Higher Education*, 42(8): 1504–19.

Tholen, G. (2012) Graduate employability and educational context: A comparison between Great Britain and the Netherlands. *British Educational Research Journal*, 40(1): 1–17.

Tholen, G. (2017) The changing opportunities of professionalization for graduate occupations. *Comparative Sociology*, 16(5): 613–33.

Ugiagbe-Green, I. and Southall, W. (2019), *Sorry (Not sorry), You're (not) hired – It's not me - it is you!....* The unspoken truths of graduate recruitment, Keynote address, Association of Graduate Careers Advisory (AGCAS) annual conference, 4th September 2019.

Ugiagbe-Green, I., Farr, A. and Bale, I. (2021), *Exploring the racialised experiences of graduates, Association of Graduate Careers Advisory (AGCAS), Phoenix, February 2021 – Race Equality.*

UKCES (2009) *The Employability Challenge*. London: UK Commission for Employability and Skills.

UK Government (2010) *The Equality Act*. www.legislation.gov.uk/ukpga/2010/15/contents

Unite Students Insight Report 2019. https://www.unitegroup.com/wp-content/uploads/2022/01/new-realists-insight-report-2019.pdf [Accessed 23.06.2022].

Universities UK and National Union of Students (2019) *Black, Asian and minority ethnic student attainment at UK Universities: #CLOSINGTHEGAP*. www.universitiesuk.ac.uk/

policy-and-analysis/reports/Documents/2019/bame-student-attainment-uk-universities-closing-the-gap.pdf

Verhaest, D. and Van der Velden, R. (2013) Cross-country differences in graduate overeducation. *European Sociological Review*, 29(3): 642–53.

Weidman, J.C. and Stein, E.L. (2003) Socialization of doctoral students to academic norms. *Research in Higher Education*, 44(6): 641–56.

Weiss, A. (1995) Human capital vs. signalling explanations of wages. *Journal of Economic Perspectives*, 9(4): 133–54.

Wilson, T. (2012) *A Review of Business–University Collaboration*. Department for Business, Innovation & Skills. https://assets.publishing.service.gov.uk/government/uploads/system/uploads/attachment_data/file/32383/12-610-wilson-review-business-university-collaboration.pdf

Wilton, N. (2014) Employability is in the eye of the beholder Employer decision-making in the recruitment of work placement students. *Higher Education, Skills and Work-based Learning*, 4(3): 242–55.

Yosso, T.J. (2005) Whose culture has capital? A critical race theory discussion of community cultural wealth. *Race Ethnicity and Education*, 8(1): 69–91.

18

Mind the Gap: Efforts to Narrow the Graduate Employment Gap for London Students from Low-participation Neighbourhoods

Richard Mendez

THE GRADUATE EMPLOYMENT GAP

In their report entitled *Widening opportunity in higher education: The third phase beyond graduation*, Universities UK (a representative organisation for UK universities) define graduate success as 'the achievement of a fulfilling role (whether in continuing education or employment) commensurate with both the innate ability and educational achievement of the individual' (Gaskell and Lingwood, 2019: 10).

With that definition in mind, the same report goes on to detail the stark (and often unfortunate) differences in successful outcomes for graduates from low participation neighbourhoods and/or disadvantaged backgrounds in contrast to other graduates (Gaskell and Lingwood, 2019: 21).

In their paper, Crawford and Vignoles (2014) found that individuals who attended private schools (an assumed marker of higher socio-economic background) earn on average 7% more per year than state-school students three years after graduation. This stark difference still applied even after factoring in other variables such as university attended, degree classification and degree subject (Crawford and Vignoles, 2014).

This is supported by economic data from the Economy Observatory, which confirms that graduates from wealthier families tend to fare better in the labour market, compared with their poorer counterparts, even in circumstances when both groups graduate from the same degree programmes (Xu, 2020). They go on to assert that graduates from poorer households will most likely experience worse outcomes compared to their counterparts during an economic downturn as and when they attempt to enter the graduate labour market (Xu, 2020).

The pandemic has most likely exacerbated these existing socio-economic outcome differences. The Office for National Statistics (ONS) reported that in 2020, the London region saw some of the greatest dips in online advertised job vacancies compared to its 2019 average (Matthewson, 2021). It even garnered the mantle of the region with the lowest volume of job adverts for several consecutive weeks, with its average being 56% of its 2019 average volume (Matthewson, 2021).

The Highflyers Research (2021) report highlights that the pandemic's impact meant that employers featured in '*The Times* Top 100 Graduate Employers' (a league table of some of the UK's biggest recruiters of graduates) cut their graduate recruitment by 15.1% in 2020, compared to the original recruitment targets for the year.

Allied to this, the report also stresses that the number of graduates recruited in 2020 was 12.3% lower than in 2019 – the largest annual fall in graduate recruitment at the UK's top employers for 11 years (Highflyers Research, 2021).

Data from The Office for Students (2019) shows that even in times when the graduate jobs market is buoyant, those from poorer backgrounds are less likely to secure graduate-level employment compared to their more affluent counterparts. Their data shows that for 2016–17, 68.9% of graduates in the most deprived quintile were employed in highly skilled jobs compared to 76% of the least deprived, which equates to a 7.1 percentage point gap (Office for Students, 2019).

A more hostile graduate jobs market, owing to a lack of vacancies, will inevitably heighten competition, resulting in the most socially disadvantaged graduates suffering the combined effects of this more hostile market and historic disadvantage, leading to a tougher time securing graduate employment.

This chapter examines the case study of a London University with a proportion of students from low participation neighbourhoods (a potential indicator of socio-economic disadvantage). The chapter will explore the university's bespoke employability interventions that have been designed, or in other cases, repurposed, to place emphasis on students and graduates from low participation neighbourhoods and/or those most likely to suffer unemployment or under-employment.

It is intended that academics and higher education careers practitioners with similar cohorts of students may benefit from some of the approaches espoused within this chapter.

All quotations included in the chapter were made by students and employers who participated in the various interventions. Students have been anonymised to protect their identities.

DEFINING LOW PARTICIPATION NEIGHBOURHOODS

The Higher Education Statistics Agency (HESA) is the UK's official agency for the collection, analysis and dissemination of quantitative information pertaining to higher education.

Amongst their portfolio of data analysis work are the UK performance indicators associated with 'widening participation'. Widening participation can be described as the aim to address discrepancies in the take-up of higher education opportunities (and their subsequent outcomes) amongst different under-represented groups of university students (Connell-Smith and Hubble, 2018).

One of the performance indicators of widening participation is the monitoring of participation rates in higher education (and progression to graduate employment) of students from low participation neighbourhoods.

HESA (2021) provides a technical definition of the term 'low participation neighbourhoods'. However, for those not familiar with the technical terminology, the definition may not provide sufficient insight.

Building upon HESA's definition, in Layman's terms, neighbourhoods are categorised into five groups from quintile 1 to quintile 5. Quintile 1 denotes postcodes or area codes with the lowest levels of students participating in higher education (i.e. most disadvantaged). At the other end of the spectrum, quintile 5 denotes postcodes or area codes with the highest levels of students participating in higher education (most advantaged). Those in quintile 1 postcodes or area codes who also fall within a category known as the 'middle layer super output' are deemed students from a low participation neighbourhood.

UNIVERSITY OF GREENWICH: A CASE STUDY

The University of Greenwich sits on a UNESCO World Heritage Site on the banks of the River Thames. Based in south-east London, UK, it has a student population of just under 19,000, and 97% of this population come from state schools according to its Access & Participation 2020–21.

As is the case with other UK universities, Greenwich compiles an 'Access and Participation Plan'. This is an institutional report that sets out how the university will improve equality of opportunity for under-represented groups to access and progress from higher education. Data from the university's Access and Participation Plan shows that progression to higher-skilled employment (i.e. graduate-level or managerial roles) or further study (e.g. master's degree) for students from low participation neighbourhoods has improved significantly over the years.

This is illustrated by the fact that the university did not witness a progression gap between those from low participation neighbourhoods and those from the highest participation neighbourhoods in 2016–17 (University of Greenwich, 2020: 4). However, it is worth noting that other measures of disadvantage (i.e. Index of Multiple Deprivation) reveals a gap of 7% between the most disadvantaged and most affluent in 2016–17. But the positives to draw from this is that the gap stood at 16% in 2013–14, meaning a 9% gap reduction over the intervening years, and the university continues to explore ways in which it can narrow or even eliminate the graduate employment gap for disadvantaged students.

However, in light of the disruption to the graduate labour market stemming from the pandemic, efforts and interventions to support disadvantaged students are more critical than ever. The university has been able to make vast improvements in narrowing the graduate employment gap for students from low participation neighbourhoods due to an intuition-wide commitment to social mobility spanning policies, recruitment practice, research on social inequalities and employability interventions. This case study will focus on some of the employability interventions specifically.

The purpose of this case study is to illustrate and share practice on some of the bespoke employability interventions established by the University of Greenwich. Whilst the interventions featured are available to all students, their impact on progression to graduate employment (namely, the bespoke in-house internships and traineeships) for disadvantaged students is noteworthy and may inform future practice at other institutions internationally.

LIMITATIONS OF THE CASE STUDY

A limitation of the case study is the methodology/measure used (i.e. low participation neighbourhood) by which to assess the disadvantage faced by the students being supported.

Even though low participation neighbourhood is a legitimate and useful measure recognised by official bodies, it can be problematic for an institution like the University of Greenwich.

A large proportion of the university's student population come from local London boroughs. This can present challenges in reliably classifying levels of student disadvantage. For example, students may be identified as disadvantaged because they live in areas where higher education participation is low but who themselves are not disadvantaged. Similarly, a student may be assumed not to be disadvantaged as they come from an area with overall good higher education participation rates when in fact they are from a deprived background.

This is a particular challenge when examining some areas in London where people who experience poverty can live in a deprived local area side-by-side with more affluent neighbours in a relatively affluent area with good higher education participation rates (University of Greenwich, 2020: 4). Given the above, the case study has limitations. However, scrutiny of secondary data sources combined with questionnaires completed by some of the students who participated in the various interventions provide the granular level of qualitative data necessary to provide reassurance that the students concerned did indeed have genuine disadvantage.

THE EMPLOYABILITY INTERVENTIONS EMPLOYED BY THE UNIVERSITY OF GREENWICH

The Employability and Careers Service (ECS) is situated at the University of Greenwich. The service works closely with all four university faculties to support students transitioning from higher education into graduate-level employment or postgraduate study. In doing so, the service will often employ a data analytics approach including the review of degree disciplines that have had historically low numbers of students entering graduate-level employment, and, on occasion, certain cohorts of students who appear to be under-represented in progression to higher-skilled employment.

In the case of degree disciplines with low numbers of students entering graduate-level employment, ECS will often approach the programme leaders (i.e. the academic staff responsible for the degree in question) and offer priority access or marketing for their student cohorts to improve take-up and, ultimately, progression rates to higher-skilled employment.

In the case of certain cohorts of students, whether that be based on, for example, socio-economic group or race, ECS treads very carefully and very rarely employs the same approach as mentioned earlier. To do so for a specific student group on the basis of their socio-economics or race and so on could be divisive. Students may feel stigmatised and/or publicly shamed for being identified as needing additional attention based on the characteristics mentioned. This in turn could lead to student disengagement and cause further harm.

In the latter case, the approach adopted is to broaden ECS's reach and awareness-raising via increased curriculum delivery (delivering degree- or discipline-specific employability content as part of the taught curriculum), working with the students' union to reach a wider number of students, including certain student societies, and also via outreach in the form of 'pop-up' drop-in career clinics in popular high-footfall areas such as the university library and cafeteria. It is worth noting that all students can access the various employability provisions available. The only exception will be for certain provisions that target final-year students. None of the employability provisions solely target students from low participation neighbourhoods or those from the lowest quintiles in the Indices of Multiple Deprivation.

Whilst all eligible students are supported and have access to the employability interventions, the service strives to support students and graduates from low participation neighbourhoods and those most likely to suffer unemployment or under-employment.

Over time, ECS has either developed new employability interventions or repurposed existing ones. What follows are examples of five such employability interventions.

THE GRADUATE WORK EXPERIENCE SCHEME

The Graduate Work Experience Scheme (GWES) is an in-house graduate trainee internship programme. It is unique amongst the employability interventions in that it is the only one that exclusively targets unemployed or under-employed final-year students and recent graduates. The participants must be unemployed or under-employed at the point of entry as part of the criteria for registering on to the scheme. In this sense, GWES immediately aligns itself to supporting students from low participation neighbourhoods and other measures of disadvantage (i.e. IMD).

GWES is a 12-week graduate-level internship that brokers finalists and recent graduates into internships with the university's faculties and professional services, such as the finance and IT departments. All successful interns are paid a salary commensurate with the university's pay grade for an early careers staff member.

ECS project manages the scheme, including initial support offered to students and recent graduates when applying to the advertised opportunities, recruitment and selection-type support for faculties and professional services during the recruitment phase, as well as inductions and on-going support for interns, faculties and professional services alike during the internship. ECS also conduct an evaluation of the scheme by surveying all parties in an effort to gauge areas for improvement.

The scheme has been very successful over its five years of operation. ECS confirm that from the 387 graduates who have participated in a GWES internship, 237 have subsequently secured higher-skilled employment. This represents a 61% success rate for those who participate in the scheme. When the scheme ran for the first time in 2014, the university's overall percentage for all graduates entering graduate-level employment was an unnerving 49%. Whilst this percentage has since risen sharply (74% in 2021), this further illustrates GWES's impact with its contrasting high success rate of 61%.

GRADUATE INTERNSHIPS (WITH LOCAL EMPLOYERS)

ECS brokers graduate internships using a very similar methodology and approach as seen in GWES. The key difference being that whilst GWES places the interns in faculties and professional services within the University of Greenwich, the graduate internships place the interns in paid graduate-level opportunities with local businesses.

ECS uses external funding that covers a proportion of the interns' salaries. To participate in the initiatives, employers are also required to make a financial contribution towards an intern's salary, the percentage of which is dependent on the level of external funding that ECS secures in any given year. However, a typical level of breakdown would be a 50% salary contribution from the employer, with the remaining 50% covered by the university.

ECS uses its extensive network of local business contacts to facilitate the implementation of this intervention. The duration and remuneration of these internships are virtually on par with GWES.

THE GRADUATE TEACHING DEMONSTRATORS TRAINEESHIP

The Graduate Teaching Demonstrators (GTD) scheme is a pilot scheme based on the GWES model. The impetus for the pilot came about via the pandemic, which forced universities to move towards online teaching. This spurred the idea of an in-house graduate traineeship scheme for recent University of Greenwich graduates, centred around teaching support intended to assist academics with online teaching. GTD is ideal for recent graduates who are interested in a career in academia.

The project management of the scheme is fulfilled by ECS, including some aspects of recruitment and selection. The traineeships are 18 months in length, and all graduates who are successfully recruited are paid a salary commensurate with the roles. They expose the graduates to aspects of academia, as they require the graduate trainees to support lecturers with preparing online learning resources (under careful supervision) and also online tutorials/seminars delivered by the lecturer.

The traineeships provide a career springboard for the graduates, as once completed, they can apply for vacancies within the university or other institutions. Alternatively, they can explore opportunities in other sectors given that the traineeship will have armed them with valuable skills and experiences applicable to a vast array of higher-level employment roles. A total of 16 GTD trainees across different degree programmes were recruited for the pilot.

GTD differs from GWES in that it does not have the strict criteria of only selecting unemployed or under-employed recent graduates. It also differs in length: 18 months versus the 12-week GWES internship.

However, both have proven to be formidable at supporting disadvantaged students/graduates into higher-level employment and thus helping to narrow the graduate employment gap for such cohorts.

THE GRADUATE INTERVIEW EVENT

The idea behind the Graduate Interview Event (GIE) was conceived in response to a common theme that was noticeable amongst many students at the university's careers fairs: low self-confidence. This manifested itself in ways such as some students being reluctant to talk to employers at their stands during the careers fair, or students only approaching employers in large groups with their peers, thus limiting meaningful one-to-one engagement between student and employer.

ECS ran and continues to run mandatory pre-career-fair preparation workshops that inform students how to navigate career fairs, how to dress, how to approach employers and, more broadly, on business etiquette.

However, over time, it was felt that a more pragmatic and impactful intervention was needed to connect students with employers and augment the students' chances of securing graduate-level employment. GIE was the solution.

GIE is a simple but effective concept. ECS made use of its employer contacts and proposed that they enter into an agreement with the university, one where they provide some semblance of exclusivity or 'first refusal' to some of their graduate-level opportunities, prioritising University of Greenwich final-year students or recent graduates for such opportunities.

Additionally, employers would guarantee conducting their interviews on the university campus so that students could attend real-life interviews for real jobs on campus instead of the conventional process of attending the employer's offices.

In return, ECS would act as a fully fledged recruitment agency on behalf of the employer, conducting the candidate preparation and sifting and shortlisting suitable candidates. ECS would also provide the interview rooms, refreshments and the order of candidates in attendance for on-campus interviews on any given day.

GIE takes place once a year over the course of six to eight weeks. It has grown in popularity, with around 20-plus employers participating and offering a total of approximately 30 graduate-level roles. This unique concept has been hugely successful. Employers benefit from immense time and cost savings, as many of the initial human resource functions are taken care of by ECS.

Students and recent graduates also benefit by being interviewed in very familiar surroundings and supported prior to interview with familiar faces (i.e. ECS careers staff). This in turn bolsters their confidence levels and performance during interviews.

Whilst GIE is a very time-consuming and logistically taxing event for a careers and employability service, the return on investment typically justifies the time and effort. In just one GIE season, between 15 to 18 final-year students have been known to secure graduate employment within the short six- to eight-week GIE period, making it one of the most efficient, evidence-based employability interventions as far as results are concerned.

It is all the more valuable as an intervention, given that it manages to address the theme of a lack of confidence amongst many students. Whilst there has been no research study at the University of Greenwich assessing the correlation or causation between students from low participation neighbourhoods and with low confidence levels, the works of Mikulaskova and Adamkovic (2018) allude to a relationship between poverty and self-esteem.

CAREERS MENTORING

Careers mentoring is the pairing of a student (mentee) with an experienced business professional from industry (mentor). The premise is that a student will gain insights into a company or a sector, establish social capital and build their confidence by having a careers mentor – all of which may assist them in gaining graduate-level employment.

The mentee is usually paired with a relevant mentor based on the degree studied and the student's career interests. ECS and faculties broker the mentoring by pairing up students with industry contacts (employees of companies that the university is engaged with in some capacity).

The mentoring period lasts between four to six months. During that period, mentees and their mentors are encouraged to meet for two hours per month. In these meetings, the mentor will typically offer the mentee advice spanning CV and interview guidance, elaborate on their experiences in their chosen profession and introduce the mentee to professional networks. Upon successful completion of the mentoring period, both the mentee and their mentor are invited to a large celebration event hosted by the faculties and ECS.

A total of 976 University of Greenwich students were paired with mentors from industry in just one year.

IMPACT ANALYSIS

Prior to the Employability Interventions

Earlier, in the section 'Graduate Interview Event', the theme of low self-esteem amongst students emerged and was indeed one of the catalysts behind the creation of GIE.

Aside from the low self-esteem amongst some students as witnessed during campus career fairs, ECS also gauged that this was a common theme during its various interactions with many students. This theme especially came to the fore during the preparation phase in some of the employability interventions covered earlier in this chapter.

To assess the impact of some of the employability interventions highlighted earlier, qualitative data was gathered via questionnaires. Some of the students who participated in the various employability interventions were asked to complete the questionnaires.

Combined with the quantitative data covered earlier (e.g., number of students going on to secure higher-skilled employment after participation in GWES and the number of students securing higher-skilled employment as a direct result of GIE), the qualitative data from the students provides greater contextual insights. This highlights the challenges students from low participation neighbourhood face and the impact of the employability interventions on their employment prospects.

Student A is a MEng Electrical and Electronic Engineering student at the University of Greenwich. Through ECS's data analytics, she has been identified as a student from a low participation neighbourhood.

Student A participated in the careers mentoring intervention. When asked why she applied for the scheme, she said the following:

> I was not self-confident in job applications. I have become introverted and less courageous about approaching colleagues and developing networks. Having endured failure a few times when applying for summer internships and graduate jobs, I felt it was time to make a change. When Emma [ECS staff member] approached us, I had no doubt about applying for careers mentoring. (Student A, author's research)

Unpacking Student A's comments, a lack of confidence, a lack of success in job applications and being introverted appear to be probable causes for her engagement with the careers mentoring scheme.

Additionally, Student A stressed that she was approached by Emma (an ECS staff member). This encounter occurred via Emma's curriculum-based seminars on the topic of 'building confidence'. Emma has also delivered non-curriculum-based workshops on the same topic.

Whilst the seminars and workshops are open to all students, the title of these sessions has been carefully crafted to entice students from disadvantaged backgrounds. During these sessions, careers mentoring is heavily promoted as a means by which to build confidence.

Student A's comments about her encounter with Emma align with the earlier point (in the section 'The Employability Interventions Employed by the University of Greenwich') regarding how ECS treads carefully when trying to engage students on the basis of their socio-economic status.

Rather than inadvertently stigmatising these students with exclusive messaging and provisions, the approach adopted is to have a broad reach (e.g. wide coverage of seminars in the curriculum) and open access to all students, though utilising carefully crafted titles that may resonate more powerfully with students from disadvantaged backgrounds.

In this case, featuring the words 'building confidence' appears to resonate with disadvantaged students. ECS was able to deduce this from its interactions with students, from which the recurring theme of 'low confidence' became apparent.

Student B studied BA (Hons) Social Work at the University of Greenwich and she was flagged up in ECS's data analytics as a student from a low participation neighbourhood. Student B participated in GTD to pursue her interest in teaching. This interest came about during her degree studies, where she realised that she no longer wanted to pursue a career in social work.

When asked what stood out to her about GTD, she replied as follows:

> It just seemed to be tailor-made as it covered my interest in teaching. The fact that I am a qualified social worker working with the social work team on the BA and MA programmes is indescribable! (Student B, author research)

Whereas Student A said:

> This opportunity would give me access to professionals that currently work in the engineering field. It would give me a chance to preview what it is like to work as an engineer and consideration whether this job suits me or not. It also gives me a chance to have someone else evaluate my CV writing and interview skills. (Student A, author research)

Unsurprisingly, the students used the employability interventions to develop employer networks and as a means to enter a specific career path: in the case of Student A, a career in engineering, whilst for Student B, a career in teaching.

After the Employability Interventions

The qualitative data collected also captured the post-intervention outcomes of the students who participated in the various employability interventions. This is especially useful for gauging the impact of the employability interventions, as the students' views and indeed their employment outcomes can confirm whether interventions such as GWES and graduate internships are genuinely impactful for students from low participation neighbourhoods.

Student C graduated from the University of Greenwich with a BSc in Finance and Investment Banking. He was identified as a student from a low participation neighbourhood. ECS brokered him into a graduate internship intervention with a financial services company as a Graduate Trainee Lending and Credit Control Officer. He has since secured graduate-level employment as an Equity Trader.

Student D and Student E have similar success stories. Student D also graduated from the university with a BSc in Finance and Investment Banking. As a student from a low participation neighbourhood, she responded to ECS's graduate internship opportunities and the pre-internship support on offer. ECS brokered her into an internship with a financial services company as a Finance Graduate Trainee. After her internship, she was employed permanently by the same company.

Student E also participated in ECS's graduate internships intervention. His degree in BSc Computer Science made him an ideal candidate for the role of Graduate Trainee Quality Assurance Analyst at a technology company, which he secured. On completion of his 12-week internship, he was recruited by the same company on a permanent basis.

In the case of Student A, whilst her intervention did not immediately catapult her into graduate-level employment, her accounts of what she gained as a result of participating suggested the intervention addressed her prior concerns of low self-esteem and set her on the path to becoming an engineer:

> At the beginning of the mentoring programme, I selected three skills to work on and improve with my mentor. We also worked through some typical interview questions where I lacked confidence. I feel more confident in front of potential employers as a result.
>
> Although we could not complete our goal in setting up a face-to-face mock interview due to covid19, I successfully applied for a few jobs and approached some employers through LinkedIn. (Student A, author research)

For Student B, she was still in the middle of her paid role within the GTD employability intervention. Student B was equally upbeat, stating the following:

> Where do I begin? I have provided feedback in regard to practice placement panels, supported my colleague who teaches law for both the BA and MA cohorts, and I am busy helping the department with admissions. The list is endless and experience invaluable. I am currently looking into the various teaching courses that are available for me to enrol. There is no stopping me now. (Student B, author research)

Student B's account highlights the 'apprenticeship' nature of the GTD traineeship, exposing the participant to on-the-job experience and continuing professional development.

All GTD trainees are offered the chance to gain a teaching and learning fellowship (i.e. GOLD Fellowship) free of charge, to enrich their experience and consolidate their teaching credentials. Similar to the much shorter internship schemes (GWES and the graduate internships), the pilot of the GTD scheme has also enabled students to venture off into other careers and secure their first graduate-level role.

Five of the original 16 GTD trainees secured graduate-level jobs with external companies midway through their 18-month traineeship. However, their premature departure from the traineeship has not been viewed as a negative. Their very participation in GTD has enabled them to secure good external positions in the private or public sector. This same phenomenon is witnessed in GWES and the graduate internships, although due to their shorter nature (i.e. 12 weeks as opposed to GTD's 18 months), most interns complete the 12-week internship before securing a graduate-level role elsewhere, or, as in the cases of Students D and E, with the same company where they completed their internship.

The graduate-level employment outcomes for Students C, D and E and the GWES statistic mentioned earlier in this chapter (i.e. 61% of all GWES interns securing graduate-level employment) illustrate the main impact of such interventions. However, statistics such as these can overshadow the other nuanced benefits gained from participation in these interventions.

Student A appears to have gained renewed confidence in herself and acknowledges the improvement in her self-esteem following her careers mentoring experience.

Student B is on the path to acquiring tangible benefits including a teaching and learning fellowship and quite possibly a teaching qualification.

What is evident is the propensity for careers mentoring to bolster the confidence of students. It also gives them enhanced social capital or key contacts within industry. These are assumed to be important qualities for success in a volatile graduate labour market.

For the more 'experiential' interventions such as GTD and GWES, the data seems to suggest that as well as directly contributing to the conversion rates of students/graduates securing graduate-level employment, the element of continuing professional development (e.g. qualifications or additional courses acquired during the traineeships and internships) appears to be a secondary benefit.

Beyond the opinions of participating students/graduates, the other key stakeholders are the employers recruiting University of Greenwich students. The opinions of students/graduates are vitally important to assess the merits and impact of the employability interventions. However, some of the interventions can only work with full participation and engagement from local businesses. Therefore, it is useful to gauge the impact and effectiveness of the interventions through the lens of the participating employers.

One such employer is MEP Ltd. The company has recruited graduates from the University of Greenwich for four consecutive years. Their line of work requires a steady pipeline of engineering graduates who are technically sound but also well-versed in skills such as teamwork.

Similarly, Sparta Global have a need for a steady pipeline of able graduates to work on technology-related projects for their Sparta Global international clients. They have been participants in GIE almost since its inception and continue to recruit University of Greenwich final-year students via GIE on an annual basis. When asked why they participate in GIE, the Managing Director of MEP Ltd replied as follows:

> The Graduate Interview Event (GIE) at University of Greenwich has a unique value as the University knows us well and understands what we do and how we do it. As the University vet and prepare these candidates, we are then able to meet with candidates who are pre-qualified which vastly reduces the non-value-added activity that often comes with recruitment.
>
> Being able to interview on campus, pre-arranged and organised by the University, cuts down on our recruitment time and costs and also makes life much easier for the candidates. We have employed four University of Greenwich graduate engineers in four years. (Managing Director, MEP Ltd, author research)

When asked the same question, the Head of Equality, Diversity and Inclusion at Sparta Global commented:

> We have been working with the University of Greenwich for several years.

> We have attended many Graduate Interview events over the years, and we are consistently pleased by how inclusively these initiatives are designed.
>
> As a result, we have always been able to work with a diverse group of students, nurturing a pool of talent that is inclusive from a perspective of gender, ethnicity, and social mobility. (Head of Equality, Diversity, and Inclusion, Sparta Global, author research)

The feedback provided by the employers reaffirm some of the assumed and intended benefits for employers when GIE was originally designed.

It needed to offer something that would entice employers to offer the University of Greenwich their graduate-level job vacancies with some semblance of exclusivity or, at the very least, 'first in the queue' consideration. As per the feedback, GIE achieves this by creating efficacy in the employers' recruitment process, saving them significant time and, very likely, money.

In the case of Sparta Global, they have leaned towards GIE's positive ability to present them with a diverse shortlisted array of talented students spanning gender, ethnicity and social mobility, the latter of those being particularly relevant when discussing the topic of supporting students from low participation neighbourhoods.

Another theme gleaned from the employers' feedback is GIE's tendency to establish 'repeat business'. MEP Ltd have used and continue to use it as a pipeline by which to recruit graduate engineers. Similarly, Sparta Global, whose business model inherently relies upon a large talent pool of graduates, were one of the earliest adopters of GIE and continue to use it annually.

That is not to say that all employers who have participated in GIE have demonstrated the repeated custom of MEP Ltd and Sparta Global. Inevitably, some employers have not managed to secure a graduate recruit from GIE after participation, with reasons such as the candidates not quite meeting their criteria or, in some cases, a lack of student interest in the employer's role(s).

Overall, there appears to be a sizable pool of employers who engage with GIE annually and continue to recruit students as a direct result.

Employers are also of significant importance for the implementation of the careers mentoring intervention. The motivations and benefits cited from employers differ from that of GIE employers.

For careers mentoring, employers have typically cited two key benefits stemming from their involvement. Firstly, it acts as a means for the employer to fulfil its corporate social responsibility pledge.

Secondly, for the employee participating as a mentor, it acts as continuing professional development. They are required to nurture and develop mentees, and this in turn develops or re-enforces interpersonal and leadership skills, which in turn can be documented and used for future promotion opportunities.

Whilst the premise of the case study is to illustrate the impact of bespoke employability interventions in narrowing the graduate labour market gap, the feedback from employers illustrates the wider impact of the interventions.

CONCLUSION

Data from the University of Greenwich's Access and Participation Plan illustrates the progress made in narrowing the graduate employment gap for students from low participation neighbourhoods.

This has stemmed from years of work to augment social mobility via its policies, research on social inequalities and employability interventions. This case study has focussed on documenting the impact of the employability interventions, amidst the backdrop of a particularly volatile graduate labour market.

Charting the implementation of various employability interventions and their associated quantitative performance data, coupled with qualitative data (i.e. questionnaire results) gauging the views of participating students, it has been possible to examine the true impact of these interventions and their contributions to the university's overall success in narrowing the graduate employment gap for students from low participation neighbourhoods.

The 'experiential' interventions such as GWES have demonstrated an impact, given the associated statistic showing its rates of conversion – that being the rates at which it has converted participating unemployed/underemployed graduates into graduate-level employment. Given that students from low participation neighbourhoods are likely to fare less well in the graduate labour market, the impact of interventions such as GWES is especially prodigious for them.

Student feedback from the questionnaires also points to the fact that the 'experiential' interventions provide the opportunity for relevant continuing professional development. In the case of the GTD scheme, trainees have the option to acquire a teaching and learning fellowship (i.e. GOLD Fellowship) free of charge. Those participating in the GWES internships are required to complete some mandatory online courses. Additionally, should they choose to do so, they can also complete optional bespoke training courses on a variety of professional topics.

Other interventions such as careers mentoring and GIE build student confidence, which is especially important given the assumed association (based on the literature and student feedback) between disadvantaged students and low self-esteem. Student feedback from the questionnaires points to the confidence boost acquired when the mentee is matched with a good mentor and both parties adhere to the mentorship for its duration.

Regarding GIE, it is felt that giving students the opportunity to attend a real graduate-level job interview within the familiar confines of university campus, coupled with pre-interview support from ECS, bolsters their interview confidence and performance. It is also worth noting that GIE's impact goes beyond confidence-building. Like some of the 'experiential' interventions, GIE also has a good conversion rate in getting participating students into graduate-level employment.

FUTURE DIRECTION

Demonstrating efforts to widen access and improve participation and employment success for students from disadvantaged backgrounds remains as one of the key talking points in the UK's higher education sector.

For the University of Greenwich, the future direction is firmly one of growth in order to positively impact more students from poorer backgrounds. Coupled with this is the need to adapt following lessons learnt from the pandemic: namely, technology-driven blended approaches to employability provisions to engage a wider body of employers and participating students. For the GIE, it will be adapted for delivery in person (as in previous years) and also for online delivery using video-conferencing technologies. This will facilitate greater numbers of employers offering semi-exclusive graduate job opportunities to Greenwich students, given that historically some employers did not participate due to the requirement of conducting interviews on campus.

The graduate internship schemes have been reviewed and contracts changed to accommodate the few occasions when the employer required the graduate to fulfil the internships as a home worker. Whilst this does denigrate the true in-person internship experience, it is felt that the home-working model is better than no internship at all.

Finally, there are ambitious plans to grow career mentees' and mentors' numbers across all faculties in the years to come, with targets alluding to 10%–15% growth (i.e. number of students participating). Once again, in adaptation to the pandemic, whilst the in-person mentoring model will always be favoured, work has been completed to allow video-conferencing mentoring to act as an alternative where necessary.

Academics whose research interests span the labour market and/or social mobility and higher education careers practitioners with similar cohorts of students may find some of the approaches espoused within this chapter of particular use to inform future practice.

REFERENCES

Connell-Smith, A. and Hubble, S., 2018, *Widening participation strategy in higher education in England*, House of Commons Library, https://commonslibrary.parliament.uk/research-briefings/cbp-8204/ (viewed 14 June 2021).

Crawford, C. and Vignoles, A., 2014, *Heterogeneity in graduate earnings by socioeconomic background*, Institute for Fiscal Studies, www.ifs.org.uk/publications/7419 (viewed 8 June 2021).

Gaskell, S. and Lingwood, R., 2019, *Widening opportunity in higher education: The third phase: Beyond graduation*, Universities UK, widening-opportunity-third-phase.pdf (viewed 9 June 2021).

HESA, 2021, *Definitions and benchmark factors*, HESA, www.hesa.ac.uk/data-and-analysis/performance-indicators/definitions (viewed 14 June 2021).

Highflyers Research, 2021, *The graduate market in 2021*, Highflyers Research Ltd, www.highfliers.co.uk/download/2021/graduate_market/GM21-Report.pdf (viewed 22 October 2021).

Matthewson, D., 2021, *Coronavirus and the latest indicators for the UK economy and society*, Office for National Statistics, ons.gov.uk (viewed 8 June 2021).

Mikulaskova, G. and Adamkovic, M., 2018, *The relationship between self-esteem, aggression, and poverty*, Clovek A Spolocnost, http://cejsh.icm.edu.pl/cejsh/element/bwmeta1.element.cejsh-f9d224c8-f621-4b51-904d-10dee9d75457 (viewed 8 June 2021).

Office for Students, 2019, *English higher education 2019: Annual Review*, Office for Students, www.officeforstudents.org.uk/annual-review-2019/beyond-higher-education-ensuring-successful-outcomes/ (viewed 22 October 2021).

University of Greenwich, 2020, *Access and Participation Plan 2020–21*, Student and Academic Services, University of Greenwich. https://docs.gre.ac.uk/__data/assets/pdf_file/0012/120603/Access-and-Participation-Plan-2020-21-to-2024-25.pdf (Accessed: 8 June 2021).

Xu, L., 2020, *How will coronavirus affect the lifetime earnings of new graduates?,* Economy Observatory, www.economicsobservatory.com/how-will-coronavirus-affect-lifetime-earnings-new-graduates (viewed 22 October 2021).

19

Are Higher Education Students from Disadvantaged Backgrounds More or Less Confident than Their Peers? A Study of Perceived Employability with First-year Students at an Australian University

Dawn Bennett, Paul Koshy and Ian Li

INTRODUCTION

Over the past three decades, Australian higher education policy has encompassed a focus on the impact of various aspects of disadvantage, or ‘equity group status’, on higher education participation, be it attributable to socio-economic (students from backgrounds of low socio-economic status (SES)), locational (students from regional and remote areas), cultural (Indigenous students, students from non-English-speaking backgrounds (NESBs)) or medical factors (disability). In addition, policy responses have also focused on related measures of disadvantage such as first-in-family (FiF) status. This has occurred as part of the increasing integration of ‘equity policy’ – those measures designed to ameliorate disadvantages associated with equity status – into overall higher education policy in Australia. Over the past decade, this has included measures to foster aspiration, access and participation in higher education across the general population through a series of measures including the expansion of university places, as well as specific measures to assist equity group students through funding for outreach and retention programmes (Koshy, 2016).

Recently, the focus in higher education policy globally has shifted towards outcomes, notably completion and post-graduate employment (Knight, 2019). In Australia, this has included a range of interventions and reporting initiatives, including the establishment of the Quality Indicators for Learning and Teaching (QILT) website, which reports on undergraduates' perceptions of their learning experience and graduate employment outcomes and salaries (QILT, 2021). An alignment of measured outcomes and funding is also taking place in Australia, with the Australian government's 'Job-ready Graduates Package' explicitly linking public funding for university places with observed deficits in the graduate markets in certain technical and professional vocations, including those relating to fields of study in the sciences, mathematics and nursing (Department of Education, Skills and Employment, 2020).

These developments have necessitated a focus on 'employability' as a critical organising concept in relation to students' educational and vocational planning. Employability can be defined as 'the ability to find, create and sustain meaningful work across the career lifespan and in multiple contexts' (Bennett, 2019a: i). Importantly, it is an attribute that is mutable and therefore subject to transformation as students gradually progress through their education journey and gain formative experiences as part of the process.

This chapter reports on the extent to which students' perceptions of the development and perceived gaps related to their employability are affected by their equity status. It draws on findings from the introduction of the employ-ability self-assessment tool – a survey instrument for student self-reflection on key employability traits, at a large, urban Australian higher education institution. It reports on an analysis of responses from first-year students and sub-samples for school-aged direct-entry students ('school leavers') and mature-age students ('non-school leavers').

EMPLOYABILITY AND EQUITY STATUS

The Bachelor degree is now the default qualification for post-compulsory education in Australia, with 41% of 19- and 20-year-old Australians enroled in a university course in 2018, compared with just 10% in vocational courses (Brett, 2018). As a result, higher education now accounts for approximately 80% of post-compulsory enrolments, compared with 67% in 2006 (O'Shea et al., 2021). This represents the culmination of growth in Australian higher education between 2008 and 2016, when undergraduate places expanded by 40% (Koshy, 2019). More broadly, it reflects the 'massification' in higher education in the developed world, with a gradual increase in higher education participation over several decades from 'elite' (0% to 15% attaining degrees) to 'mass' (16% to 50%) levels of participation, ultimately heading towards near 'universal' participation (greater than 50%) as discussed by Trow (2007).

Koshy (2019) observes that the increase in higher education participation in Australia resulted in both rising enrolments and a rising share of total enrolment in all official student equity groups: low SES students, students with disability, Indigenous students, women in non-traditional areas, students from regional and remote areas and NESB students.[1] As a consequence, around 50% of Australian students are now classified as belonging to at least one equity group (O'Shea et al., 2021). Thus, around 40% more students graduate from Australian institutions than did a decade ago, with around half the supply of graduates in the workforce now coming from equity groups.

This development necessarily focuses attention on the extent to which equity group status – which has historically been, and remains, associated with lower levels of participation – may also impact employment outcomes. Studies by Li et al. (2017), Li and Carroll (2019), Pitman et al. (2017) and Richardson et al. (2016) find that graduates from several equity groups, including those from the Indigenous, NESB and disability groups, experienced either lower rates of employment or starting salaries, or both. These effects are immediately observable in the national Australian data. For instance, the 2020 Graduate Outcomes Survey reported that in the first year following graduation, only 63.9% of graduates with disability were in full-time employment, compared with 73.6% of those without disability (QILT, 2020).

How does such divergence in outcomes translate to employability thinking among first-year equity students? Generally, a significant part of the shaping of employability expectations among equity students is attributable to perceptions among them and their influencers (e.g. parents and teachers) about their 'lower' prospects of successful performance and attainment in higher education. This is seen in the literature on higher education participation in relation to vocational education (see e.g. Becker and Hecken, 2009; Koshy et al., 2021) and in assessments of the relationship between prior academic achievement and participation, both of which suggest that in the case of some equity groups, most notably among low SES students, this relationship is a predominant factor (Marks, 2017).

Several studies of post-graduate employment outcomes find evidence for equity group difference after controlling for academic background. Richardson et al. (2016) identify the clustering of Australian equity students in 'lower status' disciplines and find that certain equity groups, such as students with disability, Indigenous students and NESB students, encounter lower overall patterns of employment. Similarly, Dockery and Bawa (2018) observe that female graduates in the science, technology, engineering and mathematics disciplines in Australia have lower levels of labour force participation and lower levels of satisfaction with the extent to which their technical skills are utilised in their jobs.

Students' perceptions of differential outcomes may also impact their self-assessments of employability. However, two recent studies utilising data from the Employ-ability self-assessment tool indicate that equity effects may be muted in relation to SES and regional location. Bennett et al. (2021a) observe that after controlling for prior academic achievement and effects associated with streaming students towards vocational education, there is limited evidence to suggest that low SES status has a key influence on perceived employability. Bennett et al. (2021b) find only limited evidence for a location effect in relation to self-reporting using the Employ-ability self-assessment measure.

Harvey et al. (2017) attribute the seemingly benign influence of socio-economic and geographical disadvantage to university selection effects, with relatively fewer low SES and regional students entering the higher education system and completing their degree to begin with, often in disciplines with stronger vocational ties to study, such as education and nursing.

MATERIALS AND METHODS

Instrument

The study reported here applied the social construction of career decision-making to career exploration and decision-making as posited by Lent et al. (1994, 2016). Students responded to a social cognitive self-reflection tool (see the Appendix) comprised of the Employ-ability measure together with six open questions (Bennett, 2019b). Demographic details comprised current work status, age in years, sex, location, highest completed level of education and their institution. The order of constructs and individual items were randomised to minimise question order bias. The instrument has been statistically validated in a sample of 10,193 students from 15 Australian universities, using exploratory and confirmatory factor analyses (Bennett and Ananthram, 2022).

The Employ-ability measure poses Likert-style scales on perceived employability and includes career decision-making, self-esteem, identity construction, citizenship, emotional intelligence and graduate capabilities. Open questions built into the survey were used to amass data on students' work background, choice of major, career intentions, self-directed development, and feedback on their academic programme. The employability traits considered in this study were as follows:

1. *Self-awareness and programme awareness*: Self-awareness is a metacognitive aspect of employability and impacts the extent to which students understand the relationship between their studies and their future careers.
2. *Career identity and commitment*: Career identity and commitment in the pre-professional context relates to students' identification with their discipline relative to career.

3 *Reconsideration with commitment*: Reconsideration of commitment in the pre-professional context relates to the extent to which students would change their study choices if they could do so.
4 *Self-esteem*: Self-esteem is an inner-value capital and reflects a ratio of realisations to expectations. A realistic assessment of self-esteem is known to influence perseverance and resilience.
5 *Academic self-efficacy*: Academic self-efficacy refers to students' perception of how well they expect to perform academic tasks and understand their subjects and whether they expect to succeed in their studies.
6 *Career exploration*: Career exploration relates to decisional self-efficacy and encapsulates exploration and awareness of career.
7 *Occupational mobility*: In the pre-professional context, occupational mobility relates to students' ability to manage disappointment and generate alternative career pathways.

Sampling and Ethics

Undergraduate university students at a university were invited to create a free personalised employability profile using the online measure; this was supported with cohort-wide educator reports and career-counsellor engagement. Ethical approvals were secured through the lead institution's Human Research Ethics Committee and student responses were anonymised prior to analysis. Students chose whether to include their responses in the research dataset and whether to respond to the open questions.

Data and Methods

For the purposes of this study, responses from the survey were restricted to first-year domestic students. This response dataset was then linked to student unit record data from the institution, to include official demographic variables such as those indicating equity status, and institution-specific data, notably weighted average marks (WAM). An indicator for Indigenous status was sought but was excluded from the variable set due to its small sample size and resulting cell count. This follows the approach undertaken by Bennett et al. (2021) in relation to this dataset and Li and Dockery (2015) in the context of looking at employment outcomes at the same institution.

The final (main) sample was comprised of responses from 5,909 first-year students, with an analysis of sub-samples also undertaken for school leavers (n = 4,465) and non-school leavers (n = 1,444). Descriptive statistics for the main sample are reported in Table 19.1. The majority of respondents in the main sample were school leavers, with around 75.6% arriving at university via the school-leaving pathway; most respondents were female (63.9%). Further, the sample was largely comprised of full-time students (with part-time students accounting for 8.6% of the sample) and those studying on-campus (90.8% of the sample).

Table 19.1 Descriptive statistics: main and sub-samples, means and standard deviations

Variable	Main sample		School leavers		Non-school leaver	
	Mean	*Std. dev.*	Mean	*Std. dev.*	Mean	*Std. dev.*
Demographic and equity status						
Female	0.639	*(0.480)*	0.622	*(0.485)*	0.689	*(0.463)*
Age	21.086	*(6.123)*	19.225	*(3.001)*	26.841	*(9.044)*
Low SES	0.159	*(0.366)*	0.149	*(0.356)*	0.190	*(0.393)*
Rural or remote	0.176	*(0.381)*	0.176	*(0.381)*	0.175	*(0.380)*
FiF	0.282	*(0.450)*	0.251	*(0.433)*	0.378	*(0.485)*
Indigenous	0.010	*(0.100)*	0.008	*(0.089)*	0.017	*(0.128)*
Disability	0.033	*(0.178)*	0.020	*(0.141)*	0.072	*(0.259)*
NESB	0.101	*(0.301)*	0.102	*(0.302)*	0.097	*(0.296)*
Pathway and participation						
School-leaving pathway	0.756	*(0.430)*	1.000	N/A	0.000	N/A
On-campus study	0.908	*(0.289)*	0.979	*(0.144)*	0.690	*(0.463)*
Part-time study	0.086	*(0.280)*	0.045	*(0.208)*	0.212	*(0.409)*
WAM	64.400	*(20.087)*	66.392	*(17.404)*	58.239	*(25.781)*
Field of study						
Natural and physical sciences	0.042	*(0.199)*	0.047	*(0.211)*	0.026	*(0.158)*
Information technology	0.026	*(0.158)*	0.027	*(0.163)*	0.020	*(0.140)*
Engineering and related technologies	0.004	*(0.060)*	0.004	*(0.062)*	0.003	*(0.053)*
Architecture and building	0.034	*(0.181)*	0.034	*(0.182)*	0.033	*(0.178)*
Agriculture and environmental studies	0.015	*(0.121)*	0.016	*(0.123)*	0.013	*(0.111)*
Health and related studies	0.386	*(0.487)*	0.422	*(0.494)*	0.275	*(0.447)*
Education	0.124	*(0.329)*	0.068	*(0.251)*	0.297	*(0.457)*
Management and commerce	0.235	*(0.424)*	0.241	*(0.428)*	0.215	*(0.411)*
Society and culture	0.093	*(0.290)*	0.096	*(0.295)*	0.082	*(0.275)*
Creative arts and other studies	0.041	*(0.198)*	0.043	*(0.203)*	0.034	*(0.181)*
Employability traits						
Self-awareness	4.762	*(0.770)*	4.740	*(0.760)*	4.831	*(0.798)*

Table 19.1 (Continued)

Variable	Main sample		School leavers		Non-school leaver	
	Mean	***Std. dev.***	**Mean**	***Std. dev.***	**Mean**	***Std. dev.***
Programme awareness	5.054	*(0.736)*	5.044	*(0.727)*	5.084	*(0.764)*
Identification with commitment	3.911	*(0.769)*	3.879	*(0.766)*	4.009	*(0.770)*
Reconsideration of commitment	3.504	*(1.002)*	3.436	*(0.996)*	3.715	*(0.991)*
Self-efficacy	2.187	*(0.493)*	2.177	*(0.488)*	2.219	*(0.506)*
Academic self-efficacy	5.362	*(0.819)*	5.337	*(0.799)*	5.439	*(0.874)*
Career exploration	6.947	*(1.371)*	6.891	*(1.358)*	7.121	*(1.398)*
Occupational mobility	6.324	*(1.626)*	6.251	*(1.589)*	6.550	*(1.717)*
Observations	**5,909**	N/A	**4,465**	N/A	**1,444**	N/A

Note: FiF = first in family; NESB = non-English-speaking background; SES = socio-economic status; Std. dev. = standard deviation; WAM = weighted average marks.

Student representation from larger equity groups broadly tracked student enrolment shares, including low SES (15.9%) and regional and remote (17.6%) students, while smaller groups such as Indigenous students (1%) and students with disability (3.3%) had lower sample shares. The NESB student share of 10% was noticeably higher than the institution's reported share of around 4%, likely reflecting the mix of fields of study, including high shares of students in *Management and commerce* (23.5%) and *Health and related studies* (38.6%).

Also reported in Table 19.1 and represented in Figures 19.1 and 19.2 are response averages for the eight employability traits for the school-leaver and non-school-leaver sub-samples, respectively. The *Reconsideration with commitment* trait, constructed as having a negative impact on employability, is inverted, such that all traits, both individually and collectively, are associated with positive outcomes in employability (Bennett and Ananthram, 2022).

A preliminary observation of the data by sub-sample indicates quite limited divergence across equity groups in relation to responses on employability traits, with the possible exception of the disability group, particularly in the non-school leavers.

Each of the employability traits represents an outcome variable in the modelling reported in this study using an identical series of explanatory variables in the main sample and sub-samples. Multivariate linear regression was conducted to examine the influence of the group of explanatory variables on each employability trait, as per the following equation:

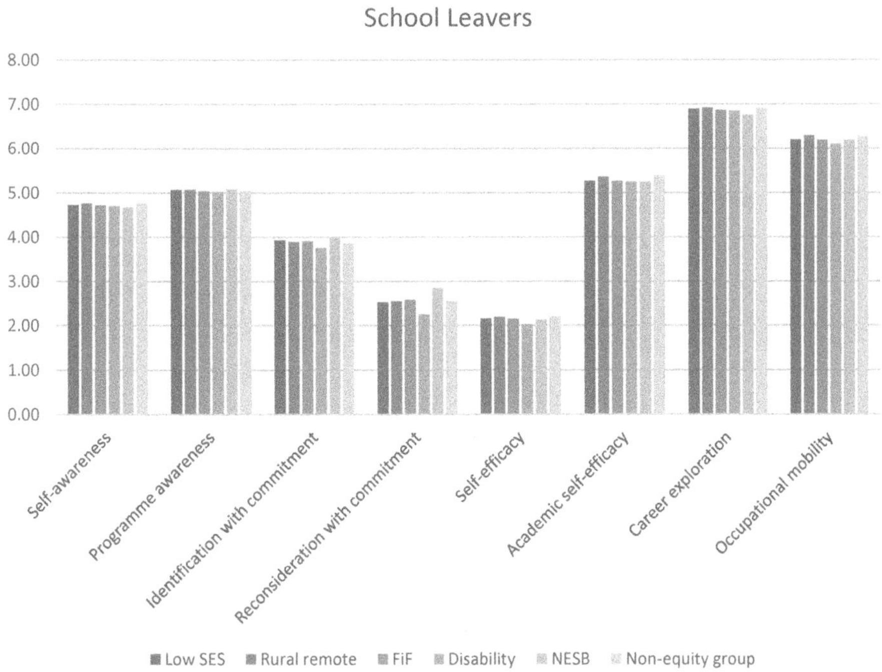

Figure 19.1 Means of outcome by equity group: school-leaver sub-sample

Note: FiF = first in family; NESB = non-English-speaking background; SES = socio-economic status; WAM = weighted average marks.

$$ET_i = \alpha_i + \beta_{ij} X_j + \varepsilon_i$$

where ET_i is one of the employability traits, X_j is the group (vector) of j explanatory variables and ε_i is the respective error term for each model.

FINDINGS

The model was estimated using data from the main sample (n = 5,909), with results from the main sample reported in Table 19.2 and results from estimations using the sub-samples for school leavers and non-school leavers reported in Tables 19.3 and 19.4, respectively.

Providing partial confirmation for the validation of the Employ-ability tool in Bennett and Ananthram (2021), the influence of the explanatory set varied across employability traits. Only *Age*, with uniformly positive and statistically significant effects, and *WAM*, with similarly positive and statistically significant effects across the first seven traits and no statistically significant effect observed in *Occupational Mobility*, exhibited a consistent pattern of influence across all traits.

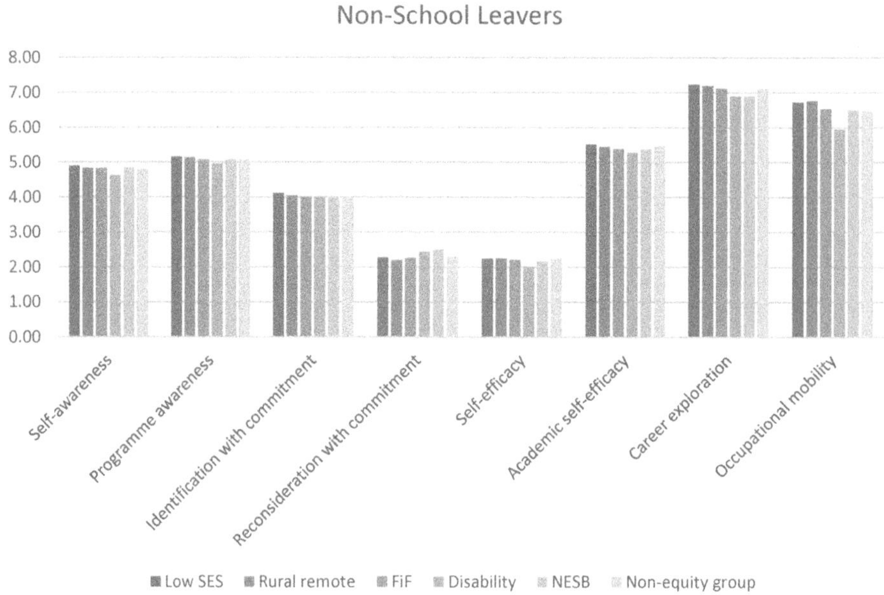

Figure 19.2 Means of outcome by equity group: non-school-leaver sub-sample group

Note: FiF = first in family; NESB = non-English-speaking background; SES = socio-economic status; WAM = weighted average marks.

Equity Group effects Varied across the Employability Traits

In relation to the *Self-awareness* trait, no statistically significant equity group effect was observed relating to low SES or locational status (see Table 19.2). This follows Bennett et al. (2021), who, in looking at a school-leaver cohort, observed no significant equity effects in relation to low SES status or an alternative measure of disadvantage using data on school sector (government, Catholic or private). However, a negative effect was observed in relation to disability status (*Disability:* –0.140, $p < 0.05$) and a marginal effect (significant only at the 10% level) in relation to NESB (*NESB*: –0.063, $p < 0.1$).

Analysis of these results in the two sub-samples indicates that the result for *Disability* was only present among non-school leavers (see Table 19.3, *Disability*: –0.244, $p < 0.05$), while the *NESB* effect was only observed in the school leavers (see Table 19.4, *NESB*: –0.081, $p < 0.05$). Also of note, the observed positive effect of WAM on *Self-awareness* (*WAM*: 0.002, $p < 0.01$) was driven by an effect in the school leavers (Table 19.3, *WAM*: 0.003, $p < 0.01$), with no statistically significant effect observed among non-school leavers in their first year.

No statistically significant effect was attributable to equity status in the model explaining *Programme awareness*, with the sub-sample analysis revealing only a marginal effect attributed to disability status in the non-school-leaver group

Table 19.2 Model results for each employability trait: main sample

	Self-awareness	Programme awareness	Identification with commitment	Reconsideration of commitment	Self-esteem	Academic self-efficacy	Career exploration	Occupational mobility
Female	0.050**	0.120***	0.117***	0.102***	−0.041***	0.025	0.121***	−0.091**
	(2.240)	(5.835)	(5.329)	(3.645)	(−2.930)	(1.063)	(3.022)	(−1.971)
Age	0.009***	0.006***	0.011***	0.018***	0.007***	0.012***	0.020***	0.033***
	(4.054)	(2.698)	(5.361)	(6.444)	(5.410)	(5.064)	(4.957)	(6.985)
Low SES	0.009	0.023	0.060**	0.042	−0.007	−0.028	0.046	0.006
	(0.313)	(0.893)	(2.199)	(1.196)	(−0.393)	(−0.916)	(0.947)	(0.102)
Rural or remote	0.000	0.012	−0.006	−0.017	0.016	0.016	0.002	0.083
	(0.001)	(0.473)	(−0.204)	(−0.503)	(0.957)	(0.573)	(0.036)	(1.501)
FiF	−0.030	−0.008	0.015	0.013	−0.032**	−0.095***	−0.037	−0.091*
	(−1.371)	(−0.367)	(0.684)	(0.457)	(−2.269)	(−3.992)	(−0.921)	(−1.930)
Disability	−0.140**	−0.085	−0.086	0.025	−0.175***	−0.126*	−0.175	−0.460***
	(−2.107)	(−1.633)	(−1.378)	(0.355)	(−4.265)	(−1.893)	(−1.465)	(−2.980)
NESB	−0.063*	0.005	0.061*	−0.270***	−0.044**	−0.092**	−0.172***	−0.037
	(−1.838)	(0.156)	(1.910)	(−6.097)	(−1.999)	(−2.448)	(−2.820)	(−0.519)
WAM	0.002***	0.002***	0.001*	0.004***	0.002***	0.005***	0.003***	0.001
	(4.439)	(4.603)	(1.865)	(6.550)	(6.316)	(8.626)	(2.979)	(0.852)
School-leaving pathway	−0.038	0.002	−0.033	−0.119***	0.000	−0.075**	−0.092*	−0.085
	(−1.299)	(0.090)	(−1.151)	(−3.269)	(0.021)	(−2.420)	(−1.739)	(−1.353)
On-campus study	−0.013	−0.017	−0.005	0.028	−0.051*	−0.032	−0.052	−0.018
	(−0.267)	(−0.388)	(−0.105)	(0.496)	(−1.805)	(−0.617)	(−0.637)	(−0.180)
Part-time study	−0.059	−0.115***	−0.006	−0.092*	−0.001	−0.103**	−0.119*	0.097
	(−1.474)	(−2.997)	(−0.156)	(−1.860)	(−0.052)	(−2.350)	(−1.721)	(1.215)
Natural and physical sciences	−0.095*	−0.032	−0.072	0.201***	−0.157***	−0.003	−0.235**	−0.174
	(−1.744)	(−0.648)	(−1.324)	(3.043)	(−4.389)	(−0.052)	(−2.195)	(−1.481)

Table 19.2 Model results for each employability trait: main sample (Continued)

	Self-awareness	Programme awareness	Identification with commitment	Reconsideration of commitment	Self-esteem	Academic self-efficacy	Career exploration	Occupational mobility
Information technology	−0.164**	−0.093*	−0.205***	0.394***	−0.111**	−0.085	−0.135	−0.180
	(−2.549)	(−1.654)	(−3.134)	(4.950)	(−2.566)	(−1.266)	(−1.258)	(−1.327)
Engineering and related technologies	0.026	0.004	−0.308	0.399**	−0.163	−0.072	0.233	−0.038
	(0.196)	(0.033)	(−1.390)	(2.080)	(−1.247)	(−0.537)	(1.081)	(−0.085)
Architecture and building	0.010	0.071	0.005	0.279***	−0.013	−0.071	0.108	−0.094
	(0.181)	(1.331)	(0.084)	(4.060)	(−0.361)	(−1.196)	(1.163)	(−0.902)
Agriculture and environmental studies	−0.149*	−0.184***	−0.179**	0.136	−0.054	−0.028	−0.000	0.028
	(−1.952)	(−2.616)	(−2.127)	(1.359)	(−1.051)	(−0.369)	(−0.001)	(0.184)
Health and related studies	0.091***	0.240***	0.086***	0.185***	−0.039**	0.035	0.206***	−0.055
	(3.396)	(9.530)	(3.244)	(5.432)	(−2.312)	(1.220)	(4.155)	(−0.979)
Education	0.104***	0.250***	0.074*	0.478***	−0.029	0.009	0.200***	−0.105
	(2.613)	(6.792)	(1.919)	(10.274)	(−1.172)	(0.217)	(2.712)	(−1.221)
Society and culture	0.023	0.070*	−0.005	0.232***	−0.010	0.036	0.123*	0.000
	(0.585)	(1.867)	(−0.130)	(4.817)	(−0.428)	(0.909)	(1.770)	(0.004)
Creative arts and other studies	−0.128**	−0.416***	−0.193***	0.288***	−0.145***	−0.104*	−0.112	−0.359***
	(−2.246)	(−7.180)	(−3.347)	(4.480)	(−4.004)	(−1.841)	(−1.067)	(−3.010)
Constant	4.407***	4.614***	3.521***	2.677***	2.014***	4.886***	6.322***	5.796***
	(51.915)	(58.024)	(43.119)	(25.241)	(38.397)	(51.694)	(41.774)	(32.928)
Observations (*n*)	5,909	5,909	5,909	5,909	5,909	5,909	5,909	5,909
R-squared	0.027	0.076	0.037	0.068	0.030	0.035	0.030	0.024
Adjusted R-squared	0.023	0.073	0.034	0.065	0.027	0.031	0.026	0.020

Note: FiF = first in family; NESB = non-English-speaking background; SES = socio-economic status; WAM = weighted average marks.

Robust t-statistics in parentheses. $^{*}p < 0.1$. $^{**}p < 0.05$, $^{***}p < 0.01$.

Table 19.3 Model results for each employability trait: school-leaver sub-sample

	Self-awareness	Programme awareness	Identification with commitment	Reconsideration of commitment	Self-esteem	Academic self-efficacy	Career exploration	Occupational mobility
Female	0.064**	0.136***	0.113***	0.103***	−0.043***	0.046*	0.143***	−0.073
	(2.559)	(5.858)	(4.557)	(3.272)	(−2.671)	(1.799)	(3.147)	(−1.404)
Age	0.012***	0.007	0.014***	0.029***	−0.001	0.006	0.013	0.022**
	(2.764)	(1.630)	(3.196)	(5.067)	(−0.184)	(1.303)	(1.589)	(2.514)
Low SES	−0.012	0.020	0.045	0.071*	−0.021	−0.079**	0.023	−0.060
	(−0.345)	(0.659)	(1.348)	(1.702)	(−0.923)	(−2.231)	(0.409)	(−0.841)
Rural or remote	0.023	0.019	0.004	−0.017	0.027	0.034	0.018	0.061
	(0.759)	(0.680)	(0.135)	(−0.443)	(1.401)	(1.070)	(0.331)	(0.972)
FiF	−0.038	−0.007	0.023	−0.006	−0.034**	−0.094***	−0.047	−0.112**
	(−1.441)	(−0.287)	(0.892)	(−0.163)	(−2.071)	(−3.386)	(−0.997)	(−2.019)
Disability	−0.066	−0.041	−0.144	0.273***	−0.155***	−0.124	−0.068	−0.184
	(−0.715)	(−0.581)	(−1.595)	(2.932)	(−2.723)	(−1.222)	(−0.386)	(−0.823)
NESB	−0.081**	0.009	0.088**	−0.315***	−0.045*	−0.096**	−0.161**	−0.034
	(−2.071)	(0.264)	(2.485)	(−6.152)	(−1.867)	(−2.261)	(−2.328)	(−0.432)
WAM	0.003***	0.003***	0.001**	0.004***	0.003***	0.006***	0.003***	−0.000
	(4.300)	(4.211)	(1.984)	(4.954)	(5.808)	(8.256)	(2.751)	(−0.306)
On-campus study	0.054	−0.046	0.009	−0.026	0.014	−0.077	−0.005	0.081
	(0.727)	(−0.559)	(0.106)	(−0.242)	(0.314)	(−0.853)	(−0.034)	(0.501)
Part-time study	−0.044	−0.116*	0.038	−0.203***	0.052	−0.048	−0.136	0.106
	(−0.722)	(−1.949)	(0.649)	(−2.679)	(1.505)	(−0.747)	(−1.246)	(0.889)
Natural and physical sciences	−0.146**	−0.070	−0.096	0.150**	−0.175***	−0.058	−0.333***	−0.212*
	(−2.456)	(−1.265)	(−1.601)	(2.097)	(−4.546)	(−0.967)	(−2.789)	(−1.668)
Information technology	−0.121*	−0.089	−0.200***	0.373***	−0.078*	−0.038	−0.094	−0.174

Table 19.3 Model results for each employability trait: school-leaver sub-sample (Continued)

	Self-awareness	Programme awareness	Identification with commitment	Reconsideration of commitment	Self-esteem	Academic self-efficacy	Career exploration	Occupational mobility
	(−1.716)	(−1.441)	(−2.639)	(4.263)	(−1.682)	(−0.511)	(−0.831)	(−1.179)
Engineering and related technologies	−0.003	0.035	−0.438*	0.407*	−0.194	−0.093	0.268	−0.064
	(−0.023)	(0.241)	(−1.679)	(1.780)	(−1.211)	(−0.669)	(1.127)	(−0.117)
Architecture and building	0.008	0.075	−0.019	0.279***	−0.005	−0.085	0.075	−0.193
	(0.119)	(1.179)	(−0.289)	(3.520)	(−0.135)	(−1.212)	(0.713)	(−1.607)
Agriculture and environmental studies	−0.173**	−0.216***	−0.174*	0.213**	−0.034	−0.029	−0.009	0.080
	(−1.996)	(−2.822)	(−1.755)	(2.023)	(−0.584)	(−0.388)	(−0.065)	(0.494)
Health and related studies	0.057*	0.218***	0.064**	0.155***	−0.049***	−0.001	0.129**	−0.135**
	(1.924)	(7.862)	(2.174)	(4.121)	(−2.638)	(−0.019)	(2.371)	(−2.171)
Education	0.108**	0.229***	0.042	0.440***	−0.045	0.053	0.185**	−0.102
	(2.235)	(5.122)	(0.859)	(7.467)	(−1.467)	(0.998)	(2.029)	(−0.939)
Society and culture	−0.002	0.061	−0.014	0.160***	−0.022	0.020	0.054	−0.023
	(−0.053)	(1.513)	(−0.323)	(2.957)	(−0.798)	(0.454)	(0.692)	(−0.259)
Creative arts and other studies	−0.146**	−0.409***	−0.206***	0.299***	−0.153***	−0.154**	−0.121	−0.398***
	(−2.271)	(−6.292)	(−3.159)	(4.147)	(−3.675)	(−2.452)	(−1.028)	(−3.053)
Constant	4.218***	4.595***	3.407***	2.418***	2.077***	4.907***	6.300***	5.947***
	(33.059)	(35.821)	(26.426)	(13.997)	(26.305)	(34.463)	(26.863)	(23.036)
Observations (*n*)	4,465	4,465	4,465	4,465	4,465	4,465	4,465	4,465
R-squared	0.021	0.073	0.027	0.044	0.022	0.029	0.016	0.008
Adjusted R-squared	0.016	0.069	0.023	0.040	0.018	0.025	0.012	0.0037

Note: FiF = first in family; NESB = non-English-speaking background; SES = socio-economic status; WAM = weighted average marks.

Robust t-statistics in parentheses. $^{*}p < 0.1$. $^{**}p < 0.05$, $^{***}p < 0.01$.

Table 19.4 Model results for each employability trait: non-school-leaver sub-sample

	Self-awareness	Programme awareness	Identification with commitment	Reconsideration of commitment	Self-esteem	Academic self-efficacy	Career exploration	Occupational mobility
Female	−0.002	0.056	0.135***	0.114*	−0.061*	−0.080	0.014	−0.169*
	(−0.045)	(1.245)	(2.778)	(1.899)	(−1.953)	(−1.554)	(0.171)	(−1.648)
Age	0.008***	0.006**	0.010***	0.013***	0.010***	0.015***	0.021***	0.035***
	(2.840)	(2.263)	(3.866)	(3.980)	(6.480)	(5.235)	(4.580)	(6.138)
Low SES	0.076	0.036	0.096**	−0.015	0.031	0.120**	0.121	0.206*
	(1.449)	(0.766)	(1.994)	(−0.227)	(0.920)	(2.074)	(1.330)	(1.846)
Rural or remote	−0.075	−0.008	−0.036	−0.024	−0.017	−0.043	−0.049	0.158
	(−1.305)	(−0.153)	(−0.645)	(−0.350)	(−0.512)	(−0.685)	(−0.507)	(1.350)
FiF	−0.011	−0.006	−0.014	0.049	−0.010	−0.081*	0.007	−0.008
	(−0.260)	(−0.152)	(−0.348)	(0.973)	(−0.372)	(−1.732)	(0.092)	(−0.086)
Disability	−0.244**	−0.144*	−0.056	−0.209**	−0.223***	−0.188**	−0.330**	−0.753***
	(−2.562)	(−1.866)	(−0.641)	(−2.114)	(−3.767)	(−2.150)	(−2.033)	(−3.566)
NESB	0.016	−0.010	−0.027	−0.103	−0.035	−0.075	−0.202	−0.051
	(0.229)	(−0.152)	(−0.364)	(−1.179)	(−0.703)	(−0.930)	(−1.545)	(−0.322)
Course-WAM	0.001	0.001*	0.000	0.004***	0.001*	0.003***	0.001	0.001
	(1.272)	(1.803)	(0.373)	(3.655)	(1.895)	(3.276)	(0.598)	(0.719)
On-campus study	−0.123*	−0.023	−0.011	0.008	−0.074*	−0.098	−0.159	−0.117
	(−1.808)	(−0.375)	(−0.172)	(0.104)	(−1.787)	(−1.309)	(−1.371)	(−0.830)
Part-time study	−0.072	−0.110**	−0.036	−0.017	−0.031	−0.137**	−0.096	0.096
	(−1.347)	(−2.184)	(−0.686)	(−0.264)	(−0.932)	(−2.268)	(−1.066)	(0.874)
Natural and physical sciences	0.162	0.134	0.009	0.471***	−0.085	0.268**	0.213	0.048
	(1.200)	(1.170)	(0.067)	(2.731)	(−0.867)	(2.003)	(0.931)	(0.151)
Information technology	−0.324**	−0.102	−0.235*	0.456**	−0.227**	−0.248	−0.291	−0.233

Table 19.4 Model results for each employability trait: non-school-leaver sub-sample (Continued)

	Self-awareness	Programme awareness	Identification with commitment	Reconsideration of commitment	Self-esteem	Academic self-efficacy	Career exploration	Occupational mobility
	(−2.117)	(−0.735)	(−1.944)	(2.398)	(−2.100)	(−1.563)	(−1.027)	(−0.708)
Engineering and related technologies	0.200	−0.094	0.286	0.368	−0.006	0.098	0.135	0.139
	(0.554)	(−0.450)	(1.482)	(1.252)	(−0.086)	(0.250)	(0.267)	(0.327)
Architecture and building	0.025	0.062	0.107	0.275**	−0.027	−0.026	0.223	0.235
	(0.257)	(0.641)	(0.918)	(2.016)	(−0.386)	(−0.230)	(1.137)	(1.129)
Agriculture and environmental studies	−0.081	−0.088	−0.205	−0.184	−0.141	−0.035	−0.011	−0.139
	(−0.513)	(−0.515)	(−1.487)	(−0.722)	(−1.274)	(−0.164)	(−0.050)	(−0.357)
Health and related studies	0.252***	0.326***	0.181***	0.312***	0.014	0.195***	0.542***	0.308**
	(3.935)	(5.451)	(2.938)	(3.937)	(0.352)	(2.869)	(4.569)	(2.349)
Education	0.135*	0.311***	0.146**	0.595***	−0.003	0.010	0.303**	−0.059
	(1.827)	(4.605)	(2.201)	(7.310)	(−0.062)	(0.126)	(2.239)	(−0.394)
Society and culture	0.151*	0.120	0.038	0.513***	0.050	0.137	0.414***	0.095
	(1.649)	(1.276)	(0.413)	(4.941)	(0.910)	(1.533)	(2.609)	(0.522)
Creative arts and other studies	−0.031	−0.438***	−0.124	0.285*	−0.117	0.115	−0.093	−0.247
	(−0.247)	(−3.381)	(−1.023)	(1.929)	(−1.590)	(0.891)	(−0.398)	(−0.838)
Constant	4.556***	4.665***	3.561***	2.736***	2.003***	4.953***	6.370***	5.634***
	(39.627)	(44.329)	(32.344)	(19.758)	(28.146)	(38.455)	(31.821)	(23.489)
Observations (*n*)	1,444	1,444	1,444	1,444	1,444	1,444	1,444	1,444
R-squared	0.051	0.089	0.055	0.116	0.071	0.064	0.064	0.061
Adjusted R-squared	0.039	0.077	0.043	0.104	0.058	0.051	0.052	0.048

Note: FiF = first in family; NESB = non-English-speaking background; SES = socio-economic status; WAM = weighted average marks.

Robust t-statistics in parentheses. $^{*}p < 0.1$. $^{**}p < 0.05$, $^{***}p < 0.01$.

(*Disability*: –0.144, $p < 0.1$) Of note to educators, the influence of equity status may be subsumed into measures of disadvantage associated with mode of study, specifically part-time study (*Part-time study*: –0.115, $p < 0.001$), with a similarly strong effect observed in both sub-samples. Academic performance, as measured by the WAM, was a more important explanator of responses on this trait among school leavers in terms of both effect size and statistical significance (Table 19.3, *WAM*: 0.003, $p < 0.01$; Table 19.4, *WAM*: 0.001, $p < 0.1$).

Positive and statistically significant equity group effects were observed in relation to the *Identification with commitment* trait, notably in relation to low SES status (*Low SES*: 0.060, $p < 0.05$), with a weaker effect observed in relation to NESB (*NESB*: 0.061, $p < 0.1$). However, the low SES effect was only present among non-school leavers (Table 19.4, *Low SES*: 0.096, $p < 0.05$), while as above, the NESB effect was only seen in the school leavers (Table 19.3, *NESB*: 0.088, $p < 0.05$).

The values for the *Reconsideration with commitment* trait were inverted, such that higher values indicate a reduced propensity for a student to reconsider their commitment to study. Other than a strong effect associated with NESB status (*NESB*: –0.270, $p < 0.01$), no significant effects were observed in relation to equity status in the main sample. However, this effect was only present in the school leavers (Table 19.3, *NESB*: –0.315, $p < 0.01$), with this variable being insignificant in the non-school leavers. The effect associated with disability was statistically insignificant in the main sample; however, strong and significant, yet opposing, effects were seen in the sub-samples: a positive effect among school leavers (Table 19.3, *Disability*: 0.273, $p < 0.01$) and a negative influence among non-school leavers (Table 19.4, *Disability*: –0.209, $p < 0.05$).

Confidence around commitment was unsurprisingly related to age and experience, with statistically significant and positive effects observed in relation to age (*Age*: 0.102, $p < 0.01$). As a result, in the main sample, the variable for school-leaver status was significant (*School-leaving pathway*: –0.119, $p < 0.01$). A strong gender effect was also observed (*Female*: 0.102, $p < 0.01$), while the effect associated with WAM was also significant (*WAM*: 0.04, $p < 0.01$). These effects were present in the sub-samples. Strong effects related to field of study were observed but not exclusively in fields with higher levels of equity student participation; for example, strong, positive effects are seen in both *Engineering and related technologies* (0.399, $p < 0.05$) – historically a low enroller of equity students – and *Education* (0.478, $p < 0.001$), which has a higher share of equity student enrolments.

In relation to *Self-efficacy*, negative and statistically significant effects were observed in relation to disability (*Disability*: –0.175, $p < 0.01$), an effect that was stronger in non-school leavers, and in relation to NESB status (*NESB*: –0.044, $p < 0.05$), with this effect only being significant for school leavers. Effects were also observed in relation to gender (*Female*: –0.041, $p < 0.01$) and mode of study (*On-campus study*: –0.051, $p < 0.1$).

Academic Self-efficacy was associated with the strongest effect attributable to WAM (*WAM*: 0.005, $p < 0.01$), but with a stronger effect noticeable in the school leavers (Table 19.3, *WAM*: 0.006, $p < 0.01$) compared with the non-school leavers (Table 19.4, *WAM:* 0.003, $p < 0.01$). Given this, it is unsurprising that the influence of demographic factors was particularly noticeable in relation to age (*Age*: 0.012, $p < 0.01$) and part-time study (*Part-time study*: –0.103, $p < 0.05$), with the educational pathway variable also being significant (*School-leaving pathway*: –0.075, $p < 0.05$). Equity group effects were observed in relation to NESB status (*NESB*: –0.092, $p < 0.05$) and FiF status (*FiF*: –0.095, $p < 0.01$).

Examination of the sub-sample results shows commonality in relation to FiF status in both sub-samples, but with the NESB effect only observable among school leavers (Table 19.3, *NESB*: –0.096, $p < 0.05$) and the disability effect only seen in the non-school leavers (Table 19.4, *Disability*: –0.188, $p < 0.05$). The statistical insignificance of low SES status in the main sample masked opposing effects in relation to low SES status in the sub-samples: a negative effect among school leavers (Table 19.3, *Low SES*: –0.079, $p < 0.05$) and a positive effect among non-school leavers (Table 19.4, *Low SES*: 0.120, $p < 0.05$).

Student responses on the *Career exploration* trait were influenced by factors associated with age and experience, characterised by a statistically significant and positive effect associated with age (*Age*: 0.121, $p < 0.01$). The only observed effect among equity group students was a marginal effect for NESB students (*NESB*: –0.172, $p < 0.01$) – although, in line with the other findings, this was only significant for school leavers (Table 19.3, *NESB*: –0.161, $p < 0.05$). A negative effect was observed in relation to disability in the non-school leavers (Table 19.4, *Disability*: –0.330, $p < 0.05$).

Occupational mobility was subject to significant effects associated with age (*Age*: 0.033, $p < 0.01$) and gender (*Female*: –0.091, $p < 0.05$), as well as disability (*Disability*: –0.460, $p < 0.01$) – although, both the gender and disability effects were only observed in the non-school leavers.

CONCLUSION

Relative to non-equity students, equity students in Australian higher education encounter reduced access, participation and employment outcomes. The influencing factors are both numerous and compounding, in the sense that disadvantage is often experienced in multiple forms. This can be seen, for example, in students from regional and remote areas of Australia, who are more likely than their metropolitan peers to have a low SES background. It is therefore unsurprising that the effects of multiple disadvantage are manifested across the student lifecycle, as measured by indicators linked with prior achievement.

Examining employability thinking in the context of equity status is therefore challenging, as much of the divergence between student groups is captured in other explanatory variables such as academic performance and school background. For this reason, studies examining self-reported data on employability thinking often find limited evidence for the influence of socio-economic disadvantage or regional location. In many ways, this evidence serves to confirm the veracity of the equity group classification system in Australia: observed outcomes across equity groups are marked before controlling for other underlying influences.

However, this study provides evidence of differences among first-year students between school leavers and those who are older, non-school leavers. These equity effects were significant and occurred in the presence of variables controlling for enrolment factors such as part-time status and WAM. Significantly, these effects were observed across a range of employability traits, ranging from study-related traits such as *Academic self-efficacy* to more future-oriented thinking around *Occupational mobility*.

We found that among school-leavers, NESB students exhibited lower rates of self-perceived employability confidence than other equity group students and those in the general student population. This provides confirmatory evidence on studies examining the reduced employment outcomes of NESB students and is a further basis for the development of specific measures to address this disadvantage. In contrast, an analysis of non-school leaver first-year students found evidence of particular disadvantage among students with disability.

Perhaps it should not be surprising that these two equity groups are particularly susceptible to reduced levels of confidence about their own employability. Both groups, as well as Indigenous students, face unique barriers to participating in and benefiting from higher education. NESB students who are, by definition, recent immigrants and arrivals have lower levels of cultural and social capital to draw on when formulating education and career plans – especially as school leavers. Harvey and Mallman (2019) point out that in a more general context of higher education pedagogy, compositional diversity on campus is important but not sufficient in and of itself to promote engagement among students with such diverse and complex perspectives and backgrounds. This applies to the development of employability traits, but it also extends to the engagement of NESB students in important areas of university life such as career guidance and work-integrated learning. As Mestan (2018: 76) attests, differences such as these encapsulate the 'disjunction between the reality of NESB disadvantage and actual university practices', particularly in relation to study outcomes.

Students with a disability often find it difficult to navigate systems developed for the general population, particularly where there are few institutional adjustments in place to meet the specific concerns and needs of people with specific needs. These concerns are well known: the 2020 Review of Disability Standards for Education (DSE) – the key document in establishing disability policy in Australia education – states that institutions should

> embed the Standards in higher education institution policies and practices across the student lifecycle (pre-access, access, participation, attainment, and transition out) at both an undergraduate and postgraduate level, as well as in workforce capability policies. (Australian Government, 2021: viii)

The evidence from this research indicates that employability-development initiatives in higher education should heed the DSE recommendations and recognise the unique journey and requirements of individual students.

Clearly, similar attention needs to be paid to NESB students, and students (equity or otherwise) in general. This will involve moving beyond broadly constructed approaches to employability in order to cater for a diverse student population whose self-perceived employability, including their confidence that they can succeed in their studies, might be lower than that of their peers from the point of admission.

REFERENCES

Australian Government (2021). *2020 Review of the Disability Standards for Education 2005*. Final Report. Canberra: Australian Government.

Becker, R. and Hecken, A.E. (2009). Why are working-class children diverted from universities? An empirical assessment of the diversion thesis. *European Sociological Review*. 25(2), 233–250.

Bennett, D. (2019a). *Embedding Employ-ability Thinking across Higher Education*. Canberra: Australian Government Department of Education and Training.

Bennett, D. (2019b). Graduate employability and higher education: Past, present and future. *HERDSA Review of Higher Education*. 5, 31–61. Available at www.herdsa.org.au/herdsa-review-higher-education-vol-5/31-61.

Bennett, D. and Ananthram, S. (2022). Development, validation and deployment of the Employ-ability scale. *Studies in Higher Education*. 47(7), 1311–1325. Published online first, 17 Feb 2021. Available at: https://doi.org/10.1080/03075079.2021.1888079.

Bennett, D., Coffey, J., Bawa, S., Carney, D., Dockery, A.M., Franklyn, K., Koshy, P., Li, I.W., Parida, S. and Unwin, S. (2021a). *Ameliorating Disadvantage: Creating accessible, effective and equitable careers and study information for low SES students*. Report submitted to the Australian Government Department of Education, Skills and Employment.

Bennett, D., Knight, E., Koshy, P., & Li, I. (2021b). Does regionality influence students' perceived employability and career orientation? A study of metropolitan, regional and remote students in Australia. *Australian and International Journal of Rural Education, 31*(3), 61-80). https://journal.spera.asn.au/index.php/AIJRE/article/view/305.

Brett, M. (2018). *Equity Performance and Accountability*. Equity Fellows Report. Perth: National Centre for Student Equity in Higher Education, Curtin University.

Byrne, M., Flood, B. and Griffin, J. (2014). Measuring the academic self-efficacy of first-year accounting students. *Accounting Education*. 23(5), 407–423.

Department of Education, Skills and Employment. (2020). *Job-ready Graduates: Higher Education Reform Package 2020*. Available at: www.dese.gov.au/document/job-ready-graduates-discussion-paper

Dockery, A.M. and Bawa, S. (2018). Labour market implications of promoting women's participation in STEM in Australia. *Australian Journal of Labour Economics*. 21(2), 125–151.

Harvey, A., Andrewartha, L., Edwards, D., Clarke, J. and Reyes, K. (2017). *Student equity and employability in higher education*. Canberra: Australian Government Department of Education and Training.

Harvey, A. and Mallman, M. (2019). Beyond cultural capital: Understanding the strengths of new migrants within higher education. *Policy Futures in Education*. 17(5), 657–673.

Jackson, D. and Wilton, N. (2016). Developing career management competencies among undergraduates and the role of work-integrated learning. *Teaching in Higher Education*. 21(3), 266–286.

Knight, E. (2019). Massification, marketisation and loss of differentiation in pre-entry marketing materials in UK higher education. *Social Sciences*. 8(11), 304–320.

Koshy, P. (2016). Equity policy in Australian higher education: Past, present and prospective. In M. Hill, A. Hudson, S. Mckendry, N. Raven, D. Saunders, J. Storan and T. Ward (eds), *Closing the Gap: Bridges for Access and Lifelong Learning*. (pp. 277–302). London: Forum for Access and Continuing Education.

Koshy, P. (2019). *Equity Student Participation in Australian Higher Education: 2013 – 2018*. Perth: National Centre for Student Equity in Higher Education (NCSEHE), Curtin University.

Koshy, P., Webb, S., Dockery, M. and Knight, E. (2021). Bachelor's degree participation in vocational institutions: Examining the determinants of participation. *International Journal of Training Research*. Published online first, 21 Jan 2016. Available at: www.tandfonline.com/doi/full/10.1080/14480220.2020.1830838

Lent, R.W., Brown, S.D. and Hackett, G. (1994). Toward a unifying social cognitive theory of career and academic interest, choice, and performance. *Journal of Vocational Behavior*. 45, 79–122.

Lent, R.W., Ezeofor, I., Morrison, A., Penn, L.T. and Ireland, G.W. (2016). Applying the social cognitive model of career self-management to career exploration and decision-making. *Journal of Vocational Behavior*. 93, 47–57.

Li, I.W. and Carroll, D.R. (2019). *Employment and Study Outcomes after Graduation: An Australian Higher Education Equity Perspective*. Perth: National Centre for Student Equity in Higher Education, Curtin University.

Li, I.W. and Dockery, A.M. (2015). Does school socio-economic status influence university outcomes? *Australian Journal of Labour Economics*. 18(1), 75–94.

Li, I. W., Mahuteau, S., Dockery, A. M. and Junankar, P.N. (2017). Equity in higher education and graduate labour market outcomes in Australia. *Journal of Higher Education Policy and Management*. 39(6), 625–641.

Mancini, T., Caricati, L., Panari, C. and Tonarelli, A. (2015). Personal and social aspects of professional identity: An extension of Marcia's identity status model applied to a sample of university students. *Journal of Vocational Behavior*. 89, 140–150.

Marks, G. (2017). Is SES really that important for educational outcomes in Australia? A review and some recent evidence. *Australian Educational Researcher*. 42(2), 191–211.

Mestan, K. (2016). Access, achievement and outcomes among students from non-English speaking backgrounds. In A. Harvey, C. Burnheim, and M. Brett (eds), *Student Equity in Australian Higher Education: Twenty-five years of A Fair Chance for All*. (pp. 125–141). Singapore: Springer.

O'Shea, S., Koshy, P. and Drane, C. (2021). The implications of COVID-19 for student equity in Australian higher education. *Journal of Higher Education Policy and Management.* Published online first, 30 May 2021. Available at: https://doi.org/10.1080/1360080X.2021.1933305

Pitman, T., Roberts, L., Bennett, D. and Richardson, S. (2017). An Australian study of graduate outcomes for disadvantaged students. *Journal of Further and Higher Education*. 43(1), 45–57.

Quality Indicators for Learning and Teaching (QILT) (2020). *QILT 2020 GOS-L National Tables*. Available at: www.qilt.edu.au/qilt-surveys/graduate-employment

Quality Indicators for Learning and Teaching (QILT) (2021). *Quality Indicators for Teaching and Learning (QILT)*. Available at: www.qilt.edu.au/

Richardson, S., Bennett, D. and Roberts, L. (2016). *Investigating the Relationship Between Equity and Graduate Outcomes in Australia.* Research Report. Perth: National Centre for Student Equity in Higher Education.

Rosenberg, M. (1965). *Society and the Adolescent Self-Image.* Princeton: Princeton University Press.

Trow, M. (2007). Reflections on the transition from elite to mass to universal access: Forms and phases of higher education in modern societies since WWII. In J.F. Forrest and P.G. Altbach (eds), *International Handbook of Higher Education.* (pp. 243–280). Amsterdam: Springer.

APPENDIX

The employability traits assessed for this study are listed below. The traits form part of the Employ-ability measure. This is a self-measure of perceived employability that is available without charge to all students. For more information, visit the educator site at www.developingemployability.edu.au.

1. *Self-awareness and programme awareness (1 = strongly disagree, 6 = strongly agree)*

- I can identify personal weaknesses in need of further development
- I can articulate my personal strengths and how these can be deployed in my career
- I am satisfied with my progress towards meeting my graduate career goals
- My degree programme is preparing me to meet the needs of graduate life
- To secure work in my discipline I will need to have graduate-level qualifications

2. *Identification with career commitment (1 = not at all, 5 = very much)*

- Does thinking of yourself as a professional in your discipline help you to understand who you are?
- Does thinking of yourself as a professional in your discipline make you feel secure in your life?
- Does thinking of yourself as a professional in your discipline make you feel self-confident?
- Does thinking of yourself as a professional in your discipline make you feel confident about the future?

3. *Reconsideration of career commitment (1 = not at all, 5 = very much)*

- If you could change your choice of becoming a professional in your discipline, would you do it?
- Do you ever think that choosing a different profession would make your life more interesting?
- Do you ever think that it would be better to prepare yourself for another profession?
- Are you considering the possibility of changing your university major in order to be able to practise another profession in the future?

4. *Self-esteem (1 =strongly disagree, 4 = strongly agree)*

- I feel that I have a number of good qualities
- I am able to do things as well as most other people
- I feel I do have much to be proud of
- I really feel useful at times
- I feel that I'm a person of worth, or at least on an equal plane with others
- I think I have enough respect for myself

- All in all, I am inclined to feel that I am not a failure
- I take a positive attitude toward myself
- On the whole, I am satisfied with myself
- I think I am doing pretty well most of the time

5. Academic self-efficacy (1 = not confident at all, 7 = completely confident)

- Judge the standard to get good marks in my assignments
- Make sense of theoretical aspects of my modules
- Explain material to a friend
- Follow and make sense of material covered in lectures
- Judge the applicability of the knowledge gained in my studies to the workplace

6. Career exploration and awareness (0 = no confidence, 9 = complete confidence)

- Figure out which career options could provide a good fit for your personality
- Identify careers that best use your skills
- Pick the best-fitting career option for you from a list of your ideal careers
- Learn more about careers you might enjoy
- Match your skills, values and interests to relevant occupations
- Make a well-informed choice about which career path to pursue
- Learn more about jobs that could offer things that are important to you
- Identify careers that best match your interests

7. Occupational mobility (0 = no confidence, 9 = complete confidence)

- Cope with the disappointment if your first choice does not work out
- Manage negative feelings if your first choice does not work out and you need to find another career choice

Notes: References for the employability traits are:

1. *Self-awareness and programme awareness*: Two items informed by Jackson and Wilton (2016).
2. *Identification with career commitment*: Eight-point commitment scale from Mancini et al. (2015).
3. *Reconsideration of career commitment*: Eight-point commitment scale from Mancini et al. (2015).
4. *Self-esteem*: Positive wording of 10-item self-esteem scale from Rosenberg (1965).
5. *Academic self-efficacy*: Adaptation of self-efficacy scale from Byrne et al. (2014).
6. *Career exploration and awareness*: Four-point decisional self-efficacy factor and four-point decisional coping efficacy factor from Lent et al. (2016).
7. *Occupational mobility*: Four-point decisional self-efficacy factor and four-point decisional coping efficacy factor from Lent et al. (2016).

20

Critical 'Employability' within the Realms of Sociology – a Movement towards 'Social Justice'

Ricky Gee

INTRODUCTION

The Browne (2010) review of higher education introduced a significant increase in student tuition fees in England and Wales, as well as providing directives on accommodating change. This report continued the heritage of neoliberal policies and marketisation of education experienced since the late twentieth century. Highlighted in the report was the importance of providing opportunities for higher education students to become 'employable', in turn proliferating a range of institutional metrices to shape endeavour (Tomlinson, 2005, 2012; Furedi, 2011; Clarke, 2018). As an academic with over 15 years of experience in higher education, the author has witnessed the rise of such quantitative metrices, in what can be described as a 'violent quantification of reality' (Gee, 2020: 104). Such metrices have a tendency to shape pedagogical practice so as to 'future proof' the market position of provision. It may not be an unfair assumption to suggest that the author is not alone in having sat through academic departmental meetings where 'employability' scores, shaped by 'Guardian metrics' and the 'Graduate Outcome Survey', are announced and scrutinised in order to invariably start to ask questions as to 'how the department can improve' (Osborne and Grant-Smith, 2017). As a sociologist, the author is left to ponder how much the academic community can influence the employability of students and their employability outcomes. How do we make students employable, and how much of this might be shaped by the social position of the student, the forms of social and cultural capital they possess or lack, the university and course they attend and the economic climate of the labour market they are entering (Roberts, 2009, 2018; Boliver, 2015)? The pedagogy to be reflected upon is based on the act of seeking to answer these questions – a pedagogy that is aware of the political and ideological dimensions of any form of career education, which is an activity that has been slowly dissolved into the narrower vista of employability (Mignot, 2001). The chapter starts by exploring the history of careers education and guidance (CEG) and how the discipline of psychology provides its theoretical basis – a discipline that lacks a consideration of social structures, thus lacking in criticality. It will then situate the parameters of the module in question: a third-year module on a BA Sociology degree at a post-1992 university in England. Doing so will highlight how the module took on board important dimensions of McCash's (2006) 'career studies' approach to CEG. This approach places the student in the role of career researcher, where their inquiry is informed via a range of career development theory as well as their home discipline of study – in this case, sociology. The sociological dimension here provides a critical standpoint against career development theory, which, as highlighted before, is predominantly informed by psychology, and thus lacking in criticality, therefore providing what is being described here as critical career studies (McCash, 2006). This chapter will provide extracts from student assignments to illustrate the impact of the learning gained. Reviewing such endeavours highlights that students are able to utilise learning to critically reflect upon their social position and how this position will provide a trajectory for career development, one that may well be counter to the students' own career aspirations (Furlong, 2009). The use of career development and critical theory is utilised to aid career narrativisation: a sociologically informed narrative to aid navigation to, if desired, challenge the perceived trajectory that is likely to be in store due to social position. Such a challenge is also considered from personal as well as collective dimensions – a desire not only to achieve one's own personal 'goals' but also provide a form of solidarity to influence the structures that position students – soon to be graduates – to move towards forms of perceived 'social justice'.

REVISITING IDEOLOGICAL DIMENSIONS OF CEG AND ITS RELATION TO EMPLOYABILITY

Careers work, traditionally via the endeavours of CEG, has continually occurred at the interface between full-time education and the world of work (Mignot, 2001). Introduced in the mid twentieth century, during the post-war industrial period, the policy goal of CEG was to ease the transition of children/young people from newly introduced compulsory full-time education into the world of work, and to provide an efficient matching process, marrying individual attributes with the demands of industrial labour to serve capital (Heginbotham, 1951; Watts, 1996; Mignot, 2001; McCash, 2006; Côté, 2014; Frayne, 2015). In line with the 'scientific management' of Taylorism and Fordism, the transfer from school to work required a speedy and efficient movement to ensure that the 'right' attributes fitted the 'right' measured industrial demands. Theorists such as Parsons (1910), Holland (1966) and Williamson (1950), utilising the unfolding discipline of psychology, shaped what is described as 'trait and factor' theory. This became a prominent theoretical basis to inform 'vocational guidance' activity, administered initially in schools via the 'Youth Employment Officer', who gave a school talk in assembly and vocational 1–1 interviews to provide 'vocational knowledge' (Heginbotham, 1951).

As western countries started to outsource industrial production and moved towards post-industrialisation (Bell, 1999; Asimakopoulos, 2009), displacing work into the service/knowledge economy, CEG thus responded via what is often described as 'developmental career theory', influenced by the human potential movement, with scholars such as Maslow (1954, 1968) moving the focus of psychology towards 'self-actualisation', influencing different 'scientific management' theories: Theory X, which had an interest in the separation of the planning and the doing of work and thus deskilling and alienating the worker, and Theory Y, which still had an underlying focus on efficiency, yet had to acknowledge the importance of workers enjoying their work, finding it 'fulfilling', to thus provide creativity and service in work activities. Such theories, embraced by career development theorists such as Super (1957) and Ginzberg et al. (1951), account for how the work role could play an important constituting aspect of identity, where CEG was to aid the movement towards fulfilling work, to unleash inner potential and move the worker to paradoxically 'become more and more what one is, to become everything that one is capable of becoming' (Maslow, 1943, in Watson, 2017: 35) whilst still serving the efficient flow of capital. Whilst the worker may well be enticed by the persuasion of fulfilling work, it is worth the critical observation that the worker is still alienated from their subsistence, and surplus value is still extracted from the worker to serve the capitalist class (Marx, 1975, in Granter, 2009: 56; Fleming, 2009). Within the post-industrial era, we witness the elongation of education via the massification of higher education to serve the knowledge economy with highly skilled 'graduates', which in turn sees a prolonging of youth and a movement from CEG administered at the end of compulsory education into forms of employability within the higher education arena. This results in an increased imperative for higher education institutions to 'embed' employability within the curriculum – a form of pedagogic input that focuses on the agency of the student rather than the social milieu that the student finds themselves within (Gee, 2017, 2019; Delva et al., 2021). What we can notice from this brief history of careers work, and how it has been shaped by contextual and social forces, is how CEG and employability are political pursuits, where the ideological stance of the policy influencing CEG will have an impact on the outcomes and experiences of its users. As Mignot (2001) expertly points out, CEG activities tend to incorporate three ideological standpoints:

- conservative: socialises individuals into employment roles and opportunities that are 'realistically' available to them – *social control.*
- liberal: raises the aspirations of individuals from deprived and disadvantaged groups to adopt the dominant value system of society – *individual change.*
- radical: acknowledges inequality is perpetuated by the existing economic structure and its power relations. The radical position holds that solutions must address this structure rather than the notion of deficits in individuals or groups – *social change.*

The application of Mignot's lens highlights how trait and factor theory has the ability and tendency to cajole and coerce individuals into positions that 'society' deems to be the best fit, providing a conservative ideological stance. The liberal stance is very much in harmony with developmental theories, seducing individuals to 'find' their 'inner potential' so as to change themselves, in order to be able to function in a knowledge and service economy, find work fulfilling and find an important aspect of 'identity'. These two stances are the most prominent to be found in practice in capitalist societies. However, the radical stance is one that this chapter argues needs to be reaffirmed, especially in a context where the labour market has experienced mass unemployment and underemployment of graduates in a post-crash and post-pandemic world (Kallerberg, 2007; International Labour Office, 2012, 2013; Petrosky-Nadeau and Valletta, 2020). The argument here is that the radical position becomes an important dimension for the contemporary context especially within the sociology curriculum, which has an interest in social change, especially since the sub-discipline of the sociology of work has moved its focus from an industrial to a public sociological lens (see Watson, 2007). Sociology will also have an interest in the social position of its students, where the sector experiences large differences in entry due to family background, level of income, parental educational status, and by other measures of 'material and social advantage' that have an impact on where graduates find themselves in the sector and are therefore likely to influence their trajectory into the precarious twenty-first-century labour market (Crawford et al., 2017: 2). The hope here is that other areas of the academy will take note of such a social justice approach – as all students have a social position, not just sociology students – and so employability can engage with its home discipline as well as prepare students for the prominent challenges of the twenty-first-century labour market.

PARAMETERS OF THE MODULE UNDER INVESTIGATION

The module under scrutiny is a core Level 6 module (final year of undergraduate degree) entitled the 'Sociology of Work and Career'. The module is the final phase of the 'Graduate employability package' within the degree, with part of the package in year 1, 'Sociology and the Real World', and part in year 2, 'Sociology and Service-Learning'. The 'Sociology of Work and Career' module provides opportunity for the students to sociologically engage with the concepts of work and career for the primary purpose of facilitating the career development of module participants. In so doing, students are encouraged to draw on their wider experience of the course and their 'career' in higher education thus far, as well as anticipating and contemplating their future. The module highlights that both 'work' and 'career' are contested concepts, the former often associated with paid work and the latter often conceptualised as linear, having either an upward or downward trajectory (hence the term 'career ladder'; see Gee, 2016, 2017). The module therefore provides space to deconstruct these narrow definitions, first and foremost sociologically, so that work can be viewed broadly to involve many activities rather than just paid work (e.g. volunteering, caring duties, education, art). Students also explore how career can be viewed sociologically as any social strand in a person's life (Goffman, 1961; see Gee, 2016, 2017, 2019). The module therefore illustrates how work and career is organised and managed, and how they influence social divisions along the lines of race and ethnicity, gender, class, disability and age. Such analytics allow for local, regional, national, international and global perspectives to be interrogated, to scrutinise how work and career have a profound connection with individual experience at the personal, familial, cultural and structural levels; as such, there are clear opportunities to facilitate career development amongst module participants.

The module has two summative assignments, both of which provide space for student reflection, to aid their own reflexive, theoretically informed learning and contemplation of future career development and enactment. The first assignment concentrates on the organisation and management of work and how this influences social divisions – for example, how the labour market might be segmented, via horizontal and vertical dimensions (Strangleman and Warren, 2008), across gender, class and ethnic lines. The students are then asked to reflect upon their learning and consider how such learning might influence their own career enactment. For example, Student M reflects on gender divisions and how they may influence her career trajectory:

> Reflecting on the world of work it is clear that gendered divisions of labour have had significant influence on my career path. I am currently studying sociology and I am working toward a career in counselling which as a result of the persistence horizontal segregation is still depicted as a female career, with female counsellors outnumbering male five to one (Brown, 2017).

Students are also able to reflect on how work is organised and managed in contemporary society, how technological 'advancement' can instil oppressive forms of practice in the workplace and how the seeking of solidarity may aid resistance:

> Advancements in technology, specifically home internet, have been extremely beneficial to me to continue working during the Covid-19 pandemic. However, I have also experienced negative effects – 'electronic panopticon' (Bain and Taylor, 2000) – whilst working for an online clothing store, which logs every action taken. I am aware that by taking actions to ally with my co-workers for example through joining a union, I can ensure that it does not result in the increased stress and lower job satisfaction that Alder (1998) discovered as a result of electronic monitoring. (Student M)

The above articulation provides an insight into an analysis of the life-career (Gee, 2016, 2017, 2022) of the student, which considers how interconnecting strands – articulations that form a trace and a narrative, of family, gender, learning and work – influence upon one another from a retrospective as well as an anticipatory lens. The student theoretically informs their reflections to not only consider the self but also their placement within a wider context, to critique such a context to consider not only their own but also collective action to resist oppressive forms of organisation and management of work.

The second assignment requires the students to place themselves more firmly in the role of career researcher in the way McCash (2006) outlines. The second assignment is a short research project where the students are to interview two willing and consenting participants for this ethically approved[1] project. The students are to construct their own interview schedule that will ask the participants useful questions, the answers to which will aid the career development of the student. As the students are sociologists, they must also investigate the participants sociologically, to ascertain useful information on their social position, their experiences of organisation, management and divisions at work. Part of the task is the students choosing and finding the participants they want to interview. This provides an important networking and learning opportunity – to build social capital as well as learn processes of accessing people before a moment of transition. The process of choosing also provokes the students to consider future career navigation, to consider which work positions would be useful to investigate to suit interest and anticipation. This provides an opportunity to explore the career development of others and maybe serve as role models to the students, providing useful information and feedback and exposing expectations within a work role – important modes of community interaction (Law, 1981). The students are to analyse the case via sociological theory, analysing the organisation, management and division of work from the perspectives of the participants, as well as utilising a range of career development theory to aid the exploration of how the participants' career develops. As with the first assignment, the students are to reflect upon the learning gained from the project, to come to conclusions upon their analysis of the participants and consider how such learning may be taken on board to influence their own career development, in terms of both perceived trajectory (Furlong, 2009) and how such terrain may be navigated, both individually and collectively.

OVERVIEW OF THE SECOND ASSIGNMENT

The students are given free range in the assignment to choose who to interview as well as what questions to ask the participants and what to focus on in the research project. As this is the case, a wide range of themes emerge when looking across the cohort's second assignment, with many choosing to focus on their social positionality and how this will influence career trajectory, the impact of the pandemic and how this influences an already precarious labour market, how emergent technology is blurring the boundaries between work and other strands in a person's life and the importance, and difficulty, of seeking solidarity within a neoliberal context.

Social Positionality

The sociology-course cohort has a strong female presence and is ethnically diverse, and many of the students are the first in their family to go to university. The social position of the participants interviewed and the learning that the students gain from such an inquiry appears to be important to the students. The students provide very nuanced and theoretically informed inquiries here, exploring how divisions occur on both horizontal and vertical dimensions and how the labour market may well provide the promise of meritocratic agency, yet where social structures still act as a force in forming career development. The extract below illustrates how a student has considered this regarding gender in the field of law:

> Roberts (1997) identifies how 'individualisation does not necessarily mean that people have been escaping from social-structures and gaining more power to determine their own career directions' (p348). An example is the glass ceiling whereby, even though women are given the same opportunities there is still discrimination in place to keep them below men. Participant 1 highlights this through identifying how she is 'often the only woman in the meeting as those higher up tend to be white male'. [...] For example, in 2017, women made up almost half the lawyer workforce but only 33% of partners (Werber, 2021).

As well as gender, ethnicity is explored by students. For example, Student O investigates participants providing support services to students in the field of higher education. Student O provides a useful analysis of these cases, informed by the literature, to inquire how ethnicity can influence career development, in relation not only to gaining access to prestigious areas of the labour market but also to career progression within such areas:

> Both participants reflect on their social position, with perceived awareness of trajectory and navigation, accounting for the differential experiences and the opportunities that they have been given [...] The Equality Challenge Unit (2015) articulated that although there has been a revised pursuit to make the workforce more diverse within universities, many BME staff remain concentrated in lower positions.

This statement provides the following reflection to inform Student O's own career development and enactment:

> Having this knowledge, makes me want to challenge these issues within a job occupation. [...] which could be hindered since I am a Black female, and I am acutely aware that I may face discrimination when entering the labour market because of my racial and gender identity. McGregor-Smith (2017) highlights that discrimination occurs through every aspect of an individual's working life, and this begins before Black people enter the labour market. [...] TUC (2020) found that 31% of Black and minority ethnic women have been unequally passed over for or rejected a promotion at work, which accounts for discrimination at the workplace.

The Impact of Emergent Digital Technologies and their Role During the Pandemic

The assignment took place in a year where all the learning took place online and where many of the participants had to adapt their ways of working, many moving their work into a virtual environment. This is particularly apparent for the participants in Student C's assignment, which explored work in the retail sector, how the pandemic had influenced work and the tyranny of technology upon alienated experience whilst serving capital:

> Jane: 'we have to fulfil customers online orders whilst running the offline store [...] it doubles the workload'
>
> [...] Technology's introduction into work has made it more efficient, allowing profit maximisation and greater speed (Granter, 2009; Virilio, 2012), triggering precarity. Now able to track physical and spoken movements, workers must constantly be ready for change (Moore, 2017) and are quantifiably measured like in scientific management. Automated technologies also cause workers alienation (Haddad and Senter Jr, 2017) by deskilling them to perform tasks. Jane experienced this within her statement:
>
> '[W]hat I do miss is touch'.
>
> This correlates with one of Fourier's (see Granter, 2009) thirteen passions making work enjoyable.

Such analysis encourages the student to explore how technology intensifies and extends the working day, where such tyranny may be unfairly distributed across the genders:

> [...] both participants reflected upon how they have become 'spatially and temporally more "available" to work' (Warhurst, Eikhof and Haunschild, 2008: p.6). Alex stated:
>
> '[y]ou've always got work to do at home'.
>
> Jane referenced having children which is evidently a significant life theme for her:
>
> 'You can fit it in around your schedule so that's why it was nice setting up a business with kids [...] you could put them to bed and start working again'.

> [...] Jane's answer corresponds with women scheduling work to fit around their unpaid emotional and caring familial duties (Smith and Elliott, 2012) by continuing it after traditional hours.

The Seeking and Difficulties of Solidarity

Many students provide insight into their perceived challenges of gaining employment and working in the digitally surveyed, precarious and uncertain twenty-first-century labour market:

> The precarious labour market leaves me apprehensive. (Student J, Gee, in press)

> I have come to expect work and home boundaries to become blurred further. This is alongside work intensification as technologies continue developing and provide constant precarity through the uncertainty of the future and what these changes entail. (Student C)

Therefore, many seek for solidarity, an acknowledgement that it is not only themselves that face such challenges, that the private troubles are linked to the public issues created by neoliberal capitalism (Mills, 1959). Therefore, students have taken the time to ask and consider the role of collective action, via informal networks of worker solidarity or via established trade unions. They have also acknowledged the difficulties this presents; see, for example, Student T's exploration of work within the police force:

> The Police Federation is the organisation set up to represent police officers. Participant 1 highlighted benefits of the union including 'breakdown cover, gadget insurance and travel insurance'. Both participants suggested they are involved due to the financial benefits, due to active participation being difficult. Participant 2 explained 'the only time you use the police federation is when a police officer is under investigation if a member of the public reports them'.

Student T explores this further to see if this is unique to their participants:

> [...] the federation supports members on matters such as diversity, mental health concerns and fighting issues that arise in the interest of the federation members (Police Federation, 2021). This lack of awareness may be linked to the decline of trade unions. Machin highlights trade unions have greatly declined in membership since 1979 corresponding with the rise of neoliberal policies (Machin, 2002).

This illustrates the importance of the research undertaken by the students, in terms of how the research can provide an insider view of what occurs and how this may differ to the literature, can consider the possible reasons for such a disparity and provide useful knowledge to inform future career navigation. Student L also considers how the individualised nature of neoliberal capitalism may well provide precarious challenges, in that it will evoke a sense of competition in a labour market crowded with graduates, creating tension between their urges to want to individually succeed and provide solidarity to others:

> The Marketisation of education has meant university is an investment in human capital (Becker, 1962) but [...] 'employers may well feel that graduates are no longer exceptionally smart' (Roberts, 2020, p.34). To combat this, it is imperative that I continue enhancing my employability, whilst maintaining a critical perspective to the neoliberal promotion of meritocracy and individual homo oeconomicus (Foucault, 2004): the assumption we are entrepreneurs of the self. [...] I will actively encourage equality AND equity for those who are disadvantaged due to their societal status, aiding progression for those who haven't experienced the privilege I have. Within wider discourse, the impact of unions must not go unnoticed as a way to collectively combat precarity within neoliberal society.

FINAL REFLECTIONS

The extracts above provide an impactful insight into the rich learning experiences that have occurred, how the students have been able to consider their social position, how this relates to their participants and how they can use a range of theories to explore career development, including the use of sociology to fill the sociological void found within many career development theories and employability practice (Gee, 2017; Delva et al., 2021), where the home discipline can aid the student to play the role of sociologist:

> As a sociologist, it is important to reflect on my own social positionality and the influence this may have on my own work career. For example, should I choose to start my own family, the question arises as to how I will balance my family and work career, without facing the 'penalties of motherhood' on my own career progression (Waldfogel, 2007, p.347, as cited in McIntosh et al., 2012). (Student E)

The students can therefore provide an informed analysis on perceived trajectory, which can inform how they will navigate the social terrain – a terrain that has been sociologically explored – to provide a coherent sense of career narrativisation, and to not succumb to the bland and overly agentic, linear lens of much employability practice:

> Completing my studies within the sociology of work and career, I have considered my future career in depth. This involved considering my current trajectory towards a job within the law enforcement sector. Career trajectory is understood by Inkson (2014) as an individual's future path towards a career based upon influential factors such as family background, social class and gender. I have considered how my gender, being female, could push me towards more caring job roles following my sociology degree (Hussein et al., 2013). Similarly, my trajectory could point towards lower-ranked jobs because women are most frequently within the lowest rank in policing and is a male-dominated profession (Home Office, 2019). To effectively navigate towards my desired role within the police and ensure success in the field, I aim to complete a Masters in International Law Enforcement. (Student T)

> Interviewing the two participants was incredibly beneficial to reflect on the trajectory and navigation of my career path. It has established a sense of reassurance as I do not know what to do professionally. I reflect on my trajectory as something that is yet to be explored and discovered, but despite this uncertainty, I want to utilise navigation as a means to end up in a career that genuinely suits my needs, even if it means not progressing in a linear fashion. (Student J)

The module not only concentrates on the future and anticipation: it also allows the student an important opportunity to reflect on their current experiences of work in flexible–precarious employment – an additional, institutionally unconsidered externality for many students within a post-1992 university-to express their concerns and experiences of exploitation. It is argued here that such an approach should not be confined to the discipline of sociology, that the academy can acknowledge that all students have a social position, and one that is likely to influence their career trajectory – that is, where they end up in the labour market once leaving full-time education (Roberts, 2018). Such an approach also allows a space to consider what work and career means to the student, to question what part they want to play within society and how they contribute to the shaping of a collective future – one that doesn't always lead them to chase a metric or money:

> Studying sociology has prompted me to take wider consideration [...] I am compelled to enter a non-profiting charity, to avoid the pressure of capitalism's competitive nature, and to use my sociological knowledge to help. Hopefully, humbling my approach to all strands of my life, not just work, and diffusing my support to consumer culture, having comprehended its role in divide.

Note

1 The module has gained ethical clearance for the module; therefore, the students do not need to individually apply. The students must follow a set of procedures to be compliant with the ethical approval, this includes having their own interview schedule approved by the module leader and also to pass on a participant information sheet and consent form, constructed by the module leader, to the participants to sign to provide consent.

ACKNOWLEDGEMENTS

Ricky would like to thank Dr Phil Mignot for his continual pedagogical guidance. Ricky would also like to thank all of the students that provided willing consent to utilise their excellent work. It has been a real pleasure taking this journey with you.

REFERENCES

Alder, G. S. (1998) Ethical issues in electronic performance monitoring: A consideration of deontological and teleological perspectives. *Journal of Business Ethics*, 17(7), pp. 729–43.

Asimakopoulos, J. (2009) Globally segmented labor markets: The coming of the greatest boom and bust, without the boom. *Critical Sociology*, 35(2), pp. 175–98.

Bain, P. and Taylor, P. (2000) Entrapped by the 'electronic panopticon'? *Worker resistance in the call centre. New Technology, Work and Employment*, 15(1), pp. 2–18.

Becker, G. (1962) Investment in human capital: A theoretical analysis. *Journal of Political Economy*, 70(5), pp. 9–49.

Bell, D. (1999) *The Coming of Post-industrial Society: A Venture in Social Forecasting*. New York: Basic Books.

Boliver, V. (2015) *Are there distinctive clusters of higher and lower status universities in the UK?* Oxford Review of Education, 41(5), pp. 608–27.

Browne, J. (2010) *Securing a sustainable future for higher education: An independent review of higher education funding and student finance*. https://assets.publishing.service.gov.uk/government/uploads/system/uploads/attachment_data/file/422565/bis-10-1208-securing-sustainable-higher-education-browne-report.pdf (Accessed 20 May 2011).

Brown, S. (2017) Is counselling women's work? *Therapy Today* [online] 28 (2) (March 2017), BACP. Available at: https://www.bacp.co.uk/bacp-journals/therapy-today/2017/march-2017/is-counselling-womens-work/ [Accessed 28 April 2021]

Clarke, M. (2018) Rethinking graduate employability: the role of capital, individual attributes and context. *Studies in Higher Education*, 43(11), pp. 1923–37.

Côté, J. (2014) *Youth Studies: Fundamental Issues and Debates*. London: Palgrave MacMillan.

Crawford, C., Dearden, L., Micklewhite, J. and Vignoles, A. (2017) *Family Background and University Success: Differences in Higher Education Access and Outcomes in England First*. Oxford: Oxford University Press.

Delva, J., Forrier, A. and De Cuyper, N. (2021) Integrating agency and structure in employability: Bourdieu's theory of practice. *Journal of Vocational Behavior*, 127, 103579.

Equality Challenge Unit (2015) *Equality in higher education: Statistical report, staff and students*. https://s3.eu-west-2.amazonaws.com/assets.creode.advancehe-document-manager/documents/ecu/Equality-in-HE-statistical-report-2015-part-1-staff_1573206770.pdf (Accessed 26 April 2021).

Fleming, P. (2009) *Authenticity and the Cultural Politics of Work: New Forms of Informal Control*. 1st edn. Oxford: Oxford University Press.

Foucault, M. ([1979] 2004) Nine: 14 March 1979. *In The Birth of Biopolitics: Lectures at the Collège de France, 1978-79*. New York: Palgrave, pp. 215–37.

Frayne, D. (2015) *The Refusal of Work: The Theory and Practice of Resistance to Work*. London: Zed Books.

Furedi, F. (2011) Introduction to the marketisation of HE. In Molesworth, M., Scullion, R. and Nixon, E. (eds), *The Marketisation of Higher Education and the Student as Consumer*. Abingdon: Routledge, pp. 2–7.

Furlong, A. (2009) Revisiting transitional metaphors: Reproducing inequalities under the conditions of late modernity. *Journal of Education and Work*, 22(5), pp. 343–53.

Gee, R. (2016) Alternative visions of employability: The role of critical pedagogy. *In School Guidance Handbook for the National Centre for Guidance in Education*. https://www.ncge.ie/resource/alternative-visions-employability-role-critical-pedagogy (Accessed: April 2020)

Gee, R. (2017) Contemplating 'career' across disciplines: reflexive explorations of 'career'. In Barnard, A. (ed.) *Developing Professional Practice in Health and Social Care*. London: Routledge, pp. 180–98.

Gee, R. (2019) Exploring 'career' via the lens of paradox: A longitudinal study of the transitional experiences of a small group of graduates. *Professional Doctorate Thesis, Document 5*. Nottingham: Nottingham Trent University.

Gee, R. (2020) Informal education as a Derridean gift: A deconstructive reading of the principles guiding youth work practice within neoliberal policy regimes. *Journal of Applied Youth Studies*, 3, pp. 103–13.

Gee, R. (2022) A critical exploration of the 'agile career': A means of exposing the politics and economy of precarity via the lens of dromology. *British Journal of Guidance and Counselling*, DOI: 10.1080/03069885.2022.2030859

Ginzberg, E., Ginsburg, S. W., Axelrad, S. and Herma, J. L. (1951) *Occupational Choice: An Approach to a General Theory*. New York: Columbia University Press.

Goffman, E. (1961) The Moral Career of the Mental Patient. *In Asylums: Essays on the Social Situations of Mental Patients and Other Inmates*. New York: Anchor, pp. 125–70.

Granter, E. (2009) Critical Social Theory and the End of Work. *Rethinking Classical Sociology*. 1st edn. Farnham: Ashgate.

Haddad, A., and Senter Jr, R. (2017). 'The Relationship of Technology to Workers' Alienation'. *Sociological Focus* [online], 50 (2), pp.159-182. DOI: 10.1080/00380237.2017.1251755 (Accessed: 23 April 2021).

Heginbotham, H. (1951) *The Youth Employment Service*. London: Methuen and Co.

Holland, J. L. (1966) *The Psychology of Vocational Choice*. Waltham: Blaisdell.

Home Office (2019) *Police workforce, England and Wales*. https://assets.publishing.service.gov.uk/government/uploads/system/uploads/attachment_data/file/831726/police-workforce-mar19-hosb1119.pdf (Accessed 5 May 2021).

Hussein, S., Ismail, M. and Manthorpe, J. (2013) Male workers in the female-dominated long-term care sector: Evidence from England. *Journal of Gender Studies*, 25(1), pp. 35–49.

Inkson, K. (2014) *Understanding Careers*. 2nd edn. London: Sage Publications.

International Labour Office (2012) *Global Employment Trends for Youth 2012: Preventing a Deeper Job Crisis*. Geneva: International Labour Office.

International Labour Office (2013) *Global Employment Trends for Youth 2013: A Generation at Risk*. Geneva: International Labour Office.

Kallerberg, A. L. (2007) *The Mismatched Worker*. New York: Norton.

Law, B. (1981) Community interaction: A 'mid-range' focus for theories of career development in young adults. *British Journal of Guidance & Counselling*, 9(2), pp. 142–58.

Machin, S. (2002) Union decline in Britain. *British Journal of Industrial Relations*, 38(4), pp. 631–645.

Maslow, A. (1954) *Motivation and Personality*. New York: Harper and Row.

Maslow, A. (1968) *Toward a Psychology of Being*. New York: Van Nostrand.

McCash, P. (2006) We're all career researchers now: Breaking open career education and DOTS. *British Journal of Guidance & Counselling*, 34(4), pp. 429–49.

McGregor-Smith, R. (2017) *Race in the workplace review. Department for Business, Energy & Industrial Strategy*. https://assets.publishing.service.gov.uk/government/uploads/system/uploads/attachment_data/file/594336/race-in-workplace-mcgregor-smith-review.pdf (Accessed 26 April 2021).

McIntosh, B., McQuaid, R., Munro, A. and Dabir-Alai, P. (2012) Motherhood and its impact on career progression. *Gender in Management: An International Journal* (online), 27(5), pp. 346–364.

Mignot, P. (2001) Anti-oppressive practice. In B. Gothard, P. Mignot, M. Offer & M. Ruff (Eds.), *Careers guidance in context* (pp. 117–132). London: Sage.

Mills, C. W. (1959) *The Sociological Imagination*. New York: Oxford University Press.

Moore, P. (2017) *The Quantified Self in Precarity: Work, Technology and What Counts*. Oxon: Routledge.

Osborne, N. and Grant-Smith, D. (2017) *Resisting the 'employability' doctrine through anarchist pedagogies and prefiguration*. Australian Universities' Review, 59(2), pp. 59–69.

Parsons, F. (1910) *Choosing a Vocation*. London: Gay Hancock.

Petrosky-Nadeau, N. and Valletta, R. (2020) *Unemployment paths in a pandemic economy*. Federal Reserve Bank of San Francisco Working Paper 2020-18. https://doi.org/10.24148/wp2020-18 (Accessed: January 2021).

Police Federation (2021) *Aims and objectives*. www.polfed.org/about-us/aims-objectives/ (Accessed 14 April 2021).

Roberts, K. (1997) Prolonged transitions to uncertain destinations. *British Journal of Guidance and Counselling*, 25(3), pp. 345–60.

Roberts, K. (2009) Opportunity structures then and now. *Journal of Education and Work*, 22(5), pp. 355–68.

Roberts, K. (2018) *Explaining education-to-work transitions: Thinking backwards, situating agency and comparing countries*. Review of European Studies, 10(1), pp. 72–83.

Roberts, K. (2020) Regime change: Education to work transitions in England, 1980s–2020s. *Journal of Applied Youth Studies*, 3(1), pp. 23–42.

Smith, A. and Elliott, F. (2012) The demands and challenges of being a retail store manager: 'Handcuffed to the front doors'. *Work, Employment and Society*, 26(4), pp. 676–84.

Strangleman, T. and Warren, T. (2008) *Work and Society: Sociological Approaches, Themes and Methods*. London: Routledge.

Super, D. E. (1957) *The Psychology of Careers*. New York: Harper and Row.

Tomlinson, M. (2012) Graduate employability: A review of conceptual and empirical themes. *Higher Education Policy*, 25(4), pp. 407–31.

Tomlinson, S. (2005) *Education in a Post-Welfare Society*. 2nd edn. Maidenhead: Open University.

TUC (2020) *BME women and work. TUC equality briefing*. www.tuc.org.uk/research-analysis/reports/bme-women-and-work (Accessed 26 April 2021).

Virillio, P. (2012) *The Administration of Fear*. London: Semiotext.

Warhurst, C., Eikhof, D. and Haunschild, A. (2008) *Work Less, Live More?: Critical Analysis of the Work-Life Boundary*. Hampshire: Palgrave Macmillan.

Watson, T. (2017) *Sociology, Work and Organisation*. 7th edn. Oxford: Routledge.

Watts, A. (1996) Socio-political ideologies in guidance. In Watts, A. G., Law, B., Killeen, J., Kidd, J. and Hawthorn, R. (eds), *Rethinking Careers Education and Guidance: Theory, Policy, and Practice*. London: Routledge, pp. 216–32.

Werber, C. (2021) 'Up or out' with no pause button: Why there's a gender pay gap in law. *Quartz at work*. https://qz.com/work/1587572/why-is-there-a-gender-pay-gap-in-law/ (Accessed 19 April 2021).

Williamson, E. G. (1950) The clinical method of guidance. In Arthur H. Brayfield (ed.). *Readings in modern methods of counseling* (pp. 22–26). East Norwalk, CT: AppletonCentury-Crofts.

PART IV

Country and Regional Differences

BACKGROUND AND CONTEXT

The five chapters collected in this part report experiences and challenges of graduate employability development in different contexts, such as the UK, Norway, Germany, Turkey, Ireland, Portugal, Australia and New Zealand.

These studies also cover a wide array of issues, including inequalities concerning employability, the role of international experience in graduate employability, factors affecting graduate employability, gender disparity and graduate employment service. Most of the chapters focus on local contexts of higher education and labour markets, which perfectly serve the purpose of this part of the book for demonstrating regional differences and country specificities.

As both higher education and labour markets are globally inter-connected, two chapters tackle some central debates regarding if and how international mobility or education help enhance graduate employability. While the chapters focus on different graduate employability issues, they (all together) offer a comprehensive picture of the transition from higher education to the world of work, involving major actors in the process – namely, students, higher education institutions, career services and employers. Although the picture is composed of experiences from different countries, many of the lessons, best practices and research findings are likely to be generalised to broad contexts or be of value as points of reference. The chapters are introduced as follows.

The Impact of International Student Mobility on Employability, Robert Coelen

Coelen's chapter deals with a paradoxical debate in the literature: whether international mobility helps students to gain certain competencies that confer their labour market advantages, or whether these competencies are already pre-existing and drive students to study abroad. He seeks to answer these questions by synthesising relevant literature by considering both the graduates' and employers' perspectives.

Coelen finds that graduates and employers have different perceptions. While students believe that international study experience enhances their employability, recruiting employers pay more attention to the sojourners' previous work experience than their international mobility. The author argues that universities offering international education programmes need to fill the perception gap. Meanwhile, he suggests that if the core value of international mobility in employability enhancement is to prepare students to work effectively with diverse individuals, such competencies should also be developed by means other than studying abroad.

Transnational, Multinational, Binational? The Role of International Education in Human Capital Development for Graduate Employability, Jessica Schueller and Filiz Keser Aschenberger

The chapter from Schueller and Aschenberger responds to a seemingly shared perception in the literature that students participating in international higher education may not have advantages in terms of employment outcomes if they return home after graduation. Through their case study of Turkish–German University in Istanbul, they find that the educational programme in the university can provide binational human capital to the students. Gaining such capital, the students have advantages in their employment in both Germany and Turkey. They suggest that international education should pay special attention to developing students' binational human capital, because it is essential to incorporate targeted employability preparation for both the host- and home-country labour markets.

***Graduate Employability during the COVID-19 Pandemic*, Belgin Okay-Somerville, Daria Luchinskaya, Pauline Anderson, Scott Hurrell and Dora Scholarios**

The authors investigate how social and educational inequalities influence graduate employability during the COVID-19 pandemic. Their work is based on a survey of graduates from higher education institutions in Glasgow in 2020 (N = 502). Their study shows that the graduates' employability is not much affected by their social background and the prestige of their graduation institutions. Instead, their findings reveal that the COVID-19 pandemic had a disproportionately negative impact on arts and humanities graduates' employability due to a sudden reduction of opportunities for skills development, networking and employment. In addition, students with health problems are disadvantageous in post-graduation employment, but those with high career competencies are likely to overcome the challenges caused by educational and health inequalities. They suggest that universities should provide better career guidance to help students navigate uncertain labour markets, especially for those students in vulnerable groups.

***Graduate Employability and the Labour-market Relevance of Norwegian Higher Education: Perspectives from Students*, Dian Liu and Siyang Kong**

Liu and Kong examine three factors that affect graduate employability in Norway: the relevance of students' study programmes to labour markets, overseas study experiences and job experience prior to or during the study period. Their study is based on the Norwegian 'Special Graduate Survey 2017' involving over 3,000 graduates from master's degree programmes. Their research finds that all three factors are positively associated with graduate employability. The survey also shows that female graduates have higher chances of being employed than male students. Based on the research findings, the authors provide relevant policy recommendations.

***Starting Points and Journeys: Careers and Employability in a Data-Rich Environment*, Bob Gilworth**

Although Gilworth's chapter is not a typical research paper, it examines a very timely issue about the use of large-scale data (based on career registration) to improve universities' support for students' employability development from a practitioner perspective. The data (concerning career thinking, experience, occupational sector preferences and outputs) are collected through Career Registration, which is a process by which information about career thinking and employability-related experience is collected from all students on an annual basis. The data can be analysed to help students to decide on options to pursue their study, to plan to acquire skills, experiences, knowledge and networks and to compete efficiently in their chosen fields, thus facilitating their career development. The author further reflects the experience of promoting and developing Career Registration in the UK, Ireland, Portugal, Australia and New Zealand. The chapter has high practical value for universities to innovate their approaches of career service and, meanwhile, suggests a new area for future research.

21

The Impact of International Student Mobility on Employability

Robert Coelen

INTRODUCTION

International student mobility constitutes a significant proportion of the activities of higher education institutes that fall under the umbrella of internationalisation. Notwithstanding the recent (temporary) reduction in such mobility because of the SARS-COV-2 pandemic (Mason, 2021) and the recent increased attention towards internationalisation at home (IaH) (Ha and Phung, 2021) and internationalisation of the curriculum (IoC) (Liu and Shirley, 2021), this chapter will limit its treatise to the potential impact of international mobility on the employability of higher education graduates. The efforts to provide internationalisation for all students, including the non-mobile majority, and particularly the examination of employability impacts of the IaH/IoC activities is in its infancy, and at present insufficient data are available to discuss this comprehensively. Some of the most recent results discussed in this chapter open the door towards a more nuanced view of the impact of international student mobility on employability, which until now has been promoted as largely positive.

There are several aspects that need further examination to establish whether and how international mobility confers labour market advantages to sojourners. Is it a case of pre-existing characteristics of students that enhance the propensity to undertake international periods of study (or internship) or is it the enhancement of certain characteristics? Is it their ability to relate the enhancement of these characteristics as added value to the work for their potential employers? Is it their ability to translate personal growth and experiences because of international mobility into actions that enhance their career progression? What about employers – what is their understanding of the effect of international student mobility on their potential new employees? This chapter aims to discuss these issues and suggest some ways forward.

INTERNATIONALISATION ACTIVITIES PROVIDE ACCESS TO ONE SOURCE OF DIVERSITY, BUT A BROADER RANGE OF DIVERSITY SOURCES ARE IMPORTANT TO EMPLOYERS

Before discussing these questions, I would like to reframe internationalisation learning outcomes from being culture-specific towards a broader concept in which they are potentially an effective vehicle for enhancing personality characteristics that are likely to have a broader appeal to employers. Effectively, this reframes these learning outcomes because of international mobility, not just in terms of intercultural competence (ICC) and international awareness but as competence in dealing (working together) with diverse others and an enhanced awareness of the benefits of diversity.

Increasingly over the last couple of decades, higher education institutes are more concerned with the employment prospects of their graduates, in line with one of the fundamental and important drivers of students electing to undertake tertiary study. Indeed, a recent survey of employers in the USA showed that the large majority agree that a degree is a worthwhile investment (Finley, 2021). Of course, for many professions, a university degree is a basic requirement. In a variety of jurisdictions, universities are now asked to report on the employment prospects and the actual employment of graduates within a certain short time frame. Thus, to better prepare graduates for employment, it would be preferable to understand how new employees could make positive contributions to organisational well-being and success and to ensure that curricula contain learning outcomes related to these aspects.

Early this century, partners at McKinsey & Company began publishing the results of investigations on the effect of increased gender diversity (Desvaux et al., 2007, 2009; Desvaux and Devillard, 2008) on economic performance and capacity of the global workforce. Sometime later, McKinsey & Company turned its view to include other sources of diversity, including race and ethnicity, age, sexual orientation, and experience such as a global mind-set and cultural fluency. Their report (Hunt et al., 2015) examined 366 public companies in Canada, Latin America, the UK, and the USA. Depending on industry and jurisdiction, different sources of diversity (e.g., racial, ethnic, or gender diversity) were more closely associated with a better financial company performance. Whilst correlation is not proof of a causal relationship, intuitively one can consider that embracing diversity is right. It is not difficult to understand, for example, that a company in the business of selling clothes understands more segments of the market if they have embraced diversity in terms of ethnicity, race, or sexual orientation and consequently is more likely to perform well than their non-diverse counterparts. The source of diversity most impactful on company performance was shown to vary by country and industry (Hunt et al., 2015). Thus, in the USA, racial and ethnic diversity were most impactful on company performance, whereas in the UK, gender diversity in the senior-executive team was most effective. The nub of this performance increase most likely relies on a greater cognitive diversity borne out of the different sources (Page, 2017). For diverse teams to be successful, they must be united in sharing a goal, whilst appreciating, encouraging, and engaging their differences (Page, 2017: 221). This applies particularly to teams that solve complex problems, or teams that require various professional inputs to create a new product or solve a multi-dimensional complex problem. After the initial study by Hunt et al. (2015), further research has demonstrated 'that the likelihood that diverse companies will out-earn their industry peers has grown' (Dolan et al., 2020).

Diversity is an interesting newcomer in the employer appreciation of important recruitment priorities, although in the QS survey (Quacquarelli Symonds, 2021), there was no strict definition of what this meant, allowing different interpretations across the world. If diversity is an important recruitment priority, it follows that companies will be populated with a greater diversity (in terms of a variety of sources) of people who need to be able to work together effectively and successfully. The ability, therefore, to interact effectively with diverse individuals becomes an important asset for a graduate.

A learner-centred definition of the internationalisation of higher education was framed as being focused on achieving the learning outcomes of international awareness and ICC (Coelen, 2016). That is to say, individuals who have experienced education that aims to achieve these outcomes have these capacities to a measurable extent. The second of these two learning outcomes, ICC, has been interpreted in converging ways, as 'the ability to think and act in interculturally appropriate ways' (Hammer et al., 2003: 422) or as 'an individual's effectiveness in drawing upon a set of knowledge, skills, and personal attributes to work successfully with people from different national cultural backgrounds at home or abroad'. (Johnson et al., 2006: 530). Examining the second definition a bit closer, in particular the aspect of working together with people of different cultural backgrounds, raises the notion that the personality characteristics, attitudes and affects, and cognitive repertoire required to work effectively with people of different cultural backgrounds may not be all that different from working together with persons who have other sources of diversity.

There are very many models (30) and related constructs (300) for ICC. These constructs, in terms of personal characteristics, boil down to three content domains of intercultural traits, intercultural attitudes and worldviews, and intercultural abilities (Spitzberg and Chagnon, 2009; Leung et al., 2014). One of the constructs of Van der Zee and Van Oudenhoven (2000), the multicultural personality questionnaire (MPQ), has gained wide appreciation and use and was regarded as one of only a few instruments as most promising for assessing ICC (Matsumoto and Hwang, 2013) based on personality traits. A more recent in-depth review of this instrument and others (Chen and Gabrenya, 2021) concluded that, in terms of content validity, the MPQ was good, but thought it missed some possibly important personality traits for ICC, such as being inquisitive, cosmopolitan, self-aware, and being non-judgemental. Relationship-based validities of this instrument (convergent, discriminant, and criterion) were also assessed as being good. It is not the intent of this chapter to provide an in-depth treatise of the various instruments, but to use the MPQ as an example.

The traits that are measured by the MPQ are cultural empathy, social initiative, flexibility, open-mindedness, and emotional stability (Van der Zee and Van Oudenhoven, 2000). A closer examination of the items used in the validated short-form of the MPQ (Van der Zee et al., 2013; Hofhuis et al., 2020) for the subscale that measures cultural empathy shows that the items do not mention anything about culture but are more related to the empathic trait. This leads to the suggestion that the MPQ might be also predictive of a broader competence – namely, the ability to be effective in working successfully with diverse individuals. Indeed, in a recent exploratory study, the MPQ was used to measure the impact of a multicultural personality towards tolerance of diversity. Korol et al. (2016) suggested that this trait and the others in the MPQ were highly associated with tolerance of diversity. The notion that this tolerance is likely to extend beyond cultural diversity is not hard to grasp. Coupling this with the current evidence that companies that embrace diversity appear to perform better than those that are not diverse (Dolan et al., 2020), it is clear that of course the individuals in a company that are effective at working with diverse others. Thus, an individual's enhanced ability in this regard augurs well for the company in which they work. As companies increasingly embrace purposeful diversity, being able to effectively interact with diverse individuals may well become highly regarded.

INTERNATIONAL STUDENT MOBILITY AND ITS EFFECT ON EMPLOYABILITY

What are the important dimensions of employability? A recent study combined and strengthened different streams of employability research from higher education and workplace learning from a Western perspective into a multi-dimensional competence-based approach (Römgens et al., 2020). The combined approach led to seven dimensions, named with terminology coming from workplace learning research and in brackets the (comparable) terminology from higher education research: dimension 1 was human capital (applying disciplinary knowledge), dimension 2 was social capital (transferable generic skills), dimension 3 was (emotional regulation), dimension 4 was lifelong learning and flexibility (career development skills), dimension 5 was reflection on self and organisation (self-management), dimension 6 was (self-efficacy), and dimension 7 was a healthy work–life balance. Graduates possessing competence in these domains would thus potentially be very employable.

Three aspects (human capital, applying disciplinary knowledge, and transferable generic skills) relate to the level of disciplinary and general expertise needed to perform a job well. Social capital and transferable generic skills, according to Römgens et al. (2020), are parallel concepts. They relate particularly well to the traits mentioned in the MPQ, including cultural empathy, social initiative, and open-mindedness. Dimension 3, emotional regulation, is well reflected in the emotional stability dimension of the MPQ (remaining calm in novel and stressful situations). Dimension 4, lifelong learning and flexibility, is seen as career development skills in higher education research, and they map well onto the flexibility dimension of the MPQ. Equally, the other dimensions could be related in similar ways to traits examined by the MPQ.

Self-management and self-efficacy have been related to meta-cognitive skills and beliefs about the capability to carry out tasks or courses of action and defined as part of motivation (Römgens et al., 2020). Indeed, an exploratory study by Petersdotter et al. (2017) showed a small increase in self-efficacy of students who underwent study abroad (those discussed in this chapter were for credit unless specifically mentioned as being for degree study) in comparison to their non-mobile counterparts. An interesting point made in this study was the apparent influence of the number of social contacts (network development) made during study abroad as a mediator of increased self-efficacy. Petersdotter et al. (2017) concluded that it was not known whether this increase was stable for the longer term after study abroad.

There are many studies that extol the benefits of a period of international study (Savicki, 2008; Lewin, 2009), including the development of important transferable skills (e.g. teamwork, critical thinking, creativity, self-efficacy, awareness of differences) as demonstrated by many (Coleman, 2001; Cushner and Mahon, 2002; Van Hoof and Verbeeten, 2005; Brandenburg et al., 2014; Potts, 2015; Yokota, 2016; Farrugia and Sanger, 2017; Petersdotter et al., 2017; Green et al., 2019, Matherly and Tillman, 2019). They all reported significant personal development because of a study abroad experience. There are papers that claim enhanced intercultural awareness because of the experience of living and studying in a foreign country (Anderson et al., 2006; Pedersen, 2009). However, some other studies have cautioned that this effect may not be as straightforward as often asserted (Vande Berg et al., 2009; Salisbury et al., 2013). Simply exposing students to a different cultural environment, as was examined in the Vande Berg et al. (2009) study, did not result in increased intercultural learning. Indeed, in this study, some students showed a decline in intercultural development. In a more in-depth study of how study abroad impacts on the ICC of internationally mobile students, using the MPQ as part of a mixed mode design, showed a more nuanced view of the enhancement of ICC. The paper reported decreases in the mean scores for cultural empathy and open-mindedness, a marginal increase for emotional stability, and no effect on social initiative or flexibility (Schartner, 2016). The decreased mean scores could possibly be attributed to the reality of intercultural interactions being more challenging than originally expected. Notwithstanding the resolution of this issue, it would appear obvious that ICC could prove to be an important asset in an increasingly globalised workplace.

The enhancement of transferable skills other than ICC and including foreign language, communication, problem-solving skills (Green et al., 2019; Potts, 2021), inexplicit employability skill development – such as managing complexity for developing agility and creativity (Hains-Wesson and Ji, 2020) – and a wider range of intrapersonal, cognitive, and interpersonal competencies (Farrugia and Sanger, 2017), which are perceived to be gained more from a longer period of study abroad, seem to be less controversial and should have a positive impact on employability, given the strong focus of employers on these skills (in addition obviously to relevant content or technical knowledge; Finley, 2021). The graduates also thought that a longer period of study abroad was more likely to be impactful in receiving a job offer. Whether this difference was the result of graduates with longer experiences of study abroad possessing enhanced ability to relate these skills due to awareness in a job interview compared to their shorter-term sojourners remains to be investigated (Potts, 2021). Farrugia and Sanger (2017) observed that students who chose study abroad based on career prospects were better able to articulate the relevant skills development and the career impact. Half of the graduates in their study reported that they thought their job offer was positively impacted by their study abroad experience and those that did not, felt their career progression was positively influenced by their study abroad experience, particularly because of the skills gained during their study abroad. This aligns well with the findings reported by Ota and Shimmi (2019). It should also be noted that Johnson and Anderson (2019) suggested that for short-term sojourners, more scaffolding might be required to link study abroad skills enhancement and relevance to their employability. Although, employers have reported recently that graduates were better able to relate their skills in job interviews (Finley, 2021). This provides some insight into the question of whether awareness of personal developments has an impact on employability. Indeed, Thompson (2004) noted a disconnect between graduates and employers on their understanding of the skills that were gained during study abroad. This was further substantiated by the observations of Farrugia and Sanger (2017), who found that employers did not systematically ask graduates about their study abroad experience. Given the type of skills that are enhanced by study abroad (Potts, 2021), this could be seen as odd, since those skills are regarded as very important by employers (Finley, 2021). There may be an opportunity here to educate employers better on the learning outcomes of study abroad (Green et al., 2019).

The studies have variously used self-assessment by students or graduates who participated in study abroad for credit or for degree (Potts, 2015; Schartner, 2016; Farrugia and Sanger, 2017; Petersdotter et al., 2017; Hubbard et al, 2018; Johnson and Anderson, 2019; Potts, 2021), though some studies used non-mobile students as a control group (Brandenburg et al., 2014; Yokata, 2016; Shimmi et al., 2016, 2017, Petersdotter et al., 2017), and others have deployed a pre- and post-test approach (Schartner, 2016; Martin-Rubió and Cots 2018). Neither the approach with a non-mobile control group, nor the pre- and post-test studies have looked at selection bias. That is to say, the mobile cohorts may possess demographic, personality, or other differences that distinguish them from their non-mobile counterparts. Could these play a role?

Indeed, Wiers-Jenssen et al. (2020) posited that self-selection into mobility plays a role. Van Mol et al. (2020) demonstrated that when controlling for selection into international student mobility using propensity score matching, the apparent labour market advantages (measured as time to transfer from study to work and salary) enjoyed by internationally mobile Bachelor's students and, to a lesser extent, Master's degree students disappeared, suggesting the absence of a causal relationship between international mobility and labour market advantage. Netz and Grüttner (2020) used a similar approach of propensity score matching and suggested that graduates from a high social origin benefit more from international mobility. Although, it remains to be investigated how such a background impacts precisely on employment skills. Students from a high socio-economic background are also more likely to study abroad (Wiers-Jenssen, 2011; Netz and Finger, 2016; Di Pietro, 2019). Jacob et al. (2019) found that the career benefits (five years after graduation) of international mobility were variable and generally larger in countries with poorer university quality, higher graduate unemployment, and fewer students abroad. The study by Van Mol et al. (2020) examined early career benefits (1.5 years after graduation). The Jacob et al. (2019) study would have the Dutch graduates of the Van Mol et al. (2020) study in a less favourable environment to derive benefit from their sojourn and may in part explain the lack of not just early career benefits but also longer-term effects.

EMPLOYER ATTITUDES TO STUDY ABROAD AS AN ENHANCEMENT OF EMPLOYABILITY

Studies by Shimmi et al. (2016, 2017) demonstrated that the longer a Japanese student spends studying abroad, the higher the positive impact on their career progression with more responsibility in management roles and a higher salary. Indeed, their self-evaluated career impact demonstrated enhanced scores on 10 items associated with career development including planning, gaining their current job, obtaining a higher salary, knowledge and skills for their current job, motivation to start a new venture or work with a non-profit organisation, value of study experience and language skills, and communicating with foreigners. These results are especially remarkable given that not half a decade earlier, Japanese companies reported being not particularly interested in employing graduates with foreign study experiences (Ota and Shimmi, 2019) due to, amongst other aspects, a decreased fit with company culture. Graduates were said to be 'too Westernised'. The graduates surveyed in these studies went abroad at a time that companies thought it was not in their interest to hire individuals with such experiences. Yet, their career progressed better than their counterparts who did not go abroad. These studies did not investigate what aspects of their performance in the company was the basis for their progression, yet it seems plausible to suggest that aspects related to company performance were at the basis of their progress. These graduates displayed performance or personality characteristics that were perceived as beneficial to company progress; however, these may not have arisen because of study abroad but may have been part of the make-up of students who choose to study abroad. This does not interfere with the notion that study abroad is able to enhance, under appropriate conditions, a range of skills relevant for employability.

Similar to Japanese employers' attitudes to study abroad, early in the previous decade, some Australian employers had concerns hiring graduates with study abroad experience, as they might present a 'flight-risk' (Green et al., 2019). Although it should be noted that employers were also positive about study abroad experiences in respect to personal development, in general they were less positive about the impact on employability in contrast to the graduates who rated this impact universally positive. A similar observation was made in Finland by Leppänen et al. (2019) comparing an earlier study by Garam (2005) with more recent observations (in 2012), where employers were much less sanguine about the foreign study experience as contributing to the employment prospects of graduates compared to the graduates themselves – 63.4% not interested or interested but not significant (employers) vs. 61.7% additional points, not decisive, gives advantage, required (students). One interesting observation that came from the study by Green et al. (2019) was that when confronted with the transversal skills enhancement as a result of study abroad, employers thought they should reconsider its value.

The current trend in Japan is a different appreciation of graduates with foreign study experience and employers generally believe that a longer period abroad is required to develop the recognised necessary career enhancing skills of foreign language ability and ICC (Ota and Shimmi, 2019). This leaves untouched the enhancement of transferable skills that is perceived to occur because of short-term study abroad, including communication, teamwork, problem-solving skills (Potts, 2021), and a wider range of intrapersonal, cognitive, and interpersonal competencies (Farrugia and Sanger, 2017), which, except for teamwork, are perceived to gain more from a longer period of study abroad. The graduates also thought that a longer period of study abroad was more likely to be impactful in receiving a job offer. Whether this difference was the result of graduates with longer experiences of study abroad possessing enhanced skills or being able to relate these skills due to awareness in a job interview compared to their shorter-term sojourners remains to be investigated (Potts, 2021). However, it should be noted that Johnson and Anderson (2019) suggested that for short-term sojourners, more scaffolding would be required to link study abroad skills enhancement and relevance to their employability.

Thus, whilst insights into the effects of study abroad and how to maximise these outcomes are becoming clearer to scholars in the field of internationalisation of education, there still appears to be a gap between what they and employers know. Several large-scale surveys on employer attitudes to study abroad have been conducted (Molony et al., 2011; British Council, 2013) and they attest to most employers indicating they are appreciative of a foreign experience. However, as Matherly and Tillman (2019: 21) point out, despite this apparent appreciation, 'some employers remain equivocal about the value of learning abroad, sometimes labelling it "academic tourism"'.

Such labelling may have its origins in the way study abroad was thought of and carried out one generation ago, at a time when many of the current employers were themselves studying at university. Indeed, a recent report by Finley (2021) provides some insight into this matter. It investigated the effect of age and educational attainment of the employer (or HR Manager) on their views of what matters most. Finley (2021) reported that, in respect of aspects related to internationalisation, employers under the age of 40, compared to those over the age of 50, were much more likely to consider hiring a graduate who had:

- Experience working in community settings with people from diverse backgrounds and cultures (53% vs. 34%)
- Exposure to global learning experiences (51% vs. 23%).

They were also considerably more appreciative of graduates who had completed a research project that was community-based, or a service-learning project. Activities that promote a range of transferable skills. Notable in this report was the enhanced racial, ethnic, and gender diversity of employers under the age of 40 compared to their more senior (age 50 and up) counterparts. It may just be that a new generation of employers has more in their sights diversity and the ability to work together with diverse individuals.

The mismatch between perception of employment readiness between education providers, employers, and students has been an ongoing issue (Mourshed et al., 2012; Collet et al., 2015; Karzunina et al., 2018; Maschião da Costa et al., 2019). In part, this may be due to the lack of a shared language about concepts thought to be important for employability. The Japanese experience (Ota and Shimmi, 2019) and the Australian insights (Green et al., 2019) also points to a lack of understanding of the outcomes of an international study experience, since these outcomes (transferable skills) are highly appreciated by employers. The apparent gap in understanding the outcomes of study abroad experiences in terms of the development of transferable skills was shown again more recently (Quacquarelli Symonds, 2021). It is interesting that for Japanese employers to change their perception of study abroad, it took this being pointed out by external campaigns, thus aligning with public learning as described in the model of Cai (2013) instead of private learning, which was available earlier in their own companies.

The latest QS Employer Insights Report (Quacquarelli Symonds, 2021) showed that international experience was selected by only 25% of companies as one of three top recruitment priorities, much less than professional experience – valuing workplace experience (66%), target disciplines (41%, especially in technical industries requiring specialised skill sets), and diversity (31%). Yet from the same survey, the transferable skills enhanced by study abroad were almost universally regarded as highly important. In the AAC&U study (Finley, 2021), an internship led the list of desirable experiences for new employees. This was also found by Pinto and Pereira (2019) in an experimental between-subject factorial design study where employers were asked to rate the employability of six fictitious resumés of business graduates of varied gender and with or without an internship both conducted locally and internationally. Having internship experience was rated highly in terms of job suitability, employability skills and starting salary, but it was immaterial whether this was an international or local experience. Indeed, work experience was already rated very highly in a 2010 survey on graduate employment carried out in the European Union (Gallup Organisation, 2010), in contrast to international experience.

China is another good example of changing employer appreciation of the value of a degree from abroad. Some time ago, returning to China with an overseas degree was sufficient to obtain a good job (Hao and Welch, 2012); however, this has been changing, and today, returning international Chinese students experience significant challenges to gain a job in an environment of increased graduate employment, competition from graduates of local elite universities (Hao et al., 2016), possession of *guanxi*, a strong social network of connections (Ferguson and Sonnenschein, 2020), limited work experience, and desynchrony with Chinese recruitment months (Singh, 2020). The paper by Tran and Bui (2021), albeit focused on Vietnam, highlights the need for some important developments with respect to support for international students intending to return home. These developments respond to similar challenges faced by returning graduates to Vietnam compared to their Chinese counterparts and may apply to international students of many other countries as well. These include the provision of graduate employability development into the curriculum (see also Johnson and Anderson,

2019), particularly in relation to their home labour market. This may necessitate the development of relationships with employers in the home country of international students, monitoring of labour conditions of these markets, and enhancement of an in-country alumni networks.

CONCLUSION

The perception that international student mobility is causally related to enhanced employability is strongly felt by graduates who have experienced one or more sojourns during their study. Several characteristics that are thought of as important for employability are enhanced by study abroad. However, recent studies increasingly point towards the possession of these characteristics prior to study abroad. In other words, students who opt to go abroad may be pre-disposed. These studies however do not preclude that the characteristics that are important for employability are in fact enhanced by a period of study abroad and thereby affect career progress.

Whilst students who have experienced study abroad are almost universally convinced that this will enhance their employability, employers are less convinced and are more interested in potential new employees having some form of work experience. Students who are internationally mobile and are returning to their home country after obtaining a degree may specifically benefit from work experience in their home country. It would be a challenge for universities that recruit international students to facilitate this, but this is thought to be very worthwhile.

There appears to be a gap in understanding between employers, students, and academics, particularly those who study internationalisation of education and what the outcomes are of study abroad. Thus, employers mostly interpret the learning outcomes of this internationalisation activity as being mostly confined to the development of foreign language ability and ICC. Even when they are able to define a wider range of outcomes including various transferable skills (Leppänen et al., 2019), this does not translate into a perception of greater employability.

One would think that the observations on increased company performance associated with embracing diversity of different sources (Hunt et al., 2015; Dolan et al., 2021) would rapidly result in a wider appreciation among employers of skills related to effectively being able to interact with diverse individuals. At least, younger employers seem to think so (Finley, 2021), both in terms of acting to create more diverse companies and their appreciation of graduates who have worked with diverse individuals or experienced study abroad.

If the development of students to be able to work effectively with diverse individuals can be engendered by activities other than study abroad, we could be on the road to enhancing employability for all students, not just the internationally mobile ones, regardless of whether this is due to pre-disposing aspects or due to a further enhancement of qualities appreciated by employers. Notwithstanding the opportunities that might be developed to enhance these characteristics using IaH or IoC, it may just be that these activities find their base in other forms of diversity-related activities, not the least of which could be interdisciplinary collaboration. The work of McKinsey & Company on the association between embracing diversity and company performance is material in this respect. One pointer towards what these activities might need to develop (at least in the way of personality characteristics) are the factors identified in the MPQ together with some other aspects, such as being non-judgemental, inquisitiveness, cosmopolitanism, and self-awareness. If we consider these personality characteristics to be traits (more or less stable by the time young people reach adulthood), we should not wait until students are in higher education to develop these, but start much earlier – for example, in primary education.

REFERENCES

Anderson, P.H., Lawton, L., Rexeisen, R.J., and Hubbard, A., (2006), 'Short-term study abroad and intercultural sensitivity: A pilot study', *International Journal of Intercultural Relations*, vol. 30, pp. 457–69.

Brandenburg, U., Berghoff, S., Taboadela, O., Bischof, L., Gajowniczek, J., and Gehlke, A., (2014), *The ERASMUS Impact Study: Effects of mobility on the skills and employability of students and the internationalisation of higher education institutions*. https://op.europa.eu/en/publication-detail/-/publication/13031399-9fd4-11e5-8781-01aa75ed71a1/language-en (viewed 1 Aug 2021).

British Council (2013) Culture at Work: *The Value of Intercultural Skills in the Workplace*. London: British Council.

Cai, Y., (2013), 'Graduate employability: A conceptual framework for understanding employers' perceptions', *Higher Education*, vol. 65, pp. 457–69.

Chen, X., and Gabrenya Jr, W.K., (2021), 'In search of cross-cultural competence: A comprehensive review of five measurement instruments', *International Journal of Intercultural Relations*, vol. 82, pp. 37–55.

Coelen, R.J., (2016), 'A learner-centred internationalisation of higher education', In E. Jones, R.J. Coelen, J. Beelen, and H. De Wit (eds) *Global and Local Internationalization*. Dordrecht: Sense Publishers, pp. 35–42.

Coleman, J., (2001), 'What is "residence abroad" for? Intercultural competence and the linguistic, cultural, academic, personal and professional objectives of student residence abroad', In R. Di Napoli, L. Polezzi, and A. King (eds) *Fuzzy Boundaries? Reflections on Modern Languages and the Humanities*. London: CILT pp. 121–40.

Collet, C., Hine, D., and Du Plessis, K., (2015) 'Employability skills: perspectives from a knowledge-intensive industry', *Education + Training*, vol. 57, no. 5, pp. 532–59.

Cushner, K., and Mahon, J., (2002), 'Overseas Student Teaching: Affecting Personal, Professional, and Global Competencies in an Age of Globalization', *Journal of Studies in International Education*, vol. 6, pp. 44–58.

Desvaux, G., and Devillard, S., (2008), *'Women Matter 2: Female leadership, a competitive edge for the future'*. New York: McKinsey and Company. https://internationalwim.org/iwim-reports/women-matter-2-female-leadership-a-competitive-edge-for-the-future/ (viewed 1 Aug 2021).

Desvaux, G., Devillard-Hoellinger, S., and Baumgarten, P., (2007), *'Women Matter. Gender diversity, a corporate performance driver'*. New York: McKinsey and Company. www.mckinsey.com/~/media/mckinsey/business%20functions/organization/our%20insights/gender%20diversity%20a%20corporate%20performance%20driver/gender%20diversity%20a%20corporate%20performance%20driver.pdf (viewed 1 Aug 2021).

Desvaux, G., Devillard, S., and Sancier-Sultan, S., (2009), *'Women Matter 3: Women leaders, a competitive edge in and after the crisis'*. New York: McKinsey and Company. www.mckinsey.com/~/media/mckinsey/business%20functions/organization/our%20insights/women%20matter/women_matter_dec2009_english.pdf (viewed 1 Aug 2021).

Di Pietro, G., (2019), 'Changes in socioeconomic inequality in access to study abroad programs: a cross-country analysis', *Research in Social Stratification and Mobility*, vol. 66, 100465.

Dolan, K., Hunt, V., Prince, S., and Sancier-Sultan, S., (2020), 'Diversity still matters', *McKinsey Quarterly*, 19 May 2020. www.mckinsey.com/~/media/mckinsey/featured%20insights/diversity%20and%20inclusion/diversity%20still%20matters/diversity-still-matters-vf.pdf?shouldIndex=false (viewed 1 Aug 2021).

Farrugia, C., and Sanger, J., (2017) *'Gaining an employment edge: The impact of study abroad on 21st century skills & career prospects'*. New York: Institute for International Education. www.iie.org/Research-and-Insights/Publications/Gaining-an-employment-edge—The-Impact-of-Study-Abroad (viewed 1 Aug 2021).

Ferguson, J., and Sonnenschein, K., (2020), 'Comparing Australian graduate employees' "use of connections" and Chinese "sea-turtle" graduate employees' use of "guanxi"', *Australian Journal of Career Development*, vol. 29, no. 1, pp. 24–35.

Finley, A., (2021), *How College Contributes to Workforce Success – Employer Views on What Matters Most*. Washington, DC: Association of American Colleges and Universities.

Gallup Organisation, (2010), *Employers' Perception of Graduate Employability*. Brussels: European Commission.

Garam, I., (2005), *International Student Mobility and Working Life. Employers' Views on the Importance of Studying and Training Abroad. (Opiskelijoiden kansainvälinen liikkuvuus ja työelämä. Työnantajien näkemyksiä ulkomailla opiskelun ja harjoittelun merkityksestä).* Helsinki: Centre for International Mobility CIMO [published in Finnish].

Green, W., King, E., and Gallagher, J., (2019), 'How can international learning experiences enhance employability? Critical insights from new graduates and the people who employ them', In R.J. Coelen, and C. Gribble (eds) *Internationalization and Employability in Higher Education*. Abingdon: Routledge, pp. 25–38.

Ha, P.L., and Phung, T., (2021), 'COVID-19 opportunities for internationalisation at home', *University World News*, 29 Aug 2020. www.universityworldnews.com/post.php?story=20200828113510793 (viewed 1 Aug 2021).

Hains-Wesson, R., and Ji, K., (2020), 'Students' perceptions of an interdisciplinary global study tour: uncovering inexplicit employability skills', *Higher Education Research & Development*, vol. 39, no. 4, pp. 657–71.

Hammer, M.R., Bennett, M.J., and Wiseman, R., (2003), 'Measuring intercultural sensitivity: the intercultural development inventory', *International Journal of Intercultural Relations*, vol. 27, pp. 421–43.

Hao, J., Welch, A., (2012), 'A tale of sea turtles: Job-seeking experiences of hai gui (high-skilled returnees) in China', *Higher Education Policy*, vol. 25, no. 2, pp. 243–60.

Hao, J., Wen, W., and Welch, A., (2016), 'When sojourners return: Employment opportunities and challenges facing high-skilled Chinese returnees', *Asian and Pacific Migration Journal*, vol 25, no. 1, pp. 22–40.

Hofhuis, J., Jongerling, J., Van der Zee, K.I., and Jansz, J. (2020) Validation of the Multicultural Personality Questionnaire Short Form (MPQ-SF) for use in the context of international education. *PLoS ONE* 15(12): e0244425.

Hubbard, A., Rexeisen, R., and Watson, P., (2018), *'AIFS study abroad alumni outcomes: A longitudinal study of personal, intercultural and career development based on a survey of our alumni from 1990 to 2017: Volume 2'*, Stamford: American Institute for Foreign Studies. Error! Hyperlink reference not valid. www.aifsabroad.com/outcomes2018.pdf (viewed 1 Aug 2021).

Hunt, V., Layton, D., and Prince, S., (2015), *'Diversity matters'*, New York: McKinsey and Company. www.mckinsey.com/~/media/mckinsey/business%20functions/organization/our%20insights/why%20diversity%20matters/diversity%20matters.ashx (viewed 1 Aug 2021).

Jacob, M., Kühhirt, M., and Rodrigues, M., (2019), 'Labour market returns to graduates' international experience: Exploring cross-country variation in Europe', *European Sociological Review*, vol. 35, no. 4, pp. 491–505.

Johnson, J.P., Lenartowicz., T., and Apud, S., (2006), 'Cross-cultural competence in international business: Toward a definition and a model', *Journal of International Business Studies*, vol. 37, pp. 525–43.

Johnson, M., and Anderson, C., (2019), 'The impact of education abroad on competency development', In R.J. Coelen, and C. Gribble (eds) *Internationalization and Employability in Higher Education*. Abingdon: Routledge, pp. 49–58.

Karzunina, D., West, J., Maschião da Costa, G., Philippou, G., and Gordon, S., (2018), *'The global skills gap in the 21st century'*. London: Quacquarelli Symonds. https://info.qs.com/rs/335-VIN-535/images/The%20Global%20Skills%20Gap%2021st%20Century.pdf (viewed 1 Aug 2021).

Korol, L., Gonçalves, G., and Cabral, M., (2016), 'The impact of multicultural personality on tolerance of diversity in a sample of Portuguese university students', *Revista Psicologia: Teoria e Prática*, vol. 18, no. 2, pp. 57–74.

Leppänen, J., Neuvonen, A., and Saarinen, M., (2019), 'Finnish employers' and students' appreciation of the effect of learning abroad on employability', In R.J. Coelen, and C. Gribble (eds) *Internationalization and Employability in Higher Education*. Abingdon: Routledge, pp. 39–48.

Leung, K., Ang, S., and Tan, M., (2014), 'Intercultural Competence', *Annual Review of Organisational Psychology and Organizational Behavior,* vol. 1, pp. 489–519.

Liu, Y., and Shirley, T., (2021), 'Without crossing a border: Exploring the impact of shifting study abroad online on students' learning and intercultural competence development during the COVID-19 pandemic', *Online Learning Journal*, vol. 25, no. 1, pp. 182–94.

Martin-Rubió, X., and Cots, J.M., (2018), 'Self-confidence amongst study abroad students in an "English as a lingua franca" university', *Language Awareness*, vol. 27, no. 1–2, pp. 96–112.

Maschião da Costa, G., Dzugan, J., Linney, S., West, J., and Philippou, G., (2019), *'2019 Global skills gap report'*. London: Quacquarelli Symonds. https://info.qs.com/rs/335-VIN-535/images/2019_Global_Skills_Gap_Report.pdf (viewed 1 Aug 2021).

Mason, L., (2021), *International Student Mobility Flows and COVID-19 Realities*. New York: Institute of International Education.

Matherly, C., and Tillman, M., (2019) 'Linking learning abroad and employability', In R.J. Coelen, and C. Gribble (eds) *Internationalization and Employability in Higher Education*. Abingdon: Routledge, pp. 11–24.

Matsumoto, D., and Hwang, H.C., (2013), 'Assessing cross-cultural competence: A Review of available tests', *Journal of Cross-cultural Psychology*, vol. 44, no. 6, pp. 849–73.

Molony, J., Sowter, B., and Potts, D., (2011), *QS Global Employer Survey Report*. London: QS Intelligence.

Mourshed, M., Farrell, D., and Barton, D., (2012), *'Education to employment: Designing a system that works'*. McKinsey Center for Government. www.mckinsey.com/industries/public-and-social-sector/our-insights/education-to-employment-designing-a-system-that-works (viewed 1 Aug 2021).

Netz, N., and Finger, C., (2016), 'New horizontal inequalities in German higher education? Social selectivity of studying abroad between 1991 and 2012', *Sociology of Education*, vol. 89, no. 2, pp. 79–98.

Ota, H., and Shimmi, Y., (2019), 'Recent trends in learning abroad in the context of a changing Japanese economy and higher education situation', In R.J. Coelen and C. Gribble (eds) *Internationalization and Employability in Higher Education*. Abingdon: Routledge, pp. 78–91.

Page, S.E., (2017), *The Diversity Bonus – How Great Teams Pay Off in the Knowledge Economy*. Princeton: Princeton University Press.

Pedersen, P.J., (2009), 'Teaching towards an ethnorelative worldview through psychology study abroad', *Intercultural Education*, vol. 20, pp. S73–S86.

Petersdotter, L., Niehoff, E., and Freund, P.A., (2017), 'International experience makes a difference: Effects of study abroad on students' self-efficacy', *Personality and Individual Difference*, vol. 107, pp. 174–8.

Pinto, L.H., and Pereira, P.C. (2019) 'I wish to do an internship (abroad)': investigating the perceived employability of domestic and international business internships. *Higher Education* 78, 443–461.

Potts, D., (2015), 'Understanding the early career benefits of learning abroad programs', *Journal of Studies in International Education*, vol. 19, no. 5, pp. 441–59.

Potts, D., (2021), 'Employability development and career outcomes from short-term learning abroad programmes', *Higher Education Research & Development*, published online first: 25 Mar 2021, doi 10.1080/07294360.2021.1901665.

Quacquarelli Symonds, (2021), *'QS Employer Insights Report 2020'*. London: Quacquarelli Symonds. www.qs.com/portfolio-items/qs-employer-insights-report-2020/. (viewed 1 Aug 2021).

Römgens, I., Scoupe, R., and Beausaert, S., (2020), 'Unravelling the concept of employability, bringing together research on employability in higher education and the workplace', *Studies in Higher Education*, vol. 45, no. 12, pp. 2588–603.

Salisbury, M.H., An, B.P., and Pascarella, E.T., (2013), 'The effect of Study Abroad on Intercultural Competence among Undergraduate College Students', *Journal of Student Affairs Research and Practice,* vol. 50, no. 1, pp. 1–20.

Schartner, A., (2016), 'The effect of study abroad on intercultural competence: a longitudinal case study of international postgraduate students at a British university', *Journal of Multilingual and Multicultural Development*, vol. 37, no. 4, pp. 402–18.

Shimmi, Y., Akiba, H., Ota, H., and Yokota, M., (2017), 'Long-term impact of undergraduate study abroad experiences on career: Comparative survey among degree-seeking study abroad, credit-bearing study abroad, and non-study abroad groups', *Ryugakukoryu (Student Exchanges)*, vol. 74, pp. 14–26 [published in Japanese]. www.jasso.go.jp/ryugaku/related/kouryu/2017/_icsFiles/afieldfile/2017/05/10/201705ryugakukoryu.pdf (viewed 1 Aug 2021).

Shimmi, Y., Ota, H., Watabe, Y., and Akiba, H., (2016), 'Studies on the development of global human resource and the long-term impact of study abroad experiences: Results from an online survey for those who studied abroad and who did not', *Journal of Asian Culture Society International*, vol. 23, pp. 3–25 [published in Japanese].

Singh, J.K.N., (2020), 'Challenges in obtaining employment in China: Lived experiences of Australian Chinese graduates', *Australian Journal of Career Development*, vol. 29, no. 3, pp. 153–63.

Spitzberg, B.H., and Chagnon, G., (2009), 'Conceptualizing Intercultural Competence', In D.K. Deardorff (ed.), *The SAGE Handbook of Intercultural Competence*, Thousand Oaks, CA: Sage, pp. 3–52.

Thompson, J.W., (2004), *An Exploration of the Demand for Study Overseas from American students and Employers*. A report prepared for the Institute of International Education, the German Academic Exchange Service (DAAD), the British Council, and the Australian Education Office. www.iie.org/Research-and-Insights/Publications/Demand-for-Study-Overseas-from-American-Students-and-Employers (viewed 1 Sep 2021).

Tran, L.T., and Bui, H., (2021), 'International graduate returnees' accumulation of capitals and (re)positioning in the home labour market in Vietnam: the explorer, the advancer or the adventurer?' *Journal of Education and Work*, vol. 34, published online first: 20 May 2020, doi 10.1080/13639080.2021.1943334

Vande Berg, M., Connor-Linton, J., and Paige, R.M., (2009), 'The Georgetown Consortium Project: Interventions for student learning abroad', *Frontiers: The Interdisciplinary Journal of Study Abroad*, vol. 18, no. 1, pp. 1–75.

Van der Zee, K.I., and Van Oudenhoven, J.P., (2000), 'The Multicultural Personality Questionnaire: A multidimensional instrument of multicultural effectiveness', *European Journal of Personality*, vol. 14, pp. 291–309.

Van der Zee, K., Van Oudenhoven, J.P., Ponterotto, J.G., and Fietzer, A.W., (2013), 'Multicultural Personality Questionnaire: Development of a short form', *Journal of Personality Assessment*, vol. 95, no. 1, pp. 118–24.

Van Hoof, H.B., and Verbeeten, M.J., (2005), 'Wine is for drinking, water is for washing: Student opinions about international exchange programs', *Journal of Studies in International Education,* vol. 9, no. 1, pp. 42–61.

Van Mol, C., Caarls, K., and Souto-Otero, M., (2020), 'International student mobility and labour market outcomes: an investigation of the role of level of study, type of mobility, and international prestige hierarchies', *Higher Education*, vol. 82, published online first: 12 Apr 2020, doi 10.1007/s10734-020-00532-3.

Wiers-Jenssen, J., (2011), 'Background and employability of mobile vs. non-mobile students', *Tertiary Education and Management*, vol. 17, no. 2, pp. 79–100.

Wiers-Jenssen, J., Tillman, M., and Matherly, C., (2020), 'Employability: How education abroad impacts the transition to graduate employment', In A. Ogden, B. Streitwieser, and C. Van Mol (eds) *Education Abroad: Bridging Scholarship and Practice*. New York: Routledge.

Yokota, M., (2016), *'Survey of global personnel development and long-term impact of study abroad'*. (Research project no. 25245078). School of Global Japanese Studies, Meiji University.

22

Transnational, Multinational, Binational? The Role of International Education in Human Capital Development for Graduate Employability

Jessica Schueller and Filiz Keser Aschenberger

INTRODUCTION

Internationalisation is one of the most prominent influences on higher education and is often regarded as key to increasing student employability. The link between international education and employability is gaining importance for a variety of stakeholders, including participating students (Nilsson and Ripmeester, 2016; Jones, 2019). Individuals and families invest in degrees abroad in the hope of favourable employment prospects. While in the past, students returning home have been able to secure advantages such as a shorter job-search period (Petzold, 2017), in the last half-decade, research has indicated more mixed findings (Bilsland et al., 2020; Craciun et al., 2020; Van Mol et al., 2020; Tran et al., 2021). In some cases, a non-local degree can negatively impact employment prospects in students' home countries. For example, China, which traditionally sent students abroad, is now developing its own education system, welcoming international students, and experiencing economic growth. As a result, Chinese graduates from programmes abroad are returning home to face fierce competition from local graduates who are increasingly favoured by local employers (Cai, 2012a; Mok and Han, 2016; Petzold, 2017; Tran et al., 2021). A possible cause for this expectation mismatch is capital development: those who have earned their degree abroad develop capital in the foreign country, which may or may not be transferable to the home country.

These developments underscore the need for a more robust understanding of the relationship between international education and graduate employability. The purpose of this chapter is to illustrate the role of international education in graduate employability by outlining a framework that emphasises focused employability preparation through the development of binational human capital. Binational human capital spans international students' home and host countries and provides a structure for students and universities concerned about developing international student employability. Drawing on a review of the literature, a conceptual framework, and a case study, we address the changing role of international education in graduate employability and its implications for scholarship and practice.

LITERATURE REVIEW: EMPLOYABILITY IN INTERNATIONAL AND TRANSNATIONAL EDUCATION

Internationalisation of higher education has two major segments: internationalisation at home and internationalisation abroad (Knight, 2012). The latter is also referred to as cross-border education or transnational education (TNE). Within internationalisation abroad, there is a further division between 'international student and scholar mobility' and 'international programme and provider mobility' (Knight and Liu, 2019). International student and scholar mobility involves students moving for education (e.g. study abroad), whereas international programme and provider mobility entails programmes moving towards students (e.g. an international branch campus). In international student and scholar mobility, students leave their home country to pursue education abroad, such as a Chinese student pursuing a degree at a British university or an American student completing a semester in France. In TNE, students remain in their home countries but receive education from foreign education providers, such as a student in Malaysia attending an Australian international branch campus. A key difference is thus between the *home* country (origin of the student) and the *host* country (destination of the student). In this chapter, international education refers to obtaining an education that requires mobility through either international student and scholar mobility or international programme and provider mobility.

Labour market outcomes are the immediate outcomes of higher education graduates who are part of the labour force, and they include indicators such as employment status, earnings, and skills-level match (OECD, 2017). Contrarily, employability is understood as the ability to find work over a lifetime and is not measurable by any single indicator. Rather, it is a contested term with several definitions (Yorke and Knight, 2004; Yorke, 2006; Rothwell et al., 2008; Tomlinson, 2017). Employability is not a set of attributes or one specific attribute, nor is it static. It is developed and used over a lifetime (Yorke, 2006). A widely accepted definition of employability, provided by Yorke (2006: 23), indicates that it is 'a set of achievements – skills, understanding and personal attributes – that makes graduates more likely to gain employment and be successful in their chosen occupations, which benefits themselves, the workforce, the community and the economy'. Due to this terminology-related confusion, employability is often equated to the ability of a student to obtain their first job after graduation. In this chapter, we primarily discuss employability, of which labour market outcomes are but one part.

INTERNATIONAL EDUCATION AND LABOUR MARKET OUTCOMES

Research has long suggested that students pursuing education abroad are motivated by the opportunity to gain skills and attributes and access certain capitals that result in better employment prospects (Salisbury et al., 2009; Crossman and Clarke, 2010; Mok and Han, 2016; Huang and Turner, 2018). Seeking a degree abroad has been touted in the literature and marketed by universities and exchange organisations as a route to a global career (Baker and Benjamin, 1994; Borjas, 1995; Chiswick and Miller, 1995; Krahn et al., 2000; Bratsberg and Ragan Jr., 2002; Zeng and Xie, 2004; Varghese, 2008; Norris and Gillespie, 2009).

Since the turn of the century, a rapidly increasing number of studies are exploring the role of higher education in graduate careers and labour market outcomes, especially the impact of a semester abroad on employability (Teichler and Janson, 2007). There is a body of research suggesting that alumni who were mobile as students are more likely to work internationally (Teichler and Janson, 2007; Varghese, 2008; Parey and Waldinger, 2011; Di Pietro, 2012; Rodrigues, 2013). One explanation for this is that individuals who are familiar with and accustomed to migrating are more likely to do so again, as their 'mobility capital' increases with each trip and becomes more valuable to them (Massey et al., 1993; Wiers-Jenssen, 2008; Rodrigues, 2013). Another explanation is that there is a greater advantage associated with international education than with local education for students from developing countries (Blaug et al., 1969; Pang and Clark, 1970; Demetriades and Psacharopoulos, 1979; Varghese, 2008; Aba, 2013).

Although an international education experience is suggested to lead to better labour market returns, research in this field is limited, anecdotal in nature, and primarily qualitative. In some cases, such research has been accused of being prone to biased interpretations (Di Pietro, 2019; Arghode et al., 2021). While studies have claimed that mobile students have better labour market outcomes than non-mobile students (Wiers-Jenssen and Try, 2005; Wiers-Jenssen, 2008, 2011; Craciun and Orosz, 2018), an international education may not necessarily always have an impact on employment prospects, since individual and contextual factors play a significant role in the education–employability link (Duvander, 2001; Støren and Wiers-Jenssen, 2010; Waibel et al., 2017; Di Pietro, 2019; Craciun et al., 2020). Graduates who were mobile as students were found to be less likely to work in the domestic labour market, but those who did find work domestically had above-average earnings, albeit not holding higher-level managerial or professional positions (Craciun et al., 2020). However, developing employability skills through study overseas could possibly make some graduates less employable at home, and returning students may find it harder to reintegrate into the local labour market (Robertson et al., 2011; Cai, 2012b). This possibility may partly be attributed to the dramatic increase in mobility, which had led employers to perceive mobile graduates less favourably (Craciun et al., 2020).

There is still a dearth of research demonstrating the measured impact of education abroad or periods of international mobility on labour market outcomes. It is often difficult to control for variables or argue causality because of a variety of confounding and hard-to-measure variables, such as individual ability, family background, selection, self-selection, and socio-economic status (Di Pietro, 2019; Craciun et al., 2020; Van Mol et al., 2020). Additionally, research on the relationship between international student and scholar mobility and labour market outcomes often does not take into account differences in labour market outcomes across international programme types, institution types, degree levels, or destination countries, and those that do so tend to focus on short-term mobility programmes (Van Mol et al., 2020). As a result, research on the impact of international mobility on labour market outcomes is limited in scope and rigour. Unsurprisingly, the graduate employability of international students was among the top three emerging areas of interest predicted to attract further interest in the next decade (Jing et al., 2020).

TNE AND LABOUR MARKET OUTCOMES

TNE differs from international education in that the core component of TNE is exporting educational structures from one country to students in another, often within the format of a locally established institution. Examples include international branch campuses and binational universities (BUs). An international branch campus can be managed independently by an institution, whereas a BU (also referred to as an 'international joint university') indicates some form of involvement at the national level (Knight and McNamara, 2017). These TNE institutions assume a 'global identity to legitimize themselves to both home country and host country stakeholders' (Farrugia and Lane, 2013: 414). Since a foreign institution or government provides education in a student's home country, TNE is situated between internationalisation at home and education abroad (Knight, 2005). Although research on the role and impact of TNE on graduate employability has increased in recent years (Matherly and Tillman, 2019), it still remains severely limited (Mellors-Bourne et al., 2015; Ashour and Allender, 2018). Three observations can be made about such research: (a) the intersection of TNE and employability is under-researched, with the majority of studies emerging after 2010, (b) there is a biased focus on Anglophone TNE in the Middle East and Asia, and (c) there is a lack of research on student perspectives.

TNE presents additional opportunities and challenges for employability and labour market outcomes, owing to the uniqueness of internationalised institutions in host countries. Thus, students may want or need to be employable within both the host- and home-country contexts. Sin (2013) established that TNE students saw a UK education in Malaysia as a way to retain ties with the home country and get a foot in the door of the local labour market while gaining an international credential and the cultural capital accompanying it. TNE can result in better employability in domestic settings in comparison to local education or education abroad, but a key determinant is whether or not employers perceive TNE programmes positively (Jones, 2019). Despite the employability benefits being at the forefront in students' consideration of a TNE programme, relatively few empirical studies have investigated the link between TNE and labour market outcomes quantitatively or been sufficiently robust to control for causality (Knight and McNamara, 2017). TNE students' voices are often not heard, although there are some studies on them (e.g. Ziguras and McBurnie, 2015). Very little is known about TNE students' preferences, outcomes, or long-term personal and professional trajectories (Hoare, 2012). This holds true even for 'traditional' TNE sending countries, such as the USA, the UK, and Australia.

Employability capital and experiences in TNE are expressed through teaching methods, curriculum, and skills reported to be different in comparison to those associated with local education programmes (Yao and Tuliao, 2019). In comparison to local institutions, examples of pedagogical differences in TNE institutions include emphasising the sharing of opinions and critical thinking, which students feel contribute to the development of their analytical skills (Knight and McNamara, 2017; Yao and Tuliao, 2019; Belderbos, 2020; Tran et al., 2021). Further, work-integrated learning (internships during studies) functions as a key boundary spanner in TNE (Bilsland et al., 2020). The high foreign-language proficiency demanded by TNE institutions ensures the enrolment of highly prepared students, but over time, this demand needs to be met through continuous language study and familiarisation with different learning contexts (Nghia and Duyen, 2019). If TNE is effective in developing employability skills, it could help students interpret their newfound knowledge and skills in the local labour market while also interpreting employability within the local paradigm (Jones, 2019).

THEORETICAL FRAMEWORK

Human capital theory, which originated in economics, asserts that education provides individuals with the skills, abilities, and attributes needed to enter and progress in the labour market (Mincer, 1958; Schultz, 1961; Becker, 1964, 1994). Becker (1964) distinguishes between specific human capital (not transferable to other employers) and general human capital (transferable to other employers). Human capital theory has an extensive history in the educational sciences, particularly in the career outcomes and employability literature, as well as in other social sciences (Sweetland, 1996; Tan, 2014). Human capital is distinct from but interrelated with other forms of capital, such as economic, symbolic, cultural, and social capital (Bourdieu, 1986; Coleman, 1988; Shumilova and Cai, 2022).

Human capital theory is often used in studies examining the associations between international educational attainment and labour market outcomes (Cai, 2012b). A branch of human capital theory that has been used frequently in the last decade to understand the relationship between international education experiences and employability is transnational human capital. Transnational human capital connects mobility experiences with labour market outcomes and international employability.

GOING ABROAD TO GET AHEAD: A PRIMER ON TRANSNATIONAL HUMAN CAPITAL IN INTERNATIONAL EDUCATION

Foreign-language skills, international work and study experience, and intercultural competencies are increasing in significance due to globalisation. The literature refers to this combination of skills and competencies as 'transnational human capital', which has been primarily applied in studies investigating immigration, employability, and international education experiences (Zweig et al., 2004; Gerhards and Hans, 2013; Medrano, 2016; Belderbos, 2020). Academic and grey literature is peppered with references to transnational human capital (Gerhards and Hans, 2013; Medrano, 2016; Delval and Bühlmann, 2020), although it is not always explicitly mentioned. The general premise of transnational human capital is that there are skills accumulated through mobility experience that translate to better labour market outcomes at home and abroad. The conceptual claim underlining this statement is that mobile students develop skill sets that are valued by employers, and these skill sets are applicable in domestic and international labour markets, thus increasing their employment opportunities (Di Pietro, 2015, 2019). Although there is some empirical evidence that employers value the skills, attributes, and competencies associated with transnational human capital (Bühlmann et al., 2018), this evidence has also been contested due to concerns of assumptive positioning and lack of methodological rigour (Medrano, 2016).

There are no universal definitions of transnational human capital or what it entails. Further, as mentioned above, the challenge with separating social, cultural, and human capital is complex because country-specific networks, knowledge, and skills can be interpreted as social capital or cultural capital (Shumilova and Cai, 2022). Building on Zweig et al. (2004), another common definition of the theory asserts that '[t]ransnational human capital refers to those stocks of knowledge and personal skills that enable a person to operate in different fields beyond the individual nation state' (Gerhards and Hans, 2013: 100). From a slightly different angle, a distinction is made between general and country-specific skills in the generation of human capital, meaning that internationals acquire skills specific to a certain country, primarily through education experiences in that country (Duvander, 2001; Chiswick and Miller, 2003; Wiers-Jenssen, 2008). A term related to transnational human capital is 'cosmopolitan capital' (Weenink, 2007, 2008; Bühlmann et al., 2013; Igarashi and Saito, 2014), which is defined as an inherited 'combinational of cultural, linguistic, social, and institutionalised resources acquired through transnational mobility of exposure to international environments' (Delval and Bühlmann, 2020: 1). Alongside cosmopolitan capital, the term 'international capital' is also mentioned in some studies (Delval and Bühlmann, 2020). The common thread binding the various terms used to define transnational human capital is that international educational mobility equips 'individuals with skills, knowledge and dispositions that constitute resources for pursuing a geographically and socially mobile trajectory' (Bühlmann et al., 2013). On this account, transnational human capital gives an individual the capital to successfully move between nation states; for this reason, it may predispose international graduates to pursue opportunities to move abroad for work.

METHOD AND RESULTS: FROM TRANSNATIONAL TO BINATIONAL HUMAN CAPITAL

In this research, we followed a combined approach to create the framework on binational human capital. Our synthesis of the previous literature and the data collected from Turkish–German University (TGU) during 2020 formed the basis of the framework. After conducting a scoping review of the literature on or using transnational human capital, we limited our scope to research that had applied transnational human capital to international education studies.

The contents of transnational human capital are presented in the literature in a fragmented fashion. For example, some authors narrow down the types of transnational human capital to fluency in foreign languages, experience in studying abroad, and international friendship ties abroad (Medrano, 2016). Others list a plethora of interrelated attributes such as knowledge of foreign labour markets, institutions, and legal systems; travel and mobility readiness; knowledge of international technical standards and norms; tolerance and willingness to adapt; and flexibility (Gerhards and Hans, 2013).

The analysis of higher education from an economic perspective, as with human capital theory, has both value and limitations, due to the complex relationship between education and the labour market. Human capital theory has been very influential in the educational sciences, but it is just one part of the higher education landscape (Marginson, 2019). Moreover, the accompanying transnational human capital theory is also not without criticism. As college students in their late teens and early 20s are at a late stage of capital development, one cannot simply assume that their later professional successes can be entirely attributed to the human capital or transnational human capital gained through their university studies – international or otherwise. The accumulation of both forms of capital, along with other forms of soft and hard (financial) capital, begins at – or arguably before – birth and is tied to the national and socio-economic contexts in which a person develops and goes to school (Gerhards and Hans, 2013; Delval and Bühlmann, 2020). Notwithstanding its limitations, human capital theory is gradually gaining momentum in scholarly discourse, despite its definitional and descriptive challenges.

This literature was then examined for descriptors of transnational human capital, which were grouped into four thematic categories as shown in Table 22.1. This categorization forms the transnational human capital framework.

THE CASE OF GERMAN BINATIONAL UNIVERSITIES (BUS)

The transnational human capital framework was used to analyse the characteristics of education and employment preparation in the case of Germany's BUs, and this resulted in evidence for a more specific form of human capital: binational human capital.

International education and TNE are primarily bilateral undertakings for students, institutions, and countries. Students study abroad for a semester or pursue a degree in *one* host country, learning the language, culture, and customs of that particular nation. They then return to the home country to pursue employment. Shin and Choi (2015), in their research on global migration from and to Korea, predicate that immigrants and emigrants create transnational bridges that help them move between their host destination and Korea, creating connections and benefits between two societies that did not exist previously (Holbrow, 2016). This is just one illustration that although referred to as transnational, the human capital developed is binational: it spans two societies – the home and host nations. Further, Saxenian (2007), in her formative study of foreign migrants in Silicon Valley, found that participants' ability to function in two countries simultaneously helped them identify and access cross-border opportunities, resulting in brain circulation between two nations. Binationally rooted and mobile individuals may leave their home country to obtain education or work abroad but maintain ties with it and thus become highly skilled potential return migrants. Thus,

Table 22.1 Characteristics of transnational human capital

Dimensions of transnational human capital	Terms/descriptions used	Sources
Linguistic ability	Multilingualism	Robson (2011), cited in Delval and Bühlmann (2020)
	Fluency in foreign languages	Medrano (2016)
Country-specific network	Friendship ties abroad	Medrano (2016)
	Tolerance and willingness to adapt and flexibility	Gerhards and Hans (2013)
Country-specific knowledge and skills	Knowledge of foreign labour markets, institutions, and legal systems	Gerhards and Hans (2013)
	Knowledge of international technical standards and norms	Gerhards and Hans (2013)
	Intercultural mindsets	Robson (2011), cited in Delval and Bühlmann (2020)
International mobility	Study abroad	Medrano (2016)
	Travel and mobility readiness	Gerhards and Hans (2013)
	Exposure to an international environment	Delval and Bühlmann (2020)
	Ease in travelling internationally	Robson (2011), cited in Delval and Bühlmann (2020)
	Mobility competence	Delval and Bühlmann (2020)
	Capital of mobility/mobility capital	Murphy-Lejeune, cited in Delval and Bühlmann (2020); Wiers-Jenssen (2011)
	Motility	Kaufmann, as cited in Delval and Bühlmann (2020)
	Migratory ability ('multiple abilities related to migratory activity, such as knowing how to depart or settle down')	Delval and Bühlmann (2020)
	International exposure	Belderbos (2019)

Source: Schüller (2020c).

binational human capital, not transnational human capital, is developed in the vast majority of employability undertakings based on international education.

This distinction is imperative because it impacts the design, execution, marketing, and enrolment of international and transnational programmes. In fact, an international education without local cultural capital may harm graduates' chances in the home-country labour market (Tran et al., 2021). The studies that were previously reviewed indicate that employers value graduates with both international *and* localised knowledge and cultural savviness. Findings from a study of a TNE institution suggest that to increase binational human capital development, and ultimately the sustainable employability of graduates, institutions should provide opportunities for students to develop binational human capital in the form of targeted linguistic preparation, study abroad, and professional international relationships (Schüller, 2020b; Schüller, 2020c). Similarly, Mok and Han (2016) argue in favour of Chinese graduates' transnational human capital development and its importance for China as a nation of brain-bridging ambassadors. The majority of international graduates apply transnational human capital traits specific to two nations – the home country and host country. Graduates seek out careers in the home or host country, though not necessarily international careers across several countries. Binational human capital affords an individual the skills and abilities necessary to move between two countries. The focused – not fragmented – development of binational linguistic, social, and cultural capital in international education leads to better employment prospects at home and abroad.

Thus, binational human capital acquired through international education or TNE provides a framework for developing the unique skills, attributes, and abilities that are valued by employers. This is because binational human capital requires the development of very specific forms of knowledge and capital (i.e. dialects and regional differences that influence a country's work culture) versus a broader skill set (i.e. intercultural communication skills). The concept of binational human capital should thus be considered an addition to and a widening of the transnational human capital theory, not a digression from or an offshoot of it. Narrowing in on these very specific forms of capital development provides for a clearer picture of binational human capital. In Table 22.2, we illustrate how the concept of binational human capital fits into and yet differs from transnational human capital.

Binational human capital may lead to a 'binational career', in which an individual moves across two countries or across companies with a binational connection (i.e. German companies operating in Turkey), developing into a binational professional within a dual 'nation-based profession' (Harrington and Seabrooke, 2020: 401). Harrington and Seabrooke (2020: 402) argue that 'mobility alone does not make a transnational professional; individuals must also possess specific forms of social and cultural capital (including language skills and habitus) and master an abstract body of knowledge applicable to phenomena that transcend

Table 22.2 Characteristics of binational human capital

Dimensions of transnational human capital	Descriptors of binational human capital
Linguistic ability	Bilingualism Fluency in the host country's language
Country-specific network	Friendship ties in the host country Professional ties in the host country
Country-specific knowledge and skills	Knowledge of host country's labour market, institutions, and legal system Knowledge of the host country's technical standards and norms Knowledge of the host country's mindset, culture, and customs
International mobility	Study abroad or travel to the host country Exposure to the host country environment Mobility and ease in travelling to the partnering country (readiness, familiarity) Intercultural competence between the host and home countries (ease in moving between cultural worlds, whether digital or analogue)

Source: adapted from Table 1 in Schüller (2021).

national boundaries'. Indeed, a 'binational' career trajectory can be cultivated and paired with a domestic life with the help of an international education or TNE. A binational career trajectory may include a few years in the home country, followed by a few years abroad, or a permanent position in the home country that requires frequent collaboration with and regular travel to the second country. Most jobs and professions are specialised and involve dealing not with the entire world but rather with a certain segment that is often based in one other country or with one population that speaks the same language. The notion of binational employability, rooted in binational human capital, can be seen as a form of 'circular and constant mobility' (Delval and Bühlmann, 2020: 1).

Since binational human capital revolves around specialised, deep knowledge, understanding, and skills useful in two national contexts, it may raise concern for countries in which programmes are not taught in the local language. An example would be master's degrees in Germany or the Netherlands. Students returning to their home countries may have similar English-language skills as locally educated students and little knowledge of the host country's language (e.g. German or Dutch). As Tran et al. (2021) found in their research, Chinese employers are finding the language skills of returnees less advantageous, since local graduates can speak at a similar level. Within the binational human capital framework, strengthening opportunities for deep interaction with the host society, language, and culture is critical in providing students with the necessary linguistic and social capital for both their host and home countries. A premier example of binational human capital development can be found in Germany's BUs.

GERMANY'S BINATIONAL UNIVERSITIES (BUS)

A BU brings together actors from two nation states to form a new university, and BUs are being developed by a growing number of countries (Knight and Liu, 2019). The German BU model has provided an exemplary framework of collaborative transnational universities since the early 2000s. German BUs are located in Mongolia, Jordan, Kazakhstan, Vietnam, Turkey, Egypt, Russia, Oman, Hungary, and Kenya (DAAD, 2020). Each BU is affiliated with one or more universities in Germany that have the primary goal of ensuring academic development. This 'academic responsibility' is emphasised as the central component, referring to the curricula, German faculty, quality assurance, and degrees awarded by a German university (Clausen et al., 2011). During the 2018/19 academic year, German TNE projects reported a total of 33,000 students enrolled in over 280 degree programmes (DAAD, 2020). A key aim of German BUs is to further the host country's development and capacity-building (Lanzendorf, 2008).

Existing studies of German TNE and BUs focus primarily on political aspects (Fromm, 2017; Kammüller et al., 2020; Raev, 2020). Although some studies have investigated the impact on host countries' innovation systems (Vogel, 2020), most are descriptive in nature (Bachmann, 2016; Furgaç, 2016; Kammüller et al., 2020). Few studies have been undertaken to explore the employability or labour market outcomes of BU alumni. Nevertheless, the Vietnamese German University conducts regular tracer surveys, and the German Academic Exchange Service (DAAD) is currently undertaking an alumni tracer survey on behalf of all German BUs.

German BUs showcase how streamlined binational education and employability could look by intertwining a home country's system with the host country's language, culture, and education system. There are four components to creating a binational education and employability framework in most German BUs: (a) German-language preparation year and courses during studies, (b) binational teaching and learning, (c) practical, research, and international experience, and (d) binational academic qualification, such as a double degree (Schüller, 2021).

To illustrate this framework, we next scrutinize the TGU in Istanbul, Turkey, founded in 2008, as a concrete example for focused binational human capital preparation (Furgaç, 2016). Students take part in a preparatory year to learn German before enrolling in a degree programme, and all degree programmes are taught primarily in German. During their programmes, students have access to study trips to and internships in Germany. Upon graduation, the alumni become competitive candidates for roles at German companies in Turkey. Table 22.3

provides an overview of the stages of a TGU binational education and the features and aspects at each stage.

The four stages can be organised into the dimensions of transnational human capital. In doing so, the binational emphasis on capital development emerges. Schüller (2021) examined the binational TGU and set the foundation for the development of the binational human capital framework. Table 22.4 illustrates the outcomes of this study, showing how the components present in German BUs come together to create a robust scheme for the development of students' binational human capital.

Table 22.3 Stages, features, and aspects of a German binational education in Turkey

Stages	Features	Aspects
Before the programme	Language	• **Preparatory year:** German language TestDaF exam • **Three taught and tested languages:** English, German, and Turkish • **Extra language courses:** Subject-specific German
During the programme	Teaching and learning	• **Flying faculty:** Lecturers from German partner universities come to Turkey to teach on-site for a limited period of time (normally using a block seminar format) • **Long-term faculty:** German and Turkish, trained in both languages and both cultures, with further education and training in Germany • **Turkish factors**: Elements of traditional Turkish higher education (history of Atatürk, Turkish language, etc.), additional higher education conditions set by the Council of Higher Education (YÖK) • **German factors:** A consortium of German universities drive the establishment and development of study programmes
During the programme	Experience	• **Practical experience:** Internships in German, Turkish, and international companies • **Research experience:** Thesis research in companies, research assistantships • **Study abroad experience:** Erasmus and Mevlana programmes, summer schools in Germany
After the programme	Qualification	• **Binational academic link:** Double-degree programmes

Table 22.4 Binational human capital development at binational universities: example of the Turkish–German University

Dimensions of transnational human capital	Binational human capital developed while at the Turkish–German University
Linguistic ability (German, Turkish, and English) • Connection to the German language[1]	German language preparatory year before studies commence Fluency in German, in addition to English, by the end of the programme
Country-specific network (Germany and Turkey) • Contact with Germans (other students and teachers, during work experience) • Alumni and degree value (in both countries)	Friendship ties in Germany due in part to study abroad experience Professional ties in Germany due in part to visiting faculty from and practical experiences in the country
Country-specific knowledge and skills (Germany and Turkey) • Students made aware of the connection with Germany • Ideological approach to teaching and research links (German teaching staff) • Typical characteristics of German higher education • Curricula developed and monitored according to German higher education standards • Certain fields and themes specifically associated with Germany (such as the environment, cars, engineering science, archaeology)	Knowledge of Germany's labour market, institutions, and legal system Knowledge of Germany's technical standards and norms Knowledge of Germany's mindset, culture, and customs
International mobility (to Germany, living in Turkey) • Extended visits to Germany (study visits, exchange of lecturers and scholars)	Study abroad in Germany Mobility and ability to travel to Germany Exposure to the environment in Germany Ease in travelling to Germany (readiness, familiarity) Mobility and intercultural competence between Germany and Turkey (ease in moving between cultural worlds, whether digital or analogue)

Source: adapted from Tables 1 and 2 in Schüller (2021b).

[1]*All* BUs have several shared characteristics that make the projects uniquely 'German', and these are listed in bullets under each of the dimensions of THC in Table 3 to indicate alignment (DAAD, 2014).

By the end of their studies, students at the TGU ideally are fluent in German and Turkish (alongside English), have had practical and educational experience in Germany, have developed deep personal and professional ties with Germans, and learned about and reflected on the unique differences between the two societies, which impact living and working within them or across both countries. Such strategic binational-employability preparation enables students to be strong candidates for a wide variety of careers in industry, government, or academia, in Germany or Turkey (Schüller, 2020a).

CONCLUSION: EMERGING FORMS OF CAPITAL DEVELOPMENT IN INTERNATIONAL HIGHER EDUCATION

In this chapter, we aimed to advance the current understanding of the relationship between international education and employability. In our key proposition, we have identified that transnational human capital may not always adequately represent the bilateral nature of international education and its outcomes. Central to international education – and graduates' resulting employability prospects – is a concentrated development of binational human capital. For both international education and TNE, it is not knowing many languages, having visited multiple countries, or having a huge network of international friends that provides students with robust employment prospects. Rather, Germany's BUs serve as an example for a streamlined, focused structure to gain the knowledge, skills, and abilities to successfully function personally and professionally in both the home and host countries.

Based on evidence from the recent returnee-employability literature, binational human capital is increasing in value among employers looking for workers with both localised knowledge and an international mindset. As international students look beyond traditional receiving countries and demand more evidence around the labour market outcomes of certain degrees, it is imperative for actors at the institutional and national levels to create policies and programmes that increase students' chances of successful binational careers. Such strategizing naturally needs to include employability preparation, but also areas such as sociocultural integration. Higher education institutions, whether international or transnational, need to develop binational-employability programmes that prepare students linguistically and culturally for careers in two national contexts. When evaluating programmes, policymakers and planners need to demand accountability from institutions in the form of robust labour market analyses. TNE institutions must serve their purpose of developing the host country's labour market and higher education system through ensuring that graduates are educated within a framework valued by employers at home and abroad.

Future directions for understanding human capital development in international education for employability remain nuanced as the types of partnership increase. A variety of location-based and location-bound combinations may exist. Beyond transnational human capital and binational human capital, these could possibly include national or intranational (urban or rural), multinational, regional, subregional, and interregional human capital. This may particularly be the case in universities where partnerships exist among three or more institutions (e.g. Swiss German University), regional universities (e.g. South Asia University), networked universities (e.g. European Universities Initiative), and universities in border regions with multiple linguistic–cultural zones (e.g. University of Bergamo). The curricula and outcomes of these international institutions require deeper inquiry.

Overall, binational human capital – not transnational human capital – facilitates employability in international education or TNE. At its core, binational human capital development nurtures the home–host country connection. Demand for binational capital formation in international education will likely increase in the coming years, especially as international student migration patterns change and fluctuate. In preceding decades, internationalisation efforts were not always approached with employability in mind. To ensure that university curricula are responsive to future international-student demands, it is vital to incorporate targeted employability preparation for both the host- and home-country labour markets. We posit that at the intersection of international education and employability, focused development of binational human capital may drive the employability of the next generation of international students. Concretely, based on these findings, universities would be poised to develop binational career services for the largest international student populations at their institutions, and provide training to all domestic and international students about how to develop streamlined – versus fragmented – applicant profiles. At the institutional level, internationalisation strategies may be better positioned to focus in on a few countries rather than many, which would result in building a robust binational human capital of students, academic staff, and administrators. Thus, this framework resonates strongly in policy making and practice, both at the national and international level. Common understanding of structure and returns of BUs, especially their contribution to employability and as a form of internationalisation, are crucial to decision makers, university administrators, and curriculum developers.

REFERENCES

Aba, D. (2013). 'Internationalization of higher education and student mobility in Europe and the case of Turkey', *Cukurova University Faculty of Education Journal*, 42(2), pp. 99–110.

Arghode, V., Heminger, S., and McLean, G. N. (2021). 'Career self-efficacy and education abroad: Implications for future global workforce', *European Journal of Training and Development,* 45(1), pp. 1–13.

Ashour, S. and Allender, T. (2018). 'Branding of Germany's transnational education and its potentials in the Arabian Gulf region', *Cogent Education*, 5(1), pp. 1–15.

Bachmann, W. (2016). 'Das transnationale Hochschulwesen im deutsch-türkischen Kontext: Eine deutsche Perspektive', in A. Küppers, B. Pusch, and P. Uyan Semerci (eds), *Bildung in transnationalen Räumen: Education in transnational spaces*. Wiesbaden: VS Verlag für Sozialwissenschaften, pp. 287–297.

Baker, M. and Benjamin, D. (1994). 'The performance of immigrants in the Canadian labor market', *Journal of Labor Economics*, 12(3), pp. 369–405.

Becker, G. S. (1964). *Human capital: A theoretical and empirical analysis, with special reference to education*, 1st edn. Chicago: University of Chicago Press.

Becker, G. S. (1994). *Human capital: A theoretical and empirical analysis, with special reference to education*, 3rd edn. Chicago: University of Chicago Press.

Belderbos, T. (2020). 'The employability of international branch campus graduates: Evidence from Malaysia', *Higher Education, Skills and Work-Based Learning*, 10(1), pp. 141–154.

Bilsland, C., Carter, L., and Wood, L. (2020). 'Beyond the degree: Graduate transitions from a transnational campus in Vietnam', *Higher Education*, 80(6), pp. 1103–1120.

Blaug, M., Layard, R., and Woodhall, M. (1969). *The case of graduate unemployment in India*. London: Penguin.

Borjas, G. J. (1995). 'Assimilation and changes in cohort quality revisited: What happened to immigrant earnings in the 1980s?', *Journal of Labor Economics*, 13(2), pp. 201–245.

Bourdieu, P. (1986). 'The forms of capital', in J. Richardson (ed.), *Handbook of theory and research for the sociology of education*. Westport: Greenwood, pp. 241–258.

Bratsberg, B. and Ragan Jr., J. F. (2002). 'The impact of host-country schooling on earnings: A study of male immigrants in the United States', *The Journal of Human Resources*, 37(1), pp. 63–105.

Bühlmann, F., David, T., and Mach, A. (2013). 'Cosmopolitan capital and the internationalization of the field of business elites: Evidence from the Swiss case', *Cultural Sociology*, 7(2), pp. 211–229.

Bühlmann, F., Davoine, E., and Ravasi, C. (2018). 'European top management careers: A field analytical approach', *European Societies*, 20(3), pp. 453–477.

Cai, Y. (2012a). *Understanding employers' perceptions of international graduates: An investigation of the employment prospects of Finnish-educated Chinese graduates in Finnish companies operating in China*. Tampere: Tampere University Press.

Cai, Y. (2012b). 'International graduates from Finland: Do they satisfy the needs of Finnish employers abroad?', *Journal of Research in International Education*, 11(1), pp. 19–31.

Chiswick, B. R. and Miller, P. W. (1995). 'The endogeneity between language and earnings: International analyses', *Journal of Labor Economics*, 13(2), pp. 246–288.

Chiswick, B. R. and Miller, P. W. (2003). 'The complementarity of language and other human capital: Immigrant earnings in Canada', *Economics of Education Review*, 22(5), pp. 469–480.

Clausen, A., Schindler-Kovats, B., and Stalf, N. (2011). *Transnational education 'made in Germany' – A policy perspective on challenges, best practices and success stories*. Available at: www2.daad.de/medien/hochschulen/projekte/studienangebote/ausgabe_ehea_2011_gesamt.pdf

Coleman, J. S. (1988). 'Social capital in the creation of human capital', *American Journal of Sociology*, 94, pp. 95–120.

Craciun, D. and Orosz, K. (2018). *Benefits and costs of transnational collaborative partnerships in higher education*. Available at: https://eenee.eu/wp-content/uploads/2021/05/EENEE_AR36.pdf

Craciun, D., Orosz, K., and Proteasa, V. (2020). 'Does Erasmus mobility increase employability? Using register data to investigate the labour market outcomes of university graduates', in A. Curaj, L. Deca, and R. Pricopie (eds), *European higher education area – Challenges for a new decade*. Cham: Springer, pp. 105–119.

Crossman, J. E. and Clarke, M. (2010). 'International experience and graduate employability: Stakeholder perceptions on the connection', *Higher Education*, 59(5), 599–613.

Delval, A. S. and Bühlmann, F. (2020). 'Strategies of social (re)production within international higher education: The case of Swiss hospitality management schools', *Higher Education*, 79, pp. 477–495.

Demetriades, E. I. and Psacharopoulos, G. (1979). 'Education and pay structure in Cyprus', *International Labour Review*, 118(1), pp. 103–112.

Deutscher Akademischer Austauschdienst (DAAD). (2020). *Binational universities, faculties, and institutes* [German]. Available at: www.daad.de/de/infos-services-fuer-hochschulen/binationale-hochschulen/

Di Pietro, G. (2012). 'Does studying abroad cause international labor mobility? Evidence from Italy', *Economics Letters*, 117(3), pp. 632–635.

Di Pietro, G. (2015). 'Do study abroad programs enhance the employability of graduates?', *Education Finance and Policy*, 10(2), pp. 223–243.

Di Pietro, G. (2019). *University study abroad and graduates' employability*. Available at: https://wol.iza.org/uploads/articles/488/pdfs/university-study-abroad-and-graduates-employability.pdf

Duvander, A.-Z. E. (2001). 'Do country-specific skills lead to improved labor market positions?', *Work and Occupations*, 28(2), pp. 210–233.

Farrugia, C. A. and Lane, J. E. (2013). 'Legitimacy in Cross-Border Higher Education: Identifying Stakeholders of International Branch Campuses', *Journal of Studies in International Education*, 17(4), pp. 414–432.

Fromm, N. (2017). *Zur Transnationalisierung von Hochschulbildung: Eine empirische Studie zur Interaktion hochschulpolitischer Akteure beim Aufbau bilateraler Hochschulen im Ausland*. Baden-Baden: Nomos.

Furgaç, İ. (2016). 'Die Türkisch-Deutsche Universität in Istanbul', in A. Küppers, B. Pusch and P. Uyan Semerci (eds), *Bildung in transnationalen Räumen*. Wiesbaden: VS Verlag für Sozialwissenschaften, pp. 279–285.

Gerhards, J. and Hans, S. (2013). 'Transnational human capital, education, and social inequality: Analyses of international student exchange', *Zeitschrift für Soziologie*, 42(2), pp. 99–117.

Harrington, B. and Seabrooke, L. (2020). 'Transnational professionals', *Annual Review of Sociology*, 46, pp. 399–417.

Hoare, L. (2012). 'Transnational student voices: Reflections on a second chance', *Journal of Studies in International Education*, 16(3), pp. 271–286.

Holbrow, H. J. (2016). 'Review: Shin, G. and Choi, J. N. (2015). *Global talent: Skilled labor as social capital in Korea*', *Work and Occupations*, *43*(1), pp. 112–114.

Huang, R. and Turner, R. (2018). 'International experience, universities support and graduate employability – Perceptions of Chinese international students studying in UK universities', *Journal of Education and Work*, 31(2), pp. 175–189.

Igarashi, H. and Saito, H. (2014). 'Cosmopolitanism as cultural capital: Exploring the intersection of globalization, education and stratification', *Cultural Sociology*, 8(3), pp. 222–239.

Jing, X., Ghosh, R., Sun, Z., and Liu, Q. (2020). 'Mapping global research related to international students: A scientometric review', *Higher Education*, 80, pp. 415–433.

Jones, E. (2019). 'Employability in transnational education', in R. Coelen and C. Gribble (eds), *Internationalization and employability in higher education*. London: Routledge, pp. 141–154.

Kammüller S., Otte, S., and Bachmann, W. (2020). 'Germany's road towards transnational provision of higher education and its footprint in China and Turkey', in B. Nickl, S. Popenici and D. Blackler (eds), *Transnational German education and comparative education systems: Research and practice*. Springer International Publishing, pp. 3–27.

Knight, J. (2005). *Borderless, offshore, transnational and cross-border education: Definition and data dilemmas*. London: Observatory on Borderless Higher Education.

Knight, J. (2012). 'Concepts, rationales, and interpretive frameworks in the internationalization of higher education', in C. K. Deardorff, H. de Wit, J. D. Heyl, and T. Adams (eds), *The Sage handbook of international higher education*. Thousand Oaks: Sage, pp. 27–42.

Knight, J. and Liu, Q. (2019). 'International program and provider mobility in higher education: Research trends, challenges and issues', *Comparative and International Education*, 48(1).

Knight, J. and McNamara, J. (2017). *Transnational education: A classification framework and data collection guidelines for international programme and provider mobility (IPPM)*. Available at: www.britishcouncil.org/sites/default/files/tne_classification_framework-final.pdf

Krahn, H., Derwing, T., Mulder, M., and Wilkinson, L.(2000). 'Educated and underemployed: Refugee integration into the Canadian labour market', *Journal of International Migration and Integration* 1, pp. 59–84.

Lanzendorf, U. (2008). 'Foreign-backed universities – A new trend'. *International Higher Education*, 51, pp. 3–5.

Marginson, S. (2019). 'Limitations of human capital theory', *Studies in Higher Education*, 44(2), pp. 287–301.

Massey, D. S., Arango, J., Hugo, G., Kouaouci, A., Pellegrino, A., and Taylor, J.E. (1993). 'Theories of international migration: A review and appraisal', *Population and Development Review*, 19(3), pp. 431–466.

Matherly, C. and Tillman, M. (2019). 'Linking learning abroad and employability', in R. Coelen and C. Gribble (eds), *Internationalization and employability in higher education*. London: Routledge, pp. 11–24.

Medrano, J. D. (2016). 'Globalization, transnational human capital, and employment in the European Union', *International Journal of Comparative Sociology*, 57(6), pp. 449–470.

Mellors-Bourne, R., Jones, E., and Woodfield, S. (2015). *Transnational education and employability development*. York: Higher Education Academy.

Mincer, J. (1958). 'Investment in human capital and personal income distribution', *Journal of Political Economy*, 66(4), pp. 281–302.

Mok, K. H. and Han, X. (2016). 'From "brain drain" to "brain bridging": Transnational higher education development and graduate employment in China', *Journal of Higher Education Policy and Management,* 38(3), pp. 369–389.

Nghia, T. L. H. and Duyen, N. T. M. (2019). 'Developing and validating a scale for evaluating internship-related learning outcomes', *Higher Education*, 77(1), pp. 1–18.

Nilsson, P. A. and Ripmeester, N. (2016). 'International student expectations: Career opportunities and employability', *Journal of Intercultural Studies,* 6(2), pp. 614–631.

Norris, E. M. and Gillespie, J. (2009). 'How study abroad shapes global careers: Evidence from the United States', *Journal of Studies in International Education*, 13(3), pp. 382–397.

Organisation for Economic Co-operation and Development (OECD). (2017). *Education at a glance 2017: OECD indicators*. Paris: OECD Publishing.
Pang, E. F. and Clark, D. H. (1970). 'Returns to schooling and training in Singapore', *Malayan Economic Review*, 15(2), pp. 79–107.
Parey, M. and Waldinger, F. (2011). 'Studying abroad and the effect on international labour market mobility: Evidence from the introduction of Erasmus', *The Economic Journal*, 121(551), pp. 194–222.
Petzold, K. (2017). 'Studying abroad as a sorting criterion in the recruitment Process: a field experiment among German employers', *Journal of Studies in International Education,* 21(5), pp. 412–430.
Raev, A. (2020). *Transnationale Bildung im Wandel: Kultur und Aussenpolitikl Grenzüberschreitende Hochschulbildung' made in Germany' (1990–2016).* Baden-Baden: Nomos.
Robertson, S., Hoare, L., and Harwood, A. (2011). 'Returnees, student-migrants and second chance learners: Case studies of positional and transformative outcomes of Australian international education', *Compare: A Journal of Comparative and International Education*, 41(5), pp. 685–698.
Rodrigues, M. (2013). *Does student mobility during higher education pay? Evidence from 16 European countries*. Luxembourg: Publications Office of the European Union.
Rothwell, A., Herbert, I., and Rothwell, F. (2008). 'Self-perceived employability: Construction and initial validation of a scale for university students', *Journal of Vocational Behavior*, 73(1), pp. 1–12.
Salisbury, M. H., Umbach, P., Paulsen, M., Pascarella, E.(2009). 'Going global: Understanding the choice process of the intent to study abroad', *Research in Higher Education*, 50, pp. 119–143.
Saxenian, A. (2007). *The new Argonauts: Regional advantage in a global economy*. Cambridge: Harvard University Press.
Schüller, J. D. (2020a). 'Binational universities: Double the opportunities'. EAIE Summer Forum, *Employability for the 21st century*. European Association for International Education: Amsterdam, pp. 37–39.
Schueller, J. D. (2020b). 'Binational universities: A model for inclusive internationalization?', *Proceedings of the WES–CIHE Summer Institute 2020*, 18, pp. 10–11.
Schueller, J. D. (2020c). 'Exploring labor market outcomes at binational universities – Two countries, one university, binational careers?', *Journal of Comparative & International Higher Education*, 12(6S1), pp. 138–142.
Schueller, J. D. (2021). 'The Role of Labor Market Outcomes in Transnational Education: A Case Study of the Binational Turkish-German University'. *Joint master's thesis*. Danube University Krems. Krems, Austria, and Tampere University. Tampere, Finland.
Schultz, T. W. (1961). 'Investment in human capital', *The American Economic Review*, 51(1), pp. 1–17.
Shumilova, Y. and Cai, Y. (2022). 'Employability entrepreneurship for leveraging employability capitals', in T. Broadley, Y. Cai, M. Firth, E. Hunt, and J. Neugebauer (eds), *Sage Handbook of Graduate Employability*. Sage.
Shin, G.-W. and Choi, J. N. (2015). *Global talent: Skilled labor as social capital in Korea*. Stanford: Stanford University Press.
Sin, I. L. (2013). 'Cultural capital and distinction: Aspirations of the 'other' foreign student', *British Journal of Sociology of Education*, 34(5–6), pp. 848–867.
Støren, L. A. and Wiers-Jenssen, J. (2010). 'Foreign diploma versus immigrant background: Determinants of labour market success or failure?', *Journal of Studies in International Education*, 14(1), pp. 29–49.

Sweetland, S. R. (1996). 'Human capital theory: Foundations of a field of inquiry', *Review of Educational Research*, 66(3), pp. 341–359.
Tan, E. (2014). 'Human capital theory: A holistic criticism', *Review of Educational Research*, 84(3), pp. 411–445.
Teichler, U. and Janson, K. (2007). 'The professional value of temporary study in another European country: Employment and work of former Erasmus students', *Journal of Studies in International Education*, 11(3–4), pp. 486–495.
Tomlinson, M. (2017). 'Forms of graduate capital and their relationship to graduate employability', *Education + Training*, 59(4), pp. 338–352.
Tran, L.T., Blackmore, J., and Rahimi, M. (2021). '"You are not as localised as I need": Employability of Chinese returning graduates', *Higher Education, Skills and Work-Based Learning,* Vol. 11 No. 5, pp. 949-965.
Van Mol, C., Caarls, K., and Souto-Otero, M. (2020). 'International student mobility and labour market outcomes: An investigation of the role of level of study, type of mobility, and international prestige hierarchies', *Higher Education*, 82, pp. 1145–1117.
Varghese, N. V. (2008). *Globalization of higher education and cross-border student mobility*. Paris: International Institute for Educational Planning.
Vogel, A. (2020). 'Transnational institutions of higher education and their contribution to the national innovation System: The case of the German university of technology in Oman', in B. Nickl, S. Popenici, and D. Blackler (eds), *Transnational German education and comparative education systems: Research and practice*. Springer International Publishing, pp. 29–41.
Waibel, S., Rüger, H., Ette, A., and Sauer, L. (2017). 'Career consequences of transnational educational mobility: A systematic literature review', *Educational Research Review*, 20, pp. 81–98.
Weenink, D. (2007). 'Cosmopolitan and established resources of power in the education arena', *International Sociology*, 22(4), pp. 492–516.
Weenink, D. (2008). 'Cosmopolitanism as a form of capital parents preparing their children for a globalizing world', *Sociology*, 42(6), pp. 1089–1106.
Wiers-Jenssen, J. (2008). 'Does higher education attained abroad lead to international jobs?', *Journal of Studies in International Education*, 12(2), pp. 101–130.
Wiers-Jenssen, J. (2011). 'Background and employability of mobile vs. non-mobile students', *Tertiary Education and Management*, 17, pp. 79–100.
Wiers-Jenssen, J. and Try, S. (2005). 'Labour market outcomes of higher education undertaken abroad', *Studies in Higher Education*, 30(6), pp. 681–705.
Yao, C. W. and Tuliao, M. D. (2019). 'Soft skill development for employability: A case study of stem graduate students at a Vietnamese transnational university', *Higher Education, Skills and Work-Based Learning,* (9)3, pp. 250–263.
Yorke, M. (2006). *Employability in higher education: What it is-what it is not*. York: Higher Education Academy.
Yorke, M. and Knight, P. T. (2004). *Learning & employability – Embedding employability into the curriculum*. York: Higher Education Academy.
Zeng, Z. and Xie, Y. (2004). 'Asian-Americans' earnings disadvantage reexamined: The role of place of education', *The American Journal of Sociology*, 109(5), pp. 1075–1108.
Ziguras, C. and McBurnie, G. (2015). *Governing cross-border higher education*. London: Routledge.
Zweig, D., Changgui, C., and Rosen, S. (2004). 'Globalization and transnational human capital: Overseas and returnee scholars to China', *The China Quarterly*, 179, pp. 735–757.

23

Graduate Employability during the COVID-19 Pandemic

Belgin Okay-Somerville, Daria Luchinskaya, Pauline Anderson, Scott Hurrell and Dora Scholarios

INTRODUCTION

The transition from higher education to employment is uncertain for most graduates. Yet, some navigate this process more effectively than others. During the early stages of the COVID-19 pandemic, graduate vacancies and work experience opportunities declined suddenly, with employers revising recruitment targets or reneging on job offers (Hooley, 2020a, b). All 2020 graduates will have experienced these events as a career shock (Akkermans et al., 2020). Nevertheless, the crisis is likely to exacerbate the impact of already known sources of early career disadvantage, such as social background, due to differential access to social, cultural and career-related resources (Lee et al., 2021). The resulting disruption to some graduates' employability could have long-lasting, multiple scarring effects, as observed in previous economic downturns (McQuaid, 2015). This chapter examines social and educational inequalities in early career graduate employability in the context of the economic crisis created by the COVID-19 pandemic. We explore the relative importance of career competencies for overcoming these inequalities.

Employability is recognised as a multifaceted concept (Behle, 2020; Tomlinson, 2017). Consistent with this, we conceptualise graduate employability as reflected in objective (employment status and salary) and subjective (perceived employability and job satisfaction) outcomes associated with securing work following graduation. This conceptualisation allows us to capture the nature of early employment quality (i.e. job satisfaction and salary), as well as graduates' actual and perceived chances of securing work (i.e. in work versus unemployed and perceived employability, respectively). Theoretically we draw on the conceptualisation of graduate employability as position, possession and process (Holmes, 2013; Okay-Somerville and Scholarios, 2017). This allows us to explore the impact of social and educational inequalities on objective and subjective employability, alongside the role of career competencies – key psychological resources relevant for navigating turbulent labour markets (De Vos et al., 2020) – during the COVID-19 pandemic.

From a 'position' perspective, some graduates are better positioned than others due to the social and cultural resources their social background affords them to navigate the transition from education to employment. A 'possession' perspective considers the role of human capital (often proxied by educational background), assuming meritocratic job markets. Finally, a 'process' view of graduate employability is concerned with how individuals, through career behaviours, navigate university-to-work transitions (Holmes, 2013; Okay-Somerville and Scholarios, 2017). Pre-pandemic research shows inequalities in graduate employability based on social and educational background (Pitman et al., 2019), with some evidence showing the importance of career behaviours in overcoming these (Okay-Somerville and Scholarios, 2017). Given these existing inequalities, this chapter assesses the extent to which career agency, in the form of career competencies, is still relevant for those who join labour markets during a pandemic.

The chapter begins by contextualising objective and subjective employability indicators as early experiences of the pandemic labour market. We then briefly review the literature on the impact of social and educational inequalities and individual career competencies in graduate employability. This review allows us to focus our two research questions as follows:

> *Research question 1 (RQ1):* What is the impact of social and educational background on objective and subjective graduate employability during the COVID-19 pandemic?

> *Research question 2 (RQ2):* How important are career competencies for explaining objective and subjective graduate employability during the COVID-19 pandemic, considering the impact of social and educational background?

We present a survey study of a cohort graduating from higher education in 2020. The findings identify arts and humanities graduates, alongside those with long-term health problems, as potentially vulnerable groups. The study confirms the heightened relevance of career competencies for navigating uncertain and ambiguous labour markets. We conclude by presenting recommendations for strategies relevant for recovery from the COVID-19 pandemic.

THE CONTEXT OF GRADUATE EMPLOYABILITY

Policies driving the expansion of higher education have been predicated on the economic, societal and individual returns of a more educated and productive workforce (McMahon, 2009). Nevertheless, empirical evidence, even before the COVID-19 pandemic, highlights an imbalance between graduate supply and employer demand, resulting in significant graduate overqualification (Holmes and Mayhew, 2015). Graduates' actual and perceived ability to secure and maintain employment (Rothwell et al., 2008) – that is, objective and subjective employability – are therefore highly relevant concepts with implications for future career outcomes, especially in the COVID-19 context. Particularly worrying are the scarring effects observed following the 2008–9 Global Financial Crisis, with some graduates trapped in low-skilled, low-paid precarious jobs up to 10 years later (Clarke, 2018).

We study objective employability as reflected in graduates' employment status and salary. For those graduating during the COVID-19 pandemic, there was a significant decline in entry-level jobs, internships and apprenticeships (ILO-OECD, 2020). International evidence shows recruitment freezes and delays by many graduate recruiters (Hooley, 2020a). In the UK, half of all graduate recruiters reduced recruitment targets, budgets and activities in 2020 (High Fliers Research, 2021). Considering such evidence of shrinking opportunities, employment status is our first indicator of objective employability. In addition to diminishing opportunities, significant earnings losses have been predicted for cohorts graduating into the COVID-19 pandemic, especially for those who experience spells of unemployment and underemployment (Frenette et al., 2020). Hence, income is our second indicator of objective employability, which we use as a proxy for ability to secure high quality jobs.

Subjective outcomes include graduates' own perceived employability during the transition to employment (Rothwell et al., 2008) and, once employed, their evaluation of job quality (James et al., 2013). Perceived employability is associated with measures of well-being, particularly stress and anxiety (Ma and Bennett, 2021), with implications for career development (Healy et al., 2022). Graduates' perceived employability is our first subjective measure. Subjective experience of work and labour markets have implications for graduates' well-being and work-related attitudes (Harari et al., 2017). Particularly for higher education leavers, subjective experience of poor job quality (e.g. due to lack of opportunities for skill use and development opportunities) is common (Boccuzzo and Gianecchini, 2015). Objective indicators of graduate employability may therefore be misleading if jobs are not conducive to skill use and development (Sloane and Mavromaras, 2020). We therefore examine job satisfaction as a subjective proxy for the ability to secure high-quality jobs (Clark, 2015).

Our conceptualisation of graduate employability thus covers a broad range of outcomes. We next consider the determinants of graduate employability.

GRADUATE EMPLOYABILITY: SOCIAL AND EDUCATIONAL INEQUALITIES

Research prior to the COVID-19 pandemic highlights the significant role that social and educational inequalities play in determining objective and subjective graduate employability. In terms of social inequalities, 'first-generation' students report higher employability-related anxieties (Okay-Somerville et al., 2020) and lower perceived employability (Kalfa and Taksa, 2015). Graduates from socially disadvantaged backgrounds are also more likely to be in 'non-graduate employment' and earn less than their more privileged counterparts (Morrison, 2019). Educational disadvantage is highly intertwined with social disadvantage; students from disadvantaged backgrounds are less likely to attend prestigious higher education institutions and study professional degree subjects (Pigden and Moore, 2020). This is important for graduate employability, because elite employers tend to focus their efforts on a select group of institutions (Browne, 2010). Students attending elite universities are likely to be aware of such labour market advantage and better able to access opportunities (Wright and Mulvey, 2021). Moreover, disciplines that are closely aligned to specific occupations or applied fields, as in science, technology, engineering and mathematics (STEM), are often associated with more successful labour market transitions (e.g. attracting higher salaries, better education–job match) than arts, humanities or social science (liberal arts) majors (Abel and Deitz, 2017). This latter group are more likely to undertake further study and take longer to settle into graduate jobs than STEM graduates (Lyonette et al., 2017).

Theoretically, systematic differences in university-to-work transitions based on social and educational background can be explained drawing on the position and possession perspectives to graduate employability, respectively (Holmes, 2013). According to a positioning perspective, graduate employability reflects a socially reproduced process (Holmes, 2013). The positional advantage gained by some graduates in higher education and employment can be explained from a Bourdieusian perspective; middle-class students, through their upbringing, are socialised into expectations of graduate employment (Edgerton and Roberts, 2014). Social class partially determines graduate employability due to the social and cultural capital it affords individuals.

Graduate employability as possession is concerned with graduates' knowledge, skills and abilities – that is, human capital. Assuming meritocratic labour markets, investment in human capital is thought to be crucial for graduate employability. In the graduate context, human capital is most explicitly proxied in educational background – for example, institution prestige and degree subject (Rivera, 2012). These proxies are also among the screening criteria for graduate jobs and have been shown to differentiate early graduate employment outcomes (Jung and Lee, 2016). Employability-related differences based on degree subject are also attributed to the structure of the labour market, especially ambiguity and availability of opportunities, with proactive career strategies unable to overcome early career disadvantage (Okay-Somerville and Scholarios, 2021). From a possession perspective, human capital and availability of opportunities to use it in the labour market explain graduate employability.

Career shocks, such as the COVID-19 pandemic, may shape career decisions and outcomes differently for different demographic groups (Akkermans et al., 2021). In this chapter, we are interested in understanding how known inequalities in graduate labour markets based on social and educational backgrounds (the position and possession perspectives) were impacted by the pandemic. Our first research question is:

> *Research question 1 (RQ1):* What is the impact of social and educational background on objective and subjective graduate employability during the COVID-19 pandemic?

GRADUATE EMPLOYABILITY: CAREER AGENCY

Pre-pandemic evidence shows that, compared to social and educational inequalities, proactive career behaviours have a greater impact on most measures of objective and subjective employability (Okay-Somerville and Scholarios, 2017). This implies that, in addition to social and human capital, career-related capital (i.e. career competencies; Akkermans et al., 2013) is also at play for securing employment and successfully managing careers. Career competencies have been studied from multiple perspectives. Akkermans et al. (2013) synthesise these under three broad categories: reflective (e.g. career insight, self-awareness), communicative (e.g. networking and seeking career guidance) and behavioural (e.g. planning and exploration) competencies. These competencies act as psychological resources to help navigate uncertain labour markets (De Vos et al., 2020) and have been shown to play a pivotal role in perceived employability and career satisfaction during university-to-work transitions (Blokker et al., 2019).

The impact of career agency on employability as described above, proxied by career competencies, resonates with a processual approach to graduate employability (Holmes, 2013). Career agency is argued to be essential in becoming employable (Allen et al., 2013), referring to the proactive career management process through which individuals gain self-awareness and environmental awareness and develop career competencies to navigate labour markets (Hinchliffe and Jolly, 2010). Career competencies therefore signal an individual's career capital and are highly instrumental in objective and subjective employability.

In a recession, career agency is particularly important to overcome employment insecurity and precarious work (Grote and Raeder, 2009). Similarly, in the COVID-19 context, characterised by ambiguity and uncertainty, career guidance and career management are ever more important to be able to identify and pursue goals (Holt-White and Montacute, 2020). For new entrants into labour markets, certain career-related behaviours – such as extracurricular activities (e.g. voluntary work) and networking – have been shown to be crucial for developing strong career competencies (Jackson and Wilton, 2017). During the COVID-19 pandemic, career guidance became extremely scarce, as most counsellors were not prepared for remote delivery (Ananiadou et al., 2020). Moreover, opportunities such as internships and apprenticeships (ILO-OECD, 2020), which are essential for building career-related skills, such as reflection and communication (Smith, 2010), disappeared almost overnight. Hence, some graduates did not have the opportunities to develop career competencies that they otherwise would have. For understanding the determinants of graduate employability during the COVID-19 pandemic, our second research question explores the relative importance of the career competencies, given social and educational inequalities:

> *Research question 2 (RQ2):* How important are career competencies for explaining objective and subjective graduate employability during the COVID-19 pandemic, considering the impact of social and educational background?

METHOD

An online survey instrument was administered to the 2020 cohort of graduates in Glasgow, Scotland, between September 2020 and March 2021. Careers advisors and alumni officers from one large college and three universities in Glasgow were invited to join an advisory board to inform survey content and facilitate access to a sample. Following initial piloting (N = 10), these representatives distributed the survey link via multiple channels, such as newsletters and social media. Participants were offered a chance to enter a prize draw for one £400 and six £100 shopping vouchers.

Sample

The study is informed by 551 graduates from one college and two universities in Glasgow. The sample was restricted to those reporting they were in work, training or unemployed at the time of data collection (N = 502: 68% were female; 75% were aged 21–24; 48% were STEM graduates; 31% were social science graduates; 23% were college graduates). Within this sample, only those at work were included in analyses related to job satisfaction and salary (N = 312: 69% were female; 77% were aged 21–24; 48% were STEM; 33% were social science graduates; 18% were college graduates).

Measures

Independent variables were social and educational background and career competencies.

Social background was proxied by asking the participants whether they were the first person in their immediate family (not including siblings) to go to university (1 = yes, 0 = no).

Educational background consisted of comparisons based on college versus university (1 = college, 0 = university) and degree subject (arts and humanities versus STEM and social sciences).

Career competencies were measured using Akkermans et al.'s (2013) 20-item Career Competencies Questionnaire (CCQ), which requires participants to respond on a five-point scale: 1 = strongly disagree, 5 = strongly agree. The CCQ is composed of six subscales: reflection on motivation (three items, e.g., 'I know what is important to me in my career', $\alpha = .78$), reflection on qualities (four items, e.g., 'I know my strengths', $\alpha = .82$), networking (three items, e.g., 'I know a lot of people who can help me with my career', $\alpha = .88$), self-profiling (three items, e.g., 'I am able to show others what I want to achieve in my career' $\alpha = .83$), work exploration (three items, e.g., 'I am able to explore my job market possibilities', $\alpha = .73$) and career control (four items, e.g., 'I can make career plans' $\alpha = .87$).

Two objective employability measures were employment status and salary. Subjective employability was captured in measures of perceived employability and job satisfaction.

Employment status was ascertained by asking participants to describe their current situation from a list of options, which was an extended version of the job search expectations commonly reported by university leavers (Okay-Somerville et al., 2020) (seven options, e.g., 'I am in/have been offered employment related to my intended career'). Those who responded 'yes' to any of the seven items were categorised as 'in work'. Those who selected 'I am unemployed (i.e. searching for a job and ready to start working)' were categorised as 'unemployed'.

Salary was determined by asking participants to indicate their current gross annual earnings in their main job before any tax and deductions.

Perceived employability was measured using 10 items from Rothwell et al. (2008) (e.g. 'My course is seen as leading to a specific career that is generally perceived as highly desirable', answered with a five-point scale: 1 = strongly disagree, 5 = strongly agree; $\alpha = .84$).

Job satisfaction was measured with a single item (Dolbier et al., 2005) (i.e. 'taking everything into consideration, how satisfied or dissatisfied do you feel about your main job as a whole', answered with a seven-point scale: 1 = extremely dissatisfied, 7 = extremely satisfied).

Control variables included known correlates of graduate employability: age, sex (0 = male, 1 = female), time elapsed between survey completion and graduation (in months), whether working in the private sector (1 = yes, 0 = public/

not-for-profit sector), have a full-time contract (0 = no, 1 = yes) and a permanent job (0 = no, 1 = yes). Additionally, we included two more controls relevant for understanding the impact of COVID-19-related health issues: perceived likelihood of having had COVID-19 (1 = definitely had it, 5 = very unlikely to have had it) and a composite measure of long-term health problems – whether they have any physical or mental health conditions or illnesses lasting or expected to last 12 months or more (0 = no, 1 = yes) and whether this condition or illness reduces ability to carry out day-to-day activities (0 = no, 1 = yes, a little, and 2 = yes, a lot); a composite score was calculated by summing the two questions. Both questions were taken from *Understanding Society: COVID-19 Study, 2020–2021* (University of Essex, Institute for Social and Economic Research, 2021). The latter composite measure reflects participants' vulnerability to the physical and mental effects of COVID-19.

Respondents were also asked free-text questions to collect qualitative data (e.g. 'How do you think COVID-19 will impact your career plans?'). We focus here, however, on the quantitative data.

Analyses

Hierarchical linear regression analyses were used for predicting continuous dependent variables (i.e. salary, job satisfaction and perceived employability). Hierarchical logistic regression analyses were used for predicting employment status. Control variables were entered in step 1, followed by social background in step 2, educational credentials in step 3 and career competencies in step 4.

Empirical evidence shows educational background to be partially determined by social background, and the effect of both on graduate employability appears intertwined (Morrison, 2014). This stepwise analysis allows us to see the distinct relative impact of social and educational background (RQ1) and career competencies (RQ2) on measures of graduate employability.

FINDINGS

Table 23.1 shows binary logistic regression analyses predicting the likelihood of being in work. This shows that the addition of educational background ($\chi^2(df)$ = 19.05 (9), $p < .05$; *Nagelkerke* $R^2 = .07$) and career competencies ($\chi^2(df)$ = 36.93 (15), $p < .05$; *Nagelkerke* $R^2 = .13$) significantly improved model fit. More specifically, we observe that those from STEM ($\beta = 2.29$, $p < .01$) and social sciences ($\beta = 3.21$, $p < .01$) degrees were more likely to be in work than arts and humanities graduates. Among the career competencies, only work exploration was significantly associated with the likelihood of being in work ($\beta = 1.50$, $p < .01$). Also notable in Table 23.1 is the persistently lower likelihood of being in work based on long-term health condition ($\beta = .71$, $p < .05$).

Table 23.1 Logistic regression analyses predicting likelihood of being in work at the time of data collection (*N* = 395)

	β	β	β	β
Aged 21–24	.62	.60	1.17	1.07
Female	.99	.99	.83	.85
Time (months)	1.90	1.90	1.13	1.19
COVID-19 likelihood	1.34	1.35	1.32	1.28
Long-term health	.66*	.68*	.71*	.71*
First generation		.78	.73	.74
College[a]			1.06	1.08
STEM[b]			2.54**	2.29**
Social sciences[b]			3.32**	3.21**
Reflection on motivation				1.13
Reflection on qualities				.93
Networking				1.08
Self-profiling				.88
Work exploration				1.50*
Career control				.89
χ2 (df)	9.03 (5)	9.36 (6)	19.05 (9)*	36.93 (15) *
-2LL	176.28	175.92	167.26	148.38
Cox and Snell *R* square	.05	.05	.09	.18
Nagelkerke *R* square	.07	.08	.15	.28

Note: β = exponential Beta, indicating the odds of being in work (in comparison to being unemployed); STEM = science, technology, engineering and mathematics.

[a]*Comparison* category is university leavers.

[b]*Comparison* category is arts and humanities graduates.

*$p < .05$; **$p < .01$.

Hierarchical linear regression analyses predicting salary, job satisfaction and perceived employability are presented in Table 23.2. For explaining salary, the only non-significant model was step 2 (inclusion of ‘first generation’). Control variables alone explained 49% of the variance in salary, especially full-time work (β = .48, $p < .001$) and permanent contract (β = .11, $p < .001$). Graduates from college, in comparison to university, report lower salary (β = –.11, $p < .05$), and STEM, in comparison to arts and humanities, report higher salaries (β = .17, $p < .001$). Networking (β = .16, $p < .001$) and career control (β = .14, $p < .01$) also positively predict salary.

For explaining job satisfaction, only the models with control variables ($F(8, 303) = 12.50$, $p < .001$, $\Delta R^2 = 25\%$) and career competencies ($\Delta F(6, 293) = 6.91$, $p < .001$, $\Delta R^2 = 9\%$) were significant (Table 23.2). Of the control variables, we observe lower job satisfaction in the private sector (β = –.11, $p < .001$) and higher among those working full-time (β = .32, $p < .001$). Only networking was significantly associated with job satisfaction (β = .24, $p < .001$).

Table 23.2 Hierarchical linear regression analyses predicting salary, job satisfaction and perceived employability at the time of data collection

	Salary (N=312)			Job satisfaction (N=312)			Perceived employability (N=502)		
	β	β	β	β	β	β	β	β	β
Aged 21-24	-.01	-.04	-.02	-.08	-.06	-.04	-.08	-.09	-.08
Female	-.05	-.04	-.01	.05	.05	.07	-.11*	-.10*	-.08
Time (months)	.17***	.12*	.13*	.10	.12	.10	.15**	.08	.12*
COVID-19 likelihood	-.05	-.03	-.03	.01	.02	.02	.07	.07	.04
Long-term health issues	-.01	0	.02	-.08	-.07	-.03	-.11*	-.08	-.06
Private sector [a]	-.09*	-.07	-.05	-.16***	-.16***	-.11***			
Full-time work [b]	.59***	.52***	.48***	.40***	.38***	.32***			
Permanent contract [c]	.15***	.13***	.11***	.01	.01	-.01	.04	.06	.05
Unemployed							-.23***	-.20***	-.12***
First generation [d]	.01	.02	.03	-.03	-.03	-.02	-.06	-.06	-.03
College graduate [e]		-.11*	-.11*		.04	-.04		.10	.10
STEM [f]		.22***	.17***		.10	.09		.24***	.18**
Social Science [f]		.15**	.10		.07	.06		.23***	.18**
Reflection on motivation			-.06			-.02			.13*
Reflection on qualities			-.06			.09			-.06
Networking			.16***			.24***			.25***
Self-profiling			-.08			.09			-.13**
Work exploration			.05			-.03			.16**
Career control			.14**			.01			.08
ΔF	.06	6.22 **	4.45***	.44	.79	6.91***	2.56	11.14***	14.16***
ΔR2	.00	.03	.04	.00	.00	.09	.00	.07	.13

Note. Column with control variables were excluded for simplicity. Variance explained (R^2) by control variables on salary, job satisfaction and perceived employability are .49, .25 and .11, respectively. Unemployment only relevant for perceived employabilty models. β refers to standardised beta coefficient; [a] comparison category is public sector or not-for-profit organisation; [b] comparison category: part-time work; [c] comparison category: self-employed/freelance, starting up my own business, fixed-term contract, temporary contract or zero-hours contract; [d] (0=No, 1=Yes); [e] comparison category: University leaver; [f] comparison category: arts and humanities graduate; * $p<.05$, ** $p<.01$, *** $p<.001$

All models, but the addition of social background, were significant in predicting perceived employability – that is, control variables only ($F(7, 494) = 8.54$, $p < .001$, $\Delta R^2 = 11\%$), educational background ($\Delta F(2, 490) = 11.14$, $p < .001$, $\Delta R^2 = 7\%$) and career competencies ($F(6, 484) = 14.16$, $p < .001$, $\Delta R^2 = 13\%$). Most notably, being female and having a long-term health condition are negatively associated with perceived employability, but these effects disappear with the inclusion of explanatory variables. Those who are unemployed consistently report lower perceived employability in comparison to those in work. Both STEM ($\beta = .18$, $p < .001$) and social science graduates ($\beta = .18$, $p < .001$) report higher perceived employability in comparison to arts and humanities graduates. Among the career competencies, reflection on motivation ($\beta = .13$, $p < .05$), networking ($\beta = .25$, $p < .001$) and work exploration ($\beta = .16$, $p < .01$) were positively associated with perceived employability, and self-profiling ($\beta = -.13$, $p < .01$) was negatively associated with perceived employability.

DISCUSSION

This chapter aimed to understand the determinants of graduate employability during the COVID-19 pandemic. We have examined the impact of social and educational disadvantage on graduates' objective (employment status and salary) and subjective (job satisfaction and perceived employability) employability (RQ1), and the relative importance of career agency (in the form of career competencies) on these outcomes, given the inequalities (RQ2). Findings show differences based on degree subject and career competencies, and they highlight a role for health inequalities and the structure of opportunities in the labour market. We discuss theoretical and practical implications of these findings below.

Theoretical Implications

For understanding the determinants of graduate employability in the COVID-19 context, this chapter makes two notable contributions to theory. Firstly, the findings contextualise the impact of social and educational inequalities on early graduate employability for cohorts entering the labour market during the COVID-19 pandemic. Secondly, the study contributes to the evidence base for the heightened importance of career behaviours, and therefore career guidance, for cohorts joining insecure and uncertain labour markets.

SOCIAL AND EDUCATIONAL INEQUALITIES IN GRADUATE EMPLOYABILITY

This study's first contribution is concerned with the known inequalities at play during university-to-work transitions. Supporting previous research (Okay-Somerville et al., 2020; Okay-Somerville and Scholarios, 2017), we found no evidence of disadvantage for first-generation graduates. This may be because the effect of social background is institutionalised and partially explained by educational background (Blasko et al., 2002), as students from disadvantaged backgrounds are also likely to have disadvantaged educational backgrounds. We can also speculate that the impact of social background may be explained by health inequalities in the COVID-19 context. Wider exploration of the data showed a positive correlation between being a first-generation student and having a long-lasting health condition ($r = .14, p < .05$), which has persistent effects on unemployment (see Table 23.2). The complexity introduced by health inequalities was observed in many of the open-ended text responses in our study, as in the following example.

> Since the beginning of the pandemic, I have developed health anxiety which now affects my day-to-day life. I now have difficulty leaving the house and being able to function in a normal routine. Financial worries since being made unemployed in the middle of March has also added to the distress of the pandemic. I am currently being treated for anxiety and depression. (female photography graduate aged 21–24 with a long-term health condition)

Traditionally, such health inequalities are rarely examined in university-to-work transitions, yet we can argue that the COVID-19 context may have heightened the importance of physical activity, social isolation and general well-being. Empirical work on student mental health during university-to-work transitions has been gaining impetus in recent years. Mental health is often studied as an outcome (e.g. related to unemployment). Our contextualisation of known inequalities of graduate employability in the COVID-19 context shows that mental and/or physical health inequalities could also be considered as correlates of graduate employability.

In terms of educational inequalities, we found that, compared to pre-pandemic research (Okay-Somerville and Scholarios, 2017), the impact of institutional prestige may have weakened, while that of degree subject may be heightened. Our results confirm a university-degree premium compared to graduating from college. This may be attributed to differences in accumulated human capital over two (college) versus four years (university). Before the pandemic, no degree-subject differences were reported in employment status, but those from non-professional degrees reported lower job quality and lower perceived employability (Okay-Somerville and Scholarios, 2017). Graduates from the 2020 cohort also report lower likelihood of being in employment. This may be partially explained by differences in timing between the two studies; the current study was immediately after graduation. Arts and humanities graduates' difficulties in accessing work, including self-employment, may also be contextualised in the COVID-19 crisis. Due to the transition to remote working, many opportunities for building work experience and/or a portfolio for arts and humanities graduates have disappeared (ILO-OECD, 2020), while those in STEM and/or social science subjects may have been furloughed (HMRC, 2021). For example, for performance artists, work takes place in crowded venues, which were among the first to shut down and the last to re-open (Marone and Resetar, 2020). Those from arts and humanities may be amongst the least likely to experience the traditional model of entry into stable work from education, often experiencing nonstandard work, such as freelancing and portfolio careers (Ashton and Ashton, 2016). This type of transition requires networking and entrepreneurial, self-directed career management (Bridgstock, 2007). Such opportunities have declined for those in arts and humanities. Our wider exploration of data showed that in the COVID-19 context, arts and humanities graduates report lower ratings on almost all career competencies, including networking. In explaining graduate employability, the context of university-to-work transitions during the COVID-19 pandemic shows us rather starkly the impact of labour market ambiguity on both objective and perceived employability. This is also evident in the persistently high impact of control variables, which shows that, especially for job satisfaction and salary, structural factors related to insecure and precarious work (e.g. hours of work and contract type) are highly constraining for some graduates' employability.

For addressing RQ1, the findings suggest that identifying social inequalities in graduate employability is not straightforward as these may be manifested through health and/or educational inequalities. In terms of educational inequalities, our findings imply diminishing effects of educational prestige, yet heightened inequalities based on degree subject.

THE ROLE OF CAREER COMPETENCIES

Our findings show that on all measures of graduate employability, the model with career competencies was significant and explained more incremental variance than social and educational background. For addressing RQ2, this indicates that career competencies have gained in relative importance for both objective and subjective employability. This supports the proposition that especially in uncertain and ambiguous contexts, career competencies act as personal resources that may shield individuals from unfavourable labour market experiences, such as unemployment or underemployment, and help craft sustainable careers (De Vos et al., 2020). This is particularly important for those at the start of careers who have little/no experience in navigating such adversities (Blokker et al., 2019). We can conclude that in a crisis, given educational and health inequalities, career competencies become more important for graduate employability.

Practical Implications

The findings highlight educational/labour market inequalities and career competencies as correlates of objective and subjective graduate employability. These findings have implications for career guidance and the availability of pathways into professions for successful university-to-work transitions.

A key practical implication of this study is the importance of career guidance for navigating uncertain labour markets. Demand for support in labour market information, job search, opportunities for reskilling and further training/education has increased since the onset of the pandemic (Cedefop, 2020). Findings from our study highlight the importance of career competencies as important personal resources for graduate employability. Supporting pre-pandemic findings (Okay-Somerville and Scholarios, 2017), for all outcomes, except for employment status, we observed that networking has a significant and positive impact. Networking has been shown to enhance social capital and career success (Wolff and Moser, 2010). In the context of graduates, we argue that networking is one of the core competencies enhancing both objective and subjective employability. In the COVID-19 context, while more organic and/or physical networking opportunities have reduced (especially for arts and humanities graduates), there remains opportunities to use social networking sites, such as LinkedIn, for accessing vacancy-related information.

This study highlights the pandemic's disproportionate impact on arts and humanities graduates, which is attributable to lack of opportunities. The importance of culture, arts, heritage and the media have been highlighted for the creation of economic and social value on the path to recovery from the pandemic (Jeannotte, 2021). This would imply policy emphasis on opportunity creation (e.g. by subsidising cultural and creative industries).

CONCLUSION

Taking a snapshot of the labour market experiences of the 2020 cohort of graduates during the COVID-19 pandemic, this study aimed to understand graduate employability, focusing specifically on social and educational inequalities in access to graduate employment, and the relevance of career agency given these inequalities. Our findings imply that the COVID-19 pandemic had a disproportionate impact on arts and humanities graduates' employability, due to a sudden reduction of opportunities for skills development, networking and employment. This study, therefore, provides evidence of heightened educational inequalities due to degree subject, rather than inequalities attributable to social background or institution prestige. Findings also highlight the impact of health inequalities for graduate employability, suggesting that future research should broaden the scope of inequalities included in analyses.

A key conclusion from this research is the relevance of career competencies as personal resources for navigating the uncertain context of COVID-19 graduate labour markets. We suggest that further qualitative work be undertaken to better understand this, and invite stakeholders involved in graduate employment to consider the interdependency of inequalities, such as social, educational and health inequalities, when designing labour market and career guidance interventions for mitigating the impact of COVID-19 on graduate employability. The findings highlight the importance of career agency alongside structural inequalities in determining graduate employability during the COVID-19 pandemic. We recognise, however, that it is also important to conceptualise graduate employability and related issues of inequality from the perspective of employers (e.g. Cai, 2013), and the absence of the employer perspective is a clear limitation of this research. Drawing on capital and institutional perspectives, Cai and Tomlinson (Chapter 31, this *Handbook*) advance our understanding here by proposing a renewed analytical framework that includes how graduates signal their employability capital to employers and how employers in turn appraise these signals. While our study is indicative of the former in the pandemic context, it provides no indication of how employers responded.

Our study is unique in its capture of the initial labour market experiences/shocks of a cohort of graduates who entered the labour market during the COVID-19 pandemic. This is a cross-sectional snapshot that provides a natural experiment to analyse individual and group differences in response to labour markets; however, this also means that we must qualify our conclusions. Future research should aim to follow up on the labour market experiences of this cohort of graduates, in particular their interchange with employers, and determine any scarring effects of graduating in a pandemic.

REFERENCES

Abel, J. R. & Deitz, R. (2017). Underemployment in the early careers of college graduates following the Great Recession. In C. R. Hulten & V. A. Ramey (eds), *Education, Skills, and Technical Change: Implications for Future US GDP Growth*. Chicago: University of Chicago Press, pp. 149–81. https://doi.org/10.7208/9780226567945

Akkermans, J., Brenninkmeijer, V., Huibers, M. & Blonk, R. W. (2013). Competencies for the contemporary career: Development and preliminary validation of the Career Competencies Questionnaire. *Journal of Career Development*, *40*(3), 245–67. https://doi.org/10.1177/0894845312467501

Akkermans, J., Collings, D. G., da Motta Veiga, S. P., Post, C. & Seibert, S. (2021). Toward a broader understanding of career shocks: Exploring interdisciplinary connections with research on job search, human resource management, entrepreneurship, and diversity. *Journal of Vocational Behavior*, *126*, 103563. https://doi.org/10.1016/j.jvb.2021.103563

Akkermans, J., Richardson, J. & Kraimer, M. L. (2020). The Covid-19 crisis as a career shock: Implications for careers and vocational behavior. *Journal of Vocational Behavior*, *119*, 103434. https://doi.org/10.1016/j.jvb.2020.103434

Allen, K., Quinn, J., Hollingworth, S. & Rose, A. (2013). Becoming employable students and 'ideal'creative workers: exclusion and inequality in higher education work placements. *British Journal of Sociology of Education*, *34*(3), 431–52. https://doi.org/10.1080/01425692.2012.714249

Ananiadou, K., Borbély-Pecze, T., Hooley, T., Jürges, A., Kadletz, F., Katayama, H., Kettunen, J., Kraatz, S., Harrison, C. M., Mann, A., McCarthy, J., McKenzie,

J., Moreno da Fonseca, P., Vlachaki, F., Villalba, E., Vuorinen, R. & Zelloth, H. (2020). *Career guidance policy and practice in the pandemic: Results of a joint international survey*. Luxembourg: European Commission, Publications Office of the European Union. https://doi.org/10.2801/318103

Ashton, H. S. & Ashton, D. N. (2016). 'Bring on the dancers': Reconceptualising the transition from school to work. *Journal of Education and Work*, *29*(7), 747–66. https://doi.org/10.1080/13639080.2015.1051520

Behle, H. (2020). Students' and graduates' employability. A framework to classify and measure employability gain. *Policy Reviews in Higher Education*, *4*(1), 105–13. https://doi.org/10.1080/23322969.2020.1712662

Blasko, Z., Brennan, J., Little, B. & Shah, T. (2002). *Access to what: Analysis of factors determining graduate employability*. Bristol: Higher Education Funding Council for England. http://hdl.voced.edu.au/10707/206846

Blokker, R., Akkermans, J., Tims, M., Jansen, P. & Khapova, S. (2019). Building a sustainable start: The role of career competencies, career success, and career shocks in young professionals' employability. *Journal of Vocational Behavior*, *112*, 172–84. https://doi.org/10.1016/j.jvb.2019.02.013

Boccuzzo, G. & Gianecchini, M. (2015). Measuring young graduates' job quality through a composite indicator. *Social Indicators Research*, *122*(2), 453–78. https://doi.org/10.1007/s11205-014-0695-6

Bridgstock, R. (2007). *Success in the protean career: a predictive study of professional artists and tertiary arts graduates*. PhD thesis, Queensland University of Technology. https://eprints.qut.edu.au/16575/

Browne, L. (2010). As UK policy strives to make access to higher education easier for all, is discrimination in employment practice still apparent? *Journal of Vocational Education and Training*, *62*(3), 313–26. https://doi.org/10.1080/13636820.2010.509549

Cai, Y. (2013). Graduate employability: A conceptual framework for understanding employers' perceptions. *Higher Education*, *65*(4), 457–69. https://doi.org/10.1007/s10734-012-9556-x

Cedefop (2020). *Career guidance policy and practice in the pandemic: Results of a joint international survey, June to August 2020* (9289631139). https://doi.org/10.2801/318103.

Clark, A. E. (2015). *What makes a good job? Job quality and job satisfaction*. IZA World of Labor, 215. https://doi.org/10.15185/izawol.215

Clarke, M. (2018). Rethinking graduate employability: The role of capital, individual attributes and context. *Studies in Higher Education*, *43*(11), 1923–37. https://doi.org/10.1080/03075079.2017.1294152

De Vos, A., Van Der Heijden, B. I. & Akkermans, J. (2020). Sustainable careers: Towards a conceptual model. *Journal of Vocational Behavior*, *117*, 103196. https://doi.org/10.1016/j.jvb.2018.06.011

Dolbier, C. L., Webster, J. A., McCalister, K. T., Mallon, M. W. & Steinhardt, M. A. (2005). Reliability and validity of a single-item measure of job satisfaction. *American Journal of Health Promotion*, *19*(3), 194–8. https://doi.org/10.4278/0890-1171-19.3.194

Edgerton, J. D. & Roberts, L. W. (2014). Cultural capital or habitus? Bourdieu and beyond in the explanation of enduring educational inequality. *School Field*, *12*(2), 193–220. https://doi.org/10.1177/1477878514530231

Frenette, M., Handler, T. & Messacar, D. (2020). *Potential earnings losses among high school and postsecondary graduates due to the COVID-19 economic downturn*. Economic Insights, 114. Statistics Canada. www150.statcan.gc.ca/n1/pub/11-626-x/11-626-x2020012-eng.htm

Grote, G. & Raeder, S. (2009). Careers and identity in flexible working: Do flexible identities fare better?. *Human Relations*, 62(2), 219–44. https://doi.org/10.1177/0018726708100358

Harari, M. B., Manapragada, A. & Viswesvaran, C. (2017). Who thinks they're a big fish in a small pond and why does it matter? A meta-analysis of perceived overqualification. *Journal of Vocational Behavior, 102*, 28–47. https://doi.org/10.1016/j.jvb.2017.06.002

Healy, M., Hammer, S. & McIlveen, P. (2022). Mapping graduate employability and career development in higher education research: a citation network analysis. *Studies in Higher Education*, 47(4), 799-811. https://doi.org/10.1080/03075079.2020.1804851

High Fliers Research. (2021). *The Graduate Market in 2021 – Annual review of graduate vacancies and starting salaries at Britain's leading employers*. www.highfliers.co.uk/download/2021/graduate_market/GM21-Report.pdf

Hinchliffe, G. W. & Jolly, A. (2010). Graduate identity and employability. *British Educational Research Journal*, *37*(4), 563–84. https://doi.org/10.1080/01411926.2010.482200

Holmes, C. & Mayhew, K. (2015). *Over-qualification and skills mismatch in the graduate labour market.* Chartered Institute of Personnel and Development. www.cipd.co.uk/Images/over-qualification-and-skills-mismatch-graduate-labour-market_tcm18-10231.pdf

Holmes, L. (2013). Competing perspectives on graduate employability: Possession, position or process?. *Studies in Higher Education*, *38*(4), 538–54. https://doi.org/10.1080/03075079.2011.587140

Holt-White, E. & Montacute, R. (2020). *COVID-19 and social mobility impact brief# 5. Graduate recruitment and access to the workplace*. The Sutton Trust. www.suttontrust.com/wp-content/uploads/2020/07/Access-to-the-Workplace-Impact-Brief.pdf

Hooley, T. (2020a). *COVID-19: Global impacts on graduate recruitment.* Institute of Student Employers and International Network of Employers and University Careers Services. https://cdn.ymaws.com/ise.org.uk/resource/collection/78C3D824-D17B-4316-8E69-15A054E40F1E/Covid-19-international_final.pdf

Hooley, T. (2020b). *Save the student labour market*. The Student Employer. http://hdl.handle.net/10545/625066

HMRC (2021). *Table 3d: Employments on furlough by sector as at 31 May 2021 (provisional).* Coronavirus Job Retention Scheme statistics: 1 July 2021 (updated 2 July 2021). HM Revenue & Customs. www.gov.uk/government/statistics/coronavirus-job-retention-scheme-statistics-1-july-2021/coronavirus-job-retention-scheme-statistics-1-july-2021

ILO-OECD (2020). *The impact of the COVID-19 pandemic on jobs and incomes in G20 economies.* Paper presented at G20 Leaders Saudi Arabia's G20 Presidency 2020. virtual meeting, 19-20 August 2020. www.ilo.org/wcmsp5/groups/public/—dgreports/—cabinet/documents/publication/wcms_756331.pdf

Jackson, D. & Wilton, N. (2017). Perceived employability among undergraduates and the importance of career self-management, work experience and individual characteristics. *Higher Education Research & Development*, *36*(4), 747–62. https://doi.org/10.1080/07294360.2016.1229270

James, S., Warhurst, C., Tholen, G. & Commander, J. (2013). What we know and what we need to know about graduate skills. *Work, Employment and Society*, *27*(6), 952–63. https://doi.org/10.1177/0950017013500116

Jeannotte, M. S. (2021). When the gigs are gone: Valuing arts, culture and media in the COVID-19 pandemic. *Social Sciences & Humanities Open*, *3*(1), 100097. https://doi.org/10.1016/j.ssaho.2020.100097

Jung, J. & Lee, S. J. (2016). Influence of university prestige on graduate wage and job satisfaction: the case of South Korea. *Journal of Higher Education Policy and Management*, *38*(3), 297–315. https://doi.org/10.1080/1360080X.2016.1174408

Kalfa, S. & Taksa, L. (2015). Cultural capital in business higher education: reconsidering the graduate attributes movement and the focus on employability. *Studies in Higher Education*, *40*(4), 580–95. https://doi.org/10.1080/03075079.2013.842210

Lee, S. Y. T., Park, M. & Shin, Y. (2021). *Hit harder, recover slower? Unequal employment effects of the Covid-19 shock*. NBER Working Paper No. 28354. www.nber.org/papers/w28354

Lyonette, C., Hunt, W. & Baldauf, B. (2017). *Occupations and skills of Arts, Humanities and Social Sciences Graduates and Postgraduates*. The British Academy. www.thebritishacademy.ac.uk/documents/2549/Flagship-Skills-AHSS-graduate-employment-outcomes.pdf

Ma, Y. & Bennett, D. (2021). The relationship between higher education students' perceived employability, academic engagement and stress among students in China. *Education + Training*, *63*(5), 744–62. https://doi.org/10.1108/ET-07-2020-0219

Marone, J. V. & Resetar, S. A. (2020). *The pandemic is a disaster for artists*. The Rand Blog, August 4. www.rand.org/blog/2020/07/the-pandemic-is-a-disaster-for-artists.html

McMahon, W. W. (2009). *Higher learning, greater good: The private and social benefits of higher education*. Baltimore: Johns Hopkins University Press. doi:10.1353/jef.0.0011.

McQuaid, R. (2015). *The multiple scarring effects of youth unemployment. Skills in Focus 11*. Skills Development Scotland. https://doi.org/10.13140/RG.2.1.1300.4964

Morrison, A. (2014). 'You have to be well spoken': Students' views on employability within the graduate labour market. *Journal of Education and Work*, *27*(2), 179–98. https://doi.org/10.1080/13639080.2012.742178

Morrison, A. (2019). Contributive justice: Social class and graduate employment in the UK. *Journal of Education and Work*, *32*(4), 335–46. https://doi.org/10.1080/13639080.2019.1646414

Okay-Somerville, B., Allison, I., Luchinskaya, D. & Scholarios, D. (2020). Disentangling the impact of social disadvantage on 'becoming employable': Evidence from STEM student university-to-work transitions. *Studies in Higher Education*, *47*(3), 545–59. https://doi.org/1.1080/03075079.202.1767052

Okay-Somerville, B. & Scholarios, D. (2017). Position, possession or process? Understanding objective and subjective employability during university-to-work transitions. *Studies in Higher Education*, *42*(7), 1275–91. https://doi.org/10.1080/03075079.2015.1091813

Okay-Somerville, B. & Scholarios, D. (2021). Job search strategies and successful university-to-work transitions in the context of labour market ambiguity. *Journal of Career Development*, *49*(1), 126–43. https://doi.org/10.1177/08948453211016058

Pigden, L. & Moore, A. G. (2020). Exploring educational advantage in the UK via graduate employment of joint honours degrees by examining pre-university tariff and degree classification. *Higher Education, Skills and Work-Based Learning*, *10*(2), 400–19. https://doi.org/10.1108/HESWBL-07-2019-0093

Pitman, T., Roberts, L., Bennett, D. & Richardson, S. (2019). An Australian study of graduate outcomes for disadvantaged students. *Journal of Further and Higher Education*, *43*(1), 45–57. https://doi.org/10.1080/0309877X.2017.1349895

Rivera, L. A. (2012). Hiring as cultural matching: The case of elite professional service firms. *American Sociological Review*, *77*(6), 999–1022. https://doi.org/10.1177/0003122412463213

Rothwell, A., Herbert, I. & Rothwell, F. (2008). Self-perceived employability: Construction and initial validation of a scale for university students. *Journal of Vocational Behavior*, *73*(1), 1–12. https://doi.org/10.1016/j.jvb.2007.12.001

Sloane, P. J. & Mavromaras, K. (2020). *Overeducation, skill mismatches, and labor market outcomes for college graduates*. IZA World of Labor 88. https://doi.org/10.15185/izawol.88.v2

Smith, V. (2010). Enhancing employability: Human, cultural, and social capital in an era of turbulent unpredictability. *Human Relations*, *63*(2), 279–300. https://doi.org/10.1177/0018726709353639

Tomlinson, M. (2017). Forms of graduate capital and their relationship to graduate employability. *Education + Training*, *59*(4), 338–52. https://doi.org/10.1108/ET-05-2016-0090

University of Essex, Institute for Social and Economic Research. (2021). *Understanding Society: COVID-19 Study, 2020–2021*, 9th edn. UK Data Service. SN: 8644. http://doi.org/10.5255/UKDA-SN-8644-11

Wolff, H.-G. & Moser, K. (2010). Do specific types of networking predict specific mobility outcomes? A two-year prospective study. *Journal of Vocational Behavior*, *77*(2), 238–45. https://doi.org/10.1037/trm0000358

Wright, E. & Mulvey, B. (2021). Internships and the graduate labour market: how upper-middle-class students 'get ahead'. *British Journal of Sociology of Education*, *42*(3), 339–56. https://doi.org/10.1080/01425692.2021.1886051

24

Graduate Employability and the Labour-market Relevance of Norwegian Higher Education: Perspectives from Students

Dian Liu and Siyang Kong

INTRODUCTION

Globally, higher education has been tasked with playing an active role in equipping students with enhanced employability in support of an innovative and entrepreneurial knowledge economy. Norway is no exception to this aspiration. To support the upgrading of industrial and technological development, innovation and entrepreneurship, and to meet the challenges posed by globalisation, Norwegian higher education has undergone tremendous reforms aimed at continuously developing enhanced employability of its population.

The nexus between higher education and the labour market in Norwegian society appears complex and multifaceted. First, the labour market for graduates of higher education is rather stable, with a low rate of graduate unemployment, a high rate of participation among females in the labour market, and relatively low mobility of student groups. Second, Norwegian university graduates demonstrated a deficiency in needed skills to support STEM activities attached to an innovation- and knowledge-based economy (OECD, 2018). Third, regardless of the initiatives to enhance labour-market relevance in higher education, institutional practices appear to lack uniformity, attributed to the multi-layered organisational governance and academic autonomy. Yet, we have seen limited research evidence, regarding the links between student employability, higher education experience, and the labour market in the Norwegian context.

Inspired by the employability literature (Hillage and Pollard, 1998; Yorke, 2006) and drawing from the specialty of Norwegian higher education (Maassen and Olsen, 2017; Støren and Aamodt, 2010), this study examines the relationship between graduate employability and the students' perspective on gaining employability. Using the national survey 'Special Graduate Survey 2017', involving more than 3,000 graduates from master's programmes in Norway, this study investigates the development of graduates' employability through a dynamic process deriving from collective experiences in and beyond higher education. This study contributes to the literature by assessing both the subjective and objective aspect of employability, which include graduates' employment opportunity, their job satisfaction, and job competence. In this chapter, the contextual information regarding Norwegian higher education and the graduate labour market is introduced, followed by scholarly work on graduate employability and the higher education aspects. It then demonstrates major findings regarding graduate employment and factors contributing to graduate employability. We summarise the chapter with discussions of policy implications and references in the changing context of higher education.

NORWEGIAN HIGHER EDUCATION AND THE GRADUATE LABOUR MARKET

Norwegian higher education is characterised by enhanced quality management (Stensaker et al., 2019), a relatively high level of autonomy (Elken et al., 2016), and relatively high level of accessibility, with a well developed student financial assistance system and strong governmental financial support. The expenditure on education in Norway accounts for about 6% of the national GDP, higher than the OECD average (OECD, 2017a). Having joined the Bologna process, Norway has adopted a joint European degree structure and the common European credit transfer system (ECTS), which supports student exchange and mobility between Norwegian and other European higher education institutions (Huisman et al., 2012). Norwegian students in higher education have a propensity for registering in business administration and law study programmes. Female students dominate the Norwegian higher education population: female students surpass their male counterparts by 18% in terms of participation in higher education. However, similar to the situation in other OECD countries, many fewer Norwegian women are enrolled in science, technology, engineering, and mathematics (STEM) disciplines such as engineering and ICT subjects (OECD, 2017a).

Norway has had stable graduate employment over the years. Due to Norway's robust economy and an inclusive labour market in an egalitarian society at large, graduates from Norwegian higher education enjoy one of the highest employment rates among the OECD countries. In 2016, the graduate employment rate in Norway was 89%, and the unemployment rate was 3%. Graduates also enjoy a government-mandated quality working environment in terms of work facilitation and employment factors (OECD, 2018). Notably, over one third of the university students study part-time in Norway, especially in bachelor programmes (OECD, 2017a). In addition, the majority of Norwegian students work part-time during their studies (Arnesen et al., 2011).

On the other hand, graduates display relatively low levels of proficiency in using numeric skills (such as formulas or statistics) that are typically required to support the STEM activities in the labour market. The overall willingness to participate in entrepreneurial activities is also rather low among Norwegian university students (OECD, 2018, 2020), indicative of the conservativeness of the group and unreadiness of higher education in terms of the global trends of innovation and entrepreneurship. In addition, employers in Norway, although expressing general satisfaction towards graduates' discipline-specific skills (TNS Gallup, 2015; Reymert et al., 2016; Støren et al., 2016), reported difficulty in getting suitable graduates to fill jobs due to the candidates' lack of work experience or deficiency in required transversal skills (OECD, 2017b).

To upgrade its innovation- and knowledge-based economy, as well as to meet the labour-market challenges posed by globalisation and technological changes, Norwegian higher education is required to play a more active role, raising and continuously developing the skills of its population (Maassen and Olsen, 2017). The government and targeted sector-led reforms have particularly encouraged institutional practices such as enhanced internationalisation and student mobility, innovative teaching and learning, extra-curricular and co-curricular activities, and career guidance, aiming at developing students' skills relevant to the labour market and their general employability (Minocha et al., 2017). Accordingly, innovative teaching and learning approaches were designed and tested in a range of programmes (Damen et al., 2017). More typically, measures were implemented to support student exchanges and study-abroad programmes, including an increased number of bilateral exchange agreements and initiatives (Norwegian Ministry of Education and Research, 2017). However, the multi-layered governance structure within higher education institutions (Ljosland, 2015), the long-embedded academic autonomy, together with the diverse organisational culture oriented towards an entrepreneurial approach or a traditional approach combine to make it complex and challenging to reach a widely accepted institutional practice model in Norwegian society.

GRADUATE EMPLOYABILITY, HIGHER EDUCATION, AND HYPOTHESES OF THE STUDY

Graduate employability has long been analysed from an individual-skill-development perspective, referring to individual graduates' ability to become employed and to keep fulfilling work after completing their higher education

(Hillage and Pollard, 1998). This stream of literature interprets employability as 'the capability to move self-sufficiently within the labour market to realise potential through sustainable employment' (Hillage and Pollard, 1998: 2). Accordingly, much work has been done investigating the development of different skill sets of graduates and trying to ascertain shared elements in such skill sets (Crossman and Clarke, 2010; Jackson and Wilton, 2017; Sarkar et al., 2016).

Following this line of argumentation, pressure to enhance employability and achieve skill outcomes for graduates has increased across cultures and placed many requirements on higher education (Bridgstock and Jackson, 2019; Sarkar et al., 2016). To date, most higher education institutions worldwide have either included or planned to include the development of students' vocational skills (Jackson, 2013; Tymon, 2013) in their study programmes to help students achieve such financial independence.

However, a mismatch between higher educational outcomes and labour-market requirements remains (McGuinness and Sloane, 2011), which could lead to unsuccessful experience in finding employment. On one hand, this mismatch is expressed by employers, across cultures, who continue to complain about university graduates' lack of readiness for employment and lack of the basic skills needed in the labour market. They also doubt the appropriateness of undergraduate programmes to prepare graduates with the skills that industry demands (Myran and Ivery, 2013). On the other hand, the phenomenon of over-education has been often observed in the graduate labour market (Carroll and Tani, 2013), contributing to yet another debate regarding graduate employability and the role of higher education.

More recently, a broader perspective has been applied in the graduate employability literature. Employability, hence, is understood as a multifaceted characteristic of graduates (Yorke, 2006), and allows more diverse dimensions to be brought in its analysis. Brown et al. (2003) regarded employability as the chances of obtaining jobs and maintaining employment. This definition implies important tasks are to be undertaken by higher education with a view to helping graduates maximise their chances in the labour market. This approach constructs employability as an institutional achievement (Harvey, 2001), which relates graduate employability to the quality of the study programme rather than the individual graduate's skill set. For example, Støren and Aamodt (2010) interpreted graduate employability as an aspect of quality in higher education – more specifically, the usefulness of the study programmes related to work tasks from the students' perception. Based on a comparative survey involving over 30,000 graduates in European countries, they found that the characteristics of study programmes (as indicators of higher education quality) play a significant role in impacting how graduates do their jobs, even if not how they obtain the jobs.

Despite the hot debate over the development of graduates' employability, and given the complexity of the concept as well as the diversity of contexts when analysing employability, there has not yet been a consensus on a definition of the concept, nor how the term can be measured in the literature (Bridgstock and Jackson, 2019; Pool and Sewell, 2007). This is particularly the case when efforts are made to align graduate employability analysis with characteristics of higher education. The changing context of higher education, the varied institutional features, and diversity of student groups combine to make the pattern even more complex. Perhaps a good starting point is to investigate the pattern in a single context, instead of making a cross-cultural comparison. This study focuses on placing graduate employability and relevance in the labour market in a Norwegian context. Graduate employability in this study is interpreted as a dynamic process, resulting from outcomes in and beyond higher education, even though higher education-related outcomes are directly related to employability in this study. In conjunction with measurements and indicators in graduate employment scholarship, we expect that:

Hypothesis 1. Students' study experience in higher education, in terms of the relevance of their study programme to labour market, has a positive impact on graduate employability.

Moreover, Aamodt and Havnes (2008) discovered another important aspect of employability, which links employability to both higher education and working life. Employability is closely related to further training as well as the working environment. For example, Jackson and Bridgstock (2021) analysed how students' participation in internships and extra-curricular activities contribute towards enhancement of employability. Such activities are useful, developing networks and improving career outcomes for the students, suggesting the benefits of more comprehensive co-curricular design in diverse learning programmes.

The heightened internationalisation of higher education also provides new insights to employability scholarship. Crossman and Clarke (2010) examined the relationship between students' international experience and employability; they concluded that students' networks and skills such as language proficiency and diverse cultural understanding grow during international experiences and increase the odds of employability.

The intensified internationalisation taking place in Norwegian higher education may impact the development of graduate employability. Therefore, we expect that:

Hypothesis 2. Students' overseas study experiences are positively associated with their employability.

Graduate employability may also be impacted by activities beyond higher education, given that a considerable portion of Norwegian students have part-time jobs during their academic careers. Therefore, we expect that:

Hypothesis 3. Students' previous and current work experience play a positive role in acquiring cumulative employability.

DATA AND METHOD

Data

We used data from the 'Special Graduate Survey 2017', which was conducted by the Nordic Institute for Studies in Innovation, Research and Education (NIFU) in 2017. The survey was distributed to university graduates who held a master's degree or equivalent in 2014, registered in the fields of humanities and arts, social sciences and law, business and administration, natural science, and technical subjects. The gross sample of the survey numbered 8,992 persons, and the net sample is 3,016 persons, with a response rate of 34.54%. We started with 3,016 graduates in the data. After a list-wise deletion based on the missing values of all variables, we ended up with 2,653 graduates.

Operationalisation

Dependent variables

We focus on graduates' employability. Due to the ambiguity of the concept and the lack of a clear definition of the term 'employability', we make use of the information of the survey on graduates' employment and current work situation and estimate employability based on three dimensions: employment, job satisfaction, and job competence.

Employment is a dichotomous variable measuring whether or not the graduate has found a job since finishing study in 2014. Graduates who reported having found a job between 2014 and 2017 (survey year) are employed ('1'), and graduates who either reported looking for a job or were inactive in the labour market are unemployed ('0'). Table 24.1 shows the summary statistics for all variables.

Job satisfaction is measured using a self-reported scale designed to ascertain 'how pleased are you with your current work?'. The subjectively measured *job satisfaction* including five categories ranging from 'very displeased' to 'very pleased'. For practical reasons, we reduced the number of categories from five to three by merging 'very displeased' and 'somewhat displeased' to 'displeased', and the same three response options for degrees of 'pleased'.

Job competence is a self-reported evaluation on the level of competence at work. It is a continuous variable ranging from 1 to 6, indicating the degree to which the graduate feels that he/she is prepared for the demands at work.

Independent variables

Two variables are used to reflect the quality of the higher education. *Study relevance* is a categorical variable that measures the extent to which graduate education reflects the skills needed in the transition from study to work. Graduates

Table 24.1 Descriptive statistics of all variables (*N* = 2653)

	Mean/Proportion	SD	Range
Dependent variables			
Employment	0.95		0–1
Job satisfaction			1–3
Displeased	0.10		
Neutral	0.07		
Pleased	0.83		
Job competence	4.89	0.84	1–6
Independent variables			
Study relevance			1–5
Very displeased	0.04		
Displeased	0.07		
Neutral	0.08		
Pleased	0.35		
Very pleased	0.46		
Study abroad	0.33		0–1
Prior work experience	0.89		0–1
Women	0.55		0–1
Controls			
Age group			1–4
27 or younger	0.10		
28–30	0.50		
31–35	0.19		
36 or older	0.21		
Marital status			0–1
Single	0.33		
Married/Have partner	0.67		
Parental education			1–6
Elementary school	0.05		
One to two years of vocational school	0.10		
Three years high school	0.08		
One to two years of university	0.11		
Three to four years of university	0.32		
More than four years of university	0.34		
High school GPA	5.14	1.13	1–7
Major[1]			1–25

[1]*Altogether* 25 majors are distributed in the fields of the humanities and arts, social sciences and law, business and administration, natural science, and technical subjects.

evaluate the relevance of their study programme to working life regardless of their current employment status. *Study abroad* measures graduates' oversea study experience within their graduate education.

Prior work experience before graduation is a dichotomous variable that measures whether the graduate had any working experience such as a part-time job or internship during the period of graduate education.

Additionally, we include graduates' *gender* in order to detect the potential gender discrepancy in terms of higher education and work experience associated with employability.

Control variables

We control several variables that may confound the analyses. Graduates' demographic characteristics, such as *age group* and *marital status*, are controlled. *Parental education* is included to control for the potential influence of family socioeconomic background on graduates' employability. The highest level of education achieved by parents is used to measure the level of *parental education*. If only one parent is available, then that parent's education level is used. In addition, we controlled for *high school GPA* and the *major* of the graduate education.

Analytical Strategy

To test our hypotheses, we investigated the overall patterns of graduates' employment opportunity, job satisfaction, and job competence in Norway. For graduates' employment, we used logistic regression and examined the influence of *study relevance, study abroad,* and *prior work experience* sequentially controlling for confounders. In the last two models, we examine the effect of gender on employment and the interaction effect between gender and higher education on employment. To investigate graduates' job satisfaction, we used multinomial logistic regression and analysed the influence of the same independent and control variables. Lastly, for job competence, ordinary least squares regressions are used.

RESULTS

Graduates' Employment Status

Some 95% of all graduates in Norway find employment after they complete their studies, as shown in Table 24.1. This echoes the OECD estimation regarding the high employment rate of Norwegian university graduates (OECD, 2018). Table 24.2 shows the influence of higher education and prior working experience on graduates' employment, after accounting for graduates' age, marital status, parental education, study major, and GPA in upper secondary school. Accordingly, graduates who are more pleased with the relevance of their study programme to the labour market are more likely to be employed. Model 1 shows that the odds of employment for graduates who are very pleased with the labour-market relevance of their study programme are about 329% higher than that of graduates who are neither pleased nor displeased with their study relevance. The odds of employment of graduates who are somewhat pleased with the study relevance are still 136% higher than the odds of employment of graduates who are neutral about their study relevance. This suggests that benefits are derived from enhanced institutional practices, involving richer labour-market information and relevant skill sets in the curriculum. Graduates who are very displeased or somewhat displeased with their study relevance are less likely to be employed; however, this correlation is not statistically significant.

Studying experience abroad is not common among graduates in Norway, as suggested by the data. In fact, Norway has a relatively low student mobility rate. The Norwegian government has set a goal of sending half of the student population on exchanges abroad, but this goal is challenging to meet at the present time. In 2016, around 15% of students participated in international exchanges, and 7% took exchange degree programmes abroad (Norwegian Ministry of Education and Research, 2017). While the alignment between overseas study experience and employability seems uncertain in the literature (Crossman and Clarke, 2010; Wiers-Jenssen, 2011), our findings suggest a positive linkage between the two. Model 2 shows that the odds of graduates who studied abroad finding employment are 80% higher than the odds of graduates who did not study abroad, after controlling for study relevance. For graduates, study experience abroad is associated with a higher probability of employment, parallel with enrolment in a study programme that is relevant for the labour market.

In addition, most of the graduates had extra work experience/part-time jobs during higher education (Table 24.1). Model 3 shows that work experience during higher education is positively associated with employment opportunity after graduation, although not significant.

Model 4 in Table 2 shows that female graduates are more likely to be employed than male graduates. Women's odds of being employed are 52% higher than men's odds. This might be explained by the well recognised gender equality enforcement, such as the female-priority principle in recruitment processes and the gender quota for corporate boards, as well as the support mechanisms such as childcare in the society (Casey et al., 2011).

We further examined whether there is any heterogeneity in the influence of higher education on employment patterns by gender. Figures 24.1 and 24.2 show that there are no significant gender patterns for the influence of higher education on employment. In other words, the influence of study relevance and studying abroad on employment reveals no differences between men and women.

Table 24.2 Logistic regression: graduates' employment as a function of perceptions on study relevance, whether studied abroad, and prior work experience (N = 2653)

	Model 1		Model 2		Model 3		Model 4	
Employment	Coef.	OR	Coef.	OR	Coef.	OR	Coef.	OR
Intercept	1.546	4.695	1.416	4.122	1.253	3.499	1.094	2.986
	(0.923)		(0.924)		(0.940)		(0.948)	
Study relevance (Ref: neutral)								
Very displeased	−0.489	0.613	−0.526	0.591	−0.530	0.589	−0.517	0.596
	(0.396)		(0.398)		(0.398)		(0.399)	
Somewhat Displeased	−0.395	0.674	−0.361	0.697	−0.359	0.698	−0.375	0.687
	(0.329)		(0.330)		(0.330)		(0.331)	
Somewhat Pleased	0.859**	2.360	0.845**	2.329	0.835**	2.305	0.855**	2.353
	(0.295)		(0.295)		(0.295)		(0.296)	
Very pleased	1.455***	4.285	1.452***	4.272	1.451***	4.268	1.467***	4.336
	(0.323)		(0.323)		(0.323)		(0.323)	
Studied abroad			0.587*	1.798	0.591*	1.807	0.564*	1.757
			(0.244)		(0.244)		(0.245)	
Prior work experience					0.274	1.315	0.247	1.280
					(0.295)		(0.296)	
Women							0.417*	1.518
							(0.212)	
Controls included	Yes		Yes		Yes		Yes	

Note: OR = odds ratio; standard errors are in parentheses; control variables include graduates' age, marital status, parental education, study major, and GPA in upper secondary school.
$^*p < 0.05$, $^{**}p < 0.01$, $^{***}p < 0.001$ (two-sided)

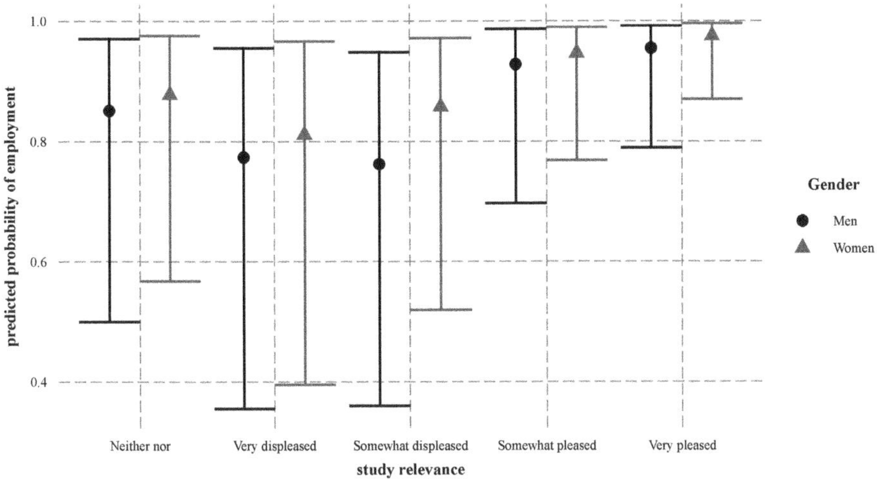

Figure 24.1 Predicted probability of employment by study relevance and gender

Note: predictions are made based on results of logistic regression; results are available upon request.

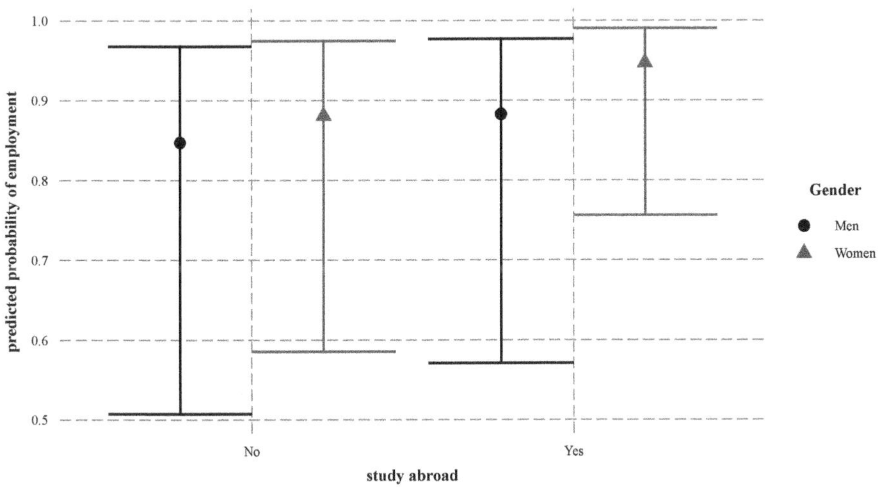

Figure 24.2 Predicted probability of employment by study abroad and gender

Note: predictions are made based on results of logistic regression; results are available upon request.

Graduates' Job Satisfaction

In the second level of the analysis, we examine the influence of higher education, work experience, and gender on job satisfaction. The focus, therefore, is on graduates who are employed. The descriptive table shows that most employed graduates demonstrate a high level of satisfaction with their current jobs (Table 24.1).

Model 1 in Table 24.3 shows who is more likely to be neutral towards their current job than displeased. Graduates who are less pleased with the labour-market relevance of their study programme are less likely to be neutral than displeased with their current work. Consistent with the analysis in the previous section, graduates who had studied abroad or had prior work experience are also less likely to be neutral than displeased with their current work, although the effects are not significant.

Model 2 shows that compared to feeling displeased with current work, the odds of feeling satisfied with one's current job are about 162% higher among graduates who are somewhat pleased with the study relevance than graduates who neutral towards their study relevance. The odds of feeling pleased instead of displeased towards their current work are even higher for graduates who are very pleased with the study relevance. Study abroad and prior work experience have no significant influence on job satisfaction.

Figure 24.3 shows that the predicted probability of being displeased, neutral, or pleased with one's current job does not differ between men and women. This

Table 24.3 Multinomial regression: graduates' job satisfaction as a function of perceptions on study relevance, study abroad, and prior work experience (N = 2523)

	Model 1		Model 2	
Job satisfaction	Neutral/ Displeased		Pleased/ Displeased	
	Coef.	OR	Coef.	OR
Intercept	1.641 (1.044)	5.163	1.772* (0.823)	5.883
Study relevance (Ref: neutral)				
Very displeased	−0.950 (0.590)	0.387	0.568 (0.375)	1.765
Displeased	−1.041* (0.357)	0.353	−0.597* (0.269)	0.551
Pleased	−0.500 (0.294)	0.606	0.963*** (0.231)	2.620
Very pleased	−0.323 (0.322)	0.724	1.821*** (0.248)	6.177
Study abroad	−0.084 (0.222)	0.919	−0.046 (0.153)	0.955
Prior work experience	−0.048 (0.348)	0.953	−0.057 (0.237)	0.945
Controls included	Yes		Yes	

Note: OR = odds ratio; standard errors are in parentheses; control variables include graduates' age, marital status, parental education, study major, and GPA in upper secondary school.

*$p < 0.05$, **$p < 0.01$, *** $p < 0.001$ (two-sided)

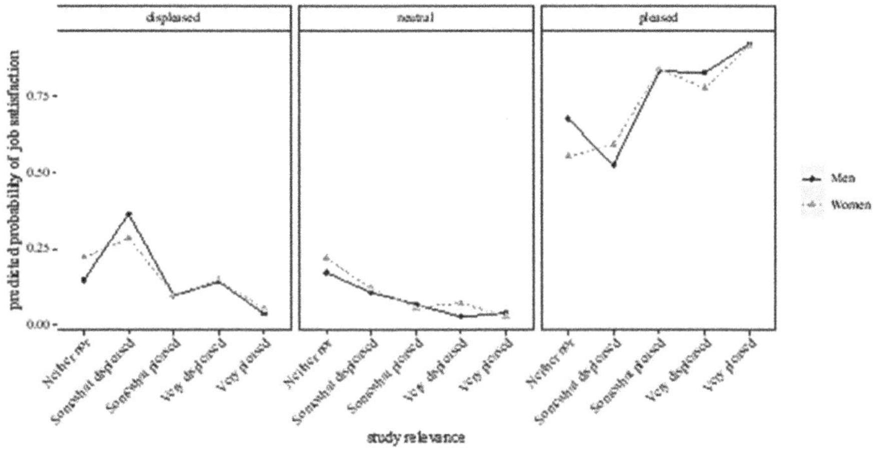

Figure 24.3 Predicted probability of job satisfaction by gender and study relevance

Note: we calculated the predicted probability of job satisfaction by gender and study relevance, holding all other characteristics to be constant.

means that gender has no significant influence on job satisfaction. The influence of study relevance on job satisfaction does not differ between men and women either.

Graduates' Job Competence

Regarding the extent to which graduates feel prepared at work, Model 1 in Table 24.4 shows that graduates who are very displeased with the study relevance of their study programme feel more prepared than graduates who are neutral about the study relevance of their programme (b = .22, p – 2s < 0.05). Graduates who are very pleased with the study relevance also feel better prepared for their work than their neutral counterparts (b = .26, p – 2s < 0.001). Studying abroad has no significant influence on graduates' job competence, as shown in Model 2, nor does prior work experience (Model 3). Women feel less prepared than men for their current work, as shown in Model 4, but the effect size is small (b = .07, p – 2s < 0.05).

Regarding gender differences, Figure 24.4 illustrates the interaction effect between study relevance and gender on job competence. The positive association between feeling very displeased towards the study relevance of their programme and job competence is evident only for women, not for men. This means that only female graduates who feel very displeased with the study relevance show a positive association with their job competence. The influence of study abroad and work experience on job competence, which are insignificant, do not differ between men and women.

Table 24.4 Ordinary linear regression: graduates' job competence level as a function of perceptions on study relevance, study abroad, and prior work experience (N = 2523)

	Model 1	Model 2	Model 3	Model 4
Job competence	Coef.	Coef.	Coef.	Coef.
Intercept	5.066***	5.058***	5.084***	5.117***
	(0.178)	(0.178)	(0.182)	(0.183)
Study relevance				
(Ref: neutral)				
Very displeased	0.224*	0.219	0.219	0.225*
	(0.112)	(0.112)	(0.112)	(0.112)
Somewhat displeased	−0.127	−0.124	−0.123	−0.115
	(0.088)	(0.088)	(0.088)	(0.088)
Somewhat pleased	0.009	0.008	0.008	0.010
	(0.068)	(0.068)	(0.068)	(0.068)
Very pleased	0.260***	0.259***	0.260***	0.262***
	(0.068)	(0.068)	(0.068)	(0.068)
Studied abroad		0.068	0.067	0.0728
		(0.037)	(0.037)	(0.037)
Prior work experience			−0.036	−0.031
			(0.055)	(0.055)
Women				−0.070*
				(0.035)
Controls included	Yes	Yes	Yes	Yes
Adjusted R^2	0.063	0.064	0.064	0.065

Note: standard errors are in parentheses; control variables include graduates' age, marital status, parental education, study major, and GPA in upper secondary school.

$^*p < 0.05$; $^{**}p < 0.01$; $^{***}p < 0.001$ (two-sided).

DISCUSSION AND CONCLUSION

In this study, we investigate the influence of higher education, as well as work experience/part-time jobs during higher education, on graduates' employability. We take into consideration graduates' experiences in and beyond higher education, and how such experience impacts their employability advancement. By doing so, we contribute to the rising scholarly discussion regarding

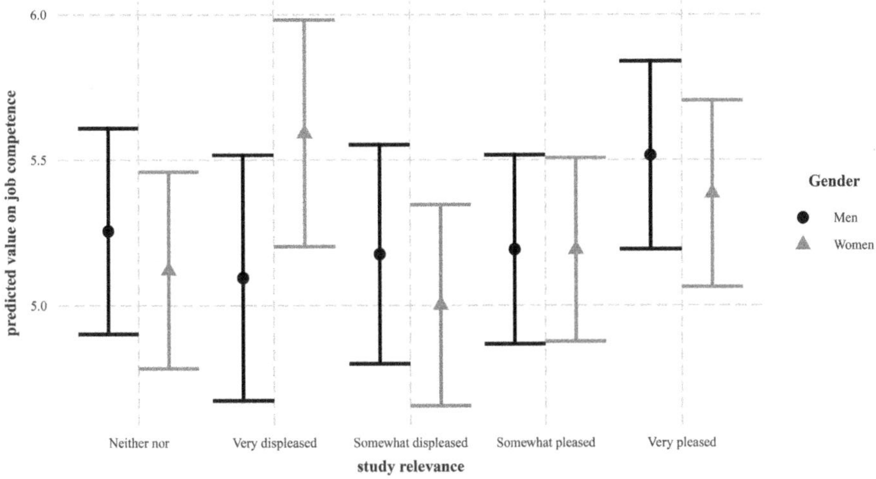

Figure 24.4 Predicted level of job competence by gender and study relevance

employability development and the higher education aspects, using a Norwegian case. This study confirms that the labour-market relevance of the study programme plays an important role in graduates' employability. Graduates who report a higher level of labour-market relevance in their study programme are more likely to be employed. Additionally, graduates who are more satisfied with the labour-market relevance of their study programme feel more competent at work. The finding suggests a positive nexus between labour-market-informed study experience, employability, satisfaction with jobs after graduation, and self-reported job competence, echoing the government initiative of enhancing labour-market relevance in the higher education system. The challenge, however, lies in reaching a consensus in institutional practices to rethink the role of higher education in better supporting the knowledge economy, both in and beyond Norwegian society. This implies joint efforts and actions of diverse stakeholders. For example, authorities and policy makers address a national guideline functioning as a framework regulating the study programmes with labour-market essences. Higher education institutions turn more active, attaching more importance in curriculum and co-curriculum design, and paving ways of university-industry contacts and collaboration. Students perform actively in co-curriculum activities and educational mobility. Industries are also encouraged to convey timely labour-market updates to institutions and students.

Our result, however, does not suggest a significant association between doing internship/having a part-time job and graduates' employability. Graduates' work experience during higher education is not associated with a higher employment probability, higher job satisfaction, or higher job competence. This might be explained by mass involvement of Norwegian higher education students in part-time jobs during their studies, which diminishes the impact of work experience in employability accumulation. Additionally, part-time jobs held by students are usually low threshold and not directly related to study programmes and hence full-time employment after graduation. It is therefore suggested to have thorough examinations regarding types of part-time jobs, length of work experience, and graduate employability in future research. This chapter also highlights that experience of studying abroad is beneficial for graduates' employability. That is, graduates participating in foreign exchanges or study-abroad experiences gain better chances in the local labour market. This implies enhanced institutional practice favouring student exchange and mobility, both at home and abroad. Institutions therefore are provoked to seek extended partners globally with rising bilateral agreements and cooperation schemes. Notably, the extent to which a short-term stay abroad can benefit the students in their search for a job was doubted in the literature (Støren et al., 2016). While this study confirms the positive linkage between international experience and employability, a better approach, perhaps, is to look beyond the short-time and immediate return from an overseas experience. This is because the added value obtained from international study experience, such as cross-cultural communication, global perspectives and understandings, and adaptation skills, are more beneficial in a longer life trajectory, and more and more recognised by both higher education institutions and stakeholders.

As a positive effect of the gender equality campaign and a sophisticated supporting system to ensure a better work–life balance for females in Norway, female students demonstrate a high level of participation in the labour market and a high employment rate, as shown in this study. However, some gender disparity remains in employability among graduates. That is, even though female graduates in general are more likely to be employed than their male counterparts, those females who are neutral about their study relevance feel much less prepared at work than male graduates. This suggests that a gender perspective should be employed in future studies, making allowances for diverse needs and hence in the preparation strategies of males and females. We also suggest combining gender with ethnicity in future explorations, as the literature suggests that female university students with an immigrant background experience more difficulty during their transition from higher education into the labour market (Brekke, 2007; Støren and Wiers-Jenssen, 2010). Due to the focus of this study, we did not include ethnic background in the analysis.

Another limitation is the absence of the employer perspective in discussions about the development of graduate employability in this study. Graduate employability analysis has long been criticised of divorcing the discussion from occupational contexts (Cai, 2013; Cai and Tomlinson, 2022). And in the literature, there has been an increasing awareness that employability is a relative term, strongly tied to organisational cultures, geographic locations, and employment fields (Benbow and Hora, 2018; Tomlinson and Anderson, 2021). While the analysis of this study draws upon survey data from the graduates' perspective, a more nuanced approach could be adopted, taking into consideration employer perception and contextual characteristics in future studies.

Note

1 Some of the data applied in the analysis in this publication are based on 'Special Graduate Survey 2017'. The data are provided by The Nordic Institute for Studies in Innovation, Research and Education (NIFU) and prepared and made available by the NSD – Norwegian Centre for Research Data. Neither NIFU nor NSD are responsible for the analyses/interpretation of the data presented here.

REFERENCES

Aamodt, P. O., & Havnes, A. (2008). Factors affecting professional job mastery: Quality of study or work experience? *Quality in Higher Education*, *14*(3), 233–248.

Andrews, J., & Higson, H. (2008). Graduate employability, 'soft skills' versus 'hard' business knowledge: A European study. *Higher Education in Europe*, *33*(4), 411–422.

Arnesen, C. Å., Hovdhaugen, E, Wiers-Jenssen, J., & Aamodt, P. O. (2011). *Studiesituasjon og studentøkonomi. Norske resultater fra den europeiske studentundersøkelsen Eurostudent IV [Study Situation and Student Finances]*. NIFU rapport 33/2011. Oslo: NIFU.

Australian Association of Graduate Employers (2010). *The AAGE employer survey*. Sydney: Australian Association of Graduate Employers.

Benbow, R. J., & Hora, M. T. (2018). Reconsidering college student employability: A cultural analysis of educator and employer conceptions of workplace skills. *Harvard Educational Review*, *88*(4), 483–515.

Brekke, I. (2007). Ethnic background and the transition from education to work among university graduates. *Journal of Ethnic and Migration Studies*, *33*(8), 1299–1321.

Bridgstock, R. (2009). The graduate attributes we've overlooked: Enhancing graduate employability through career management skills. *Higher Education Research & Development*, *28*(1), 31–44.

Bridgstock, R., & Jackson, D. (2019). Strategic institutional approaches to graduate employability: navigating meanings, measurements and what really matters. *Journal of Higher Education Policy and Management*, *41*(5), 468–484.

Brown, P., Hesketh, A., & Wiliams, S. (2003). Employability in a knowledge-driven economy. *Journal of Education and Work*, *16*(2), 107–126.

Cai, Y. (2013). Graduate employability: A conceptual framework for understanding employers' perceptions. *Higher Education*, *65*(4), 457–469.

Cai, Y., & Tomlinson, M. (2022). A renewed analytical framework for understanding employers' perceptions of graduate employability: Integration of capital and institutionalist perspectives. In T. Broadley, Y. Cai, M. Firth, E. Hunt, & J. Neugebauer (eds), *SAGE Handbook of Graduate Employability*. Sage.

Carroll, D., & Tani, M. (2013). Over-education of recent higher education graduates: New Australian panel evidence. *Economics of Education Review*, *32*, 207–218.

Casey, C., Skibnes, R., & Pringle, J.K. (2011), Gender equality and corporate governance: Policy strategies in Norway and New Zealand. *Gender, Work & Organization*, *18*, 613–630.

Crossman, J. E., & Clarke, M. (2010). International experience and graduate employability: Stakeholder perceptions on the connection. *Higher Education*, *59*(5), 599–613.
Cumming, J. (2010). Contextualised performance: Reframing the skills debate in research education. *Studies in Higher Education*, *35*(4), 405–419.
Damen, M.-L. et al. (2017). *Studiebarometeret 2016: Hovedtendenser, Studiebarometeret Rapport 2017/2*. Norwegian Agency for Quality Assurance in Education.
Elken, M., Frølich, N., & Reymert, I. (2016). *Steering approaches in higher education: Comparing Norway, Sweden, Finland, the Netherlands and UK (England)*. Report 2016/35. Nordic Institute for Studies in Innovation, Research and Education.
Harvey, L. (2001). Defining and measuring employability. *Quality in Higher Education*, *7*(2), 97–109.
Heaton, N., McCracken, M., & Harrison, J. (2008). Graduate recruitment and development: Sector influence on a local market/regional economy. *Education+ Training*, *50*(4), 276–288.
Hillage, J., & Pollard, E. (1998). *Employability: Developing a framework for policy analysis* (Vol. 107). London: DfEE.
Huisman, J., Adelman, C., Hsieh, C.-C., Shams, F., & Wilkins, S. (2012). Europe's Bologna process and its impact on global higher education. In D. K. Deardorff, H. de Wit, J. D. Heyl, & T. Adams (eds), *The SAGE handbook of international higher education* (pp. 81–100). London: Sage.
Jackson, D. (2013). Business graduate employability–where are we going wrong? *Higher Education Research & Development*, *32*(5), 776–790.
Jackson, D., & Bridgstock, R. (2021). What actually works to enhance graduate employability? The relative value of curricular, co-curricular, and extra-curricular learning and paid work. *Higher Education*, *81*(4), 723–739.
Jackson, D., & Chapman, E. (2012). Non-technical skill gaps in Australian business graduates. *Education+ Training*, *54*(2/3), 95–113.
Jackson, D., & Wilton, N. (2017). Perceived employability among undergraduates and the importance of career self-management, work experience and individual characteristics. *Higher Education Research & Development*, *36*(4), 747–762.
Knight, P., & Yorke, M. (2004). *Learning, curriculum and employability in higher education*: London: Routledge Falmer.
Ljosland, R. (2015). Policymaking as a multi-layered activity. A case study from the higher education sector in Norway. *Higher Education*, *70*(4), 611–627.
Maassen, P., & Olsen, J. P. (2007) *University dynamics and European integration*. Dordrecht: Springer.
McGuinness, S., & Sloane, P. J. (2011). Labour market mismatch among UK graduates: An analysis using REFLEX data. *Economics of Education Review*, *30*(1), 130–145.
Minocha, S., Hristov, D., & Reynolds, M. (2017). From graduate employability to employment: policy and practice in UK higher education. *International Journal of Training and Development*, *21*, 235–248.
Myran, G., & Ivery, C. L. (2013). The employability gap and the community college role in workforce development. *New Directions for Community Colleges*, *2013*(162), 45–53.
Norwegian Ministry of Education and Research (2017). *Tilstandsrapport for høyere utdanning 2017* (Status report for higher education). Norwegian Ministry of Education and Research.
OECD (2017a). *Education at a glance*. http://dx.doi.org/10.1787/888933557850.
OECD (2017b). *Getting skills right: Skills for jobs indicators*. http://dx.doi.org/10.1787/9789264277878-en.

OECD (2018). *Higher education in Norway: Labour market relevance and outcomes.* http://dx.doi.org/10.1787/9789264301757-en.

OECD (2020). *OECD employment and labour market statistics.* https://doi.org/10.1787/lfs-data-en.

Reymert, I., Aamodt, P. O., Børing, P., & Næss, T. (2016), *Hvordan ser arbeidslivet på kandidater fra Universitetet i Oslo? Resultater fra en undersøkelse i et utvalg virksomheter i 2016 (How does the business community see candidates from the University of Oslo? Results of a survey in selected businesses in 2016).* NIFU Rapport 2016/38. Nordic Institute for Studies in Innovation, Research and Education.

Rothwell, A., Jewell, S., & Hardie, M. (2009). Self-perceived employability: Investigating the responses of post-graduate students. *Journal of Vocational Behavior, 75*(2), 152–161.

Sarkar, M., Overton, T., Thompson, C., & Rayner, G. (2016). Graduate employability: Views of recent science graduates and employers. *International Journal of Innovation in Science and Mathematics Education (formerly CAL-laborate International), 24*(3), 31–48.

Stensaker, B., Hovdhaugen, E., & Maassen, P. (2019). The practices of quality management in Norwegian higher education: Collaboration and control in study programme design and delivery. *International Journal of Educational Management, 33*(4), 698–708.

Støren, L. A., Carlsten, T. C., Reiling, R. B., Olsen, D. S., & Arnesen, C. Å. (2016). *Arbeidsgivers vurdering av nyansatte med høyere utdanning og fagskoleutdanning.* Working Paper Series, 2016/16. Oslo: Nordic Institute for Studies in Innovation, Research and Education.

Støren, L. A., & Aamodt, P. O. (2010). The quality of higher education and employability of graduates. *Quality in Higher Education, 16*(3), 297–313.

Støren L. A., & Wiers-Jenssen, J. (2010). Foreign diploma versus immigrant background: Determinants of labour market success or failure? *Journal of Studies in International Education, 14*(1), 29–49.

Taylor, S., & Govender, C. M. (2017). Increasing employability by implementing a Work-Integrated Learning partnership model in South Africa–A student perspective. *Africa Education Review, 14*(1), 105–119.

TNS Gallup/NTNU (2015). *Arbeidsgiverundersøkelsen (Survey of Employers) 2015.* TNS Gallup and Norwegian University of Science and Technology.

Tomlinson, M., & Anderson, V. (2021). Employers and graduates: The mediating role of signals and capitals. *Journal of Higher Education Policy and Management, 43*(4), 384–399.

Tymon, A. (2013). The student perspective on employability. *Studies in Higher Education, 38*(6), 841–856.

Weligamage, S. S. (2009). *Graduates' employability skills: Evidence from literature review.* Sri Lanka: University of Kelaniya.

Wiers-Jenssen, J. (2011). Background and employability of mobile vs. non-mobile students. *Tertiary Education Management, 17*, 79–100.

Yorke, M. (2006). *Employability in higher education: what it is-what it is not* (Vol. 1). York: Higher Education Academy.

25

Starting Points and Journeys: Careers and Employability in a Data-Rich Environment

Bob Gilworth

INTRODUCTION

This chapter will look at the impact of the availability and use of large-scale data on the career development starting points and journeys of higher education students on careers and employability strategies and operations in higher education institutions within and beyond the UK (Gilworth, 2021).

This is an account of the impact of the Careers Registration approach, which began as a practical innovation linked to strategy development in one institution in 2012 and has gone on to form the basis of a national research project and to have international influence on careers and employability practice. This practice-based account comes from the author's direct involvement as an institutional practice leader and as the leader of a community of practice built around the Careers Registration approach.

Although there is reference to Careers Registration's roots in, and links to, career development theory and the ways in which the underlying constructs that shape the data gathering and interpretation are developing as 'career journey' models themselves, this chapter is primarily concerned with the impact of new data on day-to-day practice.

Having led the original development and implementation, the author has since had the opportunity to work with colleagues at key moments in their consideration and implementation of the approach. This chapter makes use of insights gathered from that experience to distil some key learning points about the practical impact of data-informed understanding of students' starting points and journeys.

The chapter will cover the following ground:

- What is Careers Registration?
- The origins of the Careers Registration.
- Practicalities: a brief overview of the process and indicative examples of output.
- Reflections on the UK experience.
- Some early-stage examples from outside the UK.
- Concluding thoughts, links to models of career development and potential for further research.

WHAT IS CAREERS REGISTRATION?

Careers Registration is now a widely adopted approach to generating and using data (often referred to as career readiness data) to improve understanding of the career development starting points and journeys of higher education students (Gilworth, 2021). It was originally implemented at the University of Leeds in 2012. The work was disseminated at the Association of Graduate Careers Advisory services (AGCAS) Conference in 2013 by the author and Nalayini Thambar, who was a key player in the implementation. Since then, Careers Registration has been adopted by over 80 higher education institutions in the UK and by institutions in Ireland, Australia, New Zealand and Portugal. It was the core of a national Learning Gain project led by the Careers Group, University of London, from 2015 to 2018, involving 16 partner institutions with consortium members in every nation of the UK. At its peak, the project had an anonymised dataset of 308,000 students and showed remarkably consistent patterns across very different institutions. Findings from the Learning Gain project can be found in Fiona Cobb's (2019) article 'There's no Going Back – The Transformation of HE careers services using big data'. More information on the project is available via the Careers Registration pages of the Careers Group website www.london.ac.uk/the-careers-group/careers-registration.

Put simply, Careers Registration is the process by which information about career thinking and employability-related experience is collected from all students, every year through relatively simple self-report additions to institutional enrolment systems. The data is used by institutions and particularly their careers service, to help them to understand student journeys and to provide the most appropriate impactful careers and employability support, to direct scarce resources to where they will make the most difference and to monitor the success of strategies and activities in this area.

Prior to implementing Careers Registration, institutions in the UK had the data on previous graduates from the Destinations of Leavers from Higher Education (DLHE) surveys (now replaced by the Graduate Outcomes surveys), but did not have large-scale, comprehensive data on the career development of current students. Through Careers Registration, many institutions now have comprehensive data about career thinking, experience and aspirations, which comes directly from current students and can be linked to other student data. This data provides leading indicators to sit alongside the lagging indicators (outcomes) that have traditionally been used to inform strategy and operations in the UK.

THE ORIGINS OF CAREERS REGISTRATION

Careers Registration has its roots in an institutional employability strategy with three key, student-centred aims: to help all students to

1. **Decide** on the options to pursue.
2. **Plan** to acquire skills, experiences, knowledge and networks.
3. **Compete** effectively in their chosen fields.

These aims prompted the obvious question of how will the institution know if and to what extent the strategy is working?

THE DATA GAP

The employability strategy was an education strategy concerned with supporting current students. The only large-scale dataset related to this endeavour was that derived from the DLHE survey. The DLHE was the statutory graduate destinations survey in the UK at the time. It was replaced by the Graduate Outcomes survey in 2018 (Agarwal, 2020). Destinations data has careers information and guidance value, as was its original purpose (Maynard and Kingston, 2007). Graduate Outcomes data remains a crucial element of the higher education policy landscape in the UK (Hewitt, 2020). However, the strategic requirement in this case was for data on current students.

Perhaps the best way to explain the nature of the data that was needed but not available is to consider how difficult it is to guide someone to a destination when you do not know their starting point. The key piece of information that you must obtain to direct them effectively is, of course, the answer to the question 'where are you now?'. It was precisely this 'journey-style' information for current students that would be crucial to pursuing the strategy but did not yet exist.

A comprehensive dataset showing starting points and progress was needed. This required standardised information-capture covering all students along a meaningful timeline, enabling both cross-sectional and longitudinal analysis.

Registration – the formal online university enrolment process for all students, new and returning, every year – was the only viable way to do this.

This meant convincing the university of the value of embedding careers and employability data capture into one of its most fundamental and closely guarded business processes. If successful, this would also ensure that careers and employability data would be linked to the main student record system and other important student data.

Careers Registration would never have been realised without the buy-in and assistance of key people across the organisation. Without the support of the then Pro Vice Chancellor for Learning and Teaching, and the active engagement of registry and IT services at the University of Leeds, Careers Registration would not have happened, no matter how much the careers professionals liked the idea. The centrality of the direct relationship to institutional strategy cannot be overemphasised. Careers Registration was a way of monitoring the effectiveness of the strategy, and of highlighting the issues and interventions that would be important in pursuing the strategy. Careers professionals in higher education cannot implement this approach unilaterally. The extent to which the approach has been adopted in the UK offers insight into the perceived importance of employability as a strategic imperative.

PRACTICALITIES

The process of data collection operates through the insertion of two or three forms into the annual student enrolment process. The key elements of the process are briefly outlined below. More information, including example statements, can be found in The Careers Registration Practical Guide (Cobb et al., 2019) and in David Winter's work on 'The rise of the practitioner-researcher' (Winter, 2019).

Career thinking: In the first form, students are typically presented with 10 statements about career thinking and asked to select the one statement that they feel most closely reflects their current career thinking.

The statements reflect the three main career thinking categories – three each for Deciding, Planning and Competing – plus one for the option to declare that a job, further study or business start-up is already confirmed. This last stage is often referred to as 'Sorted'. The individual statements reflect nuances within the headline categories; so, for example, the Decide category includes statements at the levels of 'not ready to start thinking about career' through 'no career ideas yet but ready to start thinking' to 'some career ideas and ready to start planning'. These categories are used to analyse responses and communicate data, but they are not presented in that way to the students at enrolment. Instead, they are presented as a set of 10 common-sense statements about career thinking. The statements were derived from student focus groups. In the original Leeds version and in numerous others, the headline categories are 'Decide, Plan, Compete', but several institutions have chosen different, local labels for the categories, such as 'Discover, Focus, Action' and 'Explore, Plan, Apply'.

Experience: On the second form, students are asked to indicate their level of participation in work experience and other employability enhancing activities usually within a time frame (i.e. the last 12 months) by selecting all statements that apply from a list.

The lists are institutionally devised, so they include offers that are specific to the institution as well as items that are relatively generic (a placement year, a summer internship, a part-time job and so on). Lists are constructed with the intention of capturing all forms of work experience that a student may have gained, whether organised by the institution or not. The latter would not otherwise be captured by institutional systems. The lists include the option for students to declare that they have no work experience to date.

Occupational sector preferences: All institutions with Careers Registration in place have adopted the two steps outlined above. Over time, some institutions have made additions, and the most common has been the introduction of occupational sector preferences.

On this third form, students are asked to indicate occupational sector preferences by choosing from a list. Students may be able to indicate multiple preferences; choosing a top three is a common approach.

As the process is linked to formal enrolment, it generates response rates at or close to 100% and therefore creates very large datasets. For example, the first run at Leeds produced responses from 31,000 students (essentially the entire student population) between the opening of enrolment at the beginning of August and the close of enrolment at the end of October. The capacity to analyse, present and interpret data on this scale is a key consideration for any careers service taking this approach (Cobb, 2019).

Outputs: Whilst a basic explanation of the data-gathering process is useful, the idea that data is not an end in itself is crucial. Change to careers and employability practice on the ground has been influenced by the presentation and application of the data, not simply by its existence. It would not be possible here to cover the full range of possibilities arising from the Careers Registration data and its potential links to other data, but some illustrations of basic outputs help to convey the idea of what is available now that was not available before.

In institutions with Careers Registration in place, careers services and academic departments can see the distribution of students across the main categories of career thinking and the subcategories within them. They can also see the nature and extent of work experience and other employability enhancing experiences acquired by students. Where included, students declared occupational preferences can also be seen. The data can be seen at every level from the whole university, through the various levels of academic units in the local structure, to individual degree programmes and year groups. The data can be viewed as a snapshot of the state of play (say, the current position in all current years of a degree programme), or longitudinally (say, the progress of a single cohort through a three-year programme) or comparatively (say, across a number of degree programmes in a School). Useful multi-factor analyses can be easily produced – say, the proportion of final-year students who are ready to apply for graduate roles and have acquired work experience in their chosen occupational sector.

Figures 25.1 and 25.2 are illustrations rather than specific examples. They represent the distribution of responses as frequently seen across a range of institutions. They are not intended to represent specific institutions or academic units.

Figure 25.1 shows the distribution of career-thinking responses for undergraduate students at the beginning of their final year at the level of a 'Faculty' (a large academic organisational unit, comprising several cognate Schools of study). The distribution of responses across the principal career-thinking categories would be typical across the multi-institutional Learning Gain project. Feedback from the UK community of practice suggests that this distribution – in which students identifying in the Decide phase are comfortably the largest group at the start of the final year – has prompted some surprise and helpful discussion when shared with colleagues in academic units. It has been frequently reported that discussion informed by data from 'students who are here right now' has been much more engaging and more likely to prompt shared planning and action than was the case with discussion of destinations data alone.

The data in Figure 25.1 can easily be disaggregated to School and programme levels and action plans formulated at those levels. Year groups can be compared and cohorts tracked through from first year to final year. The data can also be broken down within the headline categories. For example, two Schools may have similar proportions in the Decide group, but in one, the responses are dominated by 'not ready to start thinking', whilst in the other, 'some career ideas and ready to start planning' may be much more common. Situations that appear very similar

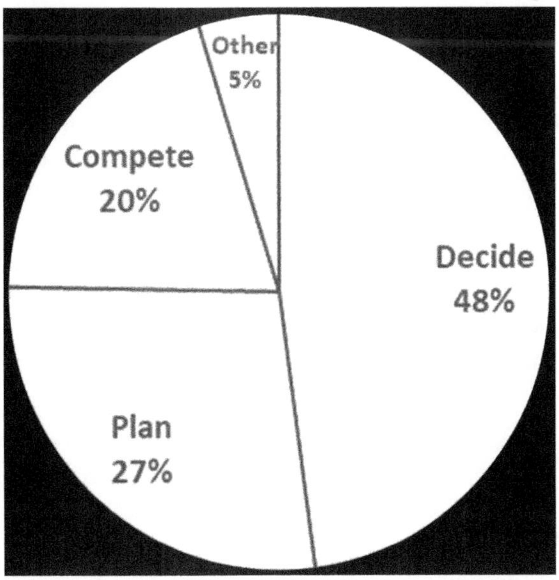

Figure 25.1 Career thinking– Faculty example – Final Year

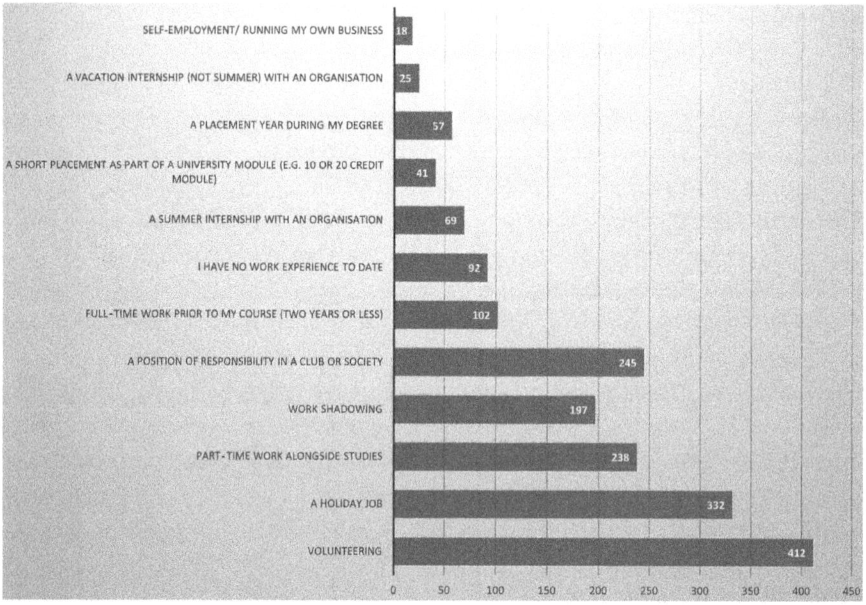

Figure 25.2 Responses on work experience at final year

at the top level of analysis may be different at the next level of granularity and different programmes of intervention might follow.

Figure 25.2 shows the distribution of responses on the acquisition of work experience at the same 'Faculty' level as in Figure 25.1. In this case, the respondents have ticked as many responses as apply to them, so the numbers are not percentages. Given the general acceptance of the benefits of work experience, the number of final-year students indicating that they have no work experience at all might be a cause for concern, prompting discussion with the students, perhaps through a personal-tutor system. The data shows the full picture of the acquisition of experience because it includes opportunities that are organised by the university and those that are not. The data in Figure 25.2 can be analysed cross-sectionally and longitudinally in similar ways to the data in Figure 25.1. Combining the work-experience data with demographic data can be powerful in terms of equality, diversity and inclusion and social mobility as it illustrates the spread of the take-up of and access to university-organised opportunities and/or structured placements and internships directly with employers.

REFLECTIONS ON THE UK EXPERIENCE

This section draws on insights gained from the UK community of practice around Careers Registration, including, but not exclusively, from the national Careers Registration Learning Gain project. Each sub-heading represents one of the topics most often mentioned by careers service leaders across the community of practice.

Transforming Conversations between Careers and Employability Staff and Academic Colleagues

This is probably the most reported change. As noted above, the impact of discussing careers and employability data that comes directly from current students has been frequently described as a much more powerful driver of action than previous more abstract discussion of destinations data. The term 'game changer' is frequently used by careers service leaders. Discussion of the support and opportunities that students might need is evidence-based rather than being based on anecdote and assumption and takes place in a time frame within which action can be taken. In many cases, this has been structurally facilitated by the ways in which careers services have become more institutionally embedded and academically aligned in recent years (Gilworth, 2019). Structures for discussing career and employability matters at the level of the key academic unit (e.g. Faculty, School) have developed and in some cases have matured to the extent that they are established, naturally occurring features of business as usual. Where this is not the case, colleagues have been more likely to report challenges in sharing the data in the context of shared endeavour.

Reinforcing (or Challenging) the Expertise of Careers and Employability Professional Staff

This has been reported as both a benefit and a challenge. Evidence-based expertise is seen to strengthen the hand of careers professional in an academic environment. However, for some, this means overcoming a cultural reluctance to see/ position themselves as expert (Thambar, 2016) and a need to engage with the interpretation of data to an extent with which they may have been unfamiliar (Winter, 2019). This latter point has been driven by multiple data sources related to regulation and institutional performance and may be true without Careers Registration.

Student Engagement and Messaging

This is another very common use of the data. Careers services can be exposed to the risk of constantly re-engaging with those students who are already engaged and failing to reach those who are not. The fact that the Careers Registration process creates a basic level of engagement with every student has been seen as a great opportunity for broader reach. The process enables careers services to identify and reach out to students and meet them at their declared starting point because they now have the answer to the question 'where are you now?'.

Careers services and the broader careers and employability eco-system within an institution can segment the student audience along lines that are genuinely career-related rather than by categories that may or may not be, such as subject or year of study. This is particularly important in the UK context, where graduate labour markets outside state-regulated professions and some science, technology, engineering and mathematics (STEM) occupations are substantially 'subject agnostic'. A recent survey by the Institute of Student Employers, which represents large recruiters with structured graduate programmes, shows that only 15% of their members specify degree subject (ISE, 2020).

Some institutions, including the University of Leeds and Ulster University, have automated responses to Careers Registration submissions, providing instant engagement and relevant advice. Both Leeds and Ulster and several others, such as Exeter and Lancaster, have configured student landing pages on their Careers Service websites to directly reflect the Careers Registration process and the idea of starting points and journeys. In the Leeds example, students click on 'Your Starting Point' to get to a page headed 'Career Planning'(University of Leeds nd) At Ulster, the page is called 'Student Employability Journey' (University of Ulster nd) and at Lancaster it is 'My Starting Point' (Lancaster University nd).The common message is that all starting points are fine and that the service will meet the student where they are. The example text and graphic shown in Figure 25.3 are reproduced with the permission of the University of Exeter.

> At the Career Zone, we want to help you with your career planning, whatever stage you are at. Whether it's a case of not knowing the sector you're interested in yet or the options that your degree offers you. Or perhaps you are very clear on your chosen career, want to skip those early stages and get help with your applications, this Career Planning section of our website should help you.
>
> At registration every year, every new or continuing student must indicate their current level of career planning by picking one of ten statements. The Career Zone aims to equip students to 'Decide', 'Plan' and 'Compete' for opportunities and follow your chosen graduate career path.
>
> This 'Careers Registration' helps us to define the support you need at your stage of career planning. (University of Exeter, n.d.)

Targeting Resources

'The introduction of Careers Registration in a growing number of HE institutions provides an unparalleled opportunity to gain an evidence-based insight into the career development needs of current students and to prioritise and target support accordingly' (Winter, 2019). Evidence-based targeting of finite resources to where they will make the most difference has been frequently cited by careers service leaders as one of the most important ways in which the data informs strategy and operations. This is linked to the point about transforming conversations with academic units, through improved, shared understanding of

Figure 25.3 University of Exeter Career Zone: Careers Registration graphic

the career-development needs of current students. This shared understanding is particularly valuable as careers and employability programmes are increasingly aligned to and take place within academic units.

This has been particularly true in tackling the persistent misconception that student needs and careers service expertise are primarily related to tactical approaches to recruitment and selection (i.e. ‘checking CVs’). This misconception has existed for a long time and is often reinforced in day-to-day discourse and implicit expectations. Resource-intensive careers programmes based entirely on recruitment and selection might be seen as logical because they were assumed to reflect the predominant student need and the core expertise/added value offered by the careers service.

Support with applications is of course a valuable offer for the right students at the right time and should always be part of the mix of careers and employability support. However, career-readiness data (as in Figure 25.1) consistently challenges the idea that support with applications is the dominant student careers support needed. Multi-institutional data from the Careers Registration Learning Gain project showed that the Decide phase accounts for the largest group of students in all three years of undergraduate degree programmes. At the beginning of the final year, the proportion in the Decide phase is typically over 40%, whilst the Compete phase (the group for whom application support would be the most relevant) accounts for around 20% (Gilworth and Cobb, 2017).

The use of data to re-frame the discussion of student needs and the attendant distribution of scarce resources and application of professional expertise has been a common feature of feedback from careers services. These conversations may involve challenging long-established orthodoxy and the assumptions of senior and powerful colleagues, but the feedback suggest that careers professionals may feel more empowered in these situations by the availability of comprehensive data coming directly from students.

The Importance of Career Choice and Career Planning

The findings from the Learning Gain project showed remarkable consistency across a wide variety of institutions and a very large student dataset in relation to the distribution of students across the main career-readiness categories, with the scale of the Decide group highlighting the importance of support with career choice and career planning as the largest area of student need. During the project, the 'Planning for Success' Report (Shury et al., 2017), was published by the Department for Education. This study of around 7,000 graduates two and a half years after graduation looked at the links between behaviours whilst at university and graduate success as determined by being in a graduate-level destination at the time of the survey. One of its key findings was this: 'Among graduates who were in employment, knowing exactly what they wanted to do or having a good idea about types of jobs and careers upon completing university was the most important factor or behaviour in determining whether that employment was in professional or managerial roles or in non-professional roles' (Shury et al., 2017). So, this report was highlighting the importance of career choice and career planning to the key metric of graduate-level employment for recent graduates at the same time as the Careers Registration Learning Gain project was highlighting the importance of career choice and career planning for current students. This was further reinforced as some members of the Learning Gain project consortium were also conducting studies comparing career readiness at the beginning of the final year of undergraduate study with the DLHE outcomes for the same cohort, which demonstrated associations between advanced career thinking and positive DLHE outcomes (Cobb, 2019).

Using Occupational Sector Data in Employer Engagement

Data from this section of Careers Registration found an immediate use in (pre-pandemic) discussions with employers about on-campus engagement. Employer Engagement teams have commented on the employer-attraction value of having data that could demonstrate a high level of declared student interest in the relevant sector. The team at King's College London was amongst the first to use the data in this way. In addition to employer attraction, they also used the data to shape on-campus employer programmes and events to fit declared student aspirations. The largely any-discipline nature of UK graduate labour markets plays a part here. In this context and with some obvious exceptions, data representing students' declared interest at scale can be a more powerful indicator of potential talent supply than subject of undergraduate study.

Examples also started to emerge that showed the value of understanding the distribution of students' occupational interests in the light of knowledge of graduate labour markets. For example, data showing a very narrow range of directly subject-related occupational interests across all three years of a degree programme may be entirely understandable where young students have chosen the subject mainly on the basis of extending successful high-school study. However, this could represent missed opportunity in a largely any-discipline graduate market and particularly so if directly subject-related jobs are scarce. In these circumstances, it is particularly important that in addition to students knowing about 'careers in' their subject area, they are helped to understand the (typically broader) range of 'careers for' students of their subject. Data on occupational interests can help to determine the extent to which there may need to be interventions around opportunity awareness in order to broaden horizons and increase opportunities.

Equality, Diversity and Inclusion

The high-level, snapshot nature of Careers Registration data cannot provide qualitative insight into barriers to engagement for disadvantaged groups, but it can be used to point to where issues exist when it is combined with data from elsewhere in the student record system. This can prompt further analysis and action. This capability is highly valued by careers service colleagues. For example, data from the experience element of Careers Registration can be used to track the acquisition of employability assets and map this on to protected characteristics to ascertain any differences in take-up of employability-enhancing opportunities and prompt action to understand and remove barriers to participation. The proportions of students from different groups in the various stages of career thinking can be analysed. This was a feature of the findings from the Learning Gain project (Cobb, 2019). Combining the career readiness, demographic and outcomes data can highlight consistencies and differences between leading indicators and outcomes. It can only be one part of the picture, but when combined with other data, Careers Registration data can play a part in addressing issues of equality, diversity and inclusion and social mobility.

Challenges

The conversations about the implementation of Careers Registration have been overwhelmingly positive, but it would be disingenuous not to acknowledge challenges. Careers Registration is a self-report process with all the potential issues that implies (Cobb, 2019). Set against that is the level of reliability suggested by the consistency of the results from the Learning Gain project across a wide variety of institutions and a very large number of students. Closing the loop at the point of graduation has been a frequently discussed challenge.

In UK universities, there is no systemic equivalent to enrolment at the point of graduation, so the Careers Registration process cannot be directly replicated at that point. A great deal of thought and energy has gone into tackling this problem and some institutions have reported notable success. It will be interesting to understand more about how this has developed and what the impact of the COVID pandemic has been, as some successful solutions have involved face-to-face data gathering. Enrolment typically happens once per year and many colleagues have been keen to find ways to update students' career-readiness status in real time during the academic year. There has been progress on this front and, in some cases, this has involved imaginative use of careers service management systems (CSMS). This would be an interesting topic for further research.

The need for the full range of staff in higher education careers services to engage with big data in day-to-day work is a relatively recent phenomenon (Cobb, 2019; Winter, 2019). This has brought opportunities and challenges. Some challenges are related to staff capacity for data analysis and presentation. Where there has been investment, this has been dealt with through the addition of new data-related posts. In some cases, roles have been re-configured to incorporate data handling and/or interested staff have volunteered and engaged in skills acquisition. It is quite common for Careers Registration data analysis to rely on central planning teams. This can work very well, but in some cases, those teams may be under resource pressure themselves, with an imperative to focus on statutory returns and external metrics. Lack of in-team data handling capacity and/or priority access to capacity elsewhere can be an inhibitor to careers services' ability to do as much as they would like to do with Careers Registration data. Careers service staff may need time and development to become comfortable and confident in interpreting and presenting the data to stakeholders (Winter, 2019). The arrival of a large volume of new data, however welcome it may be, is by no means the whole story in translating the existence of the data into impact on careers and employability practice on the ground.

SOME EARLY-STAGE EXAMPLES OF THE ADOPTION OF CAREERS REGISTRATION OUTSIDE THE UK

The following examples are of recent implementation of Careers Registration. They are necessarily brief illustrations.

Ireland

University College Dublin (UCD) was the first university in the Republic of Ireland to adopt Careers Registration. In conversation with the author, the Director of UCD Careers Network, Dr David Foster, explained the rationale for adopting Careers Registration: 'In looking for ways to reach further into the student cohort, Careers Network explored the utility of Career Registration in this regard' (Foster, 2021). He went on to explain that the introduction of Careers Registration had the benefit of directly addressing a key action in the UCD (n.d.: 15) Career Development and Employability Strategy (2015–25): '3.2 Utlilise targeted approaches to data analysis and conduct institutional research using longitudinal graduate data to inform strategic planning of career provision, both centrally and within Schools and units across the university'.

Foster suggests that 'using data to inform service delivery, when coupled with large scale evaluations of services and interventions is proving to be a robust approach to the planning, delivering and evaluating career development and employability at University College Dublin' (Foster, 2021).

UCD has adopted 'No Plan, Some Plan, Clear Plan' as its descriptors for the career-readiness stages. The student landing page of the Careers Network website is configured to reflect this in a similar way to several UK institutions, including the Exeter example quoted earlier. (UCD n.d.)

Portugal

The adoption of the Careers Registration approach by the University of Minho in Braga, Portugal, was the first example of Careers Registration being translated into another language.

The initiative was not driven by a careers service. It was driven by a group of academics, led by a Pro-Rector and constituted as 'ObservatoriUM', The Observatory of Academic Paths of Students of the University of Minho, which has amongst its main objectives: 'to analyze the impact of personal, academic and contextual variables on students' trajectories, appreciating their impact on academic success, permanence, satisfaction with courses and with the institution, and employability skills' (University of Minho, n.d.). The author is a member of the ObservatoriUM External Advisory Board.

The university implemented Careers Registration in September 2020 and shared its first set of findings across its academic community and Student Union leadership in November of that year. The data was subject to robust statistical analysis from the outset, meaning that important correlations could be included immediately in the initial report. An example would be that the report showed that

> career readiness and the number of extracurricular activities [the Minho terminology for the second part of Careers Registration] performed by students are interrelated at a statistically significant level [...] Students in the 'to Plan' phase have carried out more activities than students in the 'Explore and Decide' phase. Students in the 'Compete' phase have carried out more activities than students in the 'Plan' phase. Finally, students in the 'Sorted' phase have done more activities than the students in the 'To Compete' phase. (University of Minho, 2020)

Colleagues at Minho need to find ways to address the issues raised by the data in a resource environment that is different to the UK, Ireland, Australia and New Zealand, all of which have higher education careers service structures that are similar to each other.

Australia

Careers Registration was the subject of a symposium organised by the National Association of Careers Advisory Services (NAGCAS) and Curtin University, and led by the author, in 2019 (NAGCAS, 2019). There was much enthusiasm for the introduction of the approach, but the COVID pandemic meant that some plans had to be put on hold.

The University of Melbourne has implemented the approach, using the title 'career census'. The university uses the descriptors 'Discover, Focus, Apply and Sorted' (University of Melbourne,nd). The career-planning landing page 'How Career Ready are you?' (University of Melbourne nd) seeks to engage students with the process and the stages in a similar fashion to the Exeter and UCD examples mentioned earlier. The site reiterates for students some of the key principles described earlier in the chapter. 'When you know where you are, it's easier to plan where you're going' (University of Melbourne, nd). There is some particularly useful and reassuring language that reinforces the idea that all starting points are OK, the Careers Service will meet you where you are and that careers-readiness phases and other labels like year of study may not necessarily align and that's fine:

> There is no right or wrong phase and you may find the phases don't align to your course year level, so don't expect that just because you are in first year you will be at the Discover phase. Also, don't worry if your friends are at different phases to you – you need to develop at your own pace. (University of Melbourne, nd)

The sector body Graduate Careers Australia (GCA) is a key player in the introduction of Careers Registration in Australia. GCA has recently won a grant from the federal government to run a pilot project that is closely aligned to the Careers Registration Learning Gain project in the UK. (Australian Government, Department of Education, Skills and Employment 2020). At the time of writing, GCA is building the consortium.

New Zealand

The University of Otago is the first university in New Zealand to implement Careers Registration and has its first set of data. Otago is another university to use the structure as the way into its career-planning landing page for students, using the 'Discover, Focus, Action' descriptors.

Jackie Dean, the Head of the Careers Service, describes the implementation as follows:

> The University of Otago in New Zealand introduced Career Registration starting with their 2021 enrolments. Career Registration has given us, for the first time, an insight into the career readiness of all of our students including those who do not currently access our Career Development services. With the results of the Careers Registration survey, combined with a comprehensive database of online resources, we are now able to tailor and target resource and next step suggestions to all students. Going forward we hope to be able to work with

> Otago academic staff to identify the trends amongst their cohorts of students, and to identify the most effective interventions which can be made to result in learning gain in terms of careers and employability.Dean (2021)

The link to online resources is important. The COVID pandemic and the resulting need to move services online has accelerated a trend towards the use of digital resources by higher education careers services. Linking these directly to students' input on their own career-readiness status can be seen as an important aspect of meeting all students where they are on their career journeys.

CONCLUDING THOUGHTS, LINKS TO MODELS OF CAREER DEVELOPMENT AND POTENTIAL FOR FURTHER RESEARCH

This chapter has provided an overview of the development and adoption of Careers Registration as a practical innovation. It has also shared insights from a large community of practice into the impact to date of the addition of data on career readiness and the acquisition of employability assets in institutional careers and employability discourse, planning and action.

This account is descriptive of the data, rather than analytical. The UK Learning Gain project outputs have provided some data analysis. There will be more analytical work to come in future, from within individual institutions and across consortia where anonymised data sharing is practical, as it was in the Learning Gain project. The GCA project in Australia promises to be another interesting example. In the UK, the creation of a Data Insights Strategy Group as part of the AGCAS structure is likely to facilitate further opportunities for practitioner research.

Already emerging from practice in all the countries where Careers Registration is in place are the different ways in which institutions are constructing and presenting the career journey. Some have stuck with the original Decide, Plan, Compete model and use this as a practical vehicle for sharing the journey idea with students, as in the Exeter example quoted earlier. Others have adopted variations on the theme, such as Explore, Focus, Action, originally chosen by King's College, London, and adopted elsewhere. Others have worked on more sophisticated models to reflect the essentially iterative nature of career development. The development of Careers Registration-based models and their relationship with existing career development models and theories is an interesting area for future research.

For the moment, it may be useful to consider the existing connections between Careers Registration and established models of career development. This may go some way to explaining its resonance with and rapid adoption by a community of practitioners with some shared conceptual framing of careers and employability, arising from the theoretical bases of their professional training.

The Careers Registration approach was a practical innovation. However, it was led by qualified careers guidance professionals who, by virtue of their training, share understanding of career development theory. It is not difficult to see the implicit connection to theoretical models, notably the Law and Watts (1977, 2003) DOTS model. Careers guidance practitioners would tend to see career development as an iterative, rather than linear, process for many people, but at the same time, many see 'SODT' as a more logical arrangement, *beginning* with developing understanding of Self in terms of interests, skills, motivations and values, and continuing through the acquisition of knowledge of Opportunities, the synthesising of these into informed choices or Decisions, and learning to navigate the entry routes, gatekeeping mechanisms, personal opportunities and challenges that facilitate Transition into the desired career area.

The original 'Decide, Plan, Compete' concept underlying Careers Registration can be connected to the SODT model. The Decide component relates to developing understanding of Self, of Opportunities, and the beginnings of Decision learning. The Plan phase relates to further development of opportunity awareness, reflection on self-awareness in the light of experience and networks and confirming or revising decisions. The Compete phase is primarily about the execution of informed choices and translation of those choices into successful transitions. This hypothesis has not yet been researched, but it is possible that the speed and scale of the adoption of Careers Registration may be connected to the tacit, perhaps even unconscious, link to the DOTS/SODT model, which is so familiar to careers guidance professionals.

At the time of the original development of Careers Registration, much of the related policy and strategy discourse in and around higher education in the UK was of 'Employability' rather than 'Careers'. This was reflected in organisational change first commented upon by Watts and Butcher (2008), in which a distinction was drawn between 'non-extended' and 'extended' careers services. The non-extended service was the traditional, arguably reactive, professional services based on the provision of individual careers guidance, careers information and opportunities to interact with employers. The extended service, on the other hand, was developing to incorporate other activities, particularly the management of work experience but also volunteering or enterprise, and was much more outward facing and crucially much more strongly connected to academic units and the curriculum. This typology was subsequently updated by the author (Gilworth, 2019) to cover non-extended central service (much the same as the Watts and Butcher definition but by this time very rare in the sector), extended central service (again similar to the Watts and Butcher description but now much more common), extended and institutionally embedded service (extended services with a wide range of provision and very strong 'business-partner' relationships with academic units – probably the most common type now) and Integrated, whole-institution service (services with central and distributed provision with permanent physical presence in academic units, all of which are centrally managed).

Probably the most notable examples in the UK are the 'hub and spoke' models at the Universities of Birmingham and Nottingham. The general direction of travel for the organisation of the institutional employability effort, at least in the UK, has been towards the latter two categories for the last 10 years or so.

In a study of organisational responses to the employability agenda in English universities (Gilworth, 2019), the author explained that organisational change in some of the case studies was driven by institutional perceptions of the 'old' non-extended services as being unfit for purpose in terms of reach and scalability in order to help the institution to meet the demands of the increasingly important employability agenda. This was reflective of a broader pattern at the time. New extended 'employability' provision replaced or was built out from the old 'careers' provision. Service titles frequently changed to add employability to careers, though dropping careers altogether has been relatively rare. In two of the author's case studies, students were canvassed to ask their opinion on names for the new provision' and in both cases, they advised against the use of the term employability and expressed a preference for careers.

Against this background, the Careers Registration approach was framed in terms of a journey, where employability and careers are linked concepts understood as the 'map' and the 'luggage'. Career is the personal, potentially iterative definition of purpose and direction (the map), and 'employability' reflects the relatively linear acquisition of employability assets, such as knowledge, experience and networks (the luggage), which are taken out on the journey to satisfy the gatekeepers of opportunity and provide the basis for ongoing maintenance of employment and career success. The personal definition of career purpose translates the acquisition of assets into meaningful outcomes for the student, the institution, employers and society (Gilworth, 2021).

The link between the development of specific or generic competencies that make people 'employable' and the context of individual choices about where to apply those competencies is common to some theoretical models that are well known and widely applied by careers professionals in higher education. Knight and Yorke (2002) define employability as 'a set of achievements, skills, understandings and personal attributes that makes graduates more likely to gain employment and be successful in their chosen occupations, which benefits themselves, the work force, the community and the economy'. Dacre Pool and Sewell (2007) describe 'a set of skills, knowledge, understanding and personal attributes that make a person more likely to choose and secure occupations in which they can be satisfied and successful'.

The definition of employability that was applied to the Careers Registration Learning Gain research project was 'the capability to make well informed, realistic plans for the future and to be able to execute these in a changing world' (Cobb, 2019).

Careers Registration was intended to generate data that could be used to generate insights into both 'career' and 'employability'. The argument is that both bases need to be covered. An institutional employability strategy needs to be a careers and employability strategy in order to be effective. Careers Registration was conceived in the development and execution of institutional strategy in an environment in which graduate career success was already significant and has become more so since then. The relevance of institutional strategy and management should not be overlooked in future consideration of links to theory. Examples might include the use of data-informed insight as a resource in the alignment of environment (the external forces at work and the context in which we must operate), values (who we are and how we do things around here) and resources (those assets that we can deploy in pursuit of our strategy): E-V-R (Thompson and Martin, 2005). The use of data-informed insight to direct resources to where they will make the most difference, particularly where that has resulted in realignment from practices based on assumption and habit, is a practical illustration of this in the story of Careers Registration to date.

Through the national Learning Gain project and subsequently in various individual institutions feeding back through the community of practice, there has been a constant message about the strong association between advanced career thinking, usually referred to as career readiness, as reported through Careers Registration at the beginning of the final year of undergraduate study and graduate level outcomes as measured by the Graduate Outcomes survey in the UK. Given the emphasis on graduate outcomes in positional/status competition between institutions in marketised higher education sectors and increasingly in sector regulation (certainly in England), it is no surprise to find that attention within institutions is drawn to this element of Careers Registration as a leading indicator for a crucial performance metric.

A particularly interesting theme for future research may be around the potential for Careers Registration as an approach and through the data it generates to be aligned to the increasingly important discourse around the role of capitals in graduate employability (Tomlinson, 2017; Cai and Tomlinson, 2022).

Much of the discussion of the application of capitals to graduate employability draws attention to the tension between and importance of both structure and agency (Burke and Hannaford-Simpson, 2019). These are familiar ideas to careers professionals, both through this recent work and earlier work such as Hodkinson and Sparkes (1997). These issues and the concepts of capital – notably, social and cultural capital – are significant elements of the operating environment of the higher education careers service, through policy and strategic imperatives and professional motivation, to ensure that students from all backgrounds are not just 'getting in' to higher education but also 'getting on' to fulfilling graduate careers.

Michael Tomlinson's work on forms of graduate capital has already been shown to link to practice through the validation of the graduate capital scale (Tomlinson et al., 2021) and its connection to the work of the Careers and Employability service at the University of Southampton. As work on capitals informs practitioners about the nature of capitals which students may acquire and develop, perhaps there may be opportunities to use the coverage of the Careers Registration approach to look at engagement with and the impact of, efforts to support such development at the cohort level.

The brief accounts in this chapter of the impact of Careers Registration on practice could be seen as the beginnings of attempts to consider the question 'how do institutions construct and implement their careers and employability strategies now that they have all this data that they didn't have before?' Plans are now in place for an international collaborative project to look at this more closely.

ACKNOWLEDGEMENTS

I would like to thank Paul Blackmore (University of Exeter), David Foster (UCD), Megan Dench (University of Melbourne), Maria do Ceu Taveira and Manuel Joao Costa (University of Minho) and Jackie Dean (University of Otago) for agreeing to my using specific examples from their universities, and Jodika Gilworth for her support with format and graphics.

REFERENCES

Agarwal, N. (2020) *Don't Mistake Graduate Outcomes for DLHE. HESA*. Available online at https://www.hesa.ac.uk/blog/11-06-2020/dont-mistake-graduate-outcomes-dlhe

Australian Government, Department of Education, Skills and Employment (2020) *National Careers Institute Partnership Program Round One Projects Announced!*. Available online at: www.dese.gov.au/newsroom/articles/national-careers-institute-partnership-grants-program-round-one-projects-announced

Burke, C. and Hannaford-Simpson, S. (2019) 'Investing in Your Future': The Role of Capitals in Graduate Employment Pathways. In Burke, C. and Christie, F. (eds), *Graduate Careers in Context*. London: Routledge, pp. 17–28.

Cai, Y. and Tomlinson, M. (2022) A Renewed Analytical Framework for Understanding Employers' Perceptions of Graduate Employability: Integration of Capital and Institutionalist Perspectives. In Broadley, T., Cai, Y., Firth, M., Hunt, E. and Neugebauer, J. (eds), *SAGE Handbook of Graduate Employability*. Sage.

Cobb, F. (2019) 'There's no going back': The transformation of HE careers services using big data. *Journal of the National Institute for Career Education and Counselling*, Vol. 42, No. 1, pp. 18–25.

Cobb, F., Gilworth, R. and Winter, D. (2019) *The Careers Registration Practical Guide*. Careers Group, University of London. Available online at: https://london.ac.uk/the-careers-group/careers-registration

Dacre Pool, L. and Sewell, P. (2007) The key to employability: Developing a practical model of graduate employability. *Education + Training*, Vol. 49, No. 4, pp. 277–289.

Dean, J. (2021) *The introduction of Careers Registration at the University of Otago in conversation with the author*.

Foster, D. (2021) *The introduction of Careers Registration at UCD, in conversation with the author.*

Gilworth, R. (2019) Organisational Responses to the Employability Agenda in English Universities. In Burke, C. and Christie, F. (eds), *Graduate Careers in Context*. London: Routledge, pp. 127–139.

Gilworth, R. (2021) *Careers Registration: Starting Points and Journeys. Ed Space, University of Huddersfield.* Available online at: http://blogs.hud.ac.uk/hudcres/20-21/feb/careers-registration/

Gilworth, R. and Cobb, F. (2017) *Where are you right now? Using careers registration to support employability in higher education. HEA conference presentation.* Available online at: www.advance-he.ac.uk/knowledge-hub/where-are-you-right-now-using-careers-registration-support-employability-higher

Gilworth, R. and Thambar, N. (2013) *Careers Registration: A data revolution. AGCAS Conference presentation.* Available online at: www.agcas.org.uk/events/766-Biennial-Conference-2013-Exeter

Hewitt, R. (2020) *Getting On: Graduate Employment and its Influence on UK Higher Education*. Oxford: HEPI.

Hodkinson, P. and Sparkes, A. (1997) Careership: A sociological theory of career decision making. *British Journal of Sociology of Education*, Vol. 18, No. 1, pp. 29–44.

Institute of Student Employers (ISE) (2020) *Student Recruitment Survey* 2020. Available online at: https://ise.org.uk/

Knight, P.T. and Yorke, M. (2002) Employability through the curriculum. *Tertiary Education and Management*, Vol. 8, pp. 261–276.

Lancaster University Careers. *My starting Point.* Available online at: www.lancaster.ac.uk/careers/students/starting-point/

Law, B. and Watts, A. G. (1977) *Schools, Careers and Community: A Study of Some Approaches to Careers Education in Schools*. London: Church Information Office (pp. 8–10).

Law, B. and Watts, A. G. (2003) *The DOTS Analysis: Original version.* Available online at: http://hihohiho.com/memory/cafdots.pdf

Maynard, R. and Kingston, B. (2007) Statistics in Butler. In Butler, T. and Dane, M. (eds), *Reflection on Change*. Sheffield: AGCAS pp. 202–209.

NAGCAS (2019) *Careers Registration Forum outline.* Available online at: www.nagcas.org.au/events/event/career-registration-forum

Shury, J., Vivian, D., Turner, C. and Downing, C. (2017) *Planning for success: Graduates' career planning and its effect on graduate outcomes. Department for Education.* Available online at: https://assets.publishing.service.gov.uk/government/uploads/system/uploads/attachment_data/file/604170/Graduates__career_planning_and_its_effect_on_their_outcomes.pdf

Thambar, N. (2016) 'I'm just a plain old careers adviser': Recognising the hidden expert. *Journal of the National Institute for Career Education and Counselling*, Vol. 37, pp. 26–32.

Thompson, J. and Martin, F. (2005) *Strategic Management Awareness and Change*. Andover. South Western.

Tomlinson, M. (2017) Forms of graduate capital and their relationship to graduate employability. *Education & Training*, Vol. 59, No. 4, pp. 338–352.

Tomlinson, M., McCafferty, H., Port, A., Maguire, N., Zebelski, A., Butnaru, A., Charles, M. and Kirby, S. (2021) Developing graduate employability for a challenging labour market. *Journal of Applied Research in Higher Education*, Vol. 14, No. 3, pp. 1193–1209.

Ulster University (n.d.) *Student Employability Journey.* Available online at https://www.ulster.ac.uk/employability/journey

University College Dublin (UCD) (n.d.) *Career Development and Employability Strategy 2015-2025.* Available online at: www.ucd.ie/careers/aboutus/

University College Dublin. *UCD Careers Network Students landing page.* Available online at: www.ucd.ie/careers/students/

University of Exeter (n.d.). *Career Zone homepage.* Available online at: www.exeter.ac.uk/careers/

University of Leeds. *Careers Centre website, Career Planning section.* Available online at: https://careerweb.leeds.ac.uk/info/13/career_planning

University of Melbourne (nd) *How career-ready are you?* Available online at: https://students.unimelb.edu.au/careers/get-career-ready/how-career-ready-are-you

University of Minho (n.d.) ObsevatoriUm overview *ObservatoriUM* available online at (uminho.pt)

University of Minho (2020) *ObservatoriUM-Career Readiness of UMinho Students.* Internal report.

(n.d.) *How Career Ready are you?* Available online at https://students.unimelb.edu.au/careers/get-career-ready/how-career-ready-are-youUniversity of Otago (n.d.). Career Development Centre home page. Available online at: www.otago.ac.nz/careers/index.html

Watts, A.G. and Butcher, V. (2008). *Break-out or Break-up? Implications of Institutional Employability Strategies for the Role and Structure of University Careers Services.* http://www.hecsu.ac.uk/assets/assets/documents/PROP

Winter, D. (2019) The Rise of the Practitioner-Researcher. In Burke, C. and Christie, F. (eds), *Graduate Careers in Context.* London: Routledge.

PART V

Policymakers' and Employers' Perspectives on the Practice of Graduate Employability

BACKGROUND AND CONTEXT

This section introduces the reader to the importance of understanding the context of graduate employability from the perspective of employers, policymakers and stakeholders within regional and national settings.

The authors within this section draw upon the extensive employability literature, but through their contributions they challenge some of this thinking using a range of research methodologies, such as action research, policy analysis, conceptual research and case studies, which provide a rich investigation into the role that governments and employers play in developing human capital relevant to the labour market. The section draws upon findings from Europe, China, the UK and South Africa, demonstrating a wide range of interpretations of policymaking and different organisations.

Whilst each author takes a different approach, or lens, what brings this section together is the understanding either explicitly or implicitly of the resources that are valued by employers. Policymaking in the field of skills and graduate employability is acknowledged as fast moving with local interpretations necessary to fit the needs of the country or region or employer. As a result, this chapter builds on previous frameworks, offering new and current solutions for analysis from an academic perspective, and it offers case study examples as practical contributions to the dilemma of policy implementation.

A Renewed Analytical Framework for Understanding Employers' Perceptions of Graduate Employability: Integration of Capital and Institutionalist Perspectives, **Yuzhuo Cai and Michael Tomlinson**

Cai and Tomlinson introduce this section by considering the value of graduates by employers through their development of an analytical framework that considers how employers might perceive their role and understanding of the attributes a graduate might bring to a role. Challenging perceptions of a one-way street from education to employment, Cai and Tomlinson suggest that employers can be gate-keepers of this transition and, subsequently, this can emerge as a much promoted view of the mismatch between employer needs and graduate skills. As with other authors, Cai and Tomlinson critically examines both human capital theory and signalling theory, with both seen by policymakers as providing a useful and measurable output, which in turn is seen as a key indicator of success of a higher education experience. The importance of this chapter is to consider how the process of education and employment can be better facilitated to aid understanding between higher education institutions and employers through a novel lens integrating the perspectives of institutional theory and employability capital.

Higher Education Institution (HEI) Considerations to Support the Creation of Alliances with Small and Medium-sized Enterprises (SMEs), **Katie McAllister**

McAllister develops the theme of employer contributions to employability with specific reference to small and medium-sized enterprises (SMEs) and how a higher education institution (HEI) can leverage this local employment base to their collective and mutual benefit. In this chapter, McAllister attempts to balance the literature based on large corporate organisations with those who are small or medium-sized employers by building partnerships and allegiances through a case study in Peterborough, UK. Peterborough University College embraces its role as a facilitator of multiple partners to improve the region's problems of multiple deprivation and significant skills shortages despite being in a county that also hosts one of the UK's most esteemed HEIs – Cambridge University. McAllister shares a theoretical concept that builds HEI–SME alliances with a shared vision and joint strategy to overcome barriers and to resolve the issues linked to short-term policymaking.

A Living Agenda: The Role of Local Policy in Employability, **Catherine O'Connor**

In developing the theme of regional implementation, O'Connor uses action research from a student's perspective to understand local policymaking and implementation. The case study in Leeds, UK, takes the specific skills gap of digital skills across the local labour market and how they will be addressed from national to local policymaking. In doing so, O'Connor utilises three themes: definitions of graduate employability, details of behaviours and skills and the processes that students go through with notions of human capital. It is interesting to note how O'Connor, in gaining the students' perspective by using the traditional four stages of action research – Plan, Act, Observe and Reflect – suggests how a student can build employer relationships and develop their own ideas on individual graduate identity beyond the standard notion of graduate attributes.

The Role of Dual Education in Graduate Employability: The Comparison between Europe and South Africa, **David F. J. Campbell, Attila Pausits and Seamus Needham**

To develop policy into implementation with regional differences, this interesting case study from Campbell et al. looks at how dual education was interpreted in a project funded by Erasmus (a European fund). Dual education is defined in this chapter as having the ability to switch from academic study to vocational training within the study period, thus enabling greater transition into the world of work. This differs slightly and is explained in the case study from work-integrated learning and cooperative education. The study demonstrates how knowledge economies can develop into knowledge democracies through inter-country support and shared activities. The study suggests a platform for students to work together in teams to develop key competencies as a 'T'-shaped employee having both specialist and generalist skills. The important contribution of this chapter is the multi-national agreement to develop dual education through a collaborative funding initiative with the employer/vocational element key to its success.

All on the Same Page: The Impact and Importance of Professional Associations for Graduate Employability, **Vianna Renaud and Stéphanie Devèze**

Finally, in this section, Renaud and Delaunay introduce the concept of the role that employer associations or professional associations have in supporting graduate employability. Set within the context of a challenging environment for many higher education institutions to continue to support professional service career development staff, this chapter argues that the role professional associations have is more important than ever before. This chapter uses an extensive survey designed to elicit the views of students, employers, alumni, academics and other stakeholders in the role of professional associations. The outcomes demonstrate the impact on student experience and better communication between the various stakeholders and academic staff. It is proposed that this is particularly relevant to vocational and creative fields of practice in both the UK and France.

The five chapters all interrogate the need for a greater understanding of the perceived mismatch between the rhetoric of being 'employment ready' as the responsibility of educators only and the seemingly benign ability of employers to not play into the policy arena in order to understand the future employment needs. The authors in this section identify the need for the relationship to be built and the need to understand the multiple interpretations of government policy nationally and regionally so that the value and purpose of higher education is shared for the benefit of graduates.

26

A Renewed Analytical Framework for Understanding Employers' Perceptions of Graduate Employability: Integration of Capital and Institutionalist Perspectives

Yuzhuo Cai and Michael Tomlinson

INTRODUCTION

The literature on graduate employability has paid increasing attention to the importance of employers in gate-keeping graduates' transition to labour markets (e.g. Behle, 2020; Cai, 2012; Tomlinson and Anderson, 2021). As such, one major theme in graduate employability studies is concerned with 'the (mis)match between university graduates' competencies and employers' needs' (Abelha et al., 2020: 1). The focus on competency or skill match is often underlined by either human capital theory (Becker, 1964; Schultz, 1961) or signalling theory (Arrow, 1973; Spence, 1973; Stiglitz, 1975). Both theories presume positive relations between educational attainment and labour market outcomes but with different underlying mechanisms about the effect of education on employment (Cai, 2013). According to human capital theory, education – particularly the competencies and skills developed through education – increases individuals' productivity and therefore enhances their job performance. This proposes that employers are able to make a rational evaluation of graduates' and job-seekers' ability and consequently recruit those whose skills match the employers' needs. An alternative core idea has been developed by job signalling theory, which states that, in reality, employers often do not have perfect knowledge about the graduates' competencies. In response to asymmetries of information between employers and job-seekers, employers use educational credentials as a proxy of quality or ability. Both human capital and signalling understandings of education's role in allocating individuals in the labour market are based on a substantialist approach, where educational output is seen as a measurable or identifiable substance.

Such a substantialist approach was criticised by Bailly (2008), who argues that educational outcome, instead of being a substance that can be identified objectively (e.g. in the forms of abilities or signals), is susceptible to multiple interpretations – most importantly, employers' beliefs. In his conceptualisation, employers' beliefs are developed through a trial-and-error process. Such a perspective has a particular emphasis on individuals' cognitive frameworks and this corroborates social and cognitive psychologists' arguments that individuals use schemas, frames or belief systems to select and process information (Simon, 1957). However, Bailly (2008) has not taken into account the dynamics of social norms when elaborating on the process of developing employers' beliefs. The social norms are central in institutional theory (DiMaggio and Powell, 1983; Meyer and Rowan, 1977), which deals with interactions between human actions and institutions. By equipping Bailly's (2008) model with a theoretical engine of institutionalism, Cai (2013) developed a conceptual framework for understanding what employers conceive as the value of graduates with similar education backgrounds in the workplace. The framework was applied and verified in Cai's (2012) empirical investigation of the employment prospects of Finnish-educated Chinese graduates in Finnish companies operating in China. The framework has not only been proved useful by the empirical investigation but is arguably applicable in studies of other contexts due to its generic characteristics.

While Cai's (2013) framework helps us understand how employers in a given labour market develop and institutionalise their beliefs on the value of graduates with similar educational credentials, we argue that there are two areas for improvement in the framework. First, as the value of graduates can be seen from broad and diverse perspectives, to make the framework more operational in empirical analysis, a simple and proper lens to observe the value of graduates is expected to be provided. Second, as in the process of formulation of employers' beliefs of the value of graduates, employers are important but not the only actors, and so the framework can embrace the roles of other actors, particularly graduates, in the processes.

We also find the employability framework developed by Tomlinson (2017) can shed useful light to supplement Cai's (2013) framework in both aspects. On the one hand, the forms of graduate capital offer a simplified categorisation of the value of graduates in the eyes of employers. On the other hand, the notion of graduate capital treats graduates as central actors in increasing their value in labour markets.

Thus, this chapter aims to enhance Cai's (2013) framework for understanding employers' perceptions of graduate employability by incorporating Tomlinson's (2017) concept of employability capital. In so doing, it also helps further theorise employability capital by distinguishing the capital acquired by graduates and employers' institutionalised beliefs on the value of graduate capital. In between lies a process of signalling and feedback exchanges between employees (graduates) and employers (as two-way interactions): while graduates try to demonstrate the value of their employability capitals to prospective employers, employers try to discern the value of the capitals and how these might translate into future workplace performance and related outcomes. Moreover, how the value is enacted depends on the outcomes of a process of institutionalisation whereby the resources individuals carry through into a given employment field are framed by both a range of internal institutional dynamics (including cultural values, embedded beliefs and expectations, organisational orientation and goals) and exogenous factors that sit outside the immediate field (sector influences, immediate economic ecosystems, external organisation relations, to name a few). It becomes crucial that the resources individuals draw upon in the form of capital are recognised as helping maintain dominant institutional orders in ways that confirm incumbent members' expectations and demands.

THE RATIONALE OF INTEGRATING TWO INFLUENTIAL ANALYTICAL FRAMEWORKS OF GRADUATE EMPLOYABILITY

Our efforts to integrate the frameworks developed by Cai (2013) and Tomlinson (2017) can be justified by the compatibility between institutional theory and capital concepts (Friedland, 2009), which are the theoretical foundations of the two frameworks, respectively. Cai's (2013) framework is heavily based on new institutional theory. Tomlinson (2017) developed his framework of graduate capitals with reference to Bourdieu's conceptualisation of capitals, though not strictly following Bourdieu's forms of capital. Before discussing how institutional theory and Bourdieu's capital theory can supplement each other in their applications in graduate employability research, we first briefly present the core insights of the two theories that underline both the conceptual frameworks of Cai (2013) and Tomlinson (2017).

The new institutional theory stresses the dependency of both individual and organisational actors' actions on institutions, such as wider environmental contexts, rules and norms (Meyer et al., 2007). The central concepts in new institutional theory are organisational field and institutionalisation. An organisational field is defined as 'those organisations that, in the aggregate, constitute a recognised area of institutional life' (DiMaggio and Powell, 1983: 148). Institutionalisation is a process 'by which social processes, obligations, or actualities, come to take on a rule-like status in social thought and action' (Meyer and Rowan, 1977: 341).

In the context of recruitment, employers' beliefs on job-seekers' employability are shaped by institutional frameworks. Specifically, as further explained by Cai (2013), the employers' belief systems are developed through two intertwined processes of 'actor structuring' and 'system structuring', which are key concepts in social rule theory (Burns and Flam, 1987), an institutionalist approach to social sciences. The former is about how certain norms are internalised within an organisation and the latter is about how the norms are institutionalised within an organisational field. Moreover, Burns and Flam (1987) also argue that some exogenous factors conditionally structure actors' behaviour, social action and system development.

According to Bourdieu (1984, 1986), capital can be understood as a currency that affects the position of an individual in the social world; it can be divided into distinct yet interconnected forms – namely, economic, social, cultural, and symbolic. Bourdieu's capital is related to his theory of practice, namely the concepts of the field (Bourdieu, 1984) and habitus (Bourdieu, 1977), in which individuals accumulate economic, cultural, social and symbolic capital in order to gain a higher position within their field, with their actions being conditioned by a socially constructed habitus.

The graduate capital model developed by Tomlinson (2017) draws upon several capital forms that were outlined by Bourdieu – namely, social and cultural forms – as these constitute key resources in how individuals negotiate institutional spaces and develop cumulative advantages within the educational and economic sphere. The relative acquisition and deployment of social and cultural capital further explain the operation of inequalities based on how well equipped individuals are to exchange the value of accumulated resources into social and economic gains. This is especially pertinent for a relatively elite field such as the graduate labour market. First, intensified levels of competition to secure favourable labour market positioning means that educational credentials no longer signify exclusive symbolic status. This therefore brings into play the importance of other forms of resources in securing positional advantage. Second, the variegated nature of employment fields within which graduates look to gain a stronghold means that capitals may be differentially recognised in different institutional contexts.

Through comparing the theoretical insights of Bourdieu's capital theory and those of institutional theory, Friedland (2009) suggests that the concept of the (institutional) field can link the two theories together. As put by Friedland (2009: 887–8), 'Bourdieu has been the touchstone for a current of work that has turned towards practice within institutional fields as the site from which it might be possible to develop a new intellectual space between rational subjects on the one hand, and objective and lawful social structures on the other'. Similar to the insights of institutional theory, Bourdieu emphasises that capitals, related to individuals' positions in society, 'only exist in relation to particular fields whose profits they command' (Friedland, 2009: 898). Different fields compose society.

Within each field, 'different forms of capital – economic, cultural, social and symbolic being the generic forms – are differentially active and distributed among positions within that field' (Friedland, 2009: 898). Friedland's (2009) juxtaposition of Bourdieu's capital theory and institutional theory inspires us to renew Cai's (2013) conceptual framework for understanding employers' perceptions of graduate employability by incorporating Tomlinson's (2017) notion of employability capital.

REVISITING CAI'S (2013) CONCEPTUAL FRAMEWORK FOR UNDERSTANDING EMPLOYERS' PERCEPTIONS OF GRADUATE EMPLOYABILITY

Since the 1990s, the career success of graduates has been regarded as a key indicator to measure the quality of education. As such, universities and students have tended to become more responsive to the needs of employers, and scholarly research has started to investigate employers' views concerning the relevance of university education and the competencies of university graduates. However, the research reported diverse views on what employers considered important for graduates and this was largely due to a lack of appropriate conceptual or theoretical frameworks within which different empirical observations can be embraced. To respond to such a research challenge, Cai (2013) developed a conceptual framework for understanding employers' perceptions of graduate employability.

Cai's (2013) framework is based on the new institutional theory that understands that human actions are constrained by institutions (DiMaggio and Powell, 1983; Meyer and Rowan, 1977). Institutions can be generally understood as taken-for-granted norms and beliefs (Scott, 2001). In the context of transition from education to the workplace, employers make recruitment decisions based on their institutionalised beliefs. Cai's (2013) framework (Figure 26.1) mainly deals with how employers develop their belief systems regarding what qualities of graduates are considered valuable by distinguishing between four mechanisms: exogenous factors' influences, formation of initial signals, public learning and private learning. These mechanisms explain three stages of employers' belief evolvement, respectively.

The first stage takes place when an employer has no experience of engaging in recruiting job applicants holding similar educational credentials (e.g. Credential A) and thus the employer will make recruitment decisions based on his/her initial beliefs that are influenced by exogenous factors and initial signals. Exogenous factors are, for example, the cultural environment faced by employers, specific market conditions and the employer organisations' particular characteristics that are outside the employers' direct experience of recruiting graduates with Credential A. Initial signals can be understood as institutionalised beliefs

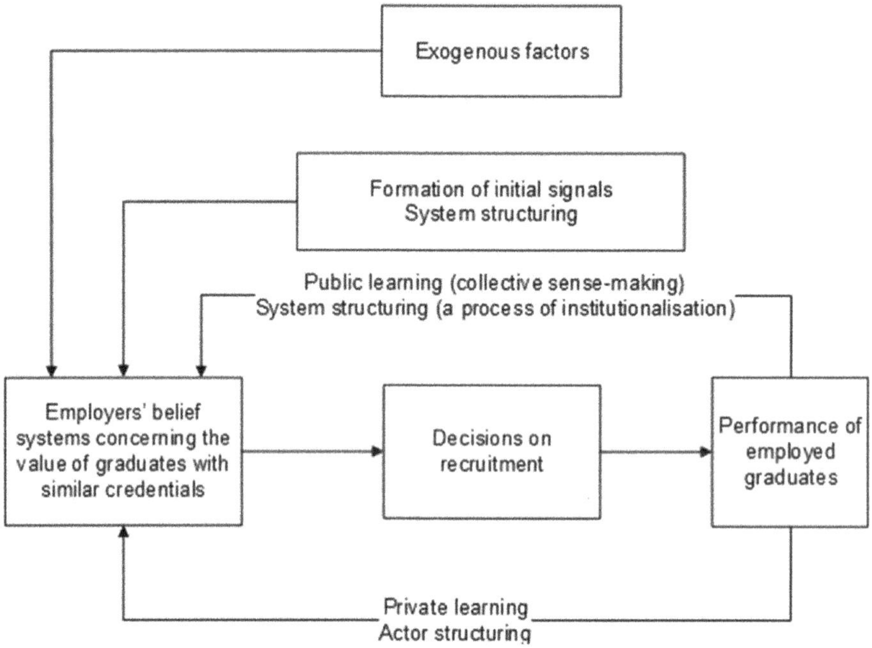

Figure 26.1 Factors and mechanisms affecting employers' beliefs

Source: Cai (2013), with slight modification for clarification.

among employers in a given specific employment field about graduates with Credential A. It is called 'initial' because the employers have no prior experience with this kind of graduates. The formation of initial signals is the result of system structuring (or public learning) by other employers in the employment field.

The second stage starts when an employer has recruited the graduates with Credential A. By observing and evaluating the employees' performance, the employer's initial beliefs will be either confirmed or corrected. The belief adjustment takes place through actor structuring or private learning. The more experiences the employer has of recruiting graduates with Credential A, the more mature his/her beliefs will be. The employer's beliefs will contribute to the system structuring in a specific labour market.

In the final stage, equilibrium will be reached. The equilibrated state of affairs is twofold. One is the internalisation of individuals' beliefs, where the employer through successive private learning processes (actor structuring) has accumulated enough experience to ascertain the candidates' 'true' value. The other is the institutionalisation of norms through public learning, where employers in the specific employment field have developed shared beliefs through collective sense-making (by exchanging information/ideas and imitating good practices of each other). As the two processes interact with and influence each other, the ideal equilibrium also requires a balance between both loops of private and public learning. This stage is an idea rather than a reality. Nevertheless, it represents a convergent end of changes in employers' belief systems.

By knowing the factors affecting and mechanisms underlying the development of employers' beliefs on graduate employability, both university graduates and their education providers can better develop their strategies to convince potential employers of their employability. As indicated by the private-learning mechanism, what eventually shapes employers' beliefs on educational output lies in a graduate's actual productivity and performance at his/her workplace. However, having competent skills does not always guarantee the graduate's success in the labour market and this has often been neglected by universities. For instance, when the graduate-producing institutions and the labour market are in different countries, a challenge is concerned with how the employers perceive the quality of the graduates (Wiers-Jenssen, 2008). Many higher education studies dealing with employers' beliefs (as well as demands and satisfactions) of graduates have tried to provide suggestions on how universities could meet the employers' needs, while little appears to have been written about how to change employers' beliefs. As implied by Cai (2013), some purposeful actions can influence the employers' beliefs, both in shaping the initial signals and in facilitating the public-learning process. For each end, universities need to have close interactions with employers and to get involved in a range of employers' networks.

Although Cai (2013) has been widely cited in the graduate employability literature, few works have systematically applied Cai's (2013) framework in empirical studies. This might be due to two constraints of the framework that may limit its application in empirical research. First, while the framework provides theoretical accounts about how the signals about employability transmitted by graduates can be institutionalised among employers in a given field, there is no simplified lens to categorise the signals, hence causing complexity in applying the framework in empirical studies. Second, although the framework implies other actors, such as graduates/students and higher education institutions (HEIs), can influence the employers' perceptions, these actors' roles are not included in the theoretical elaboration of the framework. As stated by Cai (2013), his conceptual framework building was still at a preliminary stage and further improvement is needed.

REVISITING EMPLOYABILITY CAPITALS IN RELATION TO EMPLOYER RECRUITMENT

Responding to a shift from seeing employability as skills possessed by graduates that match employers' needs to seeing it as a negotiation process between graduates and employers, Tomlinson (2017) developed the capital approach to graduate employability, in which five forms of graduate capital are identified: human capital, social capital, cultural capital, identity capital and psychological capital. Among those, the first three coincide with Bourdieu's forms of capital while the last two are beyond Bourdieu's capital framework. Tomlinson's cultural capital and human capital reflect two dimensions of Bourdieu's cultural capital (see Shumilova and Cai, Chapter 2, this Handbook).

The concept of social capital has explanatory value on a number of levels. In the graduate capital model, social capital connects to both Bourdieu's notion of relational networks (Bourdieu, 1984, 1986) and also Granovetter's (1985) notion of weak ties, as both explain how graduates can become aligned to and then integrated into a social field. In the former sense, a graduate's social capital encompasses the spread of acquaintances with significant others within a wider social field, which has the capacity to mobilise advantage through providing educationally rich knowledge and insight of social fields, including how to access and negotiate entry. The quality and veracity of such networks are important in having the power to influence how well equipped graduates are to gain a stronghold in competitive and culturally driven areas of employment. In a related sense, akin to Granovetter's (1985) approach, the power, veracity and affective qualities of social ties, often thinly spread rather than being confined to several key relations, determine how effectively individuals are able to leverage social capital for gainful outcomes. Weak ties provide a bridge between individuals and wider, hitherto unknown relational networks that enhance the flow of knowledge and information about employment fields. Crucially, the extent to which individuals are able to draw on social capital will likely determine graduates' access to positional advantages outside of formal credentials, including insider knowledge, familiarity of social fields and its key actors and signalling information on how employers recruit.

Social capital also helps mobilise another significant form of capital that is crucial for facilitating sense of place within a given employment field – namely, cultural capital. In Bourdieu's (1986) framework, this refers principally to the development and deployment of culturally relevant knowledge, dispositions and behavioural schemas that enable individuals to further develop the advantages that they may have already somewhat developed in the form of social capital. Significantly, this is often 'embodied' dispositionally in the ways in which individuals convey their socio-cultural value to others who regulate the interpersonal and inter-cultural rules of organisations. This is important because, in so many ways, the signals that both a future employee and employer convey are often 'cultural signals' (Hora, 2020; Rivera, 2011) – including attitudes, tastes, implicit cultural codes and values – that are largely referenced against a dominant social field. Much of the value of cultural capital rests on the cultural similarity between prospective employees and employers and how much the latter recognise the former as demonstrating appropriate 'social fit'. This becomes even more salient in contexts where there may be similarity in educational outcomes (human capital) and where so-called 'non-cognitive' factors (cultural signifiers) come into play in determining which candidate is desirable for a given institutional field. The relative acquisition and deployment of desired forms of cultural capital presents challenges to those who have not been able to acquire cultural capital through earlier forms of primary socialisation.

The graduate capital model further incorporates two other forms of capital that were not included in classical sociological models of capital, but which have appeared in various social science writing and have applicability to graduate employment. One of these, identity capital, connects to diverse identity approaches, including psycho-development identity formation (Erikson, 1968), reflexive modernisation and life-course planfulness (Giddens, 1991) and performative self-presentation (Goffman, 1959). Côté (2005) outlines how identity capital centres on the agential capacity to conceptualise, pursue and realise life trajectories and pathways based on the establishment of future goals and intentionality – more so, given the general erosion of pre-arranged institutional pathways. In relation to employment and careers, the concept can be encapsulated in terms of 'the level of personal investment a graduate makes towards the development of their future career and employability' (Tomlinson, 2017: 345), potentially serving to channel outlooks and behaviours that may be conducive for realising labour market goals. Moreover, identity resources towards employment also necessitate the enactment of identities as modes of social practice entailing some knowledge of audiences, role expectations and how these may be received in institutional settings.

Psychological capital is also a capital resource outlined in the model and concerns graduates' levels of career adaptability and resilience mainly in terms of 'problem-focussed coping towards developing proactive strategies in the face of challenge, mainly in the form of learning from experience' (Tomlinson, 2017: 347). Important is the capacity of individuals to withstand pressure and setbacks over the course of a career, as well as how flexible they are in the face of increased uncertainty. This also needs to be played out and enacted not just in the process of job-seeking but also when graduates are employed in workplaces, including responding to multiple workplace demands, challenges and disruptions.

A RENEWED ANALYTICAL FRAMEWORK FOR UNDERSTANDING EMPLOYERS' PERCEPTIONS OF GRADUATE EMPLOYABILITY

The proposition we explore here is that the model developed by Cai (2013) can be further enriched by incorporating a capitals approach to explain employers' behaviour in relation to graduate recruitment. The renewed model is depicted in Figure 26.2. The shapes with solid lines represent Cai's (2013) original model, which explains how the signals concerning employability of graduates with similar education credentials are internalised and institutionalised among employers in a certain employment field. Those with dashed lines indicate our

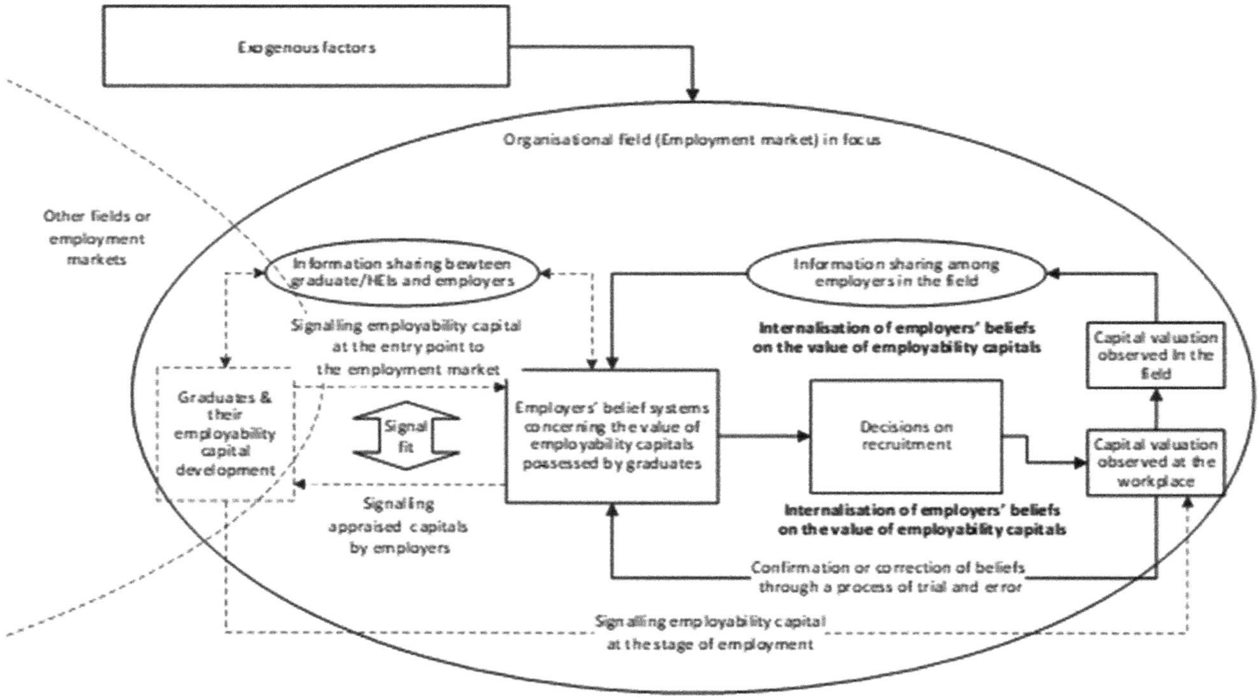

Figure 26.2 The renewed analytical framework of employers' perception of graduate employability capitals

Source: the authors.

supplemented elements by incorporating the employability capital perspective that elucidates how the signals, in the form of employability capital, are developed by graduates and transmitted to employers. Moreover, the graduates are expected to receive feedback from the employers on what aspects of their employability are appraised in terms of their future workplace value in the employment field. The renewed model centres on graduates/employee–employer exchange: employers process the signalling effects of employability capital possessed by graduates, and graduates try to convince employers of the values of their employability capitals. Among the signalling interactions between graduates and employers is signal fit, which is defined as the extent to which the signal corresponds to the sought-after quality of the signaller (Connelly et al., 2011) – a goal both employers and graduates want to achieve. The signal fit is context dependent, meaning employability capitals appraised by employers in one field might not be recognised in another. Below, we will provide some illustrative discussions about the renewed model, with a particular emphasis on the supplementary elements.

Graduates' Signalling of Employability Capital to Employers

The first level of interaction involves the signalling of capital on the part of the graduates in terms of what they convey at the point of entry in the form of a resume and job assessment event. These will have been developed and worked on before this process, but its appropriate conveyance will be important, as also important in this interaction is how these capital signals are received by employers. How such information is interpreted will be intimately connected to the beliefs employers hold about what is valuable to them and their workplace and how capital will transfer into the workplace and, consequently, how it will generate additional forms of capital that will advantage their organisations. The second process involves the decisions of employers, which are often mediated by more extensive interactional information in the recruitment process, that affirms or disaffirms their initial beliefs about the potential capital value of a job candidate. Other field actors such as extant employees or external associates may be important information-sharing resources, but the wider institutional context will provide a significant reference frame for how these decisions are determined.

A number of recent studies have integrated signalling and socio-cultural perspectives, mainly through a capital's perspective, and have shown that both graduates' and employers' constructions of graduates' employability, as well as 'talent', are largely performative (see Anderson and Tomlinson, 2021; Ashley and Empson, 2017; Handley, 2018; Tomlinson and Anderson, 2021). The ways in which graduates convey their suitability and desirability to organisational gatekeepers in the recruitment process entail some referencing to future performance or a set of intended organisational outputs. Tomlinson and Anderson's (2021) study showed that employers' conceptions of what constitutes hireable graduates rest largely on the resources that graduates are able to draw upon and convert into meaningful signals that place them in an advantageous position in relation to employers' demand-side preferences and priorities. This study also reported that the extent to which graduates can convey a skilful (and often performance-based) narration of their future potential, often through social and behavioural means, can provide a mutual social context through which their future performance as employees can be realised.

Using Employability Capital in Graduate–Employer Interactions

Social capital is important in the interaction between graduate job-seekers and employers. The process of gaining social capital may be formed before some graduates have actively approached a targeted organisation and, thus, become an important informal channel through which graduates learn about job openings and how to negotiate access. The extent to which any meaningful bond has been developed between a graduate and employer will have some bearing on how successfully a graduate is able to mobilise their existing qualifications through the formation of key initial relationships. One such activity that has been shown to be influential here is prior work experience in the targeted or related employment field, especially when this has come with proven past performance (adding to the past precedent basis of employers' beliefs). The role of both wider professional contacts and extant organisational members may be important in providing gatekeepers with potentially valuable information in terms of pre-screening a known graduate (in short, providing a 'good word' effect). This may also serve to confirm, or even challenge, pre-existing employer preferences for graduates who are drawn from an inter-connected social circle. In terms of social capital signalling in an institutional sense, a number of key reference points can be made for context. This includes the extent to which a graduate recruit is able to bond with other organisational members in order to further acquire, share or transfer important organisational knowledge. Related to this is the extent to which they can leverage additional social capital with external groups that can generate productive business advantages in the forms of profile building and enhanced client base.

Cultural capital also clearly has a strong institutional exchange value that shapes the perceived organisational value of a graduate and their potential institutionalisation into workplaces. Much of the existing research has pointed to the inequities this generates for graduates whose wider socio-cultural and educational experiences are not aligned to more socially closed, often 'elite', occupational fields, often resulting in real and perceived exclusion (Ingram and Allen, 2019; Merrill et al., 2020; Rivera, 2011). Essentially, some individuals do not have an intuitive grasp of the codes, implicit social signals and dominant cultural script within an organisation comprising of specific cultural values and practices, therefore precluding their potential to enter them. The way in which employers rationalise decisions that exclude less advantaged individuals is relevant from an institutional reproduction perspective. Much of the evidence as above indicates that employers vary in terms of how explicitly they acknowledge cultural fit as a selection criterion, although preferences towards some candidates are largely framed in terms of synergy between a job candidate and an organisation's pre-existing culture. Employers' propensities towards homo-culturalism can also be legitimated as part of a commercial imperative to gain most maximum value from recruiting the 'best' graduates and also minimising the risk of turn-over among those with fewer cultural resources.

One of the notable features of most graduate labour markets is their diversity and relative heterogeneity, including a broad range of sectors, organisational forms, sizes (small, large, medium) and business orientations (private, public, third sector). In short, not all graduates aim to enter similar fields and not all employers will adopt similar criteria given that their organisations constitute different institutional forms. Some of these will be more accommodating for graduates with less traditional (elite) forms of cultural capital. The key matter in terms of the acquisition and deployment of cultural capital is that its value is mainly contingent on the institutional field in which it is being validated and exchanged. Employers will ultimately make a culturally referenced decision based on the prevailing socio-cultural composition of their organisations and expected behavioural norms and competencies.

The two other forms of capitals in the capital model also have further explanatory scope for how graduates present and employers receive signals pertaining to capitals. Identity capital also relates to the future institutional context of a workplace and refers to the forms of social identity that graduates are able to convey about their future orientation and the claims they make about their potential: their identity capital. The identities graduates carry through into the labour market at the point of job entry remain indeterminate and aspirational before becoming actively conferred and legitimated by significant others (Holmes, 2013, 2015). The task facing graduates is convincing employers that the identities they claim to hold (e.g. a potentially competent and passionate management consultant or marketing executive who will develop ownership over their role) is going to be actualised in their performance once employed. The task facing employers is determining whether the presented identity is to be warranted based on the ways in which the identities are performed and narrated (Anderson and Tomlinson, 2021). Accordingly, the level of identity capital that graduates convey influences employers' perceptions of which graduates are likely to transition more smoothly from novice, emerging graduates to more formed early professionals. This does not just rest on graduates being able to meet performance criteria of job but also matching the identity profiles of jobs and of wider organisational members. We can also see how this corresponds to some of the other forms of capital outlined.

In terms of the final capital dimension in the model, psychological capital is not only a resource that graduates need to develop to manage complex and uncertain employment transitions, but which employers expect graduates to be able to adapt to what they perceived to be challenging and competitive workplace environments. The idea that making transitions from educational to working contexts constitutes a kind of 'reality shock' that requires active agency, deliberation and planning is again institutionally referenced as an important resource that is recognised and affirmed by employers.

IMPLICATIONS AND CONCLUSIONS

The approach we have outlined in this chapter raises some important issues concerning employer behaviour in relation to recruitment and decision-making and, more broadly, the interaction between employers and graduates. The interconnection of capitals and institutionalist approaches has the potential to shed significant light on the relational dynamics involved in how graduates and employers receive and present signals pertaining to what both can offer. In a competitive and crowded graduate labour market, employers are in the more advantageous position of being able to screen large pools of graduates with similar educational credentials. Our approach confirms what much of the existing body of literature reveals: employers' decisions are largely contextual, often highly subjective and reliant on signals about the resources and resourcefulness of future employees. These resources are framed in field-dependent ways based on how they conform to institutional dimensions of employers' organisations. For instance, the creative industries would not use qualifications as a proxy but would look at actual skills through, for instance, physical portfolios/showreels. Moreover, capitals need to be further enacted and mobilised in workplaces for both employees' and organisations' advantages.

This approach further bridges supply- and demand-side orientations to understanding graduates' employment preparedness generally and calls for a need to move empirical and practical analysis beyond the focus on how universities can 'deliver' or 'produce' employable future employees in the form of employability skills (Anderson and Tomlinson, 2021; Handley, 2018). Reframing recruitment in terms of capital acquisition and deployment within an institutional framework also carries practical implications. Within HEIs, career practitioners and those involved in employability-facing teaching and learning may need to encourage the further development and demonstration of capitals that convey their attractiveness to prospective employers. Employability programmes should encourage channelling of these towards specific organisational contexts, encouraging graduates to harness the knowledge of workplace contexts and being able to articulate how their value may translate into successful organisational performance within the dominant expectations and values. This will further enable graduates to purposefully signal their attractiveness to employers in ways that influence employers' beliefs about how resources' signals will maintain, and add to, the established institutional contexts they normatively regulate.

Work-integrated learning and formal work placements appear to be a significant way of building graduate capitals; indeed, one of the most important advantages is the development of contextual knowledge of the make-up of workplaces and being able to narrate future employability against demand-level criteria and expectations. Those facilitating the development of work-related experiences are also in a position to promote graduates' capability to package and narrate these into institutional scripts that convince employers of their workplace potential.

There are implications for those involved in graduate recruitment and workplace development at the demand side. Employers would like to discern the value of graduates at the recruitment stage. In an institutionalised employment field where employers have long experience of employing graduates with similar education credentials (often graduates from local HEIs), employers can best judge the signals conveyed by graduates regarding their employability capitals. Along with intensified internationalisation of higher education and global mobility of skilled talents, employers may more frequently encounter the situation that the education credentials of graduates as job-seekers are unfamiliar to them. Thus, employers need to enhance their understandings and mature their beliefs on targeting graduates' employability capitals. Of course, they can gain experience through trial and error in hiring the graduates, but this takes a long time and is an expensive process. Alternatively, employers could actively participate in activities involving targeting graduates as well as the HEIs where the graduates are educated, to be more aware of the graduates' employability development. Besides, they can also learn from other employers in the same employment field who have more hiring experiences of these kind of graduates.

Although the model discussed in the paper emphasises the importance of employers' beliefs on graduate employability, it must be noted that employers' views are not the only and always reliable information source for universities to predict the labour market need for two reasons. On the one hand, employers sometimes may be wrong in identifying prospective employees, understanding the competencies and potentials of graduates and predicting possible added values brought by the graduates. This is especially likely to happen in an international context – for example, when graduates are originally from or educated in systems and cultures that are unfamiliar to the employers. On the other hand, the missions of universities are not just about preparing students for the future needs in the labour market, but also about transforming the future of the labour market and bringing in new values to the society. In this respect, many employers, especially in the private sector, might be short-sighted due to their organisational mission to pursue economic profits. Universities' long-term objective on preparing students for a changing society may be inconsistent with employers' demands based on short-term needs of business development.

Finally, we note two limitations of our study. First, although the conceptualisation of both employers' perceptions of graduate employability (Cai, 2013) and employability capital (Tomlinson, 2017), on which the analytical framework developed in this chapter is based, were derived from empirical observations and analyses in diverse settings concerning both Western and non-Western graduates and job markets, the integrated model needs to be tested and evolved in empirical investigation in a wide range of contexts. Second, while our framework emphasises interactions between graduates and employers through combined institutional and capital perspectives, the insights concerning institutionalisation of capitals could be broadened to conceptualise how graduates can leverage their resources in the emerging new employment landscape (e.g. establishing start-ups). An effort in such a direction can be seen in another chapter (Shumilova and Cai, Chapter 2, this Handbook).

REFERENCES

Abelha, M., Fernandes, S., Mesquita, D., Seabra, F., & Ferreira-Oliveira, A. T. (2020). Graduate employability and competence development in higher education—A systematic literature review using PRISMA. *Sustainability*, 12(15), 5900.

Anderson, V., & Tomlinson, M. (2021). Signaling standout graduate employability: The employer perspective. *Human Resource Management Journal*, 31, 675–693.

Arrow, K. J. (1973). Higher Education as a filter. *Journal of Public Economics*, 2, 193–216.

Ashley, L., & Empson, L. (2017). Understanding social exclusion in elite professional service firms: field level dynamics and the 'professional project'. *Work, Employment and Society*, 31(2), 211–229.

Bailly, F. (2008). The role of employers' beliefs in the evaluation of educational output. *Journal of Socio-Economics*, 37(3), 959–968.

Becker, G. S. (1964). *Human capital: A theoretical and empirical analysis, with special reference to education*. Chicago: University of Chicago Press.

Behle, H. (2020). Students' and graduates' employability. A framework to classify and measure employability gain. *Policy Reviews in Higher Education*, 4(1), 105–130.

Bourdieu, P. (1977) *Outline of a theory of practice*. Cambridge; New York: Cambridge University Press.

Bourdieu, P. (1984). *Distinction: A social critique of the judgement of taste*. Harvard University Press.

Bourdieu, P. (1986). The Forms of Capital. In J. Richardson (ed.), *Handbook of theory and research for the sociology of education* (pp. 241–258). New York: Greenwood.

Burns, T. R., & Flam, H. (1987). *The shaping of social organization: social rule system theory with applications*. London: Sage.

Cai, Y. (2012). *Understanding employers' perceptions of international graduates: An investigation of the employment prospects of Finnish-educated Chinese graduates in Finnish companies operating in China*. Tampere: Tampere University Press.

Cai, Y. (2013). Graduate employability: A conceptual framework for understanding employers' perceptions. *Higher Education*, 65(4), 457–469.

Connelly, B. L., Certo, S. T., Ireland, R. D., & Reutzel, C. R. (2011). Signaling theory: A review and assessment. *Journal of Management*, 37(1), 39–67.

Côté, J. E. (2005). Identity capital, social capital and the wider benefits of learning: generating resources facilitative of social cohesion. *London Review of Education*, 3(3), 221–237.

DiMaggio, P. J., & Powell, W. (1983). The iron cage revisited: institutional isomorphism and collective rationality. *American Sociological Review*, 42(2), 147–160.

Erikson, E. H. (1968). *Identity: Youth and crisis*. New York: Norton.

Friedland, R. (2009). The endless fields of Pierre Bourdieu. *Organization*, 16(6), 887–917.

Giddens, A. (1991). *Modernity and self-identity*. Cambridge: Polity Press.

Goffman, E. (1959). *The presentation of self in everyday life*. New York: Double Day.

Granovetter, M. (1985). Economic action and social structure: The problem of embeddedness. *American Journal of Sociology*, 91(3), 481–510.

Handley, K. (2018). Anticipatory socialization and the construction of the employable graduate: A critical analysis of employers' graduate careers websites. *Work, Employment and Society*, 32(2), 239–256.

Holmes, L. (2013). Competing perspectives on graduate employability: Possession, position or process? *Studies in Higher Education*, 38(4), 538–554.

Holmes, L. (2015). Becoming a graduate: the warranting of an emergent identity. *Education + Training*, 57(2), 219–238.

Hora, M. T. (2020). Hiring as cultural gatekeeping into occupational communities: implications for higher education and student employability. *Higher Education*, 79(2), 307–324.

Ingram, N., & Allen, K. (2019). 'Talent-spotting' or 'social magic'? Inequality, cultural sorting and constructions of the ideal graduate in elite professions. *The Sociological Review*, 67(3), 723–740.

Merrill, B., Finnegan, F., O'Neill, J., & Revers, S. (2020). 'When it comes to what employers are looking for, I don't think I'm it for a lot of them': Class and capitals in, and after, higher education. *Studies in Higher Education*, 45(1), 163–175.

Meyer, J. W., Ramirez, F. O., Frank, D. J., & Schofer, E. (2007). Higher Education as an Institution. In P. J. Gumport (ed.), *Sociology of higher education: Contributions and their contexts* (pp. 187–221). Baltimore: Johns Hopkins University Press.

Meyer, J. W., & Rowan, B. (1977). Institutionalized organizations: Formal structure as myths and ceremony. *American Journal of Sociology*, 83(2), 340–363.

Rivera, L. A. (2011). Ivies, extracurriculars, and exclusion: Elite employers' use of educational credentials. *Research in Social Stratification and Mobility*, 29(1), 71–90.

Schultz, T. W. (1961). Investment in Human Capital. *The American Economic Review*, 51(1), 1–17.

Scott, W. R. (2001). *Institutions and organizations* (2nd edn). Thousand Oaks, CA: Sage.

Simon, H. A. (1957). *Administrative behavior: A study of decision-making processes in administrative organization* (2nd edn). New York: Macmillan.

Spence, M. (1973). Job market signaling. *Quarterly Journal of Economics*, 87(3), 355–374.

Stiglitz, J. E. (1975). The theory of 'screening', education and the distribution of income. *American Economic Review*, 65(3), 283–300.

Tomlinson, M. (2017). Forms of graduate capital and their relationship to graduate employability. *Education + Training*, 59(4), 338–352.

Tomlinson, M., & Anderson, V. (2021). Employers and graduates: The mediating role of signals and capitals. *Journal of Higher Education Policy and Management*, 43, 384–399.

Wiers-Jenssen, J. (2008). Does higher education attained abroad lead to international jobs? *Journal of Studies in International Education*, 12(2), 101–130.

27

Higher Education Institution (HEI) Considerations to Support the Creation of Alliances with Small and Medium-sized Enterprises (SMEs)

Katie McAllister

INTRODUCTION

Higher education institutes (HEIs) are being confronted with increased expectations of supporting their local and national economy, evidenced with the marked adoption by many HEIs of the third mission, as HEIs moving beyond the traditional missions of teaching and research to encompass economic development. HEIs wishing to support (and evidence) employability, work-based learning, graduate outcomes, entrepreneurship and their local economy must forge links with business and, in particular, small and medium-sized enterprises (SMEs), which form 99% of UK businesses (Department for Business Energy and Industrial Strategy, 2019). Yet, current literature is ignoring a dimension to HEI–SME alliances that is central to understanding them and is of vital importance to practitioners: the creation of the alliance. This chapter will explore the strategic and operational decision-making process by which HEIs create alliances with SMEs.

Large, traditional universities have a wealth of experience in creating and managing SME alliances within certain schools such as engineering or business, but this may not be evident across the whole organisation. In addition, within the government policy framework surrounding the role of the HEI in relation to regional and national development, there is an underlying assumption of the starting point of the HEI and the direction that the HEI–SME alliance will take. With the emerging global educational conversation considering HEIs as a mechanism by which to develop human capital within SMEs, higher education is viewed as a key factor in driving national SME development and economic growth. For those HEIs or schools within HEIs without a history of research or business alliance development, they are commencing this journey from a far shakier foundation. The practices currently being introduced by individual HEIs to survive and develop in this competitive market whilst meeting state- and local-initiated requirements are still being developed, leaving many HEIs grappling with how to enact this expectation.

Across the UK, SMEs account for 61% of employment (Department for Business Energy and Industrial Strategy, 2019), and 20%–30% of graduate employment (Prospects, 2020), highlighting their importance and potential for the HEI intending to develop employability opportunities, work-place opportunities, graduate outcomes, entrepreneurship and their relationship with the local economy. There is a growing national government concern being paid to the SME market, with recognition that although SMEs significantly contribute to the economy, they have been generally ignored by universities (Piterou and Birch, 2014). HEI–SME strategic alliances are expected, by the government, to redress the mounting productivity fissure and generate opportunities to develop fresh skills for businesses (Leitch, 2006). Yet, it is unclear if this can be achieved by all HEIs, with the literature relating to HEI alliances favouring large corporations and not SMEs (Apa et al., 2020). Practitioners, policy makers and scholarly literature have yet to identify how this is to be accomplished and if it truly can be fulfilled. Furthermore, with the impact of COVID-19 upon SMEs in particular, there will be an even greater emphasis upon how HEIs can identify, engage with and develop appropriate SME alliances to support employability and meaningful graduate outcomes.

TERMINOLOGY

Within Europe, SMEs are defined as ‘Enterprises which employ fewer than 250 persons and which have an annual turnover not exceeding EUR 50 million, and/or an annual balance sheet total not exceeding EUR 43 million’ (European Commission, 2016: 3). However, there is no global definition of SME, with variances in, for example, the number of employees and revenue. Literature and policy refer to partnership, collaboration, relationship, alliance and inter-organisation, with research frequently describing the university–business cooperation (UBC), industry–university collaboration (IUC) and university–industry cooperation (UIC). Yet, there is a lack of clarity regarding the terminology. This chapter will refer to:

- an alliance, implying a purposeful connection or uniting (internally or externally) in any manner – the state of being allied, and
- a collaboration, implying the cooperation with another to produce something, irrespective of ownership or co-ownership (control) of the shared purpose – the act of collaborating.

This will acknowledge that alliance is an overarching term for all connections (e.g. partnerships, cooperations, collaborations and relationships) and collaboration is any act of working together.

HEI–SME KEY ELEMENTS

SMEs are less likely to engage with HEIs (Johnston, 2020), do not perceive HEIs to be the first point of contact for knowledge or collaboration (Goduscheit and Knudsen, 2015), consider graduates to be lacking in employer-ready skills (Woods and Dennis, 2009) and perceive that HEIs are not interested in the focus of the SME (Goduscheit and Knudsen, 2015).

Whilst there has been an increase in the number of articles relating to the HEI–SME alliance over the last 20 years, most refer to individual cases or single factors to explore within the HEI–SME alliance rather than an overview of the elements to consider. In addition, recent literature reviews have centred upon HEI–business rather than HEI–SME alliance. This chapter aims to address this gap by offering theorisation about how an HEI can evolve to support the creation of the HEI–SME alliance, with consideration of Figure 27.1.

HEI'S STRATEGIC ATTITUDE AND CAPABILITY

Without a clearly defined mission or purpose that considers the dominant context of HEI–SME alliance, staff will have little opportunity to move beyond their current position, leaving this potential growth area unexplored. Yet, the academic literature regarding HEI–SME strategic considerations is ad hoc and fragmented, leaving fissures in the research relating specifically to the HEI–SME alliance creation.

HEIs should be aware of current economic, political and social developments and their potential influence (Rybnicek and Königsgruber, 2019). By scrutinising for changes to the market, the HEI can take advantage of opportunities whilst identifying the preferred spheres of activity it will engage with. For example, the HEI could detect and apply for funding to support SMEs (Moraes Silva et al., 2019). Alternatively, the HEI may redirect internal funds

Figure 27.1 Theoretical conceptual framework of HEI–SME alliance creation

to support the HEI–SME alliance creation, yet this risks significant strain upon the HEI with limited funds. By analysing the SME's actual and perceived HEI collaboration barriers (Goduscheit and Knudsen, 2015), and the HEI's own reputation in the business community (Hemmert et al., 2014), the HEI can examine the management of the SME alliance strategy to reduce risk and increase potential alliance-creation success. Kadoić et al. (2018) argue that the benefits, challenges, costs and risks should be explored to gain an understanding of the influences and dependencies upon the selected goal. In contrast, English (2013) advocates exploration of the offer, resources, benefits and challenges of the potential HEI–SME collaboration, and the additional third-party aide (i.e. not the HEI or SME). However, the HEI also needs to explore how its own strategic plan aligns with the SME's intended outcomes and objectives to gain understanding and enlighten practice.

Institutional theory highlights that the actors are strongly embedded within their wider culture, operating inside their expanded construct (Meyer, 2010) whilst resource dependence theories explore how organisational behaviour is affected by the external resources used (Kholmuminov et al., 2019). Yet, the HEI may also wish to consider the resource and power dimensions across its departments as well as those external to the institute to help examine potential discourse and articulate its vision. Strategic planning will have limited impact if the culture does not reflect the strategic aspirations. Attention should be paid to the HEI structures and inter-department connectedness in order to support staff to not only aid the SME, but also to underpin the HEI itself. Without clear metrics and sound strategic consideration relating to SME integration (Rampersad, 2015), the HEI may underestimate the time, resources, skills and requirements of the HEI–SME alliance creation or neglect its own institutional inflexibilities. Stakeholder theory can aid the HEI in recognising the value it places currently upon the HEI–SME alliance within the overall HEI strategic plans (Jongbloed et al., 2008). If the SME is considered incidental or non-essential to the HEI, this will significantly hamper the HEI's success against its strategic plan. By applying institutional theory and resource dependence theory, an organisation can ascertain the direction of its strategy, yet without the application of stakeholder theory regarding internal and external actors, the HEI is at risk of creating tension throughout the institute and negatively impacting upon performance.

THE OFFER

Much of the literature relating to the HEI–SME offer focuses upon the outcome and impact of the offer, rather than the considerations when developing the offer. In addition, considerable attention is paid to the activities that provide an economic pay-off rather than the wider and more diverse alliance-creation opportunities (Galan-Muros and Davey, 2017). In order to create value for all stakeholders, a win–win scenario is advised, adding strength to the offer and enabling SMEs to capitalise on their alliance with the HEI.

An HEI systematic and standardised package of initiatives should provide choice and flexibility to the SME whilst focusing upon how the HEI can support SMEs with minimum bureaucracy (Mourao and Goncalves-Coelho, 2016). Klofsten and Jones-Evans (1996: 187) cite that the success of their HEI–SME offer is 'related to five factors: an ability to meet real needs, a core group, a clear focus, credibility, and close relations between the stimulation organisation and the university'. Yet, consideration should also be given to how aware the SME is of the offer (Ranga et al., 2008) and the potential need to challenge perceptions held by the SME relating to HEI–SME alliances or HEIs as sources of knowledge.

The literature focuses upon the long-term benefits of the HEI–business alliance, yet the inclination of SMEs is to explore short-term impact (Fukugawa, 2005), requiring a quick-return, less complex collaboration. By considering the SME as both a customer and a supplier, the HEI can identify collaboration opportunities in a more dynamic, interactive manner (Payne et al., 2008). Within the offer, key evaluation points should be embedded to develop trust (Fogg, 2012), with opportunities for communication planned, although there is debate regarding whether an informal (Shaw and Allen, 2006) or a more formal (Peças and Henriques, 2006) process is favoured.

When engaging with SMEs, the HEI needs to explore the resourcing of the offer – a wide-ranging consideration incorporating human, financial and physical. Yet, there is an absence of suitable government funding for the HEI–business cooperation, let alone funding for the HEI–SME alliance creation. In addition, teaching-focused HEIs or HEI schools with limited or no research output compared to a research-focused school may need to plan and prioritise differently. The HEI will, therefore, need to not only evaluate the potentially significant cost of resourcing the offer against the expected outcomes but also be aware of the varying resources to consider that minimise the chance of failure. For HEIs or HEI schools new to the HEI–SME alliance creation, considerations relating to resources may be unknown territory and, if poorly addressed or not considered, will negatively impact upon the direct and indirect finances of the HEI.

HEI PROCESS CONSIDERATIONS

HEI processes denote the steps that will be taken in streamlining communication, improving efficiencies, ensuring accountability and optimising resources, yet they are hindered by the frequently archaic constructs that HEIs operate within, despite the rapid modifications that businesses are demonstrating (Lee-Davies, 2018). It appears that many HEIs lack the skills or drive to change their internal processes (Samuel et al., 2018) to ensure that the whole organisation is responsive enough to meet the contemporary needs of SMEs in a manner that safeguards and optimises an outcome whilst managing the risk. Through streamlining the process with all stakeholders in mind, such as the SME manager, student or intermediary, the HEI can remove potential and actual barriers, and overcome cultural differences and sector disparities to support the HEI–SME alliance creation (Frasquet et al., 2012).

SMEs are frequently unaware of which HEI to work with and how, which emphasises a need for heightened direct contact with improved broadcasting of successful collaborations to stimulate engagement (Ranga et al., 2008). The HEI should be mindful to promote how it creates an SME-friendly curriculum, reduces the risk, reduces costs (or accesses financial support), creates value and is flexible to SME requirements. In addition, the transparency of the offer should be considered, exploring which marketing locations will yield the highest return, such as through small business-network groups (Cumming et al., 2012). SMEs consider initial contact with HEIs to be overly complex, with identification of the correct individual being convoluted (Turkes, 2018). The one-stop shop for employers and students may overcome this barrier, as would a reduction in complex structures and inflexibility within rigid HEI frameworks that contrast to the flat SME hierarchy (Schofield, 2013). Even with bureaucracy, the SME could overlook this obligation if the value added to the business is considered to be greater than the burden (Cao et al., 2014). Clear, simple and effective communication strategies by identified HEI personnel are considered critical by businesses (Canhoto et al., 2016), and these can be supported by specifications within contracts.

SMEs may not be in a financial position to fully pursue opportunities (Buganza et al., 2014); HEIs should consider how to reduce set-up costs or provide physical/financial support to enable the SMEs' full integration into the collaboration. Processes may require updating during the collaboration to augment the outcomes (Bjerregaard, 2009), yet many HEIs are required to adhere to approved procedures, limiting their flexibility and ability to overcome cultural differences. For HEIs exploring research and development or innovation, the HEI can ensure that the SME receives financial incentives prior to academic publication (Santoro and Gopalakrishnan, 2001), provide exclusive rights in return for the full economic cost, offer a time-limited royalty-free license or delay publication (Kneller et al., 2014). In addition, the HEI must question what formalised collaborations level it requires when informal links are seen to be of equal importance by the SME (Howells et al., 2012).

Although research explores the skills required by students and graduates, there is a lack of information relating to processes required to match students to SMEs and the additional HEI considerations required to meet the needs of both students and SMEs. It is recognised that HEIs must work far harder in convincing SMEs to engage with graduates (Woods and Dennis, 2009), yet SMEs also fail to attract graduates (Heaton et al., 2008), indicating that the HEI needs to differentiate the support it offers SMEs in relation to recruitment, support and retention in its policies and practices. Processes are complex and the HEI not considering the process's impact upon the SME sector risks damaging the fragile HEI–SME alliance.

HEI HUMAN-RESOURCE (HR) CONSIDERATIONS

Given the complexity and constant flux that may occur within the HEI–SME alliance, the vital roles of the actors within the HEI must be considered, including individual duties, leadership, facilitators and administrative support. If the HEI is to develop a new management paradigm, the structure, role and responsibilities can be considered to reflect the changes, in line with grounded theory (Corbin, 2015) or role theory (Biddle, 1979). Yet, little literature exists regarding the considerations of roles within the HEI–SME alliance.

Rese et al. (2013) suggest that five crucial roles should be considered and distributed among key personnel: power management, expertise, process management, relationship promotor and communication/data gatekeeper. Alternatively, Heikkinen et al. (2007) highlight the need to consider the relationship-building role in two parts: inter-organisational connectors and the instigator of change, as well as the roles of planners and producers. This incorporates clearly defining the roles and responsibilities in a manner that supports the collaboration(s), and the development of knowledge and capabilities to efficiently and effectively succeed across the collaborations, especially where roles are shifting from being academic to more commercial (Rampersad, 2015). Collier et al. (2011) emphasise that SMEs engage with individuals, not organisations, emphasising the need for the HEI to consider the personalities and skills of their staff. The HEI may need to identify a particular skill, such as collaborative, co-creative, visionary, nurturing (Powell, 2012), a role (e.g. project manager, contractual manager or initiator) or an expertise level for a specific point in the collaboration or the duration. This is significant when considering that engagement will be frequently managed around conflicting teaching or administrative commitments, negatively impacting upon the timeliness of the action and creating what appears to be HEI stubbornness or rigidity (Edmunds, 2017). As the collaboration develops, the potential for personality clashes increases (Collier et al., 2011), further highlighting the need for skilled relationship builders and negotiators within the HEI.

RELATIONSHIP FACTORS

If an HEI wishes to create and develop SME alliances, it should appreciate what the success factors are, how they relate to each other and the influence the factors will have in delivering the HEI's strategies. For example, Krathu et al.'s (2015) detailed analysis of inter-organisational success factors includes performance, culture, relationship and connectedness, whereas Rybnicek and Königsgruber (2019) give special regard to flexibility, honesty, clarity and awareness, communication and commitment. Yet, the literature rarely makes distinctions between types of organisations (e.g. public, private), size or sector.

Each SME's alliance-creation style will be different, yet the HEI needs to identify synergies to influence SME engagement in a manner that demonstrates compatibility (Thorgren et al., 2010). Through the successful completion of shorter collaborations (Perks et al., 2012), problems can be quickly addressed whilst relationships and trust develop, cultural barriers are reduced and common language is agreed. The HEI can explore the SME's modes of operating, requirements, governance and priorities, potentially aligning to its own practices to address the tensions, differences and gaps. However, this task may be difficult for HEI staff entrenched in their own culture, highlighting the potential need for an external intermediary.

The shared feelings and perceptions, or culture, within an organisation are considered crucial factors within the HEI–business alliance, yet the lack of a business-based culture across the HEI could create cultural conflict both within the HEI and across the HEI–SME alliance (Jongbloed et al., 2008). Misunderstanding can easily increase where a common language has not been agreed (Canhoto et al., 2016), and procedures and consequences not explored to address or reduce assumptions and develop cultural convergence. HEI staff must be given the time and training to enable them to manage these differences (Karlsson et al., 2007). However, Bjerregaard (2010) highlights that cultural differences between the HEI and business do not always create barriers; therefore, it may be more appropriate for the HEI to consider the alliance both an opportunity to achieve the project as well as an opportunity to explore the contextual aspects of the alliance. In order to overcome the barriers to communication, the HEI should not only consider the channels of communication but also the frequency, openness and honesty, maintaining up-to-date information-sharing practices to foster trust (Barnes et al., 2002) between all parties. The HEI–SME alliance is reliant upon how loyal each party is to the collaboration and the effort they are ready to commit towards supporting the alliance (Attia, 2015). In the early phase of alliance development, it is recommended to have routine meetings supported by regular communication; therefore, a considerable time commitment must be planned for by the HEI.

Within the HEI–SME alliance, mutual dependency and a potential power imbalance will exist (Kern et al., 2018). It could be considered that the power moves towards the HEI where the focus is upon delivery to the SME rather than a project with the SME, yet the HEI will still be reliant on the SME to engage with it, irrespective of the project. Although it is likely that all parties will experience this within the relationship, the role of the HEI is to ensure that it is not perceived to be the more powerful (Darabi and Clark, 2012) and the HEI must consider how it influences the success factors when creating the HEI–SME alliance.

SME PARTNER CONSIDERATION

Establishing an HEI–SME alliance will be resource-demanding; the HEI will need to screen potential SME collaborators to identify those able to provide value and a higher return. If we consider that '[i]t is unrealistic to suppose that a business school could offer support to all SMEs or that it would be effective for all' (Fogg, 2012: 40), the HEI faces difficulties in identifying which SMEs to work with. The notion of the 'right SME' implies that not all SMEs will be suitable for an HEI–SME alliance and highlights the necessity for a selection criterion.

One way to view the identification of the 'right' partner is through opportune networking, allowing the HEI to explore compatibility, capability and commitment of the SME whilst minimising risk. Networking can allow for information gathering, including exploring the capabilities and strategic interests of potential partners to enable specific, targeted offers to be presented to prospective SMEs (Philbin, 2008). Alternatively, with policy driving knowledge exchange between HEIs and SMEs, the HEI can consider the absorptive capacity of the SME (Cohen and Levinthal, 1990) to identify mutual benefits and open a dialogue. However, there may be limitations to the SME's capability to engage with new knowledge, restricting the SME's ability to gain a collaborative advantage. Within the HEI–SME academic literature, the argument for absorptive capacity as a measure of suitability has significant support (Moraes Silva et al., 2019), yet there is lack of consideration for additional screening mechanisms.

Given the number of SMEs that the HEI might engage with, and the complexity of some of the collaborations, the HEI may find it necessary to develop SME selection criteria (Rybnicek and Königsgruber, 2019). Although there is significant literature regarding the criteria for exploring inter-organisational alliance selection, and SME considerations regarding university partner selection, there is little research from the perspective of the HEI and the critical elements it should consider or the mechanisms it should employ for screening potential partners to reduce risk and maximise opportunity. The HEI may wish to explore the rationale for the partnership, the compatibility with the SME (strategically and operationally), the capability of the SME and the SME's commitment. Alternatively, it may consider the SME in light of task fit, partnering fit, risk fit or dynamic fit (Cummings and Holmberg, 2012), or reputation, competence (managerial and technical) and personal compatibility (Al-Khalifa and Eggert Peterson, 1999). Barnes et al. (2002) explore areas for consideration including cultural compatibility, operational compatibility, complimentary skills, shared vision and past experience. These authors indicate the necessity to develop a criterion by which to identify SMEs for the HEI–SME alliance creation, emphasising the need for further research.

INTERMEDIARIES, THIRD PARTIES AND NETWORKS

Central to the development of the HEI's alliance creation with SMEs is the ability to access the necessary SMEs. The HEI–SME alliance-creation opportunities are significantly increased with the inclusion of additional parties, intermediaries and networks, identifying potential alliances that may have otherwise remained unexploited.

Third-party facilitators or intermediaries are those organisations outside of the HEI school or SME acting as connectors, brokers, accelerators or matchmakers (Betz et al., 2016), government organisations (triple-helix), enterprise agencies, business incubators, research foundations, innovation centres and private investors (English, 2013). Of these, the most relevant third parties are the non-government organisations that offer contacts, networking opportunities, project scoping, funding, advocacy or sector-specific representation. Indeed, it may be more cost- and time-effective for the HEI to engage with intermediaries with a pre-existing network whilst capitalising on the intermediary's relationships with SMEs (Rosli et al., 2018) to overcome the cultural, financial and operational differences across the HEI and SME. The intermediary can also help address conflict and facilitate collaborative interactions through being an independent party. In addition, 'UK firms are more likely to receive public sector financial support for innovation' (Cosh and Hughes, 2010: 89), yet the strength in focused funding for innovation may truthfully be a weak point if there is a lack of funding for HEI–SME alliance creation. The challenge for the HEI is to not only identify and develop relationships with each individual intermediary but also become familiar with their individual practices, skills/expertise, limitations, biases and motives.

SMEs consider networking connections influential for business success (Agostini and Nosella, 2019), with relationships becoming increasingly important to establish HEI credentials (Yusuf, 2008). Yet, little recognition has been paid to the limited representation of the SME community within each network (Laschewski et al., 2002), highlighting a need for the HEI to identify SME-specific/-targeted networks. In addition, large firms and SMEs have differing network patterns (Colombo et al., 2012), with SMEs experiencing limitations upon financial resources, staffing capacity and networking expertise. The HEI should be mindful of these challenges, exploring the classification or characteristics of the SME and its purpose or intentions, as a one-size-fits-all networking approach will not be appropriate. For example, the HEI could explore conferences, standard-setting forums and alumni networks to expand the exchange opportunities for SMEs, students, alumni and HEI staff, or to provide regional leadership where none exists. A further consideration is the networks within the HEI itself such as students' networks, internal business networks, the HEI business-engagement programmes and structure, innovation centres, business support centres and staff networks.

DELIVERY

Management by the HEI of the collaborative HEI–SME project is critical to success, requiring prudent monitoring of progress to ensure quality, delivery and satisfaction, whether actual or perceived. Yet, there is scant literature regarding the engagement of project management within higher education, with the focus upon research or RandD. Project management is defined as 'the application of processes, methods, skills, knowledge and experience to achieve specific project objectives according to the project acceptance criteria within agreed parameters [...] constrained to a finite timescale and budget' (Association for Project Management, 2020). The HEI can consider agile project management to allow for the uncertainty or complexity of the collaboration and need for flexibility (Collyer and Warren, 2009) across the core practices including project plans, resource allocation, team management, procedures and tools. An alternative approach is portfolio management, where a number of related collaborations are grouped to gain benefits by managing leadership, communication, workflows and resources within the portfolio (Schwalbe, 2017). Yet, this can result in limiting the dedication and time available to each project (Gallagher, 2015), and potentially reduce or even damage the individual SME relationship (Darabi and Clark, 2012).

The HEI–SME collaboration is temporary and unique, curtailed to a defined timeframe; yet, the HEI may wish to identify mechanisms by which it can explore standardisation, communication and resource allocation (Porter, 2019). The HEI–SME landscape will involve multiple, contradictory objectives and priorities that require aligning, such as competing or disconnected third-party goals from public funders or third parties, or the constraints of the SME. By considering a more explorative alliance rather than an exploitative alliance (Nielsen et al., 2018), the HEI can incorporate tangible and optimising goals regarding the current and potential alliances and collaborations, reducing possible institutional and cultural differences. Defined, agreed milestones would support this collaborative process (Peças and Henriques, 2006), with metrics that include observable and measurable behaviours, allowing agreed deviation from and reconsideration of the goals.

The HEI must carefully consider the project-related infrastructure, including the leadership, support, training and deployment, stressing potential cultural and personnel difficulties to overcome within the HEI. However, Philbin (2008) highlights that smaller projects remove the necessity for overly systematic project management, arguing that it could obstruct the collaboration. An additional consideration is the experience, capability and willingness of each SME to manage a complex project (Buganza et al., 2014), with the HEI wanting to build mutual trust and develop the collaborative alliance whilst ensuring success. Furthermore, publicly supported projects may restrain or prescribe considerations for the project management (Hemmert et al., 2014). The HEI new to the HEI–SME alliance creation may not consider adaptability (e.g. people, implementation, collaboration) to manage change but instead focus upon the control elements (e.g. planning, processes, assurance).

EVALUATION

By identifying the success of the immediate HEI–SME collaboration, the HEI can potentially expand the boundaries to develop new or additional opportunities that were not initially considered (Rosli et al., 2018). Yet, Massey (2006) contends that effective evaluation mechanisms are infrequently employed with approaches being prejudiced towards innovation or RandD, arguing that an effective evaluation mechanism possibly does not exist. In addition, the variables within the HEI–SME collaboration also create difficulties in developing key performance indicators (KPIs) for comparison of alliances (Schofield, 2013) or to evaluate the width and depth of collaborations, and there is limited research relating to evaluating the activity across several stakeholders with differing aims and objectives. The evaluation should include all stakeholders within the collaboration, such as the HEI academics, HEI researchers, HEI support staff, SME staff, students and third-party individuals. Evaluation frameworks propose various considerations such as expected outcomes, actual outcomes, impact for all stakeholders (Thatcher et al., 2016), institutional–organisational–individual evaluation (Phan and Siegel, 2006) and company–university–technical-relationship evaluation (Barbolla and Corredera, 2009). The evaluation will enable all stakeholders to identify the impact of the collaboration, highlighting whether this is a single, satisfying alliance, a sustainable alliance or one to be terminated.

Selecting an appropriate evaluation tool that can measure performance for all stakeholders whilst unifying each element of the collaboration is key for the HEI (Manville et al., 2019). The evaluation moves from reflection-in-action to reflection-on-action (Schön, 1992). The evaluation stage, following delivery, should be based upon rigorous KPIs, measuring both tangible and intangible benefits (Philbin, 2008). Performance measurement theory has resulted in the promotion of performance frameworks, with the most widely used framework being the balanced scorecard (Marr and Schiuma, 2003), measuring financial, customer and internal processes, learning and growth. Yet, this appears to exclude cultural and behavioural developments, an area that should be included to create a holistic summary for HEIs exploring a practical inventory to measure outcomes/outputs. By identifying a value assessment criterion, the value to the SME can be made explicit, leading to the SME's alliance with the HEI becoming more strategic. In addition, by monitoring and facilitating evaluation, case studies and additional collaborations can be identified (Apa et al., 2020). Monitoring and evaluating collaborations relating to students will identify the value of student engagement or graduate employment whilst allowing the curriculum to be adapted to meet the needs of the SME (Holden and Jameson, 2002). The HEI will also need to ensure that the agreed monitoring and evaluation also meets the due diligence required for its public KPIs.

CONCLUSION

Despite the enormous attention being given to inter-organisational factors, little focus has been paid to the emergence of HEI–SME alliance-creation factors in a systematic manner. Literature relating to HEI–SME alliances is increasingly focusing upon the enhancement of innovation, specific schools or industries and existing relationships rather than HEI–SME alliance creation. This chapter offers theorisation about how an HEI can evolve to support the creation of the HEI–SME alliance, with consideration of:

- strategic considerations,
- the offer to SMEs,
- operational processes,
- staffing,
- wider relationship factors,
- SME choice,
- intermediaries, third parties and networks,
- delivery, and
- evaluation.

By coalescing the elements, the wider HEI-offer essentials can be considered for the HEI–SME alliance creation. This chapter includes the manner by which different considerations weigh upon and dominate the development of the HEI–SME alliance, incorporating considerations at the concept, strategic and operational levels whilst traversing several lines of enquiry. The development of suitable strategic and operational decisions to meet the needs of the HEI and SME is a complex but vital component to the HEI's wider business alliance creation. Without this, HEIs or HEI schools new to creating alliances with SMEs are confronted with further obstacles that could hinder the HEI–SME alliance creation. HEIs must be allowed to understand the elements influencing the alliance to enable them to implement a sustainable strategy and infrastructure that not only supports the alliance but meets the delivery demands of employability, graduate outcomes, entrepreneurship and their local economy.

The chapter has provided a theoretical framework that moves beyond the current models to provide a more secure base for HEIs with no prior experience in SME alliance-building to move forward from. Empirical research is urgently required to support the HEI new to the HEI–SME phenomena, allowing the HEI to not only respond to emerging opportunities but also allowing the time to cultivate its strategic and operational processes. This highlights the need for a practice-based process model relating to the HEI's operational considerations and the exploration of impact regarding the processes that the HEI engages with when creating SME alliances.

REFERENCES

Agostini, L. and Nosella, A. (2019) 'Inter-organizational relationships involving SMEs: A bibliographic investigation into the state of the art', *Long Range Planning*, 52(1), pp. 1–31.

Al-Khalifa, A. K. and Eggert Peterson, S. (1999) 'The partner selection process in international joint ventures', *European Journal of Marketing*, 33(11/12), pp. 1064–81.

Apa, R., De Marchi, V., Grandinetti, R. and Sedita, S. R. (2020) 'University-SME collaboration and innovation performance: The role of informal relationships and absorptive capacity', *Journal of Technology Transfer*, 46, pp. 961–88.

Association for Project Management (2020) *What is project management?* Available at: www.apm.org.uk/resources/what-is-project-management/ (Accessed: 7 May 2021).

Attia, A. M. (2015) 'National innovation systems in developing countries: Barriers to university–industry collaboration in Egypt', *The International Journal of Technology Management and Sustainable Development*, 14(2), pp. 113–24.

Barbolla, A. M. B. and Corredera, J. R. C. (2009) 'Critical factors for success in university-industry research projects', *Technology Analysis and Strategic Management*, 21(5), pp. 599–616.

Barnes, T., Pashby, I. and Gibbons, A. (2002) 'Effective university-industry interaction: A multi-case evaluation of collaborative RandD projects', *European Management Journal*, 20(3), pp. 272–85.

Betz, F., Carayannis, E., Jetter, A., Min, W., Phillips, F. and Shin, D. W. (2016) 'Modeling an innovation intermediary system within a helix', *Journal of the Knowledge Economy*, 7(2), pp. 587–99.

Biddle, B. J. (1979) *Role theory: Expectations, identities, and behaviors*. New York: Academic Press.

Bjerregaard, T. (2009) 'Universities-industry collaboration strategies: A micro-level perspective', *European Journal of Innovation Management*, 12(2), pp. 161–76.

Bjerregaard, T. (2010) 'Industry and academia in convergence: Micro-institutional dimensions of RandD collaboration', *Technovation*, 30(2), pp. 100–08.

Buganza, T., Colombo, G. and Landoni, P. (2014) 'Small and medium enterprises' collaborations with universities for new product development: An analysis of the different phases', *Journal of Small Business and Enterprise Development*, 21(1), pp. 69–86.

Canhoto, A. I., Quinton, S., Jackson, P. and Dibb, S. (2016) 'The co-production of value in digital, university–industry RandD collaborative projects', *Industrial Marketing Management*, 56(C), pp. 86–96.

Cao, J., John Foster, M. and Watkins-Mathys, L. (2014) 'IT-software SMEs in China, technology transfer from universities and entrepreneurship, a successful nexus?', *Frontiers of Business Research in China*, 8(1), pp. 18–48.

Cohen, W. M. and Levinthal, D. A. (1990) 'Absorptive Capacity: A new perspective on learning and innovation', *Administrative Science Quarterly*, 35(1), pp. 128–52.

Collier, A., Gray, B. J. and Ahn, M. J. (2011) 'Enablers and barriers to university and high technology SME partnerships', *Small Enterprise Research*, 18(1), pp. 2–18.

Collyer, S. and Warren, C. M. J. (2009) 'Project management approaches for dynamic environments', *International Journal of Project Management*, 27(4), pp. 355–64.

Colombo, M. G., Laursen, K. and Magnusson, M. (2012) 'Introduction: Small business and networked innovation: Organizational and managerial challenges', *Journal of Small Business Management*, 50(2), pp. 181–90.

Corbin, J. M. (2015) *Basics of qualitative research: techniques and procedures for developing grounded theory*, 4th edn. Edited by A. L. Strauss. Los Angeles: Sage.

Cosh, A. and Hughes, A. (2010) 'Never mind the quality feel the width: University–industry links and government financial support for innovation in small high-technology businesses in the UK and the USA', *The Journal of Technology Transfer*, 35(1), pp. 66–91.

Cumming, M., Mockridge, A., Newth, O. and Sze-Yin, T. (2012) *SME too: How can HEIs and SMEs interact more effectively?* Warwick: University of Warwick.

Cummings, J. L. and Holmberg, S. R. (2012) 'Best-fit alliance partners: The use of critical success factors in a comprehensive partner selection process', *Long Range Planning*, 45(2/3), pp. 136–59.

Darabi, F. and Clark, M. (2012) 'Developing business school SMEs collaboration: The role of trust', *International Journal of Entrepreneurial Behaviour and Research*, 18(4), pp. 477–93.

De Moraes Silva, D. R., Lucas, L. O. and Vonortas, N. S. (2019) 'Internal barriers to innovation and university-industry cooperation among technology-based SMEs in Brazil', *Industry and Innovation*, pp. 1–29.

Department for Business Energy and Industrial Strategy (2019) *Business population estimates for the UK and regions 2019*. London: UK Government.

Edmunds, T. K. (2017) 'Perceived barriers to SME-College collaboration: The case of the Province of Manitoba', *College Quarterly*, 20(2): 1. Accessed June 20, 2022. https://search-ebscohost-com.libezproxy.open.ac.uk/login.aspx?direct=true&db=ehh&AN=123126313&site=ehost-live&scope=site.

English, J. (2013) 'SME university collaboration- A roadmap to success', *Annals: Series on Engineering Sciences*, 5(2), pp. 7–12.

European Commission (2016) *User guide to the SME definition*. Accessed June 20, 2022. https://ec.europa.eu/regional_policy/sources/conferences/state-aid/sme/smedefinitionguide_en.pdf

Fogg, H. (2012) 'Tracing the links between absorptive capacity, university knowledge Exchange and competitive advantage in SMEs', *Entrepreneurship and Innovation*, 13(1), pp. 35–44.

Frasquet, M., Calderón, H. and Cervera, A. (2012) 'University-industry collaboration from a relationship marketing perspective: An empirical analysis in a Spanish University', *Higher Education*, 64(1), pp. 85–98.

Fukugawa, N. (2005) 'Characteristics of knowledge interactions between universities and small firms in Japan', *International Small Business Journal*, 23(4), pp. 379–401.

Galan-Muros, V. and Davey, T. (2017) 'The UBC ecosystem: putting together a comprehensive framework for university-business cooperation', *The Journal of Technology Transfer*, 44(4), pp. 1311–46.

Gallagher, P. (2015) 'Graduate transition into work: The bridging role of graduate placement programmes in the small- and medium-sized enterprise workplace', *Journal of Education and Work*, 28, pp. 461–80.

Goduscheit, R. C. and Knudsen, M. P. (2015) 'How barriers to collaboration prevent progress in demand for knowledge: A dyadic study of small and medium-sized firms, research and technology organizations and universities', *Creativity and Innovation Management*, 24(1), pp. 29–54.

Heaton, N., Mccracken, M. and Harrison, J. (2008) 'Graduate recruitment and development: Sector influence on a local market/regional economy', *Education and Training*, 50(4), p. 276-288.

Heikkinen, M. T., Mainel, T., Still, J. and Tähtinen, J. (2007) 'Roles for managing in mobile service development nets', *Industrial Marketing Management*, 36(7), pp. 909–25.

Hemmert, M., Bstieler, L. and Okamuro, H. (2014) 'Bridging the cultural divide: Trust formation in university–industry research collaborations in the US, Japan, and South Korea', *Technovation*, 34(10), pp. 605–16.

Holden, R. and Jameson, S. (2002) 'Employing graduates in SMEs: towards a research agenda', *Journal of Small Business and Enterprise Development*, 9(3), pp. 271–84.

Howells, J., Ramlogan, R. and Cheng, S.-L. (2012) 'Innovation and university collaboration: paradox and complexity within the knowledge economy', *Cambridge Journal of Economics*, 36(3), pp. 703–21.

Johnston, A. (2020) State of the art review university-industry collaboration: Are SMEs different? Accessed June 20, 2022. https://www.enterpriseresearch.ac.uk/wp-content/uploads/2020/06/No41-University-Industry-Collaboration-Are-SMEs-Different-Johnston-FINAL-1.pdf

Jongbloed, B., Enders, J. and Salerno, C. (2008) 'Higher education and its communities: Interconnections, interdependencies and a research agenda', *Higher Education*, 56(3), pp. 303–24.

Kadoić, N., Ređep, N. and Divjak, B. (2018) 'A new method for strategic decision-making in higher education', *Central European Journal of Operations Research*, 26(3), pp. 611–28. doi:

Karlsson, J., Booth, S. and Odenrick, P. (2007) 'Academics' strategies and obstacles in achieving collaboration between Universities and SMEs', *Tertiary Education and Management*, 13(3), pp. 187–201.

Kern, A., Laguecir, A. and Leca, B. (2018) 'Behind smoke and mirrors: A political approach to decoupling', *Organization Studies*, 39(4), pp. 543–64.

Kholmuminov, S., Kholmuminov, S. and Wright, R. E. (2019) 'Resource dependence theory analysis of higher education institutions in Uzbekistan', *Higher Education*, 77(1), pp. 59–79.

Klofsten, M. and Jones-Evans, D. (1996) 'Stimulation of technology-based small firms—A case study of university-industry cooperation', *Technovation*, 16(4), pp. 187–213.

Kneller, R., Mongeon, M., Cope, J., Garner, C. and Ternouth, P. (2014) 'Industry–university collaborations in Canada, Japan, the UK and USA – With emphasis on publication freedom and managing the intellectual property lock-up problem', *PLOS ONE*, 9(3), e90302.

Krathu, W., Pichler, C., Xiao, G., Werthner, H., Neidhardt, J., Zapletal, M., Huemer, C. (2014) 'Inter-organizational success factors: a cause and effect model', *Information systems and e-business management*, 13(3), pp. 553–593. doi:10.1007/s10257-014-0258-z.

Laschewski, L., Phillipson, J. and Gorton, M. (2002) 'The facilitation and formalisation of small business networks: Evidence from the North East of England', *Environment and Planning C: Government and Policy*, 20(3), pp. 375–91.

Lee-Davies, L. (2018) 'Prehistoric process in HE: A critical review of institutional processes for business–academic partnerships in management development provision', *Industry and Higher Education*, 33(1), pp. 66–75.

Leitch, S. (2006) *Prosperity for all in the global economy-world class skills*. Final Report. Accessed June 20, 2022. https://assets.publishing.service.gov.uk/government/uploads/system/uploads/attachment_data/file/243599/0118404865.pdf

Manville, G., Karakas, F., Polkinghorne, M. and Petford, N. (2019) 'Supporting open innovation with the use of a balanced scorecard approach: a study on deep smarts and effective knowledge transfer to SMEs', *Production Planning and Control*, 30(10–12), pp. 842–53.

Marr, B. and Schiuma, G. (2003) 'Business performance measurement – Past, present and future', *Management Decision*, 41(8), pp. 680–87.

Massey, C. (2006) 'A new conceptualisation of business development for SMEs: A focus on development potential', *Environment and Planning. C, Government and Policy*, 24(1), pp. 37–49.

Meyer, J. W. (2010) 'World society, institutional theories, and the actor', *Annual Review of Sociology*, 36(1), pp. 1–20.

Mourao, A. and Goncalves-Coelho, A. (2016) Industry–university co-operation in the product and process development: Experiences with Portuguese SMEs, in *2008 IEEE International Technology Management Conference (ICE)*. IEEE, pp. 1–8.

Nielsen, J. A., Mathiassen, L. and Hansen, A. M. (2018) 'Exploration and exploitation in organizational learning: A critical application of the 4I model', *British Journal of Management*, 29(4), pp. 835–50.

Payne, A. F., Storbacka, K. and Frow, P. (2008) 'Managing the co-creation of value', *Journal of the Academy of Marketing Science*, 36(1), pp. 83–96.

Peças, P. and Henriques, E. (2006) 'Best practices of collaboration between university and industrial SMEs', *Benchmarking: An International Journal*, 13(1/2), pp. 54–67.

Perks, H., Gruber, T. and Edvardsson, B. (2012) 'Co-creation in radical service innovation: A systematic analysis of microlevel processes', *Journal of Product Innovation Management*, 29(6), pp. 935–51.

Phan, P. H. C. and Siegel, D. S. (2006) 'The effectiveness of university technology transfer', *Foundations and Trends in Entrepreneurship*, 2(2), pp. 77–144.

Philbin, S. (2008) 'Process model for university-industry research collaboration', *European Journal of Innovation Management*, 11(4), pp. 488–521.

Piterou, A. and Birch, C. (2014) 'The role of higher education institutions in supporting innovation in SMEs: University-based incubators and student internships as knowledge transfer tools', *The Journal of Innovation Impact*, 7(1), pp. 72–9.

Porter, S. (2019) 'Project management in higher education: A grounded theory case study', *Library Management*, 40(5), pp. 338–52.

Powell, J. (2012) 'The university role in the innovative leadership of small to medium sized enterprises', *International Journal of Entrepreneurial Behaviour and Research*, 18(4), pp. 396–416.

Prospects (2020) *What do graduates do? Regional Edition 2019/20.* Accessed June 20, 2022. Available at https://graduatemarkettrends.cdn.prismic.io/graduatemarkettrends/1a77ed2a-3431-4954-b8c4-d1ca3982a969_what-do-graduates-do-regional-edition-201920.pdf

Rampersad, G. C. (2015) 'Developing university-business cooperation through work-integrated learning', *International Journal of Technology Management*, 68(3/4), pp. 203–27.

Ranga, L. M., Miedema, J. and Jorna, R. (2008) 'Enhancing the innovative capacity of small firms through triple helix interactions: Challenges and opportunities', *Technology Analysis and Strategic Management*, 20(6), pp. 697–716.

Rese, A., Gemünden, H.-G. and Baier, D. (2013) '"Too many cooks spoil the broth": Key persons and their roles in inter-organizational innovations', *Creativity and Innovation Management*, 22(4), pp. 390–407.

Rosli, A., de Silva, M., Rossi, F. and Yip, N. (2018) 'The long-term impact of engaged scholarship: How do SMEs capitalise on their engagement with academics to explore new opportunities?', *International Small Business Journal: Researching Entrepreneurship*, 36(4), pp. 400–28.

Rybnicek, R. and Königsgruber, R. (2019) 'What makes industry–university collaboration succeed? A systematic review of the literature', *Journal of Business Economics*, 89(2), pp. 221–50.

Samuel, G., Donovan, C. and Lee, J. (2018) 'University-industry teaching collaborations: A case study of the MSc in Structural Integrity co-produced by Brunel University London and The Welding Institute', *Studies in Higher Education*, 43(4), pp. 769–85.

Santoro, M. and Gopalakrishnan, S. (2001) 'Relationship dynamics between university research centers and industrial firms: Their impact on technology transfer activities', *The Journal of Technology Transfer*, 26(1), pp. 163–71.

Schofield, T. (2013) 'Critical success factors for knowledge transfer collaborations between university and industry', *Journal of Research Administration*, 44(2), p. 38-46.

Schön, D. A. (1992) *The reflective practitioner: How professionals think in action*. Abingdon: Routledge.

Schwalbe, K. (2017) *An introduction to project management*, 6th edn. Minneapolis: CreateSpace Independent Publishing Platform.

Shaw, S. and Allen, J. B. (2006) '"It basically is a fairly loose arrangement … and that works out fine, really." Analysing the dynamics of an interorganisational partnership', *Sport Management Review*, 9(3), pp. 203–28.

Thatcher, J., Alao, H., A., Brown, C. J. and Choudhary, S. (2016) 'Enriching the values of micro and small business research projects: co-creation service provision as perceived by academic, business and student', *Studies in Higher Education*, 41(3), pp. 560–81.

Thorgren, S., Wincent, J. and Örtqvist, D. (2010) 'Unleashing synergies in strategic networks of SMEs: The influence of partner fit on corporate entrepreneurship', *International Small Business Journal*, 30(5), pp. 453–71.

Turkes, M. C. (2018) 'Coordination of SMEs development: Investigating their needs for external assistance provided by specialized institutions (small and medium enterprises)', *Academic Journal of Economic Studies*, 4(4), p. 12-18.

Woods, A. and Dennis, C. (2009) 'What do UK small and medium sized enterprises think about employing graduates?', *Journal of Small Business and Enterprise Development*, 16(4), pp. 642–59.

Yusuf, S. (2008) *'Intermediating knowledge exchange between universities and businesses'*, Research Policy, 37(8), pp. 1167–74.

28

A Living Agenda: The Role of Local Policy in Employability

Catherine O'Connor

THE CONCEPT OF GRADUATE EMPLOYABILITY

Graduate employability, at surface level, is a simple concept. However, beneath the surface of what has become a central pillar of higher education (HE) sits a myriad of ideas about what underpins the concept and the 'journey' students undertake to arrive at this end destination. In a review for an Institute of Employment Studies briefing, Hillage and Pollard (1998) sought to use the literature both to define employability and provide a framework to inform future policy development. They concluded that employability was 'having the capability to gain initial employment, maintain employment and obtain new employment if required' (Hillage and Pollard, 1998: 1) but also emphasised that it was not just about vocational and academic skills but also having labour market awareness to make informed decisions. Other definitions bring in organisations and the benefits of employable graduates, including Harvey (1999: 4) who defined employability as, 'the propensity of the graduate to exhibit attributes that employers anticipate will be necessary for the future effective functioning of their organization'. In an HE academic guide designed to support academics working through the complexities of employability, Yorke (2006: 8) elaborated on broader benefits, considering it as '[a] set of achievements – skills, understandings and personal attributes – that make individuals more likely to gain employment and be successful in their chosen occupations, which benefits themselves, the workforce, the community and the economy'. Taking a slightly different stance, Brown et al. (2003: 111) pointed out that employability was not an isolated notion as it included 'the relative chances of acquiring and maintaining different kinds of employment', framing their discussion around what they called 'the duality of employability' (2003: 110). The absolute dimension within this discussion was students having appropriate skills for jobs, and the relative dimension was linked to supply and demand.

The broad-ranging discussion, dialogue and, occasionally, dispute that surrounds graduate employability are more crucial than ever for two reasons:

- There is increasing policy pressure on HE to deliver graduates who are able to step in to professional-level jobs, earn salaries above a certain level and make a significant contribution to economic productivity.
- The labour market is not a static entity – it is constantly evolving and changing, and this has been accelerated and disrupted by the COVID-19 pandemic.

Tomlinson (2012) noted that governments have increasingly tried to coordinate the relationship between HE and evolving economic requirements and Edge et al. (2019) cited some of the key disruptors leading to this evolution, including big data, the internet of things and automation. Letts (2019: 23) considered the student perspective, as well as identifying that all roles in the labour market will undergo change and noted that 'graduates need a mindset to *grow into roles* and to *grow with* roles rather than simply being prepared [...] for a single, knowable role'.

In reflecting on these external pressures on HE, it is important to note that the very place of graduate employability in HE has been subject to significant dispute, with many scholars seeing it as undermining academic disciplines and forcing a generic approach to degree education. Given that the national policy trajectory, which situates graduate outcomes and graduate contribution to economic productivity as core to the perceived success of HE, can be traced back more than three decades, the discussion in this chapter does not challenge the place of the employability agenda. Rather, it accepts it is a central tenet of the HE experience and considers the challenges of engaging students with the nuances of the local labour market in the context of the demands of national policy. Using this foundation, consideration is given to the conflicts that arise out of a national policy environment that sees graduate contribution to the economy in terms of the level of earnings and a local policy environment that is framed around the value of and potential impact of inclusive growth. The challenges faced by HE institutions in their endeavour to develop students who are able to see their future broadly and beyond specific disciplines, and the potential that lies in local policy initiatives to achieve this, are also considered.

POLICY CONTEXT

National and local policy agendas that relate to HE are playing out in the context of the powerful driver of the Fourth Industrial Revolution. According to Gwata (2019), the digitalisation central to this brings challenges to traditional employment and education and a need for interdisciplinary approaches. These policy agendas have also been disrupted by the COVID-19 pandemic and the impact this has had on industry, education and society. During 2020 and for much of

2021, HE institutions were in stasis with regard to the Teaching Excellence Framework, first awaiting the publication of the Pearce Independent Review, then the response, consultation and final update on the approach to be adopted from the Office for Students. What was clear in this period, however, was that graduate outcomes would continue to play a central role in the metrics used to 'judge' excellence. In parallel to this, there has been a growing political discourse that has pitched science, technology, engineering and mathematics (STEM) subjects and their value against arts subjects deemed to be worthless and 'dead-end' (Weale, 2021).

This sits against the backdrop of discourse and pressure around the importance of digital skills and the need for industry and HE to work together to address skills gaps (BIS, 2009; BIS and DCMS, 2009; Business, Innovation and Skills Committee, 2016; Science and Technology Committee, 2016). If a clear and consistent plank of national policy is the need for education to address skills requirements, then at a local level, this should be accompanied by a need to ensure this approach is appropriately inclusive across the demographic of local populations.

This is very much the case with the local policy context in Leeds and the surrounding area where policy can be viewed in layers, with Leeds City Council policy being the first layer at the centre. The second layer is the West Yorkshire Combined Authority and third is the layer represented by the Northern Powerhouse. The COVID-19 pandemic brought significant disruption to the local policy arena with a need, in particular, to account for:

- Changing organisational working patterns brought about by home-working and the use of technology during the pandemic
- The acceleration of high-street trends in town and city centres, with a shift away from the high street towards online shopping
- Business closures and loss of jobs.

Prior to the pandemic, there was already a significant focus on the importance of digital business and skills in Leeds, with potential for further growth. The Leeds Growth Strategy 2017–23 was shaped to support economic growth and set the framework for regeneration, housing, skills, transport and infrastructure opportunities, identifying both the creative and digital sectors as areas for expansion. This was supported by The Leeds Talent and Skills Plan 2017–23, a framework for collective action to improve the supply of skills to the labour market and the Leeds Digital Skills Action Plan (Leeds Digital Board, 2017), developed by the Council working with a group of employers and education providers, to support access to digital and technology careers and foster connections between employers and education.

The second local policy layer includes The Leeds City Region Enterprise Partnership and West Yorkshire Combined Authority (2017) Strategic Economic Plan 2016–36, which identifies four strategic priorities, one of which is 'Skilled People, Better Jobs', which includes delivering a 'More Jobs, Better Jobs' programme to widen skills and progression opportunities and devising and delivering a programme of action to increase high-level skills. It also includes the West Yorkshire Combined Authority and Leeds City Region Enterprise Partnership (2021) Employment and Skills Framework, which identifies the importance of digital skills and the connection of education to employment. The outer policy layer, the Northern Powerhouse (2016) Independent Economic Review, identified four sectors where the north has 'prime capabilities' and the greatest potential for growth – digital is included in this. Education is identified as a sector with important 'supporting capabilities'.

Graduate skills and associated labour market requirements are addressed through the Leeds Talent and Skills Plan 2017–23, which has a particular focus on solutions for skills gaps. While Leeds is a city with potential for significant economic growth, the plan is clear that there are risks to growth if the need for skills in the local economy cannot be met through supply. Universities are identified as key stakeholders and are urged 'to do more to ensure the supply of labour is adequate and appropriately skilled' (Leeds City Council, 2017: 12) and 'to work more closely together with business involvement directly in the classroom and the lecture' (2017: 26). The plan makes clear the importance of apprenticeships to the local labour market and the value of skills over and above actual qualifications.

EVIDENCING THE SKILLS GAP

The need for digital literacy across disciplines in the context of the Fourth Industrial Revolution is the focus of work by Coldwell-Neilson and Cooper (2019), who also noted the lack of an agreed definition of the term 'digital skills'. Nevertheless, they made the case for its inclusion in the curriculum, for it to be contextualised in line with changing industry expectations and for the scope to be extended to include the notion of digital mindset. They defined this mindset as students 'being flexible and adaptable in all aspects of their learning development, particularly in the context of using digital technologies to support their learning, recognising these technologies will continue to change and develop' (Coldwell-Neilson and Cooper, 2019: 47). In terms of considering the place of digital technology in the labour market, the Leeds City Region is a suitable case study, as it is facing pressure on two fronts, with regard to the buoyancy of digital and technology industries and the significant number of jobs that are likely to disappear across the next two decades because of automation. The 2019 Leeds Labour Market Report indicated that 34% of jobs are at high risk of automation. The current strength of the digital and technology industries and the confidence in future growth could be a counter-balance to this. As of August 2018 102,000 people were employed in digital roles in the region and the number of digital roles is expected to grow 10 times faster than other job opportunities (West

Yorkshire Combined Authority, 2021). However, the 2019 Leeds Labour Market Report identified a 'misalignment' (2019: 62) between the subject range offered by further education and HE and the demands of the local labour market.

While universities might be assumed to be key stakeholders in work to address skills gaps, it cannot be assumed that they can guarantee that the students they attract to study will stay in the locality once they have graduated. Indeed, the movement of graduates is significant with regard to labour market health. By way of example, West Yorkshire is the largest labour market in the North of England, and the West Yorkshire Combined Authority cites a number of factors – or strengths – that are important to economic success. These include a diverse economy, growth in digital employment, infrastructure investment, diverse HE with 'a significant net inflow of students each year' and joint working to address skills priorities.

This consideration of a diverse economy clearly recognises the value of students and graduates and there have been studies that look at the retention rate of graduates in cities by the Centre for Cities. In a 2017 report, the Centre looked at the retention rate of graduates within cities, in particular identifying that Manchester has the second highest retention rate for graduates (after London) of all university cities. While Manchester was shown to retain just over half of its graduates (51%), Leeds was shown to retain only 29% (2017). The report suggested that retention rates were strongly linked to how many students the university attracts from the city itself and from the broader region. The report also showed that Leeds attracted a significant number of graduates who did not originally study in the city, with 60% of those working in Leeds post-graduation having studied elsewhere. This data reflects the value of graduates to local economies, therefore raising the question of how universities connect graduates to opportunities and support them in understanding the breadth of the labour market, beyond the boundaries of their programmes of study, and provide connections to new and evolving opportunities.

CONNECTING TO AND WITH THE LABOUR MARKET

The notion of universities connecting *to* the labour market suggests a straightforward transition from institution to organisation, from programme of study to graduate career. Connecting *with* the labour market is a more complex and multidimensional process and relationship, and one in which universities are required to navigate policy and market expectations. Tomlinson (2012) outlined three dimensions that are central to the link between HE and the labour market: the knowledge and skills that HE imparts to graduates which they, in turn, transfer to the labour market; the 'legitimisation of credentials' (2012: 26), which helps employers screen prospective employees; and the development of personal and cultural attributes. These dimensions can be seen to articulate a 'flow' between

HE and the labour market, with the connectivity between different stakeholder groups clearly outlined by Donald et al. (2018: 515) through the concept of a 'career ecosystem'. The ecosystem is built on key characteristics of interconnectedness, interactions and interdependencies, with the authors identifying the importance of establishing the student voice and ensuring it is considered as 'a major actor in the labour market' (Donald et al., 2018: 514). Donald et al. (2018) noted the constant flow of human capital resulting from these key characteristics but also what they conceived as a spiral learning process, which is essential for adjusting to the changing requirements of the labour market.

The notion of connectedness is pivotal to the work of Bridgstock and Tippett (2019), who argued that a connected approach to learning, with a focus on partnerships, groups, communities and networks, can be both an alternative and complementary approach to the familiar skill-based approaches. The work of Barrie and Pizzica (2019: 149) is also relevant here, with its focus on partnership pedagogy, which they argued focuses attention on how partners interact to shape the curriculum and can be used to develop the quality of employment through the way universities 'partner with industry and the local community to provide the authentic educational opportunities for students that will develop a future of work capabilities'. Carefully formed and maintained partnerships are suggested as ways to facilitate universities to engage with communities and networks to 'critique current trends in employment and education and to collaborate in shaping the future of work' (Barrie and Pizzica, 2019: 150–1). Crisp et al. (2019) acknowledged the fluidity and unpredictability of employability and the perception of universities as sources of skilled labour rather than a place where current thinking and social norms are challenged. They question whether universities should have a greater focus on producing individuals who challenge the nature of work and the economy rather than graduates who accept labour market expectations. In work outlining seven hallmarks that characterise a high-performing, employability-focused university, the authors noted the need for universities to make seamless connections with industry, professional organisations and the wider community, with a concentration on transdisciplinarity, action-focused learning and assessment framed around key challenges facing the world. The conundrum for universities is two-fold:

- How do they achieve the focus outlined by Crisp et al. (2019) within the context of programmes with a strong discipline focus?
- How do they work with students to encourage them to not only think broadly about their graduate opportunities but also to get them to challenge their own assumptions about post-study pathways – assumptions that may have developed throughout their secondary education and through their HE studies?

While transition to graduate employment can be seen as hugely significant, it is certainly not a simple and linear stepping-off process. The navigation is complex and calls for graduates to understand the labour market, understand how they situate themselves in it and evolve to meet its continually shifting demands. When graduates are in demand to address skills gaps, they may need to navigate sectors of the labour market that they may be unfamiliar with and which they may lack confidence in. This navigation process can be viewed as outward-looking when considering how students interact with the labour market. But factors internal to universities, particularly the way institutions support development of employability and the development of networks and partnerships associated with this, are also significant. They shape the discourse within institutions and have a direct impact on student experience and outcomes. Work to address skills gaps could, potentially, be seen as *reactive,* but this chapter makes the case for a more nuanced view. By understanding the place, significance and impact of reactions on the process that students go through at university and after graduation, universities have the opportunity to work *proactively* with students to shape this part of their experience in the context of shifting labour market demands. Key to this will be the human capital (skills and behaviours) and social capital (networks) that graduates bring into play when interacting with the labour market (Tomlinson, 2017). Social capital in particular has been linked to sense of place and sense of community (Acedo et al., 2012), and how this might connect with transition to the labour market is explored later in the chapter.

GRADUATE EMPLOYABILITY AS AN EMBODIMENT OF ACTION RESEARCH

In terms of forming partnerships, understanding and addressing the labour market and any associated skills gaps, universities could be said to be working through continuous cycles of action research. There are numerous models for the action research cycle, which originated in work developed by Lewin (Adelman, 1993). His planning, fact-finding and execution approach is just one of a number outlined by McNiff and Whitehead (2002) in a review of key theorists. The model has been unpicked and reframed by a number of scholars, including Elliott (1991), who conceptualised three repeating cycles, each involving steps of reconnaissance, planning, actions, implementation and monitoring of actions, with repeat cycles allowing for amendments and revisions. Coghlan's (2019) model added a pre-step of context and purpose and four subsequent steps – constructing, planning action, taking action and evaluating action, while Craig (2009) identified eight action research components. Where the literature shows consensus is that scholars view the process in action research and the learning through this process as key, rather than outcomes themselves. Additionally, there is recognition that action research is not necessarily a tidy and linear process (McNiff and Whitehead, 2002; McAteer, 2013), but responsive and multi-layered, with cycles repeated and actions not necessarily carried out in the same order every time. There are two key observations here. Firstly, HE cannot take the position that outcomes to develop graduate employability are *less* important than the process students go through. Secondly, national policy and the metrics-driven regulatory environment in which HE is situated means that outcomes are crucial. However, learning through the process of working through an action research cycle and making changes and adjustments as learning occurs is essential for HE if its responses to the policy environment and labour market requirements are to be timely and impactful. This presents a further challenge for the sector – how to realise change in a meaningful way and, potentially, outside of traditional and often lengthy change processes.

In viewing graduate employability as an action research cycle, it is clear the different approaches to it cannot be considered in isolation. Rather, it is the way they *connect* with one another that informs actions through a continuous cycle and which shapes the way in which universities work through the employability agenda, as illustrated in Figure 28.1. These stages can be used to align to the suggested four mainstay components of graduate employability (illustrated by the blue boxes in Figure 28.1) in normal labour market conditions and it is worth taking a moment to reflect on the complexity that is situated within these components.

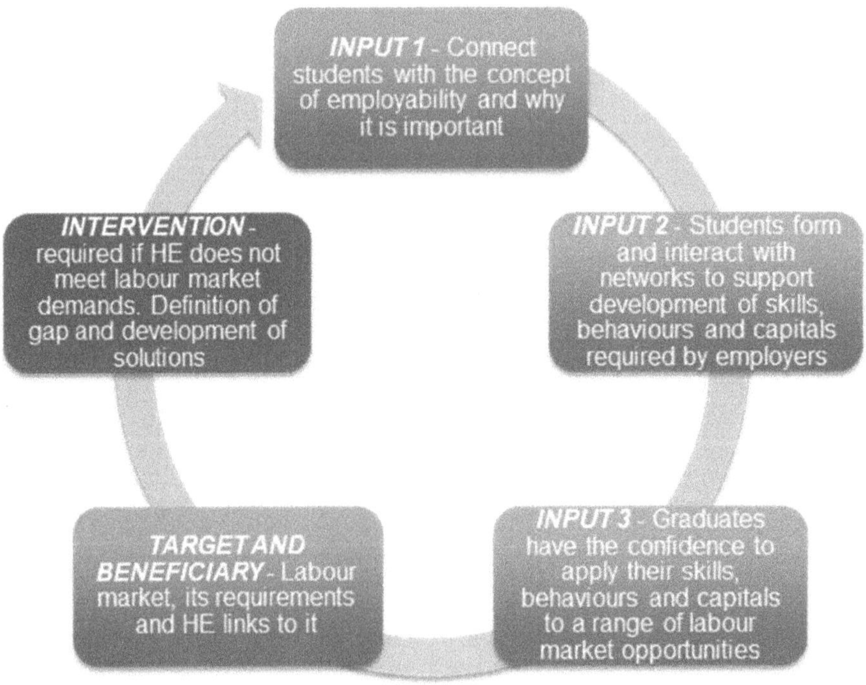

Figure 28.1 Employability action research cycle

Source: adapted from O'Connor, 2019.

In terms of Input 1, the employability agenda could be seen to be conceptualised both by universities and labour market as a single agenda but there are nuances that emerge through different understandings and through links to different sectors of the labour market. In terms of Input 2, attributes are defined and developed based on influences from both the proximal university environment and the distal labour market environment. Graduates develop skills and attributes through proximal and distal connections and through interventions embedded in the curriculum included as part of the broader university experience, or both. The challenge for HE is to bridge the gap between proximal and distal. In terms of Input 3, broader views of the development and management of employability develop when graduates and their attributes are looked at in a more holistic way and in the context of communities that graduates are, have been or could be part of. The cycle outlined here does not explicitly consider the place, influence and importance of students and graduates as individuals but they can be viewed as being central to it, with Inputs 1 to 3 being used as Harvey (2000) suggested, to empower students through, among other things, the curriculum and critical and transformative approaches to learning. His notion of the responsiveness of HE is directly relevant to interventions in the labour market to address skills gaps.

If a skills gap occurs and businesses are unable to recruit graduates with the skills they are looking for, there is a fifth component in the cycle (shown in the red box in Figure 28.1). This takes the form of an intervention. The first three components in the cycle are viewed as inputs to the labour market, which is both the target for and beneficiary of these inputs. However, where the inputs do not satisfy the labour market, an intervention (component five) is required. Such interventions can be initiated directly by HE or could be the result of policy initiatives. However, literature in the field suggests they should be informed by business, industry and community networks so that university responses are a natural part of the ebb and flow of the local economy.

This continuous action research cycle, for the purposes of this chapter, is framed around the widely accepted four-stage action research cycle of:

- Plan
- Act
- Observe
- Reflect.

Their alignment to the components in Figure 28.1 is shown in Table 28.1, which illustrates the 'messy', non-linear nature of action research but also the potential at each stage for universities to respond to issues through the living agenda in which employability is situated. It also illustrates the place of student and employer stakeholder groups in the action research cycle and makes clear that universities cannot operate in this sphere without working closely with students and employers.

The cycles outlined above, in Figure 28.1 and in Table 28.1, do not necessarily mean that the change and responses required to address skills gaps can be easily introduced but it helps to illustrate the way in which the concepts and agendas around skills gaps constantly shift, and any attempt to define them is likely to only be relevant when related to broader economic context and at a specific point in time. In addition, addressing this shifting agenda requires engagement and connections through stakeholder groups in order to create a shared understanding, approach and benefits.

EMBEDDING DIGITAL SKILLS

Just as HE must peel back the layers of policy to consider how to address labour market issues, it must also layer its responses and the speed at which these responses can be implemented and recognise that the extent to which they can be impactful will vary. Of course, all universities offer career guidance and advice but this, it can be argued, can potentially only scratch the surface of the challenge posed by the digital skills gap. A much deeper level of consideration of skills issues and potential solutions is required to address the requirements of a changing labour market and should be expected of universities if they are to play an effective role in addressing these dynamic requirements. The specialist programmes that might once have addressed the skills deployed in digital and technology industries may still have a place but they do not have the capacity to satisfy demand and they do not address the fact that the pace of technological change means that digital skills will be required across every occupation open to graduates. Universities, therefore, must consider how to embed and 'normalise' digital skills through their curriculum, as well as how to generate interest in sectors and opportunities that students might not have ever contemplated working in. The Fourth Industrial Revolution is set to 'disrupt nearly every industry in every country, creating new opportunities and challenges for people, places and businesses' (Department for Business, Energy & Industrial Strategy, 2019). The natural and assumed role here for universities in this 'revolution' would be through STEM-related research and knowledge exchange but the problem-solving and innovation required to address these changes go far beyond this and permeate into every aspect of work with students and all aspects of course and curriculum design.

Gwata (2019) argued for a shift from mono-disciplinary and increasingly narrow approaches to an interdisciplinary focus, outlining the notion of 'T'-shaped employees who possess in-depth knowledge in a specialist area, enhanced by broad knowledge alongside. To achieve this, HE in the UK therefore has to find a way to ensure students develop a broad perspective on their potential future employment, beyond the confines of their discipline focus. This goes beyond the boundaries of transition to HE and transition to the labour market. It requires

Table 28.1 Components of graduate employability aligned to the action research cycle

Employability component	Primary action research element(s)	Secondary action research element(s)
INPUT 1 – Connect students with the concept of employability and why it is important	**Plan** – Staff decide each year how to work with students to address core concepts, plan engagement with them and their use through interaction and networking	**Act, Observe and Reflect** – These elements may need to be utilised if anything disrupts planning and depending on student reaction to inputs
INPUT 2 – Students form and interact with networks to support development of skills, behaviours and capitals required by employers	**Act** – Staff and students put into practice core concepts through interaction and networking	**Observe, Reflect and Plan** – Feedback from students and employers will support this; changes may need to be planned depending on success of interaction and networking
INPUT 3 – Graduates have the confidence to apply their skills, behaviours and capitals to a range of labour market opportunities	**Act** – Students take what they have learned and practiced and apply to graduate opportunities	**Observe, Reflect and Plan** – Institutions and employers need to use data and experience to consider if additional planning is needed to inform updated actions
TARGET AND BENEFICIARY – Labour market, its requirements and HE links to it	**Observe** – Close and structured employer networks and partnerships need to be utilised to understand what is needed from graduates and how the labour market is benefiting from this (or not getting what it needs)	**Reflect, Plan and Act** – Institutions need to be continually mindful of local labour market conditions and the need to respond to these
INTERVENTION – Required if HE does not meet labour market demands. Definition of gap and development of solutions required	**Act** – Institutions, driven by national and local policy, need to move swiftly when interventions are required	**Observe, Reflect and Plan** – The efficacy and impact of interventions needs to be carefully monitored and additional responses may need to be considered

universities and the stakeholder groups they work with to consider how students locate themselves in broader communities and how they develop their sense of place during their studies so that they understand their locality, how they will transition to being active citizens and how their inputs and their actions can play a key role in positive development and change in a geographical area.

DEVELOPING A SENSE OF PLACE

The multi-faceted nature of employability and graduate transition to the labour market has been explored above and the complexities around this are intensified when the broader student journey and all levels of student transitions are considered. Literature rightly tends to focus in on particular aspects of student journey, student experience and student outcomes to support depth of understanding but connections also need to be made across different fields of study in order to encourage broader understanding and a more holistic view of the different factors at play at different points in the student lifecycle.

There is a wealth of literature looking at student belonging, with less of it considering sense of place, but these can be considered to be fields that overlap. This overlap, however, is not without its challenges when seeking to understand student journey, experience and transitions and it is worth noting a consideration raised by Imperial College London. Research on student belonging has also been a feature of work carried out by its Centre for Higher Education Research and Scholarship and the Centre (n.d.) notes that engagement focuses on what students do and is something that can be measured; belonging, on the other hand, considers perceptions and behaviours, which are more challenging to measure and evaluate.

Ahn and Davis (2020) identified four domains of student belonging at university in a study that involved 426 participants at Bangor University and which asked participants to write down 10 words or things that come to mind when thinking about sense of belonging. The results reinforced that sense of belonging is strongly associated with two particular domains – academic engagement and social engagement. However, the study also surfaced two further domains – surroundings and personal space – which the authors noted were often neglected. In the context of this chapter, it is the latter two domains that are seen to be relevant to and have commonality with the notion of place. Ahn and Davis (2020) noted the surroundings domain to cover living accommodation, geographical location and cultural location, while the personal space domain covered life satisfaction, life attitudes, identity and personal interests. The authors noted that the domains are independent of each other but that student engagement in HE needs to reflect all four domains if it is to be successful.

The differing approaches to the 'geographies of higher education' are summarised by Holton (2015: 21) and included student mobility, impact on neighbourhood, the intense experience of the first year and impact on identities. However, he also noted the tendency for literature 'to focus solely on the transition into University, ignoring that students often experience pressures *throughout* their degree pathway' (Holton, 2015: 21). Whether it can be described as a pressure or not is open to debate but moving into the labour market is certainly another key transition for students at the end of their studies. Through a study that gathered data by walking with first-year students through a city, Holton recognised that they may have more superficial associations with place but that this can strengthen significantly when they move from halls of residence to local accommodation. He also noted that 'relationships with place become layered for undergraduates as they experience different parts of the city at different times' (Holton, 2015: 27).

In a 2015 paper, Holton considered sense of place to explore how 'local' students – in the 'position of being both students *and* local residents can be challenged through the action of attending a "local" institution' (Holton, 2014: 821). Themes considered in the paper included how becoming a student could disrupt sense of place for local students, how going to university could open up 'new' places for local students and how relationship with place might be different for local and non-local students. Connecting directly to the employability agenda, Holdsworth (2006) suggested local students had the opportunity to build the social capital needed to help with boosting graduate employment prospects if they choose to stay in the area after graduation.

In considering belonging as related to place rather than just the university environment, it is useful to note the six processes related to place that were outlined by Seamon (2013): place interactions, place identity, place release, place realisation, place creation and place intensification. Seamon (2013: 19) noted that all six processes contribute to 'modes and intensity of emotional bonds with a place'. It is useful here, then, to consider how these processes might be related to student journey and, in particular, to the transition to the labour market, and this is illustrated in Table 28.2. While Processes 1–4 in Table 28.2 involve what places are and how they work, the final two processes are about how 'positive human effort' (Seamon, 2014: 18) can improve (or undermine) places.

Emerging from this, the considerations for universities would seem to be twofold. Firstly, how do the experiences and interactions linked to developing the skills and behaviours required for graduate employment contribute to the layering that Holton (2014) outlined as key to relationship with place. And, secondly, how do universities use their own role and status within their locality to further connect students with their locality and its opportunities.

For the purposes of this discussion, it is useful to consider the role of universities as anchor institutions within their localities. According to the UK Commission for Employment and Skills (2015), an anchor institution 'plays a significant and recognised role in a locality by making a strategic contribution to the local economy'. There are a number of ways that universities contribute in this regard. They are

Table 28.2 Place processes and labour market transition

Process	Seamon's interpretation	Connection to labour market transition
1: Place interactions	Relates to 'typical on-goings' (Seamon, 2013: 16), regular actions, behaviours and situations.	For students, this relates to making interactions with employers as part of their typical and regular experience. This could be through guest speakers, employer-led assessment, employer-focused events, employer challenge projects, work placements and work-based projects that are part of their programme of study.
2: Place identity	Relates to people living in an area and that place being a significant part of their lives. This is undermined if individuals or groups are isolated.	For students, this relates to them making connections and developing an understanding of the town or city they are studying in. They may not feel they are a part of all aspects of the location while they are a student but, at the very least, they need to feel that they can be part of it – that they can envision their pathway forward.
3: Place release	Relates to unexpected events – chance meetings, enjoyment of cultural events – and through them people are 'released more deeply into themselves' (Seamon, 2013 17).	Relates to the interactions outlined in Process 1 but requires specific and personal experience – for example, praise for work carried out on placement, a significant contribution being made and noted on placement, being offered further work on the basis of placement performance, choosing to explore extra-curricular work and career-related activities and having a positive or impactful experience through these.
4: Place realisation	Requires environmental and human aspects to be combined and it is this combination that gives a place its distinctiveness or 'palpable presence of place' (Seamon, 2013 17).	Students have made enough connections and had sufficient positive experiences to move away from seeing their university location as transitional to it becoming permanent and the place where they will (initially at least) develop their career.

5: Place creation	People are active in relation to place; they use their commitment and knowledge in policy, planning and design so that Processes 1 to 4 can be enhanced.	Students may be active citizens throughout their time at university but, if they transition to the labour market in their university location, they begin to be in a position to influence that place, how it operates, the issues on local agendas and the impact of these things on other people.
6: Place intensification	Relates to policy and design and how they can actively contribute to the quality and character of a place.	

Source: processes from Seamon (2013).

large employers in their own right, they may connect with employers for research and knowledge exchange and the staff and students they attract make their own economic and social contribution to the local area. Yorkshire Universities identified five core dimensions of an anchor institution: employment, procurement, land and assets, service delivery and civic contributions. The group also identified the need to focus on benefits to both institution and locality through being an anchor and the potential for individual and collective action as institutions. In Leeds, this collective approach has manifested itself in the Place-Based Economic Recovery Network (PERN), formed on the back of discussions about how universities could be involved in shaping and delivering the local industrial strategy. The network has focused on a number of key agendas around devolution, levelling-up, post-COVID recovery, health innovation, climate change and entrepreneurship, all of which are crucial to economic health and productivity.

CONCLUSION

This chapter has considered the complexities in how the graduate employability agenda is framed and operationalised in the context of national policy scrutiny and pressure. This means it is the economic contribution post-graduation, rather than civic, cultural and societal contribution, that is the default focus that national policy concerns itself with, in terms of the level of graduate job and the level of graduate salary. Local policy has a much more nuanced concern around ensuring that businesses and organisations within areas can recruit employees with the right skills and behaviours and ensuring that approaches to the labour market and benefits from it are inclusive to all. Together, they drive the living agenda that constitutes graduate employability. If universities are going to address the nuances of local needs, they need to consider deeply how they might help students understand the local labour market and the opportunities it can offer. How they might embed and 'normalise' digital skills success in this regard is not as simple as ensuring that students who arrive to study in a location all stay in that location: that is not within the gift of universities and it is not realistic in labour market terms. However, it is essential that the work universities do with their surrounding communities and business organisations is not seen by students as 'detached' from the locality but as deeply embedded in it. In embedding employability development, employer-focused content and work-based learning in the curriculum, HE needs to consider how this builds from sense of belonging, which is so important at the start of university, into sense of place, which will support connections to the labour market. Alongside this, universities need to support students to explore unexpected pathways that transcend discipline but do not dismiss it, which equip students for the continually evolving world of work and inspire them to see how they can make a difference to their communities and localities through the career they pursue and the networks they are part of.

REFERENCES

Acedo, A., Painho, M. & Casteleyn, S. (2017). Place and city: Operationalizing sense of place and social capital in the urban context. *Transactions in GIS*, *21*(3), 503–520.

Adelman, C. (1993) Kurt Lewin and the Origins of Action Research, *Educational Action Research*, 1:1, 7-24.

Ahn, M.Y., & Davis, H. H. (2020). Four domains of students' sense of belonging to university. *Studies in Higher Education*, *45*(3), 622–634.

Barrie, S. and Pizzica, J. (2019). Reimagining University Curriculum for a Disrupted Future of Work: Partnership Pedagogy in Higgs, J., Letts, W. and Crisp, G. (Eds), *Education for Employability* (*Volume 2)* pp. 143-152. Leiden: Brill.

Bridgstock, R., & Tippett, N. (2019). *Higher Education and the Future of Graduate Employability*. Cheltenham: Edward Elgar.

Brown, P., Hesketh, A. & Williams, S. (2003). Employability in a knowledge-driven economy. *Journal of Education and Work*, *16*(20), 107–126.

Business, Innovation and Skills Committee (2016). *The Digital Economy*. HC87. Retrieved at https://publications.parliament.uk/pa/cm201617/cmselect/cmbis/87/87.pdf

Centre for Cities (2017). The Great British Brain Drain: An Analysis of Migration To and From Leeds. Retrieved at 17-03-02-The-Great-British-Brain-Drain-Leeds-Analysis.pdf (centreforcities.org)

Centre for Higher Education Research and Scholarship Imperial College London (n.d.). Sense of Belonging. Retrieved at www.imperial.ac.uk/education-research/our-work/sense-of-belonging/

Coghlan, D. (2019). *Doing Action Research in Your Own Organization* (5th edn). London: Sage.

Coldwell-Neilson, J., & Cooper, T. (2019). Digital Literacy Meets Industry 4.0. In Higgs, J., Letts, W. & Crisp, G. (eds), *Education for Employability. Volume 2, Learning for Future Possibilities,* pp.37-50. Leiden: Brill.

Craig, D. (2009). *Action Research Essentials*. San Francisco: Jossey-Bass.

Crisp, G., Higgs, J. and Letts, W. (2019). Where to next with the employability agenda?. In Higgs, J., Letts, W. & Crisp, G. (eds), *Education for Employability. Volume 2, Learning for Future Possibilities,* pp. 263-272. Leiden: Brill.

Department for Business, Energy and Industrial Strategy (2019). Regulation for the Fourth Industrial Revolution. *Retrieved from Regulation for the Fourth Industrial Revolution - GOV.UK* (www.gov.uk)

Department for Business, Innovation & Skills (BIS) (2009). *Higher Ambitions: The Future of Universities in a Knowledge Economy.* Retrieved at http://webarchive.nationalarchives.gov.uk/+/http:/www.bis.gov.uk/wp-content/uploads/publications/Higher-Ambitions.pdf

Department for Business, Innovation & Skills (BIS) and Department for Culture, Media and Sport (DCMS) (2009). *Digital Britain*. Retrieved at https://assets.publishing.service.gov.uk/government/uploads/system/uploads/attachment_data/file/228844/7650.pdf

Donald, W. E., Ashleigh, M. J. & Baruch, Y. (2018). Students' perceptions of education and employability: Facilitating career transition from higher education into the labor market. *Career Development International*, *23*(5), 513–540.

Edge, N., Fitzgerald, E. & Willcoxson, L. (2019). Addressing Key Concerns in Graduate Employability. In Higgs, J., Letts, W. & Crisp, G. (eds), *Education for Employability. Volume 2, Learning for Future Possibilities,* pp.51-64. Leiden: Brill.

Elliott, J. (1991). *Action Research for Educational Change*. Buckingham: Open University Press.

Gwata, M. (2019). *To Flourish in the Fourth Industrial Revolution, We Need to Rethink These 3 Things*. Retrieved at www.weforum.org/agenda/2019/08/fourth-industrial-revolution-education/

Harvey, L. (1999). *Employability: Developing the relationship between higher education and employment*. Opening presentation at the Fifth Quality in Higher Education Seminar, Warwick University, 28 October, Coventry, UK. Retrieved at http://qualityresearchinternational.com/esecttools/relatedpubs/Employability5thQHE.pdf

Harvey, L. (2000). New realities: The relationship between higher education and employment. *Tertiary Education and Management*, 6(1), 3–17.

Hillage, J., & Pollard, E. (1998). *Employability: Developing a frame work for policy analysis*. Research Brief No. 85. London: Department for Education and Employment. Retrieved at www.academia.edu/23029127/Employability_developing_a_framework_for_policy_analysis

Holdsworth, C. (2006). 'Don't you think you're missing out, living at home?' Student experiences and residential transitions. *The Sociological Review (Keele)*, *54*(3), 495–519.

Holmes, L. (2015). Becoming a graduate: the warranting of an emergent identity. *Education + Training*, *57*(2), 219–238.

Holton, M. (2014). 'I already know the city, I don't have to explore it': Adjustments to 'sense of place' for 'local' UK university students. *Population Space and Place*, *21*(8), 820–831.

Holton, M. (2015). Adapting relationships with place: Investigating the evolving place attachment and 'sense of place' of UK higher education students during a period of intense transition. *Geoforum*, *59*, 21–29.

Leeds City Council (2017). *New Skills for the New Economy: The Leeds Talent and Skills Plan* 2017–2023. Retrieved at https://democracy.leeds.gov.uk/documents/s165032/Talent%20Skills%20Plan%20Report%20Appendix%201%20-%20Plan%20V2%20110917.pdf

Leeds City Region Enterprise Partnership and West Yorkshire Combined Authority (2017). *Leeds City Region Strategic Economic Plan* 2016–2036. Retrieved at strategic-economic-plan.pdf (westyorks-ca.gov.uk)

Leeds Digital Board (2017). *Leeds Digital Skills Action Plan*. Retrieved at Leeds-Digital-Skill-Action-Plan.pdf (leedsgrowthstrategy.co.uk)

Letts, W. (2019). University Employability Agendas, Targets and Strategies. In Higgs, J., Letts, W. & Crisp, G. (eds), *Education for Employability. Volume 2, Learning for Future Possibilities,* pp. 21-36. Leiden: Brill.

McAteer, M. (2013). *Action Research in Education*. Los Angeles: Sage.

McDonald, R. (2019). The Great British Brain Drain: An analysis for migration to and from Manchester. *Centre for Cities*. Retrieved at www.centreforcities.org/wp-content/uploads/2019/03/2019-03-22The-Great-British-Brain-Drain-An-analysis-of-migration-to-and-from-Manchester.pdf

McNiff, J., & Whitehead, J. (2002). *Action Research: Principles and Practice* (2nd edn). London: Routledge/Falmer.

Northern Powerhouse (2016). *Independent Economic Review*. Retrieved at www.n8research.org.uk/media/Overview-NP-Independent-Economic-Review.pdf

O'Connor, C. (2019). Higher Education and the labour market: the place and role of graduate attributes, identities and capitals in the context of the digital skills gap. Unpublished.

Seamon, D. (2013). Place Attachment and Phenomenology: The Synergistic Dynamism of Place. In Manzo, L. C. & Devine-Wright, P. (eds), *Place Attachment: Advances in Theory, Methods, and Applications*, pp. 11–22. New York: Routledge.

Science and Technology Committee (2016). *Digital Skills Crisis. HC270*. Retrieved at https://publications.parliament.uk/pa/cm201617/cmselect/cmsctech/270/270.pdf

Tomlinson, M. (2012). Graduate employability: A review of conceptual and empirical themes. *Higher Education Policy*, *25*, 407–431.

Tomlinson, M. (2017). Forms of graduate capital and their relationship to graduate employability. *Education + Training*, *59*(4), 338–352.

UK Commission for Employment and Skills (2015). *UKCES Explains: What is an Anchor Institution?* Retrieved at https://ukces.blog.gov.uk/2015/03/19/ukces-explains-what-is-an-anchor-institution/

UK Government (2017). *Higher Education and Research Act 2017*. Retrieved at www.legislation.gov.uk/ukpga/2017/29/contents/enacted

Weale, S. (2021). *Funding Cuts to Go Ahead for University Arts Courses in England Despite Opposition*. The Guardian. Retrieved at www.theguardian.com/education/2021/jul/20/funding-cuts-to-go-ahead-for-university-arts-courses-in-england-despite-opposition

West Yorkshire Combined Authority and Leeds City Region Enterprise Partnership (2019). *Labour Market Report 2019*. Retrieved at labour-market-report-2019-final.pdf (the-lep.com)

West Yorkshire Combined Authority and Leeds City Region Enterprise Partnership (2021). *Employment and Skills Framework*. Retrieved at employment-skills-framework-final.pdf (westyorks-ca.gov.uk)

Yorke, M. (2006). *Employability in Higher Education: What It Is – What It Is Not: Learning & Employability Series 1*. York: The Higher Education Academy. Retrieved at www.heacademy.ac.uk/knowledge-hub/employability-higher-education-what-it-what-it-not

29

The Role of Dual Education in Graduate Employability: The Comparison between Europe and Africa

David F. J. Campbell, Attila Pausits and Seamus Needham

INTRODUCTION

This contribution discusses dual education in higher education and its implications for graduate employability. Dual education is being defined as a type of higher education that focuses on the employability of graduates in different fields of practice and in different sectors of the economy and society, by requiring a study programme that is designed to enhance, in particular, such competences of graduates that support their ability to work in application contexts. These are the intended results of structures and processes of dual education within higher education, where higher education institutions (HEIs) are cooperating and networking with firms and organizations in society and in the economy. This implies, simultaneously, the involvement of practitioners within higher education – for example, for purposes of teaching. Based on this, boundaries between higher education and the context of society and economy should be made more 'transparent', and linkages between higher education and society and the economy are encouraged.

In the years 2016–2020, the Erasmus+ project LaTFURE (Learning and Teaching Tools Fuelling University Relations with the Economy in Mozambique and South Africa) was carried out, which involved four European HEIs from Austria, Germany and Finland, as well as six universities in South Africa and three universities in Mozambique. The project emphasized capacity building, based on European experiences and models, in dual education in higher education in South Africa and Mozambique, and how this can be promoted further through an international comparison and contextual implementation. To facilitate the employability of graduates (after completion or in parallel with their studies) serves as one of the crucial criteria, and the design of the LaTFURE project referred to supporting processes with the rationale of facilitating employability. The major innovation push of the LaTFURE project is to enhance the capabilities and capacities of 'self-learning' in and for dual education of the HEIs in South Africa and Mozambique, to introduce and develop tools for further implementation, to achieve an all-level institutional involvement of the participating institutions, with networks inside and outside of academia, and to help other HEIs in both countries (and elsewhere in Africa) to develop capabilities and capacities toward the implementation of further dual education. The results of the LaTFURE project are documented in a comprehensive status on the official project website (www.latfure.eu/ [Accessed: 1 July 2022]), and this website is still operative beyond the formal ending of the project (which was applied in late 2020).

From a South African perspective, with a focus on the two countries of Mozambique and South Africa, dual education involves government ministries from these two countries. Within South Africa, for example, the LaTFURE project has led to the award of a university capacity-building grant by the higher education ministry for four public universities in a region of South Africa. A key focus of this dual higher education programme Department of Higher Education and Training (DHEP) is to influence government policies on dual higher education practices and pedagogies. South African higher education has been highly influenced by its British colonial history and examples of dual higher education outside of mainstream programmes for doctors, teachers and lawyers are rare. Although South African university graduates have historically enjoyed strong employment returns on their higher education investment, unemployment of graduates has been increasing. While South Africa's public vocational sector has implemented dual education and training programmes, relationships between industry and HEIs in co-teaching and cooperation are nascent, and key learnings of dual education have been incorporated into this new dual higher education model. Particularly, the analysis here reflects on key experiences and lessons learned from the introduction and promotion of dual education in higher education in South Africa.

This contribution is structured as follows: the next section elaborates on the future of education and labour, the required future competences and dual education in advanced higher education systems, focusing on the European experience. The third section concentrates on the African experience of dual education in emerging higher education systems in South Africa and Mozambique, creating a broader overview of institutional case studies of different HEIs, while the fourth section provides a review of recent higher education policies in South Africa that aim for enhancing dual education. In the conclusion, there is a reflection on what the possible conditions are, so that a cross-national (global) mutual learning regarding dual education can take place and can be successful.

DUAL EDUCATION, THE FUTURE OF EDUCATION AND LABOUR, FUTURE COMPETENCES, FUTURE SKILLS AND LEARNING: THE EUROPEAN EXPERIENCE

Advanced societies and economies often are being described as knowledge societies and knowledge economies, but also as knowledge democracies (Veld, 2010). Knowledge and innovation (the application of knowledge) act as crucial drivers, and themselves are becoming more complex (Dubina et al., 2017). Industry 4.0 and 5.0 are emphasizing the growing importance of knowledge and innovation in industry (Carayannis and Campbell, 2021; Carayannis et al., 2021a and 2021b). Higher education and its massification are playing a crucial role here (OECD, 2021a). In reference to knowledge at HEIs or in the context of higher education systems, concepts were developed such as 'Mode 2' (Gibbons et al., 1994) or 'Mode 3' knowledge production (Carayannis and Campbell, 2009), 'Triple Helix' (Etzkowitz and Leydesdorff, 1995, 2000; Cai and Lattu, 2020; Leydesdorff and Smith, 2021) or 'Quadruple and Quintuple Helix' innovation systems (Carayannis and Campbell, 2009, 2010; Carayannis et al., 2012), the 'academic firm' (Campbell and Carayannis, 2016a) and the notion of quality of democracy as an innovation enabler (Campbell, 2019). Student-focused teaching in higher education has the implication that the goals and objectives of study programmes arrive as competences with the students and graduates (ENQA, 2015). Crucial now are the so-called 'T-competences' (or 'M-competences'), where higher education graduates and 'knowledge workers' are expected to combine 'vertical' disciplinary competences with 'horizontal' interdisciplinary competences (Campbell et al., 2019: 249). This also relates to forms of 'basic research in the context of application' (Campbell and Carayannis, 2013: 34), connecting with forms of 'transdisciplinarity' (Wagner et al., 2011), where transdisciplinarity may also be approached as an 'application of interdisciplinarity' (Campbell and Carayannis, 2013: 34). 'The future of education and labour' requires that changes and transformations of the economy (Industry 4.0 and Industry 5.0) also are reflected in transitions of the higher education systems, so that graduates can participate as knowledge workers in the economy of tomorrow (Bast et al., 2019). HEIs are challenged to teach such 'future skills' to their students and graduates, so that learning for the future can be performed successfully (Ehlers, 2020a, b). Also, the OECD (2021b) has set up in relation to such topics the initiative 'The Future of Work'. Learning (Carayannis, 2001; Leiber, 2019) may be modelled as a process in connection with innovation, then possibly resulting in the following definition: 'Learning = is a process, where knowledge is being used for the purpose of a (new) application and where also (new) knowledge is being created, and where an improvement, betterment, advancement, or a reform are being (or were) achieved' (Campbell and Pantelić, 2020: 3). Consequently, a learning organization (in context of higher education) can be defined as 'an organization that engages in innovation processes with a learning ("learning innovation processes"), meaning that these are innovation processes that are leading to an improvement, betterment, advancement, or a reform' (Campbell and Pantelić, 2020: 3). Learning can furthermore be referred to as 'policy learning' (May, 1992; Hall, 1993; compare also with Biegelbauer, 2013).

The concept of 'dual education' (in higher education) involves different considerations. A crucial reference here is the so-called 'employability', meaning that graduates can find after their completion proper work (as knowledge workers), reflecting the qualifications, skills and performances that they have acquired during their studies. In the European context, this was particularly promoted by the European Commission (2021) through the 'Bologna process'.

Dual studies generally refer to 'an academic study program combined with vocational practical training in a company/institution' (DAAD, 2015). Other terms reflecting the same idea include 'work-integrated learning' (WIL) and cooperative education. Patrick et al. (2008) define WIL as 'career-focused learning which integrates theoretical knowledge with work place practical application, within a vocationally designed curriculum'. Furthermore, WIL can be distinguished from other conceptions of learning-for-work by its emphasis on the integrative aspects of such learning. WIL could thus be described as 'an educational approach that aligns academic and workplace practices for the mutual benefit of students and workplaces' (Council on Higher Education, 2011). Cooperative education is defined as a structured programme in which periods of study alternate with periods of related work experience (Kerka, 1989). The definitions of dual studies and WIL imply that while dual studies and WIL are associated with vocational programmes, cooperative education implies a wider application of periods of work and study in programmes not limited to vocational studies. In Germany, for example, dual study or cooperative education is a type of professional higher education (PHE) in which public- and private-sector organizations directly cooperate with the higher education sector to deliver the programme (BMBF and KMK, 2008). The key feature of the cooperative dual education is that students regularly switch from their academic studies at the university to practical training by their workplace-training provider (partner company). Various actors from politics, science and industry repeatedly emphasize the advantage of dual study courses and advocate for their strengthening (Wolter et al., 2014, p. 13). Therefore, the supply of dual study programmes has increased significantly and stumbles upon a growing demand over the last decade. Driven by the public debate but also by the collaboration between the education and business sector, the reputation of graduates at the labour market and with employers has been increased as well. This development is underlined by the growing number of HEIs by offering dual education programmes, by student numbers (approximately 70,000 students now enrolled in dual programmes) as well as by growing number of programmes offered at the bachelor's but also at master's level.

Through the involvement of companies, dual education settings lead to a better students' skill development through more demand-oriented teaching and learning models. Due to the interaction with companies during their studies, students receive better opportunities for employment. First, employers get better opportunities to test and select the right graduates for open positions. Second, students can use the time during their studies to get insights from practice and learn more about the world of work. Third, the matching process in hiring practices is not limited to written applications, interviews or assessment methods. However, there are also several challenges related to dual education: the different academic and business cultures might lead to organizational as well as teaching and learning challenges for students. The specific setting and cooperation between different institutions lead to additional costs, which need to be taken into consideration. Further to this, mutual governance structures between the involved bodies are needed to handle the complexity, overcome structural and/or cultural differences during the implementation of such programmes. Dual education needs a clear commitment, but also financial support by the world of work. HEIs have not sufficient budgets to cover the extra costs of dual education. As mentioned above, besides legal challenges, quality issues related to the curriculum design and implementation might appear as focal points during planning and implementation as well. To sum up, the barriers to the future development of dual programmes relate to the cost of organizing dual programmes but also to limited places for attachment in organizations for large numbers of students, reluctance of organizations to accept or pay students, government policies and resources for supporting dual programmes, as well as legal, quality and curriculum challenges. However, with regards to the current position and future development of dual programmes, it is expected that dual programmes will continue growing due to their important role in the development of hands-on skills in the twenty-first century.

Two innovative organizational examples for dual education in European higher education are:

1. Duale Hochschule Baden-Württemberg (DHBW): Baden-Wuerttemberg Cooperative State University (www.dhbw.de/english/home).
    - This represents a concept more 'radical' than the established Universities of Applied Sciences (FHs).
    - There is a consortium of firms associated to the DHBW.
    - The consortium 'selects' the students to be sent in for studies.
    - Requirement: every student already is 'employed' by one of the associated companies. So, she or he is not in a position of having to search for employment.
    - The firm sees the study programme as a form of human development, and also commits to offering supporting conditions. This is verified and controlled by the DHBW.
2. 'Proakatemia': (Doctoral) School for Entrepreneurship with the Tampere University of Applied Sciences (https://proakatemia.fi/en/home/).
    - The school is simulating an incubator for real-term entrepreneurship.
    - Doctoral students are being trained in the competence of entrepreneurship.
    - Students are establishing so-called 'student companies', or at least crucial components of these: these consist of teams of about 20 students ('teampreneurs').
    - These students are making real business projects, involving real money and real customers.

- In addition, the students are receiving intensive training.
- After graduation, about 40% of the students (graduates) continue as entrepreneurs.

DUAL EDUCATION IN SOUTH AFRICA AND MOZAMBIQUE: THE AFRICAN EXPERIENCE

The European experience of dual education is based on advanced systems of higher education, referring to advanced economies that are evolving according to principles of Industry 4.0 and Industry 5.0. African higher education systems often are being described as 'emerging' systems, with (on the one hand) tendencies of massification, but (on the other) also being challenged by quality criteria such as the employability of graduates. Consequently, dual education should help to promote the employability of graduates – for example, in South Africa and Mozambique. Results for nine African universities (three in Mozambique, six in South Africa) are clustered on the basis of practical experience with dual education, and then the following three groups of HEIs may be identified: 'incremental' adaptations, 'new launch' and 'new programmes' (see Langa et al., 2018, and Moyo, 2020).

Incremental Adaptations and Changes in Favour of Dual Education

The University of Cape Town (UCT), University of the Witwatersrand (Wits) and University of the Western Cape (UWC) are traditional research universities in South Africa that do not have specific (comprehensive) programmes in dual education but contain dual education elements in their traditional programmes. UWC refers to dual education in the classical sense, where specific disciplines utilize dual education in programmes such as law (articles at law firms), dentistry (internships at hospitals) and education (e.g. teacher placements within schools).

UWC continues to play an important role in advocating further dual education regulatory conditions and dual education higher educational policy implementation in South Africa, particularly in the Western Cape region. The South African Department of Higher Education and Training (www.dhet.gov.za/) awarded a university capacity-building grant to the Cape Higher Education Consortium (CHEC) (www.chec.ac.za/) that concentrates on the introduction of a DHEP (https://estian1.wixsite.com/dhep) for the four major public universities in the Western Cape region (Cape Peninsula University of Technology, UCT, University of Stellenbosch and UWC). The official website of DHEP acknowledges how crucial, for example, the LaTFURE intervention was in stating

> [b]uilding on the LaTFURE project. This will be done through a series of pilot studies to determine the conditions for the successful implementation of DHE programmes in South Africa, together with a comparative curriculum analysis of similar programmes in Germany and South Africa (e.g. Social Work and Engineering). The focus will be on identifying catalysts and barriers in the South African system that may facilitate (or prohibit) the successful implementation of DHEP programmes. (Dual Higher Education Project)

The University of Limpopo, also in South Africa but located outside of the Cape region, engaged with several successful examples of dual education in programmes, involving the Department of Geology and Mining on the university side, and companies (e.g. Ivanplants) and international university cooperation partners, such as the Laurentian University in Canada.

Eduardo Mondlane University (in Maputo, Mozambique) pursued several memoranda-of-understanding based on dual education cooperations and student exchange steps with European (FH Joanneum) and South African (University of Mpumalanga) universities.

New-launch of Dual Education

The Cape Peninsula University of Technology (CPUT) and the University of Mpumalanga (UMP), both located in South Africa, can be described as universities that have programmes with an explicit orientation toward and emphasis on dual education, where the recent experience enabled them to develop these programmes further in decisive ways.

At CPUT, dual education is referred to in terms of WIL and includes the following elements and principles: students need to qualify for WIL (subject prerequisites), industry-preparedness classes (industry talks), student and employer matching (one-on-one sessions/interviews), student placement (contracts), assessment (portfolio of evidence) and feedback (presentation on return).

In the recent years, CPUT introduced four new programmes, some of which are restructured from existing programmes. These new programmes are a Diploma in Tourism Management, a Diploma in Event Management, an Advanced Diploma in Tourism Management and an Advanced Diploma in Event Management. The Diploma in Tourism Management is a result of the restructuring of a phased-out programme (National Diploma in Tourism Management). The new qualification is now a three-year qualification and sees students take up the WIL course in the third year and their final semester, making it easier for students to be integrated within the host companies. At CPUT, the assessment for the WIL courses is processed through the format of a portfolio review. During the phase of WIL, each student compiles a portfolio that is submitted to the department and marked upon completion of the course. Included in that portfolio is a review of the performance of the student via the line manager of the student while in industry. In addition, an academic supervisor visits the students at their place of work, so as to assess how they are performing and whether there are open communication channels between the student, the department and the host company throughout the period of WIL. In terms of student numbers: in 2019, there were 114 students registered for Tourism Management and there were 86 students registered for Events Management in 2020.

UMP has taken the approach to expand and to reform (improve) their programmes that refer to dual education. To realize this, UMP set-up a Diploma in Agriculture, designed and developed a curriculum toward an Advanced Certificate in Events Management (to be effective as of 2022) and restructured their Diploma in Hospitality Management.

As a consequence of this dual education intervention, UMP has strengthened relations with corporate partners in hospitality and in agriculture through the establishment of an Industry Advisory Board Committee, which sits once a semester to discuss curriculum-related issues. Furthermore, collaboration and partnerships were established with other partner educational institutions. For example, there are south–south cooperations (HEIs of Mozambique, e.g. Eduardo Mondlane University in Mozambique) and south–north cooperations (for example with HEIs in Europe – specifically FH Johanneum in Austria).

Concrete specific measures of dual learning within UMP included: learning outcomes were revised; assessment methods were revised and aligned with dual education; blended learning was adopted – for example, through a link for a UMP learning management system (https://myump.ump.ac.za/login/index.php); WIL was developed into an integral component of the Hospitality Qualification; industry was incorporated under the Industry and Programme Advisory Boards; simulations in the hotels and restaurants (newly created); project-based learning was introduced; guest lectures were invited to bring industry practitioners into the classes.

In recent times, UMP has increased enrolments in dual education programmes with qualifications such as Hospitality and Agriculture, almost doubling up their enrolments especially in 2020.

Back in 2019, Lurio University, in Nampula, Mozambique, established a new faculty – the Faculty of Social Sciences and Humanities – at Mozambique Island, offering two undergraduate programmes: Tourism and Hospitality, and International Relations and Local Development. Currently (as of 2020), there are some 205 students enrolled in the Tourism and Hospitality programme. Lurio does not offer classical dual education programmes, but the indicated two programmes have integrated dual education components that require students to work in companies in the tourism sector in Mozambique Island. Lurio has established relations with host companies in Mozambique Island, and the Faculty of Social Sciences and Humanities is in the process of redesigning aspects of the tourism programme into dual education formats. The majority of external stakeholders is referring to small and medium sizes. This situation directly impacts on the capacity of hosting students as their interns and workers.

New Programmes of Dual Education

During the performance of the LaTFURE project, Zambeze University, in Beira, Mozambique, worked together with two other HEIs in Mozambique, with an industry partner (Gorongosa National Park) as well as an overseas HEI, to set up a BioEducation consortium, which designed and launched a completely new master's programme in Conservation Biology. The Master's in Conservation Biology programme emphasizes networking among partner HEIs and the practical world of work, as it is being represented by Gorongosa National Park, via a diversification of learning and funding opportunities. The curriculum, which has been co-developed by several stakeholders, including Gorongosa National Park and partner HEIs, takes into account the present and future needs of the practice and places an emphasis on the context of employment.

The curriculum and detailed programme description (in the language of Portuguese) are posted open-access to the website of the LaTFURE project. www.latfure.eu/wp-content/uploads/2020/12/Projecto%20de%20Mestrado%20em%20Biologia%20de%20Conservac%CC%A7a%CC%83o_2018.pdf

The Master's in Conservation Biology programme extends over two years, corresponds with four semesters and has roughly about 120 credits, with the last semester being reserved exclusively for preparation and work on the thesis. The structure and duration of the courses are in line with the Mozambican National Academic Credit Accumulation and Transfer System (SNACTA) for master's-level courses. The Master's in Conservation Biology programme is anchored heavily in the Gorongosa National Park and is clustered around a didactic-pedagogical axis for professional training, where the contents are allocated and related to the conservation of biodiversity.

Policy Learning and Institutional Governance of Dual Education in the Higher Education System of South Africa

This section outlines a brief description of South Africa's Post-School Education and Training (PSET) system located under the Department of Higher Education and Training. It then describes South Africa's National Qualifications Framework (NQF) and sub-frameworks as well as governance structures for the PSET system. South Africa's education and training system is not well articulated, and key systemic, institutional and individual challenges are detailed. This section draws on the LaTFURE project to argue that the project was an important policy intervention that has the potential to address the current separation between academic learning and workplace-based education and training within South Africa.

South Africa describes PSET as education and training for anyone who has left formal schooling, regardless of the academic level achieved (White Paper for Post-School Education and Training, 2013). This definition is therefore broader than post-secondary education. South Africa's public PSET institutions are comprised of Adult and Community Education and Training Colleges, offering basic education and training; Technical Vocational Education and Training (TVET) Colleges, who offer vocational and occupational training primarily at secondary-school levels; and universities offering undergraduate and postgraduate provision.

South Africa's public higher education system is comprised of three types of universities: traditional research universities, universities of technology (UoTs) and comprehensive universities that arose from the merger of a traditional research university and a university of technology. South Africa has 26 public universities, of which 12 are classified as traditional research universities, six are comprehensive universities and eight are UoTs included two newly formed universities.

UoTs have steadily lost their historical linkages with TVET Colleges offering artisan and apprenticeship training programmes. South Africa has 50 public TVET Colleges and they used to enjoy strong linkages with the former Technikons (now 'UoTs', since 2003) that enabled the development of professional learning pathways for artisans to become technologists/technicians and technical engineers. UoTs have subsequently intensified their efforts to increase postgraduate provision and research in line with university funding incentives. There has been a corresponding decline in industry engagement and cooperative education including workplace training within the UoTs and more emphasis on disciplinary knowledge required for undergraduate degrees (Winberg 2007, Garraway and Winberg 2019). This brief background has outlined the evolution of South African public higher education and ways in which there has been an increasing focus on academic disciplinary learning together with a corresponding decline in workplace-based learning.

South Africa's PSET system is regulated through an over-arching NQF comprised of 10 levels, starting from Grade 9/NQF Level 1 to PhD/Doctoral at NQF Level 10. Within this NQF, there are three sub-qualification frameworks. The General and Further Education Sub-Qualification Framework is for formal secondary-school qualifications and some vocational qualifications from NQF Levels 1–4. All occupational programmes are located under the National Occupational Sub-Qualification Framework (NOSQF) and provide most of the industry and business-based education and training. The NOSQF operates at NQF Level 1 to NQF Level 8 (NQF Level 8 is equivalent to a four-year undergraduate degree level). The Higher Education Sub-Qualification Framework operates from NQF Level 5 (first year of university) to NQF Level 10 (PhD).

Each of these sub-qualification frameworks is under the control of statutory bodies and there is minimal interface between the education and training qualifications offered within these sub-frameworks. While the role of South African Qualifications Authority is to oversee the implementation of the NQF and ensure articulation of qualifications between these frameworks, it does not have any legal authority to enforce articulated qualifications between and across these frameworks.

South Africa has invested significant time and effort to develop articulation policies that provide for coherent learning and career pathways and progression within South Africa's PSET system. In 2013, a Ministerial Committee on Articulation was established to identify key challenges and obstacles regarding articulation between the three sub-qualification frameworks and provide recommendations. Subsequently, an Articulation Policy was published in 2017, which defines articulation as systemic (between sub-qualification frameworks), institutional (between and within education and training institutions) and individual (the individual plans their own learning pathways). Importantly, the 2017 Articulation Policy omitted a key recommendation from the 2013 Ministerial Committee that articulation needs to be programmatic and by curricular design rather than institutional articulation.

Despite significant policy progress and related research (South African Qualifications Authority, 2017), articulation within the PSET system has remained minimal, with the exception of school leavers being able to access universities if their final examination pass marks qualify them for university study. The three sub-frameworks remain as separate siloes and occupational training remains separated from disciplinary-specific learning offered by universities.

In relating all of this to the LaTFURE project, LaTFURE has been an important policy intervention. To start with, the project defined dual learning within a Southern African environment. While this was a contested and critical process, it provides an important benchmark to define dual learning as distinct to WIL policies, which remains contested in HEIs.

Second, dual learning is precisely focused on ways in which universities and business/industry can cooperate with verified learning outcomes and quality assurance processes. The implementation of dual learning (the focus of the CHEC Dual Higher Education Project and successor to LaTFURE) offers South African universities opportunities to effectively combine occupational qualifications with university qualifications and thus address a major *systemic* obstacle to articulation.

Third, the introduction of professional career and learning pathways directly addresses the parity of esteem of vocational/occupational higher education qualifications and thus addresses *institutional* articulation. Most universities in South Africa do not offer higher education vocational qualifications (other than mainstream health and teaching qualifications) and dual learning offers universities the opportunities to develop vocational higher education qualifications that they have little knowledge of. By engaging with industry in dual learning, new knowledge is created. Recently, new qualifications introduced in the TVET Colleges in South Africa – known as the Centres of Specialisation Project – promote the dual learning system. These qualifications have three components: theory (conceptual principles underpinning the trade), practical (simulated learning in a dedicated training facility) and work experience (where value-adding productive work is undertaken while learning). All three components must be learnt before the final integrated assessment can be undertaken, which in the case of the trades is a trade test (mid-term evaluation of the TVET Colleges of Specialisation, 2021).

The CHEC DHEP research team is also drawing on approaches being used within this initiative and ways in which dual learning approaches and practices can inform the development of dual higher qualifications within South African universities. Importantly, the development of dual learning approaches with TVET and HEIs opens the possibility for specialized career and learning pathways linked to business and industry that span educational institutions.

Unemployment in South Africa is particularly high, especially for young people. The recent Quarterly Labour Force Survey (Statistics South Africa, 2021) has shown an overall unemployment rate of 32.6%, and using the expanded definition of unemployment, this is 46.3%. The official unemployment rate among youth (15–34 years) was 46.3% in Quarter 1 of 2021 (StatsSA 2021). The unemployment rate was 9.3% among university graduates. South Africa currently has 17 million people who are not in any form of employment or education (referred to as 'NEETs') out of a population of 55 million (DHET, 2019).

It is acknowledged that dual learning cannot be massified as it is expensive and relies on addressing individual employer needs in a South African context, where there is a small formal economy. What dual learning does offer though is increased incentives and hope for young people to see that education and training can contribute to employment through the development of professional career paths and therefore *individual* articulation.

Current emerging DHEPs have identified a range of programmatic interventions. Programmes under consideration from the four Western Cape universities include the introduction of formal dual learning into undergraduate and postgraduate programmes in specific sub-economic sectors, such as Forestry, as well as the development of dual learning professional pathways across education and training sectors, in areas such as community development and early childhood development, that do not currently exist (SAQA, 2017; Bolton et al., 2020). The incorporation of dual learning within these professional pathways from secondary-school education and TVET Colleges to universities is currently being investigated.

The central argument of this section is that the LaTFURE project has made an important contribution to South Africa's education and training policy landscape and provided strong resources for university staff to take on new forms of self-learning in ways that increase the employability of graduates in partnership with business and industry. This is particularly important in the development of scarce and critical skills through dual learning that South African universities are currently not addressing.

CONCLUSION

Epistemic governance emphasizes that the 'underlying understanding' of HEIs are being directly addressed by governance and policy (Campbell and Carayannis,

2013, 2016b). This also applies to dual education. The 'future of education and labour' (Bast et al., 2019) requires that higher education changes, so that students and graduates are acquiring skills and competences (e.g. a disciplinary and interdisciplinary mix of 'T-competences' and 'M-competences'), so that they can engage successfully in the next-stage economy of Industry 4.0 and Industry 5.0. Dual education has the interest to promote this, so that the employability of graduates is being effectively enhanced to work as knowledge workers professionally. Dual education refers to advanced higher education systems in Europe, but also to emerging higher education systems in Africa. There is learning within national higher education systems, but there also can be a mutual learning across different national higher education systems that are operating in different contexts. This also would qualify as a 'true' cross-national and global learning. Mutual learning in reference to dual education aspects of epistemic governance is relevant, because the 'underlying understandings' also include the cultures of research, education and teaching and of innovation and learning in HEIs.

As a key proposition for institutional higher education learning in dual education, we can propose the following: dual education may imply designing and implementing whole new programmes of dual education, or, alternatively, may also imply strengthening dual education components in already existing programmes that are not comprehensively designed on the basis of principles of dual education (see the analysis in the third section, on Mozambique and South Africa).

The major focus and innovation prospect of the discussed LaTFURE project was (and is) to enhance the capabilities and capacities of 'self-learning' in and for dual education of the universities (HEIs) in Mozambique and South Africa, to introduce and develop tools for further implementation, to get all-level institutional involvement at the involved universities with the networks inside and outside academia and to help other African universities in both countries and beyond to develop capacities and capabilities toward the implementation of dual education. Therefore, dual education is expected to act as an enabler to increase employability, develop new funding models for students to attend higher education, help universities to develop and increase linkages to industry and other business sectors and establish and/or revise institutional approaches of university–business cooperation. The developed online platforms in both countries are a substantial part of the innovation and will generate more support for the HEIs in both countries to develop dual education through a more systemwide approach. The platforms are marketplaces but also important tools for data, information and knowledge sharing. Further to this, LaTFURE has created a learning space to support not only the involved partner HEIs but also all HEIs in both countries. This is an innovative approach for exploitation of the results, which is the 'translation' of project outputs (e.g. institutional framework for dual education) into learning tools and materials, which can be used by other HEIs in both countries and beyond.

Furthermore, there was a particular philosophy in place for LaTFURE. Institutions of the European member countries to the LaTFURE consortium (Austria, Germany and Finland) served as references for dual education in higher education. However, development was not understood in ways to 'copy and paste' or to 'export and import' other (successful) examples of dual education. Development was (and is) understood more in such forms that every country and every institution (e.g. in Mozambique and South Africa) must 're-invent' its own approaches to dual education. International lessons learned are crucial and should be further emphasized. However, the final answers of concrete problem-solving and implementation of dual education finally must be developed by the institutions of the higher education sectors themselves. Thus, a mutual respect was created, one that is sensitive of history and sensitive of the contexts of universities and other HEIs. This should enable and support the sustainability of and for dual education in the higher education systems such as in Mozambique and South Africa.

ACKNOWLEDGEMENTS

The Erasmus+ project LaTFURE was funded by the European Education and Culture Executive Agency and had the project number 573579-EPP-1-2016-1-AT-EPPKA2-CBHE-SP. We want to express our acknowledgement to the Agency and for the professional and collegial support by the staff. However, the authors here alone are responsible for the content of this publication; neither the agency nor the EU Commission are liable for the further use of the information contained herein.

REFERENCES

Bast, G., Carayannis, E.G. and David F. J. Campbell (eds) (2019). *The Future of Education and Labour*. New York: Springer.

Biegelbauer, P. (2013). *Wie lernt die Politik? Lernen aus Erfahrung in Politik und Verwaltung*. Wiesbaden: Springer.

Bolton, H., Matsau, L. and Blom, R. (2020). *Flexible Learning Pathways: The National Qualifications Framework Backbone*. Report for the IIEP-UNESCO Research 'SDG4: Planning for flexible learning pathways in higher education'. UNESCO, IIEP, SAQA.

Cai, Y. and Lattu, L. (2020). *Synergy Building between Triple Helix and Quadruple Helix*. Tampere: Faculty of Management and Business, University of Tampere.

Campbell, D.F.J. (2019). *Global Quality of Democracy as Innovation Enabler. Measuring Democracy for Success*. New York: Palgrave Macmillan.

Campbell, D. F. J. and Carayannis, E. G. (2013). *Epistemic Governance in Higher Education. Quality Enhancement of Universities for Development*. New York: Springer.

Campbell, D. F. J. and Carayannis, E. G. (2016a). The Academic Firm: A New Design and Redesign Proposition for Entrepreneurship in Innovation-Driven Knowledge Economy. *Journal of Innovation and Entrepreneurship* 5(12), pp. 1–10.

Campbell, D. F. J. and Carayannis, E. G. (2016b). Epistemic Governance and Epistemic Innovation Policy. *Technology, Innovation and Education* 2(2), 1–15.

Campbell, D. F. J., Carayannis, E. G. and Bast, G. (2019). Conclusion: The Future of The Future of Education and Labour. In G. Bast, E. G. Carayannis and D. F. J. Campbell (eds), *The Future of Education and Labour*. New York: Springer, 245–254.

Campbell, D. F. J. and Pantelić, I. (2020). Processes of Learning and Processes of Innovation. In E. G. Carayannis (ed.), *Encyclopedia of Creativity, Invention, Innovation and Entrepreneurship*. New York: Springer, 1–6.

Carayannis, E. G. (2001). *The Strategic Management of Technological Learning. Learning to Learn and Learning to Learn-How-To-Learn as Drivers of Strategic Choice and Firm Performance in Global, Technology-Driven-Markets*. Boca Raton: CRC Press.

Carayannis, E. G. and Campbell, D. F. J. (2009). 'Mode 3' and 'Quadruple Helix': Toward a 21st Century Fractal Innovation Ecosystem. *International Journal of Technology Management* 46(3/4), 201–234.

Carayannis, E. G. and Campbell, D. F. J. (2010). Triple Helix, Quadruple Helix and Quintuple Helix and How Do Knowledge, Innovation and the Environment Relate To Each Other? A Proposed Framework for a Trans-disciplinary Analysis of Sustainable Development and Social Ecology. *International Journal of Social Ecology and Sustainable Development* 1(1), 41–69.

Carayannis, E. G., Barth, T. D. and Campbell D. F. J. (2012). The Quintuple Helix Innovation Model: Global Warming as a Challenge and Driver for Innovation. *Journal of Innovation and Entrepreneurship* 1(1), 1–12.

Carayannis, E. G. and Campbell, D. F. J. (2021). Democracy of Climate and Climate for Democracy: The Evolution of Quadruple and Quintuple Helix Innovation Systems. *Journal of the Knowledge Economy* 12, 2050–2082.

Carayannis, Elias G. / David F. J. Campbell / Evangelos Grigoroudis (2021a). Helix Trilogy: the Triple, Quadruple, and Quintuple Innovation Helices from a Theory, Policy, and Practice Set of Perspectives. *Journal of the Knowledge Economy* 12, online first (https://doi.org/10.1007/s13132-021-00813-x) (https://link.springer.com/article/10.1007/s13132-021-00813-x).

Carayannis, E. G., Dezi, L., Gregori, G. and Calo, E. (2021b). Smart Environments and Techno-centric and Human-Centric Innovations for Industry and Society 5.0: A Quintuple Helix Innovation System View Towards Smart, Sustainable, and Inclusive Solutions. *Journal of the Knowledge Economy* 12(1), 25–55.

Council on Higher Education (2011) Work-Integrated Learning: Good Practice Guide. *HE Monitor*, No. 12.

DAAD (2015). *Annual Report of the DAAD Brussels Branch Office*. Brussels: DAAD (https://static.daad.de/media/daad_de/pdfs_nicht_barrierefrei/der-daad/daad_au%C3%9Fenstellenbericht_2020.pdf).

Dubina, I. N., Campbell, D. F. J., Carayannis, E. G., Chub, A. A., Grigoroudis, E. and Kozhevina, O.V. (2017). The Balanced Development of the Spatial Innovation and Entrepreneurial Ecosystem Based on Principles of the Systems Compromise: A Conceptual Framework. *Journal of the Knowledge Economy* 8(2), 438–455.

Cape Higher Education Consortium, Dual Higher Education Project (https://001041d6-c7f3-4f4a-9403-4585edb9a316.filesusr.com/ugd/9a731c_8b266cb7d26a474f917d936b442e58fd.pdf) https://www.chec.ac.za/higher-education-innovation/17 June 2022.

Department of Higher Education and Training (DHET) (2021). *Mid-term evaluation of the TVET Centres of Specialisation, DHET Research Bulletin on PSET*, https://www.dhet.gov.za/Research%20Bulletin%2010/documents/ArticlesandReports/5.pdf

European Commission (2021). *The Bologna Process and the European Higher Education Area*. Brussels: European Union.

Ehlers, U.D. (2020a). *Future Skills. The Future of Learning and Higher Education*. Karlsruhe: Springer.

Ehlers, U.D. (2020b). *Future Skills. Lernen der Zukunft – Hochschule der Zukunft*. Wiesbaden: Springer VS.

European Association for Quality Assurance in Higher Education (ENQA) (2015). *Standards and Guidelines for Quality Assurance in the European Higher Education Area (ESG)*. Brussels: ENQA.

Etzkowitz, H. and Leydesdorff, L. (1995). The Triple Helix – University-Industry-Government Relations: A Laboratory for Knowledge-Based Economic Development. *EASST Review* 14, 14–19.

Etzkowitz, H. and Leydesdorff, L. (2000). The Dynamics of Innovation: From National Systems and 'Mode 2' to a Triple Helix of University-Industry-Government Relations. *Research Policy* 29, 109–123.

Federal Ministry of Education and Research (BMBF) and the Standing Conference of the Ministers of Education and Cultural Affairs of the Länder of the Federal Republic of Germany (KMK) (2008). *Report on The Compatibility of the 'Qualifications Framework for German Higher Education Qualifications' with the 'Qualifications Framework for the European Higher Education Area'*. www.kmk.org/fileadmin/pdf/Wissenschaft/BE_080918_Bericht_Zertifizierung_NQF_engl_final.pdf

Garraway, J. and Winberg, C. (2019). Reimagining Futures of Universities of Technology. *CriSTaL* 7, Special Issue. Published online: 10 October. DOI:10.14426/cristal.v7iSI.194.

Gibbons, M., Limoges, C., Nowotny, H., Schwartzman, S., Scott, P. and Trow, M. (1994). *The New Production of Knowledge. The Dynamics of Science and Research in Contemporary Societies*. London: Sage.

Hall, P. (1993). Policy Paradigms, Social Learning, and the State. *Comparative Politics* 25 (3), 275–296.

Kerka, S. (1989). *'Cooperative education: Characteristics and effectiveness'*. ERIC Document Reproduction Service No. 312455

a, P., Lugendo, D., Needham, S., Pausits, A., Campbell, D. F. J., Nickel, S., Hudak, R., Wagner, G., Fernandez, A., Felix, A., Massinga, P., Daniel, L., Birch, C., Magazi, D., Makhubela, J., Charikinya, E., Lukhele-Olorunju, P. and Kivisto, J. (2018). *Final Benchmarking Report (incl. supply and demand results) and Recommendations*. Krems: LaTFURE Project Report (www.latfure.eu/wp-content/uploads/2020/11/LaTFURE_Act2.6_Final-benchmarking-report.pdf).

Leiber, T. (2019). *Theories of Learning and Teaching (TOLT) and Their Models*. Mannheim: EVALAG.

Leydesdorff, L. and Smith, H. L. (2021). Triple, Quadruple, and Higher-Order Helices: Historical Phenomena and (Neo-)Evolutionary Models. *SSRN*, published online 17 September. (http://dx.doi.org/10.2139/ssrn.3817410).

May, P. J. (1992). Policy Learning and Failure. *Journal of Public Policy* 12(4), 331–354.

Moyo, T. (2020). *Developing Content for Pilot Dual Study Programmes*. Krems: LaTFURE Project Report (www.latfure.eu/wp-content/uploads/2020/12/LaTFURE_Act4.3_Content-for-pilots.pdf).

OECD (2021a). *Education at a Glance 2020. OECD Indicators*. Paris: OECD.

OECD (2021b). *The Future of Work*. Paris: OECD.

Statistics South Africa (2021). *Quarterly Labour Force Survey Q1: 2021*. Pretoria: Government Printers.

Needham, S., Colus, F. and do Rosário, N. (2020). *Final Report on the Revised Institutional Frameworks for and the Implementation of Dual Study Programmes in Mozambique and South Africa*. Krems: LaTFURE Project (www.latfure.eu/wp-content/uploads/2020/12/LaTFURE_Act3.5_Act3.2_Revised-frameworks.pdf).

Patrick, C., Peach, D., Pocknee, C., Webb, F., Fletcher, M., & Pretto, G. (2008). *The WIL [work-integrated learning] report: A national scoping study*. Retrieved from http://www.acen.edu.au

Republic of South Africa (RSA) (2013). *White Paper for Post-School Education and Training* https://www.dhet.gov.za/SiteAssets/Latest%20News/White%20paper%20for%20post-school%20education%20and%20training.pdf

South African Qualifications Authority (SAQA) (2017). *Articulation between Technical Vocational Education and Training (TVET) Colleges and Higher Education Institutions (HEIs): National Articulation Baseline Report*. (http://saqa.org.za/docs/papers/2018/National%20Articulation%20Baseline%20Study%20Report.pdf)

in't Veld, R. J. (2010). *Knowledge Democracy. Consequences for Science, Politics, and Media*. Heidelberg: Springer.

Wagner, C. S., Roessner, D., Bobba, K., Thompson Klein, J., Boyack, K. W., Keytond, J., Rafolse, I. and Börner, K. (2011). Approaches to Understanding and Measuring Interdisciplinary Scientific Research (IDR): A Review of the Literature. *Journal of Informetrics* 165, 14–26.

Winberg, C. (2007). Continuities and Discontinuities in the Journey from Technikon to University of Technology. *South African Journal of Higher Education*, published online 18 September. DOI: 10.4314/sajhe.v19i2.25645

30

All on the Same Page: The Impact and Importance of Professional Associations for Graduate Employability

Vianna Renaud and Stéphanie Devèze

INTRODUCTION

For those working with career provision within the higher education (HE) sector, the 2019–20 and 2020–21 academic years have been a challenging time. Given the current landscape of austerity, university restructures, student expectations and increasing competition for industry placements, all taking place during a global pandemic, the role of professional bodies is even more important in supporting the sector, particularly those that are involved with work-based and placement learning. From the work of ASET, the UK Work Based and Placement Learning Association, to the Erasmus+-funded SPRINT Programme, led by the French Ministry of Education with the aim of implementing a standardisation framework for internships within the EU, there appears to be a great interest and momentum in similar initiatives taking place around the globe. One of this chapter's co-authors, Stéphanie Delaunay, is the founder and manager of SPRINT. We will present this chapter in collaboration, based upon our lens of the practitioner involved with both national and international initiatives on encouraging good practice within the sector.

Following our recent involvement in the publication of the *Student Affairs and Services in Higher Education: Global Foundations, Issues and Best Practices*, third edition (2020), we observed that similar trends were taking place across the

EU and the UK. From increased pressure from university senior management to justify financial spend, including the cost of professional memberships, other similarities included student access to quality placements and work experiences, improving student experience, increasing links with industry and ultimate graduate outcomes and employability.

In recent times, by taking part in professional association events, discussion groups and CPD (Continual Professional Development) activities, we have seen common challenges and struggles amongst our employability and placement professional peers. Whilst many commented that placements and graduate jobs seemed to have drastically declined in some sectors, other opportunities that had not been seen before were becoming viable options (e.g. ASET Regional Hubs). Now more than ever, immediate action by programme academics, placement professionals and university policy makers is needed as innovative solutions are necessary. Key concerns expressed included placement requirements and regulations, a suitable time frame, available support and online delivery, amongst others.

Amongst the uncertainty, the professional associations provided great support to their members. By providing important opportunities to discuss and explore observations taken from their institutions, many revisited any Good Practice Guidelines/Frameworks that they had created. Some associations collaborated with others to provide pandemic-specific advice, with a key example being the partnership between ASET and the QAA, with their Guidance Document on Contingency Planning for Placement Provision (2020).

We have seen that a common goal of professional associations is to impact policy within the sector by combining and utilising their collective expertise and experience. Used to create guidance and support for their members, the resulting resources can easily be the best available resources at the time for those in the field.

As to the original rationale for the creation of such documents, after promoting good practice since 1982, ASET regarding the Good Practice Handbook compiled an actual Good Practice Guide on Work Based and Placement Learning. With the goal of advancing the prevalence, effectiveness and quality of work-based and placement learning in HE, it was designed to support the work of the professional and administrative staff, academic tutors, careers teams and resource managers. Since 2014, other ASET Good Practice Guides have been released, as well as shorter publications called 'View Points' to offer guidance and support.

Based upon similar frustrations and goals around work-based and placement learning, Stéphanie came up with the idea of the SPRINT programme and that of standardising internship processes in 2018. When she was invited to join the Ministry of Education in 2019, she was encouraged to bring the project with her and was given the project to bring to completion. The idea was to be broad in territory – to cover the EU territories so that common practices could be put into place on a quicker time frame than going country by country. Now officially completed, she and the project partners have seen the impact first-hand.

Therefore, from this lens, our argument is that membership of professional organisations does, in fact, impact graduate employability through offering Good Practice Guidelines and standardisation of processes for the placement component of the academic programme. By supporting and creating capacity to those that work within the field, we feel that the benefits expand to other key stakeholders such as university senior management, placement providers, current and future students, HE consultants and ultimately the graduates as alumni.

THE STUDY

In recent years, we within the field know that (Rees, 2021) employability has become an important focus for HE (Bell, 2016), caused by globalisation and the knowledge economy (Kalfa and Taksa, 2017), increasing numbers of students (Helyer and Lee, 2014), the massification and marketisation of HE (Farenga and Quinlan, 2015; James and Yun, 2018), devalued degree qualifications (Batistic and Tymon, 2017), the Bologna Process (Sin and Amaral, 2017), government policies (Huq and Gilbert, 2013), skills shortages (Yorke, 2006; Belwal et al., 2016) and, particularly for university, the fact that graduate employability has become a publicly reportable statistic (Rae, 2007; Rowe and Zegwaard, 2017), thereby potentially impacting upon institutional ranking. Following from and in agreement with this (Rees, 2021), 'to achieve this, HE is often historically aligned with specific industry sectors where graduates are seen as human capital to be developed to support particular economies' (Yorke, 2004).

As practitioners looking at the link with professional body membership and available sector resources, we drew reference from Behle's (2020) Model of Employability within HE, particularly that which focuses on 'enabling forces'. In this part of the model, the enabling support systems include public and private labour market intermediaries and support agencies, university careers services and faculty- or subject-specific careers advisors (Donald et al., 2017). This category also includes availability of labour market information (sectoral, geographical and occupational) and students' and graduates' understanding of their self-efficacy and their job-searching skills, which very often are accessed by, and supplied from, the institutional careers and employability teams (Mason et al., 2009; Okay-Somerville and Scholarios, 2017).

In applying this concept of 'enabling forces', and agreeing that this concept encompasses the related professional bodies within HE, we felt it best to send out an informal questionnaire to our networks within the UK and the EU as the first step in the research process.

SURVEY DESIGN

The survey design was a combination of open and closed questions with a scaling system as well as the opportunity to add additional feedback. We wanted it to be informal as we felt that this would be the best way forward. The survey link was posted on LinkedIn within our respective network groups. However, there was an unexpectedly low response rate, where all respondents unanimously chose not to be named. Although, we found this to be particularly interesting upon greater reflection, as, given that the majority of university staff were still working from home at the time of the survey, their confidence may have changed without having the normal interaction and engagement with their peers. There is still a fear about ongoing restructures and job security as the sector feels the full impact of the pandemic and therefore people may have chosen to stay quiet. Given the results, we feel that this will be an ongoing research project so that we can measure any differences when the pandemic is over.

For this project, we received feedback from academic staff, professional support staff, international recruitment staff, senior management, employability consultant, placement employers, alumni and students and also international representation from France and Germany; therefore, the main stakeholders are represented. We will present the feedback as case studies.

SURVEY QUESTIONS

Good Practice Guidelines on work-based and placement learning created by related professional associations/group collaboration have:

1. Helped university staff raise their awareness in all areas related to work placements, from academic policies and procedures, risk assessments, student and employer support, etc.
2. Helped placement companies with the concept of providing a quality placement experience, supporting their process in having a mutually beneficial and effective internship structure.
3. Helped senior university managers to develop placement and internship strategies and policies, quality assurance, KPIs, management of strategic plans for the future, etc.
4. Helped students to have a quality learning experience, providing them the opportunity to achieve their learning outcomes and to better plan for their future career.
5. Helped academic staff with raising awareness and preparing students for their industry experience, setting placement assessments, providing guidelines, etc.
6. In having the above combination, given students more confidence and better preparation for the transition to life after university and therefore their graduate employability.
7. Provided much needed advice, guidance and support during the Covid pandemic as a key resource to those working in this area.

In addition, these questions were also included:

1. Are you currently a member of a professional body and/or group collaboration such as the SPRINT programme in the EU, which focuses on work-based and placement learning within the HE sector?

2. Are you aware of any Good Practice Guidelines/Frameworks around work-based and placement learning? If so, with which association/group collaboration?
3. Do you think the work of professional bodies, particularly that of the Good Practice Guidelines/Frameworks they create, can impact the graduate employability of university students? If so, how? If not, why not?
4. What benefits do you see students indirectly receiving from engaging with members of the professional body on campuses and/or within the industry?

There were a few additional open questions asking for further comments on additional benefits from having Good Practice Guidelines/Frameworks to use within the individual's role, or if they did not think there were any benefits to Good Practice Frameworks, and any additional comments regarding Good Practice Guidelines being linked to graduate employability.

THE ACADEMIC PERSPECTIVE

For one academic, Academic A,

'Yes, it goes without saying that professional bodies raise the profile of work based and placement learning which contribute to the employability of university students. Research has shown that embedding work based and placement learning into the curriculum leads to higher degree classifications and enhanced employability skills'.

She felt that the Good Practice Guidelines/Frameworks provided by professional bodies give HE institutions and practitioners who support those students 'clear guidelines and support in the delivery of work based and placement learning'.

As to any benefits,

> one can see students indirectly receiving many from engaging with members of the professional body on campuses and/or within the industry, it is felt that the indirect benefits are those that are often difficult to measure or see but are evident over time. Such benefits include greater confidence in networking situations, links to employers who may not have roles at the time but perhaps at a later time, amongst others. In addition, enhanced communication skills and being able to work through the myriad of acronyms and general language of the working world enables the student to navigate through the working world when they start the process of making applications to graduate roles. (Respondent A)

Another indirect result of engagement with professional bodies or industry professionals is that alternative options to work can be revealed. An example of this from Respondent A's experience has been 'students who had never thought about self-employment who are now exposed to new experiences and move to opening their own businesses'.

Given the recent pandemic and resulting emergency planning, she felt that the Good Practice Guidelines from these associations provided much needed advice, guidance and support as a key resource to those working in this area: '[t]he pandemic resulted in a level of cross-working between professional bodies that we have never seen before. These links were at the national and international level'.

For another academic located within the Law faculty of a different university (Respondent B), she feels that the Good Practice guidelines are 'necessary to ensure the successful access to, and the completion, of appropriate level work experience'.

She feels the key benefit to students from their institutions engaging with professional bodies is that 'this relationship underpins the importance of employability and work beyond simply being told by lecturers and parents'.

Additional benefits from staff using the Good Practice guidelines are directly linked to her role and the

> collegiality beyond a single department or institution. This can be very important for staff working within the work placement function as they may be the only person in that particular role at their department / institution. Therefore, having the Guidelines in both printed and online formats to share with one another can be incredibly helpful to them. (Respondent B)

We found this feedback to be in direct correlation to what has already been observed within the sector regarding university resourcing. With restructures, redundancies and ultimately one person taking on the role of work-based and placement learning expert, these Good Practice Guidelines have proved to be a lifeline.

THE PLACEMENT EMPLOYER PERSPECTIVE

It was felt that the work of professional bodies, particularly that who create Good Practice Guidelines/Frameworks, can impact the graduate employability of university students, as 'it contextualises the academic learning'. The key benefits that this employer see students indirectly receiving are an introduction to networking and building confidence.

Another employer stressed that the impact on students from engaging with the professional bodies and the frameworks is crucial as 'students get up to date best practice, which is important as curriculums do not update as quickly as one would like'. Students are also 'exposed to future employers and can learn about roles they had not considered. They can also find out about the specific culture of certain organisations'. One of the most important benefits in providing this information and these opportunities to students is that 'they can pick up on soft skills and other elements that are not taught; all things that they will need to know in order to be successful within the industry'.

However, it is important that universities keep the process easy for employers to engage students. The process needs to be a logical and rational one to avoid becoming disjointed.

THE STUDENT PERSPECTIVE

The student perspective, similarly to all other perspectives, is dependent upon awareness. Students in general are nominally aware that there are professional bodies in which university staff can participate. They also know that the staff structure is such that there are multiple dedicated staff members that they can see regarding their employability and placements. However, some concerns shared were more fundamental. As one student responded, 'I just want to be able to get a good placement and job when my degree is finished. Whatever it takes, from the university staff and my academics, I don't care; I just want to know that I am getting a quality education'. However, the feedback is also that 'I would have more confidence in university staff if I knew they are taking part in such professional bodies, particularly given how our academic teachers also stress the importance of joining professional associations'.

As for abiding to Good Practice Guidelines, '[t]his would make me feel more confident in my academic programme and university; just like we want to be at the top of our industry, I would greatly appreciate seeing university staff at the top of theirs'.

Whilst questions around the impact this could make on the student experience were not asked, we know that with greater confidence comes greater satisfaction. Therefore, this point will be explored in our ongoing research.

THE SENIOR MANAGEMENT PERSPECTIVE

For one senior manager based in Northern Ireland, he feels that 'the related Good Practice Guidelines ensure not only baseline standards, but also areas for quality enhancement. Students can really maximise the benefits of placement through appropriate opportunities, guided reflection and skill building'.

A different senior manager based outside of London feels that '[g]uidelines are useful internally to persuade local actors of rational courses of action and best practice – they grant authority and also help to enable the expansion of placement activity, which does improve employability'. They have greatly helped his senior management to 'develop placement and internship strategies which has been one of the most helpful elements within the context of senior management'.

Both senior managers confirmed that the guidelines have 'helped university staff with their awareness of the placement process'; however, one manager felt that they tend to support local policies and practice.

Regarding the impact upon placement companies and their awareness of how to best offer a quality learning experience, he feels that these guidelines can be a great help, and as a result, his institution points their employing organisations to them. However, he feels that those who refer to them are, '[t]hose employers who are already conscientious. It is also likely that they are already providing the best placements as they are actively staying on top of current university and sector guidance; the link could be coincidence rather than causation'.

As for students and staff, '[t]he Guidelines have been helpful for staff directly and are definitely useful for the training of academic staff, therefore raising the awareness around all aspects of the placement experience'. The guidelines are then implemented into the support offered to students. However, greater awareness could be achieved: '[w]hilst I know that my team points students to one well known Good Practice Guide and have gone so far as to provide copies to students, he is unaware of any impact that has made'.

Anecdotally we know that university staff have found the additional support given by these professional bodies to have been very important given the changing world of the pandemic, particularly those involved with the crisis management groups having to pass decisions and policy changes. However, for one manager:

> I was not really aware of any updated guidance during the pandemic however it has been a crazy year and a half. We have had to focus on business continuity so unfortunately I have not been able to stay on top of things that normally I would be on top of.

Given the previous comments on raising awareness, we feel that this feedback shows the importance of communication within teams and the sharing of knowledge.

FROM THE STUDENT RECRUITMENT PERSPECTIVE

Competition for both national and international students has recently significantly increased, and therefore 'being able to say that the university abides by the Good Practice guidelines can greatly help in the recruitment cycle; unfortunately it is something that is not currently taking place on campus'. One recruiter mentioned that it is 'quite common for one particular Department or Faculty to highlight their achievements and accreditations during recruitment drives. The knowledge that a university follows Good Practice Guidelines of a particularly professional body is lesser known'. When asked about specifically international students who may have additional drivers towards attending university, he felt that 'raising awareness could certainly help things, particular given the strong "word of mouth" concept between students, agents and recruiters in a particular area'.

THE PROFESSIONAL SUPPORT STAFF PERSPECTIVE

Both of the professional support staff included in this project feel strongly about the importance of Good Practice Guidelines. From working with the students on the ground to taking part in the professional body activities, it was felt that 'the interaction is absolutely vital to our roles. It is very easy to get into our own little silo where we are too busy dealing with the day to day instead of actually trying to see what other universities are doing'.

At the same time, there is an overabundance of professional bodies doing similar things, creating a competition between professional associations and thus limiting the sharing of information and best practice. For this exercise, we as the researchers heard this both from the UK and international perspectives.

Another key concern, and an impact seen particularly during the recent pandemic, has been the sudden halt on all CPD expenditure:

> Where we would have had a few staff members attend relevant CPD activities or workshops, now no one is allowed to go. Thankfully the association mostly aligned to my work has opened up free Regional Hub events where we can still talk and share with our peers across the sector, but it has been really hard.

At the same time, some of the feedback was quite positive:

> Having the extra free support on offer from the professional bodies, as they put on more member events during Covid, this proved to be absolutely vital to my wellbeing. With the shift to homeworking, communication was incredibly difficult and it took some getting used to using Zoom and Teams. However, as there wasn't an additional cost, I was able to attend these events and stay up to speed with the sector which proved to be invaluable when my line manager asked me for my input. Without knowing what others were doing I would have been more stressed than usual and this has been an incredibly challenging time.

Another staff member mentioned that:

> while I was working on the standardisation of internship and placement provision with different departments, everything was dropped with Covid. We had to focus on taking each day as it came as every day there was news from our institutional Major Incident Group on policy and procedure changes. I know that I will go back to that looking at standardisation but at least this has given me a better sense of just how important our professional bodies can be, particularly in such a crisis.

THE ALUMNI PERSPECTIVE

From an alumnus: 'the awareness of disciplines and practical applications in the workplace helps integration post-study, therefore the consistency in approach needs to be the same, hence any sector related Good Practice Guidelines can be very useful'. Students need to be able to engage with such resources, as 'they will be able to gain greater industry awareness, a real and specific understanding of the application of skills, a sense of perspective and context, as well as networking, making connections and having advocates'.

He stressed as well that we should look at how the sector would be if there were not any Good Practice Guidelines/Frameworks, particularly as it 'allows me to compare my practice and offering now as a potential placement provider; without it elements could be lost. Frameworks always help as it helps give a foundation and confidence which can only strengthen employability and prospects; the absence of this would impair this'.

THE EMPLOYABILITY CONSULTANT PERSPECTIVE

The HE consultant felt that students receive benefits whenever there are embedded frameworks. At the same time, he stressed that 'it is important to remove barriers to participation for employers and students from lower social capital backgrounds. If the Guidelines can support and enable this, then students will be winning'. At the time of the survey, he was working on 'placement strategy and in particular, that of Service Level Agreements between universities, employers and students to create a better quality and consistency of experience'.

Another consultant was more critical. For him, his 'perception from recent projects is that processes around placements evolve and mushroom across institutions within different departments having radically different processes. Some are massively over engineered and inefficient, whilst others do cover some of the basic legal requirements'. In his experience, 'often even teams that have been centralised are still in practice working in faculty/departmental silos'.

This echoes a senior manager and consultant in Germany: '[v]ery often different teams do different things. One member may be affiliated with one association with a colleague aligned with another association. Associations can be very competitive for membership and similar to colleagues, they may not share resources. Particularly when resources are tight and there is stress about jobs'.

The common agreement was that having institutional-level policies and frameworks greatly helps those involved. However, as one consultant stated:

> Institutions must be aware that employers will not jump through unnecessary hoops without a lot of chasing, streamlining the requirements for them is crucial as well as the need to be pragmatic. Better to have a basic process that is completed consistently than a bells and whistles process with loads of gaps in paperwork and responses.

He continues that '[a]s a general rule across all HE activity, we don't think enough about the employer experience/perception as a priority. Therefore the Guidelines can be a great help' – once again, something we need to be aware of as practitioners to help guide our processes.

DATA ANALYSIS

The results are given in Table 30.1.

Led by co-author Stéphanie, the SPRINT project – 'Standardize best PRactices about INTernships – aims at improving young people's integration into the labour market by creating a quality European framework for internships with the support

Table 30.1 Survey results

	Strongly Agree	Some-what Agree	Neutral	Some-what disagree	Strongly disagree
1. Helped university staff raise awareness of the placement process	5	4	1	–	–
2. Helped placement companies with the concept of providing a quality placement experience	4	4	2	–	–
3. Helped senior university managers to develop placement and internship strategies and policies	5	4	–	1	–
4. Helped students to have a quality learning experience	6	2	2	–	–
5. Helped academic staff with raising the awareness and preparing students for their industry experience	8	2	–	–	–
6. By having the above combination, students are more confident and better prepared for the transition to life after university	7	2	1	–	–
7. Provided much needed advice, guidance and support during the Covid pandemic	4	4	1	1	–

of standardisation. This project has been funded within the Erasmus+ Programme with the University Paul Valéry Montpellier III as the institutional base.

Starting in 2017, SPRINT was a 40-month project and strategic partnership co-funded by the Erasmus+ programme with the aim to create a European Quality Framework for Internships. It has been successful in accomplishing the original goals. The first goal was to have a framework be approved; therefore, the advisory 'Eight Criteria of Quality Internships' document has been included at the European Committee of Normalisation Workshop Agreement. This document incorporated feedback from contributing countries: Austria, Belgium, Bulgaria, Croatia, Cyprus, Czech Republic, Denmark, Estonia, Finland, France, Germany, Greece, Hungary, Ireland, Italy, Latvia, Lithuania, Luxembourg, Malta, Netherlands, Poland, Portugal, Romania, Slovakia, Slovenia, Spain, Sweden and Switzerland, including a small section on the UK, given the transition to BREXIT.

The second aim was to create a guide and a self-evaluation website for employers. The third aim was to create a guide for HEIs with a training session. All of the documents are now considered as output for the project. Recently awarded special EU status combined with great interest in potential outcomes, the support of the project will continue as, given feedback from the relevant stakeholders, it was deemed an important project.

FINAL THOUGHTS

Research will continue on the impact of the pandemic on student life, and no doubt that of graduate employability. We know this will continue to be a topic for further research that we will move into the next phase. It is important that this also is included in the employability literature as it impacts all of us, and the work of SPRINT confirms that it is of global interest and precedent.

RECOMMENDATIONS

It is clear that in our globally competitive knowledge economy (Inge et al., 2020), where change is an everyday reality, the importance of employability is generally agreed-upon by policy makers and scholars alike (Peeters et al., 2019). HE institutions need to prepare students for jobs that do not exist yet, for using technologies that have yet to be invented and for solving problems that nobody has yet thought of (Kumar, 2007).

We have also seen that the literature reaffirms the importance of design and policies for facilitating successful university–industry collaboration over time (Burnside and Witkin, 2008; Perkmann and Salter, 2012). Therefore, future research needs to delve deeper into understanding the varying perspectives and goals of university and industry partnerships between stakeholders in order to further bolster relationships and ensure progress whilst a national level analysis and supportive frameworks are developed (Dollinger et al., 2018).

Based on the stakeholder feedback at this initial stage of our study, we would like to make the following recommendations.

Greater Awareness of the Professional Bodies and of their Good Practice Guidelines

This can be done by all involved, from the professional bodies formulating targeted awareness-raising campaigns to senior management, collaborative working between the professional bodies and information sharing on campuses between faculty and central teams, amongst other activities. Whilst some associations have created a 'badge' that one can use in their signature, it would be of great help to include membership details in one's daily work duties.

For employers, university staff owe it to their students and professional practice to highlight that they are working within a certain framework. We have seen from the feedback that this knowledge can greatly empower students, staff and employers alike; therefore ensuring that all players are 'on the same page' is essential.

We agree with the literature in that there are different reasons for stakeholders engaging in work and industry learning, which can create tension and disengagement from these activities (Patrick et al., 2009). Pilgrim (2012) argues that for a clearer understanding of the motivations of other stakeholders, trying to shape processes for the benefit of all parties is critical for growing work-based opportunities. Similarly, a triadic approach, whereby students, university coordinators and workplace supervisors work in close collaboration to maximise the experience, is promoted by Dalrymple et al. (2014). The same rhetoric has been promoted by organisations such as ASET, AGCAS, Advance HE and ISE, amongst others in the UK as well as by the SPRINT programme in the EU. It is through their Good Practice Guidelines/Frameworks that this triadic way of working can be successful.

Greater Communication Between the Stakeholders

This area must continue to improve both within the UK and the EU as it is only through this that we will be successful in a truly collaborative way. Whilst sometimes the current culture may not assist, it is important to stress transparency and open communication as we all work together for the benefit of all.

Impact on the Student Experience

By staying transparent and sharing the guidelines with students, we are indirectly empowering them to potentially seek out different experiences. We are also encouraging them to start taking a more active role in their own employability, which can greatly help their understanding of their own responsibility. Linked to the current Consumer Act Law and student perception issues in the UK, maintaining clarity will greatly help all involved.

Through the pandemic, there has also been a resurgence of mental health concerns, as evidenced by Student Minds and the creation of the University Mental Health Charter. Student resilience and wellbeing are at the forefront of policy. Therefore, anything that we can do as employability professionals can only help.

We have also had it confirmed that students like knowing that they are at an institution of high repute, which comes from academic and professional support staff being actively involved in sector-specific professional bodies. We need to ensure that we work collaboratively not only with our colleagues but also with our students; this can only have positive results.

Impact on Staff Experience

Given the current stress levels those in HE are facing, by implementing time- and resource-saving measures, staff will then be able to move on to other responsibilities. We have seen from the study that Good Practice Guidelines have helped to further develop relationships amongst the stakeholders, and therefore the costs of professional memberships have been justified.

Impact on Industry Partnerships

As already highlighted, we cannot have processes just for the sake of them. Everything must have a rationale behind it, particularly when working with industry and placement providers. By sharing the Good Practice Guidelines, we can ensure that they are also empowered on how to offer quality work-based and placement learning opportunities to students.

Impact on Student Recruitment

We must not overlook the importance of having a positive student experience upon the student recruitment goals of the university. Not only important for home students (Goodwin and Mbah, 2019), university relations with work placement providers need to be nurtured within a supportive framework. HEIs need to develop links and partnerships with placement providers to enable a variety of activities such as regular feedback in order to ensure successful outcomes (Clair-Thompson, 2017), a better understanding of the obligations and mentoring role these providers can establish for a mutually beneficial basis and also a clear set of university expectations of providers (Liu and Winder, 2014). We within the sector already have the benefit of having these guidelines on hand to access through our professional memberships – now it is down to the stakeholders of work-based and placement learning to implement them.

CONCLUSION

We have seen the establishment of Good Practice Guidelines established in the UK and, through the need for something within the EU territory, that of the SPRINT Programme. Currently in development is the Task Force for Internships with The Forum on Education Abroad based in the USA. The momentum is there, so the timing is relevant.

We are confident that at this stage of the study, based upon the range of feedback, there are not any clear disadvantages or negative aspects to using resources compiled by professional bodies. The only risk that exists is a lack of awareness of these Good Practice Guidelines and lack of communication between the various stakeholders. We have seen the impact they can make at different levels, which reconfirms the notion that HEIs can no longer afford to stay in their own silo, only reflecting upon their own practice and processes. One must look to the outside sector, and sometimes region, in order to stay competitive in an increasingly competitive sector.

Contemporary professional learning (Daniels, 2017) must be a continuous process of developing practice, of 'acting in praxis' (Kemmis, 2012) in one's profession. Through having the necessary knowledge and acting well in response to the uncertain demands of particular situations that arise for the practitioners of different professional practices, one can draw upon the wisdom others have learned from reflection and similar experiences. Therefore, it is actually of greater importance and relevance to encourage staff members to join such associations and to share the specialised knowledge of the Good Practice Guidelines.

The sector must keep in mind the importance of design and policies for facilitating sustainable and successful university–industry collaboration over time (Burnside and Witkin, 2008; Perkmann and Salter, 2012). Whilst this was the first of research outputs in this area, in the next stage we will delve deeper into understanding the varying perspectives and goals of university and industry collaboration between stakeholders in order to further bolster relationships and ensure progress. As university- and program-level frameworks are mentioned to be a necessary development piece (Dollinger et al., 2018), we know that we already have such professional body frameworks in place within the UK and the EU.

REFERENCES

Behle, H. (2020) Students' and Graduates' Employability. A Framework to Classify and Measure Employability Gain. *Policy Reviews in Higher Education* 4(1), 105–130.

Behle, H. (2020). Taking stock: Employability as an outcome of higher education. Evaluating developments in the German higher education system. *Higher Education Quarterly*. DOI: 10.1111/hequ.12318

Belwal, R., & Priyadarshi, P. & Fazari, M. (2017). Graduate attributes and employability skills: Graduates' perspectives on employers' expectations in Oman. *International Journal of Educational Management*. 31. 00-00. 10.1108/IJEM-05-2016-0122.

Burnside, B. and Witkin, L. (2008) Forging Successful University–Industry Collaborations. *Research-Technology Management* 51(2): 26–30.

Clair-Thompson, D. (2017) Professional Placements in Psychology. *Phoenix*, the placements issue. Accessed June 12, 2021. http://viewer.zmags.com/publication/997093f8#/997093f8/8

Dalrymple, R., Kemp, C. and Smith, P. (2014) Characterising Work-Based Learning as a Triadic Learning Endeavour. *Journal of Further and Higher Education* 38(1): 75–89.

Daniels, J. (2017) Professional Learning in Higher Education: Making Good Practice Relevant. *International Journal for Academic Development* 22(2): 170–81.

Dollinger, M., Coates, H., Bexley, E., Croucher, E. and Naylor, R. (2018) Framing International Approaches to University–Industry Collaboration. *Policy Reviews in Higher Education* 2(1): 105–127.

Donald, W., Baruch, Y. and Ashleigh, M. (2017) The Undergraduate Self-Perception of Employability: Human Capital, Careers Advice, and Career Ownership. *Studies in Higher Education* 44(4): 599–614.

Farenga, S. & Quinlan, K. (2015). Classifying university employability strategies: three case studies and implications for practice and research. *Journal of Education and Work*. 29. 1-21. 10.1080/13639080.2015.1064517.

Fenwick, T. (2009). Making to Measure? Reconsidering Assessment in Professional Continuing Education. *Studies in Continuing Education* 31(3), 229–244, DOI: 10.1080/01580370903271446

Gertner, D., Roberts, J. and Charles, D. (2011) University-industry Collaboration: A CoPs Approach to KTPs. *Journal of Knowledge Management* 15(4): 625–647, https://doi.org/10.1108/13673271111151992

Goodwin, K. and Mbah, M. (2019) Enhancing the Work Placement Experience of International Students: Towards a Support Framework. *Journal of Further and Higher Education* 43(4): 521–532.

Hazelkorn, E. (2018) Reshaping the World Order of Higher Education: The Role and Impact of Rankings on National and Global Systems. *Policy Reviews in Higher Education* 2(1): 4–31, DOI: 10.1080/23322969.2018.1424562

Helyer, R. and Lee, D. (2014) The Role of Work Experience in The Future Employability of Higher Education Graduates. *Higher Education Quarterly* 68(3): 348–372.

Inge, R., Scoupe, R. and Beausaert, S. (2020) Unravelling the Concept of Employability, Bringing Together Research on Employability in Higher Education and the Workplace. *Studies in Higher Education* 45(12): 2588–2603.

Jackson, D., Rowbottom, D., Ferns, S. and McLaren, D. (2017) Employer Understanding of Work-Integrated Learning and the Challenges of Engaging in Work Placement Opportunities. *Studies in Continuing Education* 39(1): 35–51, DOI: 10.1080/0158037X.2016.1228624

Kalfa, S. & Taksa, L. (2015). Cultural capital in business higher education: reconsidering the graduate attributes movement and the focus on employability. *Studies in Higher Education*. 40. 580-595.

Kemmis, S. (2012) Pedagogy, praxis and practice-based higher education. In J. Higgs, R. Barnett, S. Billet, M. Hutchings, and F. Trede (eds), *Practice-Based Education* (pp. 81–100). Rotterdam: Sense.

Knight, P., Tait, J. and Yorke, M. (2006) The Professional Learning of Teachers in Higher Education. *Studies in Higher Education* 31(3), 319–339, DOI: 10.1080/03075070600680786

Kumar, A. (2007) *Personal, Academic and Career Development in Higher Education. SOARing to Success.* London and New York: Routledge.

Liu, D. W. Y. and Winder, B. (2014) Exploring Foreign Undergraduate Students' Experiences of University. *International Journal of Qualitative Studies in Education* 27(1): 42–64.

Ludeman, R. B. & Schreiber, B. (Eds.). (2020). *Student Affairs and Services in Higher Education: Global Foundations, Issues, and Best Practices*, 3rd ed, pp. 1-629. Published by the International Association of Student Affairs and Services (IASAS) in cooperation with the Deutsches Studentenwerk (DSW) Publishers, Berlin, Germany.

Mason, G., Williams, G. and Cranmer, S. (2009) Employability Skills Initiatives in Higher Education: What Effects Do They Have on Graduate Labour Market Outcomes?. *Education Economics* 17(1): 1–30.

Mbah, M. (2016). Towards the idea of the interconnected university for sustainable community development. *Higher Education Research & Development*. 35. 1-14. https://doi.org/10.1080/07294360.2016.1144570.

Okay-Somerville, B. and Scholarios, D. (2017) Position, Possession or Process? Understanding Objective and Subjective Employability during University-to-Work Transitions. *Studies in Higher Education* 42(7): 1275–1291.

Patrick, C., Peach, D., Pocknee, C., Webb, F., Fletcher, M. and Pretto, G. (2009) *The WIL (Work Integrated Learning) Report: A National Scoping Study, Final Report.* Brisbane: Queensland University of Technology.

Peeters, E., Nelissen, J., De Cuyper, N., Forrier, A., Verbruggen, M. and De Witte, H. (2019) Employability Capital: A Conceptual Framework Tested Through Expert Analysis. *Journal of Career Development* 46(2): 79–93.

Perkmann, M. and Salter, A. (2012) How to Create Productive Partnerships with Universities. *MIT Sloan Management Review* 53(4): 79–88.

Perkmann, M., Tartari, V., McKelvey, M., Autio, E., Broström, A., D'Este, P., Fini, R., Geuna, A., Grimaldi, R., Hughes, A., Kabel, S., Kitson, M., Llerena, P., Salter, A., & Sobrero, M. (2013). Academic Engagement and Commercialisation: A Review of the Literature on University–Industry Relations. *Research Policy*, *42*(2), 423-442. https://doi.org/10.1016/j.respol.2012.09.007

Pilgrim, C. (2012) Industry and university perspectives of work integrated learning programs in ICT degrees. In *Proceedings of the 23rd Australasian Conference on Information Systems* (pp. 1–9). Melbourne: ACIS.

Postareff, L., Lindblom-Ylanne, S., & Nevgi, A. (2007). The Effect of Pedagogical Training on Teaching in Higher Education. *Teaching and Teacher Education*, 23, 557-571. https://doi.org/10.1016/j.tate.2006.11.013

Rae, D. (2007). Connecting Enterprise and Graduate Employability: Challenges to the Higher Education's Culture and Curriculum? *Education and Training*, 49, 605-619.

Rees, S. (2021) Re-Imagining Employability: An Ontology of Employability Best Practice in Higher Education Institutions. *Teaching in Higher Education* 26(5): 663–678.

Rowe, A. D., & Zegwaard, K. E. (2017). Developing graduate employability skills and attributes: Curriculum enhancement through work-integrated learning. *Asia-Pacific Journal of Cooperative Education*, 18(2), 87–99.

Turner, K. & Simon, S. (2012). In what ways does studying at M-level contribute to teachers' professional learning? *Research set in an English university. Professional Development in Education*. 39. 1-17. https://doi.org/10.1080/19415257.2012.666756.

Tymon, A. (2013). The student perspective on employability. *Studies in Higher Education*, 38(6), 841-856. https://doi.org/10.1080/03075079.2011.604408

Yorke, M. (2004) Employability in the Undergraduate Curriculum: Some Student Perspectives. *European Journal of Education* 39(4): 409–427.

Yorke, M. (2006) *Employability in Higher Education: What It Is-What It Is Not: Learning & Employability Series 1*. The Higher Education Academy, York. http://www.heacademy.ac.uk/assets/documents/tla/employability/id116_employability_in_higher_education_336.pdf

Index

Note: Page numbers followed by "n" indicate endnote in the text.